Newspapers in Asia

26 March 1984

Best wishes to Chris Sterling,
whose many projects and encourage-
ments are an inspiration to us all.

John Albert

Newspapers in Asia
Contemporary Trends and Problems

Edited by
John A. Lent

Heinemann Asia
Hong Kong Singapore Kuala Lumpur

HEINEMANN EDUCATIONAL BOOKS (ASIA) LTD
Yik Yin Building, 321-323 To Kwa Wan Road,
Kowloon, Hong Kong

41 Jalan Pemimpin, Singapore 2057

No. 2, Jalan 20/16A, Paramount Garden,
Petaling Jaya, Selangor, Malaysia

Heinemann Educational Books Ltd., London
Associated companies, branches & representatives
throughout the world

ISBN 962-225-079-3

© John A. Lent, 1982

First published 1982

Cover design by Stephanie Stephens

Typesetting by Core Bookwork Company
Printed in Hong Kong by Wing King Tong Co Ltd
41-55, Wo Tong Tsui Street, Wing Foo Industrial Building
Kwai Chung, Hong Kong

For my daughter, Lisa,
who cannot "Rage Against
the Dying of the Light."

Contents

Contents   xi

Tables

Preface and Acknowledgements

Originally, this book was meant to update *The Asian Newspapers' Reluctant Revolution*, which I edited and which was published by Iowa State University Press in 1971. Permission was sought and obtained from the publishers to bring out the updated version. However, as the guidelines and later the manuscripts developed, *Newspapers in Asia: Contemporary Trends and Problems* took on a format distinct from the previous work, with more structure in content, different contributors and a wider range of countries included. For example, *The Asian Newspapers' Reluctant Revolution* did not have chapters on the Democratic People's Republic of Korea, Macao, the Mongolian People's Republic, Kampuchea (then Cambodia), Laos, Afghanistan, and Nepal, and dealt with Malaysia and Singapore together in one chapter. Bangladesh was not included because, as a political state, it did not exist when that book was written.

Newspapers in Asia: Contemporary Trends and Problems deals with daily, and in some cases non-daily, newspapers of Asia. Twenty-three countries, ranging from Afghanistan, in the area called West Asia, to Japan in East Asia, form Asia as defined here. Countries are separated into three regions. The book includes descriptions of presses of eight East Asian, nine Southeast Asian and six South Asian countries. There are two chapters each on Thailand and Vietnam. In the case of Thailand, this happened when I asked a second author to write the chapter, having not heard for some time from those originally requested to write it. When the manuscripts arrived, I decided they both merited publication since they added different dimensions to the subject of Thai journalism — one stressing original research findings on professional journalists' attitudes and newspapers' contents — the other emphasizing an historical and contemporary account of press-government relationships.

When the book was conceived, there were two Vietnams, and I sought authors for both north and south. An author for the section on the South Vietnam press was found, but my efforts to solicit someone to write about North Vietnam failed. The press, after the liberation of Vietnam in 1975, is dealt with in a separate chapter. Not included in the book are the Asian portion of the Soviet Union, countries of the Middle East and the South Pacific territories and countries.

Press freedom is described in three additional chapters, broken down by regions. These chapters synthesize some of the material on press freedom in the country profile chapters, but also include additional, more recent information on this all-important topic. Because the status of the Asian press is intricately wrapped up in the story of government-press relationships, it was believed that these chapters were necessary. Also, in some instances, they add information that contributors of country profile chapters could not present for fear of retaliation from their governments.

The time period which this volume describes is mainly from the late 1960s through the late 1970s. Some chapters contain more detailed historical sections; this is more prevalent in those chapters about countries new to this book (and not in *The Asian Newspapers' Reluctant Revolution*), such as the Mongolian People's Republic and Kampuchea, or in chapters about countries where important historical information has recently come to light or where the history was somewhat neglected in past books, including *The Asian Newspapers' Reluctant Revolution*. Most chapters were first written in 1974-75, although those on freedom of the press in the three regions and country profiles of the Democratic People's Republic of Korea, Macao, Laos, Malaysia, Philippines, Singapore and Bangladesh were written or rewritten in mid-1979.

A number of problems hindered earlier publication of this book. Let me cite a few. First, it was difficult to obtain, or retain, the services of contributors for some chapters. Afghanistan, the Democratic People's Republic of Korea, Bangladesh, Macao, North Vietnam, Singapore and the Mongolian People's Republic presented the most trouble. With the three communist states, efforts were made directly to groups in those nations, such as the Association of Korean Journalists, Association of Vietnamese Journalists and Union of Mongolian Journalists, all to no avail, and to the Prague-based International Organization of Journalists, which succeeded in finding a contributor on Mongolia. (The chapter was submitted in Mongolian and Russian; the Russian language chapter was translated and later shortened to omit considerable polemical writing.) Four other individuals who said they would write chapters later declined because of fears of political retaliation in their home countries, or the lack of remuneration, time or sufficient information on which to base a chapter.

Second, because of other press duties, and in at least one case, illness, some contributors were hard pressed to meet the deadlines. My own editing of the book was delayed because of the urgency of other responsibilities and I must confess, because of a mental block I encountered when thinking of the huge task before me.

Third, although the book was conceived in 1973 and progress was made on it at that time, some of that effort had to be duplicated after Eastern Airlines lost my baggage (including correspondence, a contract and chapters for the book), "somewhere between New York and Newark," upon my return from Penang in 1974.

To make the book current, I spent the summer of 1979 re-editing (and in some cases, rewriting) and updating the chapters. Nearly every chapter, except those I wrote, ends with an update I compiled from my voluminous files on the Asian press. Thus, the book is the result of intermittent research, writing, editing and updating from 1973-79.

All chapters, except that of Dupree and a few of my own, were written especially for this book. Dupree's chapter is largely from his book, *Afghanistan*, published by Princeton University Press. Permission to reprint those portions was obtained from the author and the publisher. Dupree contributed a new section especially for this work. Parts of my chapters on Laos, Malaysia, Philippines, Singapore and Bangladesh first appeared in *Gazette*, *Index on Censorship*, *IPI Report* and *Asian Profile*. In all cases, however, considerable editing and updating created virtually new manuscripts.

Many of the authors are Asian media scholars, some of whom worked for newspapers before entering academic life. All 21 authors are residents of Asia, or American academicians and government personnel who lived in Asia for extended periods of time. They represent United States and Asian academic institutions, government agencies, newspapers and press organizations.

All write from personal backgrounds affiliated with the Asian press; for example, the author of the Nepal chapter is editor of one of the main newspapers there and the senior contributor of the Kampuchea chapter is in exile in France for his writings in the newspaper he edited in Phnom Penh. I wrote chapters about countries where I have done research; the exceptions are the chapters on the Democratic People's Republic of Korea, Macao and Bangladesh, which I wrote when it was not possible to obtain the services of others more knowledgeable.

Contributors were given very detailed guidelines concerning content, form and style. They were asked to explore: the history of the press; characteristics of the press as an institution, covering function, structure and organization, ownership and control and concepts of the social and national development roles of the press; economics of the press, including facilities, capital, capacity of people to consume papers and other aspects; press and government/politics, including press laws, infringements upon press freedom; socio-cultural factors and the press, including language, religious issues, ethnic groups and cultural traits; contents of the average newspaper; characteristics distinguishing media systems from those in other countries; foreign influences; other contemporary trends and problems and conclusions. Each of these categories was carefully defined, including questions that contributors were expected to attempt to answer.

For the most part, the contributors to this book followed these guidelines in developing their chapters. As a result, the reader should be able to make country-to-country comparisons on many topics. There were differences in approach, as would be expected. Usually, these were caused by the availability and degree of sensitivity of data, the interests of the contributing author and the topics of chief concern in a particular nation. Thus, the Japan chapter, in particular, emphasizes an historical approach, while the Indonesia, Singapore, Afghanistan, Bangladesh (and one Thailand) chapters use a political approach. Part of the Laos chapter is made up of case studies of newspapers; part of the Malaysia chapter describes newspapers by their language of publication and the Sri Lanka chapter explains press freedom by analyzing various governments and their acts over the past generation.

There is some unevenness in documentation; some authors,

especially those educated solely in Europe or Asia, do not depend very heavily upon documentation. For the reader's convenience, citations have been incorporated briefly and parenthetically at the appropriate places in the text. These citations refer to a composite bibliography for the entire book.

Newspapers in Asia: Contemporary Trends and Problems is organized into four parts. Part 1 is an introduction to non-freedom of the press issues in Asia; Part 2 is a description of newspapers in East Asia; Part 3, Southeast Asia, and Part 4, South Asia. The placing of countries in regions was done in strict alphabetical order.

I would like to thank all authors for their diligence in meeting guidelines (and in some cases, deadlines) set for this book and for their patience in the long wait for its publication; Leon Comber, John Watson and others at Heinemann for their understanding, encouragement and patience; the hundreds of journalists in Asia, who, over the past 15 years, have given me insights into the nature of Asian journalism and Oldrich Bures, who sought authors for the chapters on Mongolia, North Korea and North Vietnam. I am especially grateful to my wife, Martha and my children, Laura, Andrea, John V., Lisa and Shahnon, for allowing me to "hole-up" in my study for hours on end.

John A. Lent

Philadelphia

Part 1
Introduction

1.1 Asian Newspapers: Non-Political Trends

John A. Lent

1.1.1. Background

The 1960s was a decade of hope for the Asian press. Regional and national institutes promoted the professionalization of the press, development of training centers and the general economic improvement of newspapers. Development journalism was conceived by the Press Foundation of Asia in an effort to report simply and in depth, the story of Asian development. Educational institutions established teaching and research centers in journalism; newly-created national press institutes seriously tackled questions of ethics and set up codes; editors and journalists in a number of countries kept a critical watch on the government sector; press councils were created; indigenous materials were experimented with for the production of newsprint, and some local printing machinery industries were started. Individuals working diligently with these projects believed that the Asian newspapers were on the brink of a revolution, at the take-off point to better journalistic practices, larger circulations and advertising volumes, and, generally, greater economic prosperity. But it did not work out that way.

John A. Lent, Professor of Communications at Temple University, is the author of nine books, 13 monographs and over 150 journal articles on mass media in the Third World. He was a Fulbright Scholar in the Philippines and later was the first coordinator of a mass communications program in Malaysia at the Universiti Sains Malaysia. He is Founding Chairman of the Malaysia/Singapore/Brunei Studies Group and Founding Editor of its bulletin, *Berita*. Two of his books, including *Broadcasting in Asia and the Pacific* (Heinemann), were awarded unprecedented double Broadcast Preceptor Awards in 1979.

At the dawn of the 1980s, a considerable portion of the optimism of the 1960s was replaced by bitterness, frustration and abject despair. Part of the problem was because of the economic recessions in the mid-1970s; part of it stemmed from increased governmental control and manipulation of the press. Certainly, the slumping economies of Asia in 1975-76 cut into the economics of journalism. For example, advertising income in Indonesia was US$15 million short of the target in 1975-76; Thailand had a 10-15 per cent shrinkage in advertising, and countries of South Asia were hit as hard. In Pakistan, as private advertising dried up and wage costs increased 200 per cent, the press turned to the government for help. As production costs grew, so did price per copy of newspapers, pushing them, in many cases, completely out of the income range of all but a limited elite (*Rye and Roy*, 1976-77, p. vi).

But, the writing was on the wall before 1975-76. The newsprint slump of 1973 definitely took its toll of newspapers. Amitabha Chowdhury, one of the founding officers of the Press Foundation of Asia and a 1960s optimist, explained that by 1973, small- and medium-sized newspapers (especially in India, Philippines and Indonesia) which had started to flourish, were left behind in the scramble for newsprint. Price hikes and page shedding ushered in press recessions in all countries; the prosperous press of Japan was hit but to a lesser degree than that of India, which had complete stagnation, or Indonesia and Thailand, where diffusion rates dropped swiftly, or Sri Lanka, where the total circulation dropped by 25 per cent (*Chowdhury*, 1974, p. 8). By 1974, the situation was dismal enough for Chowdhury to write that all the encouraging programs of the Press Foundation of Asia and other groups in the 1960s and early 1970s, "would, at best, merely prevent total paralysis of the Asian press. They would stop the worst from happening, but they wouldn't raise the curtain on a whole new stage" (*Chowdhury*, 1974, p. 6). In fact, the very progenitors of press development and professionalization, the press institutes, were in danger by 1974, according to Chowdhury, who added, that as a result, there was a poverty of research and training in journalism. He pointed out that only one press institute, with an annual budget of US$50,000-60,000, served over 12,000 Indian newspapers, and that Thailand, Indonesia and Sri

Lanka were not fortunate to have even one institute (*Chowdhury*, 1974, p. 8). Four years later (in 1978), Chowdhury seemed to have a slightly different grasp on the problem, emphasizing how Asian governments manipulated the press by promoting the axiom that the less is the freedom, the greater is the economic growth. The Sixties pushed newspaper circulations up three or fourfold. Revenues began to soar. At the same time at the top layers of the profession a lot of fat and arrogance started accumulating. We journalists were blind towards the imminent catastrophe . . . . When the independence constitutions began to lose their hold on the public, especially on the intelligentsia, we should have smelt danger . . . . Any institution that makes the relationship work between the citizen and the government, must derive its strength from the public. The value that the public attaches to the press, is the source and measure of its freedom. Once that source began to dwindle in Asia, the press had little to fall back on. Now with only the two exceptions of Japan and India, almost the entire continent is thus covered by a sad taxonomy of the various types of the disciplined press looking up to a smiling or stoic Big Brother.

Now the aim [of all Asian governments] is to remould the kultur of the intelligentsia, to make out of every citizen a new man. This undertaking, until recently, was not considered the legitimate business of the government. Now, it has become so . . . . the editor is the first pupil in the new kultur school. He then in his turn becomes the main educator, if he has himself read well the new doctrine (*Chowdhury*, 1978, pp. 8-9).

1.1.2 Production Capabilities

Most Asian nations in the late 1970s and early 1980s, did not produce all the hardware necessary for printing their newspapers, and in a number of cases, they did not have the adequate infrastructure (transportation, energy, telecommunications) for properly sustaining them. Most countries did not produce the energy they consumed; Thailand, for example, produced no more than 3 per

cent of the fuel and lubricants it consumed. Energy cost increases
in the mid-1970s, therefore, put an added clamp on the Asian
press. In Japan, for example, the prices of newspapers increased by
a third to meet staggering energy costs, and in most countries,
newspaper profits went down as a result of fuel price hikes. In
many countries where air cargo and air freight play vital roles in
distribution because of slow and poor ground transportation,
newspapers suffered even more severely because of spiralling
energy costs (*Lee*, 1976).

1.1.2.1 *Printing Technology*

Asia represents an interesting mixture of printing technology,
possessing some of the most and least sophisticated machinery.
As one source stated:

> In Japan, huge factories churn out millions of news-
> papers, magazines and a wide range of products using a
> dazzling array of the most advanced offset and gravure
> techniques. From the crowded sidelanes of many other
> Asian capitals, one hears the swish of tiny letterpresses
> and the clanging of treadle machines from one-man
> print shops (*Media*, June 1976, p. 3).

Japan has about 20,000 printing shops doing about US$5 billion
business yearly. Most Japanese newspapers use rather sophisticated
equipment. *Asahi*, for example, has incorporated NELSON (News
Editing and Layout System for Newspapers) which prepares from
copy to final page proof with computers, graphic display terminals
and high speed photocompositors. *Nihon Keizai Shimbun* has a
similar system. Since 1959, *Asahi* has used facsimile transmission
of their pages between Tokyo and Sapporo; however, there has
been some resistance from other branches which do not want to
be reduced to being mere distribution centers for Tokyo newspapers (*Lachica*, 1974c, p. 9). The Hong Kong industry has been
robust, especially with the demand for color printing (*Careem*,
1977a, pp. 3, 5).

Southeast Asian nations pushed ahead in the 1970s in printing
technology, using imported presses from the United States,
Europe or Japan to meet increased demands for better printing. As
an example, in the mid-1960s, the largest English language daily

in Thailand, *Bangkok Post*, was still set by hand; a decade later, it, like most Thai newspapers, owned offset equipment. In Malaysia, printing in the late 1970s was divided between hot and cold types; of eight Chinese dailies in Kuala Lumpur, six had gone to offset (*Media*, June 1976, p. 5). The printing industry of Indonesia has been slowly maturing. In 1977, of 300 printing houses in Jakarta, about one-half were offset. However, in the entire country, only 30 per cent of the total 1,000 printing companies used offset. Offset printing blossomed in newspapers in the early 1970s, so that about 70 newspapers use offset, 209 letterpress. Problems still plague the Indonesian printing industry, as they do those of other countries. Among Indonesia's difficulties are the lack of professional know-how, outdated equipment, cost and difficulty of procuring needed spare parts and high operating costs. Such problems have contributed to the lack of desire in the private sector to set up new and better printing plants (*Djajanto*, 1977, p. 7).

India's printing industry has lagged behind because it has received little government support. The government, in the 1970s, restricted the importing of advanced printing machinery, and did not see fit to rank printing among the 48 industries which rate a national priority. Since 1968, India has produced its own machines, a pedal-operated Platen press similar to those produced in the nineteenth century. About a hundred small industries produce a total of 300 such presses yearly. More modern presses were starting to be developed in India in the 1970s, but capital was limited. In 1973, the government, in an effort to protect the local industry, banned the importation of any printing machines that were already being produced in the country (*Bhattacharjee*, 1977, p. 6).

The Press Foundation of Asia (PFA), in the late 1960s and early 1970s, was instrumental in testing new ideas in printing technology. Its Printing Institute in Singapore was designed to study the printing, mechanical and typographical needs of small- and medium-sized newspapers, to modernize typesetting processes of language newspapers and to train printers. In a serious search for intermediate technology, the PFA encouraged the design of machines which, with print runs of 50,000-100,000, could become economically viable (*Chowdhury*, 1974, p. 6).

1.1.2.2 *Newsprint*

Rising costs of newsprint (as well as those production costs mentioned above), especially since 1971, have had a tremendous adverse impact on the growth of Asia's print media. The increased prices and shortages of 1973 forced some newspapers to close, others to reduce their column and page sizes or number of pages, and the government and other agencies to look to alternative newsprint production means. In Hong Kong, 36 newspapers closed in 1973 and 19 in 1972, mainly because of newsprint prices. Some Indian newspapers stopped publishing, while others banned Sunday publication or reduced their number of pages. Indonesian publishers appealed to the government for help, laid off printing workers and raised newspaper subscription and advertising rates. In some cases, appeals to government were futile, especially where the government had control over newsprint allocation. In a political move, the Bangladesh government in the early 1970s raised the price of newsprint by 90 per cent (*Media*, Feb. 1974, p. 4).

Compounding the problem, besides the high prices, shortages and in some cases, government monopolization of newsprint, were high import taxes and non-availability of adequate foreign exchange. Import taxes on paper were 10-30 per cent, and even 60 per cent, in some countries; Indonesia, the Philippines and Thailand had especially high taxes. Indian, Sri Lankan and Indonesian publishers drastically restricted the importation of materials such as newsprint because of the lack of foreign exchange.

Some governments, in an effort to alleviate the pressure, reduced the duty on newsprint (as in Malaysia), ordered newspapers to consume less (as in Sri Lanka), or worked with agencies such as the Press Foundation of Asia (PFA) in exploring alternative newsprint supplies. Conferences sponsored by PFA, United Nations and various Asian governments emphasized how most of Asia received very little newsprint compared to more affluent nations. The PFA in 1973-74, in an appeal to world bodies such as UNESCO, pointed out that Asian nations (except Japan) could secure only 416,000 tons of newsprint in 1973 (down from 567,000 tons in 1972), yet the world production increased in 1973 by 1 million tons (*The New Standard*, Indonesia, 23 Nov. 1974). Chanchal

Sarkar of the Press Institute of India calculated in 1975, that if the affluent world of the United States, England, Japan, West Germany and the USSR — the large newsprint consumers — reduced their total consumption by a mere 4.6 per cent, the saving would be enough to keep presses operating for a year in Bangladesh, Burma, India, Pakistan, Cambodia, Hong Kong, Indonesia, Malaysia, the Philippines, Singapore, South Korea, South Vietnam, Sri Lanka, Taiwan and Thailand (*Media Asia*, 2:3, 1975). Of the 524,000 tons used in Asia (excluding Japan) in 1974, 200,000 went to India, 60,000 to Thailand and 55,000 to Hong Kong, while Cambodia and Laos used 1,000 and 100 tons, respectively (*O'Leary*, 1974, p. 20).

Japan and South Korea were alone among nations almost self-sufficient in newsprint production. By 1974, Japan, which was being pressured to expand domestic production to keep up with demand growth and invest in the newsprint capacity of India and Indonesia, banned the export of newsprint to Southeast Asia (*Media*, Jan. 1974, p. 10). In the Philippines, the main newsprint manufacturer in Southeast Asia, the authorities ordered that any surplus should be exported to Thailand in exchange for rice.

In the 1970s, various suggestions and some efforts were made to change the newsprint situation. President Suharto of Indonesia recommended that his country and the Association of Southeast Asian Nations (ASEAN) jointly set up a newsprint factory to supply all of Southeast Asia, and occasionally, there was talk of experimenting with alternative raw materials (such as pineapple, sugarcane bagasse or vegetable waste) to make newsprint. There was some success with these experiments (*AMCB*, 1973b, p. 9). The Malaysian government in 1973 worked on the possibility of a newsprint plant; mills were started the following year in Thailand, and in South Asia, which produced some of its own newsprint, plans were made to increase productivity or develop new mills (see *Vittachi*, 1976, pp. 10-11).

1.1.2.3 Personnel

Personnel problems also hinder the production capability of the Asian press. The complaints range from poor top and intermediate management to a lack of skilled journalists and printers. Chowdhury has complained about the "notoriously irrational operational economics of the Asian newspaper industry," while others have lambasted publishers for treating their newspapers strictly as business enterprises, being much more concerned with balance sheets than newspaper contents. Japanese publishers, for example, came under severe criticism in the mid- to late-1970s, for their excessive promotional activities; some Indian, and earlier, Sri Lankan, publishers have verged on monopolization, according to government complaints.

The 1960s and 1970s spawned a number of educational, research and training institutes which helped further the professionalization of journalists. By the early 1970s, Asian Mass Communication and Information Research Centre (AMIC) reported that there were 136 such institutes in 16 Asian countries, although some were solely for broadcast personnel. Press Foundation of Asia (PFA), Nihon Shimbun Kyokai (NSK) and AMIC have been especially important in promoting professionalization of press personnel through seminars, training conferences and workshops. The PFA, conceived in March 1967 and funded shortly after by five media magnates from Korea, Sri Lanka, Singapore, the Philippines and India, listed as an aim in its charter, training in development journalism — along with freedom from newsprint hunger; the daily written word cheap enough for the poor; research for new designs of printing machines that would fit the poor-man-printer's economy of scale (*Vidura*, 1973, p. 5). A key training satellite of the PFA was the South East Asia Press Centre in Kuala Lumpur (see *Glattbach*, 1973, p. 9). About 500-600 Asian journalists were trained at various development journalism courses sponsored by the PFA. NSK, founded in 1946 to improve ethical standards of Japanese newspapers, has, since 1965, provided aid to the development of the Asian press, through seminars on management, news agencies and printing technology, and Japanese consultants in Asian countries (*Ejiri*, 1973, pp. 11-17). Between 1965-75, NSK sponsored 22 seminars with Asian journalists' participation and sent 58 Japanese consultants to other parts of Asia (*Asian Messenger*, 1977, p. 9). AMIC, started in Singapore in 1971 as an Asian media documentation center, has been involved in training, publications and as a catalyst in mass communications teaching, training and research. Many national press institutes have provided similar services to their newspapers. The Korean Press Institute publishes journalism magazines, sponsors research on newspaper readership, seminars and conferences, and since 1965, has been involved in journalism training (*Sinmun Pyungron,* 1964). The Press Institute of India has held dozens of workshops, seminars and refresher courses, published scores of books, sponsored specialist journalist seminars, arranged for the exchange of staff between Indian newspapers and instituted awards and consultancies (*Sarkar,* 1973, p. 9). Other Asian press groups also function. For example, the Indian Institute of Mass Communications in New Delhi trains journalists from the Third World; recently, IIMC sponsored a seminar to discuss training of news agency journalists.

The Conferation of ASEAN Journalists (CAJ), started in mid-1976 to coordinate cooperative efforts in research and training, has had seminars on development journalism and mass media and the Indonesian government, and has taken steps to urge cooperation among ASEAN news agencies (*AMCB,* 1976c, p. 9). In December 1978, CAJ and AMIC signed a charter of cooperation whereby, in the next two years, they would plan programs together in reporting on regional economic cooperation, urbanization and science and technology reporting. Non-Asian agencies, such as UNESCO, Thomson Foundation and Asia Foundation, have lent support to training programs.

Besides training, some of the regional and national press institutes have worked in other areas of professionalization. National institutes have promoted press councils, designed to provide a citizen check on the press, although in many cases, the councils originated as or became extensions of government (see *Rampal,* 1976).

Despite the yeoman work of these agencies, by the end of the 1970s, there were numerous pockets of journalists in Asia who had received little or no formal journalistic training, and corruption, in the form of tea money, among underpaid reporters was still rampant in many nations (*Chalkley,* 1974, p. 24). For example, a study done in Jullundur and Bhopal in India showed 86.9 per cent of working journalists had no formal training in journalism. Of the journalists surveyed, 8.4 per cent had been trained and 4.7 per cent had some workshop training. The journalists complained about the same difficulties Asian journalists have had for generations — low pay, lack of tools (such as telephones) and proper housing, and pressure from proprietors and governments (*Communicator,* 1977, p. 3). As the following chapters indicate, similar problems continue to hamper journalists throughout Asia.

By the late 1970s, concern was also expressed about the content of training programs during the previous decade and a half. Mitchell (1976, pp. 42-49) believed that Asia had fastened itself onto the hardware of development in the 1960s, and that this was reflected in the training that ensued. He thought many of the training programs emphasized Western press concepts, not those more endemic to Asia. Others thought the English language press of Asia was dominated by a Westernized elite, that Asian journalists were not perceptive to Asian problems, and, as the Sri Lankan information minister told a PFA meeting in 1978, that Asian journalists were to blame for the Western domination of news flow because they themselves did not cover Asian news (*Smith,* 1979, p. 16). In other instances, criticism was voiced against the concept of development journalism (which had its genesis in Asia), claiming it had been converted into "government-say-so" journalism; against the New World Information Order and its concepts of balanced flow of news and communication imperialism, saying these were further efforts at government control (see *Lent,* 1977a, pp. 17-26; *Harris,* 1977, pp. 27-32). Development journalism itself, according to Y. V. Lakshmana Rao, originator of AMIC and one of the optimists of the 1960s and early 1970s, was responsible for the evolving of a new type of professional journalist — "the confirmed civil servant — bent on being in the vanguard of developmental communication, thanks to the undreamt of appropriations under different headings: health, family planning, agriculture, nutrition, community development, etc." (*Rao,* 1977, p. 16).

Additionally, some of the press associations and institutes were in very painful positions in the late 1970s. Chowdhury reported in 1976 that, "Unable to resolve their moral conflict and still groping for a code of conduct, most of the press institutes' leaderships are either muted or moribund . . . . Morale of the senior editors of Asia has never been so low" (*Chowdhury,* 1976, pp. 1-2). He added that in-shop training and patrons of press professionalization efforts have nearly disappeared from the Asian scene. The very organization he worked so diligently with, Press Foundation of Asia (PFA), was in financial troubles. PFA, in 1977, divested itself of interests in *Asian Finance* magazine; sold 49 per cent of its professional monthly, *Media,* and 60 per cent equity in *Regional Reference Services* and the profitable *Datafil* (started in 1974 as one of two local versions of *Data Asia* mentioned later), to obtain capital for expansion. PFA trimmed many of its training and professionalization activities as its United Nations, Rockefeller Foundation and Thomson Foundation money ran out (*Tasker,* 1977b, p. 24; *Ali,* 1977, p. 6). One writer said the PFA foray in the tough world of commercial journalism had failed to be self-supporting (*Tasker,* 1977, p. 24). PFA has retained *Data Asia* (formerly *Data for Decision,* a weekly file of excerpts from 240 leading Asian newspapers and periodicals provided to the Asian press), the *Asian Press and Media Directory* (last published in 1977), *Data India* (the other local version of *Data Asia*) and *DEPTHnews,* model news service used to train journalists by bringing them in touch with developers, and whose product is distributed to newspapers on a commercial basis (*Santos,* 1974, pp. 13-17; *O'Leary,* 1975, pp. 43-48).

1.1.3 Consumption Capabilities

The Asian press, except for Japan, has not broken into mass circulation figures, penetrating all strata of society. Aggregate circulations have increased (e.g., from 83 million in 1973 to 106 million in 1975), but this has occurred because of the "simple force of natural increase" and steady increases in Japanese newspaper sales (*Rye and Roy,* 1976-77, p. vi). In many nations, circulations either have stagnated or have shown insignificant growth. UNESCO (1975) reported that in 20 nations, circulations increased in recent years, but in at least 10 countries, the ratio is below 20 copies of newspapers per 1,000 population. For example, India has 19, Indonesia seven and Nepal three. In Sri Lanka, print media have not penetrated more than 30 per cent of the households, and in India, a country of 605 million people, no newspaper has yet broken through the 300,000 mark (*Rye and Roy,* 1976-77, p. vi). A 1977 study showed that in Indonesia, only 15 million people (of a population of 130 million) could be reached by a newspaper. This figure was based on the nation's total circulation of 1.5 million and an assumed readership of 10 people per newspaper copy. As a final example of the paucity of newspaper circulations, five nations with century-plus traditions of print media (India, Indonesia, the Philippines, Thailand and Sri Lanka) and a total student enrollment of 135 million, have a total circulation of 14 million (*Chowdhury,* 1974).

1.1.3.1 Purchasing Power

The Press Foundation of Asia, in its charter, aimed to bring the price of newspapers within the purchasing power of more Asians. Surely, the group failed in this endeavor. For in Asia, newspapers cost five or six times more, relative to the people's incomes, than they do in Western nations. Asian newspapers are expensive because 85 per cent of what it takes to produce a newspaper must be imported from countries whose cost of living is five times higher than that of Asia. Thus, the Asian newspaper industry is caught in a vicious cycle: circulations are low because newspapers are priced too high; newspapers are priced too high because they do not have adequate circulations and advertising to meet production costs escalated because of the need to import raw materials.

In the 1970s, the prices of newspapers were raised in nearly all Asian nations because of economic recession, skyrocketing advertising rates, energy crises and newsprint shortages. The result was that, in an area where newspaper prices were always too high, by the late 1970s, they increased by two or three times what was considered too high in 1967-69. By comparison, in Tokyo, London or Washington, the average person can purchase a year's subscription to a daily for the equivalent of five days' wages. For example, in Japan, 4.6 days' earning power is enough to purchase *Asahi Shimbun* for a year. However, in Indonesia, 40 days' earning power of a teacher is required to read the *Jakarta Times,* and in India, a primary school teacher must work 15-20 days to buy *Jugantar* for a year. A semi-skilled Thai laborer would have to put in 21 days of wages to buy *Bangkok Daily*

News; a Philippine laborer, 11 days' wages for a year's subscription to a Manila daily, and in Malaysia, a factory worker would have to give up one-tenth of her daily earnings to purchase a newspaper copy on her way home from work.

1.1.3.2 Literacy

One of the problems that has been related to limited circulation growth is that of low literacy, especially in rural areas. Most of Asia has mounted campaigns to lower illiteracy rates; the success of these programs is reflected in the decrease by 7-9 per cent in Asia's illiteracy rate between 1960-70. Yet, about 47 per cent of the populations are illiterate. With the 1970s rate of educational progress and the aging of the population, the prediction was that by 1980, only 38 per cent of Asian adults will be illiterate. Because in some cultures, the social structures do not favor equality of opportunity (predominantly males and elites are educated), pockets of individuals will continue to be illiterate (*AMCB,* 1976d, pp. 13-14; see *Menon,* 1975). In other cases, where relevant reading material is not available, or where negative social pressure is placed on those who know how to read, lapses in literacy occur (*Lerner,* 1975, pp. 11-12).

However, the increase in literacy in many parts of Asia in the 1970s, confirmed the accusation of the 1960s, that the press was unable to reach the readership that *is* available. Chowdhury has argued that literacy seems to have little, if any, impact on the circulations of newspapers. He showed that in what he called the "media poverty zone" (Afghanistan, Pakistan, India, Nepal, Bangladesh, Burma, Thailand, Philippines and Indonesia), literacy rates range from 20 per cent in Bangladesh to 30 per cent in India, 40 per cent in Indonesia, 82 in Thailand and 83 in the Philippines, but the press in this zone shows similar growth patterns. For example, there are 18.6 copies of newspapers per 1,000 population and 64 per 1,000 literates in India; 34 and 36 per population and number of literates, respectively, in Thailand, and 29 and 35, respectively, in the Philippines. Chowdhury believed the picture changes in non-poverty zone areas. In Malaysia, there are 197 copies of newspapers for every 1,000 population and 271 per 1,000 literates; Singapore, South Korea and Taiwan also have high figures. Chowdhury concluded that "it is per capita income and newspaper prices — not simple literacy — that matters" (*Chowdhury*, 1974, p. 7). *Vittachi* (1976, p. 10), who would agree with Chowdhury, said that at best, outside of Japan, only two out of every 10 literate Asian households subscribe to a daily.

1.1.3.3 Relevant Contents

Because people have purchasing power and literacy does not mean they will read newspapers. Motivation to read is dependent upon relevant contents, and in Asia, as in many parts of the Third World, newspapers often lack this ingredient. Many newspapers use unattractive, bombastic writing, while the majority orient their news to urban elites, rather than rural peoples. *Vittachi* (1976, p. 10) wrote that, "Too many newspaper editors are writing for their proprietors' generation of readers and not for the new readership looming up before them. Their format and ideas of display are not sufficiently bright to attract and hold the new literate. Their writing is dull, heavy and unintelligible." Governmental "handoutitis" and the philosophy of "what the government says is news is news" have, in some instances, affected the public's credibility of, and willingness to, purchase newspapers (see Chapters 2.1, 3.1, 4.1).

In the 1970s, efforts were made to reach rural audiences with contents of interest and relevance to them. For example, in 1976, AMIC and the International Development Research Centre of Canada studied the nature of the rural press in the Philippines, Sri Lanka, India and Thailand, with the aim of disseminating development messages (*AMCB*, 1976a, p. 13), and AMIC and other groups have held conferences on the rural press. (Other conferences focused on non-formal means, such as folk or traditional media and interpersonal communication channels, to reach rural audiences.) By 1976, the Indonesian government increased its emphasis on the rural press in an effort to eradicate the 85 per cent illiteracy rate among the non-urban populations. Suharto suggested that the government should subsidize the rural press to achieve this goal (*Asian Messenger*, 1976b, p. 9). However, as the 1980s approached, not much had been accomplished to make the masses of Asia regular newspaper readers.

As Rye and Roy wrote:
> Rising costs and prices, material constraints such as
> dearth of newsprint, and a strange denial of enterprise
> and will have helped to preserve the Asian press as an
> essentially urban phenomenon, talking the urban
> language, showing urban reflexes, and imbibing urban
> likes and dislikes, while most of the people lived in
> villages (*Rye and Roy*, 1976-77, p. vi).

1.1.4 News Agencies

While the rest of the Third World complained in the late 1970s
about domination of the international flow of news by United
States and European news agencies, Asia took steps to be a more
active participant in the flow of at least its own news. In 1978,
12 news agencies from as many Asian countries (another joined
later) agreed to participate in the UNESCO-backed Asian News
Agency Cooperation. The organization aimed to expand news
networks among Asian countries, to reduce by one-fifth to one-
tenth the present news transmission charges (*AMCB*, 1978, p. 17;
Asiaweek, 1979a, p. 36), to train news agency journalists and to
work towards solving the lack of equipment, especially among
smaller agencies which could not link even with neighboring
countries (*AMCB*, 1979, pp. 5, 14). However, by early 1979, the
idea of an Asian news agency was in trouble as it had been in
the past, as the meeting scheduled to discuss its framework was
called off because of too divergent views on the nature of the
agency (*IPI Report*, 1979).

The history of initiatives to form an Asian news agency has
been fraught with disappointments. Conferences on the topic
have been held regularly but with limited results. For example,
a UNESCO conference on the development of news agencies in
Asia, held in Bangkok in 1961, set up an informal gathering of
countries called the Organization of Asian News Agencies
(OANA), but it was never very active. The idea was reactivated
many times but not as enthusiastically as in the mid-1970s when
the Third World debates raged throughout the world. In 1977,
the Philippines suggested an international news agency (International News Exchange — INEX) with funding from five Manila

government agencies, but nothing has materialized with this project (*Kulkarni,* 1977). Another meeting of news agency executives from 25 Asian countries was held in December 1977 in Sri Lanka, to develop a network for the exchange of news and features (*South China Morning Post,* 1977, p. 6), and 60 non-aligned nations met in Colombo and New Delhi in 1977 to create a non-aligned countries newspool of their press agencies. But, by the end of the 1970s, after many conference hours of discussion, many problems remained almost insurmountable to the development of an Asian news agency. A chief problem related to the nature of the agency, with some countries seeking a stronger government role than others wanted. Yet, to be successful financially, such an agency would have to depend upon large infusions of government money. Other problems related to socio-cultural differences, especially the multiplicity of languages in use by Asian national news agencies and newspapers. No matter which language is chosen for a region-wide agency, there is a need for expensive and time-consuming translation, either at the agency or on individual newspapers. Today, some national news agencies, such as those of Japan, South Korea and Taiwan, provide translations of wire copy from other services, while other national agencies, such as those of Singapore and Hong Kong, leave the translation to be done by individual newspapers (see *Lee-Reoma,* 1977, pp. 70-76).

More successful have been the domestic news services established in individual nations. Most of these, owned by government and very heavily involved in covering the development story, have been able to weather bad times because the governments think development journalism is too important to forsake for economics. And they did have bad times during the economic pinch of the 1970s, at which time, some of them complained of not getting enough help from the communications industry (postal and telecommunications). For example, in 1976, the news agencies of the ASEAN nations called for an immediate reduction in press telecommunications fees. Simultaneously, they set up a newspool and established news links among themselves (*AMCB,* 1976b, p. 4). Most national agencies are small compared to international agencies such as Reuter, Associated Press, United Press International or TASS, and cannot provide the news budgets required by some dailies. For example, Antara, the semi-government agency of Indonesia, started in 1937, issues nine Indonesian language bulletins daily of 69,000 words, and another 14 in English; Bernama, begun with Malaysian government money in the late 1960s, moves 20,000 words daily each in English and Bahasa Malay; Press Trust of India sends out 75,000-80,000 words daily, and the Philippine News Agency, started in 1973 with 60 per cent government financing, moves 150,000 words every day (*Glattbach and Santos*, 1975, pp. 13-18).

1.1.5 Conclusion

If generalizations are permissible, then one might conclude that more gains have been achieved in the production than in the consumption of Asian newspapers. The newsprint crisis is not as obvious today as in the early 1970s, and governments are mounting projects to expand the Asian newsprint industries. Many large city newspapers have adopted modern printing equipment, and in some cases, governmental and private industries have involved themselves in the manufacture of equipment. Press revenues have increased in recent years, and some efforts at professionalization of media personnel, both at regional and national levels, linger on. However, none of this progress is significant enough to warrant a belief that the production of Asian newspapers is in the throes of a complete transformation. Changes taking place are isolated in many instances to certain countries, or more specifically, to capital cities in those countries. The situation in regard to consumption of Asian newspapers continues to be bleak, as production costs drive the prices of newspapers out of the reach of the purses of most Asians and as newspapers hesitate to change their contents from a predominantly urban to a more rural orientation.

In the 1960s and early 1970s, there were enthusiastic senior editors and press institute personnel who risked making changes. With the continued governmental intrusions into the journalistic domain, replacing in the process many senior editors with young civil servants, and the drying up of some of the press institutes, little hope is held for great changes.

Part 2
East Asia

2.1 Freedom of the Press in East Asia

John A. Lent

The eight nations of East Asia, representing the bulk of the population, land and resources of the continent, have had a long history of political turmoil, attested to by two governments each claiming to be China and Korea. Resulting from these conflicts have been a number of authoritarian governments, ranging from Nationalist Taiwan and South Korea to the communist states of China, Democratic People's Republic of Korea and Mongolian People's Republic. Two other areas, Hong Kong and Macao, are among the few remaining from the colonial era. Under such political conditions, the press of East Asia can hardly be expected to be free.

This essay explores press freedom in East Asia primarily between 1975-79, taking into account the enactment of press laws, suspension of newspapers and arrests of journalists, the levying of economic sanctions and the moves to government ownership.

2.1.1 People's Republic of China

The role of the press in China, like that of the Soviet Union, is in accordance with the Marxist-Leninist concept of total integration with the government and Communist Party and in harmony with Maoist concepts of mass line, anti-intellectualism and anti-professionalism. Maoist thought calls for the press to be involved in propaganda, mobilization, organization, education and criticism, organized in an hierarchic order and evolving from each other (*Opletal*, 1977, pp. 38-39). Therefore, the press in China is totally subject to the interests and goals of society and the opinion[1] formation process as developed by the party. It is a press intricately organized both horizonally (along administrative-territorial lines) and vertically (by specialized functions) to carry out mass campaigns and often to vilify and destroy individuals.[2]

Although the Chinese Constitution of 1975 guarantees press freedom, it does so only with the stipulation that the socialist system, the laws and the leadership of the Communist Party must not be disputed or infringed. Strangely, *dazibaos* (wall posters) are explicitly mentioned and encouraged in the Constitution. The *dazibaos*, unlike formal media which are screened through various party channels,[3] make it possible to address the public more directly. In fact, one of the encouraging signs of government attitudes towards the press has been the very liberal nature of the *dazibao* campaign of late 1978, considered the most liberal thus far (*Time*, 1978, pp. 46, 48; *Asiaweek*, 1978c, pp. 36-39).

If there has been a liberalization of the formal press, its genesis can be traced to 21 January 1977, when *Jen-min Jih-pao*, the main national daily, turned over its front page to letters from readers complaining about the paper's dull image as developed under the Gang of Four. *Jen-min Jih-pao*'s self criticism said the Gang of Four dictated a style of journalism that consisted of "endless pages with long and smelly clichés"; material "overbearing and quick to label other people"; writing which was "veiled, round-about and insinuating"; "hood-winking the masses"; and articles which "stereotyped and (were) repulsive" (*Davies*, 1977c, p.7). The paper promised to change from that boring style by using a "completely new situation" with greater

1　Two different terms express public opinion in China. "Yulun" is public opinion as portrayed by Party statements; it is the content of official propaganda or the "publicized opinion" in the regular media. "Renmin Qunzhong de Yijian" is "opinion of the popular masses," or suggestions or views from the base which are at least indirectly integrated into the process of communications. *Opletal,* 1977, pp. 38-39.

2　The Chinese press uses allegory and parables in its vilification campaigns. Among other things, this makes it easier to reintegrate a rehabilitated purgee later. See *Pye,* 1978, pp. 221-246.

3　All important items of political news in China, especially if they are thought to be surprising or controversial, are first sent down through Communist Party channels some time before they are published in *Jen-min Jih-pao.* See *Harris,* 1976, p. 5.

political "liveliness," artistic creativity and economic prosperity[4] (*Butterfield*, 1977a, p. 8-c).

Later in 1977, the official press vowed to discontinue the practice of parroting itself with numerous reprints of politically significant articles in different publications. Again, the Gang of Four was blamed for this longstanding practice (London *Times*, 1977a, p. 7).

At least one foreign observer believed that by 1979 the change had been effected. Writing in the *Bulletin of the ASNE*, Ghiglione said that the regular investigative reporting in *Jen-min Jih-pao* today "tackles everything from the poor quality of Chinese television sets, to the high price of fish in Shantung province, to the exploitation of Northeast China's peasants by the electric company" (*Ghiglione*, 1979a, pp. 12-15). He, and others, (*Davis*, 1977b, p. 17), said the paper has been brightened with cartoons, drawings, more photographs, shorter articles, crisper writing and four-color spreads. A more candid style of reporting has allowed for some criticism of China and praise of the West, but this must be taken in the context of the political purposes such candidness serves — to help push the realization of the Four Modernizations (educational, industrial, scientific and agricultural) by the year 2000, and to criticize the Gang of Four[5]. Still another political motive is that there is increasing evidence that the press is being used to unload the heavy influence of Mao. For example, a *Jen-min Jih-pao* editorial in September 1977 stated that Mao's directives are sometimes contradictory and must be read in the proper context. Later that year, the newspaper stopped carrying the daily Mao quotations inserted alongside the nameplate; in their place were the sayings of Hua Kuo-feng and Teng Hsiao-ping (*Asian Messenger*, 1978b, p. 5). Thus, if a liberalization of the press is occurring, it may be of a transitory nature until the new power structure works out some of its problems.

---

4   See also London *Times*, 1977b, p. 4. Even earlier, the *New York Times* inferred that *Jen-min Jih-pao* might be changing its format as it poured out sensational matter on Chiang Ching, purged widow of Mao and one of the Gang of Four. *Butterfield*, 1976, p. 3-C.

5   In fact, on the latter point, editors who served during the Gang of Four period are now being denounced.

2.1.2 *Republic of China (Taiwan)*

Taiwan, still under "state of siege laws" enacted by the Nationalists in 1934, has been the scene in the late 1970s of a press freedom bandwagon that could augur well for the island republic's newspapers. The newly-found openness of the press resulted from the challenge of a small group of newspapers of the long-held monopoly of news by the ruling Kuomintang Party. As elections approached in December 1978, for the first time in many years, names, pictures and even campaign platforms of opposition candidates slowly began to appear in Taiwan dailies, especially the *United Daily News* (usually solidly pro-Kuomintang), *Independence Evening Post* and *China News*. But, as one writer noted,

> So far the boundaries of the newly-discovered freedom of the press are ill-defined. Authorities themselves are not yet clear about how much relaxation of control is acceptable. But it is evident that there is considerable desire among the island's press corps to keep up the momentum (*Kazer,* 1978a, p. 23).

Earlier, the *Far Eastern Economic Review Yearbook* (1978, p. 314) said 1977 was one of the most liberal periods in Taiwan's modern history. For the first time, the government allowed uncensored photographs of Mao to appear in foreign magazines sold in Taiwan. Previously, such photographs of Mao and other Chinese leaders were ripped out, obliterated beyond recognition or stamped with the Chinese word for "bandit" (*Liu,* 1977, pp. 40-41).

Encouraging as these recent events seem, one must put them in proper perspective with the laws and traditions pertaining to Taiwanese press-government relationships. Newspapers are restricted by a 1958 Publication Law requiring registration by government of all publications. The same law does not permit the press to attack the Taiwanese policy of recovering the mainland or advocacy of Taiwan's independent movement, to use demoralizing materials or to provide assistance to communist propaganda.

Regularly, publications are suspended or banned and newspeople are arrested for infringements upon the 1958 press law.

In recent years, two magazines, *Taiwan Political Review* and *China Humanist Magazine,* because of their outspokenness, have been victims of government retaliation. *Taiwan Political Review,* a liberal periodical, was closed after the December 1975 elections for "inciting insurrection" (*FEER,* 1976, p. 26); its license was revoked in mid-October 1976, at which time Managing Editor Huang Hua was sentenced by military tribunal to ten years' imprisonment. Because the authorities believed that Huang would not be subdued (he had been imprisoned for two and a half years in the early 1960s and again from 1967-75), they also arrested his brother, sister and parents (*Armbruster,* 1976, p. 19; also *Henry,* 1977, p. 57). Later, the Deputy Editor of *Taiwan Political Review,* Chang Chin-tse, was charged with minor crimes and subsequently freed on bail pending appeal, during which time he escaped to the United States (*FEER,* 24 June 1977, p. 28).

The *China Humanist Magazine* was suspended for one year as of 25 May 1977, because the publisher "did not notify the government before printing articles contrary to the magazine's previously stated purpose of publication." Any hopes on the part of the *Humanist* to reappear were stopped by a government decree of 1 March 1978, which suspended for one year registration of any new magazines. The government explained that the suspension was to prevent publication of inferior magazines and to encourage the upgrading of Taiwan's 1,577 already existing magazines. However, the issuance of the decree coincided with an application to start a magazine similar to the *Taiwan Political Review* (*Liu,* 1978, p. 22). The ban was lifted in 1979 when the government announced that because of the ban, the quality of magazines had improved (*Free China Review,* 1979a, p. 55). One writer said the tightening up of the press in 1978 was part of the domestic political control Taiwan exercised after the United States' "derecognition" (*Kazer,* 1979, p. 14). When publishing controls were eased with the expiration of the ban in 1979, a spate of opposition periodicals appeared. Many of these, which appeared to be magazines, devoted much attention to opposition views. Kazer reported, "Opposition politicians suggest that the government may be shifting its tactics, allowing opposition publications to appear but reserving the right to suspend them if they overstep their bounds" (*Kazer,* 1979, p. 14).

Other situations still exist that do not bode well for press freedom in Taiwan. For example, prior censorship is part of governmental practice in Taiwan, prompting one writer to quip that editors must commit to memory the axioms, "Thou shalt not criticize the President personally," and "Thou shalt not question basic policy" (*Kazer*, 1978b, p. 22). In 1978, the government in another ruling, stipulated that books and other materials about government officials had to be pre-censored. When something slips by a censor and is published, banning or confiscation of the publication occurs. The *Far Eastern Economic Review* claimed it is systematically and regularly banned in Taiwan (*Davies*, 1977c and d), and the *Taiwan Presbyterian Weekly* reported in 1978 that 4,000 copies of a controversial issue were "lost" in the mail. Three days before a 21 March 1978 election, a raid on a printing plant netted the entire run of *Long Live Elections!*, a book that contained sensitive pictures and copy on riots that took place on a previous election day (*Asiaweek*, 1978c, p. 24). Also in 1978, the government purchased the outspoken *Taiwan Daily News*, in the process softening its tone. The purchase took place under "threat of stern physical and financial consequences" if the publisher refused to sell (*Kazer*, 1978b, p. 22).

2.1.3 Japan

All laws restricting the press have been eliminated in Japan, except for regulations in general laws and in the special law on protection of military secrets of United States forces stationed in Japan. However, a number of self-regulatory practices, especially those of Nihon Shimbun Kyokai code of ethics, exist (*Ejiri*, 1977, pp. 11-16; also, *Ito*, 1976). Other self-imposed limitations of a more informal type are often debilitating, especially those of the so-called three "institutional inhibitions" — criticism of the royal family; exposure of the intimate relationship between rightist gangsters and politicians, and exploitation of the most sensitive area of society, "the untouchables" (*Nakamura*, 1975, p. 28). Generally, the Japanese press is hesitant to go against the Establishment; editors do not demand investigative reporting because "they think that's a job for the police" (*Forbis*, 1975, p. 10), and newspapers take a party line, opposing communism, favoring the ruling party, big business and national progress (*Huffman*, 1977). Some of this results from the group journalism prevalent in Japan where reporters use the syndicate system to cover stories:

> They have well-organized and exclusive clubs that pool questions and give them to a 'captain' to ask, with everyone sharing the answers, and all enterprise or digging made unnecessary, so that the members are left with lots of time to play mah-jongg. The reporters mutually decide what, and what not to use from interviews and stipulate which edition a story will break in (*Forbis*, 1975; see also, *Yu*, 1974; *New York Times*, 1976, p.4).

Examples abound concerning the timidity of the Japanese press. The Lockheed scandal that brought down the Tanaka government was not reported by dailies until they were forced to do so by an exposé in a monthly magazine, *Bungei Shunju* (see *Japan Echo*, 1976); the daily *Yomiuri*, for two months in 1976, sat on important information it had on Prime Minister Takeo Miki, and, in the Japanese equivalent of the Pentagon Papers case, the secret Foreign Ministry information obtained by a reporter[6] was not used even by his own newspaper.

Thus, in Japan, press freedom is hindered not by government fiat but by self-regulatory customs of publishers and journalists and by consensus reporting.

2.1.4 Republic of Korea

South Korea has some of the most restrictive press legislation in East Asia. Under the regulations, a journalist can receive up to 15 years' imprisonment for merely expressing doubts about any aspect of the Constitution; newspapers are not permitted to publish anti-Park Chung Hee material or information that could cause a crisis of national security or social or economic instability. In

---

6   At the trial of the reporter, who obtained the information by befriending a secretary in the Foreign Ministry, the Tokyo High Court ruled he had acted illegally in getting the secret documents and sentenced him to four months' imprisonment. *Brown and Lee*, 1977, p. 477.

March 1975, the National Assembly passed a bill making it punishable by up to 10 years' imprisonment for spreading distortion about the government to foreigners, either in Korea or abroad[7]. Also, under Korean law, provincial newspapers can be merged if they do not follow the Park line (*Nam*, 1978, pp. 43-45).

Total control of the South Korean press was achieved in the last five years although the campaign dates to at least 1963. In that year, President Park installed top officials of newspapers such as *Dong-A Ilbo* and *Hankook Ilbo* as his premier and vice-premier. Between 1973-75, the Park government used a variety of methods to disrupt normal press activities. Newspapers and news agencies were forced to merge or were closed; a number of journalists were arrested, and in 1973 alone, at least 20 publications (mainly magazines) had their publishing licenses revoked (see *FEER*, 17 Jan. 1975; 12 Sept. 1975, p. 18; *E. and P.*, 27 Sept. 1975, p. 13). In 1974-75, the government was responsible for an advertising boycott of the largest and oldest daily, *Dong-A Ilbo*, which resulted in a loss of 98 per cent of its advertisers in one month. *Dong-A Ilbo* relented by March 1975, firing 17 reporters, presumably as a concession to the officials who then called off the boycott (see *IPI Report*, Dec. 1975, p. 16; *Media*, March 1975, p. 22; May 1975, p. 24; *Quill*, April 1975, p. 8; *FEER*, 21 March 1975, p. 23; 11 April 1975, p. 22).

Since 1975, the South Korean press has been rather docile. Newspapers are under the surveillance of the Korean Central Intelligence Agency who "almost daily make the rounds of newspaper offices to 'chat' with editors and reporters and also may read copy before it goes to press" (*Nam*, 1978, p. 44)[8].

---

7   A number of citations exist concerning these laws. See London *Times*, 16 Jan. 1975, 3 Feb. 1975, p. 13; *Data for Decision*, 23-31 Dec. 1974, p. 2510; *Editor & Publisher*, 15 Feb. 1975, p. 13, 12 April 1975, p. 56; *The Quill*, March 1975, p. 8; *Media*, Feb. 1974, p. 24; *New York Times*, 18 March 1975, p. 7; 19 March 1975, p. 22, 20 March 1975, p. 6.

8   Former Korean high official in Washington, Jai Hyon Lee, is more emphatic on the role of the KCIA, claiming the agents are in newspaper offices on a "full-time basis to monitor and virtually edit the news." Jai Hyon Lee, "The Activities of the Korean Central Intelligence Agency in the United States," testimony before House of Representatives Subcommittee on International Organizations of the Committee on International Relations, 22 June 1976.

During the height of the Tong Sun Park controversy in the United States, the press was told not to publish anything on the affair, except for a single official announcement of 28 December 1976 (*Campbell*, 1977, p. 58).

Apart from domestic censorship, foreign news periodicals such as *Time, Newsweek* and *Far Eastern Economic Review* have for years been censored before sale or distribution, "with offending pages routinely clipped out, or short items painted over with black ink" (*Campbell*, 1977, p. 58).

2.1.5 Democratic People's Republic of Korea and Mongolian People's Republic

The press of North Korea is organized similarly to that of China, having structural and functional components. Both a national state (*Minju Choson*) and a national Korean Workers Party daily (*Nodong Sinmun*) operate, while the party committee in each province publishes a four-page daily. Each factory and enterprise has its own newspaper aimed at increasing production and maintaining worker support for ideology and the socialist revolution. As in China, most news items are provided by the national news service run by the State Administration Council. Also, most newspapers take their guidance from the national party organ, *Nodong Sinmun,* which has as its goals, the idolization of Kim Il Sung, the development of class consciousness and revolutionary enthusiasm and the propagation of the national ideology (*Vreeland and Shinn,* 1976, p. 151).

Articles must be submitted by noon of the day prior to publication to be reviewed by all members of the newspapers' editorial boards and appropriate committees of the party. Expected to act as propagandists and agitators, press personnel are called upon to contribute their efforts to governmental and party campaigns, for example, the seven-year economic development plan implemented in 1978.

The conclusion drawn from a 1976 one-month survey of *Nodong Sinmun,* which showed that 44 per cent of the space was devoted to the domestic economy and 22 per cent to history and ideology, was that,

The large number of news items and feature articles about the 'revolutionary struggle' could be indicative of a domestic propaganda campaign designed to encourage further economic sacrifices and self-denial (*Katz*, 1977).[9]

Newspapers of Mongolia are patterned after the communist model with state and party ownership and control predominating. The main dailies are *Unen* (Truth), central organ of the Central Committee of the Mongolian Revolutionary People's Party and of the government, and *Ulaanbaatoryn Medee* (Ulanbatar News), published by the Ulanbatar City Committee of the party and the executive board of the City Khural of People's Deputies. Actually, most newspapers are organs of departments and committees of the Party and state (*IOJ*, 1976, p. 96)

2.1.6 Hong Kong and Macao

Hong Kong has one of the most free presses in all of Asia despite having some of the worst possible legal restraints, such as those of the Control of Publications Ordinance. Except during infrequent emergencies, as in 1967, the authorities keep their hands off the press.[10] A law that has given the press some concern has been the Objectionable Publications Bill of 1975, designed to ward off pornography in the colony. Because the bill is vague in wording, it could be used to suppress other types of materials deemed objectionable by the authorities (*Media*, Sept. 1975). In 1977, government agents raided a magazine distribution house,

9   The same survey showed that over 40 per cent of all space on foreign governments went to the United States and South Korea, considered the country's chief enemies. For an earlier study, see "North Korean View of the U.S.S.R. and the P.R.C.: A Quantitative Analysis of the Korean Workers Party Newspaper *(Nodong Sinmun)* 1972-1973," Washington, D.C.: Psyop Automated Management Information System, Foreign Media Analysis Subsystem, 1973. That study, drawn over a 24-month sample of *Nodong Sinmun* in 1972-73, showed there were 15,372 articles on North Korea, 2,848 on South Korea, 2,769 on Japan, 2,191 on the United States, 1,359 on China and 691 on the USSR.

10   In fact, the only freedom of press incident in recent years concerned the suspension by the Chinese University of Hong Kong of its student newspaper, *Shatin News*. Three professors associated with the newspaper applied to the courts to order the university to rescind its censure resolution. *Chang*, 1976, p. 8.

presumably under the aegis of this law, and seized *Oui* and *Penthouse* magazines, banning their future sales on the grounds that they were objectionable.

In the Portuguese territory of Macao, an Ad Hoc Committee on Press and Radio was set up after the 1974 coup in Portugal to ensure that newspapers and radio stations follow government guidelines. There have been a couple of press freedom incidences in Macao recently. In mid-1974, the government tried to kill the opposition daily, *Gazeta Macanese,* by suspending its monthly subvention of US$826 (*FEER,* 16 Aug. 1974, p. 27); more recently, *Noticias de Macao* suspended publication for over two years rather than pay a fine of US$2,330 and accept a one-day ban levied by the Ad Hoc Committee. *Noticias* was accused of carrying "inaccurate reports" about the governor.

2.1.7 Summary

Recently, when press freedom in Asia is discussed, the emphasis has been on what is happening in Southeast Asia, India and Pakistan. Often ignored are the nations of East Asia. This may result because so many of the presses of this region are tightly-controlled under communist and other authoritarian governments. The usual flare-ups between government and the press just do not happen in socialist nations such as China, North Korea and Mongolia where the press is welded to the government/party apparatus. They are also less frequent in South Korea and Taiwan as those governments closed ranks on the press, in both cases claiming this was necessitated by the fact that they faced external threats from nearby communist enemies and therefore had to protect their national security. Therefore, it might seem that because these nations have so few publicized press/government conflicts, they must have a high degree of press freedom. Of course, nothing could be further from the truth.

In conclusion, East Asia is unique, having as it does four or five of the most restricted presses of Asia, as well as two of its freest — Japan and Hong Kong.

2.2 People's Republic of China

Alan P. L. Liu

The press on mainland China suffered a major shake-up during the so-called Great Proletarian Cultural Revolution from 1966-69. The effect of this major political upheaval on the press in the People's Republic can be seen in a report in the *Catalogue of Newspapers and Periodicals (Pao-k'an Mu-lu)* of 1968 which states that 58 newspapers and periodicals were then in circulation as compared with 132 in 1967 and 648 in 1966 (*Chung, 1969,* p. 12). Yet, this is hardly surprising since the press in mainland China, after 1949, has always been a subordinate public institution within the communist totalitarian apparatus. As such the Chinese press cannot avoid the effects of the stresses and strains in the elite alignment of the Chinese Communist Party. On the other hand, the relatively invariable "political culture" of totalitarian politics in mainland China also sets a limit on the extent of changes that the Chinese press underwent as a result of the Cultural Revolution.

In subsequent discussions I shall describe and analyze the major aspects of both continuity and discontinuity of the Chinese press from the outbreak of the Cultural Revolution to the present in terms of its overall structure, content and function, circulation, and conclusion.

Alan P. L. Liu is on the faculty of political science, University of California, Santa Barbara. He has written a series of monographs, books and articles on various Chinese mass media. Dr. Liu was on the research staffs of MIT and University of Michigan in the 1960s.

2.2.1 *System under Stress*

Before the Cultural Revolution, the press in mainland China was organized strictly according to the principle of unity with diversity. Unity, in the substance and organization of the press, was achieved by stamping out privately-owned newspapers and organizing a nationwide chain of "Party Press," i.e., newspapers representing the Chinese Communist Party at national, regional (provinces, municipalities) and lower (county and commune) levels. Unity in the press is ultimately achieved by establishing a single authoritative news agency, the *New China News Agency*, which supplies international news to all newspapers and broadcasting stations in China; and national news to all regional newspapers and radio stations.

Diversity within unity was accomplished by three types of (nominally) "non-Party" press. They were: ① newspapers representing a few major mass organizations such as the former *Kung-jen-Jih-pao* (*Workers' Daily*) of All-China Federation of Trade Unions, the *Chung-kuo Ching-nien Pao* (*China Youth Daily*) of the Young Communist League and the *Kuang-ming Jih-Pao* (*Brightness Daily*) of Democratic Alliance; ② newspapers about specific public interest or activity like the former *Ta-kung Pao* (*Impartial Daily*), specializing in matters on international affairs, commerce and finance; and the *Wen-hui Pao* (*Literary Gazette*) on arts and literature; and ③ a large number of newspapers published by public institutions, the most well-known ones being those for the armed forces, headed by the *Chieh-fang-chun Pao* (*The Liberation Army Daily*).

Before the Cultural Revolution, the Chinese Communist Party enforced its policy of unity in two ways. Organizationally, in every "non-Party" newspaper, a "Party fraction" was formed consisting of all Party members in the paper. This is the group that decided editorial and personnel policy of the paper. More often than not, the deputy director of a "non-Party" paper was a veteran Party member who was the actual head of the paper (*Chou,* 1963, p. 29). Professionally, every "non-Party" newspaper was required to publish, on its front page, all the important national and international news printed on the front page of the *Jen-min Jih-pao* (*People's Daily*) which, as the organ of the Central Committee of the Chinese Communist Party, heads the chain of Party press. Moreover, the specific reports published in these "non-Party" newspapers were also required to reflect and promote the official line of any subject. Often the "diversity" aspect became all but nominal. As one prominent "China watcher" commented:

> There are many days when one feels that the printing of several newspapers, instead of one, *Jen-min Jih Pao*, was a sheer waste of paper, ink and printing machines — though it may have saved labor in editorial offices (*Stewart*, 1966, p. 66).

The rationale of this kind of press structure is the Chinese Communist Party's emphasis on mass mobilization. The different types of the "non-Party Press" had made the masses of Chinese people accessible to the direction of political leaders.

Yet in 1965, as a prelude to the Cultural Revolution, Mao Tse-tung made a novel use of the unity-with-diversity principle by turning "non-Party" press against Party press. The start of this shake-up was Mao's use of the *Wen-hui Pao* of Shanghai to attack, in November 1965, the *Peking Jih-pao* (*Peking Daily*), organ of Peking Municipal Party Committee, over a play containing covert criticism against Mao. This was followed by a more spectacular event in the Chinese press, the attack on the hitherto authoritative *Jen-min Jih-pao* (*People's Daily*) by the *Chieh-fang-chun Pao* (*The Liberation Army Daily*) in May 1966[1]. The attack on the highest Party press by the military organ, of course, represented Mao's main tactics in the Cultural Revolution, to use the army to purge the Communist Party. Consequently, the then chief editor of the *People's Daily*, Wu Leng-hsi, was replaced by the chief editor of *The Liberation Army Daily*.

At the outset of 1967, as more and more regional Party establishments were subject to the "power seizures" by Red Guards and other rebels, the press throughout China suffered the same fate. Even a "Maoist" paper like Shanghai's *Wen-hui Pao* or the reorganized *People's Daily* underwent another round of shake-up. For example, *Wen-hui Pao* was taken over by an alliance of

---

1   By now, almost all published accounts about the Cultural Revolution have mentioned these initiating events; hence, I see no need to go into details. For an excellent Chinese article on this, see *Ting*, 1967.

two Red Guard groups from the colleges in Shanghai and a rebel
group organized by some staff members of the paper on 3 January
1967 (*Hung-wei Ch'an-pao,* 4 Jan. 1967, p. 4). The effect of this
and other seizures of newspapers spread so far and wide as to
provoke a similar seizure in Lhasa, the capital of Tibet. Claiming
inspiration from Shanghai, a local rebel group took over the *Tibet
Daily* on 11 January (*Radio Lhasa,* 1200 GMT, 20 Feb. 1967).
At the end of the "power seizure" movement, the Party press
survived with "scars" (which will be discussed shortly) but the
"non-Party" press suffered heavy casualties. With the suspension
of the All-China Federation of Trade Unions and Young Communist League, the *Workers' Daily* and the *China Youth Daily*
ceased publication. The *Ta-kung Pao* was at first obliged to change
its name to the *Chien-chin Pao* (*Progressive News*) and then
ceased publication altogether. Another specialized newspaper,
the *Ti-yu-Pao* (*Sports News*), formerly the organ of National
Council of Physical Exercises, also stopped publication.

Today (1974), at the national level, a skeleton of the "unity
with diversity" principle still exists in press structure. The
People's Daily, after several factional infights, remains the organ
of the Central Committee of the Chinese Communist Party. The
"non-Party" press is represented by the *Kuang-ming Jih-pao* and
the *Liberation Army Daily* has now become the most important
public institution press. While the Young Communist League and
the All-China Federation of Trade Unions have been revived, there
is yet no sign of the revival of their own organ paper. With the
People's Daily again occupying its Olympian height, the chain
of Party press at provinces and municipalities is back in operation.

In the meantime, since 1972, a campaign of rehabilitating
professional Party-line journalists has been in effect. The *People's
Daily* is again under the supervision of its former chief editor,
Wu Leng-hsi, and the *New China News Agency* is headed by one
of its former deputy directors, Chu Mu-chih, who was regarded
highly by its staff (*MacFarquhar,* 1973, p. 145; *New York Times,*
21 Oct. 1972).

Yet, as we mentioned, the Party press in mainland China has
survived the Cultural Revolution with "scars" and "wounds."
Formerly the principle of "unity with diversity" applied mainly
to Party-non-Party press relations. After the attacks on the highest

Party organ, the power seizures of regional and lower press and public denunciations of many veteran Party journalists, a force of "diversity" has now penetrated into the Party press, eroding the commanding position of the *People's Daily*. Reflecting the realignment of the elite at the top rank of the Chinese Communist Party, two regional newspapers have occasionally taken independent lines on public policy. One is the *Wen-hui Pao* of Shanghai that Mao had used in 1965 to fire the first salvo of the Cultural Revolution. In 1967, the authority of the *Wen-hui Pao* was almost equal to that of the *People's Daily*. Chou En-lai was reported to have remarked to a group of Red Guards in 1967 that: "The Central Cultural Revolution Group has to state its position through the *Wen-hui-Pao* when it is not proper for the group to do it officially. You must study the *Wen-hui Pao* seriously. The *Wen-hui Pao* has a long-time liaison station at the Center" (*Hung-chi Chan-pao,* 10 Oct. 1967, quoted in *Chao,* 1968, p. 15). Since then, the position of the *Wen-hui Pao* has declined somewhat though it is still not an "ordinary" regional or special press. As one source commented in 1970:

> A special category must be made for the newspapers and radio broadcasts of Shanghai, which since 1967 have consistently served as vehicles for points of view more radical or militant than the national media. It may be that Mao-intimates Chang Ch'un-ch'iao and Yao Wen-yuan, both long-time Shanghai propagandists and associates of Chiang Ch'ing, have been able to use the Shanghai media as their own voice.
> There were indications in 1969, however, that these media were not always more "leftist" than the national media; perhaps the term "vanguard" would describe their function more exactly (*Current Scene,* 1 Feb. 1970, p. 8).

More recently, in 1973, the radical stand of the *Wen-hui Pao* seems to have been superseded by the *Liaoning Jih-pao* (*Liaoning Daily*), organ of the Provincial Party Committee of Liaoning in northeast China. The occasion for the assertiveness of the *Liaoning Daily* in 1973 was similar to the occasion for the independence of the *Wen-hui Pao* in 1967, i.e., dispute among top Communist Party leaders over policies. In 1973 domestic Chinese politics was marked by a dispute over the examination policy and curriculum in China's colleges and universities. It took the form of a reader's letter, published by the *Liaoning Daily* on 19 July, criticizing the use of pure academic criteria to admit students to universities and a nationwide press campaign denouncing Confucius, who used to be known for his principle of "education to all regardless of class," while praising Chin-shih Huang-ti (the first Emperor of China, 221-210 B.C.), regarded as an arch-villain for his brutal treatment of scholars. What is significant is that, instead of taking a lead in these matters as its position warrants, the *People's Daily* merely echoed the radical line taken by the *Liaoning Daily*.[2] As one source commented on the significance of the independent stand of this Liaoning paper:

> If newspapers in China were competitive, the *Liaoning Jih Pao*, published in the northeastern city of Shenyang, might start advertising: "You read it first in the *Liaoning Jih Pao*."
>
> In 1971 the themes for the campaign against the fallen Lin Piao were first set out in the Shenyang paper. This past summer it was first with an attack on the examination system in China, which soon gained national currency. It was also fast off the mark in breaking the Confucius expose.
>
> The unusual influence of the newspaper is usually attributed to the unusual influence of a commander of the People's Liberation Army, Chen Hsi-lien, who is simultaneously the top military man and the top party official in Liaoning Province (*Lelyveld*, 1973).

So far only two regional newspapers have been mentioned that showed an independent line in reporting. How far this type of diversity in the press has gone in mainland China remains a moot question. However, there is evidence that diversity in the press has now affected more than just the *Wen-hui Pao* and the *Liaoning Daily*. In a visit to the *People's Daily* in late 1972, Roderick MacFarquhar was told by a member of that paper "that one

---

2   On 10 August, the *People's Daily* reprinted the 19 July reader's letter in the *Liaoning Daily* and on 28 September, an article from the *Liaoning Daily* on Chin-shih Huang-ti.

reason why local papers were not available to foreigners was that they were not always able to put over the Party line successfully." (*MacFarquhar,* 1973, p. 145)

Significant as these developments in the Chinese press may seem, they are limited by the prevailing "political culture" of totalitarianism. Substantively, one can hardly regard the independent line of the *Wen-hui Pao* or the *Liaoning Jih-pao* as a "democratizing" trend. On the contrary, both papers agitated for more "Maoist orthodoxy" in terms of primacy of politics over academics (*Durdin,* 1973). Structurally, however, the trend of local diversity can be regarded as "cracks in the monolith." The pyramid structure of the Chinese press before the Cultural Revolution, had been shaken by the events in 1967 and 1968; a process of decentralization has begun. Since Chinese press is so much a part of the totalitarian power structure in mainland China, Karl Deutsch's analysis of the inherent instability of totalitarian power applies pointedly to this discussion of the changes in the press structure. According to Deutsch:

A hierarchy of power requires that all power should be located at the apex of a pyramid, and that all power should lead downward in terms of a transitive chain of command, transmitting orders from the single power holder or the few power holders at the top to the many soldiers or policemen at the bottom. However, every such pyramid of power is inherently unstable. To maintain transitivity it must be steered by orders coming from the apex. Yet the shortest communication route to all relevant sub-centers and sub-assemblies of power is not from the apex, but from some location farther down, let us say one, two, or three tiers farther down in the chain of command, according to the size of the pyramid and the speed with which the number of power holders increases from each layer of authority to the next lower one .... The lower an officer or official is in such a pyramid of power, the closer he is to the ultimate facilities of power, the common soldiers or policemen, provided only that he succeeds in organizing for himself the support of a sufficient number of his peers on his own level (*Deutsch* in *Eckstein and Apter,* 1963, p. 502).

2.2.2 Content and Function

Compared with its effect on the press structure, the Cultural Revolution has had only marginal effect on the content and function of Chinese newspapers. At most, the press on mainland China was made to conform more literally to Mao's ideals about what a public press should do than it actually did before 1967. On this subject, Mao Tse-tung, unlike his stands on other matters, was very consistent. For example, Mao had expressed his ideal of a public press to American correspondent Gunther Stein in Yenan in 1944:

> Mao Tse-tung showed me a copy of the *Liberation Daily*. "Take the example in tonight's newspaper. Here is a long article covering a whole page which describes in detail the ways in which one of the companies of the Eighth Route Army got rid of its shortcomings and became one of the best units. The cadres and fighters of every company in our armies will read and study and discuss this article. This is the simple way in which the positive experiences of one company will be taught as policy to five thousand companies. On other days you may find similar articles about a cooperative, a school, a hospital, or a local administrative unit ....." (*Stein,* 1945, p. 117).

One might call this the pedagogic-utilitarian function of the press. But Mao went further in a talk to the editorial staff of the *Shansi-Suiyvan Daily* in 1948, in which he reaffirmed the pedagogic-utilitarian function of the press: "The role and power of the newspapers lies in their ability to bring the Party programme, the Party line, the Party's general and specific policies, its tasks and methods of work before the masses in the quickest and most extensive way" (*Mao,* 1967, p. 241). Then, Mao dwelled on two other aspects of newspaper work and function that had staged a strong comeback in the Cultural Revolution. One concerns the training of communist journalists which bears Mao's populistic and anti-intellectual stand:

> To teach the masses, newspaper workers should first of all learn from the masses. You comrades are all intellectuals. Intellectuals are often ignorant and often

have little or no experience in practical matters. You can't quite understand the pamphlet 'How to Analyse the Classes in the Rural Areas' issued in 1933; on this point, the peasants are more than a match for you, for they understand it fully as soon as they are told about it . . . . . To change from lack of understanding to understanding, one must do things and see things; that is learning. Comrades working on the newspapers should go out by turns to take part in mass work, in land reform work for a time; that is very necessary. When not going out to participate in mass work, you should hear a great deal and read a great deal about the mass movements and devote time and effort to the study of such material . . . (*Mao,* 1967, p. 243).

Secondly, Mao repeatedly emphasized the need for a militant and "pungent" style of presentation as he put it:

You must retain the former merits of your paper — it should be sharp, pungent and clear-cut, and it should be run conscientiously. We must firmly uphold the truth, and truth requires a clear-cut stand. We Communists have always disdained to conceal our views. Newspapers run by our Party and all the propaganda work of our Party should be vivid, clear-cut and sharp and should never mutter and mumble. That is the militant style proper to us, the revolutionary proletariat. Since we want to teach the people to know the truth and arouse them to fight their own emancipation, we need this militant style. A blunt knife draws no blood (*Mao,* 1967, p. 245).

To summarize Mao's conception of the content functions of Chinese press, he emphasized its pedagogic-utilitarian function and its ability to arouse readers to take immediate and resolute actions to carry out policies of the government.

It would be difficult for anyone who has been reading the *People's Daily* and other Chinese newspapers continuously since 1949, to find any serious deviation in their content from the Maoist prescription. In particular, the press before the Cultural Revolution had exercised fully its pedagogic-utilitarian function which actually accounts for its dullness to outsiders. So far as the

People's Daily is concerned, over the years the paper had become turgid in its style and compartmentalized in its content. In 1954, for example, an article in *People's China* reported that the *People's Daily* typically published the following categories of news:

1. Aids Marxist Education. Great attention is paid in the columns of the *People's Daily* to the propagation of the theory of Marxism-Leninism and the teachings of Mao Tse-tung. It has, for example, printed the full texts of Stalin's works *Marxism and Linguistics* and *Economic Problems of Socialism in the U.S.S.R.* as well as a great deal of supplementary material . . .

2. Criticism and Self-criticism. One of the special columns of the *People's Daily* runs under the general heading of 'Party Life.' This carries articles passing on experience in Party work in various enterprises and government offices, and describing the activities of outstanding Party members. . . .

3. In the Struggle for Peace. . . . Since 1950, when the Chinese people launched the great movement to resist U.S. aggression and aid Korea, the work of mobilizing the people to support this lofty struggle has become an important task of the paper. . . .

4. Popularizing the General Line. . . . . The general line provides for the gradual realization of the Socialist industrialization of the country and the carrying out of Socialist transformation by the state of agriculture, handicraft production, and private industry and commerce step by step over a relatively long period. The *People's Daily* has paid great attention to the popularization of this general line. . . .

5. Help to Peasants. . . . It makes known to them the policies of the Party and the People's government in the development of China's rural areas. It tells them why and how they should follow the road to the future pointed out by Chairman Mao Tse-tung in his work *Getting Organized.* It also reports on the achievements of outstanding members of mutual-aid teams, agricultural producers' cooperatives and collective farms. At the same time, it levels its criti-

cism against those rural cadres who deviate from the
Party line, and, because of their wrong outlook and
working style, use methods of compulsion and of
giving bald commands in organizing and guiding the
peasants. ...
6. Close Contacts with Readers. Opinions of representative people of all strata of society are fully reflected
in the columns of the *People's Daily.* It has a broad
range of active contributors from among the workers,
peasants, scholars, writers, cadres, fighters of the
People's Liberation Army and of the Chinese People's
Volunteers, model workers, students and many
others. . .(*Hsiao* 1954).

One can see from the above that the bulk of the reports in the
People's Daily before the Cultural Revolution belonged to the
"pedagogic-utilitarian" kind. Many of the reports can also be
characterized as "socialist realism," i.e., portraying an idealized
reality. Or, to use the description of Jacques Marcuse (former
correspondent of *Agence France Presse* in Peking), the reports
in the *People's Daily* provided "a form of prefabricated public
opinion" (*Marcuse,* 1967, p. 109).

The Cultural Revolution in 1967 momentarily reduced drastically the compartmentalization of reports in the *People's Daily*
so to focus its content to the campaign. To revive Mao's emphasis
on "pungent" and "clear-cut" style, a change of format came
about at the same time. As Ian Stewart reported,

... The editors appear to be making more dramatic use
of headlines and pictures, filling the front page with
bold red characters, as well as the customary black,
and large photographs of Mao and Lin, or of Tien-An-
Men Square filled with a million Red Guards. People
who regularly read *Jen-min Jih-Pao* find the content
duller than ever, but say that the packaging and presentation have greatly improved (*Stewart,* 1966, p. 66).

Yet by 1970, the *People's Daily* had largely reverted to its pre-
Cultural Revolution content and format. In principle, the layout
of the paper conformed to the formula: page one for important
and largely domestic news and commentaries; page two for
economic news; page three for academic and theoretical topics;

page four for politics, art and literature, leaving the fifth and sixth pages for international news. In actual practice, the division of reports among page two, three and four often broke down. This was largely due to the regular publication of serialized topics which had been used more frequently after the Cultural Revolution. All the serialized topics are of pedagogic-utilitarian type. The major ones are:

1. "How Should The Primary And High Schools In Cities Be Managed?"
2. "Discussion On The Management Of Primary Schools In Production Brigades That Used To Be Run By Communes."
3. "Discussion On Whether It Is A Good Thing To Let Poor And Lower-middle Peasants Manage Rural Commerce."
4. "How To Manage 'May 7' Cadre School?"
5. "Discussion On The Public Health System In Rural Areas."
6. "How Should Socialist Colleges Be Managed?"

Each of these serialized topics occupied a whole page (which can be on any page, from page two to page four) in which several reports from different localities described their actual experiences.

Aside from these serialized topics, the editors of the *People's Daily* regularly grouped reports of the same substance under banner headlines like: (1) "Our Prospering Socialist Motherland," which carried reports about new cities and general "modernization" in the Chinese countryside; (2) "Agriculture as the Foundation, Industry as the Leading Sector," which carried stories about industrial productions in support of farming; and (3) "Further Expanding the Campaign of Increasing Production and Economizing."

However, with the return of these pedagogic-utilitarian reports came the inevitable turgidities in the press. In July 1972, the *People's Daily* launched a campaign to rid the press of long, winding reports. On 24 July, it published two short reports, one about raising sheep and the other about hog breeding, as examples of shorter and livelier news writing. In subsequent days, the paper published supposedly genuine letters from readers praising the new type of reporting. A group of literature teachers at a Peking middle school wrote to say that the prevalence of long-winded articles in the press had done serious damage to students in the school,

> The teacher asserted that while their students' school life was lively, their compositions were 'monotonous in content and dry and dull in language.' "Whatever topic they write about, the style remains the same," the teacher said. "The mental outlook of our youth, who are full of vigor, cannot be seen from their compositions. From this we can see how profoundly the stereotyped writing and new dogmatism have harmed the people" (*Burns,* 1973).

To an outsider, this campaign of livelier news reports has had minimal effects on the subsequent content of the *People's Daily.* The articles on college examinations or on "the reactionary character" of Confucius which were featured in the paper in the early 1970s were long and stereotyped. But perhaps a better judge on the effect of this anti-turgidity in news writing is the regular reading public in mainland China. Yet, for the next one and a half years, no more letters from readers on this subject were published by the *People's Daily.*

Taking the content and function of the Chinese press as a whole, the populistic legacy of Mao has been slightly strengthened in the press work by the Cultural Revolution. On the international pages of the *People's Daily,* for example, a new (though irregular) column appeared in the 1970s under the title "Forum of Workers, Peasants and Soldiers." It carried reports on world affairs supposedly written by peasants in communes, soldiers of "certain units of the People's Liberation Army" or members of trade unions.

Roderick MacFarquhar reported about a more significant development, however, on the new populism of Chinese press. While visiting the *Chieh-fang Jih-pao (Liberation Daily)* of Shanghai in 1972, MacFarquhar was told by his informant, Miss Ni, of the following:

> The nearest equivalent Miss Ni has had of the Western scoop-exposé occurred earlier this year. A stringer who worked in Shanghai's No. 2 Textile Mill sent her a *ta-tzu pao,* one of a number put up by workers criticiz-

ing the neglect of quality on the part of the mill's leading cadre. Feeling that the *ta-tzu pao* made a *prima facie* case, Miss Ni discussed the question with her group head, then went to the mill, talked to the workers and read more *ta-tzu pao*. (Factory managerial staff cannot keep reporters off their premises in China.) She then went to the leading cadre and told him she wanted to publish some *ta-tzu pao* because she thought they were justified; he did not put any obstacles in her way, but she could also see that he did not like the idea. So she consulted both with her superiors on the paper and with the relevant department of the Municipal Revolutionary Committee and got their permission to publish. She then published the *ta-tzu pao* as documents and organized more senior colleagues to write commentaries on them, she being still too junior to do so. As a result of this barrage, spread out over several days, the mill's leading cadre learnt his lesson, possibly with the help of a mission from the Municipal Revolutionary Committee, though Miss Ni was not sure of that (*MacFarquhar*, 1973, pp. 151-152).

Mao's prescription for the editorial staff of the *Shansi-Suiyuan Daily* in 1948 — "comrades working on the newspapers should go out by turns to take part in mass work . . ." — has been enforced more vigorously after the Cultural Revolution. Of the 300 members on the editorial staff of the *People's Daily* in 1972, one-third was actually working on the farm in the paper's own May 7th cadre school (*MacFarquhar*, 1973, p. 145). Furthermore, according to MacFarquhar, "those who work for the *People's Daily* seem to spend much of their time helping outsiders — officials or representatives of the masses — to write their own articles for the paper" (*MacFarquhar*, 1973, p. 146). As Mao said in 1948: "With our newspapers, too, we must rely on everybody, on the masses of the people, on the whole Party to run them, not merely on a few persons working behind closed doors" (*Mao*, 1967, p. 242).

Whether this mobilized populism in press work in mainland China can persist is a moot point. In 1958, as part of the Great Leap Campaign, the same type of populism in journalistic work was carried out with fanfare. Later, it subsided with the end of the Great Leap. More recently, the so-called "Forum of Workers, Peasants and Soldiers" in the *People's Daily* that used to be published very frequently in 1967, became irregular and infrequent in the early 1970s. It is likely that populism in press work nowadays is more real in local than national press (for recent treatment, see 2.1.1).

2.2.3 Circulation

To live up fully to Mao's ideal function of the press — "to bring the Party program, the Party line, the Party's general and specific policies, its tasks and methods of work before the masses in the quickest and most extensive way" — Chinese newspapers must be made available to the majority of the population. Yet, based on the few scraps of information on the circulation of newspapers in mainland China, Mao's goal remains distant. The circulation of the entire press in China over the years is as follows:[3]

> 1950 :   3,010,000 copies
> 1959 : 20,932,177   "
> 1972 : 30,000,000   "

Taking the population figure of China in 1972 at 875 million (*Aird,* 1972, pp. 327-331), then the distribution of the newspapers on mainland China remained three copies for every 100 people, the same rate as it was in 1964[4]. Thus, in the availability of the press to its public, China still ranked below developing nations like Argentina, Chile, Mexico and Brazil, let alone industrial nations like England, Japan, the United States, France and the Soviet Union.

The most limiting factor in the restricted circulation of the

3   The 1950 and 1959 figures are from *Wang mu,* "Some Experiences in Newspaper Work Since the Great Leap Forward," *Hsin-wen Chan-Hsien,* 24 Sept. 1959, as translated in *Extracts from China Mainland Magazines* (Hong Kong: U.S. Consulate General), No. 196, p. 14; the figure for 1972 is from *MacFarquhar,* 1973, p. 148.

4   See my *"Communist China"* in *Lent,* 1971, p. 53; this chapter contains the following editorial errors: page 46, *Chung-kuo Shao Nien-pao* should be *Chung-kuo Ch'ing-nien Pao;* page 48, Table 4.2, "Combined circulation of single issue" should be "total circulation" (error in my original manuscript); and page 49, *Liberation Army Daily* should be *Liberation Daily.*

Chinese press was, of course, China's industrial underdevelopment. As the editors of the *People's Daily* informed MacFarquhar in 1972, "with 30 million copies of national and local papers being printed every day, newsprint was very short" (*MacFarquhar*, 1973, p. 148). At the receiving end of the circulation, there is the perpetual problem of low literacy. A 1972 source reported: "About 75 percent of the adult population of Taiwan is literate as compared with *an estimated 25 percent for the PRC* [People's Republic of China]" (*Aird*, 1972, p. 326) (emphasis added). It is due largely to these factors that the Chinese Communist authority has not been able to institutionalize a county and commune press which had been in a state of flux before the Cultural Revolution. In the early 1970s, there was no indication that the villagers had been served with a regular press.

To overcome illiteracy and maximize the limited circulation of the press, Chinese propaganda officials continued to rely on word-of-mouth dissemination of newspaper reports. As Marcuse reported about the *People's Daily:*

> The general public does not read the *People's Daily;* it has neither the time nor, one should imagine, the inclination, but what the morning message is, it is not permitted to ignore. Loudspeakers blare it forth in factories, people's communes, universities, public or communal eating places, dormitories, indeed every-where, and it is usually made the compulsory subject of a political discussion in the evening (*Marcuse*, 1967, p. 108).

At the moment, the Chinese Communist authority has high hopes for a new group of "missionaries" in the countryside to spread the gospel of Party press. They are the tens and millions of high school and college graduates who have been sent to the country-side and frontier for permanent settlement. They are the logical intermediary between the "great tradition" and the "little tradition." Yet, judging from the reports about these youths in the *People's Daily,* before most of them could be used by the authority to bridge the gap between literates and illiterates, the government must first cope with the low morale of these youths and the social distance between these urban-dropouts and the peasants.

2.2.4 Conclusion

"Newspapers are the weapons for carrying out the ideological struggle and the tools for building Socialism," so said a high-ranking propaganda official in mainland China. While this is clearly a partisan view, its essentially political definition has wider applications. For, if the "natural history" of American newspapers began as a device for organizing gossip as stated by Robert Park (in *Schramm*, 1960, p. 11), then the "natural history" of the Chinese press, or for that matter the press in all Third World nations, began as a device for organizing nationalist revolution (see *Liu*, 1966). In other words, "politicization" is the birthmark of the modern Chinese press (or the press in all developing nations).

While the situational stress in the development of the Chinese press is decidedly political, one must also take into account the predispositional or "cultural" stress contributing to the "politicization" of Chinese newspapers. Perhaps the most cogent statements on this are those by Pool:

> To evaluate assertions primarily by a criterion of objective truth is not a natural human way of doing things; it is one of the peculiar features of the Graeco-Roman-Western tradition. This one cultural heritage among the many in human experience has tended to make truth-value the main test of the validity of statements. And truth-value is a rather curious criterion. It is ruthlessly two-valued and dominated by the law of the excluded middle, something which classical Indian logic, for example, never accepted; statements in the latter system could be simultaneously both true and false. The Western criterion of truth-value also assumes that a statement has a validity or lack of it inherent in itself and quite independent of who says it and why. That too is something Brahminical philosophy did not accept; a statement true for a man in one Varna might be false for one in another. The Western criterion of truth assumes further that validity can be tested independently of who does the testing provided certain rituals of procedure are followed. Most cultural traditions do not make these assumptions . . .

Furthermore, most of mankind does not regard the truth-value of statements as terribly important. For most of the men who have inhabited the earth the consequences of a statement — e.g., whether it will bring the wrath of God upon you, whether it will help you earn a living, whether it will win a loved one — are considerably more important than whether it matches certain abstract rules of transformability into other statements. The Western tradition is unique in the value it has attached to the latter consideration.

So when we say that traditional societies are more concerned with the social function of communication than with its truth-value, we are only saying they are human. Yet their concern with the social function of communications is an important fact (*Pool* in *Pye,* 1963, pp. 242-243).

In a somewhat different context, yet relevant to our discussion nevertheless, Kissinger expressed similar views:

The West is deeply committed to the notion that the real world is external to the observer, that knowledge consists of recording and classifying data — the more accurately the better. Cultures which escaped the early impact of Newtonian thinking have retained the essentially pre-Newtonian view that the real world is almost completely *internal* to the observer.

Although this attitude was a liability for centuries — because it prevented the development of the technology and flexibility with respect to the contemporary revolutionary turmoil. It enables the societies which do not share our cultural mode *to alter reality by influencing the perspective of the observer . . .* (Emphasis added) (*Kissinger,* 1966, pp. 503-29).

It is the ambition of Chinese leaders and other contemporary nation-builders, to use the mass media "to alter reality by influencing the perspective of the observer" so to realize his vision of a "good society."

Thus, a combination of revolutionary era and elitist-moralistic predisposition (culture) finally culminated in the "controlled press" of the People's Republic. As such, one strength of the Chinese press lies in its mobilizational capability. The unity with diversity principle enables the Communist Party to have access to every major social group. Another strength of the Chinese press lies in what Marcuse called its "prefabricated public opinion." Momentarily, at least, the "controlled press" enables the Chinese public to rid itself of the demoralizing intellectual oppositionalism so prevalent in developing nations. As described by Edward Shils, the intellectuals in developing nations,

are extremely critical of practically all politicians and they are contemptuous of party leaders. A large part of the intelligentsia incline toward opposition — as if by their very nature. They do not give a lead to an affirmatively critical public opinion. On the contrary, their views constitute public opinion (given the narrow radius of the educated classes) and the public opinion which they represent is seldom constructive: and, when it is, it is seldom heeded. This drives them further into opposition, rather than into a relationship of positive criticism and discriminating guidance . . . (*Shils, 1965, p. 21*).

The unity with diversity principle of the press on mainland China promised to end such intellectual anarchy so that the public could focus on "constructive" public tasks.

However, drowning out *outside* "noises" by a controlled press does not mean that the latter would always provide the public a firm and constructive guide. Since 1949, the Chinese press has had to face *inside* "noises" — dissension among elite, so poignantly expressed in the confession of Wu Leng-hsi, whose editorship of the *People's Daily* was restored in 1972:

In the summer of 1956, Liu Shao-ch'i approved a *People's Daily* editorial opposing "reckless advance." The editorial was first drafted by Teng T'o, then revised by Hu Ch'iao-mu and Lu Ting-yi, and finally reviewed and approved by Liu Shao-ch'i. In the Nanning Conference in early 1958, Chairman Mao pointed out that this editorial was erroneous, that opposing "reckless advance" was erroneous, and that the editorial undermined the initiative and creativity of the masses and cadres, and resulted in the "U-shaped" development of our national economy. At that time I did not under-

stand what this was all about, so I telephoned Peking to send for the manuscript of that editorial and discovered the development explained above. Liu Shao-ch'i wrote in the manuscript, which he had reviewed and approved, that it was to be presented to Chairman Mao for review and approval. Chairman Mao wrote three words, *pu k'an le,** on it. I informed Hu Ch'iao-mu, and remarked that Liu Shao-ch'i would be implicated. Hu told me not to make these facts public at the conference, so I did not. Thus did I cover up for Liu Shao-ch'i (*Chang,* 1969/70, p. 72).
(*"I don't want to read it further.")

The Cultural Revolution reveals still another source of insecurity of the controlled press in China. The "power seizure" movement of 1967 showed that when deemed necessary, totalitarian leaders will throw the press "to the lions." The result of this is predictable. Since 1969, the Chinese Communist Party has had to contend with a prevailing view on mainland China that "it is dangerous to engage in cultural work." A conference in Hupeh province about journalistic work reported that there were views like: "When one writes too much, one's liability grows; when you write black letters on white paper, you do not know when you will get into trouble" (*Radio Hupeh,* 8 Sept. 1969, in *Chung,* 1970, p. 2, and *Dizard,* 1972, p. 9).

Against this background, one can perhaps explain the reason for the lack of success in the communist authority's fight against turgidities in the press. For, to write in turgid style behind stereotyped terms and slogans — is a way for the journalists to provide some protection for themselves. A more cynical interpretation is that many Chinese journalists have perhaps resorted to turgid writing as covert protest against a manipulative leadership.

In this respect, the controlled press in mainland China, *to a certain extent,* defeats its own purpose of providing a constructive guide to public opinion and creating new communist men by altering the perspective of the public.

2.2.5 *The Press Since Mao, by John A. Lent*

After the mid-1970s, the development or revitalization of several press phenomena foretold that possibly the role of the people *vis-a-vis* the press, and perhaps even the government, was about to change.

First, newspaper criticism groups (*ping pao tsu*), born during the Cultural Revolution and anti-Lin Piao and anti-Confucius campaigns, were developed with what was called the "rightist wind of reversal of verdict." Made up largely of workers, peasants and soldiers, the newspaper criticism groups' primary aim was to criticize newspapers' editorial policies to ensure that they followed the revolutionary line, engaged in class struggle, represented the interests of the proletariat and practised a simple and concise writing style. The opinions of these groups apparently mattered as they were published in newspaper internal publications and discussed at board meetings (*Asian Messenger,* 1976a, p. 2).

Second, after the Cultural Revolution, but especially in the mid-1970s, a new type of reportage (represented by what were termed barefoot journalists) emerged. Essentially, barefoot journalists worked alongside factory hands and commune laborers to conduct social investigation, install village correspondents and to bridge the gap between the press and readers. As a result of the efforts of barefoot journalists, one newspaper had a fleet of 2,000 worker correspondents in the Greater Shanghai area, all of whom had been trained to report and write news by barefoot journalists (*Devcom,* 1976, p. 12).

The phenomenon that had the greatest impact in China in the late 1970s was the renewed interest in the *dazibao* as a form of expression (see *McKillop,* 1978; *Bonavia,* 1978). These large letter posters were used in campaigns against Lin Piao and Confucius by the mid-1970s, but their greatest effect occurred after Mao's death on 9 September 1976. Poster and press campaigns immediately built up the cult of Hua Kuo-feng, at the same time downplaying the importance of Chiang Ching (*Mathews,* 1976). For a few months, the press and *dazibao* campaigns also investigated the role played by Teng Hsiao-ping, but, by early 1977, most campaigns severely castigated the Gang of Four or promoted the cult of Hua (see 2.1.1).

In 1978, "democratization" seemed to be in vogue as Confucius was rehabilitated. Vice Premier Teng Hsiao-ping, himself rehabilitated by then, openly suggested that the Chinese people "speak out" and "express their grievances." After December, *dazibao,* attacking many previously-held sacrosanct topics, including the Cultural Revolution and some of Mao's key sayings, were posted on Democracy Wall and elsewhere; *hsiao tao hsiao hsi* ("little road news," connoting narrow, exclusive channels) appeared, either handwritten or in poorly stencilled formats, as a form of underground political press (see *Index on Censorship,* 1979, pp. 61-63; *Asiaweek,* 1979b; *Freedom at Issue,* 1979, pp. 50-52; *Bonavia,* 1979b, pp. 37-38), and the Chinese press itself deviated from its traditional stance, indulging in investigative reporting, crisper writing, use of visual presentations, editorials often criticizing China and praising the West, and the use of more letters to the editor (*Ghiglione,* 1979b, p. 8; also *Chu and Chu,* 1979, pp. 2-7).

The authorities were tolerant until April 1979, when controversial *dazibao* were stripped from the walls, a few human rights activists, including democratic magazine publishers, were arrested, and the Chinese press attacked "ultra democracy," concluding that the people had let off enough steam and further permissiveness by party leaders was an invitation to anarchy (*Time,* 1979, p. 41). One writer said these reversals of what had become termed the "Peking Spring" showed that democracy for its own sake has no place in China (*Bonavia,* 1979a). Such actions, indicating the party did not think democracy should be pushed too hard, brought into question the sincerity of Teng's December 1978 suggestions (*Viénet,* 1979, p. 26). By June 1979, the policy swung around again to defending human rights and free speech in the press (*FEER,* 1 June 1979, p. 27).

In July-August 1979, in what the *New York Times* (29 Aug. 1979, p. A-12) described as a "campaign unusual in world journalism and perhaps unprecedented in the controlled press of Communist nations," China's newspapers admitted they had used false stories and puffery for years. The front page confessions were supposedly part of a nationwide effort to eliminate propaganda and "seek the truth from facts," the belief being that to solve China's problems, the people first have to look at them objectively. One paper, *Tianjin Ribao,* said the fault for this type of reporting lay with lazy and unethical journalists, some of whom conformed strictly to what they believed the leadership wanted, while others resorted to bribery to advance their careers.

Also, in the late 1970s, as China expanded its foreign relations, efforts were made to train correspondents for foreign reporting. In August 1978, the Chinese Academy of Social Sciences established the Institute of Journalism, partly to train journalists to serve overseas (*Chu*, 1979, p. 11).

2.3 Republic of China (Taiwan)

James C. Y. Chu

2.3.1 Historical Development of the Press

2.3.1.1 Pre-1944 Period

Situated in the far Western Pacific less than 100 miles off the Chinese mainland, Taiwan (Republic of China) has an area of 13,885 square miles. The island was a province during the Ching (or Manchu) Dynasty, China's last reigning house. As a result of the Sino-Japanese War of 1894-95, Taiwan was ceded to Japan by the Treaty of Shimonoseki.

The anniversary of the Japanese occupation, 17 June 1896, marked the publication of the first newspaper, *Taiwan Shimpo* (*Taiwan News*), in Taipei. An organ of the Taiwan governor-general, the *Shimpo* was in Japanese, which was foreign to the islanders, therefore its circulation was confined to the Japanese officials, soldiers and policemen. Nine months later, a famous literary figure from Japan, Kawamura Taka Mitu, founded the second newspaper in Taiwan. Unlike the *Shimpo,* the *Taiwan Nippo* (*Taiwan Daily*) gave great attention to literary essays and human interest stories, in order to become both an informative and amusing newspaper. The *Shimpo* and the *Nippo* competed so bitterly for readers in the rather small Japanese community in Taiwan that occasionally their staff even resorted to physical violence. The bitter rivals at last came to terms through negotiation with the office of the governor-general. As a result, the two papers merged to become the *Taiwan Nichi-Nichi Shimpo* (*Taiwan Daily News*), which published its first issue on 6 May 1898. To enlarge its readership, the new six-page newspaper contained

James C. Y. Chu is associate professor of mass communication at California State University in Chico. He is a former Government Information Office employee, World College of Journalism instructor and BCC news editor, all in Taipei.

articles in both Japanese and Chinese. It was destined to become the most powerful paper during Japanese rule until 1944.

But the newspaper faced almost insurmountable barriers during its first two years. Its troubles were mainly of two kinds.

First, although the combined circulation of the *Shimpo* and the *Nippo* totalled 4,000 copies daily, the new *Nichi-Nichi* sold only 2,500 copies because of the overlapping readership between the two papers. Also, the new daily was compelled by the government to employ the entire staff of the defunct papers. With the decline of subscription revenue on the one hand and the rise of operation expenses on the other, the paper was on the verge of bankruptcy in 1900.

Second, papermills in Taiwan did not manufacture enough to meet the demand on the island, and moreover, imports from Japan were often delayed by storms and because of the disorganized shipping industry. It was barely possible for the editor to continue regular publication of the paper.

In 1900, the governor-general ordered the reorganization of the *Nichi-Nichi* into a corporation with the Japanese administration in Taiwan as major shareholder. Meanwhile, the paper recruited well-informed Japanese politicians, professors and writers to serve on its staff as correspondents. No longer was it necessary for the *Nichi-Nichi* editor to rely upon newspapers in Japan for information. The paper featured governmental intelligence from Japan, carried colorful and vivid local news and presented essays and lyrical poems.

A significant event of Taiwan newspaper publishing took place in 1905 when the *Nichi-Nichi* began publishing a separate Chinese edition, entirely staffed by Chinese. The Chinese edition reported in detail the revolutionary movement in China under the leadership of Dr. Sun Yat-sen, which helped attract the wide attention of the Chinese in Taiwan. In October 1910, it was expanded from one and a half quarto sheets to one folio sheet. However, it was this editorial policy and the consequent expansion that gave rise to the Japanese authority's awareness of the potential influence of *Nichi-Nichi*'s Chinese editor on the native residents. In November 1911, a month after the success of the Chinese revolution, the Chinese edition was ordered to cease publication. The *Nichi-Nichi* immediately became bilingual again.

But the most significant and dramatic of all the events connected with the history of early Taiwan journalism was a young Japanese journalist-politician's challenge to the policy of the colonial government.

For many years, the press in Taiwan had been under the direct control of the Japanese governor-general, and therefore, an official organ of the colonial ruler. Sasaki Yasugordo, a well-known member of the Japanese Diet, came to Taiwan and founded the *Kosankoku Daily* (*High Mountain Daily*) in October 1899. Immediately after the publication of this first privately-owned paper in Taiwan, the liberal-minded publisher ran into direct confrontation with the ruling authority. In the first two issues, there appeared in the *Kosankoku* an advertisement calling for material concerning the corrupt and ruthless policies of the Japanese ruling class. The paper repeatedly published satirical articles featuring the corruption and incompetence of the government. However, the heavy artillery was in the main loaded with articles accusing the government of a massacre of 7,000 defiant islanders. Before the year ended, the governor-general suspended the license of the *Kosankoku,* making it the first victim of the suppression of the freedom of the press.

Although it lasted for only two months, the ill-fated *Kosankoku* did have a tremendous impact upon the future policy of the press during the colonial period. The Japanese government responded to the *Kosankoku* case with a clear-cut policy of licensing and censorship of publications in Taiwan. On 24 January 1900, the governor-general announced the "Taiwan Newspaper Publication Code." Ten days later, "Taiwan Publication Regulations" was added. Accordingly, newspapers, books, pamphlets and other forms of publications were not allowed to print and circulate without the consent of the authority. From 1902-9, three more newspapers were closed, while few new ventures were launched.

The new era in the early history of the press in Taiwan arrived in the 1920s, when the Chinese were allowed to operate and own the press. A group of Taiwanese students in Japan published a Chinese language monthly, *Taiwan Seinen* (*Taiwan Youth*) in 1920. In its first issue, the journal stated that its basic policy was "to discuss carefully the necessary improvements in Taiwan politics, and to promote Sino-Japanese friendship" (*Hung*, 1962, p. 73). More specifically, it advocated the autonomy of Taiwan, for which its copies were frequently confiscated upon arrival in Taiwan. To make itself more acceptable to the governor-general, the journal adopted a new name, *Taiwan Minpo* (*Taiwan People's Journal*), and editorially it aimed "to promote the welfare of the people in Taiwan and to attain peace in the East" (*Lin*, n.d., p. 25). The "exiled" periodical finally obtained permission to publish in Taiwan in July 1927, and later it was renamed *Taiwan Shinminpo* (*Taiwan New Minpo*) and transformed into a daily in April 1932. Two years later, an evening edition was added. During this period, the *Nichi-Nichi* and the *Shinminpo* were the two most widely read papers on the island. The former, printed in Japanese and Chinese, was designed as an organ of the government, while the latter, in Chinese only, served the interests of the islanders. The combined circulation of the morning and evening editions of the Chinese daily reached 40,000 copies in 1940.

During World War II, there were six newspapers on the island. As the war went on, shortage of newsprint gradually became serious, so that its allocation was reduced by 25 per cent in July 1940. After Pearl Harbor, supplies became even more meagre, and good printing ink was almost unobtainable. On top of these difficulties, the press suffered from a serious labor shortage. When printers, and even writers, were called to do military service, newspapers often had to be suspended. To conserve manpower and printing materials, the governor-general's office took a decisive step in March 1944 to merge the six papers into a "gigantic" daily, the *Taiwan Shimpo*, which circulated 200,000 copies, including 30,000 free copies for soldiers.

2.3.1.2 The Post-War Years

From the wreckage of war and a lack of almost everything, the press in Taiwan entered into the era of post-war reconstruction, which started with the only survivor of the war, the *Shimpo*.

From V-J Day until 25 October 1945 — the day Taiwan and the Pescadores were returned to China after 50 years of Japanese colonial rule — the *Shimpo* continued to publish, mostly in Japanese. The Taiwan Executive Governor's Office formally took over the paper on Restoration Day and renamed it the *Taiwan Shin Sheng Pao* (*Taiwan New Life Newspaper*), an official organ of the government.

When the first Japanese newspaper had made its debut in Taiwan 50 years before, the paper faced a problem of readership — the local readers could not read Japanese. Now, 50 years later, the *Shin Sheng Pao* encountered a similar problem — the new generations of Chinese on the island read Japanese rather than Chinese. Consequently, the Chinese paper had to devote 25 per cent of its space to Japanese articles; in fact, the Japanese section was not eliminated until a year later. The total circulation dropped from 175,000 in October 1945 to 73,000 in January 1947 (*Hung*, 1958, p. 107) due to the loss of Japanese readers. However, with the support of the government, the paper weathered the financial crisis, and in August 1949, was able to start a southern edition in Kaohsiung, a seaport city.

The second post-war paper in Taiwan was a party organ founded by the Chinese Nationalist Party (or the Kuomintang). The *China Daily News* was born in Tainan, a major city in southern Taiwan, in February 1946, using the plant equipment of the Tainan branch office of the old *Taiwan Shimpo*. Since then, it has been one of the most influential papers in the southern part of the island. The paper started its northern edition in Taipei on its second anniversary.

In the meantime, new independent newspapers were established in all parts of the island. According to an official survey, by August 1947, there were 30 newspapers in Taiwan. Most of them, however, succumbed to the cruel post-war economic recession. The surviving privately-owned papers included the *Min Pao* (*People's News*) in Taipei, *Ho Ping Jih Pao* (*Peace Daily News*) in the central city of Taichung, and *Tung Tai Jih Pao* (*East Taiwan Daily News*) in Hualien, the most influential local paper in eastern Taiwan.

In addition to these papers, one unique tabloid paper merits special mention. In 1948, to facilitate Chinese language education in Taiwan, the Chinese Nationalist government moved Peking's *Kuo Yu Hsiao Pao* (*Little Mandarin News*) to Taiwan and renamed it *Kuo Yu Jih Pao* (*Mandarin Daily News*). Printing the 40 phonetic symbols alongside Chinese characters, the paper was instrumental in teaching Mandarin, China's national language, to school children and the Japanese-educated populace.

2.3.1.3 After 1949

In late 1949, when the mainland of China was lost to the communists, the Nationalist government moved its seat to Taipei. With the government fled professional journalists who brought salvaged press facilities to the island. Of all the news institutions moving into Taiwan, the *Central Daily News,* inaugurated as the organ of the Nationalist Party in February 1929, in Nanking, was the most important. The paper's high-speed Goss rotary was capable of turning out 120,000 copies an hour, the well-trained staff, and the political as well as financial support of the party in power, provided it with everything necessary to become a prominent and influential paper in Taiwan. Scarcely a newspaper of this time in Taiwan was better written and offered greater variety of news and feature stories than *Central Daily News.* In particular, the paper was noted for its informative as well as entertaining literature, children and women's pages. As a voice of the central government and of the party, all public offices, schools and armed forces units subscribed; by 1954, *Central Daily News* had a circulation of 67,170 — the largest in Taiwan. *Shin Sheng Pao,* selling 62,238 a day, dropped to second (*Hung,* 1958, p. 138).

The official press continued to dominate Taiwan's newspaper industry until the mid-1950s when independent newspapers commenced.

The merger of three failing independent newspapers into the *United Daily News* in 1951 put new life into Taiwan's journalism. When the *United* was founded in Taipei, official papers all over the island shared 87 per cent of the combined circulation of the daily papers; while the *United* sold only 12,000 copies a day (*United Daily News,* 1971, p. 61). As a paper catering to the general public, especially the blue collar class, *United* stressed local news, including police stories, crime, sex and social scandals. The paper also gained a reputation for its boldness in exposing political corruption at local levels and for its concern over the welfare of ordinary people. The *United's* circulation increased steadily. When the paper celebrated its twentieth anniversary in 1971, it boasted a daily circulation of 410,000 (*United Daily News,* 1971; see Lee, 1973, p. 13), becoming the first successful independent newspaper in Taiwan.

In 1951, Taipei saw the founding of another privately-owned newspaper. The *Chen Hsin Hsin Wen Pao* (*Credit Daily News*) started in 1950 as an official bulletin of the Commission on Supplies of the Taiwan provincial government. The mimeographed sheet was devoted entirely to business and financial news, designed for the commercial circle. When the Commission ceased its subsidies to the paper the next year, Yu Chi-chung, the editor, took over ownership and changed the frail government bulletin into a strong private publication with special emphasis on business news. As a result of this reorganization, the paper became a four-page daily of regular format. Blessed with its specialization on the one hand and the efforts of a business-minded editor on the other, the *Credit Daily* steadily built itself a reputation for reliable information about daily stockmarket prices, foreign exchange rates, economic policies of the government and international economic situations. The paper did not start an extensive coverage of local news, namely police, court and other "non-business" events, until 1960. Since then the *Credit Daily,* which became the *China Times* in 1968, has given sensational play to crime and sex stories in an effort to compete with the *United Daily News.* Yet the *China Times* has continued to be the leading financial newspaper in Taiwan. By 1972, its daily circulation was estimated at 260,000 (*Lee,* 1973, p. 13), second only to the *United Daily News.*

Of the 31 daily newspapers in Taiwan, two are in English, *China Post* and *China News.* The first issue of the *China Post* hit the streets of Taipei on 3 September 1952, under the editorship of Nancy Yu Huang and her husband, Y. P. Huang. The Huangs, refugees from the mainland and their friends who were interested in publishing an English paper to serve as a channel of communication between the foreign residents and the local populace, started the *Post* in a primitive way. They could only afford to rent a flatbed press and hire a dozen typesetters. Most of the editorial staff were working on a voluntary basis; 16 of the 39 personnel were not on the paper's regular payroll. The early issues of the

Post were well edited, but poorly printed and full of typographical errors. Today, the *Post* employs a staff of more than 120. The first Taiwan newspaper to adopt offset printing, its daily circulation stands at 15,000 (*Lee*, 1973, p. 13), as opposed to the 10,000 of the *China News*.

The *China News*, for 11 years a mimeographed paper of 15 or more foolscap sheets, became a printed afternoon paper of one folio sheet on 1 July 1960. Carrying under its nameplate creed, "An Enlightened Public Is the Best Security of a Nation," the *News* dedicated itself to providing the reader with facts, a variety of opinions, and "the flavor of our special way of life" (*Tsai*, 1969, p. 27).

Most of the 16 newspapers in Taipei are distributed islandwide and because of the size of the island, the distinction between the national and local newspapers is not visible.

2.3.2 Circulation

It seems to be impossible to compile accurate circulation figures for newspapers in Taiwan, since there is no such organization as the Adult Bureau of Circulation to examine the figures claimed by newspapers. In their fight to win circulation and outdo their rivals, some Taiwan newspapers resort to exaggerating sales. Since advertising rates are based on circulation figures and upon the cost of reaching each thousand readers, this leads to many discrepancies. Despite this chaotic situation in which honest publishers are placed at an unfair disadvantage by the unscrupulous operators, few publishers, if any, are interested in correcting the problem by establishing an ABC type of agency. Consequently, the circulation of each Taiwan newspaper can only be estimated.

Yet, the increase in the circulation of newspapers in Taiwan has been phenomenal. According to research by Thomas C. Lee[1] of National Chengchi University, total circulation stood at 1.2 million in 1971 (*Lee*, 1973, p. 8), an increase of 400 per cent

1   *Asian Press and Media Directory 1976-77* showed figures at least double those of Lee for all newspapers.

in the aggregate circulation of all papers between 1952 and 1972 — at the same time the total population of the country doubled. Several sociological and economic factors have contributed to the growth of circulation during this period. Among them are the following:

1. Illiteracy declined from 42.1 per cent in 1952 to 13.3 per cent in 1972 (*Council for International Economic Cooperation and Development,* 1973, p. 7). Allied with this increase in the literate audience, was the appeal of sensational news and easily understood editorials presented mostly by privately-operated newspapers. It is this news policy that has brought the barely literate into the newspaper audience. There has also been a noticeably increased slant to the interests of women, not only because of their new importance in industry and business, but als o because of the growth of department store advertising.

2. Economic prosperity on the island has made a substantial proportion of the population new subscribers to papers; some people buy more than one newspaper daily. It is mainly people living in the south and east of the island who subscribe to a Taipei newspaper for national and international news, in addition to the local newspaper. Taipei newspapers are transported by airplanes and a special paper train, jointly operated by the 16 newspapers in Taipei.

3. The movement of people from rural areas to cities has changed the reading habits of the new city residents. In rural areas, the public is served by public billboards on which local governments and civic organizations post some major newspapers. These public billboards are usually built in front of the city hall, on the roadside of the main street and in marketplaces in small towns. Although these billboards are available in big cities such as Taipei and Kaohsiung, the busy urban life tends to discourage people from making special trips to read the newspapers on public billboards. Consequently, these new city residents become regular subscribers to a newspaper, thus increasing sales.

The aggregate circulation of newspapers in Taiwan shows an average of one copy for every 13 persons, a ratio second only to, Japan in the Far East. However, this is not as meaningful a ratio in Taiwan as in Western countries. In Taiwan, especially in the rural areas, papers are passed from hand to hand and each copy has many readers; newspapers on the public billboards also reach a great number of readers.

Circulations of newspapers in Taiwan range from a few thousand to a few hundred thousand. The circulations of the 16 Taipei newspapers account for more than 80 per cent of the aggregate circulation of all papers in Taiwan. The circulations of the major newspapers were estimated as follows in 1972:

United Daily News	280,000
China Times (formerly *Chen Hsin Hsin Wen*)	260,000
Central Daily News	160,000
Hsin Sheng Pao	60,000
Taiwan Hsin Wen Pao	60,000
China Daily News (Southern Edition)	50,000
China Daily News (Taipei Edition)	40,000
Mandarin Daily News	40,000
Young Warrior Daily News	40,000
Taiwan Daily News	40,000

Distribution within towns is by carriers, most of whom are in their late teens or early twenties. A substantial proportion of the carriers in the Taipei area are college students. The morning papers depend almost entirely upon home subscription, costing US$1.18 a month, while evening papers assign only 10 per cent to street sales (*Shen,* 1960, p. 17).

The subscription war among the Taipei newspapers is always heated, because there seem to be too many papers for a city of 1.4 million people. The papers constantly develop new promotional methods to enlarge circulations, such as gift books, chess contests, essay writing contests and beauty contests. Taipei papers all maintained a sizable department for reader services. During the excitement of a circulation campaign, the subscriptions of a competing paper may increase by a few thousand; but these are, for the most part, temporary gains. The reader chooses his paper according to its merits. In other words, good news writing and non-partisan reporting are the point of rivalry.

2.3.3 Newspaper Advertising

The decade of the 1960s was notable for the increasing use of advertising in Taiwan's mass media. The rapid growth of the

economy and promotion of the Asian Advertising Congress,
which made the public as well as advertisers aware of the value
of advertising to today's - economy, can be attributed to the
impressive increase in advertising expenditure in this period.

Expenditure on advertising grew steadily between 1965
and 1972, exceeding the growth rate of the nation's economy.
As shown in the following table, advertising expenditure reached
more than US$42 million in 1972, almost four times that of 1965,
whereas the Gross National Product in 1972 was about 2.6 times
greater than in 1965 (*Niu*, 1971, p. 58; *Yen*, 1973, p. 52; *Council
for International Economic Cooperation and Development*, 1973,
p. 18).

TABLE 1. Growth of Advertising Expenditure
and the Taiwan Economy, 1965-72

		Unit: US$1 million
Year	Advertising Expenditure	Gross National Product
1965	12.4	2,821.6
1966	14.0	3,138.8
1967	17.0	3,576.1
1968	21.5	4,199.3
1969	27.4	4,770.1
1970	36.2	5,460.7
1971	37.4	6,231.8
1972	42.0	7,181.8

Of the US$42 million spent on advertising in 1972, approxi-
mately US$15 million was for newspaper advertising. As shown
in the following table, newspaper advertising rose from less than
US$5.5 million in 1965 to US$15 million in 1972 — an increase
of 272 per cent. In 1965, newspaper advertising constituted 44.1
per cent of all advertising expenditure. However, with the introduction and growth of television in Taiwan, the established
media experienced a decline in their total share of advertising.
Despite this decline, newspaper advertising has grown faster
than the nation's economy and newspapers in Taiwan continue
to be the largest advertising medium.

TABLE 2.   Shares of Total Advertising in Taiwan by
Major Media, 1965-72

Unit: US$

Media	1965		1972	
	Expenditure	%	Expenditure	%
Newspapers	5,475,000	44.1	14,970,500	35.6
Radio	2,000,000	16.1	3,340,000	8.0
TV	1,375,000	11.1	13,625,000	32.4
Magazines	225,000	1.8	1,530,000	3.6
Outdoor	1,950,000	15.7	3,642,500	8.2
Theater	525,000	4.2	580,000	1.4
D.M.	–	–	2,479,500	5.9
Others	875,000	7.1	2,050,000	4.9
Total	12,425,000	100.00	42,037,500	100.00

Advertising gave the newspaper publisher approximately one-fourth of his income in 1966 (*Wang,* 1967, p. 26), but the general proportion rose to a little over one-half at the beginning of the 1970s. This tremendous increase meant record-breaking profits in newspaper publishing in Taiwan; almost all newspapers filled their front pages with advertising, mostly wedding announcements and department store advertisements. A few big newspapers, such as the *United Daily News, China Times,* and the *Central Daily News,* sometimes devoted nearly 50 per cent of their first page to advertisements.

Hotels, night clubs, movie theaters, airlines, book publishers, manufacturers of electrical home appliances and department stores are the chief newspaper advertisers, and patent medicines, though constantly under fire, still occupy a large space in the advertising columns. Also important are the paid wedding announcements and obituaries.

With the increase in advertising expenditure, advertising agencies have become thriving businesses in Taiwan. It has been discovered that space buying is not the only function of an agency. Most of the agencies have personnel dealing with copy and artwork which has transformed the appearance of advertisements.

Market research, used occasionally, has not become a common practice.

Prominent advertising agencies in Taiwan are Kuo-Hwa Advertising Co., which keeps close ties with such foreign agencies as Japan's Dentsu Advertising and MacManus, John and Adam in the United States, China Commercial Advertising Company, the International Advertising and Public Relations Company and the Taiwan Advertising Company (*Lin*, n.d., pp. 57-58).

2.3.4 The Government and the Press

2.3.4.1 Press Regulations

To understand the relationship between the government and the press in Taiwan, one must keep in mind that the government believes the country is under constant threat of communist attack. Nationalist China, considering itself at war with the People's Republic of China, insists, at least in official rhetoric, that one day it will triumphantly lead the people back to the mainland. Therefore, the fundamental cause of Nationalist China is not merely to defend Taiwan and its offshore islands, but also to recover China and to reconstruct the country. For this reason, the government believes that anything which undermines confidence in the regime and the morale of the armed forces is "against the national interest," and thus must not be tolerated.

According to the 1958 publication law, a publisher is required to obtain a "registration card" (license) from the government, before "publishing the first issue of his paper." Five kinds of administrative penalties are stipulated: warning, fine, seizure of publications, suspension of publication and revocation of registration. A publication deemed guilty of sedition, treason, or of instigating others to commit those crimes, is subject to the revocation of registration. The penalty is also applied when a publication continues to publish as its essential contents, indecent articles which are offensive to public morals or which incite others to commit offenses against public morals, after having been subjected to suspension for a specific period of time.

The law has been regarded by the press, private as well as official, as a great nuisance. When the International Press Institute decided in a 1960 meeting in Tokyo against admitting individual candidates from Taiwan, newspapers in Taiwan wrote editorials on the abrogation of the law, saying that it gave the country a bad name (*Gaspard,* 1961, p. 45). The *United Daily News* wrote on 26 March 1960:

> In Taiwan today it is true that much more is desired concerning freedom of the press. The best gesture will be for the . . . government to publicly announce the abrogation of the press law and replace it by some other positive legislation . . . .

On 4 April 1960 the *China News* strongly suggested:

> The Publication Law, which was huddled through the legislature in 1958 over violent press opposition, should be abolished. The law, which has not been invoked in a single case in the last twenty months after its promulgation, is just as dead and should be buried alive.

However, the government believes that the law is not designed to deter freedom of the press. "The only purpose of the law is to prevent the publication of scandal sheets [mosquito papers] and Communist propaganda," said the official circles in Taipei (*Gaspard,* 1961, p. 45). In an interview that took place when the proposed law had just been sent to the Legislative Yuan (Congress), the late President Chiang Kai-shek said:

> The government's determination to secure passage of the new Publication Law was in reality an attempt to protect legitimate newspapers, while at the same time defending the country from "neutralism" and the other effects of Communists, who assumed many disguises and who constantly abused freedom of the press. We will not make the same mistake twice (*Long,* 1958, p. 8).

As a matter of fact, the government needs no press law to accomplish this purpose as many other laws could be invoked to bring the press into line. Speaking on freedom of information in Taiwan at an annual meeting of IPI in 1964, Stanway Cheng, then publisher of the *China News,* listed such laws including the National General Mobilization Law, regulations governing the punishment of rebels and traitors (meaning the communists, the leftists, the fellow-travellers, supporters or sympathizers) and other "security" laws and regulations (*Cheng*, 1964, p. 7). Lei Chen, editor of the *Free China Fortnightly*, who challenged the government's assertion that it would retake the mainland, was arrested and convicted in 1960 of "harboring" a communist agent, his secretary, on the magazine staff. Li Ao, editor of the liberal *Wen Hsing* magazine until it was closed by a government order in 1965, was sentenced to 10 years' imprisonment in 1972. The young writer and seven other persons were convicted of having belonged to a "rebel organization," presumably one advocating a Taiwan independent of both Nationalist and Communist China (see 2.1.2).

2.3.4.2 Unofficial Censorship

The issue of freedom of the press in Taiwan has been quite controversial for the last two decades. Labels of the Taiwan press vary from "A Free and Prosperous Press," "Taiwan Press-Free with Many Controls," to "The Shackled Press" (*Teng,*1966, pp. 13-18; *Lowenstein*, 1967, p. 5; *Axelbank*, 1963, pp. 6-7). But few critics can deny that there is no official news censorship on the island. Meanwhile, even the most vigorous defenders would agree that there are certain things not tolerated by the government. These include any attacks on the policy of recovering the mainland; advocacy of the Taiwan independent movement; anything which may have a demoralizing effect; and anything which may assist communist propaganda. The absence of official censorship and the existence of taboos have put the newsmen in a perplexing and delicate position. A veteran newspaperman from Taiwan observes:

> If a newspaper is permitted to publish a story only after it is censored, the publisher, the editor and the reporter concerned can at least be free from worrying what might happen to them when that story appears in print. Unprotected by any form of official censorship, newsmen on Taiwan have to be extremely careful about what they print (*Lim*, 1970, p. 15).

Especially bothersome to the press are the last two items in the list of taboos, because there is no clear-cut definition as to what may engender "demoralizing effects," and what kind of reporting may "assist Communist propaganda." This situation leads to the practice of "self-imposed censorship" by the press. Since there are no official "do's" and "don'ts" which the journalists can follow, their pens have to be guided by experience. For instance, in the early 1960s, Nationalist pilots flew U.S.-made U-2 planes to conduct photo reconnaissance over China. When such planes were occasionally shot down by the communists, it was not acceptable to report these incidents even though the story had been carried by world news agencies. Newspapers were advised by the government not to report the news "for fear of causing international complications," (*Lim*, 1970, p. 15) but instead, to give the cause of the loss of the U-2s as "mechanical defects" during a "routine training flight."

Reporting on corruption and criticisms levelled at local governments is not considered as demoralization. However, newspapers cannot print pictures of Chinese Communist leaders and if Premier Chou En-lai were referred to in print, the word "premier" had to be in quotes. Peking must always be called Peiping, since "Peking" carries with it the meaning of capital.

The current press policy of the government can be described as "accentuating the positive and eliminating or more commonly toning down the negative," (*New York Times,* 26 Sept. 1971), while still providing readers with most essential information. For instance, in September 1971, when it became known that the United States would support Peking's claim to the China seat in the U.N. Security Council, Taipei newspapers devoted significant space on the front page to articles saying that Washington would mobilize all its resources to protect Nationalist membership. Lower down on the page, separate stories described the new American position on the Security Council seat. Take another example: Henry A. Kissinger's six trips to China were briefly and matter-of-factly reported under a single column headline.

The selection and placement of articles have often created misleading impressions. Reports of former President Nixon's China policy made by conservative American organizations and publications were widely publicized, while statements backing Nixon's foreign policy and items on the public opinion polls indicating the majority support for Nixon's China policy, were either ignored or placed much less prominently (see *Hansen and Bishop,* 1974).

2.3.5 Content of Newspapers

Most newspapers in Taiwan publish 10 pages a day, with national news appearing on the front page and international news on page two. Page three is devoted to police and court news; page four, educational news, and the other pages are allocated to business, finance, entertainment, local news and literary topics. There is no sports page, nor are there editorial or women's pages. Sports and women's stories are carried on various pages. Editorials are printed either on pages one or two.

With restrictions on reporting about national politics and policies, the papers find that they can only report fully on crime, corruption, sex and less provocative political issues. In a study of two Chinese language newspapers — the *United Daily News* and the *China Times* — and the two English language papers, Tsai found that the Chinese papers continuously devoted one-half of their page three to a single robbery-murder story, carrying it for a couple of days. In a period of two weeks, the research indicates, the Chinese papers usually focused on one or two crimes to attract readers. Interestingly enough, stories such as the Kennedy-Onassis marriage equally excited readers and were played up by newspapers in Taiwan. In October 1968, the *United Daily News* and the *China Times* devoted 20 per cent of their total news space to this particular event, and the two English language papers, 15 per cent.

Although there is no sports page, popular sports events receive much attention. For instance, approximately 24 per cent of the *Post*'s total news columns were devoted to the Olympic Games of 1968; followed by the *United Daily*, 20.2 per cent; the *Times*, 13.8 per cent, and the *China News*, 5 per cent.

The two English dailies devoted 65-70 per cent of their total news space to international news each day, while the Chinese papers allocated 30 per cent of their news to foreign topics. It is conceivable that 60 per cent of readers of English dailies are foreign diplomats and businessmen, and their dependents, who want to know more about world news and major events in their home countries.

Throughout a two-week period, Tsai came across only one news item criticizing the national government, while there were a number of stories exposing local official corruption. The critical story appeared in an English daily, which blamed the government for its failure to control vegetable prices (*Tsai*, 1969, pp. 101-109).

In a similar study, Hansen concluded that the Chinese newspapers tended to have more news stories reflecting official positions than the English dailies. While the percentage of pro-government articles was about equal between the Chinese and the English language papers, Chinese papers gave much more play to expressions of opinion which tended to confirm government viewpoints. The English papers were relatively freer than their Chinese counterparts. It is interesting to note, though the *China News* maintains close ties with the government (*Hansen*, 1972, p. 12), the *News* prints considerably more news stories and reports which contradict official government views than does the *Post*. The difference probably lies in the fact that the *Post* serves the American military community more heavily (which is more conservative), while the *News* sells more to foreign students and non-military readers in the international community. Another explanation is that the *News* feels more secure due to its intimate relations with the government (*Hansen*, 1972, p. 16). Despite the difference in their news policy, Hansen's analysis further indicates that "opposition to government policy is an empty category for both English and Chinese papers" (*Hansen*, 1972, p. 12).

Still another study reported Taipei newspapers have a great deal of similarity of news, especially with military and political affairs, and that newspapers emphasize international news (*Yu*, 1972).

2.3.6 Other Aspects of the Press in Taiwan

2.3.6.1 Newsprint and Press Facilities

The paper industry suffered great damage as a result of Allied Forces air raids during World War II, and its productivity was substantially reduced in the immediate post-war years. Taiwan imported 1,559 metric tons of newsprint a year in the late 1940s and early 1950s. The island's annual newsprint consumption stood at 2,324 metric tons in 1952 (*UNESCO*, 1952, p. 172; *Lee*, 1973, p. 9).

In 1955 the government imposed a newsprint rationing measure on the press, the "Wartime Newsprint Savings Provision." This was an attempt to save foreign exchange on imported newsprint, on the one hand, and to control the size of privately-owned newspapers on the other. Accordingly, each newspaper was forbidden to have more than one and a half folio sheets (six pages). This was expanded to two folio sheets (eight pages) in 1958, and further enlarged to two and a half folio sheets (10 pages) in 1967. Extra pages are added on special occasions such as National Day, Youth Day, and New Year's Day. The annual consumption of newsprint in the early 1970s totalled 21,500 metric tons, nine times as much as that in 1952. During the same period, the production of newsprint increased so rapidly that Taiwan was not only able to supply all its domestic needs but to export to South Korea, South Vietnam, Thailand and Malaysia. Until the worldwide shortage of newsprint occurred in 1972-74, manufacturers were compelled to sell their surplus at lower prices in the competitive foreign market as a consequence of the restriction. Both the press and the newsprint suppliers were opposed to the unnecessary restrictions on the number of pages in newspapers.

Space problems are partly overcome by using smaller type and by tighter newswriting and editing. A standard newspaper page consists of 19 or 20 horizontal columns of approximately 1,000 words each. This is two and a half times the wordage of an average page in English language newspapers.

Chinese newspapers in Taiwan made impressive improvements in printing facilities in the past two decades. One of the many remarkable developments in this area was the manufacture of a Chinese rotary press by a Taiwan machinery company in April 1960. Since then, this Taiwan-made rotary press has been widely adopted by Chinese newspapers in Taiwan and Southeast Asia.

Another development in 1965 was the use of automatic Chinese monotype, replacing traditional handsetting, by *United Daily News* and *Central Daily News*. However, this Japanese-made machine can accommodate only 2,380 Chinese characters, while a Chinese paper usually needs 2,400 frequently used and 7,000 less frequently used characters for its production. The Chinese language continues to defy a fully automatic typesetting process; consequently, work in the composing room still has to be done by hand.

2.3.6.2 Press Council

As a consequence of hot contests for circulation, newspapers in Taipei resorted to exaggerated crime news reporting and sensational, sex-oriented stories in the 1950s and early 1960s. In response to public criticisms, the Taipei Newspaper Publishers Association formed the Press Council of Taipei in September 1963, to carry out "a program of self-discipline." The council was composed of seven members, all selected and named by the Publishers Association, from among retired journalists, journalism educators and the legal profession. The constitution explicitly excluded the appointment of working journalists and government officials to the council. There were two functions that the council could perform under the constitution (*IPI Report*, 1970, p. 17): to carry on research or studies of ethical problems faced by the press, and to accept and investigate complaints, filed by the individual concerned or interested, about unethical practice on the part of the press, and then to judge their validity. Taipei newspapers usually reported findings and recommendations by the press council, although not in full text. After investigating practices of the newspaper(s) involved and judging validity of the complaints, the council forwarded its report to the Publishers Association. If deemed necessary, the publishers' organization issued a mandatory request to the newspaper(s) involved to publish a statement of correction. In some cases, the Publishers Association supported the findings but was reluctant to take action.

The 1964 sensational dispute between legislator Chen Chi-ying and the *Independence Evening Post* was a case in point. Chen, a well known writer and legislator, married Miss Wang Sui-ying, a divorcee he had known for 20 years. She had been married to a Professor Wu; they were divorced a year before her marriage to Chen. While the wedding ceremony was kept secret, newspapers quickly learned of the re-marriage and covered it in detail. The *Independence Evening Post* headlined a story, "After Chen Rattled His Sword, the Family of Professor Wu was Wrecked," stating that Chen had deliberately ruined Wu's marriage in order to marry the latter's wife.

Chen, who had been active in a "decent literature" movement, was said to have been responsible for expelling from the Chinese

Literary Association a prominent woman author who was charged with writing "too frankly of sex" (*Ting*, 1965, p. 16). In a cartoon caption, the *Evening Post* said: "While the lady writer wrote sex novels, she said it without doing it. But you [Chen] are practising it without openly saying it. If you can discipline only other persons but not yourself, then you should expel yourself from the Chinese Literary Association" (*Ting*, 1965, p. 16). Chen appealed to the Press Council accusing the *Evening Post* of malicious defamation. After a three-month investigation, the council brought in a verdict against the *Evening Post*. The council said it was highly irresponsible of the paper to print exaggerated headlines which were inconsistent with the information in the story. Furthermore, the council said the cartoons were without sufficient factual foundation and showed poor judgment. The council forwarded the report to the Publishers Association which supported the findings, yet did not ask the *Evening Post* to publish a statement of correction.

The council also made special studies concerning standards of medicine advertisements, the treatment of news of juvenile delinquency and the headlining of crime stories.

In April 1971, the press council, by then the News Council of Taipei, was expanded to include radio and television. Nine members of the new organization are selected and named jointly by the following professional journalist groups: the Taipei Publishers Association, the Broadcasters Association of the Republic of China, the Television Society of the Republic of China, the Association for News Media in Taipei and the Taipei Journalists Association (*Taipei Journalists Association*, 1971, p. 194).

2.3.6.3 Journalists

High ranking staff in newspapers, both privately-owned and government-owned, were usually trained in a journalism school in China before 1949. They moved to Taiwan with the Nationalist government during the war between the communist and the Nationalist governments, and as a result, they are anti-communist intellectuals, or in their own words, communism-fighters. Politically, they share the same conviction with the government — the recovery of the mainland — thus, they tend to identify themselves with the government. Comparing the Nationalist political and economic policies some 25 years ago with the policies of today, these newsmen in the high echelon of the press are content with the present situation on the island. As part of the establishment, they follow the party line to protect their personal interests and positions in society. These publishers and editors sincerely and firmly believe that adequate freedom of the press prevails in Taiwan, and that freedom of the press has never been infringed upon, because what the government wants them to say is exactly what they want to say. A sentiment of patriotism and loyalty dominates the interpretation of the freedom of information. Therefore, the Western concept of the freedom of the press is selectively perceived and retained, consciously or unconsciously, in order to be fitted into their own image of the government.

Most young journalists are locally trained in universities and colleges which offer journalism programs. While they desire to give more in-depth reports on vital political issues and national policy matters, internal pressure from the high echelon diverts their interests and efforts to less provocative topics. This "over-cautious" policy indeed has frustrated many enthusiastic professional journalists. On top of this situation, they are poorly paid. Monthly salaries for cub reporters with a college degree average about the same as the monthly wage of a maid servant. Consequently, journalists "moonlight" between journalism and teaching, advertising, public relations, small businesses and even public service. As one young journalist once said, "Some reporters even take three or four jobs. They evidently do not have time to think of issues. How could they make a professional reporting?" (*Overseas Scholar*, 1973, p. 58)

Restrictions on press freedom and poor salaries have compelled many young reporters to give up their journalistic careers, consequently creating a "brain drain" in Taiwan journalism (*Overseas Scholar*, 1973, p. 58).

2.3.7 Conclusions

The growth of Taiwan's economy and the development of public education have provided the press with new sources of advertising revenue and readership. Accordingly, newspapers in Taiwan are financially healthy.

However, the press is still restricted by annoying press laws and other regulations affecting its fate. Interestingly enough, some press laws contribute to the prosperity of nearly all existing papers. For example, the freezing of newspaper licenses helps the papers keep their "vested interests," by protecting them from being challenged by newcomers.

With the limitations, however, newspapers in Taiwan tend to echo whatever the government spokesmen say on vital political issues and national policy matters. Newspapermen prefer to direct their professional talents to covering less provocative issues such as corruption of government officials, crime and sex, to compensate for the lack of in-depth reporting in national affairs. This tendency has become a major concern of the public, the government and the press. A press council has been established to uphold journalistic ethics and improve standard of performance. This is certainly a forward step on the part of the press. Yet to be more liberal toward press policy on the part of the government would probably direct newsmen's interests to cover more significant news events and eventually enlighten the public.

2.3.8 Recent Press Activity, by John A. Lent

Economically, the Taiwanese press had a boom in the latter 1970s. Higher literacy and increased per capita income were responsible for elevated circulations, to the extent that in 1978, 78 per cent of Taiwan's families subscribed to newpapers (*Asian Messenger,* 1978a, p. 6), and the birth of two dailies and a weekly in February 1978.

Two of the new papers resulted from the keen competition between *United Daily* and *China Times. United Daily,* which also owns the daily *Economic News,* monthly *China Forum* and a news agency specializing in economic and financial affairs, launched *Min Sheng Pao,* in Taipei. Devoted to the promotion of the people's livelihood, according to its inaugural editorial, (*Asian Messenger,* 1978a, p. 6), *Min Sheng Pao* covers sports, health care, fine arts, film and TV, daily life and other entertainment, but omits news of politics and economics (*Free China Review,* 1978a,

p. 46). The weekly started by the *China Times, Times Weekly,* also emphasizes light news but does carry hard news. In Changhua in central Taiwan, the daily *Chih Chiang Daily,* formerly *Ta Han Daily* of Taitung, also made its debut in February.

Despite these successes, the rising costs of newsprint have adversely affected the Taiwanese press. For example, the editor of *United Daily,* pointing out that newsprint prices increased from US$165 in 1973 to US$400 a ton by the mid-1970s, said he had to step up advertising rates by 30 per cent, subscription rates 66 per cent and employees' wages 60 per cent during the same period (*IPI Report,* 1975, p. 7). Currently, each daily is limited to 12 pages because of the newsprint problem, thus requiring smaller type, and skillful editing and writing.

As for the role the press is expected to play, a revision of the Publication Law in mid-1979 and a speech by President Chiang Ching-kuo in late 1978, spelled it out rather clearly. The Publication Law revision, promulgated by the Executive Yuan, stated that applicants for new publications must make clear that purposes, nature and scope are in line with national policy, that publications pirating or imitating banned publications will be forbidden, that newspapers and magazines maligning people or extorting money will be regarded as changing the purpose of publication, and that registrations will be cancelled if the publisher does not have residence in the country, is sentenced to jail for more than two months or is stripped of his civil rights (*Free China Review,* 1979b, pp. 51-52).

In his address to the Fifth Journalists' Conference, 8 November 1978, the president suggested, among other things, that the press should: regard national salvation as a responsibility to "overcome all adverse tides"; uphold democracy and the constitutional government and teach people to "perceive and experience the true meaning of democratic government"; seek the continued development and growth of the national economy; "ensure social order and maintenance of sound customs"; "encourage and watch over the government in making administrative renovations"; "strengthen the solidarity of the whole body of the body so as to come together in coping with every adverse development" (*Free China Review,* 1978b, pp. 55-56).

2.4   Hong Kong

Chang Kuo-sin

2.4.1   Historical Background

Hong Kong is unique in many ways. Geographically, it is a tiny dot on the map of Asia; politically and economically, its influence often outshines that of some of its giant neighbors. It is different things to different people. For the aspiring, it is a halfway house to greater things or hopes of greater things; for culture, it is a meeting place for East and West, the old and the new; and for ideas, it is at once a laboratory for experiments and a marketplace for free exchange.

Hong Kong's system of government is a limited democracy superimposed on a substructure of benevolent autocracy. As a colony, it is an anachronism accepted as consistent with progress, a condemned past allowed to flourish in the present, establishing a curious reputation of being loved by few, but desired by all.

Carved from China by duress, it has been — since it came into existence in 1842 — paying its debt to China by serving as hatching ground for great Chinese reform movements and hibernating ground for movements which were slightly ahead of their times. Traditionally, it served as a place of refuge for Chinese politicians and warlords — even criminals — who had fallen out with the authorities. In the old days, it gave shelter to reformers who were hunted by the tyrannical Empress Dowager

Chang Kuo-sin is a lecturer in journalism at Hong Kong Baptist College. He has been a reporter for both Central News Agency and United Press in China, Taiwan and Hong Kong, a columnist for the *South China Morning Post* and editor of *Chinese Viewpoint Newsletter*. He was born and educated in China.

Tzu Hsi; in recent times, to Chinese Communist leaders (Peking's former Foreign Minister Chiao Kuan-hua among them) who were rebelling against Nationalist rule.

One of the Chinese reformers who sought refuge in Hong Kong was Wang T'ao (1828-97), a scholar of great talent who helped the English Sinologist James Legge to make the first English translation of Chinese classics. He started agitating for reforms when Japan was preparing for the Meiji Restoration and the Taiping Rebellion against Manchu rule was raging in China. When he supported the Taiping Rebellion a warrant for his arrest was issued by the Manchu government, so he fled to Hong Kong where in 1874 he started the first Chinese language daily, entirely Chinese owned, managed and edited. For the newspaper, he chose the name *Tsun Wan Daily News* (Tsun Wan means circulation), to symbolize his belief that, although the Taiping Rebellion had failed, its seeds would forever remain in circulation.

Wang T'ao has been called the father of Chinese journalism and the Chinese Horace Greeley. Like Greeley, he recognized the power of editorials and wrote an editorial a day, always calling for reforms in China. His paper was considered the beginning of the political press in China. Greeley's famous saying was "Go West." Wang T'ao's was "Learn from the West." He wanted China to Westernize like Japan, but with one proviso: in Westernizing, don't abandon Confucianism.

Wang T'ao visited Europe twice, the first time in 1867 when he stayed to observe the Franco-Prussian War. When he returned to China, he started a new crusade in his editorials, turning his eloquence against Czarist Russia, which he called a menace to China. He suggested that China ally herself with European powers in a bid to contain Russia. In his editorials, he also demanded the return of Macao. He was one of the visionaries well ahead of the times.

The *Tsun Wan Daily News* did not live long. Presumably because of the affinity between Wang T'ao's views and China's policy in regard to Russia, Peking tried to revive the newspaper in the 1960s, but it was published for only a few years, before being abandoned as a commercial failure.

It was also in Hong Kong that the first Chinese language daily came into being. Called *Chung Ngoi Hsin Pao* (*Sino-Foreign Daily News*), it was started in 1858 on the initiative of Dr. Wu

Ting-fang, a scholar-diplomat and a former Chinese foreign minister. *Chung Ngoi* began as a translation of the English-language *Daily Press* and was published as its evening edition. But it soon took on an editorial independence that was to leave its mark on Chinese politics. It gave strong editorial support to the reform movement in China and bitterly attacked the warlord Lung Chi-kwong who was then ruling Kwangtung. The paper also offended the British by voicing opposition against Chinese participation in World War I. As a result, it was prosecuted for sedition and fined $101.

World War I brought financial problems to *Chung Ngoi,* at the end forcing it to jettison its journalistic virtues and accept subsidies from its enemy, Lung Chi-kwong. Overnight, it turned from an enemy to a supporter of Lung. In 1919, when Lung was ousted from Kwangtung, he stopped his subsidies and the paper ceased publication.

In the two decades between the two world wars, four newspapers were started which became instant commercial successes and which constitute the mainstay of the press in Hong Kong today. They are:

1. *Wah Kiu Yat Po*: Started on 5 June 1925 as a successor to *Chung Ngoi Hsin Pao,* which had ceased publication six years earlier. Currently the oldest Chinese language daily in Hong Kong, the paper is considered the voice of Hong Kong's commerce and industry and is Hong Kong's largest newspaper in terms of number of pages, of which 28 are published daily. (The ordinary daily publishes only four or eight pages a day.) *Wah Kiu* publishes an evening edition which comes out twice a day.

2. *Sing Tao Daily News*: Started in 1938 by the Tiger Balm King, Aw Boon Haw, *Sing Tao* is now run by his daughter, Miss Aw Sian, who is building her own newspaper empire. *Sing Tao* is reputed to be the biggest money maker among Chinese language newspapers, being richly supported by advertisers. Classified advertisements alone occupy five of its 20 pages daily. In 1973, it made nearly US$3 million, about the same as the *South China Morning Post,* both newspapers probably clearing as much profit as, if not more than, the *New York Times. Sing Tao* publishes an evening edition which is one of two newspapers in Hong Kong with a circulation exceeding 150,000.

Sing Tao was part of the newspaper chain which Aw Boon Haw built, the only newspaper group that ever existed in the Chinese press. With the English language *Hong Kong Standard,* started in 1949, the chain had a total of seven newspapers scattered in China and Southeast Asia. Aw Boon Haw was a multi-millionaire who turned to newspaper publishing with an ideal. In a signed editorial published in the inaugural issue of the *Hong Kong Standard* (1 March 1949), he said his newspapers were "to speak only for the public" and their "common aim . . . is to provide a true and undistorted mirror of public opinion."

3. *Sing Pao Daily News*: The second newspaper in Hong Kong with a circulation of over 150,000, it was established in 1939. *Sing Pao* serves the lower stratum of Chinese society and is the most widely-read paper in Chinese teashops with its abundant supply of mystery stories loved by the Chinese working class. *Sing Pao* publishes eight pages a day and has no evening edition.

4. *Kung Sheung Daily News*: Started in 1925, only two weeks after *Wah Kiu Yat Po,* by a scion of Hong Kong's best-known and perhaps richest family, Ho Sai-lai, second son of Sir Robert Ho Tung. Ho was a general in the Chinese Nationalist Army and was once its general services commander. Newspaper publishing was a sideline for him, and he started the paper, not for commercial reasons, but to promote the Chinese point of view in British Hong Kong.

The years between the two world wars were a period of adjustment and consolidation for Chinese and English language newspapers alike. The *South China Morning Post,* which was to become the premier morning daily in the English language field was coming into its own. It was started by a British journalist, A. Cunningham, and a Chinese scholar, Tse Tsan-tsai, for the same purpose as *Kung Sheung Daily News,* to present Chinese viewpoints in a British colony (see *"70th Anniversary Review of South China Morning Post,"* March 1973). Its editorial policy was Chinese oriented, designed to support reforms in China. Today, it is considered pro-establishment, representing British vested interests in Hong Kong.

When the *Morning Post* began publication in 1903, there were about 19,000 English residents in Hong Kong. Only a very small proportion of the Chinese population read and spoke English and there were already three English language newspapers — *Daily*

Press, Hong Kong Telegraph and the *China Mail,* thus, it was a precarious birth for a new daily. But within two years, the *Morning Post* overtook its three rivals in circulation.

The *Morning Post* started to make a profit in 1908 and began to expand its editorial sweep in Chinese politics, crusading for more railway development, political reforms and education. It also began to call for more vigorous action against pirates who were, at the time, threatening shipping along the China coast.

After World War II, Hong Kong continued to play a unique role in the development of the press, especially the Chinese language press. In the first few post-war years, China was embroiled in civil war, ending in a communist victory in 1949. When the civil war stopped in China, the rival factions continued their fight in Hong Kong, not with guns, but through newspaper columns. Hong Kong became a new battlefield, a battlefield of ideas and ideologies. A vigorous press had grown up to serve as weapons in the new battle, a press that perhaps represented more political persuasions, more partisanship, more prejudice and bias than any other press in the world's history.

2.4.2 Freedom of the Press

Because of the circumstances of its birth, the press in Hong Kong has not always operated in the best traditions of journalism. It is no stickler for ethics. Professionally, it has not established any enduring reputation for creativeness, originality, initiative and imagination and has often been described as lackluster in performance. But in Hong Kong's tangled society, most would agree that the press has adequately discharged its duties to inform and to enlighten.

In the context of the world press, the significance of the press in Hong Kong is, however, not as much in its performance as in the extent of press freedom that it is enjoying — equalled in only one other country in Asia, Japan.

The curious phenomenon is that in Hong Kong, press freedom exists side by side with some of the worst legal restraints, many of which had been considered undesirable and repealed in England. A good example is the Control of Publications Ordinance, which the Hong Kong government, breaking the

British tradition of subjecting all citizens to the same ordinary law, made specially for the press. It contains some of the strictest restraints on press freedom. Newspapers are not to publish "false news likely to alarm public opinion or disturb public order" or news likely to persuade or induce people or organizations to commit an offense or become a member or supporter of any unlawful society or any political party or association which has been declared prejudicial to the security of Hong Kong or public order and safety in the Colony (*Control of Publications Ordinance*). Another provision empowers the government to suspend or suppress any newspaper which is substantially under the same management as a newspaper found guilty of violating the ordinance.

Other provisions govern the starting of new newspapers which have to register for permission to publish, paying HK$100 (about US$20) a year for a registration fee, and must apply to the police for a license to print. Furthermore, newspapers must pay a cash deposit of HK$10,000 (about US$2,000), to ensure the publisher's ability to pay fines or damages which may be imposed in legal proceedings.

These regulations are what had been criticized by the late A. V. Dicey, an authority on British constitutional law, as "radically inconsistent" with British jurisprudence (*Dicey*, n.d.). In Hong Kong, a legal authority commented that the regulation requiring payment of the cash deposit amounted "to a presumption of guilt as well as a presupposition that the newspaper about to be registered is bound to commit libels" (*Chiu*, n.d., p. 9).

In England, the Licensing Act had been allowed to lapse in 1695, but despite the incongruity of the regulations in today's society, the Hong Kong government has not seen fit to repeal them. The government felt that they were needed to serve as a safety valve to prevent the internal struggles in China from spilling into Hong Kong. In practice, the safety valve did not work successfully in blocking the spilling. But then neither has it restricted the growth of newspapers or curbed the exercise of press freedom in any real way.

Starting a newspaper in Hong Kong is a simple exercise of filling in some forms and paying the cash deposit of HK$10,000 (no hardship for any intending publisher) or producing two guarantors for the amount. The government asks no questions; there is never any investigation, and the whole affair is just a formality. The presses can roll as soon as the forms are handed in to the Registrar of Newspapers.

In Hong Kong, technicality and reality are carefully separated. The law is one thing; practice is another, and the two exist side by side without any insoluble conflict. Under the law, there could not be too much press freedom in Hong Kong, but the law is rarely enforced except in times of emergency, such as during the riots in 1951, 1956 and 1967. In 1967, the publishers, editors and printers of three leftist newspapers — *Afternoon News, Hong Kong Evening News* and *Tin Fung Daily News* — were convicted of sedition under the Control of Publications Ordinance. The three newspapers were ordered suspended for six months and sentences of three years' imprisonment and fines amounting to US$2,000 were imposed on the executives.

Except for the few occasions when the government has taken action against newspapers to protect public security, the press is allowed an extent of press freedom that is equal to that in any democratic country. Hong Kong is not only one of the few places in Asia enjoying press freedom in any acceptable degree; even more important, it is at present the only place — not taking into consideration the small Chinese communities in foreign countries — where the Chinese language press is enjoying press freedom. Since the modern Chinese press began in 1815, with the publication of the *Chinese Monthly Magazine* in Malacca by a British missionary, William Milne, it has lived a precarious existence, hunted, suppressed and repressed by the authorities or subjected to all kinds of pressure by politicians and warlords. Sometimes, the press had to flee China and continue to publish in foreign countries, such as Japan, as an "exile" press.

2.4.3 Scope of the Press

In Hong Kong the Chinese press has settled down to a secure existence, acquiring what is believed to be its highest readership, attributable to the high literacy rate among the Chinese population. According to the government census taken in 1971, the illiteracy rate in Hong Kong was only 17.4 per cent, while in old China, it used to be 85 per cent.

With the help of the easy laws, the great number of Chinese

intellectuals who came to Hong Kong after they were ousted from China by the communist seizure of power, turned their talents to newspaper publishing. A proliferation of the press resulted, amounting to a veritable newspaper "explosion." According to mid-1975 government statistics, there were 74 daily newspapers in Hong Kong, three English language and the rest in the Chinese language (*Hong Kong Government,* 1974, p. 147). The "explosion" gave Hong Kong the highest density of newspapers in the world, averaging one daily to every 53,000 persons, as compared with one newspaper to every 450,000 persons in Taiwan, 600,000 in Japan, 2 million in China, 1 million in India and 110,000 in the United States.

Many of the newspapers are not newspapers in the full sense of the word, only 49 of them appearing on the government's mailing list for news bulletins and press conferences. The government said 40 newspapers do not carry general news, but were "solely entertainment orientated," devoted to mystery stories, sex, novels, sports, economics, commerce and industry, horse racing or dog racing. A few were merely daily editions of movie magazines, filled with stories — real and imaginary — about Hong Kong's fledgling movieland. Many of them were what would be considered scandal sheets, carrying exotic names, such as *Precious Evening News, Sisters Daily, True Evening News, Wins Racing News, Gentlemen Daily News* and *Peace Night Evening News.*

Sixteen afternoon newspapers appeared on the government's mailing list. Presumably to soften competition for readership, they stagger their appearance on the newsstands. Two afternoon dailies appear so early in the morning (6 a.m.) that they could be called morning or mid-morning newspapers. They are the *Truth Daily* and the *Peace Night Evening News.* The English language *Star* is on the streets at 8 a.m. and has a late edition which comes out at 3 p.m. Some other afternoon papers appear on the following time schedule — noon: *Heavenly Emperor Evening News, New Life Evening Post, Wah Kiu Evening News* (1st edition); 1:30 p.m.: *Ming Pao Evening News;* 2 p.m.: *South China Evening News, New Evening News, New News Evening News* (literally translated); 2:45 p.m.: *Hong Kong Evening News;* 3 p.m.: *Kung Sheung Evening News;* 3:30 p.m.: *Wah Kiu Evening News* (2nd edition); 3:45 p.m.: *New Evening Post;* 4:30 p.m.: *Sing Tao Evening News.*

Opening a new field in newspaper publishing, the enterprising Miss Aw Sian of the *Sing Tao Daily News* began issuing giveaway newspapers, the first of which was published in 1973. Within two years, there were five such newspapers with an approximate total circulation of 54,000. They have not become as successful as their counterparts in Australia, but have begun to break even. The giveaway newspapers are named after the government built housing estates where they are distributed. The housing estates are Hong Kong's large population concentration points, each housing anywhere from 40,000 to 150,000 people.

Newspapers in Hong Kong are among the world's smallest in number of pages, most publishing only four or eight pages a day. They are also among the world's cheapest, selling at HK 70 cents (US$0.12) per copy. *South China Morning Post* sells at HK$1.50 (US$0.25), while the *Hong Kong Standard* remains at HK$1.00. The *Star* still sells at HK 50 cents.

The inexpensive price of newspapers, coupled with their fiction-oriented contents, helped to bring about the phenomenon of the multi-paper reader in Hong Kong. The majority of readers buy more than one newspaper a day for no other purpose than to read their favorite authors who write serialized novels for several newspapers at the same time. Because they are poorly paid, authors must do this in order to earn enough to live. These novels are the strongest circulation booster for newspapers, not the pornography or crime content, as was formerly thought, or even news, as it should be. All Chinese language newspapers devote at least two full pages a day to serialized novels, mostly mystery stories of gallantry and chivalry with large doses of fantasy.

2.4.4 Newspaper Economics

The proliferation of the press in Hong Kong has recently shown signs of having reached the saturation point. In terms of advertising revenue, there appears to be too many newspapers, many more than Hong Kong can support. According to a recent survey, the print media are still leading in advertising revenues; of the US$55 million spent on advertising in Hong Kong in 1973, the print media took 45 per cent, the electronic media 35 per cent, cinema 2 per cent and outdoor 18 per cent.[1]

The 45 per cent represented much less than the portion the print media had taken in the years when radio and television had not come in for their share, and indications are that the percentage is changing (or will change) in favor of electronic media. Some of the 74 dailies have begun to feel the pinch which was made all the more painful by the skyrocketing newsprint price and the recession. In 1974, at least 20 dailies closed, including the English language, evening paper, *China Mail,* Hong Kong's oldest daily, started in 1845. It ceased publication in August 1974 after nearly three years of continuing losses amounting to nearly US$1 million at the time of its closure. Other newspapers in the mid-1970s retrenched staff to cut down expenses, but the major ones, such as *South China Morning Post, Sing Tao Daily News, Wah Kiu Yat Po* and *Sing Po Daily News,* still flourished.

The closure of the *China Mail* left the English language afternoon field solely to the *Star,* a tabloid started in 1965. The *Star* aims at a young readership and gives prominence to modern trends in dancing, music and fashion which appeal to the young. It places a heavy reliance on pictures. The *Star* applies what publisher Graham Jenkins calls "psychographic skills," which is "the application of offset methods of printing, of typography, of make-up and of pictures (the graphic arts) to produce a designed effect upon the mind — and in our own case upon our target audience, that is, upon the Hong Kong Modern."[2] The *Star,* which has a Chinese language edition, is the only newspaper in Hong Kong published in both languages.

Failing newspapers in Hong Kong can expect no help from the government which adopted an absolute *laissez-faire* attitude towards the press. The press gets no preferential treatment from the government, no discount fares on buses and trams, no newsprint subsidies of any kind and no special postal privileges. In

---

1   Vincent Chow, deputy sales manager, Hong Kong Commercial Broadcasting Co., "Hong Kong's Electronic Media — What's Ahead?" lecture at Colloquium, Hong Kong Baptist College, 23 November 1974.

2   Graham Jenkins, publisher of *Star,* in a letter to Chang Kuo-sin, 30 December 1974.

a court case involving 11 reporters in September 1974, the government made sure that the press was treated more harshly than the public in a similar situation.

The 11 reporters were arrested along with 22 members of the public for illegal entry into a restricted area of Hong Kong's international airport. The reporters were there to cover a near riot by relatives of 118 Vietnamese refugees who were being deported. The government asked for the maximum penalty for the reporters who were each fined HK$200 with their convictions recorded. The 22 members of the public, who appeared before the same court, were put on bonds of HK$50 each and their convictions were not recorded (*Data for Decision,* 1974, p. 2029).

The reporters' appeal against what they considered an unfair penalty was dismissed by Hong Kong's Chief Justice Sir Geoffrey Briggs, who upheld the harsher penalty on the grounds that they, being "educated, knowledgeable and professional men," should have known better (*South China Morning Post,* 8 Sept. 1974).

The only government facility given the press is one which, legally, the government should not have provided and which, professionally, the press should not have accepted. It is the Government Information Services' daily bulletin, as much a regular news service as it is an official bulletin. The bulletin has a daily output of about 12,000 words, made up of not only official statements, texts of speeches made by government officials and official replies to press inquiries, but also news stories similar to those issued by Associated Press or United Press International. The practice is to issue an official statement in full, coupled with a news story on the statement, as well as spot news on such local happenings as fire, crime and traffic accidents.

The government bulletin is channelled to newspapers on teleprinters installed by Cable & Wireless. The newspapers pay rent for the teleprinters, amounting to about US$600 a year, but they do not pay for the bulletin. For the Chinese language newspapers, the Government Information Services started a news translation service, translating both official texts and news stories into Chinese and transmitting them to the newspapers on a facsimile service at a speed of seven minutes per foolscap page.

The news stories in the government bulletin are very professionally written, rather objective and unbiased. Even so, reputable newspapers refuse or hesitate to use them, considering them as handouts. In Hong Kong, however, they fill a need created by the shortage of qualified copyreaders, rewrite men and reporters. Editors treat the bulletins in the same way as they treat copy from the wire services, using them without editing, sometimes shortening them to save space.

Chinese editors devote more space to headlines than is considered normal, especially in view of the small size of Chinese language newspapers. Very often the headline occupies more space than the story itself, usually running to six decks. Four decks are common even for every insignificant stories. In writing headlines, Chinese editors do not usually follow the basic rules; they do not abbreviate and they sometimes inject opinion into the headlines. Thus, Chinese language newspapers are a delight for the habitual headline scanners.

Circulation of newspapers in Hong Kong is a well-kept secret. All attempts to get accurate or near accurate figures have been in vain. Asking a publisher for his circulation figure is as indiscreet as asking a lady for her age. The British Audit Bureau of Circulation is represented in Hong Kong, but it cannot operate for lack of cooperation from the press. The *Hong Kong Government Yearbook 1974* estimated circulation of English language newspapers at 102,000 and Chinese language newspapers at 1.26 million, making a total of about 1.4 million. This figure, in fact, had been more or less the estimate every year during the previous decade. It is like the age of the late Jack Benny which remained at 39 despite the passing years. The estimate of Hong Kong's newspaper circulation remained the same despite the 1.5 million increase of population in the intervening years. It cannot be accepted as a reliable estimate, but it is the only quotable one available. Calculating on the basis of this estimate, Hong Kong must have a diffusion rate of about 333 copies per 1,000 persons, the second highest in Asia, next to Japan, and higher than that of the United States.

The Chinese language press in Hong Kong is divided along lines in Chinese internal politics: anti-communist, pro-communist and neutral. Most belong to the first group, but the communists are also very strongly represented. The major Chinese communist dailies are *Takungpao, Wen Wei Pao* and *New Evening Post.* *Takungpao* was started in North China in the early 1930s as an independent paper, and was China's most prestigious daily until it was taken over by the communists. *Wen Wei Pao* is considered the official organ of the Chinese Communist Party in Hong Kong.

The Nationalists also maintain a party organ in Hong Kong, *Hong Kong Times,* launched in 1949 after the Nationalists were driven out of China. The newspapers published by the two Chinese political parties are not very popular with readers who, like their counterparts in other parts of the world, prefer newspapers without party affiliations.

2.4.5 Conclusion

Although the Chinese language press in Hong Kong is psychologically refugee-minded (ever ready to move back to China once it is possible), it has over the years established its roots in the colony. It has begun to orientate itself to a long stay and at the same time, to concern itself with local issues and, even more important, with the future of Hong Kong.

This has brought about a significant transformation in the nature of the press which has begun to identify with Hong Kong. It is making its influence felt in government and has led at least one leader to depict the press as part of the unofficial opposition in Hong Kong's system of government. Governor Sir Murray MacLehose said of the press: "You will find in Hong Kong a particularly large and lively press. Hong Kong is by any standards an unusual place; amongst other attributes history and circumstances have given it a government with an unusual constitution. In a community dominated by British liberal thought and liberal British law, the Government is forced to govern without the usual aids of a liberal constitution . . . . Without the clash of rival political parties and policies to dominate the news, the public and the Government are very dependent on a vigorous presentation of fact and commentary by the press and television."[3]

3   Hong Kong Governor Sir Murray MacLehose, speech at opening ceremony of 12th Quadrennial Conference of Commonwealth Press Union, 3 October 1974.

2.4.6 Recent Developments, by John A. Lent

Hong Kong still defies the belief that metropolitan areas can no longer support large numbers of dailies. The number of dailies fluctuates (in 1975, for instance, there were 107 newspapers) (*Hong Kong Government*, 1976, p. 144), but there is no doubt Hong Kong has the highest density of newspapers per population of any city — even nation — in the world.

The types of newspapers range from serious, pro-Peking organs to specialized dailies for devotees of sports and horse- and dog-racing, to scandal-filled "mosquito" sheets. Each has an interesting story, some of which would be suitable subjects for fiction writers. There is the *Oriental Daily News (Tung Fong Yat Pao)*, started as a "mosquito" paper in 1969 and converted into a quality publication in the early 1970s, by recruiting bright, young talent; extending its deadline to 4 a.m.; and setting up mobile reporting squads, including speedboats commanded by a central electronic communications system. By 1976, *Oriental Daily News* had the largest circulation of any daily in Hong Kong, according to the *Survey Research Hong Kong Media Index*. In 1977, its founding owner, Ma Sik-chun, was arrested as one of the kingpins of the Asian drug trade (*Yao*, 1977, pp. 19-20).

There is *Kam Yeh Pao (Tonight's Paper)*, headed by an almost one-man staff, Wong Sai-yu, who dubs himself "007." Wong, who claims he walks "on the fringes of the law," was responsible for breaking the sex-oriented story about Bruce Lee's death. He started his paper in 1972 with HK$20,000 capital and despite a three- or fourfold increase in newsprint prices, the paper annually shows a profit (*Huang*, 1976, p. 7).

There are other dailies maintained by wealthy publishers as promoters or weapons for their business conglomerates. One such paper is *Tin Tin Daily News*, owned by Alan Lau who sits on top of an empire involving financing, credit cards, laundries, handbags, shoes and watch manufacturing. Described as a publisher with a Rolls-Royce style, Lau increased *Tin Tin Daily News'* circulation from 10,000 to 90,000 within a year after purchasing it in 1977 for HK$600 and HK$1.9 million in debts. His formula included promotional gimmicks the likes of which have not been seen often since the days of Hearst. He has hopes of realizing a profit from the paper, claiming it is easy to make HK$5 to 10 million a year from a daily in the colony (*Smith,* 1978, p. 8).

Finally, there are dailies representing nearly every political hue in Hong Kong. For years, the left-wing press has acted as an outlet for information passing out of China. The dominant and oldest (dating to the Ching dynasty), pro-Peking daily is *Ta Kung Pao* which uses a more intellectual style than *Hsin Wan Pao,* an evening offspring when it began in 1949, and *Wen Hui Pao* (*Asiaweek,* 1978, p. 46a).

There are also big business aspects to Hong Kong journalism as exemplified in two large groups, Sing Tao Newspapers and South China Morning Post Ltd., both owners of an impressive array of English and Chinese publications. Sing Tao, founded by Aw Boon Haw of Tiger Balm fame, is now headed by Sally Aw Sian. The group publishes *Sing Tao Jih Pao* (morning), *Sing Tao Man Po* (afternoon) and, with a group of Hong Kong Chinese newspapers, is part of a consortium owning a television station. Sing Tao chairman, Sally Aw Sian, also has controlling interests in Pacific Communications Ltd., publishers of four prestigious English journals, is co-owner of Hong Kong *Star* (English tabloid, afternoon) and owns *Jetwind* (travel magazine) and a travel agency, among other interests. The Aws also own *Hong Kong Standard* (*Media,* 1974a, p. 4), and in 1974, started a daily in Fiji (*Media,* July 1974, p. 23). In 1978, Sing Tao Newspapers made an HK$18 million profit (*Media,* 1979a, p. 1).

Backed by powerful Hong Kong banking concerns, South China Morning Post Ltd. is also entangled in large-scale operations. Besides the *Post,* the group has *Sunday Post Herald,* 51 per cent of *Far Eastern Economic Review,* a one-third interest in *Asia Magazine,* a regional fortnightly Sunday supplement, *Television and Entertainment Times, Asian Golf Digest* (monthly) and *Welcome* (tourist newspaper) (*Careem,* 1977b, pp. 18-19). Acquisition of shares in *Asia Magazine* gave the Post group a link with the *Straits Times* organization in Singapore, another key shareholder in the magazine. Additionally, the *Post* has indirect interest in the Far East Trade Press, publishers of five regional magazines (*Kraitzer,* 1975, pp. 57-58), and at the time of *China Mail*'s death in 1974, owned 40 per cent of that daily. The group's profits in 1976 were HK$21.8 million.

The magnitude of group operations was emphasized in 1976 when an unnamed Hong Kong newspaper chain offered to go into partnership with London's *Observer* (*Geddes,* 1976, p. 1).

There were also some economical low points in the Hong Kong newspaper industry after the mid-1970s. The already mentioned *China Mail* lost US$700,000 during its last 20 months; some said it was a result of editorial and management problems, shortages of cash and mounting newsprint bills (*FEER,* 1974a, p. 13; see *O'Neill,* 1974, pp. 22-25), while one journalist attributed the death of Hong Kong's oldest paper to a glut of competitive dailies in Hong Kong and high wages paid to expatriates (*Chang,* 1974, pp. 8-9). At the time of the *Mail*'s closing, other newspapers, feeling the economic crunch, used a variety of means to survive. The *Hong Kong Standard,* for example, cut back its number of pages to conserve scarce and expensive newsprint; the *South China Morning Post* increased its capital by allowing Dow Jones to up its stake in the paper by 10 per cent (*Media,* 1975a, p. 3), and still other dailies tried to cut costs by replacing senior journalists with young reporters paid "coolie wages," by using more guest columns and stories written by government-employed journalists (*Media,* July 1974, p. 23).

The wages and professionalism of journalists continued as sore spots in the industry at the dawn of the 1980s. Despite an upsurge after 1974 of trade union activity among journalists, spurred on by the Hong Kong Journalists Association, wages remained low enough that sections of the press were affected by corruption in the form of "eel articles."[4] The Hong Kong Independent Commission Against Corruption (ICAC) received a number of complaints of palm greasing in press circles and in at least two situations came close to prosecuting.[5]

4 "The term derives from the custom of serving fattened eels as a delicacy on special occasions when the host hopes to bring influence to bear on his guests" (*Media,* 1979b).
5 An ICAC official said that many of the cases reported could be classified as offenses under section nine of the prevention of bribery ordinance but prosecution is difficult because reporters are expected to supplement their incomes and proprietors are "equivocal" in their attitudes (*Media,* 1979b).

94   John A. Lent *Newspapers in Asia*

The corruption seemed to be a manifestation of low pay, conditions of service and poor training of journalists. The director of the Government Information Service, John Slimming, told a group in late 1978 that the standards of the profession had been weakened by the number of untrained and inexperienced "youngsters" recruited by newspapers to write the "personalised story, colored or shaded by sensationalism, or prejudice, or emotion" (*Media*, 1979b). At other times, according to the ICAC, columns are used for paid attacks on individuals or companies. Reporters are tempted to take bribes because, despite the healthy profits made by a number of newspapers, their wages are kept at very low scales and their chances of moving to middle level journalism are remote (*Media*, 1979b).

Added to these problems, reporters find that even though Hong Kong has a relatively free press, there are many doors of government closed to them. Perhaps because of that, they find it easier to act as "lackeys" of vested interests in government and business, rather than investigators. The Official Secrets Act and other instructions by officials tend to keep the lid on many governmental activities. Some of this goes back to 1973 when the government introduced a series of measures to prevent leaks of confidential and restricted documents to the press (see *Media*, 1979c, p. 17; *Media*, Jan. 1974, p. 19).

2.5　Japan

Hisao Komatsubara

2.5.1　General Features of the Japanese Press

Japan has developed a mass communications system unique to itself. Newspapers, magazines, radio and television, between them, have formed what critics rejoicingly call "an informationized society," the implications of which are that information takes a greater role than ever before in the running of a highly industrialized society like Japan. In fact, these mass media have greatly influenced the molding of consciousness of Japanese people, as well as deeply embedding themselves in the cultural patterns of the country, and, more importantly, have led the nation in the right direction.

Newspapers, in an age of diversified mass media, still play, or at least are expected to play, a leading role in informing the public. Japan's newspaper press is highly developed and its combined total circulation of over 63 million daily is the third largest in the world after the Soviet Union and the United States. This is larger than the circulations of the rest of the Asian countries combined. It has grown by almost 19 million in the past decade and a half to consume 2.3 million tons of newsprint in 1977, the supply of which was entirely supported by domestic manufacturers. With over 550 copies disseminated to every 1,000 people, it serves a nation of avid newspaper readers. Newspaper

Hisao Komatsubara has been with the International Section of Nihon Shimbun Kyokai, of which he is now chief, since 1958. He has studied at New York University as a Fulbright Scholar. He teaches at Toyo University.

(This chapter was updated by John A. Lent.)

revenue from advertising in 1978 amounted to ¥570.2 billion in the overall advertising expenditure of over ¥1,600 billion. In the 1970s, however, the newspaper industry has experienced economic difficulties due to the rising cost of production, especially since the energy crisis that hit the world late in 1973. Editorially, too, a mere growth, though much of it healthy, does not seem to have reinforced the Japanese press with a journalistic thrust vital to good journalism.

But why has Japan come to have the kind of newspapers that it has today? Although much of the development has taken place in a free press, free enterprise climate since 1945, the press in Japan had already made considerable progress since its inception in the 1860s, when a modern Japan opened its doors to the outside world. Though barely 100 years old, the press was fortunate to serve, at the very beginning, a literate people who had been educated in their communities with no overall educational system in the modern sense. Of course, newspaper readers in the early days came from a limited elite, but they formed a core of people who, emerging from Japan's isolationism for two and a half centuries, were intensely curious about the outside world and about things unknown and were very acquisitive in their task of nation building. With wars every two decades (and war helps newspaper circulations) the Japanese press had newspapers in the one million circulation bracket early in the 1920s, just prior to the nation's move towards suicidal militarism. These national traits of intense curiosity, acquisitiveness and perhaps competitiveness, with the people tightly packed in an island nation, have helped develop the uniqueness of the Japanese press. Compared to some other Asian countries, Japan has the advantage of being a nation of one language and one homogeneous people, with advanced industry and other infrastructures.

The most striking characteristic of the Japanese press is the degree to which it is concentrated. A total of only 126 dailies divide among themselves a huge 63 million circulation with both national and local newspapers having a virtual monopoly in their respective markets. The trend toward monopoly and concentration can be seen in every urbanized, industrialized country as a logical conclusion of various forces at work in the last three decades. Most of Japan's consolidation resulted from compulsory mergers of newspapers during the war (Japan once had more than 1,400 dailies).

Five national newspapers, "the big three" of *Asahi, Yomiuri* and *Mainichi,* and *Sankei Shimbun* and *Nihon Keizai Shimbun* (an economic and financial daily), have a combined circulation exceeding half the nation's total. In the case of the "big three," they have publishing plants scattered in the major urban centers of Tokyo, Osaka, Nagoya, Kitakyushu and Hokkaido, reaching readers in every corner of the country. The three giants never fail to deploy their enormous resources, both financial and human, to outpace each other and local newspapers. For example. *Asahi* employs a staff of more than 9,000, including printers; maintains 82 domestic bureaux plus 196 stringers in distant places; dispatches overseas 35 correspondents, and has all the equipment needed for covering major story developments, including 11 aircraft (see 2.5.6 for more on the magnitude of *Asahi*).

Japan's national newspaper is indeed mass circulated but is by no means a low brow, popular press. Instead, it claims to be a quality press (*Ryu,* 1961). Here again, this is a peculiarity of the Japanese press and any comparison with the presses of other countries falls short (see *Academia,* 1976, pp. 32-33). Although the "big three" may resemble each other, they have distinct characteristics for many Japanese readers. True they have lost their political flavors in the pursuit of a non-partisan policy, as have all other general interest daily newspapers. But in 1977 a newspaper serving over 7 million subscribers — *Asahi* had a 7.3 million morning circulation plus 4.6 million evening subscribers — tries to offer something for everybody while annoying nobody, to use the phrase of the late Francis Williams (*Williams,* 1969, p. 236). For better or worse, the Japanese press has become part of the establishment to the extent that it has annulled frequent allegations that it is basically an opposition press.

The local press both in outlook and contents is not very much different from its national counterpart, the difference being that local newspapers serve their respective areas of circulation. In constant vigilance against inroads made by the national press, the local newspapers, within their areas, enjoy a comfortable monopoly. In fact, many of them are highly profitable, at least up to the time of the energy crisis, though those which are located in the immediate metropolitan regions are not very well off.

TABLE 3.   Major Daily Newspapers in Japan, 1977

Name	Morning	Evening	Total
Asahi Shimbun	7,310,688	4,593,083	11,903,771
Yomiuri Shimbun	7,541,216	4,473,158	12,014,374
Mainichi Shimbun	4,433,174	2,505,816	6,938,990
Sankei Shimbun	1,765,532	952,438	2,717,970
Nihon Keizai Shimbun	1,740,333	1,133,289	2,873,622
Chunichi Shimbun	2,665,817	1,515,615	4,181,432
Hokkaido Shimbun	906,207	780,315	1,686,522
Nishi Nippon Shimbun	632,600	288,816	921,416
Tokyo Shimbun	856,306	653,296	1,509,602
Kahoku Shimpo	374,870	157,427	532,297
Kobe Shimbun	416,414	249,819	666,233
Kyoto Shimbun	412,552	331,796	744,348
Chugoku Shimbun	512,880	114,570	627,450
Shizuoka Shimbun	519,324	519,572	1,038,896
English dailies			
The Japan Times	41,585	–	
Mainichi Daily News	33,746	–	
*The Daily Yomiuri**	–		
Asahi Evening News	–	35,470	
Shipping & Trade News	14,708	–	

Source: *The Japanese Press 1978.*
* *Figures not available.*

There are semi-giants in their own ranks: *Chunichi Shimbun,* Nagoya, has traditionally spurned invasions of the "big three" and built itself up as a quasi-national newspaper concern by buying out *Tokyo Shimbun* and one other local paper in Kanazawa; *Hokkaido Shimbun,* Sapporo, has developed its own facsimile transmission network to print the paper at four different plants, and *Nishi Nippon Shimbun,* Fukuoka, is circulated over the entire southernmost island of Kyushu. These three newspapers are classified as bloc newspapers because each is published in a wider area than the single prefecture to which local newspapers limit themselves. This pattern of newspaper publishing — the coexistence of national, bloc and local papers — was largely a creation of wartime mergers concluded in 1942 as franchises to publish were awarded only to national (*Asahi, Mainichi* and *Yomiuri*), bloc and local papers in their respective prefectures, finally reducing the number of dailies to 54.

2.5.2 Early Newspapers

Journalism began with the country's modernization in the 1860s. For almost three centuries (1636-1854), the Tokugawa government closed its doors to the outside world, forbidding all access to Western civilizations other than the Dutch. During that period, *yomiuri kawaraban* (title edition), a broadsheet of illustrated news, was the only thing resembling a newspaper. It was only in the 1860s, when foreign powers were clamoring at its door and the civil war was radically changing its course, that Japan began to feel an urge for modern journalism. In order to get first hand information from abroad, the Tokugawa Shogunate published *Batavia Shimbun* in 1861, which was a faithful duplicate in Japanese of an official Dutch newspaper, *Javasche Courant*.

The genesis of Japanese newspapers had other foreign influences. *Kaigai Shimbun,* the first newspaper published by a civilian Japanese, Joseph Heco (also transliterated Hiko and Hikozo), in 1865, was in a way a creation of American civilization. Heco had been brought by accident to the United States when swept off-course on a fishing expedition. There he saw what newspapers looked like. Even prior to the Japanese language newspapers, there had been English language newspapers designed for foreign residents in Yokohama, Kobe and Nagasaki. The forerunner of these was the *Nagasaki Shipping List and Advertiser,* published by an Englishman, A. W. Hansard, in June 1861. Thirteen English newspapers actually existed during the 1860s.

But, with the Meiji Restoration in 1868, an era for more steadfast newspaper publishing arrived. *Yokohama Mainichi Shimbun,* published in 1871, became the first daily and *Tokyo Nichi-nichi,* which appeared a year later, was the first daily to serve the nation's capital, clearing the way for many other newspapers that flourished in the zealous atmosphere of building a new nation.

In those days, the *shimbun* (newspaper) was classified into *ko-shimbun* (small paper) and *oh-shimbun* (big paper). This classification derived from page sizes: the former were printed on tabloid or even smaller paper while the latter were standard size sheets. But their differences went beyond their formats: while *ko-shimbun* were written and edited by lowbrows — fiction or folk ballad writers — with an emphasis on social interest stories and arts, *oh-shimbun* were produced by serious scholars and politically interested ex-samurais with a primary play on political commentary. The more seriously edited *oh-shimbun* papers dominated the dawn of Meiji journalism (*Ono*, 1922, pp. 108-111). Their language was more difficult to read (with heavy use of Kanji or ideographic characters) than the *ko-shimbun* which was highly conscious of readability, as well as legibility. They used *hirakana*, or phonetic syllabary, and illustrations.

The first major contest in editorials was developed on the subject of how soon Japan should have an elected assembly. *Nisshin Shinji-shi*, one of the earliest dailies published by an Englishman, carried the full text of Taisuke Itagaki's petition for the establishment of a parliamentary system in Japan. Also in the same camp was *Yubin Hochi* (1872-1942), which was staffed by the disciples of Yukichi Fukuzawa, the man who played the most important role in the enlightenment period of Japan. Fukuzawa and others were the liberals who believed, from their observations abroad, that Japan ought to introduce a government by the people. In contrast, the government's views had few outlets, and Genichiro Fukuchi, a moderate editor at the *Tokyo Nichi-nichi*, had to struggle as a minority, representing official opinion that an elected assembly was still premature for Japan.

In the opposition press, there were already some extremely radical newspapers, such as *Hyoron Shimbun*, a journal of political commentary started in 1873, whose editor, Editaro Komatsubara, advocated that some ministers of state should be sentenced to death for their ineptitude in running the country (*Kosaka*, 1955, p. 557). Alarmed by this extremist tendency in the press, the Meiji government began to tighten its grips on the press. Interestingly, the first press law (Newspaper Printing and Publishing Ordinance of 1869) reflected on the enlightened nature of Japan's first modern government: Article five detailed the sort of news that newspapers should report, beginning with natural disasters and fire and including business and foreign incidents. But the subsequent revision in 1873, and the Defamation Act of 1875, were both very restrictive, setting punishments for the first time for those who aimed at the overthrow of government, or attempted to instigate disorder, or slandered imperial families, public officials and the public. Newspapermen, regardless of their political leanings, were shocked at the new provisions. The following five years saw more than 200 journalists imprisoned and not a few journals closed because of the breach of the law (*Yamamoto*, 1944, pp. 20-21).

No doubt such restrictive measures tended to weaken the foundations of political newspapers which already suffered from a lack of integrity, changing their editorial stands overnight after having been sold by one political boss to another, and from not realizing that freedom of the press must stand on an economically sound base. By the middle of the Meiji era, a number of independent newspapers which had gained strength as political newspapers, lost some of their influence; among them were *Jiji Shimpo* (1882-1936), *Nihon Shimbun* (1889-1914), *Kokumin Shimbun* (1890-1942), *Yorozu Choho* (1892-1940) and *Niroku Shimpo* (1900-40) all in Tokyo; and *Asahi Shimbun* (1879-) and *Mainichi Shimbun* (1888-), both started in Osaka. There were outstanding editors at the time, among them Katsunan Kuga of *Nihon*, a nationalist writer, and Soho Tokutomi of *Kokumin*, whose fame and influence as an outstanding philosopher outlived the paper he initiated. These and other editors and their newspapers, perhaps more instinctively than professionally, were faithful to what the practice of journalism should be. When the Russo-Japanese War became imminent, for example, a group of journalists at *Yorozu Choho*, resigned when the paper changed its policy 180 degrees to support the government's preparedness. Publisher-editor Shuroku Kuroiwa was magnanimous enough to let these departing writers have a message printed in the paper in which they declared their stand was uncompromising. Two socialists among those who resigned then started *Heimin Shimbun* (1903-5), which had to meet frequent suppressions but, nevertheless, advocated their anti-war and socialist causes (*Oka*, 1969, pp. 79-83).

In contrast, their counterparts that had been started in Osaka were very much creations of their birthplace — the commercial center of Japan. As such, both *Asahi* and *Mainichi* put less emphasis on party politics and more on general news reporting. The men destined to run *Asahi* (Ryohei Murayama) and *Mainichi* (Kikoichi Motoyama) both had enterprising spirits, unlike their Tokyo counterparts. They have been regarded as the greatest newspapermen in Japan. At a time when other newspapers were managed under loose financial control, Motoyama introduced the budget system to give *Mainichi* a sound financial basis. He was a rare publisher for many decades to come, for he unhesitatingly proclaimed that his paper should, above all, be a commodity to sell. He improved the reportorial staff by establishing, for example, a network of overseas stringers who were to outrun competing newspapers during the Russo-Japanese War (1904-5).

As *Osaka Mainichi* initiated full-scale reorganization plans, Murayama conceived an ambitious expansion program for *Asahi*, buying a Tokyo paper, *Tokyo Mezamashi Shimbun* (1884), which was rechristened *Tokyo Asahi*. The other 16 Tokyo papers were hostile to the new paper owned by a stranger from Osaka and unsuccessfully attempted to boycott *Tokyo Asahi*. This was the first of many humiliations Tokyo publishers were to face because of Osaka-backed newspapers — *Asahi* first and then *Mainichi*.[1]

Between the Sino-Japanese War (1894-95) and its successor, the war with Russia, the Japanese press grew at a rapid pace in accordance with the nation's economic expansion and boom. As the Meiji era came to a close, *Osaka Asahi* in 1911, could boast Japan's largest daily circulation of 350,000, followed by *Osaka Mainichi* with 320,000. In Tokyo, *Hochi* was leading with over 200,000, taking the top position from *Yorozu*.

War alone did not increase circulation for many of these newspapers. A contributing factor was the "third page news," which now had an undeniable position in every newspaper. The term derived from the common practice of concentrating crime and other social interest news on the third pages of dailies. The trend was led by *Yorozu*, followed by *Niroku*, but eventually

---

1   *Mainichi* bought the famed *Tokyo Nichi-nichi Shimbun* in 1911, making it *Osaka Mainichi*'s sister in Tokyo. The incident was regarded as a major defeat for Tokyo pressdom.

became common for Japanese journalism. As circulation increased, advertising volume also rose, to the extent that full-page ads were seen occupying front pages of numerous papers. Classified advertising had been started by *Hochi* in 1898 and became popular among newspapers, as did advertising agencies. The first agency appeared as early as 1874 — Naigai Yotatsu Gaisha — and a great number were established at the turn of the century.

The Taisho era (1912-26) opened with a popular wave for defending constitutionalism — a political movement at first calling for the government's respect for the parliamentary process, and later for universal suffrage. The press, meanwhile, realizing its power as a watchdog of government, increasingly showered criticisms on cabinets, toppling a few in the process (for example, the Katsura cabinet and Yamamoto government). Post-World War I inflation, bad crops in previous years, and undue speculation by a handful of wealthy merchants caused soaring rice prices. On the labor front, the post-war period witnessed a rise of socialism and communism and a number of strikes were staged by laborers and farmers who were seeking better living standards.

But the incident of the decade (possibly of the century) that shocked Tokyo publishers most was an earthquake on 1 September 1923. All newspaper plants except *Tokyo Nichinichi*, *Hochi* and *Miyako* (*Tokyo Shimbun* today) were destroyed by a fire that swept Tokyo and Yokohama. Even the three surviving newspaper plants did not escape the scattering of typecases and disruption of communication lines, the latter giving birth to rumors, the worst of which indicated the fire was set by insurgent Koreans.

Because the disaster destroyed Tokyo newspaperdom, the two Osaka giants — *Asahi* and *Mainichi* — stood on a strategically better footing. At the dawn of 1924, *Osaka Mainichi* celebrated the achievement of a one million circulation mark. In the subsequent years of economic recession, the two giants enforced the survival-of-the-fittest rule by forcing a powerful cartel. When *Jiji, Kokumin, Hochi,* and other Tokyo papers were about to heal their almost fatal wounds, *Asahi* and *Mainichi* pushed them to the wall by their exclusive bilateral agreements on circulation and advertising sales. The two Osaka-born papers not only outpaced Tokyo papers in ruthless business techniques but also in reportorial zeal, which has since characterized Japan's national newspaper field. On the whole, those newspapers based in Tokyo could not catch up with the rising capitalism which changed patterns of living and, in the end, the structure of newspapers. In contrast, therefore, the rise of *Yomiuri Shimbun* from a long obscurity to sudden prominence appeared to be a miracle. Founded in 1874, it was breathing hard with a modest 50,000 circulation when Matsutaro Shoriki came to its rescue in 1924. Shoriki built its circulation — 840,000 copies daily by 1937 — by establishing popular entertainment columns of Japanese chess, sports pages, comic strips in color and science columns, as well as employing many promotional gimmicks. He defiantly removed advertisements from the front page in order to intensify the news first policy. And he did not fail to add sensationalism in a Hearstian manner.

2.5.3 *Toward Totalitarianism and a Controlled Press*

The Japanese press almost since its inception had never been without legal and administrative control especially beginning with the Newspaper Ordinance of 1869. During the 1870s, the government had displayed its restrictive measures against the press during the rising "democratic rights" movement. In the Taisho era of relative freedom, *Asahi* had to meet a crisis that shook its foundations when one of its news stories incurred the wrath of the Terauchi Cabinet in 1918. In this well-known "White Rainbow" incident, Ryohei Murayama was forced to resign as president and a group of top editors left the paper when *Asahi* ran a statement of repentance. This incident is generally interpreted as the first major blow dealt the anti-government stance of the print medium. The era ended with the passage of the Law for the Maintenance of Public Peace of 1925, that was to govern the minds of the Japanese in the following two decades. Prompted as a safeguard to expected progress in popularized democracy (by the institutionalization of universal suffrage in the same year), the law proved savagely effective in suppressing the normal functions of the press.

Japan's experience in parliamentary government was short and immature and it gave rise to frustration among the people, who thought the elected government was ineffective, preoccupied mostly by abortive debates and factional disintegrity. On the diplomatic front, the nation was not entirely united, although very few people cast doubt on the expansionist posture of their country which, most Japanese took for granted, had vested interests in China, the focus of attention during the 1930s. The civilian segment of the administration was still in favor of arriving at solutions through diplomatic channels but the nation felt it was becoming surrounded by hostile world powers.

Isolated, but growing even more chauvinistic, the military began to feel that they should supersede the elected government and mobilize the entire nation towards war goals. A group of fanatic officers and young soldiers waged a *coup d'état* on 15 May 1932, attacking the prime minister's residence and other governmental offices. It was the first major attempt of the military to coerce the civilian government with violence, but for the press, it was the last occasion to voice harsh admonition against the militarists. Critical editorials were found in the *Osaka Asahi* and *Tokyo Asahi* and in the local press, led by *Fukuoka Nichi-nichi Shimbun, Shin Aichi, Kahoku Shimpo* and *Iwate Nippo.*

Most critical of all was *Fukuoka Nichi-nichi*'s editor, Sunao (Rokko) Kikutake, who invited the wrath of the army to such a degree that local army divisions demonstrated air raid maneuvers, using the newspaper's building as the target. Kikutake reacted by warning the army to stay away from politics; he argued fascism was not the way for Japan. Calls and threatening letters came from army officers stationed in Kurume. They informed a *Nichi-nichi* reporter that Kikutake might be shot to death (*Maeda*, 1964, p. 27). By no means was he anti-military, nor was he against Japan's commitment in China. But his frequent editorials clearly demonstrated that he was an earnest devotee of parliamentarianism and civil liberties. Writing on press freedom, he urged that the public be informed of current developments and be free to criticize.

Along with Kikutake, Masatsugu (Yuyu) Kiryu stood out as one of the finest editors of the time. Kiryu was the editor of *Shinano Mainichi Shimbun*, Nagano, when he ridiculed a counter air raid maneuver staged in 1933 by the army in Tokyo. His reasoning was that it would mean defeat for Japan if the country ever countered an attack from the air — the argument that was to be proven precisely 12 years later. Like *Fukuoka Nichi-nichi*, Kiryu's paper had to meet an organized boycott by the local veterans' association, which was very powerful in the days of militarism. In the end he left the paper, which succumbed to the coercion. Kiryu subsequently started a personal journal, *Tazan no Ishi* (meaning an example one may profit by), in which he unleashed violent criticism against the way Japan was outraged by the military. The kind of journalism Kiryu wanted to display could not be sanctioned by censors; in fact, it is remarkable that he endured more than eight years with the journal, until shortly before the outbreak of the Pacific War. He died without knowing his farewell address to his readers, written in the last issue, had been suppressed by censors.

Perhaps Kikutake and Kiryu were the only examples of courageous journalism of the day. The supply was short and it quickly dried up. It was Kikutake who observed a few days after the attempted *coup d'état* of 1932:

Reading editorials of various newspapers in Tokyo and Osaka and writing on the incident, one does not fail to see in many of them an attitude as if they were fearful of and intimidated by someone, thus unable to express freely what they believed (*Kimura*, 1975, p. 195).

He also noted sympathetically that being the center of politics, editors and journalists in Tokyo must have felt physical intimidation more frequently. "If they should let coercion go as far as to prostitute their pens," he warned, however, "the nation would be driven to the precipice with no freedom of choice" (*Kimura*, 1975, p. 195).

Physical intimidation certainly existed. During the 26 February 1936 Incident, soldiers attacked not only the statesmen but the Tokyo office of *Asahi Shimbun*, causing it to miss its evening edition. Insurgent soldiers at the same time raided *Hochi*, coercing it to print articles favorable to the army. A state of emergency was proclaimed, banning all relevant news reports, except those officially announced by emergency headquarters. This dealt the final blow to discordant public opinion and to the anti-military attitude of the press. When Japan waged open war with China in the Marco Polo Bridge Incident of 1937, liberal journalists had already shut their mouths; other papers had climbed on the bandwagon in praise of the war. Yoichi Wada, dean of journalism at Doshisha University, noted: "The battle of journalism was finished 90 per cent by the 15 May 1932 Incident and 99 per cent by the time of the 15 February 1936 Incident" (*Wada,* 1974, p. 127).

At this juncture, one must note the aspect of "collaboration" by the press. To begin with, reporting from China, for most of the press, was nothing more than a big feat of sensational reporting. It was already apparent at the outbreak of the Manchuria Incident of 1931. The big city press took advantage of its resources to report news stories and pictures depicting brave deeds of Japanese soldiers who "dared fighting in self defense" against the Chinese soldiers who "arrogantly challenged our vested interests" in China. In the editorials, too, there was positive support of the Japanese Army, although many editors were wary of the free-wheeling of the military. "By this incident the nation's endurance has gone beyond limit," wrote *Tokyo Nichi-nichi,* "we urge again the Government to take tough measures against the Chinese." In the final analysis, the press had helped create hostility to the Chinese and fanatical support of the Japanese military, thus restricting the alternatives of the government which still had tried to avoid magnifying the Incident (*Toriumi,* 1973, pp. 20-21).

As Japan went into open war with China in 1937, most of the press began to give more positive backing to the military with *Tokyo Nichi-nichi* and *Kokumin* leading the way. "Let us punish the Chinese," *Kokumin Shimbun* demanded, "for there are limits to our endurance." Even *Asahi,* which apparently compromised its non-expansionism stand after the 26 February 1936 Incident, wrote that "the only recourse left now is to give a heavy blow" to the Chinese. On the dawn of the fall of Nanking, a group of 44 newspapers around the nation, including *Asahi, Mainichi* and *Yomiuri,* published a joint declaration on 14 July 1938, attacking Great Britain for aiding Chiang Kai-shek. Their various extramural activities amply demonstrated that they were now in full support of the invasion in China. Many newspapers took to campaigns such as the "home-front patriotic movement" or "home-front resource conservation movements" in which they either appealed for contributions to build aircraft or they organized a public contest for military songs (*Takagi,* 1972, pp. 97-98).

A series of laws and ordinances were created in the ensuing decades of Showa (up to 1945) in order to fortify already stringent legislation. As the laws were put into practice, however, it became obvious they were not just meant to tighten controls on the media, but to brainwash the people to nullify any thought imcompatible with the imperialistic order and to forcibly change the media along the lines of fascism.

Communism had been outlawed in 1923 before the Law of the Maintenance of Public Peace, but an outrageous purge took place during 1931-34, when more than 10,000 writers, teachers and other activists were arrested. Many of them, including Takiji Kobayashi, a communist writer, were tortured to death in prison. Liberalists were the next target: a law professor of Kyoto University was banished because he had written that the civil code was lopsided, and Tatsukichi Minobe was badly attacked by the military, as well as the rightists, for his emperor-as-an-organ theory. But the most atrocious was the so-called "Yokohama Incident" of 1942-44, when 44 scholars, researchers, magazine editors and newspaper reporters were arrested in a frame-up fabricated by the special secret service police. No proof had been established that they had engaged, as alleged, in organized dissemination of communistic thought, but they had to undergo severe torture which resulted in death to some of them.

Government's attempt to actively control thought and turn the mass media into its propaganda mouthpiece was materialized in the creation of Domei News Agency and the Bureau of Information. The basic strategy of the military was that modern warfare could not only be fought by force on the battlefield, but by all-out efforts of economy, thought and propaganda. Born out of the merger of Dentsu (established in 1901) and Rengo (born out of Kokusai and Toho in a 1926 merger) in 1936, Domei was used to carry propaganda announcements to Southeast Asia and China. Under the close supervision of the government's information Committee, Domei received one-half of its operational cost as a subsidy from the government, in order to carry out its function of "Japan's voice through Domei to the world, the world's trends through Domei to Japan." As Japan failed to secure a favorable world opinion, the government felt a need for a great national news agency capable of countering "anti-Japan propaganda." At its zenith, Domei had more than 3,000 staff members and over 50 bureaux throughout the world.

The advent of the second Konoe Cabinet enabled governmental information activities in 1937 to be reorganized into the Bureau of Information which exerted powerful influence through censorship and "guidance of the press." Restrictions of both news contents and newsprint were further strengthened by the National Mobilization Law of 1938, which proved very effective in mobilizing the press towards war goals. Based on the law, the various restrictive ordinances were put into effect, notably the Newspaper Enterprise Ordinance of 1941. This ordinance had two distinct functions: to set up a control organ to collaborate with the pursuit of national policies and to force the merger of daily and non-daily newspapers.

As a result, Nihon Shimbun-kai was established in 1942 (towards the end of the war it was reorganized as Nihon Shimbun Kosha, a distinctly public corporation). The association was given powerful authority to interfere with editorial and business operations of every newspaper, but above all, it was authorized to screen all journalists by forcing them to register. Involuntary mergers had been in progress since 1938 by the prefectural police under the directive of the government's Information Bureau. Initially a number of non-daily newspapers suspended publication; then many inefficient dailies by 1940, so that the number of dailies was reduced from 1,422 to a mere 355 at the end of 1941 (*Takagi,* 1972, pp. 109-110). The governmental policy then called for only one daily per prefecture, and, as a result, the number of dailies was reduced to 54 in 1942, greatly easing the job of censorship officials. After 1938, newsprint was also controlled under the Material Mobilization Plan. At first, a 12-15 per cent reduction was applied to all papers but an additional 10 per cent reduction went into force from July 1940. Thus, the consumption of newsprint fell from the peak 6,955 million pounds in 1936 to 5,296 million pounds in 1941.

Wartime gags became farcical as the tide of war turned against Japan. Expressions such as the "invincible Imperial Army" or the "Anglo-American devils" filled the pages, and "retreat" was always camouflaged by the word "transfer." Whereas Japan's "magnificent victory" had never materialized with the defeat at the Battle of Midway Sea, it was reported in the press as a victory for the Japanese by a margin of six to three in damage when the truth was, the U.S. Navy inflicted a 10:2 damage rate (*Matsuura*, 1975, pp. 50-51). At the end of the war, a United States Strategic Bombing Survey Mission made an extensive survey of Japan's propaganda efforts during the Pacific War. One of its conclusions was that Japan had failed, first by awkwardness and, second by excessive secretiveness beyond its capability, to hide the dark side of the story (*Matsuura*, 1975, p. 67). Ironically, the Hitlerite censorship and propaganda machine approached its completion when the nation suffered total defeat. An anecdote of this period remains that Premier Hideki Tojo was so outraged by a story that appeared in *Mainichi* with the headline, "Bamboo spears not enough, let's have aircraft," that he punitively conscripted the 37-year-old reporter, Takeo Shinjo, in the army.

2.5.4 *Japan's Defeat and the Press*

On 15 August 1945, Japan surrendered to the allied powers with the acceptance of the Potsdam Declaration, which laid down basic conditions for the dissolution of old orders and for a new and democratic Japan. A new Japan, as the allied powers envisaged, would uproot aggressive militarism, dismantle the *zaibatsu* (gigantic industrial combines), separate Shintoism from politics, reinstitute freedom and human rights, and, in the end, obliterate Japan's potential threat to the world.

Officials under Douglas MacArthur, the Supreme Commander of the Allied Powers (SCAP), were given "history's greatest experiment" to restructure the defeated nation; but the job eventually ended up half finished. On the one hand, there was a fervent desire to change this totalitarian nation into a democratic one, and, on the other, there was the strategic consideration to preserve Japan's national potential to be used as a bulwark in a forthcoming world power struggle. The latter gained strength in the course of events immediately after the war, in what Winston Churchill phrased "the cold war." While the civilians in SCAP were extremely idealistic, hoping to bring about what the New

Dealers failed to do in the United States, those in uniform were cautious of the new power represented by the Soviet Union, to the extent that they had second thoughts about raking up all the values that military Japan represented. Such hopes and fears reflected on the Japanese press and its struggle for a democracy.

During the first two months of occupation, MacArthur issued a series of memoranda concerning the press, in which he ordered the abolition of all restrictive legislations regarding the press, film, and communications; declared freedom of speech and press to be established; and called for the disassociation of the press from government.[2] Contrary to policies laid down by the Allies in Germany or Italy, SCAP's press policy in Japan did not entirely disband existing newspapers, magazines, or radio stations, the sole exception being Domei News Agency. (Domei was disbanded in October 1945, and two separate news agencies were created — Kyodo News Service to serve general dailies and Jiji Press to supply economic and financial news to business concerns.)

SCAP supervision of the press was divided into three sections. Reorientation of the press was in the hands of the Civil Information and Education (C.I.&E.); censorship of the press was given to the Civil Censorship Department of the Civil Intelligence Section, and press labor affairs were handled by the Labor Department of the Economic and Scientific Section.

A new power took over the press and a number of people who had served the imperialist government were banned from the media, including Inosuke Furuno, president of Domei News Agency; Matsutaro Shoriki, owner of *Yomiuri Shimbun,* and Taketora Ogata of *Asahi,* who had headed the government's Bureau of Information. Some publishers stepped down either voluntarily or by popular demand from the hastily organized labor unions.

2   "The Memorandum on the Freedom of Speech and Press," 10 September 1945; "The Press Code for Japan," 19 September, 1945; "The Radio Code for Japan," 22 September 1945; "The Memorandum Calling for Disassociation of Press from Government," 24 September 1945; A memorandum on "Further Steps toward the Freedom of Press and Speech," 17 September, 1945; "A Memorandum to Abolish All Restrictive Legislations Regarding the Press, Film, and Communication," 29 September 1945; and "A Memorandum to Abolish Newsprint Allocation," 26 October 1945 (see *The Japanese Press 1949,* pp. 48-53).

Ensuing developments in the post-war confusion helped raise the question of "the right to edit" a newspaper. In terms of what has been taking place in the mass media in Europe or in the United States today, the issue may better be called the question of editorial participation or internal democracy within the press. In the light of the propaganda role that the Japanese press had played during the war, it was only natural for the Allied powers to eliminate collaborators from the media and to institute freedom of speech and press, enabling the Japanese people to be liberated from the constraints of Japanese imperialism and militarism. That the press was the only area where SCAP had direct control showed the gravity occupation policies placed on it in the democratization of Japan.

Indeed, it was a kind of revolution that took place in the newspapers; of 56 dailies published in the immediate post-war period, 44 replaced their heads, including *Asahi, Mainichi* and *Yomiuri.* A vacuum thus created had to be filled and it would not have been too unusual for the unions, as a newly-formed democratic force, to have taken over the situation. The gravest incident took place at *Yomiuri Shimbun.* As at the other newspapers, the union demanded the resignation of President Shoriki and other executives held reponsible for the war and urged "structural democratization" by instituting a self-management system. Shoriki stubbornly refused but he had to resign eventually when he was dragged to the Sugamo Prison as a war criminal in December 1945. Tomin Suzuki, a radical who had been forced to retire in his home town during the war, was appointed managing editor and proudly announced that *Yomiuri* would become the people's journal and the true friend of the public (*Yomiuri,* 12 Dec. 1945). Indeed, in the next five months, the newspaper called for a united popular front to replace the old order of government-bureaucracy-capitalist regime, demanded the voluntary resignation of Emperor Hirohito, and welcomed enthusiastically Sanzo Nosaka, a communist leader who returned to Japan from 16 years' exile (*Masuyama,* 1972, pp. 113-119).

SCAP had already begun to be wary of the extent to which a new Japan was being democratized, and its Press Section, headed by Colonel Daniel C. Imboden, a former California newspaper publisher, openly interferred with the press. *Yomiuri's* new publisher, Tsunego Baba, was summoned and told to oust Suzuki and five other editors. A second round of the strike thus developed; SCAP supported management this time, and its omnipotence made the union's defeat almost self-evident. "The trouble at *Yomiuri* and other papers is caused by the division of editorial decision-making," Imboden told the Japanese publishers, "this is the right that belongs to the owner of the newspaper." In the first six months or so after the war, popular control was possible at a few newspapers. But by the middle of 1946, the leftist groups were dismissed from these newspapers, notably *Hokkaido Shimbun, Nishi Nihon Shimbun,* in addition to *Yomiuri.* Many Japanese, including communists, mistook MacArthur's occupation forces for "the liberation army" of Japan, but it was clear by mid-1946 that SCAP was no longer interested in eradicating the remaining vestiges of imperial Japan. Stability, instead of reform, and reconstruction, instead of democracy, took over SCAP's policy in Japan (*Gayn,* 1974, p. 327).

As the Cold War intensified and as world crisis returned to the Far East in the form of the Korean War, SCAP's policy assumed a further change to the right. MacArthur suspended the Communist Party newspaper, *Akahata,* on grounds it instigated irresponsible, illegal factions, disturbed order and injured public welfare (*Arai,* 1966, pp. 77-79). Subsequently, the mass media were asked by SCAP's Public Office Examination Section to expel all communists from their editorial offices. SCAP did not issue any order but verbally told the publishers that the "red purge" must be carried out as part of the publishers' responsibilities, guaranteeing the papers SCAP's full support (*Nihon Shinbun Kyokai,* 1956, p. 91). According to Nihon Shinbun Kyokai statistics, 700 staff members and editors were dismissed from 47 newspapers, news agencies and NHK (Japan Broadcasting Corporation). Of all industries, the "red purge" in mass media yielded the highest percentage of dismissals: 2.3 per cent of mass media personnel were purged as compared to an average of 0.38 per cent for 18 other industries (*Arai,* 1966, p. 85).

The imposition of censorship by the occupation forces was the other side of the story. Many Japanese newsmen felt Occupation censorship was often as unreasonable as the gag rule imposed by the Japanese bureaucracy and military (*The Japanese Press,* 1958, pp. 9-10). Most censors were clumsy and inexperienced in handling news articles submitted to them before publication, and thereby caused considerable delay. Any news implying rising hostility between the United States and the Soviet Union was blue-pencilled, as were dispatches critical of Occupation policies in Japan. Even articles which appeared in American newspapers, or those distributed by Associated Press or United Press, were suppressed by SCAP censors. References to rape and other misconduct of American soldiers were not allowed, regardless of their validity. One source has written: "The very considerable extent of the censorship may be judged from the fact that in one newspaper alone the censors suppressed 251 articles, made 811 deletions in others, changed 56, and held up 180 without action (*Coughlin,* 1952, p. 57). Prior censorship was terminated on 15 July 1948, and three months later, censorship after publication was lifted.

Also victims were many of the foreign correspondents stationed in Tokyo. General MacArthur was hated by the Tokyo press corps and he also hated these newsmen (*Gunther,* 1951, p. 106). He was extremely sensitive to news dispatches from Tokyo and his "inner circle" of immediate followers did not hesitate to resort to whatever means they considered necessary to retaliate against newsmen. Some foreign correspondents, returning from home or from assignments out of Japan, found their re-entry refused; and still others learned protests were filed with their editors by SCAP about what was reported from Tokyo. On the black list of SCAP were correspondents of *New York Herald Tribune, Chicago Daily News, Christian Science Monitor, Nation, CBS* and *Times* of London. For example, the *Times* of London's Frank Holey dispatched a story of a labor demonstration in which he wrote the Japanese police were violating the constitution in their handling of the demonstrators. One of the generals at SCAP was so outraged that he demanded the British government representative in Tokyo to expel Holey but was flatly told His Majesty's Government had nothing to do with the *Times* (*Matsuura,* 1969, pp. 82, 105-106).

2.5.5 *The Press as an Industry*

The Japanese press was barely breathing when the Pacific War ended. Many of the newspapers were destroyed by American air raids; newsprint and other material supplies were painfully short, and newspapers could publish only two pages daily towards the end of the war. The press freedom gained after the war had, by 1946, encouraged 126 new newspapers to mushroom. For the first time since 1938, when the government-instigated merger diminished the number of newspapers, the press looked diversified enough to reflect every shade of public opinion. Unfortunately, however, few of them could survive the ensuing free competition. To begin with, they were not attractive to advertisers because of their limited circulations and lack of tradition. Moreover, most of them did not have their own printing presses, the lack of which had handicapped the speedy transmission of news. Between 1948 and 1951, most of the new publications were either merged with the older papers or closed.

Economies of scale were again at work very much in a Japanese way. The pattern of publishing returned to concentration and monopolization, with the big national newspapers dominating the entire nation and the local dailies monopolizing their respective areas of circulation. Competition does exist among the "big three" and between the national and local newspapers, but the rewards of the phenomenal growth that has taken place since 1945 have been divided among these papers allowing few newcomers.

It began when newsprint production increased and its control was lifted in 1951. Earlier in November 1950, the resumption of sister evening newspapers was led by *Kobe Shimbun,* followed by *Asahi, Mainichi* and *Yomiuri.* Hitherto, they could publish only one edition daily (during and after the war under the newsprint control), but after 1951, they were able to publish both morning and evening editions, which as a set readers were forced to buy. The battle was not engaged in without time-worn promotion techniques. Sales and delivery of newspapers in Japan have been handled by distribution agencies which, in the main, are exclusively contracted by one or two newspapers. They are the basis on which the Japanese press maintains a large circulation and very efficient home delivery system (91 per cent of daily newspapers are home delivered). Newspaper sales rely very heavily on gimmicks. Not only are newspaper copies distributed free but potential subscribers also receive soaps and detergents, sugar and kitchen utensils, and more recently blankets and pocket-sized computers. At one time, the people ridiculed this practice, calling it "the pot and kettle competition."

A grand-scale circulation war occurred in Osaka in 1952 when *Yomiuri* started a sister paper there. As a latecomer in the national field, the newspaper must have thought it could not penetrate the already established market of Osaka, without resorting to extraordinary means. The *Osaka Yomiuri* sponsored in the fall of 1953 a readership lottery with a fund of ¥100 million unprecedented in its scale and very effective in boosting its circulation to 900,000 copies in a little more than a year. Publishers in the Kansai area were both shocked and outraged by what they considered unfair practices, and *Osaka Yomiuri* was expelled from the membership of Nihon Shinbun Kyokai in 1955. The ostracized paper not only ignored repeated warnings of the publishers association but increased its lottery to ¥200 million and started distributing to readers free copies of the thrice weekly *Children's Newspaper*. At length, the Kansai publishers filed a suit with the Tokyo High Court, which ruled that *Yomiuri*'s conduct was in violation of the anti-monopoly law.

Newspaper publishers painfully realized the folly of excessive competition among themselves, but they were no longer confident of self regulation within the realm of Nihon Shinbun Kyokai. As a result, they resolved to appeal to a legal framework by which unfair sales competition would be forestalled, and the Fair Trade Practice Commission, in response, specified "unfair trade practices in the newspaper industry" (*The Japanese Press 1956*, p. 111). Except morally, it had no binding powers and what followed was that newspapers contrived evasive methods, finally leading to more restrictive provisions under the anti-monopoly law in 1962.

What had happened was that despite the steady growth of total circulation, the market had reached saturation point with gains barely following the population increase. For the *Asahi-Mainichi-Yomiuri* league, moreover, their percentage share in the aggregate circulation had been witnessing a significant recession, from 69.9 per cent in 1942 to 59.2 per cent in 1945 and 44.3 per cent in 1959. The credit for this must go to the healthy growth of the local press despite the gigantic sizes of the national papers.

The aggressive sales campaign engaged by the "big three" was meant to restore the pre-war balance of power in their favor. Just before *Yomiuri* started its Osaka paper, *Asahi, Mainichi* and *Yomiuri* jointly withdrew from Kyodo News Service in September 1952. The "big three" explained that their extended news-gathering networks had lessened their need for Kyodo's services. But the move was interpreted as an attempt on the part of the "big three" to weaken Kyodo, and ultimately the entire local press, whose dependence on Kyodo was extremely essential. The membership dues for the three at Kyodo had accounted for 25 per cent of the news service's total revenue (*Arai*, 1966, p. 58).

In 1959, the "big three" invaded the far North to inaugurate the printing of their papers locally in Sapporo. Previously, the island of Hokkaido had been geographically impossible for the Tokyo giants to dominate in circulation; their dailies got there one day after publication and after travelling 1,000 kilometers. But modern technical breakthroughs have enabled them to transmit news material almost instantaneously and have it appear in print in Sapporo within one hour of leaving Tokyo. On 1 June 1959, *Asahi* became the first newspaper in the world to introduce facsimile transmission, connecting Tokyo and Sapporo by micro-waves, with the printing done by offset. Next to Hokkaido is the north central Honshu island of Hokuriku area, where *Chunichi Shimbun,* a Nagoya-based provincial newspaper with a circulation well over a million, joined the league of facsimile publishers with local publishing in Kanazawa in 1960. *Yomiuri* followed in 1961 by launching its local version in nearby Takaoka, the home town of its owner, Shoriki. Facsimile transmission has proved so effective that it has become widely used, not only by the national newspapers connecting their respective publishing plants, but by other newspapers aiming at faster production and delivery in remote areas.

For the local newspapers belonging to Kyodo (in the wake of facsimile transmission utilized by their gigantic opponents), faster transmission of Kyodo's news services had become of vital importance. In 1960, Kyodo inaugurated the Kanji teletype transmission, a Japanese version of TTS which enabled local newspapers to greatly reduce typesetting needs and to receive Kyodo's dispatches faster and in greater quantity.

In fact, technical innovations are probably among the highlights of the Japanese newspaper industry. In addition to keen competition, the rising wages and material cost and the increasing labor shortage during the 1960s accelerated the Japanese press to adopt better production techniques to yield greater productivity. Unlike Great Britain, and the United States, to a lesser extent, the labor unions in general were not very antagonistic about introducing new techniques, for they did not face dismissals as the result of redundancy or reduced working conditions. This was thanks to a booming economy which required newspapers to increase both the number of pages (from 16 pages in 1960 to 36 pages in 1970 in the case of a national daily) and circulation. Computerized photo typesetters of various models are extensively used, very often jointly with plastic plates to replace the conventional lead stereotype plates. The most outstanding innovations were *Asahi's* NELSON (English abbreviation for the News Editing and Layout System of Newspaper) and *Nihon Keizai Shimbun's* ANNECS (Automated Nikkei Newspaper Editing and Composing System), both of which had been jointly developed with IBM's Federal Division in the United States. The core of these systems is the IBM-2680 photo composing machine, which automatically produces one-third of a page in film with all typesetting done by means of digital dots sent from the central computer. Previously, the use of complex and numerous ideographic characters had been the bottleneck for Japanese newspapers in their efforts to improve production efficiency.

Nihon Keizai Shimbun is more ambitious in the use of computers in that the publishing house has launched specialized information services (Nikkei Economic Electronic Data Services), now sold abroad as well as in Japan, a marketing weekly and several periodicals — all on the basis of vast information resources the main newspaper gathers. Its business diversifications do not stop there; the paper has interests in a television station, a short-wave broadcasting station, a printing house and a film production company; has joint ventures with McGraw-Hill of the United States; and operates three economic research institutes, in addition to having real estate and small advertising agencies.

At the time of EXPO 70, *Asahi*, *Yomiuri* and *Mainichi* all demonstrated home facsimile newspapers, a system where newspapers are transmitted electronically from newspaper offices by landline or radio into the home of subscribers who can read the newspapers in printed form. *Asahi Shimbun* is the most ambitious in this experiment, still continuing a demonstration at a Tokyo hotel, but the cost of the paper that must be used and the receiving device are so prohibitive, and the printed quality is so inferior, that the system is not yet commercially viable for the average household. Newspapers in the early 1970s showed great interest in cable television, both as a possible extension of their service via the home facsimile, and as a two-way communication potential.

Traditionally, the Japanese press had depended for its revenue more on circulation than on advertising. This was particularly true of the large circulation national dailies. In post-war days, however, the society changed, becoming more consumer-oriented, and improved marketing concepts helped increase the importance of advertising. Newspaper advertising grew more than tenfold in less than four years from 1947 and registered substantial growth during the 1950s, averaging an annual rate of 24 per cent. Hand in hand with the booming national economy in the following decade, it continued to increase by 14 per cent per annum, and in 1962, for the first time in history, the press got a larger income from advertising than circulation: 50.4 per cent from advertising, 49.6 per cent from sales of newspaper copies.

However, commercial radio's advent in 1951 (previously semi-governmental, non-profit, NHK-monopolized), and television's debut in 1953 (both NHK and commercial stations), created new problems for the printed medium. Previous to the electronic media, the press had a virtual monopoly of advertising, taking 71.6 per cent of the pie in 1950. In 1955, the press proportion dipped to 55.3 per cent, and in 1960, to 39.3 per cent, while radio-TV advertising soared from 10.7 per cent in 1955 to 32.5 per cent in 1960 and to 36.9 per cent in 1965. The decreasing advertising share must not however, be construed as a decline of the press as an advertising medium; actually, in volume, the 1955 to 1965 decade saw advertising expenditure with the press increase almost four times. Percentage shares of various media came to a standstill, with the press and television taking about equal shares of the pie. Unlike many advanced nations, where the printed media were badly affected by the encroachment of the electronic media, the coexistence of both media in Japan was made possible because of the tremendous growth of the national economy in the 1950s and 1960s. Besides, instead of looking at the new media as enemies, the Japanese press from the beginning, joined broadcasting as a cooperative partner in capital investment, management and news personnel supply. The total circulation for all Japanese dailies has gone up steadily, despite broadcasting's inroads: from 14,180,000 in 1945 to 26,848,000 in 1950, to 37,039,000 in 1960. Even during the 1960s, it had an average annual growth of 3.4 per cent with an aggregate circulation of 53,022,000 in 1970.

TABLE 4.   Advertising Expenditure in Various Japanese Media, 1947-78

				Unit: ¥ billion (percentage share)	
Year	Newspaper	Magazine	Radio	Television	Others
1947	1.1 (75.4%)	0.16 (10.9%)	–	–	0.2 (13.7%)
1950	12.0 (71.6)	0.7 (4.2)			4.05 (24.2)
1955	33.7 (55.3)	3.5 (5.7)	9.8 (16.1)	0.9 (1.5)	13.0 (21.4)
1960	68.4 (39.3)	10.0 (5.7)	17.8 (10.2)	38.0 (22.3)	39.0 (22.5)
1965	123.3 (35.8)	19.2 (5.6)	16.1 (4.7)	111.0 (32.2)	74.4 (21.7)
1970	265.3 (35.1)	41.8 (5.5)	34.5 (4.6)	244.5 (32.3)	169.9 (22.5)
1974	394.5 (33.7)	62.6 (5.4)	55.4 (4.7)	391.7 (33.5)	265.3 (22.7)
1975	409.2 (33.1)	67.0 (5.4)	60.7 (4.9)	420.8 (34.0)	202.4 (16.4)
1976	460.0 (31.2)	80.0 (5.5)	70.0 (4.8)	510.0 (35.0)	(15.8)
1977	506.8 (30.9)	87.7 (5.3)	81.1 (4.9)	584.7 (35.6)	
1978	570.2 (30.9)	95.1 (5.2)	90.8 (4.9)	651.8 (35.4)	

Source: *Nihon Shinbun Nenkan* (Japanese Newspaper Yearbook) 1970, 1975, 1976, 1977, 1978.

TABLE 5. Growth of Japanese Daily Newspaper Circulation, 1942-78

Year	Population ('000)	Circulation ('000)	Growth (%)	Copies per 1,000
1942	73,450	14,687		199
1943	73,980	14,276	2.8	193
1944	73,865	15,518	8.6	210
1945	72,410	14,180	−8.7	196
1946	76,155	17,411	22.7	229
1947	77,551	19,940	14.5	257
1948	80,217	19,337	−3.1	241
1949	82,220	26,620	37.6	324
1950	83,200	27,848	4.6	335
1951	83,200	29,922	7.4	360
1952	84,636	31,998	6.9	378
1953	86,559	34,435	7.6	398
1954	88,622	33,957	−1.4	383
1955	89,837	33,956	0.0	378
1956	90,810	34,927	2.8	385
1957	91,817	35,982	3.0	392
1958	92,970	36,656	1.8	394
1959	94,024	36,076	−1.6	384
1960	95,052	37,039	2.6	390
1961	95,909	39,139	5.6	408
1962	96,688	40,218	2.7	416
1963	97,368	41,730	3.7	429
1964	98,367	43,802	3.2	445
1965	99,483	44,134	0.7	444
1966	100,555	45,399	2.8	451
1967	101,362	47,555	4.7	469
1968	101,988	49,704	4.5	487
1969	102,747	51,498	3.6	501
1970	103,521	53,022	2.9	512
1971	104,540	53,402	0.7	511
1972	106,958	55,845	4.5	522
1973	108,202	58,016	3.8	536
1974	109,574	57,820	−0.4	528
1975	110,949	58,580	1.3	528
1976	112,145	60,782	4.0	—
1977	113,226	62,220	2.8	550
1978	114,276	63,732	2.7	558

Source: *Nihon Shinbun Nenkan* (Japanese Newspaper Yearbook) 1975, p. 440; *The Japanese Press*, 1976, 1977, 1978, 1979.

Note: Circulation counts morning and evening papers (a set newspaper) separately.

2.5.6 Changes in the Japanese Press, by John A. Lent

One must be struck by the hugeness of the Japanese press. To talk about a daily such as *Asahi,* with 9,069 employees scattered in five major Japanese cities, 23 overseas offices and 281 local news bureaux, who have at their disposal the use of 125 company owned cars, 82 motorcycles, 53 radio-equipped jeeps, 13 vans equipped with radiophoto transmission, three jet aircraft, four helicopters, a 300-bed dormitory, plus other amenities, is indeed mind-boggling. The magnitude of *Asahi*'s operations is further emphasized by its publishing of 18 major morning editions, 10 afternoon editions, another 105 designed for localities; by its ownership of an English language daily, three weeklies, three monthlies, 10 yearbooks and interests in 60 other enterprises including radio and television stations, travel agencies, real estate firms and All Nippon Airways (*Malcolm,* 1978, p. F-3).

When we realize *Asahi* is running a close circulation war with *Yomiuri* and has competition from at least three other giants, the vastness of the Japanese newspaper industry becomes even more apparent.

In a country with numerous newspapers with circulations in the millions, very well developed advertising, printing technology far surpassing most of the world, a newsprint industry that makes the nation self sufficient, and legislation that omits all restrictive press laws, it would seem publishing problems would be minuscule. However, that has not been Japan's experience in the 1970s. In fact, striving for vastness may have been a negative feature of the Japanese press.

Since 1973, the internecine competition among newspapers, coupled with an economic environment racked by severe recession, has meant there had to be changes made in the Japanese press. In 1975-76, for example, the print media tried to combat recession by delaying the addition of new technologies of production, by reducing the number of pages in dailies and by laying off personnel, the latter being extremely ticklish in Japan because of the permanent status workers have (see *Yamada,* 1978, p. 47; *Time,* 9 Aug. 1976, p. 56). One giant newspaper, *Sankei Shimbun,* enforced a drastic retrenchment plan in 1976, hoping to cut its 3,600 member work force by half in 1979. *Sankei* planned to relocate the workers in some of their other publications (*Sakurai*, 1976). By 1978, there were sharp decreases in the number of employees at most newspapers, one (*Mainichi*) thinking it might have to reduce its 6,700 payroll to 1,200.

In 1977, *Mainichi*, which for generations was one of the three largest dailies, admitted on its front page to virtual bankruptcy, having been vanquished in the fierce circulation wars. The paper owed US$258 million, for which it paid US$64,000 in interest daily; in 1976 alone, *Mainichi* lost US$29.5 million. Upon hearing of its plight, two banks rallied around *Mainichi* by freezing its interest payments and by creating a new, debt-free company (*Saar*, 1977, p. 4-A). Earlier in 1974, the president and all 16 members of the board of directors of *Mainichi* had resigned because of the serious financial position of the company.

Pinched by inflation and only a moderate advertising growth rate (although 1978 was the first time since 1953 that newspapers generally outstripped television in growth rate of advertising), *Asahi* led the big dailies in March 1978 in upping its subscription rate. *Asahi* raised its rate for the set of morning and evening editions to US$8.33 a month, an 18 per cent increase.

Part of the reason for the financial problems faced by national newspapers can be traced to managements that allowed their dailies to engage in non-profitable (in fact, deficit producing) circulation wars. To entice subscribers, newspapers gave away gifts, some as expensive as electric blankets and watches. However, these subscribers were not usually permanent; many switched their loyalties to the newspaper offering the biggest gift at any given time. In 1977, Nihon Shimbun Kyokai convinced its member newspapers to rationalize sales activities to slow down gift giving practices.

In other instances, once a national daily started an edition in a remote region, all other national newspapers felt compelled to set up a plant and publish there. The result was all would operate in the red. As one *Mainichi* staff member said: "If one paper builds a printing shop in a new area, we cannot help but take the same action. Otherwise, it will affect the morale of our staff" (*Sakurai*, 1975, pp. 66-67).

At other times, national newspapers sold editions at different prices to garner circulation. In the mid-1970s, *Yomiuri* started an edition at Nagoya and sold it at the giveaway price of US$1.70 monthly, when other *Yomiuri* editions sold for US$4.30. *Yomiuri*'s competitors filed a complaint with Nihon Shimbun Kyokai and the High Court. In 1975, Japan's Fair Trade Commission raided the offices of *Yomiuri Shimbun* (Tokyo) and *Chubu Yomiuri Shimbun* on the suspicion that the paper was breaking anti-monopoly laws. *Asahi, Mainichi* and two local newspapers had complained that *Yomiuri* sold its papers at different subscription rates.

In 1977, changes were also made in the editorial policies of most major national newspapers. The changes came on the heels of numbers of complaints that Japanese newspapers did not have individuality — that they all looked alike — and that they were too meek to perform their watchdog role effectively (see 2.1.3). Changes in 1977 brought an increase in the use of interpretative articles, investigative reporting and readers' criticisms, and for the first time, bylines over articles (*The Japanese Press 1978*, p. 14).

Japanese newspapers traditionally lacked individuality because of the spirit of neutrality and impartiality in which basic news was reported. Also, some critics believed that the papers were too bureaucratized to have distinctive voices of their own, that they did not indicate clearly where they stood on issues (*Sakurai*, 1975, pp. 66-67). Some of the blame for sameness in news coverage was attributed to the Kisha clubs (reporters' organizations) which operate all over Japan (see *Burson-Marsteller Report*, Aug. 1975, p. 4). The clubs exercise exclusive rights over many news sources, barring non-establishment journalists such as freelancers, magazine writers and foreign correspondents. They have jealously protected their news sources to the extent that they have lost the "critical edge by which they are supposed to conduct their journalistic mission" (*deRoy*, 1977, p. 23). The daily operations of the press clubs are met by member papers while the basic facilities are provided by government and business sponsors, making the press vulnerable to pressure when the interests of the sponsors are threatened (*Nakamura*, 1975, p. 28).

The credibility of the Japanese press has been lowered in the past generation partly because of the incestuous relationships that have developed with government and other institutions (see *Komatsubara*, 1976). Numerous favors granted the press by the government might be considered bribes to blunt the pen in other societies; in Japan, they are considered special rights built into the system. For example, many sites where newspaper offices stand were once government property bought by newspapers at far below market rates (*Nakamura*, 1975, p. 28).

The government has also facilitated the press by exempting it from various taxes: enterprise tax, exemption from or reduction of taxes on material used in newspaper production; exemption from commodity tax for photographic material (a reduced tax rate is applied in case of import duties on newsprint); discounts on public rates and tariffs; railway transportation for newspapers is discounted by 20 per cent; postal rates for newspapers are reduced to 50 per cent (*IPI Report*, Sept. 1974, p. 5). In 1979, newspapers appealed to be exempt from the general consumer tax the government planned for 1980 (*NSK News Bulletin*, 25 March 1979, p. 3).

2.6 Democratic People's Republic of Korea

John A. Lent

The organization of the press of the Democratic People's Republic of Korea (North Korea) is both along structural and functional lines (see 2.1.5). At the apex are the Central Committee of the Party daily, *Nodong Sinmun,* and the official government daily, *Minju Choson.* In addition, there are eight other dailies published in Pyongyang, as well as four-page Party dailies in each province. Every factory or enterprise has its own newspaper aimed at increasing production and maintaining worker support for the ideology and socialist revolution. Kim Il Sung University and all colleges publish newspapers designed for the ideological education of students (*Vreeland and Shinn,* 1976, p. 151). Thus, all newspapers are under the control of the Party, government ministries or official organizations such as the army or Ministry of General Education.

Nodong Sinmun, with a circulation of about one million, publishes six pages daily with the primary goals of idolizing Kim Il Sung, developing class consciousness and revolutionary enthusiasm and propagating *chuch'e sasang* (independence). The paper's editor, always a high ranking Party member, heads the influential Korean Journalists' Union. *Nodong Sinmun,* started on 17 July 1945, serves as a guide for the provincial press. The second most influential daily is *Minju Choson* which has a limited circulation of about 200,000. Other important papers are *Nodong Ch'ongyon,* organ of the Socialist Working Youth League; *Nodongja Sinmun,* voice of the General Federation of Trade Unions and *Kyowon Sinmun,* a daily of the Ministry of General Education used to issue Party directives to teachers. The other Pyongyang dailies are: *Jokook Tongil,* Committee for

Peaceful Reunification of Korea; *Joson Inyingun,* Korean People's Army; *Nongup Keunroja,* Central Committee of the Korean Agricultural Working People's Union; *Pyongyang Shinmoon,* Pyongyang Municipal Administration Committee; *Saenal,* League of Socialist Working Youth of Korea, and *Pyongyang Times,* published in English and French (*Asian Press and Media Directory 1976/1977,* p. 141).

All communications in North Korea, meant for political education and indoctrination, are controlled by the Party's Propaganda and Agitation Department. Great reliance is placed on meetings, groups, the educational system and traditional communications systems to get the message to the people. The State Administration Council exercises overall management over the media through its agencies: General Publications Bureau, Central Broadcasting Committee and Korean Central News Agency. As indicated, one of its subordinate agencies publishes the government daily, *Minju Choson* (*Vreeland and Shinn, 1976,* p. 149).

Korean Central News Agency (KCNA) provides the majority of news items used by the newspapers. It issues a daily bulletin in English and Korean and exchanges services with TASS, Hsin Hua and agencies of other communist countries.

Copies of articles selected from KCNA or written by daily newspaper reporters are usually submitted to the newspapers a day in advance for review by members of the editorial board and the appropriate committees of the Party. Editors follow instructions of the Party concerning placement of articles, choice of type and length of time for feature news stories. *Vreeland and Shinn* (*1976,* p. 151) wrote:

> Journalists are disciplined in the Party's ideology and policies and are trained to write in a style that always emphasizes the benefits of Party practice and Kim's leadership. Although written under narrow limits of freedom, each article is screened: first internally by publication officers; and finally by the Propaganda and Agitation Department of the Party.

The ideological education and journalistic training are provided by the Korean Journalists' Union (founded 10 February 1946), which all journalists are required to join. The Union, divided into propaganda and organization, international reporting and editorial and training, operates an institute that provides both two-year and six-month courses of study. Continuing education of its 6,000 members is provided by weekly and monthly courses. KJU also strives to improve the work of journalists by sponsoring reportorial contests and other events (*Treffkorn,* 1978, pp. 4-5). Because of the uniformity of press goals and journalists' training, most newspapers look alike in style and content. The first two pages are usually devoted to speeches, policies and directives of Party leaders, while page three is generally provincial and departmental news and page four, international. A content analysis of *Nodong Sinmun* in the mid-1970s showed the content primarily featured the domestic economy (agricultural methods, land reclamation and economic management). Over 44 per cent of *Nodong Sinmun*'s stories were on economic topics. Twenty-two per cent dealt with history and ideology — political socialization and all forms of ideological work and its role in the life of North Korea. Of the space given to international news, over 40 per cent represented the activities of South Korea and the United States, considered the chief enemies of North Korea (*Katz,* 1977).

The North Korean press, as all media, promotes the personality cult of Kim Il Sung, to the extent that one writer believed it was attempting to outdo Stalin, Mao and Lenin in this regard. The word "communism" has been replaced by "Kimilsungism," a doctrine which the official press claims liberated hundreds of thousands of people in the world. Press articles emphasize that Kim is the greatest revolutionary thinker of all time and that everything is possible under the guidance of his "inspiring thoughts" (*Hazelhurst,* 1976, p. 8). *Rodong Sinmun* occasionally devotes an entire page of its few pages to singing Kim's praises and uses statements that he was "sent by Heaven, and foreseeing everything, never makes a mistake in anything." An editorial in *Far Eastern Economic Review,* labelling this type of writing "crapulous drivel," said the press is daily "transfiguring Kim into a godhead" (*Far Eastern Economic Review,* 4 July 1975, p. 7). In the 1970s, the government spent huge sums of precious foreign exchange reserves to place whole page advertisements (some costing US$15,000 each) to idolize Kim in West European and United States dailies such as the *Daily Express* and *Times* of London and *New York Times.* Later, these advertisements were reprinted in the North Korean press to make North Koreans think the Western press also had high regard for their leader (*Hazelhurst*, 1976, p. 8). Similarly, the North Korean press reserves phrases such as "puppet clique" and "ferocious human scum" for discussions of South Korea and other nations considered enemies. One writer concluded that, "While its credibility abroad is generally poor, the North Korean press may be accepted at face value in North Korea's highly controlled society" (*Saar*, 1976).

2.7 Republic of Korea

Sunwoo Nam

2.7.1 History

Even with a long tradition of movable type printing (in fact preceding Gutenberg's invention by several decades) Korea did not see its first regular newspaper until 1883. That was *Hansung Sunpo,* the official gazette of the Yi dynasty court, published once every ten days. The first civilian newspaper was *Tokrip Shinmun* (*The Independent*—1898) which was rather revolutionary in a number of ways. It was the first newspaper published in the Korean alphabet, understood by commoners, rather than in cumbersome Chinese characters, the written language of the elite. It also advocated democratic principles such as civil rights. More than anything else, the paper was for the continued independence of the country, free from foreign encroachments (*Choe,* 1960; see *Oh and Won,* 1976).

As Japanese aggressive intentions towards Korea became more apparent, a few other newspapers were started, again to fight for the continued sovereignty of Korea. However, the Korean dynasty succumbed to the forced annexation by the Japanese in 1910. The Japanese Government closed down Korean language newspapers, except for one used as its mouthpiece, and, instead, started a number of Japanese papers (see *Dong-A Ilbo,* 1964, *Nam,* 1965).

Sunwoo Nam is associate professor at Norfolk State College and former assistant professor at the University of Hawaii. He was a journalist with *Dong-A Daily News* for five years. A Fulbright and East Asian Studies Scholar, Dr. Nam received his Ph.D. from the University of Wisconsin.

The March 1st Independence Movement of 1919 was the first organized uprising on a nationwide scale against Japanese rule. Japanese military police opened fire on the demonstrators, killing about 7,500, and later arresting 47,000 (*Dong-A Ilbo,* 1964, p. 12). After this show of nationalistic spirit, Japan switched its colonial policy from a harsh, militaristic rule to a more conciliatory one. As one of the conciliatory gestures, the authorities permitted Koreans to publish three daily newspapers, *Dong-A Ilbo* (*Oriental Daily News*), *Chosun Ilbo* (*Korea Daily News*) and *Sisa Shinmun* (*Current Newspaper*). The Japanese hoped that the first would stand for Korean nationalism within limits, the second would be neutral, and the third would represent a pro-Japanese view. However, shortly after their inception, all three became more or less nationalistic. The three guiding principles or the policy statement of the *Dong-A Ilbo* would illustrate the nationalistic tinge and self-assumed leadership role: (1) We take it upon ourselves to be a means of self-expression for the Korean people; (2) We advocate democracy; (3) We stand for cultural enlightenment (*Dong-A Ilbo,* 1964, p. 12).

Naturally, the Korean language newspapers manifesting anti-Japanese tendencies were dealt with harshly. Censorship, post-publication punishments ranging from confiscations of copies to indefinite suspensions for the newspapers, and ranging from arrest or intimidation, to incarceration for the staff; all these methods of control were employed. The example of the *Dong-A,* the foremost nationalistic paper, will suffice. From its beginning in 1920 until it was closed temporarily in 1940, along with the *Chosun Ilbo, Dong-A Ilbo* suffered the following treatment:

Indefinite suspension ranging
    from two to nine months: 4 times
    Prohibition of sales   63 times
    Confiscation of copies   489 times
    Item deletion: 2,423 times
        editorial   269 times
        political   281 times
        city desk   150 times
        photos   73 times (*Dong-a Ilbo,* 1964, p. 44).

After World War II, Korea was divided into two parts, with the northern half under Russian occupation and the southern half under American military rule. The American authorities granted near-full freedom of expression of the press at first, resulting in a mushrooming of newspapers both right and left. However, when the excesses of that freedom became manifest in terms of political terror and strikes fanned by the extremist newspapers, the U.S. military government enacted a registration act for periodicals which in effect functioned as a licensing act.

The Republic of Korea was established in 1948 in the southern half of the Korean peninsula, and its constitution, like many constitutions of the world, guaranteed freedom of expression and of the press. This freedom was hollow, because, to begin with, the old dynasty decree on licensing of newspapers was retained by the autocratic government of President Syngman Rhee. Also, a set of specific instructions on taboo items was forwarded to all newspaper offices by the Office of Public Information (*Choe,* 1960, p. 380).

During the three years of the Korean War, most newspapers lost the meager facilities they had and all newspapers were subject to customary wartime censorship. The end of the Korean War did not bring freedom of the press because Syngman Rhee and his party wished to remain in power indefinitely. They amended the constitution to enable the continued presidency of Rhee, and the opposition parties and newspapers that opposed such dictatorial schemes were dealt with promptly. At least two papers were suspended for typographical errors reflecting on Rhee, and a major opposition paper, *Kyunghyang Shinmun,* was closed down in 1959.

The April uprising of students, in protest against the rigged presidential elections, snowballed into a popular revolution, overthrowing Rhee's Liberal Party government. Premier Myun John Chang's Democratic Party government was installed through the freest elections ever held in Korea. Under the short-lived Chang cabinet, the Korean press enjoyed the greatest degree of freedom. First, the license system was replaced by a registration system. Anyone with money, a nominal sum at that, could start a paper. Thus, the number of news agencies rose from 14 to 276, and daily newspapers from 41 to 131 (*Kim,* 1964, p. 111), most of the newcomers not publishing a single issue. They simply wanted to extort money from officials and citizens. Alarmed, the Korean Newspaper Editors Association was about to establish an ethics commission when the military *coup d'état* toppled Chang's government on 16 May 1961. The military government sharply limited freedom of the press, closing down 76 dailies, among other publications. During its first year, the military regime arrested more than 960 reporters; 87 per cent were charged with being fake reporters or extortionists; the rest were charged with errors in reporting or editing (*Kim,* 1964, p. 112). However severe these measures were, responsible newspapers welcomed some of them as steps in ridding the profession of its bad name.

In 1962, the military government, alleviating its strict control of the press, formulated "Standards for Implementation of Press Policy." This decree limited dailies to single editions rather than the two normally published. Newspapers without specified minimum printing equipment were required to close "voluntarily" or to merge with other papers within a short period of grace. The government offered loans for equipment expansion and management costs to publications meeting its requirements, and also reduced tariffs on imported pulp and newsprint.

In December 1963, a civilian government of the Democratic Republican Party, the party of President Chung Hee Park, who had been the chief of the military junta, was installed through popular election. Since then, the shifts in the fortunes of the press have been directly related to the whims of the ruling elite and the changing currents of the political situation. There have been brief periods of respite for the press, when President Park and his party professed to lead the country along the pathway of democracy while mobilizing it for economic development. However, their avowal of democracy has been proved to be nothing more than a thin veil behind which they constantly maneuvered to solidify their hold on power to stay in office.

Thus, since the military takeover in 1961, the Korean press has fared much worse than under the authoritarian regime of President Syngman Rhee, with brief periods of respite when Park and his party had to go through the motions of elections, at which time, the press was allowed to reflect what the opposition party members were saying, within limits.

2.7.2 *Characteristics of the Press as an Institution*

The Korean press, by tradition and inclination, may be characterized as a press with a political mission — a mission of leading the nation to independence during the Japanese colonial period, and of helping democracy to gain a foothold after the liberation. The newspapers assumed the leadership role; rather than reflecting "public opinion," the press served as the catalyst of public opinion. The self-assumed opinion-making role can be detected by the fact that there are unusually large editorial writing sections at all major newspapers — numbering about 10 staff members on most Seoul dailies. Newspapers in Seoul are also saddled with large editorial/reporting sections, usually numbering more than 100, because of editors' penchants for exclusiveness in the style and kind of stories. Journalists in Korea are very well educated. In fact, for a time, newspapers attracted the top college graduates, mostly from Seoul National University, in tough competitions where there would be 100 applicants for every cub reporter position.

2.7.3 *Ownership*

In general, newspapers are owned privately. However, one Korean language daily and one English daily are regarded as being outrightly owned or controlled by government, and another daily in Seoul is suspected of having close ties with the Korean Central Intelligence Agency (KCIA). In addition, a major morning paper is owned by a key member of the government; rather, the publisher of the paper was recruited for a major government post — first as the vice premier of the government — and later as the vice chairman of the negotiating team for North-South Korea talks on reunification. Under such circumstances, the paper's leaning is not hard to detect, even though there may be occasions when reporters revolt against the publisher's line. Also, a mass communication empire, consisting of a daily, monthly, women's weekly, and radio-TV network, is owned by a major figure in Korean industry. Another major daily, the *Chosun Ilbo,* recently built new offices, and a hotel, with Japanese money. Therefore, the publisher of the paper cannot be expected to be independent of the government which approved the loan in the first place. In a sense, with the possible exception of *Dong-A Ilbo,* all papers are more or less beholden to the government. As one editor put it,[1]

> The government doesn't have to bring pressure to bear upon an editorial stance; rather the publisher himself, whose position is compromised by the favors he received from the government, be it a bank loan or an honorific title with a governmental commission, anticipates what the government wants to see in editorials or news columns on crucial issues and transmits his predilections through the channels in the editorial hierarchy.

The government is not even satisfied with this low profile; what it wants is a completely subservient press doing its bidding without question. The government recognizes the tremendous power of publicity, either in favor of or against government policies and programs, and it wants to ensure that the critical role of the press is completely subjugated by the constructive role. This tends to emphasize the positive needs of society and to aid and encourage the developmental goals of government. Perhaps, towards that end, government encouraged mergers of provincial newspapers so that there would be one newspaper in each province with the exceptions of big cities such as Seoul, Pusan or Daegu. Even in Seoul, rumors circulated for some time that the government planned to encourage mergers of some papers, perhaps such threats serving as a sword of Damocles to publishers. In 1973, the government had a good chance to kill a newspaper when its publisher, who also doubled as president of a private university, was indicted for bribing a general out of favor with President Park at the time, and for appropriating some of the charitable funds collected ostensibly for flood victims. The wife of the publisher agreed to close the paper "voluntarily." The paper was not missed. It was not of good quality with a very limited circulation. In fact, one major complaint is that all newspapers look alike because of the severe control of the press by the KCIA and the timidity of publishers and journalists alike.

1   Personal interview, editor-in-chief, major daily, Seoul, January 1971. Source granted anonymity.

2.7.4 Economics of the Press

As far as facilities go, the Korean press as a whole is in good shape, partly because of the minimum requirements set by government, and partly because of the competitiveness of newspapers. Practically all the daily papers own their rotary presses, in addition to other equipment. Some Seoul papers boast a fleet of two to three light airplanes or helicopters and two-way, radio-equipped cars. Typesetting is still by hand because of the problem of Chinese characters, over 1,000 of which are still used by newspapers. All big city dailies receive teletype transmission of wire services, including Reuters and AFP.

One of the most closely guarded secrets in a business whose main concern is openness of all other segments of society, is its own economics. Accurate figures of circulation, advertising and subsidy, if any, are hard to come by. The *Dong-A Ilbo* is supposed to be the leader in terms of circulation with more than 500,000 copies, followed by *Chung-ang Ilbo* with about 400,000. The two morning dailies in Seoul, *Chosun Ilbo* and *Hankuk Ilbo,* are reported to have circulations of between 200,000 and 300,000.

There is no doubt that advertising is the biggest source of a newspaper's income. When the *Dong-A Ilbo* was the major opposition paper under the Syngman Rhee regime, advertisers considered it the best medium for their wares simply because of its enormous popularity. Not anymore. Because of the uniformity of content, and availability of other media, advertisers are more discriminating these days. Advertising agencies are a relatively unknown phenomenon in Korea because most manufacturers have their own advertising bureaux which deal directly with their counterparts in newspapers. Some newspapers are known to resort to a form of extortion, billing manufacturers for advertisements they print without the advertisers' consent. Because of competition among papers for advertising money, advertisers' influence should be considerable, but the strong tradition of editorial independence among newspapers prevents much advertising meddling. At worst, advertisers pressure news staff to withhold accident stories which may unfavorably reflect on the company, or to substitute the company's name with an English initial if the story is too big to ignore. The biggest advertisers are pharmaceutical firms which promote everything from simple cold remedies and antibiotics to hormone tablets for sexual potency. Newspapers must share some of the blame for the abuse of these drugs. The proportion is about 40 per cent advertising to 60 per cent news in South Korea.

2.7.5 Capacity to Consume

Newspapers had to raise their monthly subscription rates from US$0.87 to US$1.12 in January 1974. In a country where the reported per capita income is about US$350 a year, newspapers can only be afforded by the average wage earner dwelling in a big city.

Readers complain about the lack of individuality of newspaper content, claiming they all look the same if you hide the mastheads. They blame the control of papers by the KCIA and the "gutlessness" of the papers for the blandness in news stories and editorials.

Some newspapers resort to the circulation tactic of delivering unsolicited copies for a couple of months and then asking householders to sign up. The criss-crossing of the nation with superhighways, the relative smallness of the land area and a literacy rate of about 90 per cent could be catalysts for increased circulation; however, a drawback is that most of the papers do not mean very much to the general public.

In view of the rising cost of newspaper publishing, because of many increases in the necessary materials (including an insufficient amount of newsprint production in South Korea which necessitates import with tariffs, giving leverage to the government), newspapers should streamline their operations and, perhaps, share printing facilities. However, because many newspapers, at least in Seoul, have a number of side businesses, such as publishing children's dailies and sensational weeklies, and because of the intense jealousy concerning use of equipment, seemingly rational solutions do not work.

2.7.6 Content of Average Newspapers

Because of the newsprint shortage and a stipulation of the Korean Newspaper Publishers' Association which, in effect, functions as a cartel, a daily is limited to eight pages a day for six days a week. Unlike their American counterparts, Korean papers have a rigid format. A typical daily would have political and internationally significant news on the front page, which may also have a short one column commentary. The second page, usually reserved for economic news, also carries editorials, while page three has various analyses and background stories on national and international developments and foreign news. Serial articles and essays by intellectuals may appear on the fourth page, and the fifth page is a mixture of women's features and cultural/academic articles. Since all the dailies published in Seoul are national newspapers, either in reality or in aspiration, one page is devoted to regional news, depending on the province for which the particular edition is designed. Second in importance to the front page is page seven, which carries soft news, meaning city desk coverage. Page eight is generally sports news mixed with coverage of the entertainment scene. No two papers are exactly alike, but the rigid departmentalization and use of serial novels (usually two per issue, one a historical yarn; one a contemporary love-affair story) are always the norm.

The format of Korean papers may result from a conscious or an unconscious imitation of the Japanese press. Another parallel exists in terms of the range and frequency of cultural/entertainment activities sponsored by newspapers. One paper in Seoul sponsors the Miss Korea beauty pageant, others realize sizable profits from backing art exhibitions, sports events, concerts and "go" tournaments. Unlike American papers, Asian papers tend to use staff-generated columns and articles, with the exception of foreign news. It is a rare Seoul daily which does not maintain two full-time correspondents — one each in Tokyo and Washington, D.C. — in addition to a number of stringers elsewhere.

Also, most Seoul dailies publish weekly magazines which contain many lurid articles, some of which constitute invasion of privacy. Most of them are little more than girlie magazines. One reporter on a major newspaper reported of the pressure from editors on serial novelists to make their stories more intimate and salacious; he characterized such pressure as collaboration with the efforts of the powers-that-be to stupefy or drug the public (*Kim, 1973,* p. 141). Even the *Dong-A,* which resisted the temptation to enter the weekly field, sometimes includes titillating materials, or scenes totally irrelevant to the story telling, in its novel columns.

2.7.7 The Press and Government

Government control is the single most important factor affecting the press in Korea. What follows is a brief account of political developments with their implications for the press in the 1960s and 1970s, without an understanding of which it is impossible to comprehend the plight of the Korean press. President Park and his associates may have been motivated by a sense of patriotism, wanting to see a stable and economically viable nation, when they staged their *coup d'état* in 1961. Whatever their motivations, promises have been broken repeatedly with regard to restoring democracy. They range from Park's 1963 statement that, "I am an unfortunate soldier — I am not going to run for presidency at the end of the military rule," to his repeated assurances that he would not serve more than two terms, to the eventual coup against his own constitution by making himself eligible for life presidency in the so-called October Revitalizing Reforms of 1972. Undoubtedly, the trend has been inexorably towards one-man rule.

By definition, the military which deals with matters of secrecy, tends to be antagonistic towards the press which pushes for openness. Therefore, during the military rule of May 1961 to December 1963, it was hardly surprising that the press was controlled; one of the control measures, "the purification" of the press by getting rid of fake publishers and reporters, was, in fact welcomed by the established newspapers. In retrospect, the return of civilian government under, by then retired General Park, should have been no cause for rejoicing by the press.

The constitution which declared "all citizens shall enjoy freedom of speech and press, and freedom of assembly and association" (Chapter II, Article 18, Paragraph I) also said "the standard for publication facilities of a newspaper or press may be prescribed by law" (Chapter II, Article 18, Paragraph 3). There is a law concerning the registration of newspapers and news agencies which incorporates the minimum standards of facilities. This law has been invoked a few times against smaller papers, making other publishers of small provincial papers (which also may not measure up to the standards) extremely pliable to the slightest suggestions coming from the authorities.

As for the well established Seoul newspapers, the government used more subtle methods. The ruling party succeeded in tapping the retired president of *Dong-A Ilbo,* Doo-sun Choi, for the premiership during the first six months of civilian rule; his cabinet was nicknamed "the bullet-proof cabinet," warding off criticism, if not immunizing the government from critical journalists. In addition, the ruling elite recruited a number of bright middle-echelon journalists, thereby learning about the inner workings or "secrets" of the press which could be used later to force collaboration of newspapers and individuals. The practice of "handouts" of money to reporters by various ministries and politicians continued for a time, even to the point of making a number of reporters wealthy. Some editors also were not immune from this temptation, especially because of the relatively low salaries they earned.

Meanwhile, President Park and his government pushed ahead the vigorous economic development of South Korea through re-opening of diplomatic relations with Japan, which some opposition leaders called the "sell-out" treaty. In the process, the government acted much like a bulldozer obliterating all the obstacles in its path. Those obstacles were the intelligentsia; (broadly defined, including university students and journalists) as well as the splinter opposition parties; and the two treads of the bulldozer were the army and the Korean Central Intelligence Agency. Once the goal of "the modernization of the fatherland" was defined and apotheosized under the leadership of President Park, all the means to achieve the end became justified. The authorities reiterated that the demand for quick industrialization and development was urgent, and that the country faced a powerfully armed enemy in North Korea. In this context, the government has said it cannot tolerate critics and gadflies who are regarded as impediments to the economic development necessary to "win victory over Communism." The line proceeded that if newspapers are left alone, they most certainly dwell on the failures of government's efforts to develop. The criticism of the developmental movement would engender cynicism and distrust of the ruling elite, finally wrecking the goals of government. Therefore, contents of newspapers should be controlled.

In short, when the development is apotheosized, there could not be much room for freedom of press, which is the antithesis to planned and quick-paced developmental efforts. Actually, developmental politics seem to be an antithesis of liberal democracy, with its sometimes long-winded deliberations in the decision-making process, and its independent press and judicial review.

There was frequent invocation of the martial law rule and rewriting of the constitution to ensure the continuation of the Park regime in the 1960s, culminating in the "October Revitalizing Reforms" of 1972. These "reforms" eliminated all checks on presidential authority, including civil rights safeguards such as *habeas corpus* and such limited powers as the legislature and courts once enjoyed. Campaigns for the referendum on the Revitalization Constitution were conducted under rules which prohibited any debate about the constitution in the press, in public or even, as the rules were applied, in private letters. The next step was the re-election of President Park for a six-year term by a new body (itself newly elected) called National Council for Unification. The vote was 2,357 for and two invalid. Incidentally, the Revitalization Constitution stipulates that, "All the people will not be limited in their freedom of the press, publication, assembly and association without in accordance with the law."

Credit for creating conditions leading up to the "Revitalizing Reforms" goes to the Korean Central Intelligence Agency, whose Korean name, Chungang Cheungbobu sends a chill through Koreans at every level and in every institution of society. Its functions are defined by law as intelligence and the maintenance of public safety, but, in practice, its range is unlimited. Dae-jung Kim, opposition party presidential candidate in 1971, was quoted by the *Manchester Guardian* as saying:

This country is an absolute national dictatorship, completely controlled by the Central Intelligence Agency. In other countries news reporters write the news, but in this country the CIA does the writing . . . its agents have interferred in student-teacher relationships in schools, creating a credibility gap, and intimidated professors and intellectuals so that they no longer dare to write freely . . . The CIA has even infiltrated into the opposition party, causing strife and division (Honolulu Sunday *Star-Bulletin* & *Advertiser,* 28 Jan. 1973).

Even with the opening of the dialogue with the North Korean leadership that started in 1972, with Lee Hu-rak, the then KCIA director, as the prime mover, the anti-Communist Law remained unchanged, which provides, among other things, that "Persons praising, encouraging or cooperating with anti-state organizations or their constituent members, or engaging in acts otherwise favoring anti-state organizations, shall be punished by penal servitude for not more than seven years." In the past, a number of reporters and editors were charged with violation of this clause and brought to trial, some being sentenced to imprisonment with others being exonerated. But the cases always ended up in the lower courts, or even worse, at the investigative stage where there is ample room for extra-legal intimidation and harassment. However, what makes journalists' lives miserable, much more than the existence of such laws, is the persistent pattern of extra-legal or informal control exercised by the KCIA.

Almost every day, KCIA agents stop by their assigned newspaper offices to "chat" with editors and reporters, and it is suspected that KCIA has paid informants within the newsrooms. One large newspaper knows the identity of the informer on its staff, but tolerates him because he is useful in securing the release of reporters who are detained by the KCIA for interrogation.

The following is a brief sketch of the ordeals suffered by *Dong-A Ilbo* journalists in recent years, partly because the paper epitomizes the Korean press, and the KCIA seems to resort to a tactic of selective intimidation. As Keyes Beech, in his dispatch from Seoul, said: "When the CIA cracked down on *Dong-A Ilbo*, Seoul's leading, most independent daily, other newspapers automatically fell in line" (The *Honolulu Star-Bulletin*, 10 April 1972).

When *Dong-A Ilbo*, even under the tight surveillance of the KCIA, dared to print two editorials mildly critical of the declaration of the state of national emergency in 1971, the publisher of the paper, Sang-man Kim, was detained and interrogated by agents for four hours. What transpired in that session is not known, but shortly thereafter, the newspaper dismissed Dong-Wook Lee, the editor-in-chief and Kwan-woo Cheon, a managing director who had many encounters with the KCIA when he was editor-in-chief. How "offensive" were the editorials?

Sample passages read like fundamentals of democracy normally found in textbooks: e.g., "However, under the pretext of liberal democracy, we have seen that a number of developing countries resorted to a contradictory policy of suppressing the very advantages of liberal democracy. If all of us are careful not to fall into that kind of contradiction in the process of confrontation with the Communist dictatorship in North Korea, it will be difficult for the declaration of the national emergency to bear the fine fruits" (*Dong-A Ilbo,* 7 Dec. 1971) and " . . . Democratic social system avoids monolithic conformism, and pursues diversity . . . If under the context of monolithic conformism, the press is subject to a certain control, the society cannot be expected to actively purify itself; instead, the corruption will be further ripened . . ." (8 Dec. 1971).

An AP dispatch from Seoul in January 1972 reports of one hapless *Dong-A* editorial writer who was grilled by CIA agents for 17 straight hours for writing the following comments, in part: "Excessive control of the press in a modern society will lead to the undesirable consequence of unrest among citizens . . . . Those in power tend to control or regulate public opinion . . . . They tend to find social stability in uniform public opinion. The control of conflicting interests causes pain and frustration . . . . Needless to say, much frustration is quite incompatible with the cause of societal security. Public opinion . . . cannot exist where there are no press activities" (8 Jan. 1972). Even the fact of his detention could not get into his newspaper, which is hardly surprising because when the president of the paper was detained, the paper dared to print a short item in an edition for a province, only to be forced to delete it in the main edition. The impact of such suppression is calculable: all other papers took cues and behaved. Critical editorials and articles completely disappeared, resulting in a bland uniformity of contents in all newspapers.

Dong-A Ilbo did not endorse the reforms in its initial editorial following President Park's declaration of martial law on 17 October 1972. Later on, it seems the paper was forced to support the Revitalizing Reforms, as indeed all publications in the country were required to carry hortatory slogans supporting what some Western reporters described as Park's "coup by constitution." Because editorial writers could not oppose the revitalization openly, they tried to register their disapproval by not mentioning it much. One KCIA agent was reported to have inserted the word "Revitalization" many times when he read a proof of a commentary. Elizabeth Pond of the *Christian Science Monitor* wrote:

Those who demur receive the penalty. Three *Dong-A Ilbo* editors were held overnight by the Korean CIA and beaten, according to one report. In another report they were simply intimidated by being held, but were not beaten. (In the past, this was the more usual treatment of anyone of editorial rank; rough handling was reserved for lower ranks of reporters.) (11 Nov. 1972)

According to Amnesty International, the KCIA does resort to brutal tortures, both mental and physical, for extracting confessions (especially on those suspected of being Communist spies), but the extent of rough handling of journalists is not known because they are warned not to discuss their treatment with others.

How does the press respond to such pressure? The South Korean press developed esoteric ways to outwit its adversary. Because it cannot write about the dictatorship of Park, it runs instead a series of articles on the excesses of the autocratic Syngman Rhee regime, which, if read between the lines, reveals that those were the good old days in comparison with the more systematic and thorough control of civil liberties today. Because the press is not allowed to write about student demonstrations in Korea, instead it plays up student demonstrations abroad, for example, how Thai students were successful in bringing down that strong military regime. Indignant about the excesses of the KCIA which cannot be mentioned, the press carries a series of articles about the brutalities of the Russian secret police apparatus under Beria. Still, South Korean journalists cannot completely escape the feelings of frustration and impotence simply by these oblique means of expressing themselves. Thus, when a focal point or catalyst is provided, their frustration explodes.

The beginning of the catalyst was provided when the self-exiled, opposition presidential candidate in the 1971 elections, Dae-jung Kim, was kidnapped in broad daylight from a Tokyo hotel and taken to Korea in August 1973. Assuming and asserting that only a Korean government organ, perhaps the KCIA, could do such a job, the Japanese lodged a strong protest against the Korean government, which, of course, denied the involvement of any official body in the incident. The Japanese continued to put pressure on the Korean government, threatening to withhold economic aid. During this time, the newspaper editorials were silent; indeed, any editorial on Kim's incident scolded "the irresponsible remarks" by Japanese authorities and the Japanese press.

Then, beginning 2 October 1973 students from Seoul National University started demonstrations against the Park regime – its handling of the Dae-jung Kim case, as well as the iron-clad control of all segments of society by the KCIA, including the surveillance on academia. It took six days for Korean newspapers to mention the demonstrations and arrests. The *Dong-A* had the temerity to write two consecutive stories on the demonstrations on 4-5 October, only to be forced to delete them from the stereotypes. Student demonstrators then included in their slogans a demand for the return of freedom of speech and press.

In early November, the Korean government decided to send Premier Chong-pil Kim as the presidential emissary to Japan to apologize for the Dae-jung Kim incident and consented to the deportation of several Korean diplomats suspected of being involved in the kidnapping. Even members of the emasculated opposition party began to ask tough questions which were reported daily in the press. When a new wave of student protest broke out and continued daily in almost every campus of the nation, newspapers insisted on reporting them. But the stories were printed only on city pages under small headlines, and no pictures were allowed. According to a Washington Post News Service story, the government put heavy pressure on editors to stop even such limited reporting, but working journalists began newsroom sit-ins and threats of mass walkouts, insisting that the reporting continue.

Once again, the historical spearhead of the opposition tradition, *Dong-A Ilbo,* took the lead. According to one report, "Journalists at the *Dong-A* held three sit-in protests at strategic moments. Their counterparts at the *Hankook Ilbo* held four all-night protests. The *Chosun Ilbo* reporters staged a protest" (*The Honolulu Advertiser,* 9 Jan. 1974). A modest victory for the students and press seemed imminent when Park ousted much feared KCIA director Hu-rak Lee and promised not to punish the students. Simultaneously, KCIA agents were withdrawn from newsrooms, and "the Ministry of Information, which is not empowered to haul in journalists for interrogation or to beat them up, took over press monitoring" (*The Honolulu Advertiser,* 9 Jan. 1974). Premier Chong-pil Kim even said that the government's new policy is to assure a "self-controlled" press through constant dialogues.

Encouraged by the Park government's seeming change toward softness or flexibility in dealing with dissent, a fundamental political ferment became manifest. A group of prominent individuals, including a former civilian president, began calling for restoration of the democratic system in Korea, and this was reported on the front page. The government retorted by setting up criteria of self-control which forbade any opposition or challenge to the October Revitalization, items that bring grave dangers to national security and diplomacy, and those that create social disorder and demolish the foundation of the economic stability.

That did not stop the press from reporting the activities of the opposition leaders, including the nominal opposition party in its launching of a nationwide drive to obtain a million signatures to petition President Park for an amendment of the constitution guaranteeing the restoration of democracy in Korea. One of the prominent leaders in the movement was Kwan-woo Cheon, former editor-in-chief of *Dong-A Ilbo,* who was expelled from the post by KCIA pressure. When this restoration of democracy movement began to gain momentum, Park, on 9 January 1974, invoked emergency powers again, specifically aimed at banning any attempt to amend the constitution. Park's order made it illegal to "deny, oppose, misrepresent or defame the constitution" or to "assert, introduce, propose or petition for revision or repeal of the constitution." Further, it banned all acts of informing other persons of any such prohibited activities by means of *broadcasting, reporting* or *publication* (emphasis is author's). Park created military courts to mete out sentences of up to 15 years to anyone violating or criticizing the provisions of the declaration. Anyone suspected of violating any of the above mentioned could be arrested and searched without warrants. Probably more ominous and chilling was the announcement that the KCIA would "coordinate and supervise" those procedures. This then was the darkest hour for the press and for the people, whose freedom of expression was so completely proscribed. The government also made it clear that the ban on reporting the suppressed activities applied to foreign correspondents.

On the day the announcement was made, "Kobawoo," a character in an extremely popular comic strip that alluded to the student demonstrations of October 1973 before the news columns did, was shown tearing down the traditional New Year greeting of, "In the spring, great tidings," from the gate of his house, and posting a new writing which said, "Silence is golden." That may represent the feelings of many reporters and editors: If they cannot speak out against dictatorial manifestations, they might as well close their papers to register a resistance of silence. Obviously, their desires do not coincide with the interests of the publishers.

2.7.8 *Recent Events, by John A. Lent*

South Korea in the 1970s had one of the highest economic growth rates in the world, which bode well for the economic side of journalism. The increased wealth and rising purchasing power allowed print media to renovate the technical side of production and increase circulations, although doing next to nothing for journalists' professional standards or the quality of contents. One writer reported in mid-1979 that the press had gone from an "erstwhile respectable, elite industry to just another form of profit-seeking enterprise" (*Kim,* 1979, p. 59).

Reflecting the expansive mood of the economy, the number of television sets went up 4.7 times between 1972-78, while the number of newspaper copies sold increased 1.6 times to a rate of 203 copies per 1,000 population. By the mid-1970s, at least three newspapers claimed circulations of over half a million. The youngest of the three, *Joong-Ang,* established in 1965, is the fastest growing, with 510,000 subscribers, making it the largest evening daily. *Joong-Ang* is also the largest mass communication group, owning a weekly, two student journals, one general audience monthly, a women's magazine, an AM/FM radio station and one of the two commercial television networks. (The other commercial television network is a financial prop for *Kyunghyang Shinmun.*) The older, prestigious *Dong-A Ilbo,* which also has other media properties, had a circulation of 650,000 by the mid-1970s, while *Choson Ilbo* had 561,000. Most of the 13 national dailies (all published in Seoul) have gone to offset printing during these economic good times. The rest of the Korean press is made up of two or three local newspapers in each of the nine provinces.

Editorially, the South Korean press is not doing so well. The public is critical of newspaper content, saying it seldom tells the truth and that it is on the side of special interest groups (for an earlier study of journalists' perceptions of their roles, see *Oh,* 1977-78, pp. 10-48). The weeklies are entertainment-oriented to the point of being sensational, while dailies have joined together to give a type of journalism that is safe and bland. Publishers have agreed to devote half of their eight pages daily to "soft, sketchy, non-controversial" articles concerned with groups and individuals, but not issues (*Kim,* 1979, p. 60). Of course, some of these trends are dictated by big companies that provide the advertising money.

Part of the problem stems from the brain drain newspapers suffered during the 1970s. Probably because they can no longer report truthfully on government and politics without incurring the wrath of the Korean Central Intelligence Agency and other Government supporters, senior journalists leave their jobs when they get an opportunity to enter government or industry. They have been coopted. Junior reporters entering the profession are not the cream of the crop as in the past. Recruiting is still done through open examinations coinciding with university graduations, but now top students are attracted to fast growing trading companies which can provide better pay, prestige and job security (*Kim,* 1979, p. 59).

Ten mass communications schools continue to educate journalists, although realizing they cannot base this education on the traditional concept that journalists are watchdogs and crusaders. Instead, the present generation of journalists is being socialized to view its role within the government framework. Molding them is a group of former, senior journalists who are now in government and public relations posts.

The struggle some newspapers and journalists had with government in the mid-1970s — fighting advertising boycotts, arrests, harassment, forced mergers and suspensions, censorship and restrictive laws with strikes, sit-ins and critical writing (see *Crabbe*, 1975, p. 13; *Hazelhurst*, 1975a; *Whang*, 1975 a and b; *Nam*, 1978; *Quill*, 1975, p. 8; *Thorpe*, 1975 a and b) has left them battered and gun shy. Many journalists have decided either to leave the profession for more lucrative government or business posts or to play it safe writing non-controversial drivel; most of the newspapers seem to have opted for the economic rewards of a fast developing nation, forsaking some of their traditional values in the process.

The situation has not improved much since the assassination of Park in October 1979.

2.8 Macao

John A. Lent

Macao is seldom taken into consideration when the Asian press is discussed. Yet, newspapers such as *A Abelha da China* and *Gazeta de Macao,* both edited by friars as political sheets, published there as early as 1822 and 1824, and missionary printers — such as the Jesuits in the mid-sixteenth century and the London Missionary Society agents in the first generation of the nineteenth century — used Macao as printing headquarters (*Teixeira,* 1965; Lent, 1979).

In the mid-1970s, the 10-square mile Portuguese territory had six dailies, two in Portuguese sold mainly by subscription, and four in Chinese, sold mainly on the streets to a population that is 98 per cent Chinese. Additionally, a twice weekly general interest newspaper, a weekly official bulletin and a few religious newspapers, all in Portuguese, plus some Chinese language periodicals devoted mainly to tourist interests, round out the publications (*UNESCO,* 1975, p. 316).

The press played a role in the 1974-75 political turmoil which started when a group claiming to be promoters for a better Macao, bickered with the Macao government. Formed shortly after the 1974 coup in Portugal, the group, Centro Democratico de Macao (CDM), aimed at instilling a democratic spirit into the 300,000 Macanese. CDM scathingly attacked the administration, most of which was reported in the press, until in mid-1974, the government cancelled a weekly CDM program on government-controlled Radio Macao, because the program was said to include half truths on "corruption, inefficiency and abuses of power in high Government offices." The banning of the program caused protests against the governor's curb on freedom of expression; in the process, the two-man, Lisbon appointed Ad Hoc Committee on Media, which had approved the program, resigned. Originally, the committee's main job was to see that no newspaper violated the guidelines laid down by the military junta for publishing news of troop movements and other matters. When a new committee was formed, its aim was "to assist, not to control, the media." During the same protests, the editor of one of the two Portuguese dailies, *Noticias de Macao*, resigned because his publisher refused to print the full text of the CDM program. The paper's new editor, Dr. Antonio Maria da Conceiçao, reportedly received two telephoned death threats during his first three days in office (*Yao*, 1974b, p. 31).

Until this incident concerning the controversial radio program, the press had been thought by some CDM personnel as a key weapon against the government. Political cartoons ridiculing officials and their misconduct appeared frequently in the press, and some were openly sold on news-stands with the approval of the Ad Hoc Committee. A CDM official stated the role he expected the press to play, by saying, "With the freedom of the press, we're confident that we can have a government which is responsive to the real needs of the people and which will improve the living conditions of the masses" (*Yao*, 1974a, p. 27). One Portuguese daily, *Gazeta Macaense*, was punished for its strong anti-government stand when the governor suspended its monthly subvention of US$826 in May 1974.

The Chinese language press, largely under the sway of pro-Peking interests, remained relatively uncommitted during the fracas, its few and timid comments often showing concern about the effects of the political squabbles upon tourism and the colony's sagging economy. In mid-1975, however, the Chinese press mounted its largest campaign against the Portuguese Communists, classifying them as revisionists. They openly attacked the leftist slant of the Portuguese government and gave extensive coverage to anti-Communist riots in Portugal (*Yao*, 1975b, p. 26).

In February 1975, the other Portuguese-language daily, *Noticias de Macao*, was accused of carrying inaccurate reports on the Governor, Colonel Garcia Leandro, appointed the previous November. *Noticias'* punishment was a US$2,330 fine and a one-day suspension, both imposed by the Ad Hoc Committee, which earlier claimed its aim was not to control the media. In a signed editorial, the editor, da Conceiçao, said he was resigning and the newspaper was suspending operations rather than "work with the sword of Damocles always hanging over our heads" (*Media,* April 1975, p. 4). *Noticias* did not resume publication until June 1977, after a successful appeal to the Supreme Court of Lisbon.

2.9 Mongolian People's Republic

D. Urjinbadam

Since the Mongolian People's Republic was formed in 1921, the Mongolian people, under the guidance of the Mongolian People's Revolutionary Party (MPRP), have changed a backward nation into an agro-industrial, cultural nation, with a flourishing economy and educational progress.

2.9.1 Background

Today, in the Mongolian People's Republic, the same productivity is accomplished in one and a half months that was done in the whole of 1940. Every fourth citizen is engaged in some form of education, and for every 10,000 people, there are 99 hospital beds and 19.8 doctors. Over the years, the population has increased 2.1 times.

The omnipotent people's will has been developed in the print media. The MPRP has given regular attention to the organizational strengthening of the organs of print media, bettering their material base, raising the ideological level and the content of material published. Besides the main central newspapers, every county, city and factory has its own newspaper. For this reason, the average family receives four or five different publications regularly.

As in other countries, periodical publications in Mongolia come into contact with facets of political, economical and cultural life. The difference is that, in Mongolia, they commenced at a much later date — in the twentieth century. From the beginning of its

D. Urjinbadam is secretary of the Union of Mongolian Journalists. He wrote this chapter in Russian and Mongolian. The Russian version was translated by Michael Schilenok and was shortened, omitting a great deal of the ideological content, by John A. Lent.

appearance, the press received pressure from the feudalists, since most publications were of a democratic nature, defending nationalistic independence, the interests of the working class and overall enlightenment.

The history of the Mongolian press is closely tied to that of the MPRP. Mongolian revolutionaries, with D. Sukhe-Bator at their head, released the first edition of *Mongolyn Unen* (Mongolian Truth) outside the borders of Mongolia. It was published in Irkutsk (USSR) on 10 November 1920 and smuggled into Mongolia. Its presence was illegal in Mongolia until April 1921. *Mongolyn Unen* explained the meaning of the October Revolution to the Mongolian people and called upon them to rise up in the name of freedom against reactionary feudalists, Chinese militarists, foreign occupiers of Mongolia and White Guard bandits. The front page of the first issue called for the establishment of contacts with nations great and small for support in the battle for revolution. In this issue, under the headline, "Mongolian People Beware," "traitorous ministers who sold Mongolia to Chinese occupation" were criticized. Incidences of animalism, rape and pillage inflicted by Chinese soldiers upon the citizens were related. The newspaper wrote that only if the people armed themselves could they win freedom and independence. *Mongolyn Unen* praised the successes and gains of the first Soviet government and called for friendly ties with it and workers and peasants throughout the world.

Actively praising the revolutionary ideas and decisions of the First Congress of the Mongolian People's Revolutionary Party, *Mongolyn Unen* publicized revolutionaries' activities, especially with a series of articles popularizing Lenin's ideas of not following the capitalistic path of development. The newspaper wrote that power in Mongolia must be chosen from the bottom up and leaders of the country had to be selected carefully and be held answerable to the people for their actions. "Only in this manner," underlined the paper, "can there be a guarantee of freedom and happiness for the country." In the third issue, *Mongolyn Unen* stated that in the armed battle against foreign occupiers, Mongolia could count on Russia. In this manner, the newspaper fulfilled a huge role in the course of politics and the decisions of the Party, mobilizing the people for the revolutionary battle, driving out foreign powers, liquidating the feudalist system and establishing the people's will. After the victorious revolution, there appeared other newspapers, such as *New Capital, People's Right* and *Summons*, all started between 1921-25. These publications dedicated a great deal of attention to the political awareness and activeness of the masses. Today, *Mongolyn Unen* is the most widely read daily in Mongolia.

The theoretical organ of the Central Committee of the Party, "Party Life" (*Namyn Amdral*), was established in 1923, but under the name, "Mongolian People's Party." Since 1924, the Central Committee of the Union of Mongolian Youth, has published the newspapers, "Young People's Truth" (*Zaluutchuudyn Unen*), and "Young Generation," and since the spring of 1944, the Mongolian Pioneer Organization has published Pioneer Truth (*Pioneriin Unen*), and the magazine, *Change*. The latter newspapers and magazines, directed to children and young adults of Mongolia, fulfill a large role in educating them in the revolutionary, working class traditions of the Party.

In 1924, the Army newspaper, *Red Star* (*Ulaan-Od*), was established. It pays great attention to the education of soldiers, aiming to heighten their preparedness and strengthen the military's friendship with the Soviet Union and other socialistic nations. A year later, the first edition of the magazine, *Women's Opinion* (later changed to *Women of Mongolia, Mongolyn Emegteitchuud*), appeared. In its first issues, the magazine was dedicated to the enlightenment of women workers in Mongolia, liquidating the bondage of the feudalist system and educating women in revolutionary ideology. In 1944-45, the Party committees and deputations also began publishing a mutual publication.

Still published are the newspapers, *Labor* (*Khedelmer*), *Literature and Culture* (*Utga Zokhiol Urlag*), *New Village* (*Shine Khedee*) *Sports News* (*Sportyn Medee*) and *Education*. Some of the magazines are *People's Government and Life, Professional Union, Teacher, Health* (*Eruul Mend*), *Small Flame* (*Tsog*), *Builder* (*Barilgatchin*) and *Socialistic Laws,* plus other central and lesser publications.

2.9.2 Goals of the Press

Central and local newspapers and magazines are distinctive as to direction, specialty, readership, identity and history. But their goal is one: popularizing the politics and decisions of the Party and government.

The Mongolian revolutionary press, from the day of its creation, stood firmly behind the policies of the Party and the direction of the working class. The press leads a strong battle against all "bourgeoisie ideology," and, following the guidelines of the Party, wages an unending war against "imperialist reactionary forces." The Party ideology defends the thoughts of Marx and Lenin, putting them to use daily. For this reason, the press counts as one of its main objectives, the unification of the ideology of Marx-Lenin, with the policies and decisions of the Party and the socialistic structure of the country. The press arms the readers ideologically, helping them to better understand and know the obligations of the entire socialistic ideology, to foster the spirit of international socialism and communist ideology and to battle against the backward past.

The MPRP demands from journalists a complete knowledge of the works of Lenin. By the constitution of the Party, every citizen has the right to free use of the press and to participation within it. All newspapers and magazines are tied to the Party and are its ideological organs. This means that the newspapers are the products of the workers themselves. The main themes for publication are the decisions of the Party and government, heroic labors of the people, joyful and happy life in Mongolia, Communist education, among other things. The MPRP, by propagandizing its policies and decisions through the press, advises people on topics of politics, economics and culture and listens to opinions and criticisms from the public. A wide use of criticism and self-criticism is one of the major demands of the Party which the press firmly holds to. Criticism in the press is directed towards defending the Marxist-Leninist principles.

Historically, at the end of the 1930s, the Mongolian press helped the Communist Party educate the young people, calling on them to prepare for the defense of their freedom and independence against foreign aggressors. During World War II, the press, using the slogan, "All for Victory, All for the Front," helped the efforts of the Soviet Red Army against German fascism and Japanese militarism. The main themes of the newspapers were the growth of the Leninist policy of cooperation, united with international Communist movements and policies, and the course of the MPRP. Since 1960, when the nation went through a "socialistic building," the press has performed with honor its mission of collective agitator, collective propagandist and collective organizer.

2.9.3 Additional Information, by John A. Lent

The press of Mongolia dates back to 6 March 1913, when *Shine Tol* (New Mirror) was published as a 40-page journal devoted to science, education, history, political science and literature. With its fifth issue, *Shine Tol,* which lasted until 21 August 1914, expanded to include a weekly newspaper of six to ten pages. *Mongolyn Unen (Mongolian Truth),* started in 1920, laid the ground work for the revolutionary press in the country (see 2.9.1), followed in 1928 by *Bukh Mongolyn Ulaan Uildverchin (All-Mongolian Red Trade Union)* as a herald of the working class. On 1 September 1929, *Azhiltchny Zam (Workers' Road)* appeared, aimed at explaining Party and government policy to Chinese workers living in Mongolia, and between 8 January 1930 and October 1932, the Central Committee of the MPRP and Central Council of Mongolian Trade Unions published the daily, *Mongol Ardyn Unen (Mongolian National Truth) (IOJ,* 1976, p. 95).

One source, writing on the history of the Mongolian press, categorized three stages of development:

Between 1921-40, the press struggled for the nation's non-capitalist development and was involved in national liberation. Much attention was paid to political propaganda. By the end of the 1930s, the press had expanded to include five newspapers and seven magazines for a total circulation of 90,000, or one copy of a publication to 10 people.

In the second stage, 1940-60, the role of journalists was for the socialist construction of the nation, and for a time, the development of a nationwide movement to aid the Soviets against Germany. In the 1940s and 1950s, the press was redesigned to include not just central and local papers, but also publications for most economic and cultural enterprises. The Union of Mongolian Journalists was started in this period, as was the press agency, MONTSAME, meant to provide foreign and domestic news to all media. By the end of the 1950s, there were 30 central and local newspapers and 26 magazines with an overall circulation of 700,000, or two publications for every three people. Directives of the Central Committee in 1947 and 1952 improved *Unen*'s political and ideological level and the work of publishers generally and solidified the principles of collective leadership. Another 30 directives dealing with the development of the press were issued between 1954-61.

The third stage, 1960-74, saw the press involved in the advanced building of socialism and the conversion of the economy from agrarian industrial to industrial agrarian. By the 1970s, there were 38 newspapers and 27 magazines with a total circulation of 1.3 million, or one publication per person. Journalists' jobs during this stage were more difficult as they had to propagate progressive work experience, arm the working people with economic knowledge and explain to the masses their responsibilities and duties to society (*Deleg*, 1974, pp. 6-7; *Vidura*, 1975, p. 71; see also *Munchzargal*, 1976, pp. 95-100).

Today, 42 newspapers are published in Mongolia with a total circulation of 730,000. Of these, 19 are published by *aymak* and city committees of the Party and executive boards of the Khurals of the People's Deputies. There is one newspaper each in English, Russian and Kazakh. Chief newspapers are *Unen,* central organ of the Central Committee of the MPRP and the government, and *Ulaanbaatoryn Medee* (*Ulanbatar News*), published by the Ulanbatar City Committee of the Party and the Executive Board of the City Khural of People's Deputies. *Unen* has a circulation of 120,000, while *Ulaanbaatoryn Medee*'s is 27,000. Still others are *Zaluutchuudyn Unen* (*Young People's Truth*), published twice weekly since 1924; *Khedelmer* (*Labor*), two or three times a week, press organ of Central Committee of Mongolian Trade Unions since October 1947; *Ulaan-Od* (*Red Star*), thrice weekly organ of Ministry of Defense and Ministry of Interior since 1924, plus others that represent additional government or Party agencies, such as the Ministry of Transportation, Central Council of Mongolian Pioneers, Ministry of Agriculture, Central Council for Physical Culture and Sports and others. In addition, 31 journals with a combined circulation of 530,000, are published, as are newspapers in each town and *aymak*. Except for *Ulaanbaatoryn*

Medee and *Nairamdlyn Darkhan* (*Darkhan — A Town of Friendship*), both of which appear three or four times weekly as city "dailies," other *aymak* papers appear two or three times weekly (*IOJ*, 1976, pp. 96-100). A large percentage of the contents of these papers comes from MONTSAME (Mongolian Telegraph Agency, founded March 1921), which disseminates 14,300 words daily and publishes weekly bulletins in Russian and English. MONTSAME exchanges information with 14 foreign agencies. Approximately 450 journalists belonging to the Union of Mongolian Journalists also add to the newspapers' contents, as do 15,000 voluntary correspondents who cooperate with newspapers, journals and radio. Contents of newspapers are expected to promote Party and governmental campaigns (see *Sanders*, 1975, p. 30).

Part 3
Southeast Asia

3.1 Freedom of the Press in Southeast Asia

John A. Lent

3.1.1 Overview

Freedom of the press in Southeast Asia has faced serious threats during the 1970s as the authoritarian governments of the region promote the new concept of developmental communication and redefine older concepts such as freedom and democracy. Officialdom has taken the previously meritorious notion of development journalism (reporting impartially on a nation's development) and has converted it into government-say-so or commitment journalism, used in some cases to push ideologies and campaigns of controlling governments or political parties. Simultaneously, national leaders and their entourages have redefined goals of journalists, saying they should be cooperative and guided by government, rather than be adversaries. The same authorities point out that press freedom is not a priority of Third World nations which are trying to feed and keep healthy their growing populations, that actually press freedom is a Western-borrowed value — a luxury that their nations cannot afford because of "national security," or "stability," or "public welfare," or ethnicity problems, etc.

Apparently, even some of these leaders do not fully believe what they are espousing, for, at various times, they do temporarily loosen their strangleholds on media, allowing some freedom of expression. The martial law government of Marcos, for example, has at times encouraged a more lively press criticism (most recently before the 1978 election);[1] however, once the government feels the slightest tinge of insecurity, the screws are tightened

---

1 Philippine authorities at various times have accused the press of being too servile and have invited editors to be more critical. Francisco Tatad, information secretary, in February 1977, told Manila editors that the press was made up of a bunch of servile incompetents running sycophantic sheets. The journalists do not take the bait because they know that Tatad is Marcos' chief censor and they recall what happened to their colleagues when they became critical.

again (*San Juan,* 1978, pp. 39-47). Editors in Indonesia have faced similar highs and lows of press freedom in Suharto's regime. Indonesian newspapers were relatively free until the January 1974 student demonstrations after which they were subdued (*Southerland,* 1976b, p. 26). By mid-1976, the Indonesian press seemed to regain its former élan so that until January 1978, most Southeast Asian governments exercised far more control over their presses than did the Indonesian authorities. In fact, Suharto took some pride in this, telling his Parliament in August 1977, that he believed the press had sufficient freedom and adding, "at least it is not among the worst in Asia." One source believed the government felt assured that Indonesian newspapers would not stray too far out of line because of Army regulations on them, record levels of advertising revenue, proprietors who had grown fat under the New Order government and because of the ruthless 1974 clamp-down on the press (*Asia 1978 Yearbook,* p. 198). But, in early 1978, the Indonesian press was seriously restricted. Because the government is acutely aware of its overseas image, the situation took another about-face (*IPI Report,* 1978, pp. 5-7) and the papers regained much of their former vigor faster than had been expected.

In Thailand, press freedom has been an up-down affair for decades. More recently, Thai journalists had one of their freest periods between October 1973 (when student riots overthrew the government of Thanom Kittikachorn) and October 1976. Press regulations were loosened and a 1974 constitution guaranteed press freedom, denied closure of newspapers for political reasons, forbade censorship, limited press ownership to Thais and disallowed government financial support of private papers (*Lent,* 1977b, pp. 45-50). However, all of that ended after the bloody 6 October 1976 coup. The new head of government, Thanin Kraivichien, was accused of being repressive and often contemptuous of the press. As one writer noted:

> From Thanin's standpoint, in fact, the biggest enemy of all was the press. His inability to use the media as a gauge of public opinion forced newspapers to play heavily on lurid crimes and sex scandals — but rarely on political issues. Even so, national police chief General Montchai Phankongchuen signed no fewer than

23 closure orders on newspapers for criticising govern-
ment policies and 'endangering national security' —
offences judged by the Thanin government's Press
Advisory Board and Censorship Committee....
Attempts to settle media problems with Minister Dusit
(Siriwan) created rather than avoided confrontations.
Yet the military seemed to be courting the crippled
press (*Asiaweek,* 1977a, pp. 20-21).

When the military returned to power in 1977 in still another
October coup, the press was allowed to breathe more freely
again. The ruling Revolutionary Party, under General Kriangsak
Chamanand, issued a series of orders, one of which stated that the
party, mindful of the importance of the press, would allow
publishing without censorship or control (*The National Review,*
1977). An accompanying announcement explained the conditions
of the relaxation, saying the party:

... will not yet censor newspapers. Newspapers may be
published and sold without censorship or control by the
Press Advisory Council as before because the Revolutionary Party believes that the press will support this
revolution by disseminating reports of developments
with truth and justice, will give opinions with honesty
of heart in a way that will build up the nation and the
people. Any action by a newspaper that creates trouble,
disseminates falsehood to the public, or without justice,
will be halted by revolutionary power since this is
necessary for the safety of the nation and the people
and good behaviour of the people. This is so especially
for newspapers that act as spokesmen of foreigners, or
speak for elevate [*sic*] doctrines that are dangerous to
the nation, the people or the monarchy, or try to sow
disunity within the nation, whether directly or indirectly by whatever method. They will be suppressed
absolutely (*The Nation Review,* 1977).

In Malaysia and Singapore, with much more stable governments
than that of Thailand, newspapermen are guided by the regular
admonishments of officials as to what their roles should be, as well
as by legislative and other controls. Singaporean journalists were
given clear indication in 1971 of what can happen if Lee Kuan

Yew takes a dislike to sectors of the press. Lee purged the press by exposing the *Eastern Sun* as a Communist-financed paper, thus forcing it to close "voluntarily"; withdrawing the publishing permit of the *Herald* and sealing its fate forever, and detaining, for at least two years, four owners and editors of *Nanyang Siang Pau,* on accusations that they whipped up emotions among the Chinese (see 3.8.3.1). The result in Singapore, and in Malaysia, is that although sections of the press remain privately-owned, for the most part, they respond in harmony with other government spokesmen (*Lent,* 1975c, pp. 663-669; *Lent,* 1975d, pp. 7-16; *Casady,* 1975, pp. 3-7).

Because of the socialist nature of the governments of Burma, Laos, Kampuchea and Vietnam, the mass media are controlled by strict structural and functional designs which do not allow even the wavering degrees of press freedom seen elsewhere in Southeast Asia. The governments own the presses and use them as they wish; the societies themselves, especially those of Indochina, are virtually closed to the outside world.

3.1.2 *Ownership Control*

In every country of Southeast Asia, governments have insured that newspapers be locally owned. It is understandable that these newly-emergent nations wish to work out their problems without the influences of foreign-owned newspapers on their soil. However, in many cases, foreign (and local group and individual) ownership has been replaced by that of the ruling party or the government.

In Singapore, the potential for government ownership is there in the form of the August 1974 Newspaper and Printing Press Bill which restructures newspaper ownerships, creating two classes of shares — management and ordinary. Management shares, carrying more voting weight than ordinary, can be owned by only those approved by the Ministry of Culture (see 3.8.3.3). The law, which permits the government to be an owner of print media, also forces newspapers to become public corporations and breaks up large share ownership by individuals and families (*Chopra,* 1975, p. 4). No person is allowed to have more than 3 per cent of the ordinary shares issued by a newspaper (*Asiaweek,* 1977b, pp. 34-35).

One writer said that, although, on the surface the act seems designed to keep out foreign owners, it is actually meant to keep out anyone who has fallen foul of the government (*Chopra,* 1975, p. 4).

Amendments to the Malaysian press laws also disallow foreign ownership and force newspapers to go to public ownership. Ownership of the press in the 1970s has shifted in growing numbers to political parties and government agencies, especially among English and Malay language newspapers. New Straits Times Group (three dailies plus magazines) is 80 per cent owned by Pernas (the state trading corporation which has ties to United Malays National Organization, the predominant political party); the Utusan Melayu Group (two dailies plus magazines) and Star Publications also are UMNO-owned, while other papers have Malaysian Chinese Association and Malaysian Indian Congress backing. In East Malaysia, the press is almost entirely supported by political parties, although the press of Sarawak is less closely tied to parties than that of Sabah.

For years, Ferdinand Marcos decried the oligarchic control of Philippine media by families such as Lopez, Soriano, Elizalde and Roces. Once martial law was promulgated in September 1972, Marcos confiscated existing media properties without remuneration and established the strongest media conglomerates in the nation's history, making the media the private monopoly of those in authority, their close relatives and business associates. For example, Philippine Daily Express Company (at least four publications) is owned by Marcos through Roberto Benedicto and is financed partly through the president's contingency fund; the five *Bulletin* publications are owned by Marcos former aide, Hans Menzi; the combine of *Evening Post, Focus Philippines* and *Orient Express* is the property of the husband-wife team of Juan Tuvera and Kerima Polotan, the former a presidential assistant and the latter a biographer of Imelda Marcos; *Weekly Examiner* is the possession of Leon Ty, a Marcos appointee serving as governor of the Development Bank of the Philippines; *United Daily News* is headed by Ralph Nubla, Marcos supporter in Chinatown, and *Times-Journal* and *Manila Journal* are owned by the First Lady's brother, Benjamin Romualdez (*Lent,* 1976a, pp. 5, 12).

In socialist Burma, all dailies are state owned. As such, they print the same stories verbatim, leading one source to quip that their sole purpose is to employ people (*Philadelphia Bulletin,* 20 June 1976, p. 8-B). The structure of mass media is rather elaborate in Burma with a Ministry of Information that includes a Press Management Board (which directs nationalized papers), Nationalized Printing Presses Supervisory Committee, the Sarpay Beikman (main government publishing element), the Printers and Publishers Central Registration Board and the Journalism School. Under a Directorate of Information, there is the News Agency of Burma and the Press and Publications Scrutiny Section (see 3.2).

The military management of what was formerly South Vietnam in May 1975 forbade all private publishing of newspapers, magazines and books. The Vietnamese press resembles those of other socialist states with an official daily, *Giai Phong;* a party organ, *Nhan Dan;* an army daily, *Quan Doi Nhan Dan,* and a theoretical journal, *Hoc Tap,* among others.

Laos and Kampuchea, which have always been somewhat slow in press development, have, since 1975, centralized under government ownership the few publications allowed to exist. The Laotian press, before the Pathet Lao takeover, was city-oriented, elitist, and above all, politically-financed (*Lent,* 1974d, pp. 31-34; *Lent,* 1974c, pp. 170-179). Under the Communist regime, the press has been whittled to two newspapers — the official *Siang Pasason* (*Voice of the People*), begun 11 August 1975, as the central organ of the Lao People's Revolutionary Party, and the semi-official *Viangchan Mai* (*New Vientiane*), started on 1 November 1975, by the government. Laos also has a news agency, Khao San Pathet Lao, owned by the Ministry of Information, which publishes government bulletins (*Asian Press and Media Directory 1976-1977*). Kampuchea does not have a mass-circulated newspaper under the new government; instead, a few journals are circulated to selected government officials. The government uses loudspeakers to communicate with the people (*Philadelphia Inquirer,* 17 April 1977, p. 18-A).

Additionally, most news agencies of Southeast Asia are either owned or controlled by the government, this being the case especially in Malaysia, Indonesia, Philippines, Burma, Laos and Vietnam.

3.1.3 Legislative Control

Most Southeast Asian countries have either legislated new press laws or radically changed old ones during the 1970s. In almost every nation, licensing of newspapers and indigenous ownership have become the norms.

The 1971 and 1974 amendments to Malaysia's Printing Presses Act (1948), which requires annual licenses and permits for news papers, state that a license can be withdrawn if a newspaper distorts public order incidents or inflames or stirs communal hostility and if a publication is not Malaysian-owned. The Sedition Ordinance (1948) was amended in 1971 to prohibit all discussion of four sensitive issues – the Bahasa Malaysia language policy, special rights of the Malay ethnic group, special roles of sultans and other royalty and the policy which denies citizenship to certain non-Malays. Singapore's latest press law is discussed in 3.1.2 and 3.8.3.3.

Philippine law since 1972 decrees that all newspapers must be Filipino-owned and must have publishing permits. Numerous presidential decrees have limited media reporting, informing the press what they can and cannot publish. One of the latest, Presidential Decree 576 of 1974, stated that mass media must control themselves through government-established bureaux, both of which are headed by pro-Marcos journalists. Indonesia's Basic Principles of the Press also requires a license to publish and states that the press cannot use material contrary to the national ideology. Further, it stipulates that censorship cannot exist, that media must be Indonesian-owned and that the "right of control, criticism and correction of a corrective and constructive nature" is assured. It has already been seen how the law has been bent, especially in 1974 and 1978, by Indonesian authorities to mean something completely different (*Lent,* 1978c, pp. 41-60). Under the Thanin government, Thai journalists also were affected by Press Advisory Council-implemented laws that allowed for censorship and suspension of papers and arrests of journalists. Especially fearful in 1977 was a bill requiring all journalists to apply for a work permit from the Ministry of Interior (*Asian Messenger,* Autumn/Winter 1977, p. 18). Upon assuming office in October 1977, the Revolutionary Party abandoned many of these restrictions, although, as already mentioned, it cautioned journalists on what was expected of them.

The State Party Protection Law of Burma, passed in the People's Assembly in 1974, states firmly that citizens can be punished with three to 14 years' imprisonment for conspiring, collaborating or publishing with the aim of opposing party principles and for publishing documents classified by the party as secret (*IPI Report*, March 1975, pp. 1, 3). An earlier press law requires annual registration of newspapers.

Indochina had extremely harsh press laws even before 1975. Vietnamese press laws of 1969 and 1972 required, among other things, that journalists possess a registered press card, that each newspaper deposit with the authorities a security bond of US$47,000, that 100 copies of each edition of every newspaper be delivered to the Ministry of Information for censorship purposes. Since the Communist takeover of the South, 1976 regulations forbid publication, distribution or sales of papers directed against the government, exposure of the government, party or Army or praise for the former South Vietnamese governments. Newspapers in Kampuchea after May 1974 were required to deposit US$3,875 in the national bank to insure their financial stability. Further, a June 1972 Ministry of Information law stated it was against the law to cast a slur on a person's honor or on national security or on morality. Laos, before 1975, also had licensing laws for the press. Although little is known about the press in Kampuchea and Laos today, it can be assumed that they operate under as stringent regulations as newspapers in Vietnam and other socialist nations.

3.1.4 Control by Suspensions, Harassment and Arrests

When newspapers violate the press laws or otherwise run into difficulty with officials, they are often suspended and/or their publishers and editors are arrested and jailed. In other instances, journalists have been harassed in many ways; some have been murdered.

Extreme cases of banning of newspapers occurred in Indonesia in 1965 when Sukarno closed all Chinese dailies; in the Philippines in 1972 when Marcos obliterated the press, except for his own *Express* and *Bulletin Today;* in Thailand in October 1976 when all newspapers were temporarily closed; in South Vietnam in 1970, 1971 and 1972 when the Thieu government confiscated newspapers 250, 718 and 907 times, respectively (*Tin Sang* was confiscated at least 166 times in 1971) (*Sussman,* 1974, p. 5); in Kampuchea in 1973 when all papers were suspended after an assassination attempt on President Lon Nol; and again in Kampuchea and South Vietnam, as well as Laos, in 1975 when the Communist governments killed off the private presses.

Indonesia has banned newspapers on a few occasions since the January 1974 riots during the visit of Japanese Premier Tanaka. At that time, licenses of seven dailies and four weeklies were revoked because of their critical writing (*Budiardjo,* 1974, pp. 73-76). The government, to provide employment for journalists of the banned papers, decided to grant licenses for three new dailies on the condition that publishers and editors of the 11 banned papers could not be associated with them. The government announcement also stated that journalists applying for positions would be screened by the Kopkamtib, the Command for the Restoration of Security and Order, and that the three dailies would follow three principles — embody the spirit of the New Order and the ideology of *Pancasila,* omit news that might incite or distort facts, and refrain from creating racial, ethnic, religious or political strife or discredit the national leadership (*Goldstone,* 1974, pp. 27-28). In January 1978, on the eve of national elections, the Suharto government closed seven leading Jakarta papers in what it proclaimed was an effort to maintain security and order. The papers were accused of tending to incite the population (*Jenkins,* 1978b, pp. 13-14). When the military lifted the ban after two weeks, the papers were only pale shadows of their former selves, prompting one journalist to write, "it seemed clear that it would be a long time before the Indonesian press would enjoy the same sort of freedom again" (*Jenkins,* 1978a, p. 19). Before being allowed to resume publishing activities, however, the editors of the banned papers had to sign statements saying their newspapers, being co-responsible for maintaining public stability and public interest, would put public and state interests above personal ones, would maintain the good reputation and authority of the government and national leadership, would fulfill, execute and respect stipulations laid down by law, by the

Press Council and by other regulations of government, and would engage in introspection, correction and internal improvements. At the same time, the national security chief told the editors not to cover student political activities or give space to statements from six prominent Indonesians who had been critical of the Suharto government (*Jenkins,* 1978a, p. 19). The January 1978 suspensions had their effects on all newspapers, to the extent that by May-June, some officials said they thought the press was too quiet and possibly even boring. Adam Malik and others tried in 1978 to initiate a dialogue between government and the media, but as one Indonesian writer said, the trust had not yet been restored (*Anwar,* 1978, p. 90; *Kamm,* 1978, p. 17).

For the first time in Thailand's history, all newspapers were banned immediately after the October 1976 coup. The military junta that came to power ordered all publications to cease and reapply for licenses through a newly-developed Committee for Re-Licensing Newspapers. Most liberal and leftist papers were ordered to remain closed. By March 1977, after only four months in office, the Thanin Kraivichien government ordered temporary closures of several other newspapers (*Far Eastern Economic Review,* 4 March 1977, pp. 9-10), including the *Daily News* and former Prime Minister Kukrit Pramoj's *Siam Rath.* In February 1977, one of Kukrit's columns made wrong accusations against the government, it was charged (*Asiaweek;* 11 March 1977, p. 34). In the same month, the *Daily News,* the nation's second largest in circulation, was shut down because a columnist had written an open letter to his old classmate, the prime minister, lambasting the lack of press freedom during his regime. As Thai newspapers have spare licenses as buffers in case of closure, the *Daily News* appeared three days after its shutdown under the name, *Daily Mail.*[2] When the police confiscated the first edition of the *Daily Mail,* Thai newsmen became extremely jittery over the hard line of Thanin and his Interior Minnister, Samak Sundaravej. It was apparent the police were enforcing Act 44 of the Printing Law that stipulates that publications must bring out a paper within

2   *Dao Siam* did the same thing when it was banned, appearing the following day as *Dao Dara Yuk Siam. Dao Siam* was closed because the police said a columnist had made a snide remark about the prime minister, stating he likes spaghetti, is married to a Dane and has given his children foreign names.

60 days of being issued a license or lose that license. Act 15 of the same law revokes an editorship if a publication does not appear for 30 consecutive days (*Asiaweek*, 18 Feb. 1979, p. 37).

Besides suspending all but two of Manila's newspapers at the outset of martial law, the Marcos government in the Philippines more recently in December 1976 and January 1977, raided and padlocked the offices of more ephemeral publications such as the Roman Catholic mimeographed weeklies, *Communicator*, *Signs of the Times* and *Ang Bandilyo* (*Far Eastern Economic Review*, 17 Dec. 1976, pp. 14-15).

As noted in 3.1.1, Lee Kuan Yew, in his purge of the press in 1971, was responsible for the closure of *Eastern Sun* and *Herald*; with his government's latest strictures on ownership, other newspapers may fold. In Malaysia, only minor newspapers, usually in East Malaysia or political party newssheets, have been banned in recent years. In October 1976, the *Kinabalu Sabah Times* and *Sandakan Jih Pao* were closed for a short time by Chief Minister Harris Salleh who said the two papers engaged in subtle campaigns by "distortion of facts and fabrication" of reports to discredit the government.[3]

Oftentimes, when newspapers are closed, staff members face arrest and/or detention, and at other times, journalists are maimed or killed for their writings. South Vietnamese journalists were beaten and killed by Thieu goons in the early 1970s; similar terrorism existed in Kampuchea, and during Thailand's liberal period, 1973-76, a number of violent acts were committed against journalists and newspaper property.

The arrest and/or detention records of some Southeast Asian journalists would put James Franklin or John Peter Zenger to shame. In Laos, *Lanxang Kaona* editor, Liam Phommarath, said he was taken to prison on at least 20 occasions — spending a total of five years there — in the 1960s.[4] In the Philippines, Eugenio Lopez, jr., owner of Chronicle Publications, was in prison from

---

3 This author's interviews in Kota Kinabalu in November 1977, gave him the impression the whole issue revolved around longstanding political feuds. Personal interviews, Tan Sri Yeh Pao Tzu, managing editor, *Daily Express*, Kota Kinabalu, Malaysia, 28 November 1977, and Haji Jasnie Gindug, director, *Sabah Times*, Kota Kinabalu, Malaysia, 28 November 1977.

4 Personal interview, Liam Phommarath, Vientiane, Laos, December 1973.

1972 until he escaped in 1977; others among the hundred arrested and jailed without formal charges still languish there. On the prison island of Buru in Indonesia, there are enough journalists among the 13,000 political prisoners to form a club. At least 24 of these journalists have been in prison for as many as 13 years; most of them have not been formally charged, let alone tried (*Content,* Feb. 1978, p. 1). One Indonesian editor who has had his share of difficulties with governments is Mochtar Lubis, formerly proprietor-editor of *Indonesia Raya.* Lubis served approximately nine years under house arrest during the Sukarno years, was re-arrested in February 1975 for subversion in relation to the January 1974 riots and served over two months in prison before being cleared (*Editor and Publisher,* 1 March 1975, p. 15). His newspaper, banned at the time of his arrest, had not reappeared in 1979.

More recently, in February 1978, the editor of *Duta Masjarakat,* an Indonesian Moslem daily which no longer publishes, was arrested for alleged involvement in student agitation against the uncontested election of Suharto, and in April 1978, other journalists were arrested for subversion. Numerous journalists have been arrested in Thailand during the past five years, one of the most recent incidents involving Prom Tippumee, editor of *Dao Siam,* who was detained in early 1977 for publishing an editorial and a column attacking the prime minister's curbing of the press. And, during the late 1970s in the Philippines, *Communicator* editor, Fr. James Reuter, S.J., had been charged with subversion and the entire executive board of the Association of Major Religious Superiors (publishers of *Signs of the Times)* had been indicted (*Butterfield,* 1977b, pp. 7, 26). They have since had their charges dropped.

Singapore and Malaysia authorities, separately and cooperatively, have taken numerous actions against editors and reporters in the 1970s. On 2 May 1971, four senior executives (Shamsuddin Tung, Lee Mau Seng, Ly Singko and Kerk Loong Sing) of the Chinese language daily, *Nanyang Siang Pau,* were arrested in the early morning hours and ordered detained without trial for two years. Accused of stirring up racial issues and glamorizing communism, the four Singaporean journalists were released after serving terms varying from six months to over two years, but only after confessing to the original charges, and in a case or two, on the condition that they leave Singapore. A fifth *Nanyang Siang Pau* editor, Lee Eu Seng, was detained originally for two years in January 1973; he was finally released in February 1978, when the authorities said that because of new press ownership laws, Lee did not pose a threat because, in fact, he no longer owned *Nanyang Siang Pau* (*Asiaweek*, 17 Feb. 1978, p. 15). One of the first four detainees, Shamsuddin Tung, was back in jail in 1976, detained on election night for playing on the sore point of the Chinese language issue. He tried to secure his release in late 1977 by saying he abhorred violent revolution and Communism, but, in this rare case, a confession did not satisfy Lee Kuan Yew. Shamsuddin Tung was released in early 1979 (see 3.8.3.2).

Numerous other pressmen have shortened their stays of detention by consenting to stage-managed confessions, usually televised and carried verbatim in the press. In mid-1976, the Singapore government revealed an alleged plot by four editors, two each in Singapore and Malaysia, to promote communism either for the overthrow of the Malaysian government or to stir up the ethnic groups in Singapore. Top Malaysian journalist Samad Ismail of *New Straits Times* and Samani Mohamed Amin of *Berita Harian* were detained under the Internal Security Act, while simultaneously in Singapore, two *Berita Harian* editors were arrested for using stories, at Samad's request, to cause disruption among Singapore's Malay population (see *Lent*, 1978d, pp. 9-18). Within six months, the former editor of *Sin Chew Jit Poh* in Kuala Lumpur, Chan Ken-Sin, was detained for indulging in communist activities. He has since been released. All five made televised confessions; there is considerable doubt in the minds of some Malaysian and Singaporean intellectuals about the truthfulness of these confessions (see also 3.8.3.2).

3.1.5 Censorship Control

Both positive and negative censorship abound in Southeast Asia. In the former, governments, using a guidance philosophy, "suggest," "guide" or "advise" editors about the types of stories preferred. They emphasize that the press must cooperate with the officials by stressing positive, often development-inspired news, by supporting governmental ideologies, plans and campaigns, and by downplaying negative news. On the other hand, negative censorship is more overt; censors bluntly inform editors that certain materials must be deleted, or upon publication, blacken or cut them out of the publications or ban the issues. Examples of covert censorship are plentiful in the region. In Malaysia, newspapers, guided by the tenets of the economic plans and the *Rukunegara* (*National Ideology*), practice strict self-restraint, steer away from investigative reporting, fill pages with government speeches and campaigns, ignore the opposition, de-emphasize foreign news and use a high ratio of government press releases (*Lent*, 1975c). Singaporean journalists are advised to meet the needs of a developing society, to promote Lee Kuan Yew's campaigns and to act as government mouthpieces. For example, in mid-1974, editors were politely "advised" to overlook a growing squabble between students and the vice chancellor of Singapore University. In fact, the advice was that students should receive zero publicity. Indonesian newspapers promote *Pancasila* (*National Ideology*) and, like the Philippine press, practice self censorship and take guidance from government officials' speeches and from angry phone calls if they overstep the fine line between what is and is not allowed in print. Stories go unreported in the Philippine press on a regular basis because of the timidity of reporters who practice self censorship. Editors rationalize that they do not have some stories covered because of the psychological control that the government wields over them; they do not want to be invited by the military for discussions about aggressive reporting. For example, some editors were called in by the First Lady in September 1976, because of the manner in which they covered the trial of Marcos political arch-rival, Senator Benigno Aquino.

Burmese dailies receive pre-publication counsel provided by the Ministry of Information, usually indicating the government's preference for national development and support of government news. Because of such guidance, the former editor of *Working People's Daily,* U Soe Min, went into exile in 1977 because he said he was "sick of lying" (*Asiaweek,* 11 March 1977, p. 35). In Thailand, under the Thanin government, journalists in an act of survival, moved away from investigative reporting and political analyses. The government itself set up a model newspaper, *Chao Phya,* to do battle with and set an example for the private press. Of course, the model newspaper went all out to support the model government. After the 1977 change of administration, *Chao Phya* went out of existence (*The Nation Review,* 4 Nov. 1977).

Indochinese presses, like those of most socialist nations, promote government and party ideology through mass campaigns, but in all three countries, radio and loudspeakers have been more widely used for this purpose. Media in all three nations have urged people to leave the cities, to abandon their Western ways and to support developmental programs. Vietnamese dailies that formerly wrote of military victories over the United States, now play up road building and food production in the South.

Overt censorship appears from time to time in all Southeast Asian countries. Malaysians, Singaporeans, Indonesians and Filipinos, among others, regularly receive newspapers and periodicals they subscribe to with pages blackened or ripped out (*Media,* April 1976, p. 21). While living in Malaysia, I received the *Far Eastern Economic Review* (Hong Kong) with an entire section pulled out that I later discovered dealt with Malaysia. Before being banned in Malaysia, *Playboy* was scrutinized by censors who airbrushed out pubic areas on nudes. One day in 1978, subscribers to Singapore's *Straits Times* in Indonesia received their papers with black ink splattered over one-fourth of a page which contained an Indonesia election story (*Andelman,* 1976a, p. 6). The examples are endless.

Thanin's short-lived government in Thailand had a propensity for censorship, banning and burning books it considered politically subversive or pro-communist and establishing a strict seven-point censorship code that allowed for virtually no criticism of the government. Former Prime Miniser Kukrit Pramoj, addressing the first meeting of Thai press organizations called to protest governmental censorship in early 1977, termed the situation nearly intolerable; he was particularly upset that government censors cut pages from foreign periodicals. In Laos, a committee was set up in early 1977 to censor everything (*Media,* Feb. 1977, p. 12).

Despite guaranteeing freedom of the press and expression in at least three sections of its constitution, Burma in 1976, developed elaborate guidelines under which private publications were to be scrutinized (Burmese way of saying censored). These principles stressed that any publication opposing the Burmese socialist system and economy is to be banned, that criticism of personal shortcomings in executing socialist aims is tolerated only if it is constructive, that slanderous writing causing religious squabbles or supporting landlordism and capitalism is eschewed and that crime, sex and Western decadence are taboo. The guidelines even suggested that caution should be exercised in revealing accurate facts when to do so was detrimental to Burmese interests (London *Times,* 28 Aug. 1976, p. 4).

3.1.6 Conclusion

In the past, when writing about press freedom in Southeast Asia, this author has attempted to end on a bright note, pointing out encouraging aspects of the problem. At the dawn of the 1980s, the search for positive features about press-government relationships in Southeast Asia is a tiresome one. As the use of the press for developmental (read governmental or political in most instances) purposes becomes deeply entrenched in the region, as critical local and foreign newsmen are kept under tow and as governments continually redefine democratic principles to suit their own ends, there is not much to encourage a hopeful conclusion. Southeast Asian journalism has become a sterile wasteland, and the sad part is that a group of young, opportunistic journalists, who may not know much about the rich, independent tradition of the Asian press, seem to be taking it all in their stride, while the warnings of older newsmen seem to fly off into the silent air.*

---

* This chapter is reprinted from *Human Rights Quarterly.*

3.2 Burma
Paul P. Blackburn

3.2.1 Background

Once among Asia's liveliest and most outspoken, the newspapers of today's Burma have become muted organs of that nation's doctrinaire socialist/military regime. In its present form the Burmese press is seen as a "weapon" in the Burmese Government (GUB) arsenal of resources for achieving its national policies: Burman dominance over the economy, continuing progress in handling the ethnic and political insurgencies that still plague the country, consolidation of single-party government under Ne Win's Revolutionary Council (RC) and the Burma Socialist Programme Party (BSPP), passive neutralism in foreign affairs, and overall strengthening of national unity in line with the "Burmese Way to Socialism."[1]

Prior to the 1962 takeover by General (now Mr.) Ne Win's RC, the Burmese press was described by one observer as "a brawling infant in a fluid, overcrowded field largely centered in Rangoon.... The press can be checked but not directed by government. It is uninhibited and courageous, sometimes to the point of folly" (*Hollstein,* 1961, p. 351).

1   For an articulation of GUB ideological foundations, see Burma Socialist Programme Party, *The System of Correlation of Man and His Environment,* Rangoon: Ministry of Information, 1963; and Union of Burma, Revolutionary Council, *The Burmese Way to Socialism,* Rangoon: Ministry of Information, 1962.

Paul P. Blackburn is with the United States International Communication Agency. Dr. Blackburn was director, Tokyo American Center; United States Embassy cultural attaché in Japan, and served five years with USIA in Thailand. He studied communications and national development in Burma, Malaysia and Thailand.

With a total circulation of about 247,000, (*UNESCO*, 1964, p. 202)[2] pre-RC Burma had about 32 dailies, of which three were published in English, seven in Indian languages (two Tamil, two Urdu, two Telegu, and one Hindi), six in Chinese, and 16 in Burmese (with five of these published in Mandalay, four in Moulmein, and the remainder in Rangoon) (*Hollstein*, 1961, p. 352). In contrast, the press of Burma today consists of only seven dailies, all of them operated by the GUB. Five are published in Burmese and two in English, and their combined circulation is estimated at about 284,000 (*USIA*, 1972, p. 2).[3]

The history of Burmese newspapers offers few precedents that might have foretold this startling transformation of the one-time "brawling infant" into a tamed, government-dominated press. However, perhaps the tradition of colonial restrictions on newspaper activity has carried over in the thinking of modern-day administrators of Burma. In addition, the repressive clampdown by the RC upon seizing power in 1962 from U Nu's democratic government may find some parallel in the harsh measures towards the press adopted by King Thibaw after succeeding the more tolerant King Mindon Min in the 1870s. In any event, Burmese history contains numerous instances of drastic changes in policy when one regime has replaced another, and certainly the present government has been no exception to this pattern.

Burma's first papers appeared about 1836 in Moulmein, in what was then British-controlled territory. These were the English language *Moulmein Chronicle,* the Karen *Morning Star,* and the Burmese *Moulmein Times* (*Hollstein in Lent,* 1971, p. 140).[4] The first to be published in Burmese-controlled territory was the Burmese language *Ranabon Naypyidaw (Mandalay Gazette),* which appeared in Mandalay in 1874, in the period before the final British takeover of upper Burma in 1886. This paper had royal patronage and enjoyed relative freedom during King Mindon's reign. Of the 66 newspapers started between 1871 and

2   UNESCO figures covering 1960-62 listed Burma as having 39 dailies, seven more than indicated by Hollstein.

3   *Asian Press and Media Directory 1976-77* (p. 27) reported total circulation as 800,000, but when one adds circulations of individual newspapers listed in the directory, the total is closer to 280,000.

4   These and the following remarks on the pre-1962 press draw heavily on Hollstein's chapter in *Lent* (1971), especially pp. 140-51.

1941, only *New Light of Burma,* founded in 1919 and nationalized in 1969, has survived in one form or another. Most of the
others were very short-lived. Some, however, showed considerable
staying power, and a few distinguished themselves during various
phases of the independence struggle, despite colonialist restrictive
measures such as the Emergency Powers Act of 1931, which
proscribed statements undermining civil authority or creating
divisions within the society.[5]

Following the repressive World War II Japanese occupation, a
period in which Burma experienced its only direct pre-publication
censorship, 56 newspapers of all types quickly emerged on the
scene. Faced with government controls and scarcities of machinery
and newsprint, difficulties of news-gathering (particularly in the
areas of insurgency), and lack of managerial experience, only a
dozen of these had survived by 1950.

The 1950s were a "golden age" of Burmese journalism. In that
period, newspapers constructively played the role of "loyal
opposition" to the government by sharply analyzing and ques-
tioning official policies and activities. Among the noteworthy
dailies of the time were the English language *New Times of Burma,
Nation* (edited by U Law Yone, a prominent intellectual), and
Guardian (established by scholar Dr. Maung Maung), and the
vernacular dailies, *Kyemon* (Mirror), *Rangoon Daily, Oway* and
Hanthawaddy.

From 1958 to 1960 U Nu, who had been prime minister continuously since Independence in 1948, voluntarily turned power
over to a "caretaker government" headed by General Ne Win.
During this period, which presaged the post 1962 era, though at
the time it was thought to be only a temporary authoritarian
interlude in Burma's democratic development, the Ministry of
Information stepped up its scrutiny of publications and expanded
the placement activities of its Press Branch, and the regime used
an Emergency Powers (Temporary Amendment) Act to initiate
sanctions against papers considered pro-Communist or anti-
government. With U Nu's return to power in 1960, a more relaxed
and tolerant attitude towards the press reappeared. However, even

5   As reported in *Guardian,* 3 December 1970, p. 2, a history of the Burmese press
written by U Po Kyaw Myint credits the newspapers with an influential role in the fight
for independence during the 1930s. For contrary view, see Butwell, 1975.

this period saw considerable squabbling between press and government over a press reform bill, which ultimately was passed only four days before the Ne Win coup, thereafter to fall into oblivion.

When it captured total control of the reins of government in March 1962, the 15-member RC's writ extended only to the major cities and most of the Irrawaddy Valley, while ethnic and Communist insurgent groups held sway over much of the outlying countryside. Within the cities, moreover, commerce was still dominated by Chinese and Indian traders, a situation galling to the Burman majority which viewed it as an unwelcome legacy of the colonial period. The RC has been willing to accept some economic stagnation (there has in fact been minimal if any increase in per capita GNP during the decade that the RC has been in power, and rice exports have fallen to a small fraction of former levels) as a necessary price of breaking the grip of the "alien" merchants. This policy is justified in terms of a strong "self-help" attitude heavily permeated with a fear of over-involvement with foreigners. It is based on socialist economy, neutralism and political power in the hands of the BSPP in alliance with affiliated Workers' Councils and Peasants' Councils. Movement towards increased political participation, as exemplified by the 1973 constitutional referendum and the 1974 elections for a People's Congress, is intended to be a gradual extension of political participation within the context of a single-party (i.e., BSPP) system (*New York Times,* 19 Sept. 1973, p. 8).

3.2.2 *The Press Today*

Following the coup, the RC arrested offending journalists, started its own newspaper (the *Working People's Daily,* in English and Burmese), nationalized others and forced the suspension of all non-dailies and many of the dailies, either by indirect tactics — such as selective use of GUB advertising — or direct closure. In January 1966, the government proscribed the four Chinese and five Indian dailies still in existence, which at that point had an estimated circulation of about 27,000 (*USIA,* 1966, pp. 16-17). *Kyemon* (*Mirror*), *Botataung* (*Vanguard*) and *Guardian* were nationalized in September 1964, and *Hanthawaddy* and *New Light of Burma* in January 1969. The last newspaper to remain in private hands, *Rangoon Daily*, gave such undeviating support to the GUB as to be virtually indistinguishable in content from the nationalized papers. It limped along in precarious financial condition longer than the others, but finally had to close in August 1972 when its publication permit was withdrawn by the GUB. The only non-Rangoon newspaper now publishing is *Hanthawaddy*, which was moved to Mandalay in October 1969 to replace the pro-Peking *Ludu*, the one-time leading journal of upper Burma, closed in July 1967 during a period of worsening Sino-Burmese relations.

Thus, in contrast to the geographical dispersal, linguistic variety and wide ideological spectrum of the Burmese press of the 1950s, Burma's newspapers today are published only in Rangoon and Mandalay (with the former accounting for 95 per cent of circulation) and only in English and Burmese, and confine themselves to reporting on the achievements of the GUB. Critical comment consists of occasional stories, editorials and letters to the editor which point out shortcomings in the implementation of government programs, but never go so far as to question the validity of the Burmese Way to Socialism. Despite known ideological proclivities of individual writers and editors, and the subtle expressions of dissenting opinions which sometimes appear in print, idiosyncratic behavior is rather marginal. Essentially, the Burmese press today is an unalloyed instrument of official policy.

In addition to putting the lid on dissenting press content, the GUB has deprived the well educated Chinese and Indian minorities of access to newspapers in their own languages. In fact, no publications of any kind are allowed in Chinese and Indian languages, nor are they used for any programming on the Burma Broadcasting Service. The government in this way attempts to enhance national unity and its other development objectives through strictly controlling not only the political content of the newspapers but also the linguistic format within which ideas are circulated in the society.

3.2.3 Financial Woes

The major GUB arm affecting newspaper operations is the Ministry of Information, over 70 per cent of whose budget is devoted to the Central Press activity (e.g., see *Union of Burma,* 1966, pp. 116, 121-122). This division of the information pie reflects both the unusually low priority given to broadcast activities (Burma has no television, and conducts all of its broadcasting out of a single Rangoon facility) and also the total GUB control of the press. Despite the funds allocated for their management, however, the nationalized newspapers are supposed to be self-supporting. The following profits were reported for 1968-69; *Working People's Daily* (Burmese and English editions), K1.2 million (at that time the official exchange rate was US$1= 4.76 kyats); *Kyemon,* K2.0 million; *Botataung,* K800,000; *Guardian,* K60,000; and *New Light of Burma,* K50,000 (*Botataung,* 10 Dec. 1969, p. 2).[6] *Kyemon* was reported to have earned in the neighborhood of K2.0 million in 1970-71, but at the same time was criticized for taking too much of the very limited advertising available to the Burmese press and thus opening itself up to the charge of being an "advertisement paper" (*Working People's Daily,* 29 Feb. 1972, p. 1).

Among the Ministry of Information's press-related elements are the Press Management Board, which directs the nationalized newspapers, the Nationalized Printing Presses Supervisory Committee, the Sarpay Beikman (successor to the Burma Translations Society and the main government publishing element), the Printers and Publishers Central Registration Board and the Journalism School. Coming under the Directorate of Information is the News Agency Burma (NAB). NAB (Domestic) collects and distributes national news and issues official pronouncements and announcements, while NAB (External) screens, reproduces and provides the sole legal distribution channel for the daily intake from the international wire services. The Directorate of Information also supervises the Press and Publications Scrutiny Section, a post-publication review mechanism for newspapers and magazines.

The RC's 1962 Press Law (Printers and Publishers Registration Act) delineates the requirement for annual registration of newspapers, the rules for submission of publications for scrutiny

6   Despite these published figures, *Guardian* and *New Light of Burma* are believed to require heavy subsidization, and the seventh nationalized daily, *Hanthawaddy,* apparently suffered heavy losses before its relocation to Mandalay in late 1969.

and punishments for violations of the law. Though there is no pre-publication censorship (a requirement imposed, however, on materials put out by foreign embassies), pre-publication counsel is given to the press by Ministry of Information officials who periodically provide guidance on the priority and handling of major stories. Finally, broad responsibility for ensuring that the newspapers observe "the code of ethics of the press" belongs to the GUB-sanctioned Burma Press Council (*Union of Burma,* 1968, p. 151).

Between 1962 and 1973, daily circulation remained in the 245,000-285,000 range. Apparently, the figure had not changed by 1976. With a population of perhaps 31 million, Burma consumes less than one newspaper per 100 population, well below the "UNESCO minimum" recommended level of 10 newspaper copies per 100 of population. The low figure has persisted despite the fact that with an adult literacy rate of perhaps 70 per cent Burma is one of the most literate of the developing countries. The explanation for Burma's modest performance in newspaper output is related to the constraints imposed by antiquated equipment and shortages of imported newsprint, particularly the latter, added to an official policy which decrees that newspapers, as a social service in the cultural sector of national development, "shall flourish in direct proportion to the tides of socialist success like the lotus and the water's height" (*Working People's Daily,* 11 May 1973, p. 2). In other words, newspaper circulation expansion should be carried out in proportion to progress in other areas of economic development.

Describing its frustrations with putting out a newspaper in today's Burma, the *Working People's Daily* has commented with self-deprecating humor:

When the paper is delivered late to its subscribers some of the readers aptly dub it the Waiting People's Despair. The name sticks. As for us at the transmitting end of the paper, we are unhappy about the late delivery and, though we are fully sympathetic to readers when they complain about it, there is hardly anything we can do when the aged machines sometimes stubborn-ly refuse to work in spite of hard work and ingenuity of the engineers and workers. The machines are

TABLE 6.   Burma's Newspapers and Circulations

	1972	1976
English language papers: *Guardian*	14,000*	17,000**
Working People's Daily	18,000	17,000
Burmese language papers: *Kyemon (Mirror)*	73,000	51,000
Locktha Pyithu Nezin (Working People's Daily)	73,000	75,000
Botataung (Vanguard)	70,000	70,000
Hanthawaddy	18,000	22,000
New Light of Burma	18,000	30,000

Sources: *U.S. United States . Information Agency. "Country Data: Burma."
  Washington: USIA, 1 November 1972. (Mimeographed).
  **Asian Press and Media Directory 1976-77*. Hong Kong: Press Foundation of
  Asia, 1976-77.

fatigued. Spare parts, newsprint and ink are not plentiful. The Editors often find it difficult to put in all they want and have to be satisfied with publishing what they consider to be the most deserving. The technical staff are always hard-pressed to keep things going (*Working People's Daily*, 11 May 1973, p. 2).

If there was to be an unlimited supply of newsprint, estimates vary as to the increase in circulation that would result. In any event, it would probably be considerable. In 1969, *Botataung* offered the following comment:

It is known that the people are unable to subscribe to the papers they want to read .... Look at the *Botataung*. Many have criticized us for insufficient circulation. In a way, they are right. Today, our circulation is 60,000 daily. This is a limited quantity. If all the demands were met, circulation would reach the 150,000 mark. This is a wide gap, and to fill it is a problem. It is because of the budget allotted to newspapers. We have to use newsprint and other raw materials, all of which have to be bought with precious foreign exchange. Our allotments depend on the financial situation of the country. We have to function within our means, for which circulation has to be limited (*Botataung*, 10 Dec. 1969, p. 2).

Likewise, the *Working People's Daily* has said that though it wants to raise its Burmese language circulation from the 70,000 level to 150,000 "within three or four years . . . due to financial condition the circulation will not be increased beyond the present level in the immediate future" (*Working People's Daily*, 6 Jan. 1970, p. 2).

3.2.4 Government Controls

In addition to holding down circulation levels of indigenous newspapers, GUB is extremely selective about printed materials imported into the country in newspaper or magazine form. Although some international dailies are brought in for use by the government and foreign embassies, the only foreign newspaper to which members of the public may subscribe is the *Statesman* of Calcutta, and its daily circulation in Burma is not more than a few hundred.

The great bulk of the news in a typical issue of any of the seven Burmese newspapers comes from the NAB, which serves as both a government information service and a national news agency having general reporting as well as official news dissemination responsibilities. While NAB (Domestic) does not control all internal news, its coverage of national events is the basic staple of the press. The extent of reliance on this source is indicated by the following description:

> Gone are the days when individual newspapers competed in the mad hunt for scoops and sensations. All that the Burmese newspapers do today is to collect the daily news bulletin of the News Agency, Burma, make a selection out of its contents and publish the selected pieces according to their respective ideas of display. They do maintain reporting staff of their own but the reporters are generally used for routine assignments such as covering the arrival and departure of foreign visitors at the Rangoon Airport (*Tun*, 1970, p. 48).

NAB (External) subscribes to some 15 international wire services, representing all shades of international opinion, and issues its own selected compilation of these files in English for the local newspapers and other interested offices. In making this selection, NAB prides itself on the fact that it "has scrupulously maintained a standard of impartiality and a sense of objectivity in presenting coverage between news connected with opposing world blocs as well as between conflicting strands in international opinion" (*Union of Burma,* 1968, p. 151). Though there are occasions where contrasting, sharply-variant versions of the same international news story are presented side-by-side, the newspapers have some discretion regarding which accounts to publish. Moreover, NAB itself does not attempt to give equal space to Communist and non-Communist sources. In an analysis of 712 NAB news file items from 13 wire services distributed during a one-week period in June 1970, the writer found that only 57 (8 per cent) were from news agencies of Communist nations, whereas AFP had 254 items, AP 156, UPI 117 and Reuters 86. The GUB's use of the NAB as a funnel for all international news (except for that carried by international radio broadcasters and in the few foreign dailies and magazines allowed into the country) and most domestic news is consistent with its desire to exercise maximum governmental control over all messages, from whatever sources, reaching the general Burmese population.

The Journalism School, established in 1967, provides mainly in-service training for newsmen, armed forces personnel, BSPP cadre and various departments of the Ministry of Information. The basic course runs about 10 months, and normally involves from 30 to 40 students at any one time. Reflecting the GUB policy that journalistic ability and ideological correctness should go hand in hand, the course represents an attempt to simul-taneously train the students in the practical aspects of their profession and to inculcate them with the ideology of the revolution (*Working People's Daily,* 16 May 1968, p. 1).

Because the GUB regards the press as "the principal means of informing the working people of the country of the advances and progress of the revolution" (*Working People's Daily,* 16 March 1966, p. 2), the newspapers are given a key role in citizen mobilization efforts. For example, calling journalism "an effective

weapon in organizing and educating the people," Information
Secretary, Lt. Col. Tin Tun, in 1972, asked newspapermen to be
"able organizers and liaison officers" in order to "draw the entire
people to participate in drafting the new constitution and in the
successful implementation of the economic plan" (*Forward,*
1 Feb. 1972, p. 3). Journalists are also expected to keep firmly
in mind the distinction between common popularity and socialist
responsibility, as drawn in the following official comment:

> . . . winning the public confidence is the most primary
> requirement for the socialist press if it is to succeed in
> its objective of organizing the people for the socialist
> cause. Only when the people have faith in the socialist
> press will they yield to what it advocated . . . . To work
> up an image of the socialist press worthy of public
> confidence, socialist journalists must manifest their
> stand on the side of the people, feed them the truth
> and must do away with subjectivism, always reporting
> things objectively. Merely increasing the circulation
> by sensational journalism which appeals to the dark
> impulses of the people does not amount to building
> up a prestigious image of the socialist press; it is merely
> making the newspaper popular, which socialist journa-
> lists must avoid at all costs.[7]

Thus, Burmese newspapers are expected to give full support to
the national task, first by building their own image, second by
imparting information the GUB deems appropriate, and third
by inspiring the enthusiastic cooperation of the people.

3.2.5 Contents of Newspapers

With the papers' single-minded aim of gaining support for national
objectives, now almost completely absent are the light-hearted-
ness, the eye for sex and scandal, and the tenor of controversy
on matters great and small found in many newspapers elsewhere
in the region. The GUB feels that the concept of a free press
operating in symbiotic relationship with the government should
be rejected as an exploitative, divisive aspect of capitalism. In
contrast to this discredited theory of the press, current GUB press

7   Speech by Lt. Col. Tin Tun, reported in *Working People's Daily,* 23 July 1968, p. 1.

policy is seen as a significant step forward:

Whereas the press before 1962 liked to call itself "responsible" and "democratic," it actually did more harm than good to real public interest. The generally vague concept of journalism and the role of the Press, even among the newspapermen themselves, also led in some cases to the publication of undesirable items such as those emphasizing the sex angle. There was also the belief that a piece of news was news and must therefore be published regardless of its possible effect on public welfare. Now these ideas are no more (*Working People's Daily*, 5 Aug. 1969, p. 2).

Despite emphasis on ideological purity and the need to build support for official policies, some latitude — and even encouragement — is given to newspapers to make criticisms of certain aspects of GUB performance through news reports, editorial comments and letters to the editor. However, the press is not permitted to question the wisdom of the leadership or the RC's intentions of bringing about a socialist transformation of Burmese society. To make this point clear, the government has warned that "people's forum columns" are designed solely for "well-meant suggestions for the success of the socialist cause," and "must not be allowed to degenerate into a platform for anti-socialist elements" (*Working People's Daily*, 23 July 1968, p. 2). Moreover, journalists are expected to support the government in thought as well as deed. As Lt. Col. Tin Tun put it in a speech to newspaper workers: "It is not enough just to pay lip service by saying that the Party leadership is correct, but the conviction must stem from the mind and the heart" (*Working People's Daily*, 24 May 1970, p. 1).

In an effort to determine the relative amount of attention given to various issues, the writer conducted a content analysis of 595 *Working People's Daily* editorials published between 1 January 1968, and 30 September 1969. (Although this survey is rather old, its findings probably resemble the situation today.) Of these, 23.9 per cent (142 items) dealt with political matters, 8.4 per cent (50) with foreign policy questions, 28.4 per cent (169) with economic development programs, 9.1 per cent (54) with education, 3.5 per cent (21) with internal insurgency, 5.4 per cent (32) with medicine, 3.4 per cent (20) with mass media and 13.1 per cent (78) with other matters such as Burmese customs, traffic accidents and sports.

With less than 10 per cent of its editorials focusing on international .relations — and the great bulk of these dealing not with specific contentious issues but with the work of international organizations or else reaffirming the nation's neutralist posture — the inward looking focus of the Burmese press is clearly indicated.

Furthermore, in examining the 142 items falling under the general rubric of "political," the writer found only 17 that treated internal politics per se, a finding not surprising, given the absence of both partisan political activity and also any "cult of personality." On the other hand, however, this category contained 63 editorials classified as "ideological statements," in which the content was essentially an exhortation to the readers to change their ways of thinking. That an average of three editorials a month of this type appeared in the sample newspaper underlines the strong ideological permeation of the Burmese press. Related to these findings was the discovery that nearly all subjects — from national customs and culture to sports to education to ethnic minorities to specific economic activities — were given a national development angle and treated as having direct relevance to broad GUB aims. The overall impression received from a close reading of Burmese editorials is that they reflect a very sober and introspective press, which considers a wide spectrum of human activity relevant to national development, and which does not hesitate to use its facilities as a vehicle for exhortation and mobilization of the readership.

3.2.6 Conclusion

Though GUB often refers to mobilization of the populace through the press its placing of heavy constraints on circulation shows that it is not attempting to reach a wide mass audience. Instead, it seeks to program the press (and other already existing communications channels) in such a fashion as to impart to elite party, bureaucratic, military and academic audiences — and presumably through them to the people as a whole — the major ideological components of the Burmese Way to Socialism. Burmese mass media, then, are best described as being part of an elite-oriented, ideological system, in which the press plays the major role *vis-à-vis* the other media (see *Blackburn,* 1971, pp. 333-36).

The Burmese system, with its emphasis on control, cadre-contacts, mobilization and ideology, has some obvious features in common with other socialist countries, though some of these may place greater stress on the electronic media and may be more willing to permit media content in minority languages. Burma's reluctance in this latter regard is probably a function of the underlying fear by the dominant Burman group that in conditions of unbridled economic competition it might lose its pre-eminence. Lacking confidence in its ability to deal with domestic dissent and ethnic diversity, a strategy of single-community (i.e. Burman) dominance has been felt essential.

With passage in 1973 of a new constitution (albeit one formalizing BSPP single-party rule), circumscribed elections in 1974, and increasing widening of the BSPP base to embrace more of the nation's workers and peasants, it is possible that the Burmese press will gradually lose its present elite character through broadening of its readership and an opening up to a greater variety of opinion. These developments seem unlikely in the short term, however, given the government's policies of curtailing newsprint imports and its desire to continue to use the press as an unambiguous "weapon" in the struggle to achieve a socialist transformation of the society. On the other hand, Burmese history is replete with drastic shifts in policy accompanying changes in leadership, and it is plausible to speculate that the future may bring a Burmese mass media system very different from the one in existence today. About the only prediction one can safely make is that the GUB will not (in truth, cannot) take further steps to exercise greater control over the press. Surely, Burma can know no more complete press control than it is experiencing today.

3.2.7 *An Update, by John A. Lent*

Economically, newsprint problems continued to dog the Burmese press in the 1970s. In August 1973, for example, all newspapers halved their sizes; the country had to import newsprint because the only paper mill (state owned) did not produce any newsprint. By the mid-1970s, the state owned Trade Corporation 8 was distributing to print media an average of 150 tons per month, all of which was purchased at relatively high prices from neighboring countries, especially Bangladesh.

Politically, all media still follow President Ne Win's "Burmese Way to Socialism." When they do not, they pay the consequences. For example, in late 1975, the printing licenses of three publication houses — Moe Kyaw Aung Press, Pyi Shwebo Press and Thamadi Press — were revoked for printing unauthorized literature (*Asian Press and Media Directory 1976-77*, p. 27). The following year, a correspondent for Agence France-Presse was expelled for focusing on "the dark side" and omitting successes. The expulsion order included this statement on journalism:

> A good journalist is one who strives to report what he sees or what he knows after meticulous authentication, whether he likes what he sees and agrees with what he hears, irrespective of his personal belief and ideological conviction. One who does not report true facts, who blacks out the good side and focuses on the negative side is no longer a journalist but one who insults the world's reading public (*Media*, May 1976, p. 3).

This view of what a journalist should be coincides with some comments made by the Burma scholar, Richard Butwell. Writing in 1975, Butwell said that perhaps there have been a few myths built around the Burmese press. First of all, he doesn't believe the press was ever as free or important under U Nu as is generally claimed. Second, he thinks that the press today is not that different from what it was a generation ago when U Nu and the "independence-winning Anti-Fascist People's Freedom League politicians" were in power. In fact, his belief is that Burmese newspapers may be freer than those in any other single-party or non-party dictatorship.

Concerning the contents of the Burmese press today, Butwell said most news is "government accounting of what it is doing (or exhortations by government leaders to the population to do something or not to do something)"; that there is no news on political rivalries, ambitions or relationships, but that reporting is usually "straight and apparently accurate." Citing June 1975 student demonstrations against the Burmese government, Butwell said the rioting was given front page for several days, and the government response to the riots was treated objectively. Most domestic reporting is not on politics, but on development, taking the form of accounts of reports to workers' and peasants' groups by high government officials. Foreign news is more balanced with several sides to an issue presented, and stories on foreign policies of Southeast Asian neighbors seem to illustrate in detail the value of other strategies other than that of Burma. Finally, according to Butwell, the press today is a "no-nonsense press," not publishing rumor or conjecture as bona fide political news as was done previously. What are the characteristics, then, of the Burmese press? Butwell said:

> It is not seriously a dialogue or discussion press, it is not a politically competitive press, and it is not a critical press. It is, however, a press that prints most of what can still be called political news and that is surprisingly free to report what actually takes place in the country — despite the fact of dominantly government ownership (*Butwell*, 1975).

3.3 Indonesia
Michael H. Anderson

Under the authoritarian regime of the late President Sukarno, Indonesia was an impoverished nation — socially, politically, and economically — in which press freedom and independence did not exist. The charismatic founder of the republic believed that an inquiring press was incompatible with the "Guided Democracy" he and his Marxist-oriented supporters wished to build.

Today, there is change in the tropical Indonesian air, and Indonesian leaders and journalists are hard at work trying to rehabilitate the country after the frenzied 1950s and 1960s. Despite a setback brought about by violent riots in January 1974, the "New Order" (Orde Baru) military government of President Suharto appears to be on the road to developing a progressive, stable society.

Suharto has brought stability to the often-turbulent archipelago, and the press — like other institutions — is beginning to revive in the fresher air of freedom. Caution and realistic action — not instability and ideological trappings — are features of the "new" Indonesian political scene, and newspapers are displaying the vigor and independence associated with societies in a state of resurgence following a period of repression (see 3.1.1).

In 1971, the country's first national elections since 1955 were held, and the large majority for Suharto's GOLKAR alliance is cited as evidence that Indonesia is on the road to recovery.

Michael H. Anderson spent three years in Malaysia where he was associated with the South East Asia Press Centre and University of Penang. He has professional newspaper experience in the United States and has travelled extensively in Southeast Asia, including Indonesia. He has finished a Ph.D. at the East-West Center, Honolulu.

Indonesians — tired of political unrest and flamboyant leadership — demonstrated approval of Suharto and the major policy changes which have occurred since 1965 when Sukarno was turned out. The veteran Asian journalist, Tarzie Vittachi, who has studied the Indonesian scene since independence, says the current Indonesia experiment in parliamentary democracy is the most "home grown" of any in Asia:

It is by no means perfect — it is still experimental and will evolve through experience into something recognizable to existing reality rather than to ideological niceties. It provides a forum for varied opinion and criticism without stultifying national effort through the kind of permanent opposition that is established by the Western parliamentary models (*Vittachi,* 1973, p. 3).

David B. H. Denoon has observed that a characteristic of the current political system is "a remarkably free but ideological and unsophisticated press" and that "criticism of the government is certainly more open and biting than that allowed in Singapore, Thailand, Hong Kong, or the Indochinese states" (*Denoon,* 1971, pp. 337-38).

Indonesia — at least until the 1974 press crackdown following the first major rioting since Suharto came into power — had become a notable exception to the recent move among Asian nations towards more — rather than less — press controls. It was also an exception to the rule that once a country has experienced severe press restrictions, its journalists at first find it difficult to live without them.

3.3.1 The Indonesian Scene

Indonesia — the strategically placed "sleeping giant" of Asia with about 130 million people and the natural resources to become a great power — is beset with numerous difficulties as it strives for modernization and a return to constitutional government.

Any discussion of the contemporary press in this sprawling island-nation must take into account two basic facts of Indonesian life: it is still very much a developing society, and Sukarno had an enormous impact on journalism and the general political environment.

In 1973, this writer commented:

Perhaps the best way to think of Indonesia is as the classic, textbook example of 'the developing country.' Mention a development problem and chances are Indonesia is struggling to overcome it. Regardless of the factors considered — economic, social, education, political, or communication — the country is among the least developed in the world today (*Anderson,* 1973, p. 15).

Christopher Lucas, calling Indonesia "a Happening," has observed: "In this mind-blowing tumult, the anthropologist can stop off anywhere between the Stone Age and the Space Age" (*Lucas,* 1970, p. 42).

A brief list of the more critical problems facing this vast, complex country includes:

Overpopulation. Indonesia is the fifth most populous country in the world, and its 2.8 per cent growth rate is among the highest anywhere (*UNDP,* 1973, p. 1). Population distribution is extremely uneven, and about two-thirds of the people crowd onto Java with 5 per cent of the land. More than 80 per cent of the people live in rural areas, but urbanization is progressing rapidly as jobs and the glamor of big-city life are attracting people into urban areas from the *kampongs.* The influx of rural migrants into Jakarta — one of the world's fastest growing capitals, with about 5 million people — has become so great that the government has had to declare it a "closed city."

Poverty. Seventy per cent of the people are subsistence farmers, and the per capita annual income — about $100 — is one of the world's lowest. In 1974, Sydney Schanberg of the *New York Times* wrote about the gap between the haves and the have-nots: "There are two worlds in this vast Asian nation along the equator — the rarefied world of government balance sheets that show billions of dollars and the human world in the teeming villages and city streets where per capita income is still 25 cents a day or less" (*Schanberg,* 1974, p. 13-A).

Cultural pluralism. "Unity in Diversity" is the motto of incredibly diverse Indonesia, where several hundred ethnic groups with a variety of languages, customs and religions are found.

Eapen wrote about the rich Indonesian cultural fabric:
> The sophistication and intellectualism found in Jogja-
> karta, the elegance and refinement of the Balinese, the
> Christian orientation of the people in Flores, the mod
> culture of Jakarta youth, the modernizing Toba Batak,
> the slowly changing tribes of West Irian, etc. provide a
> complex heterogeneous cultural pattern and pose many
> problems for those involved in communications (*Eapen,*
> 1973b, p. 51).

Geographic isolation. The third largest Asian nation, Indonesia
consists of 13,677 islands (about 1,000 are inhabited) spread
across 3,200 miles from Sumatra in the west to West Irian in the
east.

Inadequate education system. Literacy is estimated at about 65
per cent in urban areas and 41 per cent in rural areas (*Read and
Woods,* 1971, app. 1, p. 2). School has been made free and compulsory through sixth grade, but a 1973 United Nations report
indicated why Indonesia's education problems are among the
world's most difficult:
> In the 6 to 24-year-old group, it is now estimated that
> '40 per cent have not had the opportunity of attending
> school, while of the remaining 60 per cent, more than
> half fail to reach the sixth grade. Most children attend
> school only for two or three years at most. There is a
> crucial shortage of teachers, facilities, and supplies. The
> small percentage of students who go on to college or
> university face scant employment opportunities, and
> there is a sizable "brain-drain" to other countries. Even
> more extensive is the brain-drain from rural to over-
> crowded urban areas by students having secondary
> school education (*UNDP,* 1973, p. 6).

Each of these, among other, problems worsened during the
upheaval of Sukarno's one-man rule. Schools, for example, were
virtually closed for several years in the 1960s, and the country's
already weak politico-economic infrastructure fell apart as
Sukarno stressed ideology and high-sounding objectives, rather
than realistic policies that would help the people.

The press, too, deteriorated during these years, and only now has some stability and confidence been injected into the "fourth estate."

3.3.2 Press Profile

Anyone who does not believe there is a correlation between underdevelopment of mass communications and underdevelopment in general ought to take a close look at the Indonesian situation.

UNESCO has suggested that every nation should try to provide at least the following facilities for every 100 persons: 10 copies of newspapers, five radio receivers, two television receivers.

In Indonesia, low levels of literacy, personal income and urbanization have contributed to a low demand for all media. Consequently, the country falls below each of the minimum UNESCO-suggested levels. An optimistic evaluation of current media facilities shows these unofficial results for every 100 Indonesians: one newspaper copy, two radio receivers, 0.2 television receivers.[1]

It should be emphasized that Indonesia — more than many nations — suffers from a dearth of reliable press statistics. Sumono Mustoffa, head of the Press Foundation of Indonesia, has understated the problem: "Real, comprehensive work on the Indonesian press, let alone research on it, has yet to be done. Whatever raw data available are scattered and in Bahasa Indonesian [the national language]."[2]

Data about the press must be treated cautiously because — regardless of their source — they are often incomplete and inconsistent. Newspaper circulations, for example, have been exaggerated so that editors could charge higher advertising rates and gain a larger share of scarce newsprint.

Despite this major difficulty in acquiring reliable information about the press, it is obvious that newspapers have still not fully

1   These unofficial figures are based on an estimated 2,550,000 radios, 200,000 television receivers, and 1.5 million daily newspaper circulation. For data about Indonesian mass media, see Press Foundation of Asia, *The Asian Press and Media Directory,* Manila: PFA, 1974. In 1975, the number of radios was estimated at 4,227,530, the number of television receivers at 399,271, and daily newspaper circulation at 1.8 million (*Asian Press and Media Directory 1976-77,* pp. 82-83.)

2   Personal correspondence with Sumono Mustoffa, head, Press Foundation of Indonesia, 10 Dec. 1973.

recovered from the oppression and the chronic economic problems of the Sukarno years. In early 1974, newspaper circulation was still almost 700,000 less than its 1966 peak of 2 million copies daily, and the press continued to be weak and in a state of flux (see *Agassi, 1969*). Newspapers come and go, circulation fluctuates greatly and most editors operate on very small budgets due to the generally slow rate of economic development.

Clearly, Indonesia is not awash in newspapers. According to unofficial 1972 figures, the country had about 130 dailies with a circulation of about 1,362,050 and about 424 weeklies/periodicals with a circulation of 4,074,800.[3] If each copy of a daily paper were shared by six persons, the newspaper reading public would be about 8 million, or 6 per cent of the population. Most of these readers are in urban areas since newspapers do not reach many rural areas where the vast masses live. Figures for 1975 listed 285 newspapers and periodicals, 65 of which were dailies, 114 weeklies (*Asian Press and Media Directory 1976-77, p. 82*). Even if the country's physical infrastructure permitted papers to reach remote areas regularly, the average person could not afford them. Even the average urban dweller cannot afford a regular subscription, although he might occasionally buy a paper, especially if it features some sensational news. Most papers cost about US 6 cents or 25 rupiahs. A 1972 study of three villages near the major provincial city of Bandung revealed how little Indonesia's poor masses are exposed to mass media. For example, 50 per cent of the villagers said they had "never or nearly never read a newspaper"; 62 per cent said they "either have never read a magazine or have read one only once or twice in a lifetime"; and 69 per cent said they had no contact with the movies. Radio fared better; 57 per cent listened to it daily, 21 per cent at least weekly (*Jackson and Moeliono, 1972, pp. 19-21*).

An important characteristic of the Indonesian press, then, is that it addresses itself primarily to elite, urban Indonesians rather than to the masses. According to Eapen,

> Members of this public are the consumers of the printed medium, the people with political awareness and with

3   This data appeared in a PAB report in *Bek's Daily,* 19 March 1973. The agency's report attributed these figures to a "statement of account submitted by President Suharto" to the People's Consultative Assembly (MPR), 12 March 1973.

some education. They include teachers, members of the small business community, and the middle and lower ranges of the civil and commercial services. They form the bulk of the articulate public serving a relay function in the communication processes. It is difficult to assess their size (*Eapen,* 1973b, p. 51).

In 1973, Jakarta, the country's news center, had 22 dailies which accounted for more than half of the country's total daily circulation. (At the end of 1975, there were 17 dailies in Jakarta.) The provincial press, however, was sizable, and most provincial capitals had at least two dailies and a number of weeklies. Medan, the capital of North Sumatra, for example, had about 10 dailies.[4] Bandung boasted *Pikiran Rakyat,* one of the country's best provincial dailies.

The most successful papers are the so-called "independents" with the government-linked newspapers a distant second. Highly nationalistic, most papers are affiliated with one of these major interest groups: the military, the Moslems, the Christians, the Nationalist Party (PNI) or the intellectuals. By law, all newspapers must be owned and managed by Indonesians.

Another characteristic of contemporary journalism in Indonesia has been the growing strength of the Abri (Armed Forces) press since 1965. The country has no official government newspaper, but military publications and many so-called "independent" publications maintain close ties with the Suharto government.

The leading military paper is the army's *Berita Yudha (War News* — cir. 30,000), but other Armed Forces dailies have played important roles in Indonesian journalism since Sukarno's overthrow.

Although opinions differ on this point, *Kompas (Compass* — cir. 190,000) appears to be the country's largest and most respected newspaper. It is associated with the small Catholic Party and is highly regarded for its professionalism, including its serious news coverage and constructive editorials. *Kompas,* also published in an attractive, 16-page offset format, continues to gain circulation and advertising.

4   For a list of dailies, news agencies and foreign correspondents in Indonesia, see Republic of Indonesia, Department of Information mimeograph list, No. 013/H.O/4/71, April 1971. For a later listing of Jakarta publications, see Republic of Indonesia, Department of Information Handbook 6, *Pers Ibukota Data Hasil Inventarisasi: 1972-73.*

Another of Indonesia's better papers is *Sinar Harapan (Ray of Hope* — cir. 110,000), the major afternoon paper. Affiliated with the Christian political party, the paper is considered liberal and financially sound. Its flamboyant coverage sometimes verges on the scandalous and gets its editors into trouble with authorities. Unlike most Jakarta papers which are staffed by Moslem Javanese, *Sinar Harapan* is staffed by enterprising Protestant Bataks from North Sumatra and Menadonese from North Sulawesi (*Bangkok Post,* 15 Jan. 1973).

One of the country's prestigious older dailies was the *Indonesia Raya (Greater Indonesia* — cir. 30,000 before its suspension) (see 3.1.4). Its internationally renowned, award-winning editor, Mochtar Lubis, is a long-time Sukarno foe and the country's best-known journalist. The paper resumed publication in 1968 and continued until its death to be critical of the government and to have close ties with intellectuals. Unlike most other dailies which relied on outside printers, the *Indonesia Raya* had its own presses.

KAMI (Ours — cir. 15,000) had been, journalistically, one of the best papers. Started by the "Generation of '66" independent youth movement which opposed Sukarno, the paper was an intellectual, cosmopolitan publication until its publishing permit was revoked in 1974. Its influence extended far beyond its small circulation because of the important role students play in Indonesian politics. *KAMI*'s editors had strongly supported press freedom, including the right of anti-government papers like *El Bahar (The Sea*) and *Suluh Marhaen (Torch of Proletariat*) to exist (*Agassi,* 1969, pp. 41-42). These two pro-Sukarno papers ceased publication in 1971.

Rosihan Anwar's intellectual paper, *Pedoman (Compass* — cir. 15,000), is the voice of the banned Socialist party. The paper is a strong advocate of non-alignment and — unlike Indonesian papers generally — features excellent coverage of foreign affairs. Its publication was suspended in 1974 by the government.

Publisher M. B. Diah, former Minister of Information under Suharto, is Indonesia's Hearst or Pulitzer. He runs *Merdeka (Freedom* — cir. 100,000), a daily which reflects "neo-Sukarnoism" and is often strongly anti-U.S. The paper is inexpensive (less than US 3 cents a copy), and its sensational news coverage and attractive offset format make it popular. Diah's publishing empire also includes *Topik* (cir. 20,000), one of the country's three *Time*-style news magazines which have become increasingly popular since the first appeared in 1970. The two other news magazines are *Tempo* (cir. 32,500) and *Express* (cir. 24,000) (*Hayward,* 1973, p. 4). *Express* was suspended by the government in 1974.

Nusantara (*Archipelago* — cir. 10,000) was a progressive, pro-Western paper that was banned between 1960 and 1967. In 1972 its chief editor, T. D. Hafas, was convicted of libel for insulting Suharto and the government with his paper's zealous coverage of high-level corruption (*Samson,* 1973, pp. 128-29). Later, in 1974, the paper's permit was revoked by the government. (Corruption is widespread in Indonesia, and students, editors and intellectuals have long battled to stop it.)

Pos Kota (*City Post* — cir. 150,000) is extremely popular with the average newspaper buyer in Jakarta. The paper concentrates on local news and is sex- and sensation-oriented.

Newspaper mortality rate is very high, and few editors can afford to operate truly independent publications. Few papers have circulations above 50,000 and most have circulations under 10,000. Economic and political pressures have forced many weak papers to merge, and some of the country's economically weak papers and scandal sheets have had to fold. In 1973, there were only half as many newspapers publishing as there had been three years before, and local papers had been especially hard hit by competition from the large Jakarta dailies (*Hayward,* 1973, p. 4).

Many papers have to depend on circulation since advertising revenue is very limited. Indonesian businesses are simply too weak to afford advertising space. In 1972 they spent only US$10 million on all forms of advertising, and about 60 per cent went to newspapers (*Effendi,* 1973a).

National news dominates the content of most Jakarta and provincial newspapers. Newspapers generally appear in four-page editions. According to the Indonesian Department of Information, one page is usually filled with news reports of national interest; another is allocated for advertisements; one half page is devoted to foreign news reports, and the remaining one and a half pages are devoted to problems of local interest and sundry issues (*Sukarno*, 1970, p. 1).

Nearly all Indonesian newspapers are published in the national language, Bahasa Indonesia. Indonesia differs from many of her neighbors which have lively non-vernacular newspapers, usually English and Chinese. English has surpassed Dutch as Indonesia's second language, but there are only two English language papers in Jakarta, neither politically significant. A few provincial papers also appear in regional languages, such as Sundanese, but they, too, are insignificant.

Although the country has a Chinese population of about 3 million, the government has not allowed independent Chinese language publications since 1959. Government officials fear that Chinese character papers would carry propaganda harmful to Indonesian unity. *Harian Indonesia* (*Indonesian Daily* — cir. 75,000), the only Chinese paper in the country, is a Jakarta-based, army publication. Indonesian Chinese, however, are allowed to own and operate publications, but they must print in the national language.

The presence of a large, unassimilated Chinese community in Indonesia continues to be a sensitive issue, and anti-Chinese feelings are widespread. Many Indonesians resent the relative affluence of many Chinese businessmen and affiliate them with GESTAPU — the abortive communist coup of 30 September 1965. Several hundred thousand Chinese were killed in the bloody purge of communists and their "sympathizers," and the government has placed severe restrictions on the Indonesian Chinese of this generation.

3.3.3 The Political Climate

Press development is always closely intertwined with political development, and any discussion of Indonesia's journalism must include political, as well as economic, social and cultural, factors.

Sukarno, the individual most responsible for press development, or its lack, ruled Indonesia from independence from the Dutch in 1949 until his overthrow by army officers with the support of students and intellectuals after the abortive coup.

The economic chaos, violence, corruption, xenophobia and authoritarianism of the Sukarno post-independence years are well-documented,[5] and they inevitably contributed to press instability. As Sullivan has written:

> Under Guided Democracy, the press found the soil poisoned, the air polluted and itself all too vulnerable to the capricious storms which raged over the Indonesian landscape. In a speech to Indonesian journalists, Sukarno once totally rejected the idea of a free press. 'I definitely declare now that in a revolution there should be no press freedom. Only a press supporting the revolution should be allowed to exist.' The others, he added, must be eliminated. And so they were (*Sullivan,* 1967, p. 105).

One of those "eliminated" was Mochtar Lubis of *Indonesia Raya.* He dared to criticize Sukarno and to expose government corruption and, consequently, found himself in jail or under house arrest for nearly 10 years. Later, he was to win one of the first Ramon Magsaysay Awards for his editorial crusading on behalf of human rights and press freedom (see 3.1.4).

Another prominent editor, Rosihan Anwar, has said: "From 1959 until the emergence of the present new order, Indonesia was ruled under President Sukarno's Guided Democracy, and for about six years the press was completely emasculated, with journalists who were sycophants of the 'great Leader of the Revolution' " (*Anwar,* 1973, p. 4).

Antara[6], the national news agency, was taken over by the PKI (Indonesian Communist Party), and newspapers were forced to become obedient "tools" of the government in its fight against colonialism, liberalism and imperialism. All traces of professionalism disappeared, and "cooperative" journalists signed a pledge of loyalty to Sukarno or were arrested and forced to stop publishing.

5   For details about the early days of Indonesian journalism, see van der Kroef, 1954, pp. 337-46. For details about the press during the Sukarno years, see Oey, 1971.

6   Antara (Between) is the most widely used Indonesian news agency, but the country has two others — an army news agency (Pusat Pemberitaan Angkatan Bersendjata, or PAB) and a private agency (Kantorberita Nasional Indonesia, or KNI). Indonesia's foreign minister, Adam Malik, was a journalist in 1937 and helped establish ANTARA as a crusading agent of the anti-Dutch, independence movement. KNI was formed as an independent agency in 1966 by a group of Jakarta journalists. For details, see Eapen, 1973a, pp. 1-12.

The erosion of press criticism was disturbing to many journalists, who since independence days had enjoyed a tradition of vigorous liberalism and muckraking. Sullivan explained what the press was like before the crackdown:

> The halcyon years of Indonesian journalism were the three or four immediately following the end of the colonial struggle with the Dutch. The native press has been an important integral part of the revolution. Its journalists had prestige, a feeling of their own significance, a place in the new Indonesian society. The press was free in the sense that it was not subject to formal, government-backed restrictions. It was, moreover, recognized as an important force in shaping public awareness and public opinion in Indonesia (*Sullivan*, 1967, p. 99).

Rosihan Anwar, in *IPI Report,* has said:

> During the 1950s until towards the end of that decade Indonesia was known as one of the few countries in Asia with a free and lively press. It was also a press with strong political direction. No government under the then prevailing liberal political system could afford to ignore the press which had toppled a Cabinet, over a foreign policy issue such as happened when the Indonesian Foreign Minister in 1950 moved too closely to the American side, acting against the non-aligned policy of the republic (*Anwar,* 1973, p. 4).

But non-alignment, constitutional government and a critical press gradually were eliminated as Sukarno declared that parliamentary government was not possible in his fragile, young nation. Dutch and Chinese papers were banned, foreign and local journalists were brought under control of the Ministry of Information and newspapers took on a certain sameness as they were all filled with Antara "news" releases.

By 1965, *Editor & Publisher* (6 March, p. 37) could report: "In the springtime of Indonesian independence from the Netherlands, newspapers blossomed and flourished in a chaotic profusion of political hues. But the fall of democracy has brought a narrower, duller spectrum: non-committal brown, craven yellow, and Chinese Red."

While the government was tightening its control on the press and other key social institutions, it was losing its control on the economy, and the country verged on bankruptcy. According to the *Area Handbook for Indonesia — 1970,*

> When General Suharto assumed control of the government in 1966, the economy lay in ruins. Industrial production had reached its nadir, with plants either idle or operating at a small fraction of capacity; government finances were in chaos; inflation was raging; the country had become isolated internationally in the economic as well as the political sphere and was unable to meet its foreign debt obligations (*U.S. Army, 1970*, p. 367).

Newspapers were hard hit by economic instability and by the deteriorating transportation and communication facilities. Newsprint was in short supply, equipment was sadly out-of-date and the price of a newspaper skyrocketed as a result of run-away inflation.

The over-all effect of government mismanagement was a dramatic decline in both numbers of papers and daily circulation. According to Agassi, "In August 1959, there were 94 dailies in all languages with a total circulation of 1,036,250; by the end of 1960 this was reduced to 47 dailies in all languages with a total circulation of 576,000" (*Agassi,* 1969, pp. 14-15).

Journalism under Sukarno's Guided Democracy was both politically and economically risky and, as one Indonesian student wrote, people preferred to buy rice, rather than newspapers (*Pardede,* 1972, p. 13).

3.3.4 *Transition to Stability*

What is the situation in Indonesia today?

The painful Sukarno experience is still fresh in the minds of many Indonesians, and predictions about the future of the country are risky, epsecially in the light of the 1974 student demonstrations and the continued gap between the haves and the have-nots (see. 3.1.1).

However, most Indonesia-watchers agree that the country is on the way to achieving her potential after years of instability and turmoil. Neill, for example, wrote in 1973 that "regardless of how impatient anyone may be to see further change, in broad historical

view General Suharto has done a remarkably good and rapid job
of rebuilding Indonesia and has permitted as much of the democratic process as is feasible in this country which was not heir
to a democratic tradition (*Neil,* 1973, p. 374).

"Major economic and political changes have occurred in
Indonesia since 1966," Denoon has written. "During this period,
caution, skill at political manoeuvre, and pragmatism have
characterised the Suharto government's choices in its domestic
political, economic, and foreign policy moves" (*Denoon,* 1971,
p. 332).

The end of "confrontation" with neighboring Malaysia,[7] the
return of international agencies to Indonesia, the growth of
regional cooperation through the Association of Southeast Asian
Nations (ASEAN), the booming tourist business, and the increase
in petroleum production are but a few specific signs of progress.

The press, too, has undergone major changes with the arrival
of the "new order." The political demagoguery, severe press
restrictions and constant state of economic unrest are gradually
diminishing, and journalists, at least until the mid-1970s, were
able to operate in a climate that gave them more room to
maneuver than at any time since the early 1950s, when political
parties and newspapers of all viewpoints operated unhampered.

In addition, the gentlemen of the Indonesian press seem to be
talking more about the need for a responsible, forward-looking
press as a cornerstone for the "new" Indonesia. More than two-
thirds of the population is under 25, and editors generally are
gearing their coverage to the new generation of readers who were
born after independence was achieved.

Like other institutions in Indonesia, the press is in a difficult
period of transition, but there seems to be reason for optimism
that the press can become a free and vigorous institution within
an egalitarian Indonesian society.

Agassi, for example has said:

> With the stabilization of the rupiah and a more liberal
> import policy, the technical and financial situation of

7   The end of Indonesia's campaign to "crush" Malaysia meant that the traditionally
close ties between the two predominately Malay-Moslem nations could resume. In 1972,
the two governments finally reached agreement on a common spelling system and the
flow of information between them has increased dramatically since then.

the press should eventually improve, and it should be able to produce dailies whose price will be within the reach of the average literate Indonesian. Adding to this a significant improvement in the transportation system — and a large market of the small town and rural literate population could open up (*Agassi*, 1969, p. 19).

Government censorship and other restrictive policies had nearly disappeared until the mid-1970s. M. Sivaram, an International Press Institute consultant, had argued: "Now that these controls and guidance have been abandoned, to a large extent, and Indonesia thrown open to the world, the resultant winds of change have begun to sweep the newspaper front in this country" (*Sivaram*, 1967, p. 6).

Mochtar Lubis had said that the "process of recovery has been very painful and slow because of the depressed economic situation and the deterioration of transportation, communication, and printing facilities which have been the legacy of the Sukarno regime" (*Lubis*, 1968, p. 2).

Many problems — including obsolete equipment, the absence of business management techniques, scarcity of advertising,[8] newsprint shortage, corruption, poor distribution system and lack of trained journalists — remain, but the Indonesian press has survived.

Not only does the press survive but it is moving ahead. Several of the financially strong papers in Jakarta, Surabaya, Semarang and Bandung have switched from letterpress to offset printing; there seems to be a new emphasis on objective reporting; the government is trying to improve the transportation and communication facilities upon which good journalism depends, and a new breed of journalist interested in a full-time, non-political professional career is slowly replacing the old order, "Generation of '45" journalist who probably got into journalism through political activism.

8   Indonesia-operated advertising agencies have complained that the big foreign agencies now operating in the country are forcing them out of business. They have asked the government to help encourage foreign corporations — with their large advertising budgets — to have accounts with Indonesian rather than foreign agencies. The indigenous agencies complain that it is difficult to survive on small Indonesian business accounts only.

In addition, organizations like the Indonesian Journalists Association (Persatuan Wartawan Indonesia); the semi-official Indonesian Press and Public Opinion Institute (Lembaga Pers dan Pendapat Umum); the Press Foundation of Indonesia (Yayasan Pembina Pers Indonesia), and the Newspaper Publishers Union (Serikat Perusahaan Suratkabar) are struggling to raise professional standards and stimulate the growth of a strong newspaper industry.

And some of the prestigious liberal papers banned by Sukarno have resumed publication, and a new — but ambiguous — press law has been passed to provide a legal framework within which journalists can operate.

3.3.5 The "New Order"

The 1966 law — "The Basic Principles of the Press" — bans censorship, establishes a press council under the Minister of Information, requires local press ownership and guarantees the press "the right of control, criticism and correction of a corrective and constructive nature" (*Republic of Indonesia*, 1966, p. 7).

The new law, however, is subject to wide interpretation, and critics point out that the Department of Information, local military commanders and Kopkamtib (The Operation Command for the Restoration of Security and Order) continue to have undue influence on the press.

The law, for example, says that "during the transitional period" newspapers must still have a government license to publish (*Republic of Indonesia*, 1966, pp. 14-15). It also prohibits publication of Communist or anti-*Pancasila* material. *Pancasila*, the country's basic official ideology, includes five principles: belief in one God, nationalism, humanitarianism, social justice and democracy.

During the first six months of 1973, Reuter reported, Indonesian authorities burned 18 tons of banned Communist and pornographic material. This reportedly was only two tons less than the amount destroyed in all of 1972 (in *Christian Science Monitor*, 17 Aug. 1973).

Suharto has said that the press is one of the major vehicles through which the people can participate in Indonesian development and that the government will guarantee free expression. But not everyone agrees that the press has become its old, free self again.

A *Far Eastern Economic Review* report (9 Oct. 1971, p. 50) of the Asian press scene said,

> The let-up under President Suharto is, as far as the law is concerned, more in form than in substance. Indeed, new government regulations promulgated in the wake of the abortive coup in 1965 formally buried the concept of independent newspapers. Demanding uniformity from all newspapers, the regulations decreed that every paper should become the official organ of a recognized political party and that provincial newspapers should change their names to match those of the capital editions representing their respective sponsors.

It remains to be seen how far conventional press freedom will be tolerated in the "new" Indonesia. The government, after all, is dominated by the military, and generals have never been known for their tolerance. They have, however, been known for "guiding" public opinion and for keeping a close eye on the news media.

At least through 1973, the Indonesian press had managed to remain comparatively free and frank. According to the *Far Eastern Economic Review* (9 Oct. 1971, p. 50):

> After all, it is a country where students still demonstrate, and effectively. The independent spirit of the Indonesian is reflected in many of the newspapers. Reporting often is lively and cartoons are a staple diet. There is no official censorship. But there are lines which may not be crossed.

Foreign correspondent Henry S. Hayward, writing from Jakarta, has said: "While editors sometimes criticize the government for genuine or supposed shortcomings, the government does not hesitate to slap back at the press when it appears to get out of line" (*Hayward*, 1973, p. 4).

Sinar Harapan has been "out of line" several times recently. For example, in 1973, the government shut down the paper for 10 days in what some considered an arbitrary manner. Kopkamtib authorities muzzled the paper after it had prematurely published budget figures that Suharto was to have announced to Parliament several days later. The government said that the newspaper's "scoop" was irresponsible and had discredited both the president and members of Parliament (*Bangkok Post,* 15 Jan. 1973).

In late 1973, Kopkamtib commander General Sumitro warned the press not to emulate the "criticizing mania" of Western newspapers. In an open letter to the highly critical *Indonesia Raya,* Sumitro called on papers to stop modelling themselves on foreign papers that cultivated the habit of regarding government critics as heroes and its supporters as stooges (*Agence France-Press,* 29 Dec. 1973).

Other incidents involving the government and the press at odds with one another were reported in the 1970s. The International Press Institute, for example, has commented on the detention of about 20 journalists for several years and, in 1973, reported that "all foreign news agencies must now submit their copy to the official Indonesian news agency" and that "the most serious example of government harassment of the press was the arrest and interrogation of newspapermen who criticized a tourist project sponsored by President Suharto's wife" (*IPI Report,* Jan. 1973, p. 10). But the major press-government "konfrontasi" came in early 1974 when the 11 publications were banned and the Minister of Information, Mashuri Saleh, vowed that the government would "put the press in order." Later that year, Mashuri's Indonesian Press Council was busy discussing how to define the limits and responsibilities of the press in carrying out its duties to society.

The government's anti-press measures in 1974 led Derek Davies, a Hong Kong journalist, to comment:

> It must be tempting for a journalist who has been gagged to start shouting from the rooftops when the gag is loosened, but pressmen in Indonesia today must be pondering guiltily on the thin red line which divides freedom and licence and whether they would not have done better to have eased their way more responsibly into their new function as media for a national debate.

But, he continued, "One effect of closing down the newspapers is of course that the Government is denied an important means of communication and damaging rumours begin to proliferate" (*Far*

Eastern Economic Review, 25 Feb. 1974, p. 17).

3.3.6 Is the Press "Free"?

In Indonesia, where an elite group of generals and intellectuals dominate public opinion and the decision-making process, and where most people are still inadequately educated and owe their loyalty to a particular region, religion or ethnic group rather than to the nation, many of the conditions which would justify a free, Western-type press do not exist.

Journalists, for example, still have low professional standards. "Too many of us are not committed to anything, except to our own freedom," Mochtar Lubis has said. "And there are even newspapers which are not committed even to that. As long as they earn good money, they are well satisfied to sell their sensational stories, their pornographic or paid reports. And some newspapers are still content to sell their soul to the highest bidder" (*Lubis,* 1971, p. 2).

Therefore, after years of instability and authoritarianism, it is unreasonable to expect Indonesia to achieve press freedom overnight. It will take time to get adjusted to democracy, and Sumono Mustoffa of the Press Foundation of Indonesia predicts the government and the press will continue to debate press freedom. "I can promise you there is bound to be more press quarrels here as we go on," he said. "But they are more like the quarrels of a mother and a doctor on how to save the life of the sick child" (*Mustoffa,* 1971, p. 3).

While a more open atmosphere exists today than during the later Sukarno years, Indonesian journalists — like their colleagues in other developing societies — have had to proceed cautiously to avoid stepping on some still-sensitive toes. An Indonesian journalism educator summarized the situation by saying that the Indonesian press finds itself in "a highly volatile situation in which it must carefully watch its actions" because of government-press confusion and disagreement over the 1966 press law and the lack of clear laws on such issues as libel, obscenity and blasphemy (*Susanto,* 1971, p. 31).

An editor, for example, clearly would think twice before writing about such issues as Communism, Chinese minority population, political detainees,[9] the role of Islam, the future of the army and high-level corruption. Attacks on the president and his family are also risky. An editor of a Jogjakarta weekly, for example, was arrested in 1968 for calling Suharto "General Togog" (General Stupid) (*IPI Report,* Oct. 1968, p. 11). And press "liberalism" is not equally distributed throughout the archipelago. Anwar has observed:

> Not a few Indonesian pressmen have experienced that the farther you are from Jakarta, the center of government, the more liable you are to become the victim of all kinds of pressures, subtle as well as unsophisticated, perpetrated by the local power. Thus the press carried stories about provincial journalists getting rough physical treatment for news published that was not amenable to the local authorities, military as well as civilian. Or they would be summoned by the police, interrogated and taken into custody. (*Anwar,* 1973, p. 4).

But despite occasional pressure from officials, many journalists in Indonesia are relatively free of the blatant political interference and the arbitrary action they knew so well under Sukarno. Indonesian specialist Arnold C. Brackman summarized the current situation: "Under Suharto, newspapers were given a new lease on freedom, but not completely. However, criticism of the government abounds in the press, in editorials, reports by the non-communist opposition and so forth. The only real bar is on the communist party."[10]

And — compared to such neighbors as the Philippines, South Korea, Singapore, and Burma who have opted for a more controlled press in recent years — Indonesia's press system is relatively free of government interference. Anwar agrees:

> The Indonesian pressmen when they look across the border, and observe the situation and the plight of the

---

9   Estimates are that 10,000 "hardcore" Communists from the attempted 1965 coup are being held as political detainees on Buru Island. A 26 November 1973 Reuter report stated that the government planned to set up a radio station to give these detainees development news, education and music programs.

10   Personal correspondence with Arnold C. Brackman, author and Indonesian specialist, 7 Jan. 1974.

press in the other Southeast Asian countries have certainly no reason to lose heart with their own conditions, because they still retain their useful role in exercising social control, and are still relatively effective" (*Anwar,* 1973, p. 5).

3.3.7 The Press and Development

President Suharto has given rural development top priority in REPELITA, the government's five-year development plans, and the potential for utilizing communication — including newspapers — to help with rural development is great.

The important question, of course, is whether Indonesia — which has always been in a more or less constant state of crisis — can maintain an independent press system which is able to criticize and, at the same time, aid the government's economic reconstruction and rural development efforts.

The Area Handbook for Indonesia — 1970 said, "Relations between rural communities and the urban areas are essentially relations between the static world of tradition and the world of dynamism and change" (*U.S. Army,* 1970, p. 128). The biggest challenge facing the urban-oriented press, then, is how to promote peaceful, purposeful change in rural areas where the bulk of the people live and traditionally have depended upon face-to-face communication. But, Indonesian newspapers have generally operated only in the cities and the towns because of "the extremely bad physical communications with the countryside, lack of attention to the expansion of readership among the rural population, and lately a newspaper price which is far too high for the urban low income groups and even more so for the extremely low cash income of the average villager" (*Agassi,* 1969, p. 35).

In addition to the normal hazards of newspaper publishing, Indonesian editors have been plagued by newsprint shortages and spiralling prices, and some dailies have had to temporarily suspend publications or at least limit the size of their papers. *The Jakarta Times* reported that for June 1973, Indonesia had only 20 per cent of the monthly, 2,500 tons of newsprint it required (*Effendi,* 1973b).

The newsprint shortage and the worldwide inflation crisis have hurt all papers in Asia, and agencies like the Press Foundation of Asia and FAO have been studying ways of making cheaper newspapers. In Indonesia, a working group of government and foreign forestry firms has been investigating the establishment of a US$200 million regional newsprint mill that could produce 400,000 tons a year for Indonesia and other members of ASEAN (*Agence France-Presse,* 1 Sept. 1973). In the meantime, Indonesia must continue to spend millions of rupiah in foreign exchange each year so that the bulk of its costly newsprint and other newspaper ingredients can be imported from the West.

The government has tried to subsidize transportation of newsprint from the main ports to the regions, and the cost of cutting reels into sheets, but such assistance is always "too little, too late" and has been phased out.

The Indonesian Newspaper Publishers Union (SPS) argues that the government has a responsibility to guarantee an adequate newsprint supply and points out that the government has a long history of direct aid to needy newspapers that began at independence with funds to help them compete with Chinese and Dutch papers (*Effendi,* 1973b). Suharto, however, has favored the use of private capital to bail newspapers out of their financial troubles, but private investors have not been interested. In addition to modest subsidies, the government is trying to promote better provincial papers by encouraging mergers so that the smaller papers can survive the rapidly increasing production costs and the severe competition from the Jakarta papers, which are expanding their operations into the countryside.

The problems of the press in a developing society, of course, cannot be solved by government action alone. For example, increased literacy or more government subsidy would not necessarily guarantee more and better Indonesian newspapers or greater service to the rural masses. More attention needs to be given to the modernization of all levels of the press and to finding ways to help smaller, non-urban papers survive economically. Unless these difficult problems — basically economic in nature — can be solved through the joint efforts of the government, press and international agencies, the Indonesian peasants will continue to be forgotten and the press will remain overwhelmingly urban and elitist.

3.3.8 Narrowing the Gaps

The problems of improving communication and of modernizing Indonesia are staggering, and newspapers will never be able to do the job alone.

Indonesian officials — like those in many developing nations — seem to be saying more and more that the press ought to concentrate on the decision-makers and the urban people, while broadcasting and interpersonal communications, including traditional Indonesian forms such as the *wayang kulit* (shadow puppet play), under government aegis, will try to reach and mobilize the rural peasantry (see *Adhikarya,* 1972).

Broadcasting — rather than the print media — seems to hold the potential for becoming Indonesia's only truly "mass" medium. Because of the country's wide geographic spread and its economic backwardness, shortwave radio is probably the only realistic answer to Indonesia's mass education and development communication problems.

Villagers are always more "listening minded" than "reading minded," and a report of a UNESCO mission said "that bearing in mind Indonesia's unique problems — its geography and its acute shortages of books, paper, and trained teachers — only the extensive use of broadcasting will provide both a speedy and efficient solution to this wastage of human resources" (*Koch,* 1968, p. 6).

Imaginative use of radio and, eventually, television — coupled with more personal, one-to-one communication through rural extension officers — could reach all of Indonesia's peasants directly with information from the "outside world" to help fight illiteracy, spread the family planning message, alleviate malnutrition and other basic health problems and promote national unity by improving communication between islands and between ethnic groups.

While the major responsibility for closing the urban-rural gap realistically must rest with broadcasting, newspapers certainly have the major role to play in preventing another Indonesian gap — the one between the military leaders and the civilians — from growing. The press should do all it can to see that the army does not stifle internal political development and eliminate the chance that Indonesia might someday become a prosperous nation under a more representative government than now exists. The current political and economic difficulties in Indonesia seem to justify strong military leadership, but the press should be preparing the country for the day when political leadership can pass into civilian hands and when competition between responsible political parties can be possible.

The generals-turned-politicians must create a political process that will be responsive to the changing and conflicting interests of a diverse population, and journalists must work harder at providing more and better independent newspapers that encourage self-help and democratic participation throughout Indonesian society.

Failure of the politicians and the journalists to meet these challenges and to stimulate free discussion of national goals and policies could well lead to another terrifying outbreak of political instability and violence.

John Hughes of *The Christian Science Monitor* has written that the fall of Sukarno meant that strife-torn Indonesia had won a second chance (*Hughes*, 1967, p. 295). Not all nations get such an opportunity, and what Indonesia under Suharto does, will depend to a great extent on how the politicians and the journalists can exist — and work — together.

3.3.9 Additional Information, by John A. Lent

The issue of freedom of the press remained unresolved at the dawn of the 1980s. Because of the closures of newspapers in 1974 and 1978, editors were cautious in what they reported, even after a few government officials requested a more critical stance. Perhaps, memories of government suppression were too fresh in the minds of journalists; perhaps, the fluctuating nature of government-press relationships and the sometimes vague "guarantees" of press freedom were too intimidating. High government officials, such as President Suharto, Adam Malik, Mashuri Saleh and Admiral Sudomo, in the mid-1970s especially, stated in public that press freedom existed in Indonesia, based on *Pancasila* and Article 28 of the 1945 Constitution, which assures, "the freedom of society to express its opinion and thoughts orally as well as in writing." The article adds that in accordance with *Pancasila,* there should be a balance between individual and social rights (see *Susanto,* 1977, p. 268). In a speech in March 1975, Suharto placed all responsibility upon the national press to foster the dignity of press freedom. He believed, however, that the press had a responsibility to report upon developmental topics; if the press differed with government on national development goals, it had an obligation to offer alternatives (*Indonesian News and Views,* April 1975). About the same time, Malik (see *AMCB,* March 1975, p. 17), Sudomo and Saleh pointed out that it would be detrimental to Indonesian interests to accept the alien concept of unlimited press freedom.

In the area of production capability, there were important advances for newspapers in the 1970s. Starting from a very limited base in 1960, the growth of printing and publishing in Indonesia has become steady, partly because of an increase in per capita income, the doubling of school enrollments and the government emphasis on literacy. There were some stumbling blocks — especially the sharp rise in newsprint prices in 1973 — but by 1975, the publishing industry had made a comeback. Newsprint consumption of dailies quadrupled between 1970-80 and the amount and value of equipment used in producing newspapers increased. As late as 1971, for example, Indonesia did not have a firm capable of doing four-color process; by the mid-1970s, there were several. Additionally, other newspapers had expansion plans underway in the latter part of the decade. Modern printing equipment is still imported although some platen letterpress machinery is manufactured domestically to meet the needs of rural newspapers for inexpensive equipment not requiring electric power. Thus, the range of printing equipment on which Indonesian newspapers are published extends from presses that would be antique dealers' delights, to four-color, offset operations using computerized typesetting.

The largest printing combines, all located in Jakarta, are the commercial companies, Granmedia (*Kompas,* two bestselling magazines and books), P. T. Sinar Kasih (*Sinar Harapan* and a women's magazine) and Merdeka (*Merdeka,* the weekly newsmagazine *Topik,* monthly *Keluarga* and *Indonesian Observer*), and the government owned Percetaken Negara N.I., considered one of the largest printing facilities in Southeast Asia. *Sinar Harapan* is considered one of the most advanced newspapers in use of modern technology. It started in 1961 with subcontracted printing and a circulation of 2,500; today, the daily uses two four-unit offset presses, cold composition, computerized typesetting and a sophisticated transportation system to bring out its 110,000 copies daily (*Printing and Publishing,* 1977, pp. 20-28).

In the mid-1970s, the Information Ministry commenced a project to circulate newspapers designed for rural audiences, which was in line with the adult education program of REPELITA II (National Plan). The first of these newspapers, *Tandang,* was a success, achieving a circulation of 25,000 within a year. However, the project was temporarily shelved when the decree was issued banning the establishment of newspapers.

3.4 Kampuchea

Soth Polin and Sin Kimsuy

3.4.1 Historical Evolution

3.4.1.1 Political Role

The history of the Khmer press, which has lagged far behind that of developed countries, can be divided into three distinct periods according to the political upheavals and transmutations of the country: the period before national independence; the transitional period between independence and the events of March 1970, and the period from 1970 to 1973. Of course, there is the contemporary period which this essay does not discuss.

For a long time, public opinion was not taken into account because the public did not present political pressure to the authorities. During the protectorate, which ended in 1953, Cambodian[1] newspapers were more or less considered non-existent because, on the one hand, there were not many (in Khmer or foreign languages), and on the other hand, because of their presentation (they were considered .more as a novelty than an institution), they did not interest the public. The slow evolution of the Khmer press can also be attributed to a colonial policy

1 The country underwent two name changes in the 1970s — from Cambodia to Khmer to Kampuchea. Because this chapter treats different time periods before it was called Kampuchea, Khmer and Cambodia are used interchangeably.

Soth Polin resides in Paris. Before he fled Kampuchea in 1974, he was president of l'Association des Editeurs, founding editor of *Nokor Thom,* editor of *Khmer Ekareach* and *Koh Santepheap.* Sin Kimsuy taught in various Kampuchean schools and was associated with *Ponleu Angkor, Nokor Thom* and *Khmer Ekareach.*

that avoided establishment of newspapers by implementing a very severe censorship.

The Khmer press began in 1936 with the creation of *Nagaravatta* (*The Country of Pagodas*). At that time, there were also some papers in French and Vietnamese, started for French colonists and for the Vietnamese who were already in the country in large numbers as French auxiliaries. The circumstances in which *Nagaravatta* was born were marked by the extreme hostility of certain Khmer circles towards the French — then masters of all Indochina — who had to face the national consciousness of the Khmers for the independence of the country. To begin a newspaper at that time, one had to go through the very complicated formalities set up by the French who insisted that applications be filed to the "General Governor" of Indochina in Hanoi through the "Superior Resident" in Cambodia. The promoters of *Nagaravatta* were mainly Son Ngoc Thanh, Pach Chhoeurn and Sim Var, assisted by a team of militant nationalists. The first twice-weekly political newspaper in Cambodia, *Nagaravatta*'s main task was to initiate the Khmer people to politics and to draw their attention to national consciousness in preparation for the movement of national liberation. Not many people read newspapers in Khmer at that time; instead, the privileged classes, bourgeoisie, higher civil servants, royal families and businessmen read them in French (*La Vérité, Opinion, Presse de Saigon*) or in Vietnamese. The mentality was that to read, speak or write in one's own language was almost a dishonor or humiliation.

Nagaravatta, with Pach Chhoeurn as publisher and Sim Var as editor-in-chief, was only "read at the start by people of the lower social classes, wage-earners, and minor civil servants, whose national feeling was very alive" (*Kouk Noyobay*, 1971, p. 21). However, the success of this newspaper grew very quickly, its effect being that of a bomb released amidst the sleeping masses and aimed at the colonial policy. After a year, the newspaper had an unfavorable reaction from the French authorities, who in 1937, banned it and arrested and jailed the publisher and his staff. The banning of *Nagaravatta* left a void in the newspaper world of Cambodia, thus ending the period of the Khmer press before national independence.

From 1953 to 1970, newspapers were still not important

(although the country had received its independence), partly because freedom of expression was not possible in the reign of the then chief of state, Prince Sihanouk. However, the opposition newspapers, *Khmer Krok* (*Khmer Who Rises*), *Prachéa-Thippatay* (*The Democracy*), *Khmer Thmei* (*The New Khmer*) and *Meatophum* (*Mother Country*), were the most widely read, because they spread political ideas contrary to those of the regime, even daring to publish violent articles blaming the regime for society's problems. Especially between 1955 and 1963 (which coincided with the struggle of the opposition party against the regime), strong suppression of opposition newspapers again led to another gap in the life of the Cambodian press.

One had to wait for some years, until 1968, to witness the publication in great numbers of Khmer language daily newspapers and twice-weekly magazines (actually about 10 to 30), which, on the whole, were interested in the fate of the country. However, these papers did not have freedom of expression, their function being restricted to reporting the official and foreign news. Some newspapers in that year, notorious for their taste for anything sensational (especially *Sochivathor*), were known as "muckrakers" or "rags." Writing about blood and sex (written in very obscene language), they were the most read because they were accessible to the uneducated public. In 1967, a new opposition paper, *Khmer Ekareach* (*Khmer Independent*) was started, edited by former Prime Minister Sim Var, a redoubtable opponent of Prince Sihanouk. The main objective of this daily was to ridicule the regime, denouncing everything from corruption to abuse of power to incompetence, and quietly attacking the Prince. With a precise and satiric style (Sim Var is a polemist), and strong and determined language, *Khmer Ekareach* quickly became a threat to the authorities, and on several occasions, it was suspended. By 1969, newspapers had two faces, that of serious politics and that of sensational playfulness.

At the end of 1969, the Khmer language *Nokor Thom,* edited by a staff of intellectuals, was started as a new opposition paper. The feelings of *Nokor Thom* (expressed in virulent and hostile language to the regime) were those of the majority of the dissidents. The success of this daily was also prodigious and by 1970, it had the largest circulation in Cambodia. Its regular readers came from among the educated class, academics, students and civil servants.

After the beginning of 1970, Khmer newspapers, except for a few, could be characterized by their open hostility to the regime. On the whole, the papers tried to be serious spokesmen for the public's opinion, especially those living in towns. From 1970, the Khmer press took on a national consciousness, playing a constructive role through criticism and proposals concerning government activities. They seemed, in a relatively short time (between March 1970 and March 1973) to have more freedom and independence. Their common attention was centered on the so-called "enemy invaders" and the restoration of the monarchy. But, after March 1972, the press even stopped supporting the new regime, attacking it instead for its incapacity and anarchic traits. Despite these criticisms, the press remained patriotic and nationalistic, fighting the nation's enemies — the Vietnamese Communists. By 1972-73, one could speak of a new spirit of the Khmer press, interested in the political affairs of the country, weak but full of initiative, maturity and more confidence.

The constant deterioration of the national situation after Cambodia went to war did not help the Khmer press in its survival struggle, no matter how meritorious it had become. March 1973 was tragic: assuming that newspaper freedom was in the way of authority, the government decreed emergency measures, put the country under martial law and indefinitely suspended all private newspapers.

3.4.2 *The Khmer Press as an Institution*

3.4.2.1 Structure and Organization of Newspapers

If the history of the Khmer press was short, then that of each individual newspaper was ephemeral. Newspapers' lives were spasmodic: they were born and a few years later they died, so that in 1974, not one Khmer newspaper established a decade before, existed.

Obviously, the Khmer press had not yet found its way. It remained poor and ineffectual, and its organization was not elaborate. The director of a Khmer newspaper was often both owner and editor, which in Cambodia meant that the editor was not a necessary man. In fact, frequently, an editor's name was listed in the newspaper as decor. Definitely the editors played secondary roles on the three main dailies in 1973-74: *Nokor Thom* (*Big Country*), *Khmer Ekareach* (*Independent Khmer*) and *Koh Santepheap* (*Island of Peace*). *Khmer Ekareach* had two directors: the political director (Sim Var, later Khmer ambassador to Japan) assumed the moral responsibility, while the publishing director, who was really a working editor, was responsible before the law for all articles published. This subterfuge was used because the political director, who was also the owner, was abroad most of the time and could not, according to the common statute of civil servants, assume any responsibility in a paper not always in accord with government.

Sometimes the director of a newspaper was just a figurehead; that was the case of *Koh Santepheap*. Its director, Sou Sorn, was not the real patron, although he was responsible before the law. The owner, Chou Thani, an infantry officer in the 13th Brigade, actually handled the political line of the newspaper.

These exceptions apart, the director was always the owner of his paper. He was sometimes assisted by a political advisor, who helped by writing occasional editorials; some editorial writers; five to 10 staff members who dealt with the news and reports, as well as doing secretarial work; and a dozen reporters. Not many newspaper correspondents existed in the provinces. Khmer newspapers were reluctant to employ them, for on the one hand, the correspondents often misused the editor's confidence in them by bribing and blackmailing people. Owning a press card in the province made one as powerful as a policeman, and its holder often deviated from the mission he was supposed to perform. He could easily be bribed by the provincial authorities dominated by the *chef militaire,* who behaved like a feudal warlord. So, special correspondents were dispatched to report what was going on in the provinces.

The editorship also relied on the collaboration of outsiders such as civil servants and employees in the Ministry of Information, who from time to time, wrote articles for the papers or acted as informants or magazine suppliers.

3.4.2.2 Property and Control

Except for the party newspapers created just before the July 1972 legislative election, a Khmer newspaper rarely belonged to a group of entrepreneurs. The profits were so small that it was nearly impossible to share them. Moreover, the establishment of a newspaper needed such modest capital that almost anyone could handle one. This explains why there were many newspapers in Phnom Penh after 1968, and why the director-owner often controlled his own newspaper.

Faced with governmental power, the Khmer newspapers were very weak because of a lack of institutional character. The papers' opinions often reflected their constant dread of authority, rather than their own personality. That is to say, that private newspapers were manipulated by the government, especially before March 1970; and those governments which succeeded one another between 1970-74 wanted, if not to suppress the newspapers, then at least to control them. In November 1967, because of a telegram, from the Association d'Amitié Chine-Cambodge in Peking to the Association d'Amitié Khméro-Chinoise in Phnom Penh, which was hostile to Sihanouk's rule and published in *La Nouvelle Dépêche du Cambodge,* all newspapers were closed by the authorities.[2] *La Nouvelle Dépêche du Cambodge,* which had leftwing tendencies, and the rightwing *Phnom Penh Press* never reappeared. Instead, the state newspaper in French, *Le Cambodge,* and another in Khmer, *Reastr Sangkum* (People's Society), took their places. A month later, owing to the National Congress, the private newspapers were given the right to publish again, but servile as they had been, they just appeared crushed and repentant.

It was this kind of hybrid newspaper which gave rise to a phenomenon rarely seen in Southeast Asia — the coexistence of the government and independent newspapers. This way of living in peace with each other was not a compromise, but rather a constant threat to the private press which was appreciated and more professional than the government press.

Some private newspapers were simply started and controlled

2   Telegram published in *La Nouvelle Dépêche du Cambodge,* 9 Sept. 1967. Sihanouk was angry about Peking's reaction.

by powerful men in government: military chiefs and millionaire *princes-seigneurs,* who did not know what to do with their money, and therefore hired people of humble birth to discredit rivals or to lavishly praise them. Without reader support, these newspapers did not last long, but they did a great deal of harm to the reputation of the press in general.

In December 1970, the government imposed censorship on all private newspapers and then suspended *Nokor Thom* for a month and *Khmer Ekareach* for 10 days for disobeying censorship codes. This censorship was stopped, however, because public opinion was against it. Finally, in March 1973, a pilot of the Khmer Air Force bombed the Presidential Palace at Chamcar Mon, and the government took this opportunity to decree emergency measures, suspending all private newspapers, including those of the party.

3.4.3 Social Role of the Press

For years in the 1960s, the role of the press had remained negative or passive. Newspapers were reduced to reporting news in brief, car accidents, abuses and rapes, robbery, divorce and other civil and penal instances. The previously mentioned *Sochivathor,* edited by Nouth Chhoeurm, was in this category. The taste for the sensational saw its climax from 1967 to 1969 and coincided with the economic decline of the former regime. The beginning of war in March 1970, however, gave rise to a new kind of public thought marked by the awareness of the difficulties being met by the country. The newspapers, especially private ones, wanted to be aware, realistic, objective and effective, trying their best to be spokesmen of the public. *Khmer Ekareach,* edited by Sim Var, was of this category. The daily *Khmer Ekareach,* which supported the 18 March 1970 coup, fought various social evils, such as corruption, left by the former regime. Immediately, other newspapers followed its example, sparing no one, but really directing their criticism against high government and society personalities whose loose lives were well known. Taking the opportunity of the transitional era after 18 March 1970, when the government was chalking a new political line, when reforms were called for in all areas, when public power was still unsettled, and when there was a relatively short period of freedom, the newspapers, without respite, exposed the abuses and incompetence of an administration inherited from the colonial era, putting the new government on guard against any eventual mistakes. Actually, the press was manifestly inclined towards bringing about national change and stability. As a matter of fact, after 1970, the press was tied to a new discipline: avoiding private stories and only publishing stories of great use to the general public. The first half of 1973 was marked by new social difficulties, owing to the spread of war and the increasing number of refugees in towns. The press intervened, drawing government attention to the growing difficulties of the population, requesting and helping officials solve problems and warning them against eventual misfortunes. In effect, the press denounced the evil doings of some civil servants, the dishonest actions of some Chinese dealers and speculators who illicitly raised prices and hoarded essential goods. Thus, the theme of the press during the first part of 1973 dealt with the wartime economy.

In March 1973, the Khmer press showed sympathy for school teachers who were striking for a wage increase. This proved fatal for the press, for when the Presidential Palace was bombed that month, the government used this event to silence newspapers. The press ban plunged the country into great consternation as there was a tomblike silence everywhere. A government without an independent press became more and more alienated from the people, who were not interested in the government press, usually operated by incompetent civil servants who considered it as a means and not an end. Without the powerful balance of an independent press, corruption raged unchecked in the country.

3.4.4 Economic Aspects

3.4.4.1 Facilities

Khmer press operations were rudimentary. The small printing machines imported from Japan, specifically for newspapers with small circulations, were old, and it was difficult to obtain spare parts for them. Furthermore, the ink available in Phnom Penh was not consistent, being so diluted that it did not leave a clear impression, or so sticky that it caused blots on the pages. News-print, imported from abroad at exorbitant prices, was also of the very lowest quality. Additionally, there were not many varieties of printing types, causing newspapers to appear unattractive. No wonder, then, that in a country of 7 million people, the largest newspaper had a circulation of less than 20,000 before March 1970, and of 30,000 after that date.

3.4.4.2 Capital

To finance a newspaper in 1974, one needed a starting capital of 8 million Riels (US$20,000), 5 million for equipment, machinery and installation and 3 million as working capital. This assumed that the newspaper was an immediate success, or else one had to spend more than that — perhaps 10 million Riels. Before March 1970, the establishment of newspapers cost about 200,000 Riels (US$3,000), because they were not well developed and had small staffs. Newspapers had very little reporting to do as local news was, after the manner of *Sochivathor,* provided gratuitously by informants and correspondents. Other information was obtained from official agencies or monitored from national radio. But, after 18 March 1970, with the advent of war, there was a rush for news, and dailies modernized themselves. The capital needed to finance a daily at that time increased.

To be economically viable, a newspaper had to have a circula-tion of over 20,000, 70 per cent of which had to be sold. Income from advertisements was absurdly low and the daily Khmer papers did not rely on this means to subsist. The government press in Khmer or in French and Chinese, not to mention the semi-official reviews such as *Cambodge Nouveau* or *Khmer Republic,* mono-polized scarce advertising that existed in the nearly non-existent Khmer economy. Yet, two dailies, *Nokor Thom* and *Khmer Ekareach,* were fortunate to get from 120,000 to 160,000 Riels per month (US$300 to $400) in advertising, an amount far from sufficient to meet all expenses, but enough to keep them alive. The banks, small factories making powdered milk, soft drinks or sandals, and various ministries of the government were the sources of this income. Thus, compared to the press in neighboring Thailand, or even South Vietnam, whose pages were full of advertising, the Khmer press played the part of poor relatives. In addition, advertisements were considered by the Khmer public as a sign of a newspaper's servility to the commercial society. Some newspapers were condemned for publishing immoral advertisements, such as those for dancing bars showing naked women dancers, when the country was still at war. Obviously, advertisers did not have any control over the Khmer press, for it was not dependent upon them for income. In fact, advertising agencies did not exist.

3.4.4.3 Consumption Capacity

Without proper advertising resources, the price of newspapers was very high, thus prohibitively expensive to the general public. In Cambodia, the people who read the newspapers were the rich. They purchased several dailies; even the sensational papers were accessible only to the wealthier or middle class people.

3.4.4.4 Distribution

In peacetime, the newspapers were sent to the province by bus and readers waited a day to receive them. After the war began in 1970, all the main routes leading to the capital were regularly cut and distribution had to be done by plane. The newspapers reached the provinces on the day of publication, but the very high expenses were staggering to the editorship.

In Phnom Penh, newspapers were distributed to bookshops and newspaper stalls by a dozen adult news distributors on motorcycles; other copies were distributed by children who sold them in restaurants. For a newspaper of 10,000 circulation, 500 copies generally were delivered to homes and administration offices, 1,000 were sold by newsboys, 4,000 were sold in bookshops and stalls in Phnom Penh and 2,000 were sent to the provinces. About 25 per cent usually was unsold, providing a surplus which was often wasteful. A newspaper with 10,000 circulation was sure of being read by at least 100,000 persons. Cambodians did not exchange newspapers as in Hong Kong, but they were keen on lending them. In an office or household, a paper went from hand to hand until everyone had read it. Newspaper stalls were crowded with people who read the evening papers for free when they arrived. In addition, many bookshops rented newspapers, which was detrimental to management.

3.4.4.5 Other Aspects: Newsprint Crisis

The shortage of newsprint was a big worry for the editorship. As the riel lost value after the beginning of 1971, the price of newsprint continually went up, the result being newspapers raised their selling price nearly every two months in order to recover the loss.

During peacetime, Cambodia possessed a papermill in Chhlong (Kratié Province), but after the hostilities began, the factory was in the enemy zone. The country, then, fully depended on imported paper which had a 15 per cent purchase tax used as a contribution to the war effort. Still, the imported paper was not sufficient to meet local consumption. Some officers in the Ministry of Commerce and Chinese dealers acted with concerted planning to maintain a paper shortage, assuring them of good profits. Newsprint was available on the black market at exorbitant prices which created difficulties for the press and publishing trades. The most alarming paper crisis occurred in December 1973, when, over a period of four months, the price quadrupled.

The war kept readers interested in dailies which provided news of combat and attacks; yet, there was a limit to this rise in prices of newspapers beyond which the public was not willing to go. By March 1973, it took 8 per cent of the monthly salary of an average Cambodian to purchase a month's subscription. There was very little hope of good newspapers surviving in Cambodia as a result.

3.4.4.6 Printing Presses

Before March 1970, the printing presses, generally Japanese-made, were imported free of tax. Later, however, very few importers existed. The increasing difficulties which the press and publishing trades met closed the doors of many printing houses. However, the four largest Phnom Penh newspapers in Khmer — *Nokor Thom, Khmer Ekareach, Koh Santepheap* and *Ariyak Thor* — retained their printing presses, as did the Government Press, which was far better equipped.

3.4.5 Government and the Press

3.4.5.1 Press Laws

Like the liberal press of the West, from which it took a great deal of inspiration, the Khmer press wanted to be an opposition force, but the task was far from easy. In June 1972, the Ministry of Information published a very severe press law, which said that the press was free but must not cast a slur on any person's honor, on the national security or morality. The "honor of persons" related to the dignity of individuals and especially their private lives (Articles 2 and 21). The snag was that in Cambodia, the power holders hardly distinguished their public responsibility from their private lives. When the press accused a higher civil servant of corruption, for example, he invariably reacted by counter-accusing, saying the press uttered personal, mean attacks aimed at ruining his reputation.

The "blow to morality and to the national security" was not clearly explained. One did not know the limits which separated the "can" and "cannot." Journalists had to know how to adapt themselves to circumstances, to self censure, to weigh their words in order to avoid too much being said. The dangers can appear at any time. For disobeying the press laws, one could have found himself on his way to prison or ruin, not to mention risking the vengeance of powerful men. For instance, on 9 January 1972, the director of *Nokor Thom* received a plastic charge which destroyed his car, because the paper ridiculed a politician friend of a general. Vath Van, one of the publishing directors of *Khmer Ekareach,* was struck on the head with an ax for criticizing the same person.

Article 22 of the press law specified that the press could freely criticize government politics and actions, as long as it was not injurious. Also, criticism which was not injurious but "done with insincerity to impede the action of the Government or justice" was not authorized. Article 32 prohibited the use of the press "to outrage:

    a. The President of the Republic, the Vice-President of the Republic, Buddhist Chiefs and clergies of the two Orders; b. The Chief of State, the Ambassador, the

Chargé de Mission or the Consul of any country maintaining diplomatic relations with the Khmer Republic;
c. The deputies, the senators, the members of the
Government, the members of the Supreme Court, the
Superior Council of the Bench, of the Constitutional
Court, the High Court of Justice and of all other
constituted bodies, the agents of administrative or
electoral mandate, concerning activities involving the
mission or function of the interested parties; d. Private
bodies, which are individuals or legal entities; e. The
deceased, with the intention of casting a slur on the
honour and prestige of heirs, relatives or mandatories
who are still alive . . . . Any contemptuous or injurious
words are considered outrageous."

One can see how narrow the options were for journalists who
wanted to carry out their tasks diligently. The vague words,
"outrage," "contempt" and "injury" could be interpreted in
different ways. A journalist could be condemned or acquitted
depending on the will of the authorities.

3.4.5.2 Libel

Proceedings instituted against the press for libel were used by
persons of high office or by the government itself to subdue
journalists. Yet in their indictment before the tribunal, higher
civil servants often deviated from the questions raised in the
papers. To clear themselves of the charges, they endlessly underlined their competence, magnified the good achievements of their
work, but obstinately abstained from answering the charges raised
against them. Instead, they tried to counterattack in the aggregate
by repeating that the press libelled them. They watched for weak
spots in the words to see whether there were any possible
mistakes, any careless usage which might give them the opportunity to grasp the journalists by the throat. One can say they
searched for the grammar mistakes. For example, during Prince
Sihanouk's absolutism in 1969, *Sovanphoum* (*Golden Village*)
was fined 104,000 Riels (US$2,080 at the time) for libelling Kou
Roun, then director of security; its crime was to call him "asura"
(the ogre).

Prince Sihanouk himself, as chief of state, lodged a libel complaint in August 1969 against Sim Var, director and owner of *Khmer Ekareach*. The accused had written in an editorial supporting the new government (named Government of Salvation by Sihanouk): this government was supposed to "end anarchy, social disorder and corruption which are sapping the country while foreigners are invading it" (*Khmer Ekareach,* 17 Sept. 1969). The last part of the sentence incriminated Sim Var. In reality, Sihanouk was angry about another article published a day later in *Khmer Ekareach,* accusing Khek Vandy, president-directeur-general of many state-owned companies and friend of Mrs. Monique Sihanouk, of corruption. Sihanouk would have claimed only one riel in damages if he won the proceedings. The tension was so great that Queen Kossomak (Sihanouk's mother), Lon Nol, president of the Ministers' Council, and Cheng Heng, president of the National Assembly, combined their efforts to beg Sim Var to soften his position. Sim Var should have scuttled his newspapers.

In 1971, Thon Ouk, president-directeur-general of an oil refinery, lodged a complaint against *Nokor Thom,* which had exposed with supporting proof the defective management of this state-owned company. Thon Ouk objected to the words used by the paper; for example, "He (Thon Ouk) is really so servile to them that one might believe he should bring them the toilet paper himself . . . ." The County Court acquitted *Nokor Thom* in this case.

Mrs. Ung Mung, former minister of tourism, also instituted libel proceedings against *Nokor Thom,* for calling her a cook and her Ministry of Tourism "Samlâr Kâko" (a kind of Cambodian soup with various ingredients). The serious criticisms were just ignored by the minister.

3.4.5.3 Infringements upon Press Freedom

The code law, written without the participation of journalists, constituted a violation of press freedom. As Sim Var noted, and rightly so, if this code did not let people criticize and blame their rulers, whom they pay to their last farthing, then a dictatorship prevailed.

Throughout the history of the Khmer press, there have been violations against the persons and property of journalists. Director of *Prachea Chon* (Communist tendency, pro-Hanoi), Nob Bophan, was shot dead on 9 October 1959 (*Khmer Ekareach,* 17 Sept. 1969), by an unknown person (said to be an agent of Sihanouk). In April 1960, Khieu Samphân, a "Docteur ès-sciences économiques" and progressivist, and director of the French daily, *l'Observateur,* was stripped while walking on the street and tortured by Kou Roun, then Sihanouk's minister of security.[3] He had praised poor little bread sellers. In 1958, a famous writer, Sang Sawath,[4] director of *Khmer Thmei* and partisan of the Khmer Sérei (Free Khmer) Movement, was killed on Kirirom Mountain. In 1967, a demonstration was provoked by Sihanouk's entourage aimed at destroying the office and printing press of *Khmer Ekareach.* Damages were enormous: 3 million Riels (at that time, US$60,000).

After 18 March 1970, the repression of journalists was never relaxed. Several journalists were jailed without trial, as in the case of Bouy Sreng, director of *Sankruoh Khmer* (*Save the Khmers*) in July 1972. In general, if the newspapers failed to please the government, they were suspended. The suspension could be temporary or final.

3.4.5.4 Journalism as a Stepping Stone

In short, journalism in Cambodia revealed itself as a harassing, devouring profession, a daily exercise of high acrobatics. The journalists were like tight rope dancers; dangers could occur at any time, dangers in breaking their journey, in looking back. If they fell into step behind the government, their papers lost readers, which was financially disastrous. If they acted for the

3   On 13 April 1960, while motorcycling along the street in front of Lim Kry's house, not far from Police Preah Sihanouk, Khieu Samphân was molested by a gang of assailants who were police agents of the government. Everyone knew about the incident and Khieu Samphân, indignant about it all, published articles in the paper accusing the police. Kou Roun summoned him to his office where he hit Khieu Samphân with a cane until his sphincters let out excrement. The irony is that Khieu Samphân later became prime minister for Sihanouk, his former torturer.

4   Sang Savath was a very talented novelist. He published in 1955, *Moha Chaur Neou Toul Dèn* (*The Pirates at the Frontier*) and *Dècho Krâhâm* (*The Red Lord*).

public good, they lost friends and laid themselves open to the anger of the men in power, who could and did take drastic measures. When the circulation of a paper increased quickly, this was hardly a sign of good health or prosperity, but rather a sign indicating that it would not last long. A talented, dutiful journalist had no great promise for his own future.

However, journalism could lead to success, providing that one left the profession. Many journalists became ministers, among them, Trinh Hoanh, Chau Seng, Tep Chhieu Kheng, Keam Reth and Khun Thay Li. Four became prime ministers or heads of state — Song Ngoc Thanh, Sim Var, Long Boret and Khieu Samphân. Some of them forgot their journalistic pasts very quickly once in public office.

3.4.6 Socio-Cultural Factors and the Press

3.4.6.1 Languages and Minorities

After the nationalization of the press by the government at the end of 1967, private newspapers were authorized to publish only in Khmer. Government newspapers, on the other hand, were published in Khmer, English, French and Chinese. Newspapers in Khmer were more numerous than those in other languages, and the circulation of government newspapers in French and Chinese was greater than that of newspapers in English. The latter point is explainable in that: (1) as a second language, French was used in the administration together with Khmer. Civil servants, school teachers and students constituted the market of readers in French, whose number diminished after the "Khmerisation" policy of the Ministry of Education was enforced in 1967. (2) There were large numbers of Chinese in Cambodia, whose immigration began far back in history. Of an overall population of about 7 million, about 350,000 to 400,000 were Chinese, most of whom still lived, spoke and thought the Chinese way. With their vocation and aptitude for commerce, they found in the press excellent opportunities to promote their businesses. The Chinese were keener on reading than Cambodians, and generally, each Chinese household subscribed to one or two Chinese language newspapers. The Chinese press served Chinese interests exclusively, for the Khmers generally did not understand Chinese. Thus, instead of insuring the social integration of Chinese into Khmer society, the Chinese press encouraged cultural and social barriers.

The other social and religious groups, the Vietnamese and Cham, were barely influenced by the national press and did not have newspapers in their own languages. Finally, the two government papers in English were relatively new and reached a very limited audience.

3.4.6.2 Contents of Newspapers

Except for *Nokor Thom* and *Le Republicain,* with eight tabloid pages each, Cambodian dailies generally had four pages. The first and last pages were for editorials, local news, world news and analysis articles about problems concerning national topics and public interests. Local news included reports on the activities of the chief of state and government, communiques from different departments, civil affairs having reference to acts of corruption, and sometimes the right to answer. In general, important articles were illustrated with photographs and cartoons. There had been an evident effort to adapt the press to satisfy new demands of readers. The reverse phenomenon was also true: the adaptation of readers to the changing tendencies of the press. It was this mutual stimulation which made the Khmer press progress. It followed that the articles which pleased the public before 1970, might have been ill-considered later by the majority of readers.

Advertising rarely appeared on the front page which was more political than commercial. Above all, war news provided a large part of the local news from 1970-74. Daily, the press published news from the battlefield, through reporters and press releases from the general staff of the National Armed Forces. Especially through the political commentaries, whose themes were usually concerned with state affairs, one appreciated the worth of papers in Cambodia. These analytical articles were seen in only a few dailies and weeklies, especially, *Nokor Thom, Khmer Ekareach* and *Bulletin de Jeunesse.*

The inside pages of the newspapers were reserved for less important information. Stories, local or translated from foreign languages, traditionally came first. They were of all kinds: classical or modern, sentimental or philosophical. Scientific and historical news was also dealt with and was popular with the intellectuals, academics, students and civil servants.

3.4.6.3 The Readers

Readers were divided into several categories, according to their tastes and interests. For example, there were those interested in fresh news, those who looked for intelligent and deep analysis of economic, political and social issues, and those keen on the sensational. The first category included dealers and businessmen who constituted the enterprising class of the country, while the second included the intelligentsia (professors, students and civil servants), and the third was made up of readers of low academic backgrounds. Nevertheless, the second category of readers increased every year while the third decreased gradually, relative to the progress of the national awareness of the press.

3.4.7 Conclusion

On the whole, the press in Cambodia remained until 1974 a combative one. It was more political than commercial or technical and even its information role was secondary. Most newspapers were founded when the country was seething with political upheaval, and therefore, their fate was linked to the development of the political circumstances from which they were born. Their lives were not stable at all and, consequently, their political influence was never long-lasting. Nevertheless, some newspapers succeeded in influencing the course of historical events, through their prestige and talent, through the impact of their articles on public opinion. Among these were *Nagaravatta,* prior to the advent of independence, and *Khmer Ekareach,* on the eve of March 1970. After 1972, despite their ephemeral life, private newspapers in Cambodia took advantage of the period of freedom granted by the new regime to enjoy their new role as a fourth power. But the suspension of all newspapers by the government after 18 March 1973, put an end, perhaps permanently, to this new born freedom. It can be concluded that in Cambodia, the participation of the press in the guidance of state affairs was never guaranteed by any consensus of interests between authority and the private papers.

This participation was, in fact, tolerated only when the authorities expected there would be full support for and blind obedience to their main political lines. In this climate of conditional and controlled freedom, many newspapers were forced to exist on the opportunities afforded by circumstances. Nevertheless, this weakness and the political instability of the Khmer press can also be explained by the fact that most newspapers were not worthy of the name; their lack of organization and their irresponsibility prevented them from becoming efficient institutions which could shield themselves against the eventual pressures of government.

As for its role of providing information, the Khmer private press only half succeeded in doing this, despite some progress made in 1970-74. With no professional background, Cambodian journalists, generally prompted by political enthusiasm, launched out into business with the hope of carrying the job through and improving it later through experience. Inefficient and slow reporting, a lack of scientific news and analysis and insufficient technical means needed for the proper functioning of newspapers, all helped explain why the Khmer press was not considered a significant social institution compared with the presses of other countries.

3.4.8 Since 1974, by John A. Lent

After Soth Polin wrote the above chapter, the Cambodian cabinet passed a resolution allowing newspapers to reopen in May 1974. However, publishers were required to post US$3,875 in the national bank to guarantee the financial stability of their newspapers (*Philadelphia Inquirer,* 18 May 1974). Among the first on the streets were the English language *Phnom Penh News,* a non-official government newspaper, two French language dailies and a weekly, a Chinese daily and a Khmer daily published by the Army. The influential *Nokor Thom* and *Khmer Ekareach* were not allowed to resume. This number of newspapers was small compared to the 20 or 30 in 1972 and the 18 in 1973.

Shortly after, in July 1974, Soth Polin himself became one of the most controversial figures in Phnom Penh when he published a farewell edition of *Nokor Thom,* attacking the power structure and pointing the finger at high officials for the assassination of a former education minister and his deputy. *Far Eastern Economic Review* (15 July 1974, pp. 13-14) wrote:

The paper created such a sensation that all 5,000 copies sold out almost immediately, before the Government had a chance to ban them. The going rate for a black market edition climbed to Riels 500 (US$1.10), five times the normal price. Officially, the government chose to ignore the issue, but privately many politicians and others were seething . . . . the fact that the charges did not come from one of the many Phnom Penh smear sheets caused a lot of surprise. Not only is *Nokor Thom* highly regarded, but Soth Polin is perhaps Cambodia's most renowned man of letters.

In a letter to this author (6 Sept. 1974), Soth Polin wrote:

I have been struggling in the swirl of Cambodian politics. I tried particularly to have the government authorize again the publication of private press, circulating my paper *Nokor Thom* in pirated editions. I could thus put out six numbers irregularly. It was lucky for me that I did, for it was an extraordinary success. They found it impossible to check the impact of my paper, the copies of which had been pulled away before the forces could intervene. They could not succeed in either having me condemned and gave up finally all efforts to open wide the cock, ready hereafter to seek troubles for me personally. Therefore all the Cambodian newspapers function since June 15, 1974, except mine and *Khmer Ekareach* . . . . Then happened the extraordinary event of June 4: Education Minister, Mr. Keo Sangkim and his assistant, Mr. Thach Chia were assassinated. As their murderers are among the most powerful Phnom-Penh politicians, they had the investigation suspended quickly. I was exhausted and disgusted of this regime and this injustice. I decided to say the truth. I had prepared my attempt for one month and put out my last number, the most incendiary of all. One hour after distribution I took a plane to Paris. At this moment they have confiscated my press and here I am outlawed.

Suspensions continued when newspapers did not follow the government line. On 13 January 1975, the Lon Nol administration closed for one week three Khmer newspapers for reprinting excerpts of a Swedish television interview with the deposed Prince Sihanouk. As it became apparent in early 1975 that the Khmer Rouge would be victorious, newspapers such as *Koh Santepheap* and *Ariyathor* expressed anger over what they believed was a betrayal by the United States (*Schanberg*, 1975, p. 10-C).

One of the leaders who emerged after the Khmer Rouge take-over on 17 April 1975, was Khieu Samphân, a former journalist who had been harassed by the Sihanouk government when he edited a French language newspaper (see 3.4.5.3), banned by the authorities in 1961 as a Communist propaganda outlet. He became deputy minister in April 1975, and soon after, president of Kampuchea.

The new government has not relied heavily upon print media; instead, Radio Phnom Penh has become the chief vehicle of communicating with the people through loudspeaker hookups. By 1977, there was no mass circulation newspaper, only a few journals circulated to selected government officials. In 1979, one of the few publications in Kampuchea was *Padevat* (*Revolution*), the organ of the Communist Party. Certainly, the human right of freedom of expression was denied. As one source reported:

> Freedom of expression or opinion is non-existent in such a climate of fear, even for the old population but especially for the new. There is no legal recourse for anyone charged with any crime — only death or escape. Probably never in modern history has the national character of a people been changed on such a radical scale (as in the Pol Pot regime) (*Asia 1979 Yearbook*, p. 166).

3.5 Laos

John A. Lent

3.5.1 Historical Development

Because Laos has been in a state of turmoil for so many years, not much time has been expended on the preservation of the nation's press history. In one of the few documents that mentions the Laotian press, Raymond Nunn and Dô Vân Anh found evidence of 41 newspapers or periodicals published in Vientiane, the capital city. Of these, 11 were dailies, 18 weeklies, one monthly and 11 of undetermined frequency. Where it was possible to determine the language of publication, 16 were in Lao, three each in French and English, and one, a trilingual in French, Lao and English. The known dailies to these authors, all published after 1958, were *Agence Lao Presse, Coordination, Daily News Bulletin, Khao Khosanakan, Khao Pachamwan, Lao Lane Xang, Lao Presse, Sien Mahason, Sieng Lao Quotidien, Sieng Se Ree* and *Xat Lao.* The oldest publication the authors could determine for Laos was the monthly *Bulletin Administratif du Laos,* which appeared in 1902. Other publications before 1950 were *Chot Mai Het Lao* (1939), *Lao Nhay* (1941-45) and *Pathet Lao,* a Laotian supplement of *Lao Nhay* (1941-44) (*Nunn and Anh,* 1972; see also *National Library of Australia,* 1969; *Pelissier,* 1964; *Schwegman,* 1967).

A survey conducted by the United States Information Agency (*USIA,* 1958, p. 1) reported that in 1958, only 12 news-sheets served as newspapers in Laos. Two of these were printed tabloids and 10 were mimeographed pages stapled together. The report added that circulation was limited by a literacy rate of 15 per cent, by primitive transportation and communication facilities and by contents that were impartial, biased, unreliable and untimely. Most newspapers served as organs for government officials or the wealthy elite who wanted to promote particular political viewpoints. All foreign news was supplied by Agence France Presse which allowed the Lao Ministry of Information newspaper, *Agence Lao Presse,* to reproduce articles without giving credit. Some newspapers collected news by monitoring foreign radio broadcasts or by reproducing articles from Bangkok dailies. At least four groups were prominent owners of newspapers. A leftist and neutralist, Bong Souvannavong, published *Lao May* and *Santiphab* and owned a second press used for commercial printing. The other groups were controlled by Katay Don Sasorith, a former prime minister who had *L'Avenir du Laos* and *La Voix du Peuple;* the wealthy Voravong family, which owned *Sieng Lao* and *Prachathipatay,* and Phouy Sananikone, leader of the Independent Party, who had *Mahasan* and *L'Hebdomodaire Independente.* The Pathet Lao (Neo Lao Hak Xat) published a "concise and informative sheet which is popular among low income groups" (*USIA,* 1958, p. 1).

The constitution of 1949, which guaranteed "freedom of speech, writing, and publications," was revised on 26 December 1957, at which time these rights were omitted. However, journalists' rights had been recognized in a law passed in October 1957, "The Law to Guarantee the Democratic Rights of the People," which provided for press freedom as long as it did not "jeopardize the King, the religion of the state, the aim of peace, neutrality, democracy, or unity of the nations" (*USIA,* 1958, p. 2).

Lao language newspapers published in 1958 were *Lao Hakxat,* pro-Communist organ of the Pathet Lao Movement (established 1957); *Lao Lane Xang,* of the Nationalist Party (daily; 400 circulation); *Lao May,* organ of Santiphab Party (established 1947; weekly; 1,500 circulation); *Lao Presse,* published by the Information Service as the official daily of the Royal government (established 1953; 2,000 circulation); *Mahasan,* leader of Independent Party (established 1954; semi-monthly); *Prachathipatay,* neutral but followed Communist line (established 1957; semi-monthly; less than 500 circulation); *Santiphab,* an organ of Santiphab Party (weekly; 1,000), and *Sieng Lao,* mouthpiece of

Voravong family interests (established 1948; biweekly; less than 500). Of the four French language newspapers, three were designed to promote the views of former Prime Minister Katay Sasorith: *La Tribune des Jeunes,* a youth newspaper established in 1950 (biweekly; less than 500 circulation); *L'Avenir du Laos,* a biweekly established in 1957 (circulation of less than 500), and *La Voix du Peuple,* a biweekly of less than 500 circulation, established in 1950. The other French language newspaper, *L'Hebodomodaire Independente,* was started in 1957 as a weekly by the Sananikone family to serve as a Royal government and Independent Party organ.

3.5.2 The Press in the Early 1970s

3.5.2.1 Dependence on Government

Observing Laotian newspapers in the early 1970s gave the impression one had stepped back in history to a time when flatbed presses were in use, type was hand set, trained staff were non-existent and ideas about press freedom were tested regularly in an effort to form a workable model.

The six dailies, handful of weeklies and monthlies that existed in Vientiane in 1973 barely survived. The largest circulation of a newspaper in a country of over 3 million people was 2,500-3,000, that of *Xat Lao.* Pon Chantharaj, *Xat Lao* editor, said to publish more than this number of copies was unprofitable because of high newsprint costs and limited readership, the latter concentrated in Vientiane.[1] To distribute newspapers in outlying areas was prohibitive, affected mainly by high air freight costs and wartime conditions. The mobility of war-torn populations and restrictions placed on information flow by the Pathet Lao further hindered successful gathering and distribution of news in provinces outside the capital.

As for physical plants, the average Lao editor worked in cramped, dingy, ramshackle quarters without the benefits of teleprinters, adequate type fonts or presses. The four printing presses in use were old flatbed types, some predating World War

1   Personal interview, Pon Chantharaj, editor, *Xat Lao,* Vientiane, Laos, 21 December 1973.

II. The calibre of personnel Lao editors worked with was pitifully low, the average staff member having barely a primary school education.

Despite such formidable problems, the six dailies — *Xat Lao, Sieng Seri Daily News, Lao Hua Daily, Vientiane Post, Sai Kang* and *Agence Lao Presse* — carried on in a highly competitive spirit. Each claimed to be politically and economically independent, at the same time accusing its competitors of being political party or government puppets. For example, the editor of *Sieng Seri* emphasized his paper's independence, pointed out which parties other dailies supported and then, as an afterthought, said the whole Lao press worked under a system whereby politicians supported papers they agreed with.[2]

Whether they admitted it or not, Lao editors depended on government or political party help; the economic instability of the press did not allow otherwise. In gathering international news, Lao newspapers, when they were not monitoring Voice of America, BBC or Radio Australia, relied on the two possessors of press association teleprinters, *Agence Lao Presse* and National Lao Radio, both government-owned and controlled. *Agence Lao Presse* was a mimeographed newspaper issued Monday through Friday by the Department of Information. The paper, issued in both French and Lao editions, had the use of an Agence France Presse service. In fact, because of its dependence on AFP, the Lao Department of Information in the early 1970s was called the Department of Confirmation, confirming everything AFP transmitted.

To cover domestic news, Lao dailies nurtured government cooperation. For example, the editor of *Vientiane Post* said he held morning briefings with his staff during which time he told reporters which governmental departments had extended invitations for press coverage.[3] In other words, press coverage of most government functions was by invitation. Another daily, *Lao Hua,* published for the Chinese community, had been ordered by the authorities to run verbatim *Agence Lao Presse* stories for its domestic news coverage. According to its editor, *Lao Hua* was

2   Personal interview, Thip Thammavong, editor, *Sieng Seri Daily News,* Vientiane, Laos, 20 December 1973.

3   Personal interview, Prisa Trichanh, editor, *Vientiane Post,* Vientiane, Laos, 20 December 1973.

not trusted by the authorities to report on government because of an incident a few years before when the paper was known as *Lao Samay*. At that time, *Lao Samay* ran a verbatim account of the My Lai massacre, taken from a news service. The story was embarrassing to the United States Embassy in Vientiane, which had *Lao Samay* closed.[4]

In other aspects, the Lao press was heavily dependent upon government help. When newspapers circulated to provincial communities, they were often transported by military planes. Also, newspaper subscriptions, being expensive, were restricted to elites, and the largest groups of elites in Laos were the civil servants, politicians and military personnel. *Xat Lao* figures that about 95 per cent of its copies were purchased by the government, military and police; *Agence Lao Presse* survived partially through ministerial subscriptions.

3.5.2.2 Press Freedom

Such help from government or political parties usually came at a price. For example, *Sieng Seri* thought nothing of publishing government advertisements free of charge; all newspapers believed it was part of their duty to run government announcements, usually under the guise of supporting national development. If Lao editors seemed to be a mellow lot in 1973, it was because they had seen what had happened to crusading colleagues. They were also aware that their licenses to publish were in effect, only as long as they did not get into trouble with the authorities who censored daily. Suspensions of newspapers had occurred frequently, happening when newspapers carried "rude articles against the government," according to the *Sieng Seri* editor.[5] There also had been cases of reporters who were expelled from Laos, and of others who had been hauled before military authorities and "threatened with menacing words." The latter happened with *Lane Xang* in the mid-1960s, according to that publication's editor.[6] But these incidents seemed minor compared to what

4   Personal interview, Somphon, director, *Lao Hua Daily News*, Vientiane, Laos, 20 December 1973.
5   Interview, Thip Thammavong, *op. cit.*
6   Personal interview, Colonel Khamsavang Chanthryasak, police commissioner and editor, *Lane Xang*, Vientiane, Laos, 20 December 1973.

happened to one journalist, Liam Phommarath.

Liam Phommarath in 1973 had finally become a member of the Lao National Assembly. At the same time, he was retained as sole agent for the only provincial weekly, *Voice of the People*. The latter position, which paid US$40 per month, he held through the sympathy of *VOP*'s editor who realized Liam's financial plight and appreciated the stand the journalist-politician had taken against the officials in the 1960s. For approximately a decade, Liam strove to publish his *Lanxang Kaona* and at the same time, keep out of prison. In the end, he was not very successful in either endeavor; his paper died and Liam himself logged about five years of prison life, having been taken in at least 20 times[7] (see *Lent, 1974d*, pp. 31-34).

3.5.3 Case Studies

The following interviews conducted by the author in December 1973, give an indication of the seriousness of the problems faced by editors in Laos (see *Lent, 1974c*, pp. 170-179).

3.5.3.1 Xat Lao

In 1973, 10-year-old, Lao language *Xat Lao* claimed to be the largest circulation and oldest continuously-published daily in Laos. However, the newsprint shortage and a doubling of newsprint prices in 1973 hampered the paper severely. For one thing, *Xat Lao* cut its circulation from a high of 5,000-6,000 in 1970 to about half that figure. Additionally, staff members were dismissed, the number of pages decreased from 12 to eight and frequency of publication reduced from six to five days weekly. Uneconomical subscriptions in provincial areas were dropped so that *Xat Lao* maintained only 100 to 200 subscribers in five major cities; the copies were sold in bulk to agents in those cities who had to sell them all, as returns were not allowed. Before the newsprint hike, *Xat Lao* could afford to lose money by circulating to small villages as advertising revenue made up the deficits. By late 1973, however, advertising only accounted for 80 per cent of the

---

7   Personal interview, Liam Phommarath, member of Lao National Assembly and former editor of *Lanxang Kaona*, Vientiane, Laos, 20-21 December 1973.

daily's production cost.

Xat Lao, as well as the other newspapers, was limited in its circulation range by the purchasing power of the Lao people. "The average government official earns 15,000 kip (about 800 kip to one US dollar) a month when the price of rice can go to 22,000 kip a sack during the rainy season. So, not even all officials can afford to purchase newspapers," the *Xat Lao* editor said.[8]

On the topic of press freedom, the editor of *Xat Lao* said:

> Editors make criticisms but editorials are loyalist or government oriented. But in news reporting, we give both sides. People here don't care about editorials; they are meant for embassies or the journalistic tradition, not for the masses.[9]

In 1973, *Xat Lao* had six editorial staff members who had been trained on the job through trial and error. Unlike other Southeast Asian nations, Laos did not have a formal training center for journalists, a result of which was that newspapers copied items from each other. For example, 95 per cent of the contents of the weekly English language *Vientiane News* were direct translations of *Xat Lao* items.

Obviously, contents of Lao newspapers were rather similar given this set of circumstances. Taking *Xat Lao* as an example, page one was always devoted to domestic news, while the second page was made up of editorials and the popular and powerful letters to the editor. Page three was commentary while the fourth page dealt with theater and art, as well as lovelorn columns. Romance and adventure type novels were serialized on page five which also carried the "social random notes." *Xat Lao*'s editor described the notes in this fashion:

> If someone of importance goes to a bar, we tell the people in this column. That's how we get officials to read the paper — to see if their names are in the social random notes. Of course, the page is of interest to the wives who wonder what their husbands are doing. The officials do not quarrel with us on these items or it may get worse for them.[10]

8   Interview, Pon Chantharaj, *op. cit.*
9   *Ibid.*
10   *Ibid.*

The sixth page consisted of a travel article written by an editor who had been abroad. Usually the article was serialized and contained subtle, editorial notes.

3.5.3.2 Vientiane Post

Started in mid-1973, the *Vientiane Post* circulated to approximately 2,250 people, 500 of whom lived in the provinces. The five-day-a-week paper was initiated with the editor's personal money, which he in turn obtained from the Development Bank of Laos. Insisting the *Post* was independent, the editor said his paper favored national reconciliation of the Lao people and government and a neutralist political line.[11]

Of the 30 *Post* employees, seven were reporters who gathered international news by monitoring radio and picking up USIS bits of information. The main problem of the *Post* related to the newsprint shortage, because of which the paper had miscalculated potential profits. In late 1973, the *Post* was breaking even financially. According to the editor, the 400,000 to 500,000 kip monthly advertising revenue of the *Post* was barely enough to feed the staff; subscription money was used to pay about US$550 a ton for newsprint. When staff members did receive their pay, they got about 20,000 to 30,000 kip per month.[12]

3.5.3.3 Sieng Seri Daily News

Sieng Seri's main problem was also a financial one. As with other Laotian newspapers, *Sieng Seri* sold for 60 kip per copy. On a typical day, the eight-page daily received 60,000 kip in circulation money. About 200 copies of the paper were flown to outlying provinces through what the editor termed "the Lao way of circulation," bribing an airline clerk with a couple of free copies of *Sieng Seri* for the privilege of free airfreight. Advertising brought in another 200,000 kip monthly. Although *Sieng Seri*

11   Interview, Prisa Trichanh, *op. cit.*
12   *Ibid.*

received no government subsidy, the editor said his paper, as well as all others in Laos, was favored with donations from politicians who agreed with the editorial policy.[13]

Sieng Seri usually did not have enough money to pay the staff; some of the reporters (as with other Lao reporters) supplemented their meager, salaries by working as compositors for Thai printers across the Mekong in Nong Khai.

3.5.3.4 Lao Hua Daily News

Lao Hua was the chief Chinese language daily, the only other being *Sai Kang*. Most of the contents of *Lao Hua* dealt with commercial news of the Chinese community, the majority of whom could not read Lao language dailies. The paper published news of overseas Chinese but refrained from taking a pro-Peking or pro-Taipei line. International news was obtained by monitoring Radio Australia or BBC broadcasts. Of 22 *Lao Hua* employees, only one was performing a reportorial function in 1973; he was the social reporter. Upon invitation, the social reporter participated in Chinese activities which he later wrote about.

Publishing seven days a week, *Lao Hua* made 1.2 million kip monthly from circulation, another 1.5 million kip monthly from advertising. Staff expenses amounted to about 1 million kip per month.[14] The paper carried 12 pages but increased to 16 or 18 if "a rich man gets married and we have a lot of congratulatory advertisements," a director of the company said. Congratulatory and condolence advertisements accounted for a large proportion of the paper's budget.

3.5.3.5 Other Publications

The five-day-a-week *Lao Presse,* a mimeographed newspaper with French and Lao editions, was published by the Lao Ministry of Information. Formally titled *Agence Lao Presse: Bulletin Quotidien,* it was said to be more of an agency than a newspaper,

13 Interview, Thip Thammavong, *op. cit.*
14 Interview, Somphon, *op. cit.*

because it was purchased only by government, business and ambassadorial personnel, not the public.

Voice of the People, a weekly published in Pakse, was the only newspaper not published in the capital city. Although the editor in 1973 was a military man, the rest of the staff was made up of civilians and the paper insisted there was no connection with the army.[15]

Lane Xang was the other publication in 1973. It had a long history of problems. A daily in the latter 1950s, the newspaper was closed for five years by the government following the 1960 coup. In 1965, *Lane Xang* adopted a neutralist line and remained a daily until heavy floods in late 1966 wrecked the plant. A year later, the paper resumed as a weekly, but promptly ran into difficulties with the military. In 1968, an employee who needed money to study in France, stole *Lane Xang's* year's supply of newsprint and sold it. As a result, the paper quit publishing until 1972 when it resumed as a monthly.[16]

Faced with these bleak prospects, why did Vientiane have as many newspapers as it did in 1973-74? The editor of *Lane Xang* explained what all Laotian editors said: newspapers were maintained as hobbies of journalists as well as organs of political factions.[17]

3.5.4 The Press after 1974

By December 1975, the Pathet Lao had control of Laos, and 650 years of monarchy was replaced by the Democratic People's Republic of Laos, in what some periodicals called the "polite" or "jolly song and dance" revolution.

The Communists organized their propaganda machine rather quickly. The Ministry of Propaganda, Information, Culture and Tourism became the chief authority for media; existing news-

15 Personal interview, Colonel Khamsouk S. Rajphakd, editor, *Voice of the People,* Vientiane, Laos, 21 December 1973.
16 Interview, Colonel Khamsavang Chanthryasak, *op. cit.*
17 *Ibid.* Other interviews conducted with Bouaphet Sygnavong, directeur de la presse, Ministry of Information; Khamchong Luangpraseut, editor, *Lao Presse;* Kath Ditthavong, director of propaganda and information and director of National Lao Radio and Ouphet Souvannavong, deputy director of programs, National Lao Radio.

papers were suspended and replaced by two official or semi-official papers, and foreign correspondents and foreign news agencies were expelled from Laos. The Ministry of Propaganda, Information, Culture and Tourism publishes the daily government bulletins issued by the Khao San Pathet Lao news agency (*Asian Press and Media Directory 1976-77,* p. 142).

Among newspapers which ceased publishing in 1975 were the 10-year-old *Sai Kang,* a pro Souvanna Phouma daily (ceased 8 October); the conservative *Xat Lao* (ceased 14 November); *Sieng Seri Daily News,* owned by the rightist, General Vang Pao (ceased 9 May); the three-month-old *Viangchan Kao Na,* right wing weekly tabloid (ceased 2 May); the three-year-old *Viangchan Phot* which became *Viangchan Mai* in early 1975; the English tabloid, *Vientiane News* (ceased 5 May), and *Khao San Pathet Lao,* daily newsletter of the Pathet Lao which ceased under that title on 9 August, to be replaced two days later by *Sieng Pasason.* Thus, by 1976, the press of Laos, never formidable in numbers and circulation, was reduced to *Sieng Pasason* (*Voice of the People*), the official voice of the Lao People's Revolutionary Party with a circulation of 12,000, *Viangchan Mai* (*New Vientiane*), daily broadsheet of the government with a circulation of 6,000, and two small Chinese newspapers. Shaplen, in mid-1976, reported that foreign, English language newspapers (not magazines) had been banned, and the nation depended upon rumors and radio. He said loudspeakers on every block blared "forth revolutionary exhortations and songs — the latter traditional Laotian tunes with new words" (*Shaplen,* 1976, p. 76).

At first (in mid-1975), Laos required that foreign newsmen have sponsors in Laos and entry applications approved by the foreign ministry. A blacklist was started at that time of unwanted journalists who wrote "biased and distorted" articles. Everingham said "journalistic blunders, topping some biased and shoddy reporting about Laos," gave the government the pretext it needed to issue press controls. In mid-1975, two foreign newspapers were banned and a third was censored (*Everingham,* 1975, p. 22).

A year later, the two government newspapers engaged in a press war with sensational Thai newspapers, which they believed were hostile and inaccurate in their reporting of Laos. *Sieng Pasason* and *Viangchan Mai* at the time poured out a huge amount of anti-

Thai propaganda (*Everingham*, 1976, pp. 18-19). Late in 1976 (November), the government closed the Agence France Presse bureau, refused visas to United States correspondents wanting to cover the first anniversary of Laos as a Communist nation and ordered all diplomatic missions in Laos to submit for censoring, six hours before publication, their published daily news bulletins (*Far Eastern Economic Review*, 15 July 1977, pp. 34-35).

Censorship became more stringent in early 1977 as a committee was set up to censor everything written, sung, recited and danced in an effort to uphold "the quality of progressive artistic works."

Perhaps the extent to which government agents were ready to go in their efforts to oust foreign journalists was exemplified in the case of *Far Eastern Economic Review* correspondent, John Everingham. Everingham was expelled from Laos in July 1977, after being accused of being a spy. Among the 16 charges made against Everingham were that he took pictures of Lao government leaders; dispatched news to many newspapers around the world, besides those he was accredited with at the Ministry of Propaganda; associated with Lao people for the purpose of gathering news (the agents said foreign journalists had the right only to speak to government officials, not private citizens); trafficked in opium; corrupted the morals of youth and illegally possessed foreign exchange and a lethal gas weapon (later found to be a BB gun) (*Far Eastern Economic Review*, 15 July 1977, pp. 34-35).

3.6 Malaysia

John A. Lent

Malaysia, a former British colony of approximately 11 million people, is diversified by ethnic origins, languages and religions. According to 1970 population figures, Malaysia is made up of 46.6 per cent Malays, 8.72 per cent other indigenes, 34.1 per cent Chinese, 8.97 per cent Indians and Pakistanis and 1.5 per cent other immigrants. The four main languages in use are Bahasa Malaysia, the language of the Malay ethnic community (now considered the national language), Chinese, English and Tamil. Malaysia is much better off than its neighbors, having huge rubber and tin resources to draw upon; however, the nation is still considered underdeveloped. Politically independent since 1957, the nation is governed by a parliamentary system, made up mostly of representatives of the National Front, an alliance of all the strong political parties.

Historically, the press had been patterned along linguistic and political party lines; its loyalty, for the most part, was to the motherlands of ethnic communities, not to Malaya (later renamed Malaysia).

3.6.1 Historical Perspective

3.6.1.1 English Language Press

The first newspaper in what is now Malaysia appeared in English, and from its beginning in 1806 until 1970, there were at least 122 others in that language. Fifty-one originated in Singapore, 27 in Penang, 25 in Kuala Lumpur, nine each in Ipoh and Malacca and two in Taiping (*Lim,* 1970).

It should not come as a surprise that the first newspaper was in English, even though only about a hundred English merchants, planters and government personnel were included in the total population of 30,000. Like most colonial periodicals, *The Government Gazette* of Penang served as a house organ for the foreigners, advertising their wares, printing government notices and keeping them abreast of happenings in England. Merchant and auctioneer, A. B. Bone, established the *Gazette* on 1 March 1806, under "certain conditions" laid down by the East India Company which had granted the publishing permit. Although not specified, the conditions were probably those common to the company at that time: "no gossip, no criticism of government, individuals or policies and submission of proof sheets before final publication" (*Byrd,* 1970). *The Government Gazette* was published at a commercial press, unlike the first newspapers of Singapore and Malacca (the other two Straits Settlements) which came off missionary presses. All of the early newspapers had one thing in common — they were subsidized. *The Government Gazette* received monthly subsidies in exchange for printing government announcements, and on a few occasions, was granted government loans which were to be repaid in job printing.

In Malacca, the Anglo-Chinese Press, operated by the London Missionary Society personnel, dealt with Chinese language newspapers first, but between September 1826 and October 1929, the Society published the weekly *Malacca Observer* in English. Like so many of his contemporaries, *Observer* editor, John Henry Moor, ran into trouble with the authorities; he was duly punished; pressure was placed on the Anglo-Chinese Press to keep him in line and finally the officials closed his paper (*Gibson-Hill,* 1953, pp. 174-199).

Most significant to the contemporary press scene in Malaysia (and Singapore) was the birth of The *Straits Times and Singapore Journal of Commerce* on 15 July 1845. The paper survives as the largest-circulated daily in both nations. The *Straits Times* was financed by Martemus T. Apcar and edited by lawyer Robert Carr Woods, described as a "pompous, self-important and frivolous writer" who thought so highly of his sense of humor that he underlined his printed puns (*Kennard,* 1970). Woods promised to uphold "the integrity of national institutions, laying bare to the eyes whatever abuses spring up or exist . . . and by faithful advocacy of public rights secure to the governed protection against the innovation or misrule of the governing." Revamped in early 1858, the *Straits Times* began daily publication in a new format.

After 1890, English language newspapers appeared on the scene much more regularly – and disappeared nearly as quickly. Whereas there were 35 papers in the first 84 years of the history of the English language press, 88 others were published between 1890 and 1970. The fact the Malay Federated States produced newspapers after 1890 accounted for some of this increase. For example, Kuala Lumpur did not have its first English language paper until the *Straits Budget* appeared as a weekly in 1894, followed two years later by the daily *Malay Mail*. Taiping's first newspaper was published during the same decade, while Ipoh published its first English newspaper after the turn of the century (*Lim,* 1970). Most of these newspapers were short-lived and left very little impact. Of course, exceptions existed, such as the *Malay Mail, Straits Echo* and *Malayan Tribune*. The *Echo,* published in Penang, claimed to be the first English language paper to represent the Chinese in the Straits Settlements; it was designed to disseminate information about Sun Yat-sen's movements. Started in either 1903 or 1911, the *Echo*'s most glorious years were the 1930s, when it waged circulation battles with the Singapore giants for control of northern Malaya (*Saravanamuttu,* 1970).

That decade before World War II was a key time for English language journalism in Malaya and Singapore. During those years, the big business practices which had been common in Western nations for decades were finally replacing personal journalism. Previously, editorial policy and content were all-important, but in the immediate pre-war years, newspaper people noted the importance of sales and circulation. Tops in circulation was the *Malayan Tribune,* followed by *Straits Times* and *Straits Echo.*

By February 1942, the Japanese had complete control of mass media in the area. All newspapers were confiscated and converted into Japanese propaganda organs. For example, the *Straits Times* was made into *Syonan Shimbun;* the *Malay Mail* in Kuala Lumpur became *Malai Shimbun;* the *Malayan Tribune* plant in Perak was changed into the *Perak Shimbun* and the *Penang Gazette* became the *Penang Daily News* and later *Penang Shimbun (Onn,* 1946, p. 2). These dailies remained in the English language although in most cases, they printed editions in Malay, Chinese and Tamil as well, or as in the case of the Malacca paper, they devoted separate pages of the same issue to other languages. The contents were basically the same in all of these papers, resounding the themes of a new Malai, down with Anglo-Americanism and Asia for Asiatics.

As was the case in most of Southeast Asia after the war, Malaya and Singapore witnessed a mushrooming of new papers, at least 13, between 1945 and 1950, and most pre-war leaders were re-established. The *Straits Times* resumed as a single sheet on 7 September 1945, although it had been forbidden by the British Military Administration. BMA wanted its own newspaper to be the chief English language paper in the region for the first six months of liberation (*Straits Times,* 20 Sept. 1970). On the other hand, Penang's *Straits Echo* was encouraged to commence in September 1945, the BMA even granting a loan for that purpose. The *Tribune* also resumed with the aid of a loan.

While most newcomers failed to make the grade, the *Straits Times* seemed to do everything right. With its purchase of the *Malay Mail* in 1952, the paper gained a Kuala Lumpur office and plant, from which it initiated Malayan editions of the *Straits Times* in June 1956, and *Berita Harian* in 1957. Its purchases soared so that by 1958, the Singapore *Straits Times* published ten periodicals, while the Kuala Lumpur branch had the *Straits Times, Malay Mail* and *Berita Harian* (*Abisheganaden,* 1970). Among the newest English language newspapers in Malaysia is *The Star,* started in Penang in September 1971 (see *Lent,* 1975b, pp. 95-113).

3.6.1.2 Chinese Language Press

Malaysia's first Chinese language newspaper is considered the first modern Chinese periodical anywhere in the world. Nine years after the English language *Government Gazette* appeared in Penang, British missionary, William Milne, on 6 August 1815, established the *Chinese Monthly Magazine* or a *Monthly Record of Social Manners* in Malacca. Designed to proselytize for Protestantism

in China, the *Chinese Monthly* would have appeared in China had
there not been a ban on missionaries there (*Britton*, 1933, p. 17).
However, it might be justifiable to think of *Lat Pau*, started in
Singapore in 1881, as the first Chinese newspaper in what is now
Malaysia. Operated by a wealthy merchant, See Ewe Lay, it was
the first newspaper created and published by a Chinese. Although
the paper lasted 51 years, finally facing liquidation in 1932,
Lat Pau was not without problems, chief of which were recruitment of staff and gathering of authentic news. Because Chinese
intellectuals were not willing to leave the homeland for the Straits
Settlements, See relied on translations from Chinese newspapers in
Hong Kong and Shanghai, the local English language press and
agents throughout Southeast Asia, for his news content (*Chen*,
1967, p. 13).

The first 80 years of Chinese journalism in the Straits Settlements were not very fruitful. Newspapers were started on a
hit-or-miss basis, not oriented so much towards the local Chinese
community as to foreign missionaries, not interested so much in
creating a local Chinese public opinion as to report on activities
in China. The situation changed drastically during the next period,
1895-1911, which Lin Yutang (1936, p. 80) called the golden
age of Chinese journalism. As Singapore became a rendezvous for
political refugees from China, a public opinion press, espousing
the causes of either the reformists or revolutionaries, was the
result (*Purcell*, 1967, p. 209). When the revolutionaries exhausted
their Singapore resources, they moved on to Penang. Sun Yat-sen
resided in Penang in 1910-11, during which time he helped found
Kwong Wah Yit Poh, which still survives. *Kwong Wah* was Sun's
main propaganda vehicle during its early years. Other newspapers
were set up in Penang or Kuala Lumpur during this golden age
(see *Lent*, 1974a, pp. 397-412).

The next period that saw a blossoming of Chinese newspapers
in what was then Malaya, was the 20 years just before World War
II. For example, of the 44 Chinese papers in Malaya/Malaysia
(excluding Singapore) published between 1815-1970, 11 were
started between 1921-30 and six others in 1931-40 (*Lim*, 1970).
Some of this growth can be attributed to the accession of the
Kuomintang to power in China during the mid-1920s, which,
according to Cady, had profound changes on the typically

apolitical attitude of Malay Chinese. Heretofore, the Peking government had paid virtually no attention to the overseas Chinese; the new regime solicited the political and financial support of Southeast Asian Chinese (*Cady, 1964, p. 453*). After 1930, the Malay Communist Party began wooing the Chinese and agitating against the British. Thus, as they had done during the golden era, newspapers developed to support a movement: this time either Kuomintang or Communist. Surviving newspapers begun in this period were Penang's *Sing Pin Jih Pao,* Ipoh's *Kin Kwok Daily News* and the Singapore editions of *Nanyang Siang Pau* and *Sin Chew Jit Poh,* both of which circulated in Malaya until separate editions were created in 1962 and 1966, respectively.

During World War II, although the Japanese did not encourage the use of Chinese and Tamil, their *Shimbuns* published pages in those languages. Underground newspapers that operated during the Japanese occupation for the most part were in Chinese. In the 1945-47 period, at least 10 Chinese newspapers were started, including *China Press* (1946) which survives.

3.6.1.3 Malay Language Press

Compared to its English and Chinese language press, Malaysia's national language newspapers are relatively young. The first recognized newspaper in the Malay language appeared in 1876, seven decades after the *Government Gazette* in English and 61 years later than the *Chinese Monthly Magazine.* However, once developed, the Malay press grew quickly. Between 1876 and 1941, at least 162 Malay language newspapers, magazines and journals were published; at least another 27 appeared since 1941 (*Roff, 1972, pp. 1-2; Lim, 1970*). The most prolific period of the Malay press in the century was between 1906-41, when 147 periodicals were issued, nearly one-half of which were published in Peninsular Malaysia. Very few of the publications lasted long, to the extent that today, in Malaysia, there are only three Malay dailies, the oldest of which, *Utusan Melayu,* dates only to 1939.

Malay journalism owes its beginnings to the locally-born Indian Muslims of Singapore, called Jawi Peranakan. As Roff explained, the Jawi Peranakan were locally-born offspring of unions between indigenous Malay women and South Indian Muslim traders. In late 1876, this group formed an association in Singapore, which in turn published a weekly called *Jawi Peranakan (Roff,* 1972).

A writer of the time described *Jawi Peranakan* as having a circulation of 250 by 1880, "ably and punctually edited, having with only one exception, been issued consistently on the day on which it professes to come out" (*Birch,* 1879, p. 52). The paper was also responsible for spawning other newspapers. Roff claimed that most of the 17 periodicals that appeared between 1876 and 1905 were sponsored or edited by *Jawi Peranakan* personnel (*Roff,* 1972, p. 3). Most of the first periodicals were hand lithographed weeklies, modelled initially after English language newspapers, and later using Egyptian and Arabic news content. The result was that most of the content did not relate to the Malay community.

In July 1906, the mood of Malay journalism began to change with the appearance of *Al Imam (The Leader),* a religious periodical published in Singapore. Previously, Malay media dealt with literary and social interest contributions, but *Al Imam* had a drastic effect on the trends in content and outlook of periodicals. During its three-and-a-half-year existence, *Al Imam* pushed for social and religious reforms in Malaya, setting an example for successors such as *Neracha (Scales), Saudara (The Brethren)* and *Al Ikhwan (The Brotherhood).* Another development of the period commencing in 1906, was the birth of major national Malay dailies. Operated as a Malay edition of the *Singapore Free Press, Utusan Melayu,* started in 1907 publishing thrice weekly, was the closest thing to a daily in Malay. For seven years, it had no Malay language competition; in 1915, *Utusan Melayu* became a daily and continued until 1921. A second daily, *Lembaga Melayu,* appeared in 1914 as a somewhat Malay edition of the *Malayan Tribune;* it died in 1931.

During the 1920s and 1930s, the Malay press gradually moved out of Singapore, increased its numbers considerably and offered a diversified field of daily and weekly newspapers. Malay media portrayed more and more the growing Malay consciousness on the peninsula, part of which could be gleaned in the correspondence columns of newspapers which were filled with controversies over language, idiom, custom and religion (*Zainal,* 1941, p. 245).

Between 1930 and 1941, at least eight daily Malay newspapers appeared, five of which were particularly significant. They were: *Warta Malaya (Malaya Times)*; a new *Utusan Melayu* started in 1939; *Majlis (The Council)*; *Lembaga (The Tribune)* and *Saudara*, all important for their political content. During World War II, most Malay papers were suspended. The Japanese confiscated *Utusan Melayu* on 15 February 1942, and eventually merged it with *Warta Malaya* to form *Berita Mâlai (Malaya News)* (*Nik*, 1963, p. 69). From the end of the war until independence in 1957, at least 20 Malay language newspapers were published. Whereas pre-war newspapers strove for the rights of Malays against Chinese and Indian encroachments, those appearing in the immediate post-war period fought against British colonialism. Since independence, about a dozen Malay newspapers have been initiated. Two months before independence, *Berita Harian (The Daily News)* was started as a Malay edition of the *Straits Times;* the Kuala Lumpur edition was established shortly after. Still others have been *Mingguan Bahru*, Penang weekly in 1958; the short-lived *Merdeka* of Kuala Lumpur in 1964 and papers in Ipoh and Kota Bahru. *Utusan Melayu*, noting that more people were learning Malay because of a constitutional clause of 1957 making it the national language, started its weekly *Mingguan Malaysia* in 1964 and a Romanized Malay daily, *Utusan Malaysia*, in 1967. (see *Lent*, 1978b, pp. 598-612).

3.6.1.4 Indian Language Press

Birch mentioned two Tamil language newspapers in the Straits Settlements before 1880; one, *Tangai Snahen*, was published in Singapore between 1876-79 (*Birch*, 1879, pp. 51-54). A few others appeared sporadically during the next 40 years, but it was the reformist movements of Malayan Indians after 1920 that sparked a lively journalistic tradition. The immigration of more educated Indians and Ceylonese into Malaya during this period provided the experienced journalists necessary to sustain a press (*Ambalavanar*, 1970, p. 2). The newspapers they created began the gigantic task of upgrading the political, labor, social and intellectual conditions of Malayan Indians. The Tamil papers, using South Indian dailies as their models, took up nationalist and reformist causes, campaigning for better immigration policies, working conditions and political rights previously denied to Malayan Indians. Spearheading the reformist movements was *Tamilaham,* founded in 1921 by Narasinha Iyengar. In its very first issues, the paper broached the subject of Indian immigration to Malaya, and by its second year, was discouraging Indians from coming to work the plantations. *Tamilaham* lost some of its power when Iyengar left in 1924 to start *Tamil Nesan.* A number of left-wing publications in Tamil were started immediately after World War II, "spreading anti-colonialist propaganda of an extreme kind" (*Arasaratnam,* 1970, p. 113). But most Indian newspapers, e.g., *Tamil Nesan* and *Sangamani,* contented themselves with promoting Tamil nationalism and unity on the basis of culture and language.

There were also sporadic issues of Malayalam and Punjabi newspapers in Malaya before and immediately after World War II. No Malayalam newspaper exists in Malaysia today, and the Punjabi press exists in name only.

The past quarter century has seen a number of shifts in Indian journalism in Malaysia. New immigration laws have dictated against employing Indian nationals and the surviving newspapers are now edited by Malaysian Indians. With the governmental aim of creating a national unity, Tamil newspapers, like their English and Chinese counterparts, are being implored to broaden their scopes and not just serve the campaigns of the ethnic group (see *Lent,* 1974b, pp. 344-49).

3.6.2 Contemporary Press

Unlike most other Southeast Asian nations, Malaysia possesses a diversified, financially-sound and wide-reaching mass media apparatus. The 50 daily and Sunday newspapers, with a total circulation of over a million, are subdivided by language with about 25 in Chinese, 12 in English, six in Bahasa Malaysia, five in Tamil and two in Punjabi. Additionally, six radio networks, a national news agency, two television channels and an educational television system, all under government ownership and control, operate. As an indication of the security of the press, in 1974, when Malaysia was having numerous economic problems, the newspapers announced record profits. Competition has remained keen, especially between the English language *New Straits Times* and Penang *Star* and among the Chinese dailies.

The New Straits Times Press is the largest media conglomerate in Malaysia, owning *New Straits Times, Sunday Times, Malay Mail, Sunday Mail, Berita Harian, Berita Minggu, Business Times,* a magazine group and a book company. New Straits Times Press also has equity participation in the *Asian Wall Street Journal.* By 1978, New Straits Times Press was owned by Fleetprint, a Malay dominated group which included among its holdings a Sarawak bank, Bian Chiang (*Asiaweek,* 19 May 1978, p. 39). The *New Straits Times* became the first Asian newspaper to completely computerize its editorial operations, doing so, in 1976 (*Letchmikanthan,* 1977, p. 18).

Another large group, Utusan Melayu Group, publishers of the daily *Utusan Melayu* in Jawi and *Utusan Malaysia* in Romanized Malay, weekly *Mingguan Malaysia* and at least 10 magazines, was important in the 1970s for its spectacular increase in readership. Between July 1973-June 1974, readership of *Utusan Malaysia* rose by 200,000 to 547,000 readers; *Mingguan Malaysia* readership went up to 717,000, and the group's monthly women's magazine, *Wanita,* became the most widely read periodical (*Coats,* 1975, p. 10). For the first time in the history of the nation's press, Bahasa Malaysia language newspapers surpassed those in English and Chinese in readership.

3.6.2.1 Ownership

A governmental decision of 1972 has changed the ownership structure of the Malaysian press; the trend is now against foreign holdings in Malaysian media. An amendment to the Printing Presses Bill in January 1974, officially established that Malaysians must maintain majority shares in all newspapers. In introducing the bill, the then Minister of Information, Ghazali Shafie, said that in a developing nation, it is important to insure that mass media are above suspicion, and that papers owned by foreigners are not likely to play genuine and truthful roles. According to Ghazali Shafie's figures, in 1972, only 13 of 34 papers were wholly Malaysian owned, another 16 were instituted with foreign capital having less than 50 per cent of the shares, and five were totally foreign owned (*Media*, March 1974, p. 24). Few would argue for the foreign ownership of a nation's mass media; however, what is debatable, and somewhat suspicious, in the case of Malaysia, is the manner in which local ownership has been implemented. As the leader of the opposition in Parliament said, newspapers switched from foreign ownership to ruling political party control, leading to future diminution of press freedom (*Media*, March 1974, p. 24). There are examples to support this claim. In 1972, the Straits Times Press was renamed New Straits Times Press and 80 per cent of its shares were placed in the hands of the government trading corporation, Pernas. As a result, control of New Straits Times Press lies indirectly with United Malays National Organization (UMNO), a Malay dominated political party in the National Front government. Later, Fleetprint, also dominated by Malays was listed as owner of New Straits Times Press. Utusan Melayu Group is owned by UMNO, and indications throughout the 1970s were that *Nanyang Siang Pau*, largest Chinese language publisher, had also come under the party's sway. A second large Chinese daily, *Sin Chew Jit Poh*, and its Penang sister, *Sing Pin*, is owned by Pernas (*Suara Pemau*, 15 Sept. 1975). Star Publications (daily *Star*, *Kwong Wah Yit Poh* and magazines) is bankrolled by UMNO and the Malaysian Chinese Association (both elements in the National Front), and since 1974, has been chaired by former prime minister, Abdul Rahman. Former *Star* chairman, Dato Hussein Nordin, also chairman of Utusan Melayu Group, is now deputy chairman of the publishing firm, and former chief minister of Sabah, Tun Mustapha, also owns shares in Star Publications. At least one of the two remaining Tamil language dailies is owned by a high official of the Malaysian Indian Congress, another political party member of the National Front. The latest newspaper to appear in the country, *Watan*, although professing to be independent, is owned by former cabinet minister and ambassador to the United States, Mohamed Khir Johari. Finally, political party ownership of newspapers is very prevalent in the East Malaysian states of Sabah and Sarawak.

3.6.3 *Press Legislation*

The 1970s also saw the enactment of numerous laws and amendments that affected the Malaysian press. The Printing Presses Act, promulgated in 1948, was amended in 1971 and 1974. The act stipulates that a potential publisher must secure a license to use a printing press and a permit to publish a newspaper. Both must be renewed annually through the Ministry of Home Affairs which can withdraw either without cause at any time. Since 1970, all license holders must guarantee that their publications will not distort facts relating to public order incidents in Malaysia, will not inflame or stir communal hostility or use material likely to prejudice public order or national security. The 1974 amendment insures local ownership of newspapers (see *Lent, 1978b,* pp. 155-56).

The Sedition Ordinance of 1948, and its 1971 amendment, is especially feared by Malaysian press personnel. The law itself is not that different from sedition laws elsewhere, making one liable to fines or imprisonment for acts, words, speech and publication which have seditious tendency. What is unique is the 1971 amendment forbidding mass media discussion of four broadly-defined sensitive issues: the Bahasa Malaysia language policy, special rights granted to the Malay ethnic community under the Second Malaysia Plan, the special roles of sultans and other royalty and the citizenship policy regarding non-Malays. The act has been used twice in the past decade.

Other laws have intimidating effects upon press people. Under the Control of Imported Publications Act, the Minister of Information has absolute discretion in restricting the importation of any publications he deems prejudicial to the public order, morality or security of the country. The act has been applied mainly to pro-Communist publications, and others such as *Time, Newsweek* and *Far Eastern Economic Review* were banned or censored for carrying stories that the government found unfavorable to its programs and policies.

Probably the act used most frequently in recent years to suppress oppositionist views has been the Internal Security Act (1960). Under it, the Minister of Information can prohibit the printing or possession of any material which, in his opinion, may lead to violence, cause public disorder or promote hostility between races. Rights to normal court procedures are violated in the enforcement of the act. Initially, no public charge is lodged against the accused who may be held for 60 days before a charge is placed and his case is heard by a special administrative board. The accused may be placed in confinement for up to two years at the sole discretion of the hearing officer. In 1976-77, the act was used to detain at least editors of *New Straits Times* (Samad Ismail) and *Berita Harian* (Samani bin Muhamad Amin) and the former editor of *Sin Chew Jit Poh* (Chan Ken-sin). In each of these instances, the individuals were detained without trial until they agreed to make public confessions over government television. During the televised proceedings, they stated that they were tied to Communist or Marxist groups or individuals, worked against the best interests of Malaysia and were now ready to denounce their actions and beliefs. They were then questioned by a group of journalists or government selected inquisitors, and their confessions were subsequently used in the local press (see *Lent*, 1978d, pp. 9-18).

3.6.4 *Press Freedom and a Guided Press*

Complementing controls by the government through ownership and legislation is the idea that all aspects of information and entertainment in the Malaysian press must be guided by the government. The premise is that Malaysia, a newly-emergent nation, needs time to develop; the mass media must provide this time by not touching upon sensitive issues, by stressing positive and conversely, ignoring negative societal characteristics.

Goals which the press is implored to promote are written into the Second and Third Malaysia Plans and the *Rukunegara* (National Ideology). The former, calling for a restructuring of society, is meant to upgrade Malays economically and to eradicate poverty nationwide. The *Rukunegara* is based on the beliefs of a united nation, democratic, just, liberal and progressive society, and the principles of loyalty to king and country, belief in God, upholding of the constitution, rule of law and good behavior and morality.

Thus, with stringent legislation, as well as the national policy guidelines of the economic plans and *Rukunegara,* Malaysian newspapers practice strict self-restraint. All newspapers, for instance, steer away from investigative reporting, fill pages with government speeches and campaigns and generally ignore the opposition. As one Bahasa Malaysia newspaper editor said, "it is not the newspapers' role to check on government. The papers here are not pro- or anti-government, but supporters of government."[1] Print media, operating under virtually a guided press concept, stress developmental news through statements made by officials and press releases issued by the Department of Information, press agents of various ministries and Bernama News Agency. Content analyses have borne out that Malaysian newspapers use large proportions of developmental information supplied by — and supportive of — the government. Studying 24 issues of *Utusan Malaysia, Utusan Melayu* and *New Straits Times* in 1974, one researcher showed that these dailies devoted 52.3, 52.4 and 32.4 per cent, respectively, of their news content to national development projects (*Hamima Dona Mustafa,* in *Lent and Vilanilam,* forthcoming). Also, in line with the objectives of the Second Malaysia Plan, the two Bahasa Malaysia dailies promoted the policy of increasing Malay involvement in business. Other analyses show similar findings (see *Lent,* 1978b, pp. 157-158). In a 1976 study of two months of Bernama copy and contents of three major dailies, it was found that all carried between 54.5 and 67 per cent government news and 33 to 45.5 per cent non-government news (*Safar Hasyim et al.,* 1976). A content analysis of election news in 1974 found that the Malay language *Utusan Melayu* used eight times as much, and the English language *New Straits Times* four times as much, news favoring the government coalition, as they carried for the opposition (*Meor Zailan et al.,* 1975).

3.6.5 Economics

As indicated earlier, most Malaysian newspapers are economically viable enterprises. Circulations and readership have generally been

---

1   S.H. Tan, former editor, *Malay Mail,* to Universiti Sains Students, Kuala Lumpur, Aug. 25, 1972.

on the upgrade in the 1970s, and as late as 1978, newspapers still garnered 56.4 per cent of all advertising money in Malaysia. The latter point is important since in most nations, television has surpassed newspapers and other media in grabbing the advertising dollar. In Malaysia, television gets 16.9 per cent, followed by periodicals with 14.7 per cent (*Wong*, 1979, p. 25; see also *Middleton*, 1977, pp. 19, 21). Writing in the mid-1970s, Coats emphasized the remarkable ability of Malaysian newspapers to prosper even in dire economic times:

> After a year in which the press in the West shuddered under the weight of rising newsprint costs, wage demands and falling revenue, and those in less developed parts of the world, such as India, saw the rapid reduction in the size of their newspapers and even the disappearance of some, the three leading groups in Malaysia announced record profits.
>
> And, at a time when advertising agencies were sent running for cover as budgets were decimated and living standards declined, Malaysia felt the draught a little but its agencies remained resilient and stalled on cutting back staff until, in a couple of instances, the turn of the year (*Coats*, 1975, p. 10).

In conclusion, the Malaysian press can be defined as economically sound but nearly bankrupt when it comes to political freedom. By relinquishing their watchdog posts, the newspapers have become less than credible champions of governmental priorities. There seems very little chance of this latter trend being reversed.

3.7 Philippines
John A. Lent

3.7.1 Pre-Martial Law

No one could quibble with the statement that the press of the Philippines until September 1972, was the most free in Asia. It was a fact of which Filipinos were extremely proud and to which Asian journalists pointed when it was said press freedom in Asia was dead (see *Lent*, 1971, pp. 191-209). Since September 1972, however, the Philippine press has become one of the most controlled presses in Asia, a region where governments traditionally allow media very little leeway.

Since independence in 1946, all Philippine governments have levelled protests against the press, but most of these protests were not taken very seriously. The press was strong and freedom of expression was unrestricted to the extent that no politician or public figure could hope to escape permanently from press revelations. Irresponsible acts were conducted throughout these raucous times, but in the 1960s, efforts were being made by the press, through the Philippine Press Institute and others, to make itself more socially responsible.

3.7.1.1 Governmental Media Apparatus

As the deliberately-guided press theory of the developing world caught up with Manila in the 1960s, the government began building its own information structure to compete with the private mass media. Cries rang out consistently against the increasing use of government handouts to control press content.

But the government, especially that of Marcos, responded by telling the people to worship new gods and adopt new creeds which said that developing nations such as the Philippines could not afford the luxury of a free press.

In order to bring the press under control, the Marcos government of the late 1960s and early 1970s launched one of the largest government media operations in Asia, seducing lowly-paid journalists into the government information services in the process. Through a system of public financing, the comprehensive Marcos media network by mid-1971 included the National Media Production Center, which by then had been placed under the Office of the President; the Malacañang (Presidential Palace) Press Office; and the public information offices budgeted under all departments of the government. The total budget of these government media centers was said to equal that of at least four of the six major dailies in the Philippines.

Besides these operations, Marcos also acquired control — directly or through relatives and friends — of some of the commercially-operated mass media. For example, a top military aide, Hans Menzi, acquired the *Manila Bulletin* and its broadcasting outlets, and other Marcos interests took over the Kanloan Broadcasting System. In April 1972, a new paper, *Philippines Daily Express,* appeared with the purpose of playing down crime, sensation and political muckraking and stressing positive news, especially that relating to national development and the good image of the government. The publisher of the *Express* was Juan A. Perez, jr., a former Malacañang assistant; the editor was Enrique Romualdez, cousin of the president's wife.

To man these government information enterprises, Marcos raided the commercially-operated media for staff members. Additionally, Marcos used newsmen on a part-time basis, installing them or their wives on the board of censors and other official agencies. Top journalistic mudslingers of only a few years before, such as *Manila Times* columnist J. V. Cruz (who became an ambassador), found themselves in important and lucrative government posts.

3.7.1.2 Criticism of the Press

As the Marcos information complex expanded, so did the criticism levelled at mass media practitioners. The Marcos administration increasingly accused the press of actions designed to subvert and bring down the government. Nearly every time the president and his wife, Imelda, spoke, they blasted the press. Some of the charges bordered on the ridiculous. For example, when Imelda Marcos had a miscarriage in 1971, the president attributed its cause to press attacks accusing the First Lady of bribery.

Marcos was also hitting out at the media oligarchies long before martial law came into effect. For years the Philippine media had been owned by the giant business concerns of a small number of families, especially the Lopez, Soriano, Roces and Elizalde families. One of the largest, the Lopez conglomerate, included the *Manila Chronicle* and ABS-CBN radio-TV networks owned partly by Fernando Lopez, who had been vice president of the Philippines under Marcos. But, after Marcos and his vice president split in late 1970, administration officials intensified their criticisms of the mass media owned by large vested interests. Marcos suspected the Lopez family of financing student activists in an effort to embarrass him. In other instances, Marcos took to name calling, terming the newspapers "whiners, gripers and time-wasters."

This continual haranguing of the press had its effect: criticisms were being toned down by the press and many journalists switched to less controversial subjects, such as environmental pollution. A series of libel suits initiated by the government — the largest against *Time* magazine for 50 million pesos — added to the tension. One paper, the *Dumaguete Times,* died even though acquitted of the criminal charges brought against its editor and staff by the government.

As a result, self-restraint was being used by some editors. Thus, when Marcos suspended the writ of habeas corpus after the August 1971 grenade bombing at a political rally in Plaza Miranda, only the *Manila Times* and *Manila Chronicle* were totally opposed, while the *Evening News, Philippines Herald* and *Daily Mirror* agreed with the president's move. The *Bulletin* played it safe and did not comment.

As 1972 approached, the press-Marcos battle was reaching fever pitch. By barricading himself from public inquiry, the president had become the least accessible chief executive in the nation's history. Newsmen complained of the distortion and misrepresentations flooding their offices and carrying Malacañang datelines. Marcos was blamed for creating credibility problems by saying one thing and doing another.

Other direct pressures were brought to bear upon the press during the pre-martial law period. On one occasion, the Marcos government paid movie exhibitors not to advertise in the vehemently anti-Marcos *Manila Times*. In December 1971, a former National Press Club president complained that the government was trying to make the availability of newsprint so prohibitive that papers would be at the mercy of the government.

Probably the most shocking action the Marcos forces took against the press occurred in mid-1970 with the arrest of journalists Rizal and Quintin Yuyitung, brothers who published the *Chinese Commercial News* of Manila. The Yuyitungs had been harassed by other Philippine governments, having been accused of everything from being pro-Kuomintang to pro-Loyalist, pro-Japanese (during the occupation), and most recently, pro-Communist. But, early on the morning of 5 May 1970, they were taken from their homes and deported to Taiwan under very suspicious circumstances by the Philippine immigration director himself. In his deportation order, Marcos accused the Yuyitungs of committing "overt acts favorable to the communist cause." Despite an outcry from world press organizations, the Yuyitungs received prison sentences as recommended by the military court that tried them in Taiwan. Evidence against the brothers was very scanty; it was explained they were pro-Communist because they monitored the New China News Agency and used certain language that was communistic. Quintin Yuyitung was released from a Taiwanese prison in August 1972, after serving two years. He was told he was free to go anywhere except back to his Philippine homeland. Rizal was released a year later.

Meanwhile, Manila pressmen and politicians were keenly aware of what was happening to them. The Philippine Press Institute point out the increasing dangers the press was facing and campaigned for passage of legislation such as the Padilla Press Freedom

Bill, which sought to penalize public officials who refused to show public records to the media. Constitutional Convention delegates approved a bill in January 1972 which held that a committee on public information should be established, that the right of every citizen to have full access to public records should be insured, that the state should not nationalize the mass media, and that censorship should not prevail.

But, by January 1972, it was too late to do much about the government. Realizing that he, the only re-elected president in the Philippines, was also becoming its most unpopular chief executive, Marcos moved to secure his power base. More and more, he used his critics as scapegoats for the mounting number of bombings, the increasing crime wave, the July 1972 floods, the devaluation of the peso, the Muslim-Christian fracas in Mindanao, the attempted or planned assassinations of administrative personnel and the drubbing his Nationalist Party received at the 1971 Senate elections. On 22 September 1972, he put the Philippines under martial law rule.

3.7.2 *Martial Law and Government-Press Relationships*

3.7.2.1. Death of Manila Press

Citing the media as a prime enemy and target, Marcos wasted very little time in killing newspapers and broadcasting stations. Without warning, police walked into newspaper offices and broadcasting studios, ordered staff members to leave and posted announcements stating: "This building is closed and sealed and placed under military control." They were operating under a letter of instruction from the president to the press secretary and national defense secretary. In that letter, dated 22 September 1972, the president ordered that all media of communication be taken over for the duration of the national emergency. Such drastic action was rationalized by one military official as necessary to prevent subversives from being warned about operations to pick them up. Thus, by daybreak of 23 September, Marcos had wiped out the entire news media of the Philippines in a fashion reminiscent of the Japanese occupation of the 1940s. All he exempted were his own *Daily Express,* his KBS radio station and a few others of his supporters.

On 26 September, an announcement by Executive Secretary Alejandro Melchor sealed the fate of a number of papers. Melchor said some newspapers would never resume, claiming Manila had too many dailies (15 in pre-martial law). Marcos, in a *New York Times* interview of 27 September, said the publishing rights of six dailies would be withheld indefinitely. His reason was different from Melchor's but quite familiar by that time: the press and radio had been infiltrated by Communist propagandists "and have been guilty of distortions, tendentious reporting, speculation and criticism that have damaged society and weakened resistance to Communism." Two weeks later, Marcos denied what appeared then (and increasingly so later) to be his only reason for suspending the papers, saying they were locked up "not because they were critical of me, but because they participated in a conspiracy, a conspiracy of the Communist Party." At other times, when the government was receiving criticisms for its unpopular actions against the press, Marcos officials relented enough to say these were only temporary measures.

Immediately following the introduction of martial law, a Department of Public Information was established, replacing the Presidential Press Office. This new department of the executive branch was designated to merge all the public information offices of the various branches of government. Named as Secretary of Public Information was 33-year-old Francisco Tatad, a former diplomatic correspondent and columnist of the *Manila Daily Bulletin.*

On 25 September, the new department issued its first two decrees. The first decree laid down guidelines for the conduct of the news media and instituted a formidable array of government controls and censorship devices. The second decree dealt with the operation of printing presses, informing printing firms they could not print any matter for mass dissemination without prior approval of the department and that they could not print any of the prohibited items mentioned in the first decree.

Besides suspending mass media operations, strengthening the governmental information office and issuing stringent censorship rules, the Marcos regime also arrested its chief opponents, charging that they had been involved in a Communist conspiracy. The government originally announced that these individuals would be held for the duration of the national emergency or until Marcos ordered their release. By mid-1973, a large number of the detainees had been released and some placed under house arrest. Despite Marcos' claims to the contrary, the main reason most of these individuals were imprisoned related to their anti-Marcos writings.

3.7.2.2 Birth of Marcos Press

Whereas some other Asian nations instituting martial law have allowed the media to resume within a few days, Marcos' government favored a whole new set of politically-acceptable newspapers instead. After a month of martial law, publishers, editors and broadcasters grew pessimistic about their chances of operating. Government papers expanded operations; the *Daily Express,* for example, started an afternoon edition, a second morning edition in Filipino and a weekly *Expressweek.* The second paper allowed to function, the *Times Journal,* was published for the first time in October 1972 and, like the *Express,* was financed by a friend of Marcos, Edmundo Ongsianko, particularly at the outset. The *Express* was reportedly paid for by Roberto Benedicto, ambassador to Japan.

Being the only papers available for the initial months of martial law, the *Express* and *Times Journal* were placed in extremely advantageous positions. From a circulation of 110,000 on 25 September, the *Express* had risen to 520,000 by mid-October, about three weeks after martial law. Advertisers queued up for space, even though advertising rates had been increased from 15 to 45 pesos per column inch. Post-martial law newspapers also had the advantage of low capital overhead costs — in most cases they simply leased or took over the premises of defunct newspapers.

Being government-sanctioned, the press failed to report activities that could reflect on Marcos. And when, in late October 1972, a new constitutional provision was adopted making it possible for Marcos to remain in power indefinitely, Filipinos were unaware of this because *Express, Business Day* and the broadcasters passed over it in silence.

In mid-November, Marcos talked about permitting pre-martial

law dailies to resume but emphasized that a "wide dispersal of ownership by public subscription" was necessary. New rulings stressed that no one person or family could own more than 20 per cent in any one medium. He hinted that some of these newspapers might be permitted to set up shop if they drastically changed their management pattern and capital structure. But those publications that in the eyes of the military had participated in a "conspiracy to overthrow the republic" were permanently disenfranchised. Apparently, all pre-martial law publications, save the *Bulletin Today*, were in this category as it was the only paper to resume.

By the mid-1970s (and continuing into the 1980s), Marcos had converted the oligarchic control of the press by families such as Lopez, Soriano, Roces or Elizalde, into a conglomerate owned and operated by relatives and personal and political friends. Among these were the Philippine Daily Express Company (*Daily Express, Filipino Express, Expressweek, Sportsexpress*), owned by Marcos through Roberto Benedicto and financed partly from the president's contingency fund; Bulletin publications (*Bulletin Today, Balita ng Maynila, Liwayway, Hiligaynon, Bannaway*), owned by former Marcos aide, Hans Menzi; the combine of *Evening Post, Focus Philippines, Orient Express*, owned by the husband-wife team of Juan Tuvera and Kerima Polotan, the former a presidential assistant, the latter the biographer of Imelda Marcos; *Weekly Examiner*, owned by Leon Ty, a Marcos appointee serving as governor of the Development Bank of the Philippines; *United Daily News*, the Kuomintang paper headed by Ralph Nubla, Marcos supporter in Chinatown; and Times Journal publications, owned by Benjamin Romualdez, brother of Imelda Marcos.

3.7.2.3 Plethora of Regulatory Bodies

On 16 November 1972, the president signed his 36th decree, calling for the establishment of the Mass Media Council, with Tatad as chairman and the secretary of national defense as co-chairman. MMC set guidelines for the reopening of media and was to supervise and control the "performance and conduct of all mass media relevant to the promotion of closer coordination with the objectives of the government." MMC ceased functioning in spring 1973 with the formation of the Media Advisory Council.

In May 1973, the Media Advisory Council, a civilian body, was established by presidential decree to supervise all mass media and replace the Press Consultative Panel. MAC was to undertake the encouragement of responsible opinion writing dealing with social and economic conditions, the freeing of media from monopoly ownership and a national and orderly allocation of radio and TV frequencies, among other things. Marcos claimed its purpose was to relax government control of the media and authorize media operations subject to his approval, but the appointment of the National Press Club President, Primitivo Mijares, as its head revealed how much autonomy was destined for the media. Mijares was an *Express* columnist-reporter and one of the men closest to Marcos. After his defection to the United States in 1975, Mijares described himself as Marcos' "chief censor" (*Mijares,* 1976). The very comprehensive, 45-page MAC guideline set rules on what constitutes responsible opinion writing, honor and freedom of others, independence and integrity of media personnel.

By September 1973, MAC had submitted to Marcos a proposal to take over the Philippine business activities of Reuters, Agence France Presse, Associated Press and United Press International. MAC also tried to take over the functions of the Department of Public Information, the Bureau of Posts and the Textbook Board in a bid to become the supreme authority on anything remotely related to the mass media. By late 1974, MAC was disbanded, partly because of attempts by Mijares to expand his power at the expense of the Department of Public Information. At the time, Marcos told the world the "media is [*sic*] no longer controlled by government," but rather from within by the mass media themselves. Presidential Decree 576, issued then, specified that mass media would control themselves through a Philippine Council for Print Media and a Philippine Council for Broadcast Media. However, both councils were headed by and stacked with pro-Marcos journalists. Although the councils continued to function in the late 1970s, the dominant voice in Philippine media affairs was (and is) the Department of Public Information, which, with an annual budget of US$17 million, coordinates a number of agencies, directs all government propaganda, produces media content and has the power to oversee press licenses and renewals, screen employees and accredit foreign correspondents (*San Juan,* 1978, pp. 43-44).

3.7.2.4 Newspaper Content

Press content after martial law definitely portrayed the goals and aspirations of government. The print media reflected positive and passive news, usually ignoring negative societal and governmental characteristics. Thus, after relationships with China were established, the Manila press became cluttered with praise of Mao and China. But, during the February 1976 labor unrest in the Philippines, the papers were ordered by the information secretary to ignore the demonstrations, and instead, to rely on government releases about parades, dances and other government spectaculars, designed as diversionary tactics. A number of the extravaganzas were also designed to generate a favorable world opinion for the Philippines, among these being the Miss Universe pageant in 1974, the Ali-Frazier boxing match in 1975, the Karpov-Korchnoi chess tournament in 1978 and several international conferences.

At various times Defense Secretary Juan Ponce Enrile, Information Secretary Tatad and Marcos himself, among others, have urged editors to be less timid. In one two-month period in 1975, Enrile made three appeals to the press not to be shy, all to no avail (*Gonzaga,* 1975, p. 28). In 1977, Tatad complained that new blood was not seeping into publishing, that old competents pass on and are not replaced by new competents. Claiming journalism was a "sterile wasteland," he predicted that the situation would worsen (*Philippine Times,* 16-18 Feb. 1977). Manila editors, however, have not taken the bait, are still very cautious and not willing to overstep that fine line between what is and is not permitted in the New Society. They point to colleagues, especially on *Times Journal* and *Bulletin Today,* who wrote about protest marches and illegal detention of political prisoners in 1975 and were hauled before the military to explain their actions. They remember that Imelda Marcos chastized the *Bulletin Today* for its coverage of the subversion trial of former Sen. Benigno Aquino in the mid-1970s, and that the president spoke to the *Bulletin Today* publisher about a story on the surplus-laden sugar industry.

In mid-1978, Marcos called the publishers and editors together to voice his concern with the growing "fascination" with crime reporting. Simultaneously, an order is said to have gone out telling publishers to tone down crime stories and to relegate them to inside pages (*Dalton,* 1978, p. 3). Similarly, there was some outrage in 1979 over the exploitation of sex in the media, including movie advertisements in dailies and the bold pictures of movie stars in Sunday supplements (*Media,* Feb. 1979, pp. 1, 7). The result of this fear has been that the Philippine press, according to one foreign newsman, "is so scandalously servile the only possible source of reliable domestic news is the classified ads." By the late 1970s, the press, as a private monopoly of those in authority, suffered from psychological, rather than direct, control. Some critics blamed the restraint exercised by journalists on laziness; others said it resulted from the fear of repercussions from aggressive reporting (*Asiaweek,* 29 July 1977, p. 9). A 1977 White Paper on the press, commissioned by the Philippine Council for Print Media, pointed to corrupt practices among journalists as part of the problem; some press personnel rebounded by claiming the publishers were the culprits for raking off huge profits and not sharing them with underpaid reporters. One columnist suggested that publishers should declare their assets at the time of martial law with the present to see how they enriched themselves at the expense of junior reporters who continued to make US$100 a month (*Asiaweek,* 28 Oct. 1977, p. 49).

Wherever the blame rests, press personnel in the Philippines know how precarious their positions are. Publishers may quarrel with each other in print, but they all observe the rules, written or unwritten, of the Marcos government that there should be no criticism of the First Family. Columnists, in the late 1970s, kept policymakers on their toes with sharp digs at their wrongdoings, but only dished out servile praise for the Marcos family (*Far Eastern Economic Review,* 1 Dec. 1978, pp. 22-23).

3.7.2.5 Government and Foreign Correspondents

At various times in the 1970s, Philippine officials reacted to reports of foreign correspondents writing about the New Society. In 1978, the president and Imelda Marcos said in numerous speeches that they believed biased and malicious stories on how they ran the country were being written for the foreign press. The sycophantic local press even implied that foreign correspondents were secret agents of other governments. One columnist, Teodoro Valencia, wrote that because they were secret agents, foreign correspondents should be shot. Valencia and Foreign Secretary Carlos P. Romulo, himself an editor at one time, thought the foreign press was biased and brutally unkind to Marcos, and was leading an orchestrated drive to vilify the president (see *Philippine Times*, 22-28 June 1978, pp. 5, 16). In April 1978, during and after the elections in the Philippines, foreign correspondents were told to wear identification tags when covering events to distinguish themselves from "agents provocateurs masquerading as journalists." The government called upon the Foreign Correspondents Association in Manila to screen its membership of subversive foreign agents (London *Times,* 11 April 1978, p. 7). The Marcos government's main complaint was that the foreign press ignored good news and featured negative aspects about the country (see *Far Eastern Economic Review,* 8 April 1977, p. 19). Correspondents countered by saying that after six or seven years of reading the most glowing accounts of the regime in the local press, Marcos and his officials were not used to objective reporting. The government, in 1978 and before, took measures to present the good news by supporting a Third World news agency which would feature positive, development-oriented information; by taking out special advertising space in Western publications, and by introducing, through the secretaries of defense and information, an Official Information Act into the interim national assembly, which, if passed, would penalize government authorities for disclosing information endangering "national security." The act would have broad scope and a powerful wallop, according to one source (*Media,* Oct. 1978, pp. 1, 4-5). In early 1979, a parliamentary committee threw out a move, aimed mainly at United States correspondents, to bar foreign newsmen from the country for alleged false reporting (*Indian Press,* Feb. 1979, pp. 23-24).

There were other forms of retribution taken against foreign newsmen and media. Associated Press chief, Arnold Zeitlin, in November 1976, was given 24 hours to leave, without the benefit of a hearing, for writing critically about the government. In

February 1977, *Far Eastern Economic Review* correspondent, Bernard Wideman, was denied an extension of his visa for his anti-Marcos writing. He, however, was absolved of the charges against him, the government declaring that a foreigner writing for a foreign audience could not incite Filipinos against their own government (*Salonga,* 1977, p. 11). Wideman was allowed to remain in the country, partly because the authorities were attempting to project to the world a new image of the Marcos government (*Tasker,* 1977a, p. 14). In another case, Defense Minister Enrile in late 1978 filed a US$865,000 libel suit against the *Far Eastern Economic Review,* at the same time ordering the seizure of the Manila properties of the Hong Kong-based magazine; the arrest of *Review* correspondent Rodney Tasker if he re-entered the Philippines, and the banning of the publication from the country (*Media,* Nov. 1978, p. 1; *Far Eastern Economic Review,* 10 Nov. 1978, p. 28). In April 1979, the government delayed indefinitely the exit visa of the *Review*'s new Manila reporter, Sheila Ocampo (*Media,* May 1979, p. 12).

It seemed that the government, in an effort to build a good international image, wanted to control the outgoing information about the country in the same fashion that it had earlier controlled the domestic media.

3.7.3 Renewed Competition

As the 1980s dawned, the Philippine press was in a competitive spirit reminiscent of pre-martial law days. Although they certainly did not display the political sting of old, the dailies did bring back other features — e.g., the society page and reporting of crime and scandal — which led to circulation wars. Leading the fray were the Times Journal Group and Bulletin publications. At stake was the number one position in daily circulation in Manila.

Until 1979, *Bulletin Today* had the largest circulation, having overtaken the *Express.* In December 1978, the Times Journal Group created a tabloid, populist daily, *People's Journal,* as its catalyst to unseat *Bulletin Today. People's Journal* had immediate appeal with its low price (15 centavos compared to 50 centavos for other dailies) and racy content; in two days, its circulation went to 85,000. However, after a week, the paper was killed off by the Philippine Council for Print Media, headed by *Bulletin Today* publisher, Hans Menzi. The council ordered the paper closed because it did not have a valid publishing permit. The Times Journal Group explained that the new paper was actually a resurrection of a monthly published between 1973-76, but terminated because of an inadequate printing plant. After five days of controversy, *People's Journal* was allowed to resume. After that, the Times Journal Group, which had moved into new headquarters in early 1978, escalated the circulation war, and by mid-1979, *People's Journal* topped the circulation figures with 400,000 (*Malloy*, 1979, p. 9). The *Times Journal* itself had been revitalized between 1977 and 1978 when, because of a number of supplements it began to carry, the circulation went from 70,000 to 120,000. Among the *Times Journal* supplements were *People*, a Sunday supplement; *TV Journal*, a Friday supplement; *Sports Journal*, Saturday; *Nation's Journal*, a fortnightly. *Bulletin Today*, shortly after, started its own supplement called *Who* (*Asiaweek*, 29 Dec.-5 Jan. 1979, p. 11; *Asiaweek*, 15 Dec. 1978, p. 9).

Despite the renewed competition, the Philippine press cannot be compared to its pre-martial law predecessors in liveliness, critical stance, irreverence and irresponsibility. Perhaps a leading government opponent summed it up best in 1978: "Before martial law, people wrote and talked without thinking. Today, people think and think without writing or talking" (*Media*, April 1978, p. 14).

3.8 Singapore

John A. Lent

3.8.1 Brief History

Until the past decade, mass media of Singapore and Malaysia were almost indistinguishable. They shared the same historical roots, corporate structures and names; correspondingly, they were subjected to the same governance and control.

This was understandable in that Singapore was, for most of its history, a part of the administrative apparatus of what is now Malaysia — early on as one of the Straits Settlements (along with Penang and Malacca), later as a segment of the Federation of Malaya, Singapore, Sarawak, North Borneo and Brunei, and after 1963, as a state in the Federation of Malaysia. In August 1965, Singapore was expelled from the federation and became a sovereign and independent republic.

Because of its entrepôt status, Singapore gave the Malay peninsula many of its first newspapers. It produced the first Malay language periodical, *Jawi Peranakan,* in 1876, and until the 1930s, remained the main publishing center in that language. The first Tamil language periodical was established in Singapore between 1876-79; English and Chinese periodicals also flourished there. Although Penang, now a part of Malaysia, is credited with the first newspapers of the Malay archipelago, early Singapore papers lasted longer. (The first newspaper in Singapore, started by missionaries on 1 January 1824, was *Singapore Chronicle or Commercial Register.*) The most successful and oldest newspaper of both Singapore and Malaysia is *Straits Times,* founded in Singapore on 25 July 1845.

As Kuala Lumpur was established as a key city, some Singapore newspapers started sister editions there, but it was really after Malaya became independent of British rule in 1957, that there was a mushrooming of these satellite editions. For the most part, these newspapers were considered Singapore corporations with main administrative officials and facilities located in that city. Until the 1970s, newspapers such as *Straits Times, Sin Chew Jit Poh, Nanyang Siang Pau* and *Eastern Sun* fed news, and in some instances, entire pages, via facsimile to Kuala Lumpur for production in their Malaysian editions. Among other newspapers which printed editions in Malaysia were *Berita Harian, Utusan Melayu, Tamil Murasu, Tamil Malar, Shin Min Daily News, Malay Mail* and *Tamil Nesan*.

With increasing pressure from both governments, the corporate structures of the eight surviving dual nation newspapers were separated. In Malaysia, the big push in this direction came in the mid-1970s with the successful governmental efforts to force Kuala Lumpur branches of such papers as *Straits Times, Nanyang Siang Pau* and *Sin Chew Jit Poh* to offer at least 51 per cent of their stocks to Malaysians.

3.8.2 The Contemporary Press

3.8.2.1 Circulation and Readership

In 1977, 15 newspapers (12 of which were dailies) published regularly in Singapore with a daily combined circulation of about 527,000. Because of Singapore's multi-ethnic and multi-lingual characteristics, four newspapers are in Chinese (total circulation of about 246,500); three in English (total circulation 218,500); three in Tamil (total circulation 31,500), and one each in Bahasa Malaysia (circulation 28,100) and Malayalam (*Singapore Bulletin,* March 1978, p. 7). The newspaper with the largest circulation is *Straits Times* with 172,000. Straits Times Press is a conglomerate which owns the English language daily, *New Nation* (42,000) and *Sunday Nation* (83,200); *Sunday Times* (179,000); *Berita Harian* (28,100); *Berita Minggu* (38,100) and *Business Times* (4,500). An offshoot of Straits Times Press, Times Periodicals, is the leader in periodicals with *Her World, Fanfare, Singapore Business, New Directions, Straits Times Annual* and *The Craft of Sound.* Besides Straits Times Press, *Sin Chew Jit Poh* (largest Chinese daily with 96,100) has also been part of a group ownership, that of Aw Boon Haw with dailies in Malaysia and Hong Kong.

English and Chinese newspapers are the largest and most active, mainly because of the predominance of English as a lingua franca and the large proportion of the population which is Chinese. At the end of 1975, the population of Singapore was estimated at 2.25 million, 76.1 per cent being Chinese, 15.1 per cent Malay, 6.9 per cent Indian and Pakistani and 1.9 per cent, other races (*D'Cruz*, 1979, p. 15). The problem in Singapore has been that as a multi-lingual state, all languages are expected to be treated equally in principle, but Bahasa Malaysia is the national language and English the dominant (see *Kuo*, 1976, p. 34).

Unlike in Malaysia and the Philippines, English language has been in the ascendancy in Singapore for many years, partly because of Lee Kuan Yew's English first campaign. Chinese newspapers have felt the pinch as the English press cornered the high income audiences; the future, according to an article in *Media* (May 1979, p. 35), could mean "flagging sales and ad revenues, followed by a possible shutdown of one or more of the Chinese-language papers." The author added that English language papers have advantages of being "slick, professionally laid-out and edited, containing a greater amount and variety of reading, as well as up-to-date international news and . . . more complete and accurate coverage of local beats." The Chinese press, it was suggested, will have to improve reporting standards, provide better training and pay for journalists and break down the deep hostility between *Nanyang Siang Pau* and *Sin Chew Jit Poh,* which does not allow for cooperation. Bilingualism has also been suggested and has been implemented in the *Straits Times,* which thrice-weekly carries a bilingual page (*Media,* May 1979, p. 36).

In other actions, the Chinese press seemed no longer to resist the greater use of English, but instead, tried to cope with (and even exploit) it. The fact that most students begin their education in institutions where English is the chief medium of instruction led *Sin Chew Jit Poh* (followed immediately by *Nanyang Siang*

Pau), in May 1979, to switch to a more Westernized writing style
— presenting stories left to right along horizontal lines, rather
than from top to bottom, right to left (*Asiaweek*, 20 July 1979,
p. 16). It is probable that the switch resulted because of a government request to that effect made a few years before (*Media*, April
1974, p. 25).

In 1979, the Chinese press pushed ahead to start an English
language daily the following year to break the monopoly of
the *Straits Times* (*Far Eastern Economic Review*, 1 June 1979,
p. 7), and to help subsidize and preserve Chinese language dailies.
At a seminar held by Chinese language editors in 1979, to
discuss the plight of their papers, criticisms were levelled at the
Chinese press for its "lack of depth and aggressiveness and
regurgitation of official press releases" (*Awanohara*, 1979a,
p. 26). Other editors added that a problem is created when
older Chinese journalists retire and are not replaced because
younger reporters cannot be recruited. Also, with government
and business using English as the medium, reporters from the
Chinese press not proficient in English cannot obtain the stories,
or if they do get them, they face the time-consuming problem
of translation. Added to these difficulties is the *Straits Times*
efforts to pre-empt competition, by placing correspondents in
major world capitals and forming an "elite task force" of reporters
to generate its own in-depth analysis of important events.

Apparently, the *Straits Times* took seriously, criticisms levelled
by the government and others in the 1970s. One author, claiming
in 1978, that the word was out that the government sought
another paper to challenge the *Straits Times,* said there were
three theories to explain the government stand:

> One is that the *Straits Times'* monopoly frustrates
> the Government — it is unable to use the threat
> of closure effectively since the group's main product,
> the daily *Straits Times,* fills a commercial need . . . .
> With another English newspaper, the Government's
> control of the press could be strengthened.
>
> Related to this is the second theory, concerning lack
> of competition for the century-old group. Politicians
> and bureaucrats constantly moan about the lack of

quality in local news coverage . . . . In effect, a 'quality'
English newspaper would add to the Government's
'best of everything' basket — which sums up the third
theory (*Lee*, 1978, p. 22).

3.8.2.2 Big Business Press

The affluence and economic growth of Singapore are reflected
in media penetration figures and advertising budgets. For example,
in 1970, one in nine Singaporeans owned a radio set, one in 15 a
television receiver and one in six purchased a newspaper regularly.
Fifty-seven per cent of the adult population of the city state read
newspapers daily. That same year, the following were the advertising budgets of Singapore media: press, S$16.8 million; television,
S$9.6 million; radio, S$1.8 million, and Rediffusion, S$0.8 million
(*Glattbach* and *Anderson,* 1971, pp. 5, 10). By the end of the
1970s, broadcasting reached 70 per cent of the population and
in 1975, two-thirds of the population 15 years old or older
reported they normally read at least one newspaper. The Chinese
papers had the largest readership (38.3 per cent); English (28.7
per cent), Bahasa Malaysia (7.8 per cent) and Tamil (2.9 per cent)
(Kuo, 1978, p. 1070).

In 1978, newspapers still maintained a strong grip on advertising
revenue — 59 per cent — with English language newspapers getting
at least two-thirds of that (*Media,* May 1979, pp. 32-33). One of
the Chinese newspapers, *Nanyang Siang Pau,* for example, saw
advertising and lineage revenues increase by 34 and 74 per cent,
respectively, between 1973 and 1977. The financial soundness
that resulted from newspapers such as the Straits Times Group was
mentioned by Health Minister Dr. Toh Chin Chye in his reaction
to negative *Straits Times'* remarks about a bill he had introduced:

> The *Straits Times,* with only a paid up capital of
> S$4.3 million, made S$3.6 million (US$1.57 million)
> profit before tax (in 1977), paying a dividend of 30%,
> and issued a bonus issue of one for two (*Lee,* 1978,
> p. 23).

That Singapore newspapers have become big business enterprises (more so than dailies in most neighboring states, except for Malaysia and Philippines) is attested to by the equipment expansion programs of organizations such as Straits Times Press and Nanyang Press. In 1978, the Straits Times Press signed a US$1 million contract for a T-410 electronic copy processing system to be used by its four dailies and three Sunday newspapers (*Editor & Publisher,* 29 July 1978, p. 22). The following year, Nanyang Press ordered the largest "Urbanite" web offset press yet to be built, consisting of 10 single color printing units. The press can print 60,000 copies an hour, compared to 20,000 of the old Nanyang press. It allows *Nanyang Siang Pau* to print later and still be on the streets before the rival *Sin Chew Jit Poh* (*AMCB,* March 1979, p. 11).

However, Lee Kuan Yew, believing there must be veiled interests where there is big business, introduced legislation in 1974 and 1977 (see 3.8.3.2), designed to break up the media empires operated by a handful of people, by offering most of the shares on the open market to small-time operators. First to go public in 1977 were *Nanyang Siang Pau* and *Sin Chew Jit Poh,* both of which were owned by families accused by the government of power-broking. Competition for the shares, offered at significant discounts (see *Rowley,* 1977c, pp. 120-121; *Business Times,* 30 Nov. 1977, pp. 1, 7), was so intense that a lottery was organized for them. The lottery became necessary because *Nanyang Siang Pau* was 14 times oversubscribed, and *Sin Chew Jit Poh,* 22 times. At the end of the first day of trading, a S$1 (US 41 cents) share in *Nanyang Siang Pau* had risen to 150 Singapore cents, while a share of *Sin Chew Jit Poh* soared from S$1 to 250 Singapore cents. *Nanyang Siang Pau* shares settled at 210-215 Singapore cents, while those of *Sin Chew Jit Poh* hovered at 235-240 (*Asiaweek,* 23 Dec. 1977, p. 34). The previous owners, even though they lost by having to sell up, also profited. The principal owners of *Sin Chew Jit Poh* (the Aw family) sold 5.3 million shares at S$1, while the 50 owners of *Nanyang Siang Pau* (mostly heirs of Lee Kong Chian) put up 4.98 million shares, taking in more than US$2.2 million, less commission.

3.8.2.3 Contents of a Guided Press

An analysis of the contents of the *Straits Times* gives some indication of the effects of a guided press, where newspapers are used to meet the needs of a developing nation, to promote the campaigns of Lee Kuan Yew and to act mainly as mouthpieces of the government. In the *Straits Times*, 58.2 per cent of the news is local, 31.7 per cent is news from Asia and 10.1 per cent is news from outside Asia. As one author wrote, the international news "reflects Singapore's heavy dependence on international and regional activities" (*D'Cruz*, 1979, p. 15); the local news deals mainly with social and community news, not political. Most government news is informational and educational, rather than political, and the heavy emphasis on sports is in keeping with the image of a rugged society. Chinese newspapers also emphasize social and community affairs (*D'Cruz*, 1979, p. 15). Thus, newspapers are used as socialization agents in this multi-racial state to maintain a sense of national identity and unity and to highlight government policies and campaigns.

In 1978, there was speculation that the government was dissatisfied with the *Straits Times* for not filling its pages with news officials wanted to read. One government official was quoted by *Lee* (1978, p. 23) as saying,

The *Straits Times* does not have enough good writers. Much of its news comprises reprints of ministers' speeches, and the rest is trivia . . . . What the Government would like is intelligent coverage of economic and financial developments in the EEC, Japan and the United States. In order to do that, they've got to have people with training in economics and finance. The field of development economics, which is important to Singapore, is very complex.

As an example of a newspaper whose content emphasis was determined by government suggestions, the *Sunday Nation* (which has built its circulation partly on the soccer mania in Singapore) played up that sport on the advice of the authorities who wished to fill the huge national stadium.

At other times, newspapers have been advised not to investigate matters that might be embarrassing to the authorities. For example, in mid-1974, editors were "advised" politely to overlook growing squabbles between students and the Singapore University vice-chancellor and to not give publicity to protestors. On other occasions, important national events have been ignored until the official word was given (see *Far Eastern Economic Review,* 22 July 1974; 13 Sept. 1974). The *Asia 1974 Yearbook* (p. 268) stated that if politicians are not government leaders, they are not likely to be heard in Singapore newspapers which had got "over the unprofitable habit of devoting valuable space . . . to any comprehensive coverage of politicians who did not matter either in terms of state power or entertainment value."

Various premises underline Lee Kuan Yew's press policy. One, combining the foreign influences and multi-ethnic theses, assumes Western liberal traditions are dangerous to a beleaguered nation such as Singapore — a Chinese city surrounded by poor Malay Muslims. This premise holds that Singapore is in a uniquely delicate position, with only its human resources to fall back on, and as such, cannot subscribe to the same rules as other nations. The best and most relevant of all philosophies, therefore, is the government line, which, among other things, points out dangers in uncreative and unhealthy imitation of the West.

To get his philosophies over to the press (and other social institutions), Lee takes to the podium occasionally. The press has learned to listen to these sometimes-fierce speeches; Lee made one on press freedom in April 1971 which went unheeded, and the following month a press purge occurred. In one of his most significant public pronouncements on press freedom — at the IPI in Helsinki in June 1971, Lee laid some of the groundwork for his press philosophy. Discussing the impact of foreign media contents, he said,

> At a time when new nations require their peoples
> to work hard and be disciplined to make progress,
> their peoples are confused by watching and reading
> of the happenings in the West. They read . . . and
> see . . . . violent demonstrations in support of peace,
> urban guerrillas, drugs, free love and hippieism. We
> want the mass media to reinforce, not to undermine,
> the cultural values and social attitudes being inculcated
> in our schools and universities . . . (*Lee in Josey,* 1971,

pp. 15-18).

More recently, there have been government seminars or pep talks by Lee Kuan Yew himself that have resulted in editorial changes at newspapers. A February 1978 seminar for top civil servants, for example, concluded that newspapers should "elicit public opinion on the Government's intentions before certain matters became public policies" (*Lee,* 1978, p. 23). At about the same time, the prime minister voiced his impatience with the *Straits Times'* "Preoccupation with London as the centre of the outside world," saying he wanted local coverage of news from the EEC, Japan and the United States. Within six months, *Straits Times* met some of this request by stationing reporters in London, New York and Washington and with Euromoney. Reacting to a recent statement by the Minister of Culture that the role of the press is "to generate original and considered viewpoints and not to contribute to useless controversy," one writer said, "In practice, this means that the papers of Singapore will have to learn to criticise without being anti-establishment" (*Lee,* 1978, p. 23).

Self-censorship of contents is practiced thoroughly in Singapore, the results being, as reported by *Media* (May 1979, p. 33), that,

> Direct, aggressive criticism of the government and important government personalities is rare. Reporting of important issues tends to be circumspect with few strong viewpoints expressed in editorials and the press acting as a vehicle rather than a participant in dialogues . . . . When the Singapore press does pull its punches, and water down government criticism, at the back of editors' minds is always Lee himself, brilliant, autocratic, and when it comes to journalists, sometimes downright mean . . . . All in all, Singaporeans read well-produced, informative newspapers that, aside from profit-making, lean more heavily towards rendering a service to the community than to fulfilling what some might consider a duty as the fourth estate in a democratic country.

3.8.3 Government-Press Relationships

3.8.3.1 The 1971 Purge

If there had been any doubts about Lee Kuan Yew's sensitiveness regarding the press, they were put to sleep after 1971, the year he purged his island republic's press and set the tone for press performance for years to come. In a sweeping campaign that year, described by one writer as the "most remarkable public controversy since full independence . . . in 1965" (*Polsky,* 1971, p. 187), Lee closed two dailies, detained editorial executives of a third and expelled from Singapore several foreign journalists. It was a culmination of over a decade of power wielded by Lee and the PAP over Singapore's press.

As early as 1960, newspapers such as Singapore *Standard* and *Straits Times* had been intimidated by Lee Kuan Yew and the PAP. The *Standard* editor, in fact, blamed threats by the prime minister as part of the reason that a successful daily, owned by Aw Boon Haw, folded in 1960 (*Ooi,* 1971). Fearing Lee's government, the *Straits Times,* at about the same time, lessened its criticism of the authorities, and simultaneously, strengthened its Kuala Lumpur branch as a safeguard. Other victims of this period were numerous publications suspended because they practiced yellow culture — a type of journalism distinguished by its sensationalism and banned by Lee Kuan Yew.

Also suffering from governmental interference almost from its beginning in July 1966, was the *Eastern Sun,* owned by Dato Aw Kow, eldest son of Aw Boon Haw. After the 1965 Malaysia-Singapore split, both nations carefully controlled the importation of printed materials — Singapore authorities not permitting the circulation of Malaysian newspapers and vice versa. Singapore dailies were asked to develop separate Kuala Lumpur editions if they planned to circulate in Malaysia. The *Eastern Sun,* published in Singapore, received such a request from the Malaysian authorities; when it did not oblige, an ultimatum was given Dato Aw Kow. Preferring to ignore the request, and later ultimatum, Dato Aw Kow closed the Kuala Lumpur office of the *Eastern Sun* in December 1968. Advertisers withdrew their support and *Sun* staff members resigned (*Ooi,* 1971); thus, even before its closure by Lee in 1971, the paper was in dire financial trouble, without any hope of being bailed out by the PAP.

Still another daily to suffer the wrath of the Lee government was *Utusan Melayu,* its Singapore office closed by authorities in late 1969 because the Malay language paper originated outside Singapore (in Kuala Lumpur) and was supported by the United Malays National Organization.

But, Lee Kuan Yew's real war with the island press began on 2 May 1971, when four senior executives of the Chinese language daily, *Nanyang Siang Pau,* were arrested in the early morning hours and ordered detained without trial for two years. They were accused under the Internal Security Act of stirring up racial issues and glamorizing communism. *Newsweek* (7 June 1971, p. 49) reported that the executives — Shamsuddin Tung Tao Chang, editor-in-chief; Ly Singko, chief editorial writer; Lee Mau Seng, managing director and general manager; and Kerk Loong Sing, public relations officer — were thrown into jail for running a front page photograph of Mao Tse-tung playing ping pong. According to the United States news magazine, Lee Kuan Yew was disturbed because he considered himself as head of the overseas Chinese communities. But, Lee Kuan Yew's punitive action against *Nanyang* cannot be explained in such simplistic terms; it had been conceived much more systematically, as part of a governmental campaign. As one writer correctly surmised, Lee and his party were aware, from the beginning of the republic, that they had to create a Singapore identity for the indigenous Chinese and to build a government on multi-racial foundations (*Polsky,* 1971, pp. 183-187). By 1971, these goals seemed almost impossible, what with the favor shown post-Cultural Revolution China by Singapore Chinese, the 1969 race riots in Malaysia, and the discontent of Singapore Chinese over the language and education issues.

Nanyang Siang Pau was therefore used as a launching pad for Lee's campaign against "black operations," domestic and foreign intrigues inimical to Singapore's general interest. Some of this is reflected in the specific charges levelled at *Nanyang*'s Lee Mau Seng, accused of consciously veering his paper's editorial policy to: glamorize communism and stir up chauvinistic sentiments over the Chinese language, education and culture; highlight more unsavory aspects of Singapore life; create the impression the government was hostile to the Chinese, and, refer to Singapore's 150 years of colonial fetters, i.e., Singapore is still not independent, thus, echoing the communist line.

What must have surprised the prime minister was the reaction of *Nanyang*. For years, Lee threatened and the media cowered. Instead, *Nanyang* organized a public campaign calling for the release of their editors, or at least a public trial for them. As a diversionary tactic, the government escalated the "black operation" scare, implying that *Nanyang* was an example of a subversive plot against national stability (*FEER 1972 Yearbook*, pp. 281-82). By mid-May 1971, the authorities disclosed the activities of the *Eastern Sun* to further prove their point of outside interference. The *Sun* was accused of having received US$1.19 million in loans, at very low interest rates, from Communist sources in Hong Kong. When Dato Aw Kow did not reply to the charges, seven senior expatriate staff members walked out of the *Sun* on 16 May, and the paper folded. Strangely, Dato Aw Kow was questioned by the authorities on a few occasions, but was never charged with any crimes. Also, it was never stated just what the Communists expected to gain from a pro-government, anti-Communist paper such as the *Eastern Sun*.

Lee Kuan Yew's next target was the Singapore *Herald* which, according to one source, "managed to incur his hostility almost from the moment it began publication" (*Polsky*, 1971, p. 189). The *Herald*'s editorial intention to be pro-Singapore, as distinct from pro-government, irritated Lee, and he reacted. Even before the May 1971 confrontation, the prime minister and his press secretary, Li Vei-chen, were denying normal press facilities to the *Herald*, banning its reporters from official press conferences and briefings, withdrawing governmental advertising and refusing to give the paper government press releases. Additionally, members of Parliament and all government agencies cancelled their *Herald* subscriptions; even teachers tried to pressure children to have their parents stop buying the paper.

In February 1971, the *Herald*'s founding editor, Francis Wong, who had had a long standing battle with Lee, was forced to resign. Investors in the paper were told their difficulties with the government would cease once Wong was removed. Lee explained to the

International Press Institute General Assembly in June 1971, that Wong was fired because he was half politician and half journalist. Attending the same meeting (where international attention was focused on the Singapore situation), Wong denied being a member of any political party or being fired; he said he quit to restore the confidence of prospective investors who were understandably perturbed by the government pressure. Accusing the prime minister of harassing the paper from its beginning, Wong challenged him to call a commission of inquiry into the allegations against the *Herald* (*E&P* 19 June 1971, p. 14). In an interview with this author two years later, Wong said he left the *Herald* because the Singapore press situation was absurd, and there was no possibility of a lessening of restrictions for a long time. He added that in Singapore — and Asia, more generally — it was not a matter of press freedom, but rather the fact that the government "can suspend your paper or arrest you without any charges."[1]

On 17 May 1971, the government intensified the feud with the *Herald* by refusing to renew the work permits of three expatriate staff members, two of whom were the husband-wife team of Bob Reece, foreign editor, and Adele Kho, features editor. The three were ordered out of Singapore on 48-hour notice. Lee then proceeded to accuse the paper of receiving funding from unfriendly outside sources. He showed concern that US$490,196 was invested in the *Herald* by Tan Sri Fuad (Donald) Stephens, a noted Borneo politician, and charged Stephens of investing via a Hong Kong-based nominee company, thus concealing the real ownership. The *Herald* replied it had no intention of concealing anything. Other principal shareholders were also subject to harassment. Sally Aw Sian, cousin of Dato Aw Kow of *Eastern Sun,* had US$166,000 invested in the *Herald* which Lee Kuan Yew said was not her own money. After insisting otherwise in several interrogations at Lee's hands, she terminated her support for the paper, saying she could no longer tolerate the government's hostility. The *Herald*'s chief creditor, Chase Manhattan Bank, which had loaned US$600,000 to the paper, was also brought into the fray. Hoping to make the bank foreclose on the loans, Lee sent government officials to Chase Manhattan to examine

1   Interview, Francis Wong, Penang, Malaysia, 12 May 1973.

records pertaining to the *Herald*. He then summoned Chase Manhattan and *Herald* executives to a hastily-called meeting to find out more about the financing.

As the attacks by Lee and his foreign minister, S. Rajaratnam, intensified, the *Herald* replied in kind, initiating a major self-defense under the headline, "Our Right To Live with Dignity." For the 10 days, beginning 19 May, when the *Herald* fought the government, circulation increased from 12,500 to nearly 50,000, and thousands of Singaporeans donated money to a "Save the *Herald*" fund. But Lee had the last word, revoking the paper's license to print on 28 May 1971. Although the Singapore government can withdraw the annual printing press permit and publishing license at any time, with no reason necessary, the *Herald* case was the first such use of the power on a full-scale newspaper (*Straits Times* Malaysia, 30 Sept. 1971).

The effects of Lee's May press offensive were obvious and expected: press laws were strengthened, newspapermen pulled their heads in further, and self-restraint was the guiding policy of most media. As for the *Nanyang Siang Pau* executives, they were released after confessing to the original charges, and in a few instances, on the condition they leave Singapore. Kerk Loong Sing was released in December 1971, and expelled from the island the following August (*Straits Times* Malaysia, 27 Jan. 1973). After 20 months, Shamsuddin Tung Tao Chang and Ly Singko were released on 27 January 1973, after confessing they had tried to stir up communal tensions over the Chinese language and culture issues. Ly "confessed" that he wrote inflammatory editorials with misgivings because proprietor Lee Eu Seng raised his salary. Within hours of this "confession," Lee Eu Seng's printing license was withdrawn and re-issued in the name of the senior editor, and Lee himself was ordered detained for two years under the Internal Security Act. After his arrest, Lee Eu Seng was taken to the *Nanyang* offices which were then searched by the Internal Security Department (see *Straits Times* Malaysia, 31 Jan. 1973; 5 March 1973).

Meanwhile, Lee Mau Seng, one of the original four detainees, was given two additional years when his detention order expired in mid-May 1973 (*Straits Times* Malaysia, 24 May 1973). Finally, after admitting his "mistakes," Lee Mau Seng was released in

October 1973 on the condition that he emigrate to Canada with his family (see *Straits Times* Malaysia, 14 Oct. 1973; *IPI Report,* Jan. 1975, pp. 13, 19). He was kept under house arrest until his departure, during which time he was not permitted to see visitors, except for close relatives. On his way to Canada six weeks later, Lee Mau Seng said he had been made to sign a "Russian confession" to obtain his release.

3.8.3.2 Another Purge? Then Liberalization?

The battle for press freedom in Singapore took another dip down-wards in 1976-77. Between February and June 1976, the *New York Times* reported that in Singapore, 50 persons had been arrested as part of communist conspiracies, most of whom were freed after confessing their crimes on television (*Andelman,* 1976b, p. 13).

Typically, the scenario involved critics of the government — many of whom were journalists — detained without trial under the Internal Security Act until they agreed to make public confessions over the government television station. During the televised proceedings, they stated that they were tied to Communist or Marxist groups or individuals, worked against the best interests of Malaysia or Singapore, and were now ready to denounce their actions and beliefs. They were then questioned by government selected inquisitors or a group of journalists, and their confessions were subsequently printed in full in the local press.

During the national elections of late 1976, Shamsuddin Tung, former editor of *Nanyang Siang Pau,* who had been dismissed from his paper in August 1974 when the Newspaper and Printing Presses Act was passed, was detained without formal charges or trial, for playing on the Chinese language issue during his bid for political office. After protests from worldwide bodies, the Minister of Home Affairs implied that Tung was part of a "black opera-tion" (*IPI Report,* Feb. 1978, p. 15). Tung attempted to secure his release in July 1977 through a public renunciation of the use of force to overthrow the government; however, a confession was not enough at that time (*Rowley,* 1977a, pp. 34-35).

The incidents that caused the greatest uproar were the March-April 1977 "confessions" involving a lawyer and two *Far Eastern Economic Review* correspondents, and the mid-1976 "confessions" of the most prominent Malay language editor in Malaysia and three other journalists, two from Singapore, accused of being his cohorts.

In January 1977, *Far Eastern Economic Review* correspondent Ho Kwon Ping was arrested and charged under the Essential Regulations of Singapore, with disseminating protected information without the consent of a competent authority. Ho had discussed the manufacture and export of M-16 rifles in Singapore. At first, he pleaded not guilty. Rearrested in the same month, Arun Senkuttuvan, another *Review* correspondent, was detained under the Internal Security Act. When he made his televised "confession" in March, he said he had used half-truths in his articles to portray the government as "undemocratic, totalitarian, autocratic and oppressive." He also implicated *Review* editor, Derek Davies, in a plot to cause a rift between Singapore and Malaysia (for fuller details, see *Lent,* 1978d, pp. 9-18). On the day of Arun's "confession," Ho Kwon Ping was detained again without trial under the Internal Security Act, for alleged anti-government activities. He "confessed" a month later to using his articles to discredit the government. Both Arun and Ho were released shortly after their "confessions," but Arun's citizenship was revoked.

There was wide speculation that the arrest of Malaysian editor, Abdul Samad Ismail, on 22 June 1976, was prompted by Singaporean concerns. The *New Straits Times* editor was arrested for communist subversion, along with Samani bin Muhamad Amin, news editor of *Berita Harian* Malaysia. Six days earlier, the editor and former assistant editor of *Berita Harian* Singapore, Hussein Jahidin and Azmi Mahmud, were detained for "consistently and diligently" carrying out activities "aimed at influencing a number of people to carry out certain prejudicial activities." On the day of the Kuala Lumpur arrests, the Singapore authorities issued a statement, prominently displayed in Kuala Lumpur and Singapore dailies, linking the previous week's arrest of the two Singaporean journalists to a communist scheme masterminded by Samad "to work up discontentment and despair among the Malays and to influence them towards communism as an acceptable ally to solve their problems." The link was also prominently mentioned in the "confessions" all four made. Malaysian and Singaporean dailies carried full transcripts of the "confessions" and lent full support to their governments; other Asian newspapers and regional and international press bodies called for high level judicial reviews to insure that there had not been miscarriages of justice (see *Das*, 1977, pp. 8-9; *Davies*, 1977c, p. 7).

The episode was possibly the worst shock in Singapore-Malaysia relations since the August 1965 split. Also, the television "confessions" in both nations were of utmost concern to many individuals who feared they were further serious erosions of the remaining civil rights, especially freedom of expression, in the two states (see *Lent*, 1978d). In Singapore, in mid-1976, 64 persons were still in detention for political reasons, five of whom had been held without trial for ten years and three for more than 13 years (*Stockwin*, 1976, pp. 10, 15).

Two of these longest-serving political prisoners — Said Zahari, former journalist on *Utusan Melayu* (see *IPI Report*, Jan. 1977, p. 6), and Dr. Lim Hoch Siew, both of whom had been arrested in February 1963 — were released in 1978, but ordered to live in exile on separate islands. Their releases, as well as other events, left the impression as the 1970s came to a close, that Singapore was in a liberalization period. (*Asiaweek*, 1 Dec. 1978, p. 18) reported that some observers believed that Lee Kuan Yew's motive stemmed from Singapore's relative isolation from countries already pushing the human rights cause. Earlier, in February 1978, Lee Eu Seng of *Nanyang Siang Pau*, detained under the Internal Security Act since 1973, was released on the condition that he retain his old address and avoid overseas trips without the permission of the Internal Security Department. In his case, some observers felt it resulted because of a visit to Singapore by the US coordinator for human affairs, while the government said he was released because, under the Newspaper and Printing Presses (Amendment) Act of 1977, he could "no longer make use of the *Nanyang Siang Pau* against the public interest" (*Asiaweek*, 17 Feb. 1978, pp. 14-15; see *Richardson*, 1978, pp. 18-19). In a further sign of political liberalization, essential at a time when it was believed that Singapore was breeding new leadership, Shamsuddin Tung was released in January 1979, on the condition he does not participate in politics or leave the country. Three months earlier, his citizenship was revoked, rendering him stateless (*Awanohara*, 1979b, pp. 14-25; also *FUEMSSO News Service*, 9 Feb. 1979, p. 4). Finally, a 1979 publication of the Singapore Students' Union, after surveying the *Straits Times*, thought that it was "adopting a more critical stance which has been expressed in various ways such as a forum page, more 'open' editorials, a slightly greater emphasis on happenings of a social nature." The feeling was that the *Straits Times* was making an effort to accommodate alternative views or mild criticisms on the advice of the government, which in turn wished to siphon off some potentially dangerous frustrations of the public (*FUEMSSO News Service*, 23 Feb. 1979, p. 2). (For more on press freedom in Singapore, see *Casady*, 1975, pp. 3-7; *Lent*, 1975d, pp. 7-16).

3.8.3.3 Newspaper and Printing Presses Bill

Perhaps, as already indicated, a showcase liberalization of the press was possible, because the government had built up its legal machinery to handle most dissidence from that quarter. The law that was most effective in guaranteeing that the press will not get out of line is the Newspaper and Printing Presses Act of 1974 and its 1977 amendment.

Repealing the Printing Presses Act of 1920 (amended 1970), the 1974 law retained old restrictions, such as the annual licenses required to own a printing press and to issue a publication. But the big difference in the new law concerned the creation of two classes of newspaper shares — management and ordinary. Management shares, carrying heavier voting weight than the ordinary, cannot be owned by anyone not approved by the Ministry of Culture; once such approval has been obtained, a newspaper cannot refuse management shares to that individual. Further, non-Singapore citizens cannot hold management shares without the minister's explicit permission. If any newspaper fails to meet the minister's requirements, then the government has the power to put in its own nominee.

Another section of the act states that directors of newspapers must be Singapore citizens and that foreign financial backing must first be declared openly and then approved by the Ministry of Culture, which will assure that it is for bona fide commercial purposes. If the Minister of Culture refuses to allow the retention of such funds, they must be returned to the sender, or donated to a charity specified by the minister. Still other conditions state that the government has the power to authorize searches of premises, with or without a warrant, for outlawed publications, and Malaysian publications can only circulate in Singapore with the Ministry of Culture's permission. Penalty for violation of any section of the Newspaper and Printing Presses Act is three years' imprisonment or US$4,273 fine, or both; certain clauses can bring punishments of two years in prison and US$5,000 fine (see *Data for Decision,* 2-8 Sept. 1974; 18-24 March 1974; *Far Eastern Economic Review,* 15 April 1974, p. 16).

Shortly after passage, the act was amended by a parliamentary select committee to punish, with prison terms up to 10 years and a fine up to US$2,000, journalists failing to report receipt of funds from foreign sources for publishing news items or for following particular biases (*PCI Review,* India, Oct. 1974, p. 7; see *Josey,* 1974b, pp. 17-18). One of the accomplishments of the Newspaper and Printing Presses Act was to force newspapers to become public corporations, thus breaking up individual or family ownerships (see *Chopra,* 1975, p. 4).

Newspapers which the 1974 act was aimed at, have already gone public, for example, *Nanyang Siang Pau, Sin Chew Jit Poh* and *Straits Times.* Others, such as *Shin Min* and *Min Pao,* with 53 and 42.5 per cent, respectively, of Hong Kong ownership, also were affected, as was *New Nation,* previously owned on a 50:50 basis by the Straits Times Press and Melbourne *Herald* (*Sharp,* 1974, p. 16).

The 1977 amendment to the act, which went into effect July 1977, limited individual holdings in publishing companies to 3 per cent of the shares, the remainder going on the open market to small-time investors (*Asiaweek,* 23 Dec. 1977, pp. 34-35). Culture Minister Jek Yuen Thong said the government, in promoting the amendment, wanted to curb the potential of newspaper owners "to manipulate public opinion" (*Rowley,* 1977c, p. 120). Affected most severely were the family owned *Sin Chew Jit Poh* and *Nanyang Siang Pau,* which, as indicated previously, were forced to divest their shares (*Rowley*, 1977b, p. 112). By the end of 1977, other newspapers had been given extensions to dispense of surplus shares, among them being *New Nation, Business Times, Shin Min* and *Min Pao* (*Straits Times* Singapore, 1 Dec. 1977, p. 12). Surplus shares not disposed of by the deadline would be forfeited to the government. Small newspapers with a paid up capital of less than US$1.6 million were exempted from the amendment.

3.8.3.4 Other Regulations

If the Newspaper and Printing Presses Act and amendment, Internal Security Act and the press purges are not enough to keep journalists in line, the authorities have other regulations they can use. For example, the Undesirable Publications Act of 1967 specifies that imported publications and recording discs be examined carefully by the Ministry of Culture (*Singapore Government*, 1971, p. 239); libel laws, used and abused by high officials, keep the opposition in its subservient role, and the Essential Regulations Ordinances, as well as sedition laws, protect national security. Other press laws are promulgated from time to time to meet governmental campaigns and policies. For example, when a bill was introduced to prohibit smoking in certain public places in 1970, a corresponding law was passed prohibiting advertisements relating to smoking from use in all media.

Libel suits have been used by high officials in recent years to suppress opposition parties and their journals. Leong Mun Kwai, People's Front Party secretary general, was jailed for six months for a July 1972 article he wrote in that party's weekly organ, *Barisan Rakyat*. Leong was accused of libelling President B. H. Sheares, in an article in which the official was called a "puppet" and "slavish." Leong's appeal was thrown out because the libel was committed against the head of state (*Straits Times* Malaysia, 31 Oct. 1972).

In 1973, Lee Kuan Yew was awarded S$50,000 in his successful libel suit against *Barisan Socialis* and its publisher, Yeo Ah Ngoh. Yeo was accused of "personal, scurrilous, unfounded and vicious attacks" against the prime minister, that, if left unrefuted, would have reduced his effectiveness in governing Singapore and maintaining law and order. Later, Yeo was jailed for one month for contempt of court; he reportedly described Singapore courts as "instruments of oppression" in his journal (*Straits Times* Malaysia, 11 July 1973). Still others have brought libel charges against the opposition press in an effort to stifle it (see *Straits Times* Malaysia, 22 July 1972).

Nanyang Siang Pau letters editor, Goh Seow Poh, was fined S$500 in 1973 for publishing a letter by a "group of soldiers" without first verifying their names, identities, residences and whether they, in fact, had written the letters. The charges, filed under the Essential (Control of Publication and Safeguarding of Information) Regulations of 1966, were the first of their kind since the law was put into effect (*Straits Times* Malaysia, 8 June 1973). The soldiers, in their letter, inquired how they might be discharged from their national service training to gain admission to a university. Singapore law stipulates that newspaper editors who publish letters of complaint about the Singapore Armed Forces or other prohibited information, even though they are unable to verify the senders of the letters, run the risk of a S$4,000 fine or up to a year in prison. Editors are required to inform the Defence Ministry of their inability to trace senders of letters and are not allowed to publish the letters without prior consent of the Ministry (see *Straits Times* Malaysia, 12 April 1973).

In another case that points out the stringency of controls in Singapore, Pang Cheng Lian, a part-time *Newsweek* correspondent, was found guilty in November 1974 of contempt of court and fined S$1,500 for supplying information to the United States news magazine. The resultant article alleged that Singapore courts were biased and partial in favor of the government. In sentencing Miss Pang, the Chief Justice said he imposed the fine to "emphasise the necessity for parttime reporters of foreign publications, imported here, which have no responsible editor or manager in Singapore to send accurate . . . complete material to their foreign employers" (*Josey*, 1974a, p. 30).

In conclusion, the Singapore press, like its counterpart in neighboring Malaysia, is one of the best endowed financially and worst endowed when it comes to freedom. With the number of laws that exist to control the press, it is unlikely that a liberalization period will have much effect.

3.9 Thailand

Guy B. Scandlen and Ken Winkler

There is a Thai belief that in "years of a comet, Kings die," which is to say that comets accompany social change. The reader may need to be reminded that 1973-74 (the period in which this chapter was researched) was a year of momentous change in Thai society.

The most prominent change was the "student revolution" which overthrew a military dictatorship, replacing it with an interim, benevolent, caretaker government and finally an elected one. It was during this revolution that the press assumed a greater credibility in the eyes of the Thai people. In addition, there were labor problems — culminating after years of repressive treatment by former governments — political scandals and a worldwide newsprint shortage that threatened the existence of many newspapers.

Though the data in this study are based on primarily intensive analyses from July to October of 1973, the development and ramifications of the material collected stretch far into the 1970s.

We feel that Thailand is a case study of a developing press where the printed media — the only information media not controlled by the government — have been given new freedom's tremendously responsible dual role: having established credibility, to play ombudsman to masses of people without influence in a society structured upon influence; and to diffuse information and

This chapter was researched while both authors were working at the Faculty of Communication Arts, Chulalongkorn University. Scandlen is now a UNESCO communication research advisor in Kuala Lumpur, Malaysia and Winkler, a freelance writer and teacher based in San Francisco. Both authors wish to acknowledge the invaluable assistance of Bumrongsook Siha-Umphai, Dean of the Faculty of Communication Arts.

opinions to the people, thereby helping to create more informed participants in the political and economic processes of development.

This chapter is presented in four parts: a brief background summary of Thai newspapers; a study of articles in which newspapers write about themselves; a survey of newsmen in order to obtain a profile of the status and opinions of average journalists and a content analysis of urban, compared with rural newspapers.

3.9.1 Background

Thailand is a developing nation, according to UNESCO, one with a daily newspaper output of 1.4 copies per hundred people, far below the minimum adequacy of 10 daily newspapers per hundred people suggested by that organization. The Thai literacy rate of 68 per cent is, however, among the highest in Asia and suggests a large potential readership (*UNESCO, 1964*).

According to the "Rural and Urban Populations of Thailand: Comparative Profiles" (Chulalongkorn University, 1972), newspaper reading occurs with greater frequency among urban than rural male household heads, and availability of newspapers (and journals) plays as important a role in the urban-rural differences as the ability to read does.

More women than men "never" read newspapers. This was noted by USIS in 1964, and again by Deemar, a local marketing company, in 1972 and 1973 (*Deemar, 1972, 73*). Daily reading is more frequent for individuals of higher socio-economic status than for those of lower. In 1964, USIS reported that "educated respondents read more often than those who were not so well educated. Government officials, students and professional people read newspapers most often; laborers, housewives and farmers least often."

In 1972, Deemar reported that newspaper reading occurs with much greater frequency in provincial urban regions, as well as in Bangkok-Thonburi, than in rural areas. For whatever reason, it is obvious that newspaper reading, daily or otherwise, is not a habit for a majority of Thai nationals, although it is increasing. USIS (1971) noted that among the highly educated, news reading

TABLE 7. Exposure to Newspapers by Migration Status,
Thailand
Rural and Urban Male Household Heads

	Rural	Provincial Urban		Bangkok-Thonburi (Urban)	
Newspaper Reading (Rural) or Purchase (Urban)		recent rural migrants	all provincial urban dwellers	recent rural migrants	all Bangkok-Thonburi dwellers
Everyday	4.7	22.0	27.8	23.2	39.2
Almost daily	6.8	15.3	10.3	14.3	12.5
Once in a while	36.8	23.7	23.3	26.8	19.8
Never and can't read	50.9	39.0	38.5	33.9	27.3
Don't know, no answer	0.8	0.0	0.1	1.8	1.2
Total percent	100.0	100.0	100.0	100.0	100.0
(N)	(1112)	(59)	(670)	(56)	(858)

Source: Chulalongkorn University, 1972.

in general has increased as a daily habit from 62 per cent in 1964 to 73 per cent in 1969, and among those with little or no education, from 22 per cent to 37 per cent.

That a great potential for newspaper reading exists has been further legitimized and institutionalized by the Adult Education Division of the Ministry of Education. In 1971, newspaper reading centers were founded at the village level to aid new literates in retaining and improving their reading ability as part of the Functional Literacy Program.

The centers are built by villagers and the ministry provides funds for chairs, tables, newspaper stands, bookcases and bulletin boards. The ministry subscribes to three newspapers chosen by villages, one of which must be from the local region. By early 1973, 832 villages had established such centers and within two years, the number had increased to over 1,300 centers in as many villages. The ministry hoped to "foster a sense of (national) awareness" and "create a newspaper delivery network to cover the entire nation" (*World Education* 1973).

The price of newspapers makes them a luxury for a high percentage of the population. E. Lloyd Sommerlad said that a Thai has to spend the equivalent of two weeks' earnings to buy a subscription to a newspaper and "the price of a single paper is what a man may spend on his mid-day meal" (*Sommerlad,* 1966). The "Comparative Profiles" underscores this further by showing that of common household possessions, newspaper subscriptions rank seventh among Bangkok-Thonburi households with 25.2 per cent subscribing; seventh among provincial-urban households with 21.7 per cent subscribing, and sixth among rural ones with 3.5 per cent of households subscribing (*Chulalongkorn University,* 1972).

Mitchell has written that the first thing one learns of Thai journalism is that, until recently, not very much has been known or written about it (*Mitchell,* 1965). His exhaustive historical account (*Mitchell in Lent,* 1971), a recently published history and historical content analysis in Thai by Sukanya Teerawanit of Chulalongkorn University (*Teerawanit,* 1974), and the *1971 Directory of Mass Communication Resources* by Thammasat University's School of Journalism and Mass Communications (*Kaviya,* 1971) help fill this gap.

In the limited literature available one theme recurs: that historically the Thai press, and newspapermen in particular, have tended to be irresponsible and unprofessional by Western standards. Alexander MacDonald, founder of the English language *Bangkok Post,* wrote that "(journalism) was not a profession: it was a happy-go-lucky, unprincipled, catch as catch can game, played by ink-stained saints and sinners. The saints were few, the sinners legion" (*MacDonald,* 1949).

Somkuan Kaviya of Thammasat University has commented that " . . . . . most media in Thailand have little financial or organizational stability. For example, one newsman assigned to an editorial staff may work on the advertising or marketing staff at the same time. Furthermore, there is no guaranteed employment and fast change-overs in staff occur frequently" (*Kaviya*, 1971). But according to the International Press Institute, more and more journalists are joining one or more professional organizations and there is evidence of even greater responsibility and professionalism in press performances (*Anant*, 1968). A recent survey by the authors listed seven active news associations.

The problem of ethics remains, however, and questionable practices are reported frequently in the newspapers. It is not unusual for public figures to be approached (as happened to the relative of one of the authors) even by one of Thailand's most prestigious newspapers with offers to withhold a story in exchange for a fee. The same author was approached by another journalist with an offer to withdraw a story if provided with sufficient remuneration.

A frequent accusation against provincial newspapers is that the printed news is merely filler for space not occupied by the national lottery results; probably because, as Mitchell has explained, "the most consistently timely content of the papers (is) the list of the winning numbers" (*Mitchell*, 1965). Scandlen has noted, however, that if people were interested in lottery results only, they needed only to secure the listing from any hawker at a fraction of a newspaper's cost. Or, more simply, the results could be checked free of charge from listings pasted outside shops selling lottery tickets and newspapers (*Scandlen*, 1975).

Provincial newsmen themselves see their papers as "playing an increasingly important role in the life of up-country folk." Citing circulation and response from readers, rural publishers claim that provincial circulation is greater than the Bangkok dailies, and that newspaper offices have become "public grievance houses" for people with problems, especially against the government. This is certainly a trend among certain popular urban papers, as will be discussed later. Rural newsmen, especially, feel that their readers enjoy reading about local events and about themselves (*Kumragsa*, 1971).

In his study of Thai peasant personality, Mosel found that expectations regarding the accuracy of newspaper news were "uniformly low . . . all respondents believe radio news is more reliable" (*Mosel in Pye*, 1963). This has been confirmed in the past by USIS (1961, 1964, 1967). However, in 1971, USIS found for the first time that people attributed far greater credibility to newspapers than they had in previous surveys, and broadcast credibility lessened (*USIS,* 1971).

Although Thai language, popular newspapers see their role as providing entertainment as well as information, there seems to be a trend towards greater responsibility and, therefore, perhaps, greater credibility. The "Comparative Profiles" states that for provincial urban dwellers, newspapers are read not only as entertainment, but as sources of practical information (*Chulalongkorn University,* 1972).

Pongsak Phayakavichien, a newsman of great sensitivity and dedication, argues that the press is becoming more responsible. His comparative content analysis of urban newspapers in 1960 and 1969 found especially great increases in column inches devoted to politics and small increases in column inches devoted to the monarchy, corruption, rural development, human interest and sports (*Phayakavichien,* 1971). Blackburn, on the other hand, has commented that "while Thai papers seemed to surpass those of (Malaysia and Burma) in giving the citizens a sense of participation in the major events of the day, they were noticeably less effectively programmed to build support for officially-determined national development ends" (*Blackburn,* 1971). Phayakavichien found marked increases in stories relating to crime, catastrophes and entertainment.

Most newspapers are privately owned while all electronic media are government operated and controlled. All radio and television news and opinion is written and composed by the government Public Relations Department (PRD) and distributed throughout the kingdom every day. Phayakavichien wrote in 1971 that, "newspapers are the only medium in Thailand through which people can talk back to the government while the government-owned radio and television are clearly propaganda tools." This has never been more clearly demonstrated than during the events of 14-15 October 1973, the student revolution. During this time, some of the most respected and well-known radio newscasters helped the soon-to-be-removed government compose news releases that were blatantly untrue and clearly designed to mislead the public. These statements were broadcast nationwide, while the newspapers reported events as they happened, however sensationally. (It must be said that the revolution, sensational by its very nature, lent itself to colorful reporting.) In newspapers, advertisers are finding new marketing channels, as evidenced in the content analysis of *Phayakavichien* (1971), *Scandlen* (1975), *Thammasat University* and, most recently, *Scandlen* and *Winkler,* all of which indicated large amounts of space devoted to advertising. Mitchell feels that with the energetic interest of advertisers, newspapers will acquire greater freedom than they have ever had (*Mitchell in Lent,* 1971).

Compared with the rest of the developing world, Thailand is not a very urbanized country. Registry figures in 1970 indicated that only 14.6 per cent of the total population lived in municipal areas and, according to the *Christian Science Monitor* (15 Feb. 1969), it is the rural population which, in 1969, displayed particularly heavy voter turnouts.

David A. Wilson, a political scientist, felt that "public opinion is a political force of some consequence (in Thailand) (and) . . . the communication process within the political public . . . serves as a dynamic element" (*Wilson,* 1962). Of the Thai electorate, H. Carrol Parish, Jr., another political scientist, wrote "whenever the public has spoken out forthrightly with a strong voice on any issue, changes in the direction indicated by that opinion have resulted" (*Parish,* 1968), the most recent example being the student revolution of 1973. Later, we shall try to assess what information is available to the rural 85.4 per cent of the population, who pursue rather active voting behavior. We shall try to compare it with the newspaper information in the highly urbanized Bangkok-Thonburi center. Do rural newspapers use facilities to concentrate on local news, thus stimulating local interest, or are they merely carbon copies of urban newspapers, a tendency in developing countries noted by Wilbur Schramm (1964). How do urban and rural papers differ in news emphasis?

Writing in 1965, Mitchell found the "future non-daily up-country dailies might come and go, by the end of the 1960s the idea of upcountry dailies had become a persistent one." In 1971 one Thai writer prophetically noted that, "local news-papers, as evidenced by their continued popularity, do play a significant role in the community and papers which ignore that fact may be faced with the sudden opinion [*sic*] of shutting down their press" — an imminent possibility even confronting some of Thailand's large metropolitan newspapers, such as *Pim Thai* and *Siam* (*Kumragse,* 1971). *Pim Thai,* prior to 1973, was an established, conservative daily of dwindling circulation. *Siam* was a brash, popular, sensationalistic paper, whose ownership had just changed hands, illustrating clearly the routine through which mastheads, not newspapers, changed hands. Both papers were closed because of financial pressures. The mastheads lived on, however, a process which is discussed below.

3.9.2 Article Study

In order to ascertain how newspapers view themselves, 13 daily Bangkok-Thonburi papers were chosen, according to highest published circulation figures, for the sample. The newspapers were: English language — *Bangkok Post, Bangkok World* and *The Nation;* Thai language — *Siam Rath, Thai Rath, Ban Muang, Chao Thai, Daily News* and *Prachatipatai;* Chinese language — *Sakon, Siri Nakorn, Tong Hua Daily News* and *Sing Sien Yit Pao.*

Articles were clipped, read and grouped into categories by frequency of occurrence. These were divided into five categories of the newsprint crisis, government statements and restrictions, press comments from Deputy Prime Minister Prapass Charusathien, charities and service actions by the newspapers themselves and press responsibility as seen through their editorials. Specific articles cited below are identified by month and day of 1973.

The shortage and higher price of newsprint hit Thailand quickly and severely, because most pulp and print is imported. Papers of all three languages were concerned over the government proposals for new mills, price changes and taxings. Of articles studied in the Chinese press, 58 per cent dealt with the problem, as did 40 per cent of the Thai and 65 per cent of the English language press. Major problems arose, because existing paper mills do not have the capacity for producing the needed 180-200 tons for everyday use. In Kanchanaburi, the government closed down a mill for "financial losses" only to approve a joint Thai-Taiwan venture to use some 1,000 square kilometers of bamboo forests in the same area (*Post,* 21 Sept.). Several businessmen wanted to re-open the mill, but after the revolution, it was decided to open it on a "tender only" basis (*Post*, 23 Oct.). Also, at Bang-pa-in, the government paper mill had to raise print prices from Bh.7,400 a ton to Bh.10,000, while at the same time their chief purchasing officer was arrested for "falsifying [*sic*] official documents" (*Post*, 22 Sept.). Fears that student textbook prices would be higher were laid to rest when the government allowed printing companies to buy print at the former rate (*Siam Rath*, 15 Sept.). Import overtures were made to Russia, Bangladesh, People's Republic of China and the Philippines with mixed promises and results. The Philippines refused to sell 7,000 tons, because what they had already sold "was enough for Thailand." Even though the Philippines wanted 14,000 tons of rice, and "even though they haven't paid their bill" for the previous year, Thailand would "agree to sell the rice if the Philippines sells us the paper" (*Siri Nakorn*, 30 August). To solve the problem, ASEAN officials decided that a regional paper mill should be placed in Java, but experts later disagreed and felt Sumatra would be better and there the matter rested. On 1 August 1973, all Chinese language papers stopped their evening editions due to rising costs. The English papers had previously raised their prices and were soon followed by the Thai press. *Thai Rath* and *Daily News* both stated they would no longer print advance copies of their editions. (Thai language newspapers frequently print inner pages a day or so in advance, saving the cover pages for latebreaking news. Popular newspapers post-date every edition; that is, today's newspaper is published using tomorrow's date.)

Credibility about the real crisis was brought into question, when one journalist remarked that a company known as the "Five Tigers" told Press Association members that if they ordered newsprint by 25 August, they would have no problems with delivery or credit (*Siam Rath*, 15 August). This company was criticized by the magazine *Business in Thailand* (Dec. 1973) as having "a monopoly on paper" in the country and for manipulating "the market to suit themselves." The charge was underlined in January 1974, when police and students raided warehouses in an anti-hoarding drive and uncovered almost 6,000 tons of unregistered newsprint. Since newspapers in Thailand use almost 200 tons a day, this hardly seemed like hoarding; however, the police seized it intending to auction it off. On 25 February, *The Nation* said the government was announcing price controls, trying to reduce the cost from Bh.7,000 (US$350) a ton to the previous year's range of Bh.3,000 to 6,000 (US$150-$300). This was because of the assurance they had from exporting countries that there "will be a sufficient supply at a reasonable price." If Thailand could have a viable pulp mill, capable of producing an adequate daily amount of bamboo or pine pulp, then its dependence on imports would be lessened. But conservative estimates said it would take two to five years to make planned facilities adequately operational. Even if the ASEAN plan were feasible, Thai participation would be uncertain, considering daily Thai needs multiplied by the needs of other member countries, and given current nationalism trends.

Deputy Prime Minister Prapass Charusathien was the bogeyman for the Thai press before his ouster by students in October 1973. His attitude towards the press varied from "they're full of lies" (*Post,* 21 Oct.) to they bring "disunity" (*Siam Rath,* 11 Sept). Though his comments rated a small percentage in actual coverage, the effect was weighty because he was also chief of police and assistant commander of the Army. He asked the press not to "write to their taste" (*Siam Rath,* 11 Sept.) and not to print solely for "high circulation" (*Ban Muang,* 12 Sept.). He did, however surprise a news conference in July, by saying permits would be allowed for new Thai language papers *only,* as there were "enough English and Chinese language ones" (*Sakon* and *Siri Nakorn,* 23 July). This was not publicly commented on until 8 August when *Thai Rath* said "favoritism" would play a "decisive role in granting permission to newspapers, we will not be surprised if (permits are) granted to certain individuals and withheld from others." This was confirmed when *The Nation* (7 Oct.) reported two new papers were coming out, one Thai language and the other Chinese language, each having as "Chairman of the board . . . . . . the secretary to the Interior Minister."

In a content analysis of Thai papers, Scandlen in 1975 noted that newspapers, especially Thai provincial ones, looked upon themselves as ombudsmen for the public. This is partially supported by the amount of help and assistance Thai newspapers claimed that they offered the people. Following the 1973 October revolution donations poured into *Daily News* (25-28 Oct.) and *Thai Rath* (28-30 Oct.), which in turn were given to the National Student Center of Thailand (*Thai Rath* 22 Oct.). During the period of this study, *Thai Rath* ran the greatest number of "assistance" stories: farmers (30 Aug., 23 Sept.), slum people (23 Aug., 10 Sept.), strikers (11 Aug.) and a prostitute (25 Oct.) used *Thai Rath* as a medium for airing their grievances. *Daily News* also assisted flood victims in the north with money and clothes collections (11-13 Oct.) and scholarships to journalism students, while *Ban Muang,* as did the previous two, hosted visiting monks and students (7, 16 Oct.) and held charity benefits (14 Aug., 7 Sept.). Chinese papers frequently asked for public help for destitute families (*Sing Sien Yit Pao,* 26 July) and got results. English papers did not report any similar charitable functions during that time period. Also, together with the Bangkok Bank, several newspapers were working on an agricultural assistance program (*Daily News,* 10 Aug.). It is significant that the editors took these situations seriously as evidenced by their appeals for justice and the prominence they gave charities by page placement. Self-aggrandizement (*Thai Rath,* 20 Sept.; *Chow Thai,* 1 Sept.; *Ban Muang,* 10 Oct.), although subtle, usually appeared as enumerations of the good works the papers performed. Chinese papers emphasized how "our papers" aided the community. In one case, *Ban Muang* organized a charity boxing match (10 Oct.), and readers were well reminded about who did the sponsoring.

Government news releases dealing with press responsibility, although not published frequently (20 per cent Thai language, 10 per cent Chinese language and English language), seemed to have had a strong effect due to the editorial comments they inspired. The Public Relations Department vied with General Prapass in ordering newspapers to take responsibility and described itself as "presenting the right news" to the public, as being "close to the newspapers" and as being accepted as an "important source of news" (*Ban Muang,* 8 Sept.). *Ban Muang* stirred controversy by criticizing a government TV station whose director subsequently wanted to close the paper for "five years." The paper vowed "to fight to the end" (*Ban Muang,* 27 Aug.). When the Public Relations Department asked for an apology, *Ban Muang* went to court where it was cleared by the argument that it had criticized "for the benefit of the people" (*Ban Muang,* 4 Oct.).

On 22 October, *Thai Rath* reported that the Special Security Police would not let the paper print certain news and photographs about the revolution. Between 14-15 October a word battle raged. The Public Relations Department fretted that newspapers were using color words to describe events to "create more destruction." *Thai Rath* countered by saying the Public Relations Department should not worry and should "try to solve more immediate problems." The papers themselves were considered "not the tool of government, we stand for the people" (*Thai Rath,* 26-28 Sept.), and on 14 October *Chao Thai* said Prapass had given an interview asking for "understanding between the government and newspapers," and the paper said the government "should create good understanding between students and themselves."

The Public Relations Department warned about writing news that "excites" and "sensationalises the situations" (*Post,* 13 Oct.), and *Thai Rath* answered two days later that newspapers have "a duty to present facts," even if the Public Relations Department "doesn't want them to do so." Evidently the paper was backed by the public, for its circulation on revolution day soared to one million (*Thai Rath,* 19 Oct.).

The restraint shown by the papers editorially during and after the revolution is noteworthy. True, the Public Relations Department tried to assert itself by issuing warnings, but the papers policed themselves. After the government had fallen, some lurid sex stories and many charges of corruption were printed (*Nation,* 23 Oct.) as traditionally follows the fall of a regime, but they were relatively free from tabloid sensationalism. In the end, when the Thanom government was searching for someone to blame for its downfall, it said the newspapers "incited" the people. Newspapers replied that they had "an allegiance to the people" (*Chow Thai,* 14 Oct.).

Also significant, the new interim government dropped the usual requirement of waiting for official clearance for articles through the police press officers. The stringent requirements for new papers were waived also. (Previously, new papers bought the mastheads from non-operating papers officially registered, but not publishing. Thus for an exorbitantly inflated price, one could buy the masthead from *The New Thai Daily* and change it by downplaying part of the title to *Daily*, creating a new paper from the ashes of the old.) However, the government, still watchful of the Thai press law, revoked the license of the *Siam Rath* editor for publishing an article from the Sweden-based Thai Liberation Movement which had attacked the king. Though only revoked for a month (*Post*, 20 Dec.), it served notice that the newly-allowed freedoms had their limitations despite the fact some citizens believed the editor had "good reasons" (*Nation*, 30 Nov.) to inform the public of the existence of such an organization.

After the student revolution in 1973, the restriction on establishing newspapers was lifted. In July 1974, the police reported issuing licenses for 736 newspapers and magazines: 144 for daily newspapers of which 114 were for Thai language, 21 for Chinese language and nine for English language. The remainder included weekly, fortnightly and monthly publications. All of these have not yet appeared on news-stands and the list is still incomplete for there have since been licenses granted to Japanese language newspapers as well.

Violence dogged newsmen throughout the country during the period of this study. One provincial editor had his ear burned (*Sakon* and *Siri Nakorn*, 24 Aug.; *Chow Thai*, 25 Aug.) because of his stories concerning "outlaws," while the editor of *Pak Tai* in the South found his car in flames. He suspected the police, for he had run a series of articles exposing their gambling control and protection rackets and he had no other "known enemies" (*World*, 28 Aug.). *Ban Muang* had its northern office raided by "twenty unknown men" (*Ban Muang*, 13 Nov.) and another crusading editor was gunned down in Udorn after writing stories about illegal logging operations in "protected forests" (*Nation*, 1 Aug.). On the other side of the coin, two scandal writers were jailed for extortion against an Indian merchant (*Post*, 11 July).

Labor problems only involved the Lord Thomson (British) owned *Post* and *World*. The management was accused of discrimination against Thai employees (*Post*, 16 July), as well as the hiring of unqualified aliens "who even higher-placed Nationals have to take direction from" (*Nation*, 28 July). This is compared to the welfare program of *Thai Rath*, where workers "divide" up the voluntary small monthly saving each contributes (*Thai Rath,* 3 Aug.). Also, the *Post-World* syndicate was somewhat singled out in the newly proposed constitution by the regulation that "newspaper proprietors must be persons holding Thai citizenship" (*Nation,* 5 Jan.). Earlier charges against these papers that they "violated journalism ethics" by turning over interview tapes on their own initiative on a suspected visiting revolutionary and then "boasting" about it later (*Nation,* 5 Dec.) went unanswered. Other papers received criticism too, but usually the charges and the answers were printed.

3.9.3 Attitudes of News Professionals

The authors attempted to survey the attitudes of newsmen among urban Bangkok-Thonburi and provincial papers. Lack of funds prohibited in-depth personal interviews. Questionnaires were designed and pre-tested in three languages: Thai, Chinese and English. A random sample of 75 per cent of the news gathering and editorial staff of each Bangkok-Thonburi newspaper was drawn and questionnaires deposited at the desk of each selected professional. A cover letter explaining the purpose of the survey was included. The questionnaires were to be collected on an appointed day, but the response was not encouraging. Originally, newspaper editors were suspicious of this survey, perhaps because it carried the university letterhead. Universities are government institutions and therefore suspect. Only after intervention by several Thai colleagues, were the authors allowed to deposit their questionnaires. Fear of the military government's pressure and reprisals may have been the basis for this. As will be seen, those who responded to the survey also chose not to respond to many of the opinion questions, even with assurances that all questionnaires were confidential. Student research assistants visited each Bangkok-Thonburi newspaper three times to speak to reporters, requesting them to complete the questionnaires. In total, 95 questionnaires were returned from all sources. Provincial newspapers were sent five questionnaires each with return stamped enveloped and a cover letter requesting that the editor and 50 per cent of the reporting staff complete it.

The 95 respondents were predominantly male (79 persons)

between the ages of 20 and 40 (72 respondents), from Bangkok-Thonburi (73 persons), married (55 persons), with three children or fewer (71 persons). Forty respondents had a Bachelor of Arts degree, 12 had completed vocational training, 11 had finished high school, 20 had from eighth to twelfth grade educations. Nine had a Master of Arts degree. Educational training tended to be lower on provincial papers than on Bangkok-Thonburi papers. Training of news professionals is a popular controversy in Thailand. Newspapers complain that universities, for example, do not adequately train journalism graduates, and, on the other hand, universities and vocational schools respond that their mandate is to educate broadly and not to simply turn out skilled technicians. Eighty-four of the 95 respondents said they were trained on the job; seven cited academic preparation.

3.9.3.1 Newspapers in Thai Society

Twenty of the respondents felt that the role of newspapers in Thai society was to inform and "benefit" society. Twenty-five commented that newspapers were not developed enough yet and lacked responsibility. Over a third chose not to answer. There were other miscellaneous comments, but we feel it is significant in view of earlier comments and the content analysis to follow, that no one felt the role of newspapers was to entertain. This, of course, may be due to sampling bias. By far, the majority of respondents felt they had freedom to comment, print material and investigate issues (the survey was made towards the end of the military dictatorship). In commenting on the above, 10 persons said that press freedom depended on society, seven felt it depended on the government. Four respondents felt press freedom should be limited, three said the press needed ethics. Seventy-three respondents reported never having felt pressure from any source.

Of those who *had* felt pressure, 36, by far the largest number, cited editorial staff and newspaper management as the source of the pressure, while 17 pointed to advertisers and 16 cited businessmen and local government authorities. Fourteen mentioned national government authorities as sources of pressure; 12, religious sources; 10 mentioned politicians out of government.

Other sources, briefly stated, included private parties, the military, government organizations, self-censorship, foreign governments, family and friends and the courts. But these were cited by not more than nine respondents and usually many less than that. What were the reactions to these pressures? Seventeen stated they felt frustrated; 10 said they had no feelings; 14 tried "to correct it," to get management to take action; four accepted the pressures and one fought against them.

Sixty respondents expressed support for media labor organizations, although not all of them were members; 50 were not members of any organization. The remaining 45 respondents were members of two or more organizations.

TABLE 8.   Memberships in Professional Associations, Thailand

Name of Association	*Number of Members*
Reporter's Association of Thailand	17
Provincial Journalists Association of Thailand	
Provincial Press Association of Thailand (Dual Memberships)	15
Press Association of Thailand	6
Provincial Press Association of Thailand	5
Journalists Association of Thailand	4
Sigma Delta Chi	1

Eighty-nine respondents felt that provincial news is important, but in enumerating the most important pages, not one person mentioned a page which might contain provincial news. These are multiple response answers to an open ended question.

There seems to be very little support, exchange or cooperation between newspapers. Fifteen respondents mentioned that they occasionally exchanged news and pictures.

What sources do these news professionals use? Fifty-five

Table 9. Most Important Pages in Thailand Newspapers
by Frequency of Responses

Page	Number of Responses		
	Total	Urban	Rural
Back page*	33	21	11
Editorial, opinion and thought page	23	19	4
Science, medicine page	15	10	5
Business page	12	8	4
Sports page	11	8	3
Society page	9	8	1
Foreign news page	8	8	0
Women's news	5	5	0
Education	5	5	0
Entertainment	3	3	0
Front page	3	2	1

*customarily used as a jump page

respondents reported (in multiple answers) using their own observations in collecting news, while equal numbers of respondents used personal contacts, both in government and out of government, as sources for news. Fifty cited each of these sources. Extremely few (15) used contacts in foreign governments; 26 used foreign embassy press releases. The use of wire services broke down as follows: 34 used Associated Press; 29, Agence-France Presse; 27, United Press International and 22, Reuters.

The future of the Thai press is very conditional in the view of these respondents. Twenty-four said it depended on press freedom; 19 said the future was solely in the hands of the attitude and practice of newspaper management. Fifteen felt the future depended upon the audience's education; 14, the ethics of newspaper people; 13, on the press ability to regulate itself and on the strength of the news associations to enforce those regulations.

Table 10.   Rank Ordering of "Important News" in Thailand
Newspapers by Percentage* of Responses

"What kinds of news does your newspaper consider
to be important for its readers?"

URBAN

Ranking	News Categories	Degree of Importance**			
		Very Imp.	Imp.	Not Sure	Not Imp.
1.	International, foreign news	35.21	54.93	9.86	0
2.	Thai government affairs	42.25	45.07	9.86	2.82
3.	Economic activity, commerce	23.94	59.15	16.90	0
4.	Education, educational activities	25.35	53.52	1.41	19.72
5.	Accidents, crimes, natural disasters	30.99	46.48	14.08	8.45
5.	Editorials, letters to the editor, religion, ethics, morals	38.03	39.44	19.72	2.82
5.	Labor, agriculture	23.94	53.52	2.82	19.72
6.	Advertising, announcements	19.72	52.11	12.68	15.49
7.	Space, science, medicine	11.27	60.56	22.54	5.63
8.	Sports	15.49	3.52	22.54	8.45
9.	Arts, culture, entertainment, fiction	1.41	63.38	30.99	4.23
10.	Women's news, home, fashion, domestic advice	2.82	32.39	23.94	40.85
11.	Human interest, gossip, astrology, solicited advice, biography	4.23	29.58	40.85	25.35
12.	Lottery, sweepstakes	4.23	8.45	64.79	22.54

N = 71

RURAL

Ranking	News Categories	Degree of Importance**			
		Very Imp.	Imp.	Not Sure	Not Imp.
1.	Editorials, letters to the editor, religion, ethics, morals	55.55	40.90	4.55	0
1.	Thai government affairs	22.73	72.73	4.55	0
2.	Accidents, crimes, natural disasters	22.73	63.64	9.09	4.55
3.	Advertisements, announcements	27.27	55.55	0	18.18
3.	Education, educational activities	36.36	45.45	18.18	0
3.	International, foreign news	9.09	72.73	18.18	0
4.	Human interest, gossip, astrology, biography, solicited advice	31.82	45.45	9.09	13.64
5.	Economic activity, commerce	31.82	9.09	27.27	0
6.	Arts, culture, entertainment, fiction	18.18	50.00	29.27	4.55
6.	Space, science, medicine	9.09	59.09	9.09	22.73
7.	Labor, agriculture	22.73	40.90	36.36	0
8.	Women's news, home, fashion, domestic advice	0	40.90	40.90	18.18
9.	Lottery, sweepstakes	4.55	9.09	36.36	50.00
10.	Sports	9.00	0	22.73	68.18

N = 22

* Sums may not equal 100% due to rounding error.
** Rankings according to the combined percentage of very important and important responses.

3.9.4 Reading Preference and the Content of Newspapers

Over a three-year period, *Thai Rath* was clearly the most popular paper among Thais, followed by *Daily News* and *Siam Rath*, a distant third. The choice of newspapers in the newspaper reading centers reflects the popularity reported above, although at this writing, the information on the reading centers is still incomplete. The greatest number of reading centers received *Thai Rath*, followed by *Siam Rath*, *Daily News* and *Ban Muang*, in declining order.

In response to the USIS question in 1971, "Which newspaper is most consistent with your point of view?", 47 per cent of respondents answered *Siam Rath*, 9 per cent answered *Daily News* and 1 per cent each answered *Pim Thai*, *Bangkok Post* (English language) and *Sin Sieng Yit Pao* (Chinese language).

Table 11. Stated News Reading Preferences, Thailand
(General Population Survey)*

News Category	daily	twice a week	once a week	never
National news	55**	5**	18*	1*
Crime	45	6	25	7
Local news	44	4	24	10
International, foreign news	41	6	24	12
Social problems, society	34	4	24	16
Columnists	30	4	29	24
Sports	27	5	22	16
Finance and business	20	4	34	27
Science and space	20	5	28	21
Cultural events	18	5	34	22
Editorials	15	3	25	36

Source: USIS, 1971
   (N = 1,000)
*   reported by percentage of respondents answer.
** percentage may not equal 100 because of non responses not reported here.

Table 11 reports the kinds of news stories USIS respondents in 1971 said they read most frequently. National and international news are the stories most frequently mentioned, followed by columnists, social problems, editorials and science and space.

3.9.4.1 Content Analysis of Newspapers

It is interesting to compare the stated news reading preference with the actual content of the papers, although it must be said that the amount of news offered may not be related to the *quality* of news. The (English language) *Bangkok Post*, for example, was seen in our analysis as offering great quantities of soft news and advertisements. A 1973 survey of university instructors, however, showed that of all newspapers in Thailand, *Bangkok Post* was considered the most credible and dependable for national and international news (*Prachachart*, 16 Dec. 1973).

However, before analyzing the news content of specific papers, it might be useful to ascertain what kinds of news have been available to both urban and rural peoples, irrespective of specific newspapers. To measure this, the authors subscribed to every Bangkok-Thonburi daily newspaper publishing during the summer and fall of 1973. A statistical week was constructed over a period of three months and each paper was sampled. Provincial papers do not usually publish daily, so subscriptions were purchased for every provincial paper publishing at the time, and each edition received was sampled. Not every paper responded, however, so this universe of papers is a self-selected one. (A detailed description of the methodology may be obtained from the authors.) Units of news were tabulated and a Chi square analysis performed to detect significant differences in the relative proportions of space dedicated to various kinds of news content. (Detailed lists of news content per paper may be obtained from the authors.) The data were further analyzed by rank-ordering news categories according to percentages of space dedicated to them.

In 1970, Scandlen (1975) did a content analysis between urban and rural papers and found significant differences in the relative proportions of space dedicated to all the content categories except the following: (see Appendix I) accidents, disasters, crimes and unlawful acts; Thai governmental affairs; economic activity and commerce; human interest, gossip, astrology, biography, solicited advice.

In terms of percentage of space, the following three categories of news were found not to differ significantly in terms of relative proportions of space in both urban and rural papers: (see Appendix II) advertising — 22.2 per cent of urban papers, 37.2 per cent of rural papers; arts, culture and entertainment — 9.2 per cent of urban papers; 12.3 per cent of rural ones; human interest — 9 per cent of urban papers and 8.6 per cent of rural papers.

In the category of governmental affairs, urban papers gave significantly greater amounts of space to national news while rural papers gave significantly greater space to local news. There seemed to be more similarities between urban and rural newspapers in 1973 than there had been in 1970 in terms of kinds of news, but this may be attributed to better sampling procedures in the second study, as well as possible changes in direction of news content. In 1973, employing a much more controlled sample of papers, the authors found eight categories of news in which there were no significant differences. Urban and rural papers were similar in the amounts of relative space devoted to advertising, economics, human interest, miscellaneous, women's news, arts and accidents. Significant differences were found in the relative proportions of space devoted to editorials, labor, education, sports, international news, Thai governmental affairs and blank space.

In 1973, the highest percentage of space was again given to advertising and announcements: 30.9 per cent in urban papers and 31.4 per cent in rural ones. Human interest ranked second in both types of papers, 19.7 per cent in urban papers and 16.6 per cent in rural ones. Thai governmental affairs ranked third with 12.4 per cent of space in urban papers and sixth in rural papers with 5.8 per cent. The lottery ranked fifteenth in urban papers with 0.5 per cent, and eleventh in rural ones with 1.6 per cent (see Table 12).

Table 12. Rankings of News Categories in Thailand Newspapers
by Percentage* Basic Space Units, 1973

Rank	Urban	Percentage	Rural	Percentage
1.	Advertising	30.88	Advertising	31.40
2.	Human interest	19.71	Human interest	16.57
3.	Thai government affairs	12.35	Miscellaneous	10.91
4.	Miscellaneous	8.14	Blank space	9.97
5.	Arts	5.51	Accidents	6.19
6.	Sports	4.59	Thai government affairs	5.79
7.	International News	3.94	Editorials	4.31
8.	Economic Activity	3.81	Arts	3.09
9.	Accidents	3.15	Economic activity	2.96
10.	Blank space	1.97	Education	2.96
11.	Editorials	1.83	Lottery	1.61
12.	Women's news	1.70	Sports	1.34
13.	Space, science, medicine	1.05	Space, science, medicine	.94
14.	Education	.78	International news, labor, agriculture	.67
15.	Lottery	.52	Women's news	.53

* Percentages may not total 100 because of rounding.

The greatest differences between Thai, Chinese and English language newspapers were found in four news categories: advertising and announcements; accidents; sports, and human interest. In Chinese language newspapers, there were two and one half times more advertising than in either their Thai or English language counterparts. There was more news about accidents, crimes, natural disasters in English language newspapers than in the other two languages, and the English language press also contained twice as much sports news as the Thai or Chinese press. Chinese papers carried over six times more human interest stories than the English language press and two and a half times more than the Thai press. Papers of all three languages carried nearly identical

amounts of news devoted to arts, culture, entertainment (ranking
fifth collectively in percentage of space devoted to this category);
space, science and medicine ranking thirteenth collectively with
1.05 per cent of space. (Refer to Table 13.)

Table 13. Differences Between Thai, English, Chinese Language,
Bangkok Newspapers
By News Category, 1973

News Category	x^2 Chi Square	p Level of Significance
1. Arts, culture, entertainment, fiction	.05804	.995*
2. Space, science, medicine	2.18792	.90*
3. International, foreign news	3.20187	.75*
4. Education, educational activities	3.38075	.75*
5. Lottery, sweepstakes, related stories	3.90252	.50*
6. Economic activity, commerce	4.31928	.50*
7. Editorials, letters to the editor, religion, ethics, morals	5.84380	.25*
8. Women's news, home, fashion, domestic advice	7.75620	.25*
9. Blank space	10.98669	.05
10. Thai government affairs	15.20526	.01
11. Advertising, announcements	17.79770	.005
12. Accidents, disasters, crimes unlawful acts	19.68788	.005
13. Sports	22.02261	.005
14. Human interest, gossip, astrology, biography, solicited advice	29.79434	.005
15. Miscellaneous	33.11772	.005
16. Labor-agriculture, no news about this topic was sampled during the period of content analysis.		

* No significant difference or association.

Regional papers (Table 14) tended to be very much alike, but most alike in space devoted to advertising and announcements; space, science and medicine; the lottery, and international news. They are least alike in space devoted to stories of sports; economic activity and commerce, and women's news. All regional newspapers had a great deal of advertising (collectively 31.4 per cent) and very little news about science, space and medicine (0.9 per cent collectively). They devoted the same amounts of space to the lottery (1.6 per cent) and international news (0.67 per cent). The South was the only region that carried sports news during the course of this study. Northern papers carried much more news of economic activity than did the other regions. Only papers in the Central region carried women's news.

3.9.4.2 Analysis by Individual Newspapers

In view of the fact that certain urban newspapers had been singled out more than others as being widely read or having points of view with which people agreed, it may be instructive to see what sorts of news were found in those papers. In 1973, advertising, human interest, sports and Thai governmental affairs ranked first through fourth in amounts of space for *Thai Rath,* which was consistent with the 1970 analysis (*Scandlen,* 1975) that found the same rankings except for the fourth which was accidents. At that time, Thai government news ranked eighth. *Daily News* in 1970 contained the following top five rankings: advertising; human interest; sports; accidents, crimes, disasters; arts, culture and entertainment. In 1973, advertising and human interest were both first with equal percentages of space, followed by miscellaneous, women's news, and news of Thai governmental activity.

In 1970, *Siam Rath's* news categories ranked in the following order: editorials, letters to the editor; advertising; international, foreign news; Thai government news. Three years later, Thai government news and women's news shared first rank, followed by advertisements, editorials and foreign news tied for third. This seems to be in keeping with the reputation of *Siam Rath* as being the elite, intellectual newspaper. However, it is being challenged by two others: *Prachatipattai* and *Prachachart.* The latter was established after this analysis was performed but a look at the rankings of *Prachatipattai* showed "serious" news first, followed by miscellaneous; economic, commercial news and human interest, tied for third; advertising and announcements, fourth.

Table 14.   Differences Between Newspapers Across Regions (North, South, Northeast, Central) of Thailand in Each News Category, 1973

	News Category	Chi Square	Level of Significance
1.	Advertising	.72839	.995*
2.	Space, science, medicine	1.08528	.995*
3.	Lottery, sweepstakes, related stories	2.76806	.90*
4.	International, foreign news	3.36923	.90*
5.	Editorials, letters to the editor, religion, ethics, morals	3.83895	.75*
6.	Human interest, gossip, astrology, biography, solicited advice	4.95517	.75*
7.	Arts, culture, entertainment, fiction	5.12381	.75*
8.	Labor, agriculture	5.38023	.50*
9.	Blank space	5.99729	.50*
10.	Miscellaneous	6.94461	.50*
11.	Thai government affairs	7.24680	.50*
12.	Education, educational activities	7.56244	.50*
13.	Accidents, disasters, crimes, unlawful acts	11.43249	.10*
14.	Sports	13.97034	.05
15.	Economic activity, commerce	15.85290	.025
16.	Women's news, home, fashion, domestic advice	16.42728	.025

* No significant difference or association.

No analysis of *Ban Muang* was performed in 1970 but a 1973 analysis showed that advertising and miscellaneous both ranked first, followed by news of arts; human interest and Thai government news tied for third. All other categories ranked far behind. Although *Pim Thai* no longer publishes, it may be interesting to see the kinds of news its readers were exposed to in 1970 (concurrent with the USIS survey that asked the question about newspapers and people's points of view): advertising ranked first; sports, second; arts, culture, entertainment, third; and human interest, fourth.

The two non-Thai language newspapers mentioned by respondents were analyzed in 1973 as follows: *The Bangkok Post* (English language) ranked advertising first; sports second; human interest third; and miscellaneous fourth. The Chinese language *Sin Sieng Yit Pao* placed advertising first; international, foreign news and human interest both ranked second; arts third; and all other categories far below.

3.9.5 Reading Preferences, Professionals' Attitudes and Content Analysis

Observers have stated that the Thai prefer to read crime and sensational news material. The Thammasat University study, for example, commented that, "the most popular (news story) is local crime news followed by entertainment and social news. People are not interested in political or provincial news" (*Kaviya,* 1971). USIS stated that "most readers throughout the country preferred commentary style of journalism to factual content, except for crime or domestic news" (*USIS, 1971*). That same organization reported that crime news ranked second to national news in frequency of readership in 1971. What did professional news people feel was important for their readers? Provincial news professionals surveyed, ranked news of accidents, crimes, natural disasters, second in terms of what they believed was important for their readers, while urban professionals felt it was fifth in importance (along with editorials, labor, etc.). Provincial papers in 1973 devoted nearly 6.19 per cent space to accidents, crimes, natural disasters, and urban papers devoted 3.15 per cent. In 1970, both urban and rural papers devoted equal amounts of space (7.7 per cent) to accidents, crimes, natural disasters, more than they did in 1973. The content analysis of both years indicated that this type of story, by no means, dominated the news; earlier. Phayakavichien also found a reduction in space devoted to sensational news (*Phayakavichien,* 1971). Even though a reduction has been noted, there is still a strong interest in crime and sensational news on the part of news professionals, as well as readers, and rural papers may be giving readers more of what they want to read in regard to this kind of news.

Observers may not have been accurate about the amounts of space devoted to news of crimes, accidents and natural disasters, but they seemed to have been entirely correct in their comments about human interest news, whatever its components: social problems, gossip, society columnists, social news, etc. In fact, the amount of space devoted to human interest had increased from 1970 to 1973. In 1970, urban and rural papers devoted 9 per cent and 8.6 per cent, respectively; in 1973, the increases were to 19.7 per cent and 16.5 per cent, respectively.

The USIS survey (if the categories of social problems, society and columnists are noted collectively) reported extremely strong daily readerships of human interest items. Rural news professionals ranked human interest news fourth in terms of importance to readers, but their urban colleagues ranked it eleventh. Rural news people may be more realistic than their urban colleagues in terms of what they provide their readers.

However, it must be remembered that the "Comparative Profiles" found that provincial urban dwellers used newspapers to get practical information, as well as for entertainment, and that USIS found that national news, local news and international, foreign news each received a large number of daily readers, and collectively, commanded a far greater reported daily readership than other news categories combined (*Chulalongkorn,* 1972). Further, the newspaper people interviewed for this chapter seemed to take a rather serious view of the kinds of news their readers should be exposed to. Certainly, hard news outranked soft news.

Rural news professionals believed that editorials, letters to the editor, along with news of Thai governmental affairs, were the most important kinds of news for their readers. This might support the contention that rural papers see their role as that of ombudsman to the people (although this is nowhere mentioned in response to an open ended question about the role of rural newspapers, nor did very many respondents cite the editorial, opinion pages as being particularly important). The 1973 content analysis showed that rural papers ranked editorials seventh with 4.3 per cent of news space, which is more than in 1970, when editorials ranked thirteenth with 1.5 per cent of news space. The concept of and the intent to be ombudsman may be very alive for rural papers, but the practice, obviously, was not as strong as the desire.

In the views of urban news professionals, editorials ranked fifth in importance, but the editorial pages seemed to be extremely important, ranking second only to the back page. However, urban papers devoted only 1.8 per cent of space to editorials in 1973, as opposed to 6.1 per cent in 1970. Intent far outweighed practice. USIS reported that people said they read editorials least frequently of all other categories, ranking it last of the eleven categories of news.

For the urban papers, news of Thai governmental affairs was given great importance, both in the practice as well as in the intent of the professionals who wrote it. This conformed to the USIS findings that the greatest number of people reported reading national news daily. It ranked second in terms of importance in the minds of urban newspeople and tied for first (with editorials) in the views of their rural colleagues. The 1973 content analysis showed that this category comprised 12.35 per cent of urban news space, ranking third, a large increase over 1970. In rural papers, it occupied 5.79 per cent of the space, ranking sixth, a slight increase over 1970.

Urban professionals believed foreign news was the most important item for their readers, and surprisingly, rural professionals ranked it third in importance. The USIS survey also reported that readers ranked foreign and international news fourth in reading frequency. In terms of printed news, however, in 1973, foreign news comprised only 3.9 per cent of urban news space, ranking seventh, and 0.69 per cent of rural news space, ranking thirteenth. In 1970, urban papers devoted 5.8 per cent of space to foreign news and it occupied 0.4 per cent of rural news space. In 1973, eight urban respondents cited the foreign news page as being important, while no rural news people mentioned it. Obviously, rural papers did not devote much attention to foreign news while urban papers did, although the amounts were not very large despite news professionals' belief that it was so very important. Educational news was another case where intent was more elevated than practice. News people ranked educational news rather high in terms of importance for their readers (fourth among urban respondents and fifth among rural), but it was never mentioned by readers in the USIS survey as a category they ever read. In both the 1970 and 1973 content analyses, the amounts of space devoted to news of education were minimal. It ranked thirteenth among urban papers in 1970 with 3 per cent of space, and fourteenth in 1973 with 0.78 per cent; in the rural press, it ranked twelfth with 1.3 per cent of the space in 1970, and ninth in 1973 with 2.96 per cent.

Arts and culture ranked low in terms of what people said they read. Urban news professionals ranked this category ninth in importance for readers, and rural newspeople ranked it sixth. However, the 1973 content analysis showed news space for arts and culture ranking fifth in urban papers and eighth in the rural press. In 1970, art and culture ranked much higher in terms of space devoted to this kind of news: second in both urban and rural papers.

We would like to look at two final categories of news: economic news and labor-agriculture news. USIS reported that economic news was among that least frequently read by respondents. Out of 11 categories, it was eighth in terms of frequency of reading. In 1973, news of economic activity was given 3.8 per cent of space in urban papers (ranking eighth) and 2.9 per cent in rural papers, ranking ninth. It had been much lower in 1970. In the views of urban news professionals, however, economic news ranked third in terms of importance for readers and fifth among their rural counterparts.

USIS did not report the category labor and agriculture. Urban professionals ranked it fifth in terms of importance for readers, along with accidents and editorials, but rural papers ranked it seventh. It does not appear to have been given any space in urban papers during the month of our content analysis, possibly due to sampling error; the category ranked thirteenth in terms of space in rural papers. It ranked fifteenth in 1970 among urban papers; tenth for rural ones.

As for winning lottery listings, it is true that rural papers devote more space to them than the urban press, but it is not an inordinate amount of space. Further, rural professionals ranked the lottery listings next to last in terms of importance to readers and their urban colleagues ranked the listings last.

3.9.6 Conclusion

The authors have attempted to outline for the reader the place journalism has occupied in Thai society and the gradual evolution of journalism into an increasingly credible and activist role. This role has been documented by a survey of Thai journalists, a content analysis of published news and summaries of other research and opinions dealing with Thai journalism. Of course, any conclusions drawn are transitory, for, as shown, Thai journalism is still struggling for identity, credibility, respectability and acceptance by society as a whole.

The government may have been realizing the press' institutional value all through the 1970s. There are indications that criticism of the government, even before the revolution, did not result in severe repercussions. Seventy-six per cent of the journalists interviewed reported never having been intimidated by the government. Also, the government may have been heeding the increasing credibility gained by the press during the revolution — as well as editorial pleas for national unity and hard work in building the new democracy. Also, newspapers generally have supported the new governments' efforts in redirecting the country. But political awareness and economic sophistication cannot be created through heavy doses of arts, culture, entertainment, human interest, crime and disasters, alone. More important to the political and economic stability of a country and to the task of mobilizing human resources behind the national effort, must be news of its government's affairs, news of commercial activity, as well as news channels for public debate.

Our research has shown that news professionals seemed aware of this: respondents cited "hard news" as far more important for their readers than "soft news," and USIS showed more people mentioned reading national news and foreign news daily than other kinds of news. Further, the USIS respondents said they identified most closely with the views expressed by *Siam Rath,* a paper of hard news and opinion, the "intellectual" newspaper. There seemed to be a difference, however, between what people said and did. Perhaps they wanted to be seen as reading papers such as *Siam Rath* (and later, *Prachatipattai* and *Prachachart*) but in fact, the greatest circulations were found in newspapers such as *Thai Rath* and *Daily News.* These two publications, whose content is largely "soft news," are most frequently mentioned in readership surveys as read daily.

Even so, the content of these publications may be shifting as evidenced by an increase since 1970 of space devoted to news of Thai governmental affairs and a subsequent decrease in news content devoted to accidents, crime and natural disasters. There has also been an increase in human interest news, perhaps related to a strong readership preference for it, as noted by USIS. Thus, newspapers seem to be searching for the delicate balance between entertainment and information, attracting attention and providing the necessary tools people need when economic development and the political processes are yet new and fragile experiences.

Undoubtedly, the most unique aspect of the Thai press is in its role of ombudsman of the people. This is a dynamic and increasingly complex role, incorporating two recent observations: Blackburn's that Thai newspapers create a sense of participation in the major events of the day and Pran Chopra's that the Thai press takes itself seriously in providing forums for public opinion, which distinguishes it from the other presses in the region, "the only light in the dark situation of the press in Southeast Asia."

Thailand is ripe for responsible newspapers. With a high literacy rate, increasing newspaper readership in the urban and rural sector, active support and promotion by the Ministry of Education, as well as local and national commercial interests' use of the press as an advertising media, newspapers could be the developmental multiplier for the market of ideas so badly needed.

3.10 Thailand

Boonrak Boonyaketmala

With a succession of political changes, triggered by the students' revolution of 6-15 October 1973 (commonly referred to as "The Ten Days") and the ultimate downfall of the United States' foreign policies in Southeast Asia in early 1975, the destiny of the Thai press is launched towards several historically unfamiliar courses. Against the inevitable arrival of the new rules of the game for the press, possible because of the mentioned monumental episodes, there is a stubborn prevalence of the traditionally so-called "journalisme à la siamoise" (*Pickerell*, 1960, p. 83), a term subject to many interpretations except that of socially responsible journalism. Contemporary Thailand, under an unprecedented political context, thus witnesses a sudden and hostile coexistence between at least two journalistic mainstreams: on the one hand, the emerging series of journalism styles unknown in over a century's historical heritage of journalism and, on the other hand, a perpetual expansion of a bizarre and capricious mode of journalism historically evolved from a peculiar combination of the uniquely Thai political, economic and cultural environment (*Pickerell*, 1955, p. 6).

Major trends related to Thai newspaperdom that arose in the mid-1970s included: the sudden availability of an uncertain freedom of expression; the prospect of a probably feasible system of self-censorship for the press through a press council; the con-

Boonrak Boonyaketmala is a Ph.D. candidate at the East-West Center. He is also a lecturer and researcher affiliated with Thammasat University, Bangkok. He has worked on three major dailies in Bangkok and is the author of a prize-winning book on the Thai throne.

troversial mushrooming of diverse kinds of newspapers; an appearance of the avowed leftist-ideologically-oriented publications; the rise of a new generation of journalists to prominence; an awakening of the public awareness regarding the "proper" role of the press; an extensive public criticism of the overall national policy of communications; among many others. Amidst such manifest phenomena, which undoubtedly represent a distinct pattern of growth, indicating a revolutionary point of departure for newspaperdom as a social institution in Thailand, there are also in existence various stagnant elements which hinder its complete cycle of revolution. In reference to this dilemma, one commentator noted: "Although political changes since mid-October 1973 have had a direct and positive impact upon the profession of journalism in this nation, Thai newspapers seem to be the slowest to make necessary and progressive adjustments for good" (*Prachachart Weekly,* 10-17 Jan. 1974, p. 46). One of the leaders of the new journalists in Thailand bitterly criticized the dominating group of irresponsible newspapermen as being unable to cope with the atmosphere of democracy available since the deposition of the "terrible trio," meaning Field Marshal Thanom Kittikachorn, Field Marshal Prapat Charusathien and Colonel Narong Kittikachorn, the most powerful figures in Thai politics prior to the October students' revolt. The irresponsible newsmen only caused chaos while the few journalists who have been freedom fighters willingly accepted the new level of responsibility. He intimated that the new sense of freedom in Thailand did not automatically improve the newspapers, because it did not bring with it an instant awareness of responsibility (*Yoon,* 1974, p. 27).

This climate of contradiction, as a result of the Thai political vacuum, is indeed the central theme in relation to the future direction of journalism in Thailand. Noteworthy changes within press circles are metaphysically rooted to both the general process of social changes accelerated in Thailand in the first half of the 1970s, and the international political changes which occurred in this region early in 1975, due to the American disengagement in Indochina wars. Physically, however, the relatively liberal atmosphere connected with the Thai press is a direct consequence of "The Ten Days," without which the fate of Thai newspapers would have taken a different path. The psychological importance of this historical period is truly pervasive, because it is intimately interconnected with the fundamental dynamics of the Thai political momentum. According to a discerning observer, the incident has exerted an immense symbolic influence on a nation-wide scale and, thus, "a line can be drawn from here to distinguish one age from the other" (*Arpapirom*, 1975, p. 213). For two political scientists who have done thorough research on this particular period, the students' revolution of October 1973 altered the future direction of the Thai political system. They asserted that "The Ten Days" will be remembered as the most important event in Thai political history since the "revolution" of 1932 (*Prizzia and Sinsawasdi*, 1975, p. 30), when the People's Party toppled the absolute monarchy in a bloodless coup. After the bloodshed of October 1973, pointed out another scholar, there can be no going back to the naked army rule of past decades, even though the Thai military may retain a considerable role in national affairs. If Thailand is fortunate, he continued to predict, the melancholy events of "The Ten Days" may propel the nation out of a 40-year interregnum and towards fulfillment of the ideals of the 1932 revolution (*Race*, 1974, p. 203).

Thus, viewed in political terms, "The Ten Days" has been a landmark not only in Thai political history but also in journalistic history. The historical development of the Thai press may be roughly classified into three interwoven periods: the period from the appearance of the kingdom's first newspaper to the abolition of the absolute monarchy (1844-1932); the period from the rise to supremacy of the People's Party to the fall of the National Executive Council of Field Marshal Thanom Kittikachorn (1932-73); and the period from the royally appointed interim government of Prime Minister Sanya Thammasak to the constitutionally elected coalition government led by Prime Minister Kukrit Pramoj (1973-76). This chapter is an endeavor to locate and evaluate chief streams related to Thai journalism since the so-called neo-Field Marshal Sarit coup of 1971 (*Girling*, 1972, p. 534) by the Revolutionary Party of Thanom's military oligarchy. The following section is intentionally devoted to an analytical history of newspapers, aimed to serve as a conceptual basis throughout this chapter.

3.10.1 Thai Press During 1844-1971: An Historical Sketch

Politically, the development of Thai newspapers during the period before the revolution of 1932 was threefold: (1) the initial birth of the press was an indirect product of Western expansionism in the context of the nineteenth century's international political gravity, which forced Thai leaders to design a foreign policy construed to reluctantly appease the more immediate appetites of Western innovators through a tactic of maximum appearances and minimum concessions (*Prizzia,* 1968, p. 49); (2) the consequential acceptance of and involvement in journalistic activities on the part of the royal institution, symbolically paved the way for Thai newspapers to flourish into an obscurely influential social institution, locally unknown in the previous centuries of Thai history; and (3) the increasingly-swelling world of the press spontaneously expanded the size of the political public, which dramatically produced diverse effects upon the political tendency of the Thais.

In many dimensions, the relationship between the press and politics in this country has been from its very beginning, intimate. In the earliest past, observed one scholar, the press and politically-important propaganda were inexorably entwined. The American founding father of the press in Thailand, Dr. Dan Beach Bradley, thus, "hoped to influence King Monkut" (Rama IV, reigned 1851-69) through his newspapers and "through the king, the kingdom" (*Mitchell* in *Lent,* 1971, p. 211). And, moreover, when newspapers were exploited by the Thai monarchs as a means of public communication, the royal newspapers seemed to be unconsciously used as political tools. The royal press in general, therefore, displayed a distinct trait of Thai journalism: "journalism as a means of disseminating the official, authoritative word, journalism as disputation rather than journalism as the reporting of information" (*Mitchell* in *Lent,* 1971, pp. 212-213).

The *coup d'etat,* organized by a group of middle-level officers in the military and civil services, which ended the control of the royal family over the government in 1932, was ultimately the climax of Thailand's voluntary and involuntary exposure to Western political concepts through various channels. The decades since the formal abolition of absolute monarchy brought Thailand under a number of quasi-parliamentary constitutions and dictatorial regimes. Political instability as a result of constant political struggles, within the military and civilian cliques in and out of power at a given time, became an established tradition in Thai political culture since 1932. The technique of *"coup d'état"* was repeatedly refined by Thai political experiences as a formalized means of seizing complete control over the government. A political scientist generalized that the Thai political life of the era was "the persistence of the same leaders, much of the same law, and most of the same institutions year after year." The most extreme *coup d'état,* he continued, brought to power not the same people but their protégés or former associates. New constitutions repeated much of the old, word-for-word (*Wilson,* 1962, p. 274).

Distinct characteristics of the Thai press in such a politically struggling age, according to one scholar, were that: "(1) individual papers were frequently published as outlets for particular individuals who led cliques within the complicated pattern of politics-in-government; (2) papers much more interested in sensation and entertainment than news as such were published; and (3) the press concentrated in Bangkok, a pattern that did not change significantly for non-daily papers until well after World War II and remained undisturbed for daily papers until the 1960s" (*Mitchell* in *Lent,* 1971, p. 220). Up to the 1960s, press controls in Thailand "fluctuated almost wildly between complete freedom and virtually complete repression, depending on the particular views of the individuals in power at any given time." But the overall trend of those days was clearly towards controls (*Mitchell* in *Lent,* 1971, p. 216). This fact is certainly paradoxical when one looks back to the relatively freer press in Thailand under the absolute rule of kings. When asked which period between the absolute monarchy and the age of "democracy" was freer for journalism, a veteran editor instantaneously answered: "the period before the coming of democracy" (*Paritanondh,* 1972, p. 24). An historian explained this apparent paradox by the fact that the more traditional Thailand had a press "either so minor or so clearly under royal direction that there was no need for the Throne to take notice in terms of legalistic controls." He assessed that the emerging press during the reign of King Chulalongkorn

(Rama V, reigned 1868-1910) "was largely free to criticize, although there was no question of the Throne's right and power to control and even censor directly, if the monarch so decided" (*Mitchell* in *Lent,* 1971, p. 215). Furthermore, under King Wachirawut (Rama VI, reigned 1910-25), Thailand witnessed the so-called "Golden Age of Thai Journalism," in which the king "welcomed fair criticism of his government but reacted with vigor to what he believed to be unfair or groundless attacks on his administration" (*Minetrakinetra et al.,* 1965, p. 10). Such a paradoxical situation was perhaps highlighted by King Prachatipok (Rama VII, reigned 1925-32), the last monarch, who ruled Thailand with absolute authority, when he pointed out that the Thai people did not enjoy an authentic freedom of expression as a result of the declaration of the first Thai constitution in 1932. He said the People's Party monopolized political power, and opposition newspapers were deliberately eliminated or punished. The king insisted that full freedom of expression must be guaranteed by the People's Party (*Bunnag,* 1972, pp. 193-144). King Prachatipok's call, however, was not answered by the members of the People's Party, who continued to suppress a large number of opposition newspapers on vague grounds of legal justification (*Boonsa-ad,* 1974, pp. 104-112).

Since the rise of the People's Party, the press was more often than not operating under fear, while political instability was gradually transformed into a way of life for Thais. This may have been because of a fundamental political fact observed by an analyst, that the "revolution" of 1932 lacked several basic preconditions to lead to a durable political takeover. The leaders of the People's Party were not even genuine representatives of public opinion (*Phongpanich,* 1973, p. 89). This analysis is consistent with a view held by a political scientist who does not value the actions of the People's Party as a "revolution" in the real sense of the term (*Siffin,* 1966, pp. 141-142). The abolition of absolute monarchy in 1932, therefore, was in no sense a part of a popular uprising. These elementary factors have undoubtedly formed a springboard for the political instability experienced by virtually all governments since 1932, resulting in a series of uncertain policies towards newspapers.

The decades after 1932 saw the intimacy between newspapermen and politicians being confirmed. Exceedingly political and partisan, nearly all leading newspapers of any given time since 1932 were reported as linked to some active politicians. In the very beginning, Pridi Phanomyong, one of the most powerful leaders of the People's Party in the 1930s, and of the Free Thai Movement in the 1940s, was accused by a political historian as having manipulated two newspapers as tools of political propaganda (*Samuttawanich*, 1974, p. 45). Field Marshal Pibulsongkhram, Pridi's associate and rival, published a number of newspapers in competition with the newspapers which opposed him. The pro-Pibulsongkhram newspapers were labelled by various independent newspapermen of the period as the "prostitute's sheets" (*Boonsa-ad*, 1974, p. 124), meaning the newspapers unashamedly promoted the dictator. During Pibulsongkhram's World War II administration, all newspapers in Thailand were forced to print on their first page: "Believe in the Leader, the Nation will be out of Danger." After the war, however, Pibulsongkhram was to fade from the Thai political arena.

The so-called "Dark Age of Thai Journalism" came with the dictatorial rule of "strong man" Field Marshal Sarit Thanarat, who was prime minister from 1959 to 1963. With Sarit's age of martial law, the press was continuously threatened by the well-known Announcement No. 17, issued by his Revolutionary Party in 1958. The Announcement provided that all prospective newspaper publishers had to apply for a license and that "any newspaper publishing statements of a certain character shall be warned, impounded, and destroyed or undergo punishment in the form of withdrawal of the license of its publisher, printer or proprietor." Statements subject to punishment under the Announcement were those which "offend the King. . . . discredit the government, . . . contribute to the popularity or desirability of Communism . . . or constitute Communist subversive tactics; . . . those which are vulgar; . . . and likely to undermine the morals . . . of the nation; . . . those which divulge official secrets" (*Moore*, 1974, p. 337).

Compared to all post-1932 governments, Sarit's was much more authoritarian. "Until the seizure of power by Sarit," declared an analyst, "no government after 1932 claimed to be absolute. Modest opposition to the government was usually permitted, and some limits were maintained on executive rule" (*Darling,* 1960, p. 348). Thus, Sarit, during his supremacy, was the sole source of political authority; his regime was similar to the absolute rule of kings in the past. For many commentators, therefore, Sarit was primarily responsible for the state of decay of Thai news-paperdom after his dictatorial administration late in the 1950s. An editor in Bangkok concluded that, "the revolutionary age of Field Marshal Sarit was the casual origin of weaknesses still visible in the press." During his administration, "virtuous newspapermen who respected their profession were disturbed and many of them flew away from journalism as a result" (*Social Science Review,* March 1973). Among the most distinguished who disappeared from Thai journalism because of Sarit's terrorism was perhaps Kulab Saipradit, one of the most respected figures in Thai modern literature. Kulab spent his life in exile in Peking from 1958 until his death in 1974 (*Jeung-anuwat,* 1974, p. 42). Kulab's literary efforts have now become a symbol of revolutionary spirit, not only among progressive journalists, but also among the general political public.

Announcement No. 17, to a newsman, was the symbol of the ultimate withering away of press freedom in Thailand. In Sarit's days, "Thailand became the weirdest country in the world because newspaper licenses turned out to be commercially profitable products." Since no new newspaper was permitted to publish because of his repressive law, "there was a wild economic speculation of the existing newspaper licenses, even among professional bankers. Some bought such licenses for millions of baht each for rent to those who wished to publish newspapers" (*Prachachart Weekly,* 15-22 Nov. 1974, p. 39).

During Sarit's government, observed an author, the Thai press served little need, other than entertainment and escapism. Further-more, an extreme degree of inaccuracy and irresponsibility that did not merit the privilege of freedom was apparent (*Pickerell,* 1960, pp. 88, 96). This fact is probably rooted in both Sarit's dictatorship, which forced the press to dwell on the least sensitive matters to avoid possible "problems," and a tradition of "journa-lisme a la siamoise," embedded in the history of journalism. In Sarit's rule, perhaps only *Siam Rath* could be classed as a quality "news and opinion" newspaper. Owned by one of the most prominent and colorful pressmen in the history of modern Thai journalism, M.R. Kukrit Pramoj, later prime minister of a coalition government, *Siam Rath* rose steadily to fame among the expanding political public as a pro-royalist newspaper.

3.10.2 The Press Under the Thanom Administration: 1963-73

The end of Sarit's authoritarian rule as a result of his sudden death in 1963, saw most of the backward elements endemic in Thai newspapers being carried over into different dimensions in the government of his military heir, Field Marshal Thanom Kittikachorn. The development of Kittikachorn's one-decade rule may be divided into three periods: (1) the period from the death of Sarit to the gradual relaxation of military absolutism (1963-68); (2) the period from the declaration of the constitution to the abolition of the parliamentary mechanism (1968-71); and (3) the period from the neo-Sarit *coup d'état* to the fall of the National Executive Council (1971-73).

Press controls under the Thanom government were less stringent compared to the era of Sarit. Following the death of Sarit, the press was "allowed for the first time in five years to clearly express opinions" (*Mitchell* in *Lent,* 1971, p. 219). Press exposés in connection with the late prime minister's extramarital love life and financial affairs were carried without interference by the government (*Mitchell* in *Lent,* 1971, p. 219). The first period of his rule by martial law saw the rise of newspaperdom as an industrial enterprise. Equipped with modern technology, the popular press of this era was consciously geared towards a profit-oriented industry. The increase of circulation became the prime goal for the popular newspapers, while professional excellence was almost completely ignored. Shocked by the conditions of the Thai press under the Thanom regime in the mid-1960s, an observer noted that Thai newspapers used excessively exploited sex and sensationalism while unable to deal with political issues. Compared to the press in Asia in general, he ranked Thai newspapers among the exceptionally least serious (*Lyons,* 1965, p. 8). Because of the prevalence of severe press laws, Thai newspapers for the most part, seemed reluctant to develop themselves into an effective watchdog of the military dictatorship.

In 1968, when a new constitution was declared which resulted in a general election the following year, the Thanom regime did not abolish Announcement No. 17 handed down by Sarit, despite many conscientious voices of protest in and out of Parliament. A combination of severe legal restrictions and uncertain legal applications, pointed out an experienced reporter, forced Thai newspapers to develop a form of self-censorship for the sake of their continued survival (*Worapong,* 1973, p. 114). Late in 1970, a new press act was presented to the National Assembly for passage by the United Thai People's Party (UTPP), led by the Thanom clique. This act included stringent regulation of the press which was opposed by spokesmen of Thai mass media. In an unprecedented display of solidarity, all Bangkok newspapers refused to cover the official visit to Thailand of United States Vice President Spiro Agnew, as a protest against the proposed press act. The act was not voted on until the arrival of the neo-Sarit *coup d'état,* sometimes called the silent *coup d'état,* on 17 November 1971, which symbolized a revival of military dictatorship. The rationale of this particular coup was deeply rooted to the changing political scenes at both the national and international level (*Lee,* 1972, pp. 36-43).

After the coup late in 1971, the Revolutionary Party of the Thanom junta issued Announcement No. 3, which provided that "the Revolutionary Party will not for the moment censor the newspapers." This was reasoned that the Revolutionary Party "believes that all newspapers will cooperate with this revolution." However, "newspapers representing the voices of foreign nations or upholding the doctrines dangerous to the nation, the religion, the king, or attempting to bring a division into the nation's unity by a direct, indirect or any other method will be suppressed" by the power of the Revolutionary Party (*Bunnag,* 1972, p. 195). The *coup d'état* of 1971 was a reminder for Thai newsmen that the military dictatorship had not withered away from Thai political life. This fact certainly imprinted several negative effects upon the press circle. Under a revised atmosphere of fear, Thai newspaperdom under the Thanom oligarchy tended to over-emphasize its commercial role by exploiting many editorial and marketing techniques. The question of qualitative improvement was rarely tackled. Obsessed by the idea of increasing circulation,

Thai newspapers became followers, rather than leaders, of public opinion. The state of "consumer sovereignty," asserted an economist, was the primary cause of low quality of Thai newspapers (*Thanapornpan,* 1973, pp. 18-24). The pursuits of the Thai press in the early 1970s were labelled by a critic as "journalism of conformity," which inclined to lead the public towards political passivity (*Arpapirom,* 1974, pp. 185-204). The decay of political morality resulted in unimaginative journalism which tamely conformed to the political whims of the military men in power. Businessmen who invested in newspaper enterprises in this political setting seemed to seek merely commercial ends from newspaper publishing. Thus, the main tendency of newspapers in this period was to imitate all popular features adorned by the mass mind. *Thai Rath,* the former pro-Sarit newspaper founded in 1958, served as an ideal model since it had been the giant of the popular press in terms of circulation. In 1972, when two new newspapers were started, *Siam* and *Ban Maung,* they obviously aimed to compete with *Thai Rath* in all imaginative ways. In fact, *Siam* was a direct copy of *Thai Rath,* except for the nameplate.

In the middle of 1971, however, there was an interesting change in the Thai press. The beginning of the English language *The Nation* as the first only English daily owned by Thais, was indeed the initial step towards a creative mode of journalism among the new generation of journalists. In terms of quality, *The Nation* was a landmark in Thai journalism because it professed to practice objective journalism comparable to foreign owned newspapers in Bangkok. This mode of journalism was known later as the "New Journalism" (*The Nation,* 13 Oct. 1974). Steadily rising to fame among the English reading public concentrated in Bangkok, *The Nation* served not only as a spearhead of responsible journalism for local journalists, but also as a storage bin for the works of a new generation of newsmen.

Another wave of responsible journalism appeared on the Bangkok scene when *Prachathippatai* was taken over by a new group of journalists early in 1973. Printed in Thai, *Prachathippatai* pulled together a number of promising pressmen who were "under the age of thirty." Before "The Ten Days," *Prachathippatai* was the only Thai language newspaper competing with *Siam Rath* in readership. *Siam Rath* found itself relatively conservative compared to the new *Prachathippatai,* which gradually became popular among politicized students on university campuses. Up to the period before "The Ten Days," *The Nation, Siam Rath* and *Prachathippatai* served as the main currents of quality-oriented newspapers avowing to feed the hungry political public. Whereas these three newspapers were widely read among the potential political force in Thailand, *Thai Rath, Daily News, Siam* and *Ban Maung* were very popular among less articulate readers. Marked by sensationalism, escapism, sex and violence, the latter group of newspapers, with rare exceptions, merely touched upon politically important issues in a gossip fashion. Thus, the Thai popular press tended to play a reactionary role in relation to the political health of the country. After a long history of suspected and confirmed blackmail and extortion, concluded Winkler and Scandlen, Thai journalism, prior to "The Ten Days," seemed to have moved towards a professional "ombudsman" position in Thailand (*Winkler and Scandlen,* 1974, p. 38).

With its longer tradition, Thai journalism in general has been the only relatively free medium, compared to radio and television (founded in 1931 and 1955, respectively), which from their conception have been government monopolies. Although most of the 192 radio and nine television stations in the early 1970s were operating on a commercial basis (*Bennett,* 1974, p. 176), they had been little more than the mouthpieces or weapons of influential officials and competing government agencies. A political analyst noticed that various radio and television stations openly served as organs of rival units in the Thai bureaucracy (*Riggs,* 1966, pp. 150-151). Thus, the structure of information flow in Thailand has been, in essence, conflicting. On the one hand, there has been a communication network directly controlled by a number of public agencies and, on the other hand, there has been a print medium, obscurely controlled by the powerful figures in the political arena. By Western standards, the notion of objectivity, except in special circumstances, has been almost foreign to the Thai mass media in general. In the context of information flow, the press has been the primary source to reflect and lead "some" public opinion. Past experiences illustrated the fact that if united, the press was generally tolerated by the

Thanom administration. During the pre-students' revolt, a frequent critic of press laws claimed that the Thai press under the military regime led by Thanom had more freedom than any other in Southeast Asia (*Yoon*, 1974, p. 27).

The middle of 1973 saw an increasingly apparent waning of psychological power of the Thanom military faction. The politically-articulate university students became increasingly active and powerful in their protests aimed at the top men in the military pyramid. The students' endeavors to balance the political monopoly held by a few in the military establishment were, for the most part, allied by the press which was sympathetic to the students' protest programs. By late 1973, the Thai press was politically prepared to the extent that it was not reluctant to reflect political dissastisfactions echoed by the ever-expanding, politically-conscious public in and out of Bangkok. With the ultimate arrival of "The Ten Days," the Thanom regime, which used to brush aside the press as an insignificant journalists' toy, awakened to its influence. According to a report, the press rallied the hitherto non-political masses to the student rallies. Many of the 250,000 who attended one of the student rallies, and several of the 66 killed and 865 wounded during the rioting, were not students (*Media*, Jan. 1974, p. 3). *Thai Rath* on the revolution day, 14 October, sold as many as one million copies, an unprecedented record in the history of Thai journalism (*Winkler* and *Scandlen*, 1974, p. 37). On 13 and 14 October 1973, the Thanom government sent the army to *Thai Rath* and the *Daily News* to attempt to censor news at the desk but, by this time, things were out of the government's control (*Media*, Jan. 1974, p. 3).

The fate of the Thanom military dictatorship was, to a noticeable extent, decided by newsmen who chose to ally with the ideals proclaimed by the young revolutionaries who, with spontaneous support from the people, turned Thai political events upside-down for the first time in the long history of the nation. Remarked an eminent intellectual, without the ample press coverage of the events leading to and surrounding the students' revolution of October 1973, they could not have toppled the Thanom military junta (*Media*, Jan. 1974, p. 3). In the end, one scholar observed, when the Thanom government was searching for someone to blame for its downfall, it said the newspapers "incited" the people, and the newspapers reacted by saying, they had "an allegiance to the people" (*Winkler* and *Scandlen*, 1974, p. 37). Such a claim was not always the case, however, for many opportunistic newspapers which were either politically naive or reactionary. One commentator, therefore, noted that 15 October 1973, was a doomsday for the Thai press, except for a precious few. The Thai newsmen for the most part did not know how to handle the situation when the students and citizens had already overthrown the military dictatorship (*Yoon*, 1974, p. 27). Another observer of the Thai press pointed out that the newspapers published during "The Ten Days" were much a part of the establishment to be destroyed. "Angry and overwhelmed students who saw themselves pictured as villains while their colleagues were being cut down by government fire" thus tore their "opposition" newspapers to shreds (*The Nation*, 13 Oct. 1974).

3.10.3 The Press Under A democracy In Transition: Sanya's Interim Government, 1973-75

The bloodshed of October 1973, was, in a sense, a signal that Thai society has evolved to such a level of complexity, wealth, literacy and sophistication that no one group has a monopoly of political power. The immediate appointment of the interim government by King Bhumibol Adulyadej (Rama IX, reign from 1946-present) in the moment of political crisis, resulted in a civilian-dominated government led by Professor Sanya Thammasak, former rector of Thammasat University. His accession to the prime ministership was meant to create a social order that would form a basis for the democracy idealized by the uprising's activists. In the course of his prime ministership, Sanya was perhaps most popular among the journalists. Sanya had been an avid reader of the Thai press and, according to a leading newspaperman, was considered one of the most responsive men in Southeast Asia to opinions voiced by the press. He even went on record that he would resign if the Thai press wished him to (*Yoon*, 1974, p. 27). With him in power, the ban on issuance of new newspapers was almost immediately lifted. The latest Thai constitution, written and promulgated during his administration, contains a clause granting the long overdue press freedom. Article

40 of the longest of the dozen constitutions of Thailand since 1932, provides that "All persons are to enjoy freedom of speech, writing, printing and publication." It went on to say that, "Abridgement of such freedom may be made only by virtue of the provisions of law particularly enacted for safeguarding the right, freedom, honour, or reputation of others, or for maintaining public order or good morals or protecting youth against moral degeneration." Furthermore, "Closing of a printing press or prohibition of printing in a manner to affect freedom under this section is void." Regarding press censorship, "No requirement of submission of articles or contents in a newspaper for prior censorship by officials can be required unless the nation is engaged in battle or war or there exists a state of emergency or martial law, provided however such requirement may be made only by virtue of the provision law enacted under paragraph 2." In terms of ownership, "Only Thai nationals can own newspapers in accordance with the condition stipulated by law." And, moreover, "Financial support to a private newspaper shall not be given by the State" (*Prizzia* and *Sinsawasdi,* 1974, p. 192).

Amidst the new sense of freedom enjoyed after the October uprising, there were many notable changes in press circles which revealed internal institutional reform, whereas all the familiar myths haunting Thai newspaperdom continued to exist. The sudden freedom to publish newspapers after long years of legal restrictions imposed by the military oligarchies, unmasked the fact that military dictatorship was not the only cause which obstructed a proper development of a free and responsible press. The boom of newspapers in terms of quantity saw the re-enactment of an age old problem in new dimensions. In an era when freedom of the press was not for a moment doubted by the most demanding critic of government, features of the so-called "journalisme à la siamoise" thus developed at a pace unbearable for many observers. In the middle of August 1974, the Thai press witnessed one of the most shameful incidences in the history of Thai journalism, when an entertainment columnist of *Thai Rath* was questioned at the Press Association of Thailand, regarding the accusation that he had taken bribes, kickbacks and even extortion money. The "court of hearing" was ended by a shoot-out. The episode puzzled very few people in Thailand, especially not the men of the press, for the fact that corruption had long existed in the newspaper business was well-known. "It was inevitable," said a newspaper's editorial, that this incident had to be settled by gunmen. The shoot-out was symbolic of how journalists in Thailand, whether crooked or honest, have been unable to settle their conflicts sensibly.

Sanya's one-and-a-half-year role as the leader of the caretaker government was not only one that guaranteed complete press freedom, but also tolerated a widespread irresponsibility among pressmen. In fact, his government was reported as "against press control." The Interior Minister of his administration said in an interview that the government did not want to use Announcement No. 17, still legally effective, to deal with the abuse of press freedom (*Bangkok Post*, 23 April 1974). His cabinet decided to urge the press not to publish "fanciful, groundless and factless stories and rumours" which might affect the stability of the government, but to publish "responsible and factual reports" that were deserving of full freedom of the press (*Bangkok Post*, 11 April 1974). A religious personality, Sanya personally demanded from the press that they help improve morality of the general public by publishing short poems about Lord Buddha's teachings. "The Buddhist poems could go something like: Do only good; be honest; don't assault anybody," Sanya pointed out, adding, "there would be much happiness in the society if this is done" (*Bangkok Post*, 4 July 1974).

Sanya's toleration of Thai newspapers resulted in a "license boom" early in 1974, when almost 400 people all over the country applied for licenses to publish newspapers and other periodicals (*Media*, April 1974, p. 3). Up to 6 December 1974, the numbers increased to 806, 16, 30 and one, for Thai, English, Chinese and Japanese newspapers, respectively, making altogether 853 licenses permitted. Among this number, 177 licenses were issued for the daily newspapers (*Nugkhow Yearbook*, March 1975, p. 168). Such a license boom, due to a radical change of press policy by the Sanya administration, practically ended the monopoly of newspaper publishing previously possible because of tight press policies of the military regimes of Sarit and Thanom. In reality, however, not even 10 per cent of all the licenses permitted were used by those who applied for them. Probably most of the applications for newspaper licenses were meant to satisfy the Thai whimsical speculation of the political return of military dictatorship. It had been very expensive to rent a newspaper license in the era of military supremacy. During Sanya's administration, a "New Journalism" was formally declared. Objective news reporting, responsible comment and a new approach to the affairs of the nation were promised as essential features (*The Nation*, 13 Oct. 1974). The old guard of journalism came under sporadic attacks from the new generation of journalists, according to a commentator, in a style not unlike hatred campaigns in China; no names were overtly mentioned and there was no individual target in the new journalists' attacks (*The Nation*, 13 Oct. 1974). At the height of the campaign, a journal entitled *Revolution of the Flies, the Newspaper Coup d'état* was published, in which 13 reporters from eight Thai daily newspapers who formed the "fly society," called for improvement in standards of both newspaper administration and Thai journalism generally (*Media*, April 1974, p. 26). The reference to flies goes back to a very old Thai observation that a fly does not feed or swarm over its dead peer, that it is not cannibalistic; thus, journalists of old never attacked or criticized fellow journalists (*The Nation*, 13 Oct. 1974). The breaking of this golden rule of Thai journalism, therefore, needed a revolution of the flies. Although ineffective in its attempt to purify the black spots of Thai newspaperdom, this movement resulted in a series of similar movements by other groups of journalists and non-journalists. Early in 1975, a club called "Newspapers for the People" was established to promote a conscience of responsibility among newsmen and to protest against professional malpractices of newspapermen (*Siangmai*, 4 March 1975). The members of the club included some 20 new-generation newsmen who aimed not only to purify Thai journalism but to attack foreign domination of Thai political, economic and cultural life (*Prachachart*, 4 March 1975). Also involved in similar activities were students of journalism at Thammasat University, who had created a public exhibition against "irresponsible" journalism (*Prachachart*, 5 March 1975). Such revolutionary movements have been the major sources of inspiration for a widespread public initiation and participation in several protests against a number of Thai newspapers, such as *Siam Rath, Ban Maung, Siam Rart, Dao Siam, The Bangkok Post* and *The Bangkok World,* each for different charges. Three common themes seemed most apparent: that newspapers had supported foreign powers to dominate Thailand's destiny; newspapers had called for a return of the military dictatorship; and newspapers had committed serious irresponsible practices regarding journalistic ethics. In all cases, the government of Sanya did not interfere with the conflicts between protesters and pressmen, but left them to be resolved in court by legal procedures. Such a phenomenon has paradoxically aroused many dissatisfactions on the part of the overwhelmed and angry activists who, in most cases, demanded immediate action from the government. To this extent, the mushrooming of newspapers since Sanya's administration has been a springboard to an unprecedented degree, for many public controversies regarding press freedom and press responsibility.

The most remarkable new styles of journalism have been perhaps reflected in *Prachachart, Prachathippatai, Siangmai, Athipat* and *The Nation.* Printed in black and white, these five newspapers were distinctly different from their counterparts which were fancifully published in many eye-striking colors. The exceptions were the two English newspapers, *The Bangkok Post* and *The Bangkok World,* and a score of Chinese newspapers in Bangkok which have chosen to be less sensational in their appearance. *The Nation* and *Prachachart,* since their inception in 1971 and 1973, respectively, have been loyal to their promises to print objective news reports and responsible commentaries. Operated by the same group of associates, the twin English and Thai newspapers have been increasingly well-respected by intellectuals and the general political public concentrated in Bangkok. *The Nation* and *Prachachart* have had, perhaps, the most mature editorial policies of any newspapers owned by Thai publishers. Committed to libertarian journalistic concepts, *The Nation* and *Prachachart* have also emphasized the principles of political democracy, national sovereignty and economic independence. Accused by many socialistically-inclined commentators as being too Westernized in their orientation, *The Nation* and *Prachachart* have managed to stand on the forefront of nationalistic lines.

Half a year older than *Prachachart* and two years younger than *The Nation*, *Prachathippatai* changed its editorial line in the course of time. Half a year before the ultimate downfall of the Thanom military junta, *Prachathippatai* practiced a journalism that may be best termed fairly objective in news reporting and mildly anti-military absolutism in commentaries. *Prachathippatai* was, therefore, steadfastly pro-students' political efforts before, during and after the October revolt. This was exceptionally rare when compared to other newspapers. Because of political changes triggered by "The Ten Days," which brought a favorable atmosphere of freedom into the country, *Prachathippatai* became increasingly leftist in its political outlook.[1] This editorial policy seemed to change again in late 1975 when the managing staff of *Prachathippatai* fired a number of its editorial staff members for a series of vague reasons (*Square Weekly*, 16 Sept. 1975, p. 41). *Prachathippatai* shifted its posture from a formerly leftist newspaper, in the sense that it had served as a platform for anti-establishment opinions, to a more middle of the road stand. A lack of sufficient and able editorial staff and its uncertain editorial policy seemed to be *Prachathippatai's* main problems. Many of its staff left to join the more stable *Prachachart.*

Siangmai, like *Prachachart,* was a direct product of the new atmosphere of democracy in Sanya's term in government. Edited and managed by a former columnist of *Thai Rath* and *Siam*, *Siangmai* always had a small editorial and managing staff. Steadfastly anti-authoritarianism, *Siangmai,* in its early days, frequently published articles containing socialist political messages. Its political stand, however, changed in the course of time. Possibly because of excessive competition, *Siangmai* turned out to be rather inferior compared to other newspapers intended for serious readers.

Under Sanya's interim government, Thai journalism encountered another notable, unprecedented development, with the appearance of the biweekly newspaper *Athipat*, owned and administered by the National Student Center of Thailand

1   The word "Leftist" in this context is broadly used to mean an attitude which is against the establishment. This does not necessarily lead to a conclusion that *Prachathippatai* advocates a dictatorship of the proletariat. Seeking real democracy in Thailand has often been considered leftist by the establishment.

(NSCT), the central organ which brought to reality "The Ten Days." Serving as a catalyst of political changes, NSCT published *Athipat* since late 1973, as a forerunner of "cultural warfare" committed "to progagate right thoughts, to lead public opinions against the enemies of the people and to support the people's movements against the imperial invaders and national traitors." "Our standpoint is one and the same with that of the people," declared *Athipat,* "our objectives in fighting are only those for the people" (*Athipat,* 24-31 July 1975). During its idealistic existence, *Athipat* proved to be consistent in its journalistic efforts to bring a new consciousness into Thai political life. News reporting and social commentaries were geared to building up nationalistic and socialistic sentiments among the expanding number of young political activists and their sympathizers. *Athipat* was extremely anti-militarist and anti-colonialist. In fact, this was the very *raison d'être* of *Athipat.* Many observers have seen it as a politically progressive newspaper, while others have accused it of being "too Maoist" in orientation. Circulated among a limited group of readers, *Athipat* was the nucleus of NSCT's leadership. Edited and managed by non-professional journalists, the student idealists turned out one of the most alive newspapers on Bangkok's newsstands. Apparently, NSCT manipulated *Athipat* as its machinery for a "thought reform" program consciously pursued by NSCT. Two scholars pointed out that student leaders in Thailand had realized that the success of their "cultural revolution" would determine the permanency of the political changes they had already achieved since "The Ten Days" (*Prizzia* and *Sinsawasdi,* 1975, p. 51).

Despite all the dramatic events which occurred in the press after "The Ten Days," there had been little change in radio and television in Thailand. In fact, Radio Thailand, the main government mass medium, came in for a lot of hostile criticism during the students' revolution. The Department of Public Relations has repeatedly been called the "Department of Lies"[2] by several

2   After "The Ten Days," during which time Radio Thailand broadcast information attacking the student revolt, the Department of Public Relations has been under constant attack by both students and journalists. Journalism students at Thammasat University protested against Radio Thailand by presenting it with a wreath made of trash.

conscientious critics of government. One reporter suggested that the Department of Public Relations would run into problems if it continued to be a staunch mouthpiece of the government. If the fundamental attitudes of the Department of Public Relations are not overhauled, he said, "the people will have to execute both the government and the Department of Public Relations" (*Prachachart*, 10 May 1975).

Considered in the context of past experiences of Thai journalism, the role of Sanya as the prime minister in such a politically critical and transitional period was essentially twofold: he liberated the Thai press from the "kingdom of fear" familiar during the decades of military rule, guaranteeing for the press complete freedom of expression unprecedented in the nation's history, and he also tolerated all kinds of journalistic activities exercised by the men of the press. No longer was the bogey of Communism used as a notion to threaten journalists. Noted one newsman, the press can, from now on, rest secure that unless they are brought to court no newspaper will be closed down or a journalist imprisoned for his views. In his days as prime minister, those involved in journalistic activities thus had an opportunity for the first time in many decades to experiment with and propagate any form and content of ideas they deemed worthwhile. The freedom extended to what people could read. The publication and readership of "new left" and traditional Communist literature, observed one scholar, increased a hundredfold after the students' revolution of October 1973 (*Prizzia*, 1975, p. 7).

The end of Sanya's administration in February 1975 (after the coalition government of M. R. Seni Pramoj was approved by the Parliament), saw a number of highly responsible newspapers walking hand in hand with a score of irresponsible ones. In Thailand, where the bounds of responsible journalism have been often overstepped in the name of press freedom, the commercially-oriented press had begun to exploit sex, sensation, violence, extortion and rumor to a degree that caused all conscientious men to worry. Alarmed by widespread irresponsible practices among many journalists, the publisher of a foreign-owned English newspaper, *The Bangkok Post,* called for stronger libel laws in the face of the misuse of freedom (*Media*, April 1975, p. 25).

Nearly all newspapers published after the license boom were

those which were more than willing to do service for politicians and businessmen, who had always played dirty games for the sake of their own personal interests. At the cost of journalistic ethics, the old guards of stagnant elements of the Thai press continued to betray their professional responsibility. In general, most of the old line journalists did not think of themselves as instruments of change among the masses; in fact, they were willing to print anything that sold, or brought occasional rewards to them. Many newspapers, such as *Dao Siam, Raiwan Bunterng, Siam,* and even the most well-established and prosperous, *Thai Rath* and *Daily News,* therefore, print a regular column concentrating on obscenity, to compete for the hungry and frustrated mass of readers. A sense of social responsibility has really been a foreign notion for many Thai journalists. A sex columnist at *Dao Siam,* in an interview with a student of journalism at Chulalongkorn University, went as far as saying that, "I do not care a bit for being criticized by many as irresponsible to the society" (*Nisit Nugsuksa Monthly,* 1 July 1975, p. 29).)

The Sanya administration left the political arena in February 1975, when Thai political life was at the peak of confusion. Newspapers were filled with speculation as to the results of the general election held on 26 January 1975. This resulted in a coalition government led by M. R. Seni Pramoj, the leader of the Prachathipat Party, after three weeks of power bargaining among 30 political parties which had seats in parliament. Rumors of the political return of military dictatorship were printed in newspapers day after day. The major question amidst this new political atmosphere, according to a political scientist, was how far the revolution of October 1973 would go. Included in this question was another: how long would the new constitution itself last? (*Race,* 1975, p. 157). The game of power bargaining among all the power brokers concerned, which resulted in the leadership of Seni, was by no means conclusive. The first Thai coalition government lasted for only a few weeks because of the rapidly changing political momentum prevailing at the time. The resultant political vacuum was finally resolved by a substitution of a new coalition government under the direction of M. R. Kukrit Pramoj, the leader of Social Action Party and Seni's brother.

3.10.4 Newspapers Under A Newspaperman's Government

A well-known politician, banker, scholar, teacher, dramatist and novelist, the next Thai prime minister, Kukrit Pramoj, was certainly best known as a journalist. The first Thai newspaperman to become prime minister, Kukrit founded *Siam Rath* in 1950; he still directs it today. A serious opinion-oriented newspaper, *Siam Rath* enjoyed a stable reputation among the politically-conscious public of Thailand during its more than two decades of life. A pro-royalist evening newspaper, it had begun to decline after "The Ten Days," when the Thai political route started to change. Writing two regular columns for *Siam Rath* for over two decades, Kukrit, as a result, had some fame and a wide political base. He had gained a reputation as one of the bravest voices to criticize the military regimes (*Peagam,* 1975). His writings in *Siam Rath,* according to one of its reporters, were the newspaper's "heart." Many readers bought *Siam Rath* just to read him, thus, without his writing, it was not a complete newspaper (*Klinsoonthorn,* 1975). There can be no doubt that Kukrit has been one of the most respected and famous newspapermen produced by Thailand.

The decline of *Siam Rath* after "The Ten Days" seemed to have sprung from a number of reasons. Firstly, Kukrit's image in relation to the students' revolution was not a good one. When the students rose up to demand the collapse of the Thanom military regime during street demonstrations in October 1973, Kukrit was nowhere to be seen and offered no encouragement to the demonstrators. Student esteem for him rapidly withered, and the loss of support from students wounded Kukrit, according to his friends (*Peagam,* 1975). Many key student leaders were therefore highly critical of his government (*Thompson,* 1975). Secondly, after late 1973, when Kukrit was appointed speaker of the National Assembly, he ceased to write his two regular columns in *Siam Rath.* He explained that he had not written in his newspaper during the time he was speaker of the National Assembly because he believed he should not have his views expressed in public (*Siam Rath,* 6 Feb. 1975). Kukrit returned to his career as a journalist for about a month before he was approved by the constitutional parliament as prime minister in the middle of March 1975. Thirdly, after his accession to prime minister of the coalition government, *Siam Rath* began to lose its image as an objective and fair newspaper. In fact, the editor clearly confessed that the newspaper would stand with Kukrit as the leader of the coalition government (*Siam Rath,* 3 April 1975). And, fourthly, the period after "The Ten Days" saw many new newspapers published, so that it was normal for *Siam Rath* to lose some readers. Hence, *Siam Rath* finally fell from its long-established status as the most popular newspaper among the political public in Thailand. Many of Kukrit's faithful readers repeatedly called for him to resume his role as a journalist, but Kukrit said the country was more important than *Siam Rath* (*Klinsoonthorn,* 1975).

Early in his accession to the role of prime minister, Kukrit, in a speech, ranked the press among the most important political groups in the country, along with university students and professors, the military, the parliamentarians and the public. Kukrit suggested that his government would not tolerate irresponsible journalism born out of emotion and thoughtlessness. As a manipulator of public opinion, he said, the press could obstruct the growth of democracy by exaggerating unimportant issues. The prime minister insisted that the Thai press learn the meaning of "responsible press," and he reiterated that his government would respect freedom of the newspapers (*Prachachart,* 31 March 1975). His first formal statement regarding the Thai press was seen by all spokesmen of the newspapers as being a threatening message from the government. As a result, nearly all newspapers carried editorials attacking him as an enemy of the press. Newsmen reminded Kukrit that he should remember his past role as a journalist who staunchly fought for freedom of the press. From then on, Kukrit seemed to be increasingly unpopular among Thai journalists. He often attacked individual newspapers as being irresponsible in interpreting and quoting interviews with him, accusing them of "twisting" his words. The newspapers fought back by declaring that Kukrit hold his tongue. A columnist at *Siam Rath* wrote that Kukrit was the most frequently attacked prime minister by the newspapers (*Siam Rath,* 25 Aug. 1975). At one time, Kukrit even took it as his duty to declare in Parliament that he would be more careful in giving interviews to the press. Kukrit's usual intimacy with the press disappeared after he formalized all his interviews, giving short answers to questions posed by newsmen. According to a reliable source, such a change did not arouse press hostility, but rather, amused the newsmen, who found themselves having a special relationship with the prime minister (*Siam Rath*, 25 Aug. 1975).

Generally, the Thai press under Kukrit's administration enjoyed freedom of expression at the same level given to the newspapers by the interim government of Sanya. Because of a political crisis in his administration (one month after his accession to the prime ministership), Kukrit refused to abolish Announcement No. 17 handed down by Sarit. This attitude towards press freedom was an outright contradiction of his own words late in 1974: "From now on," he said, "the closing of a printing press or prohibition of printing in a manner to affect the freedom of the press is void" (*The Nation*, 6 Oct. 1974). But, in 1975, he reluctantly accepted the proposal from journalists that his government abolish the Announcement No. 17.. "Why bother with it?" asked Kukrit, "Throughout my career as a journalist I never spent a moment thinking about the existence of Announcement No. 17" (*Prachathippatai*, 20 April 1975).

In October 1975 Kukrit said that his government had always respected press freedom: "The government has permitted the newspapers to freely criticize and opinionate despite the fact that some newspapers are at times irresponsible." He suggested that the Thai press should use its freedom with dignity for the sake of the country, pointing out that there had been a distinct improvement on the part of the press "compared to the past" (*Prachachart*, 4 Oct. 1975). However, this seemingly favorable indication of press freedom did not mean that his regime had not attempted to control Thai press by some "extra" regulations which contradicted the constitution of 1974. In September 1975, when the National Security Act was proposed by his government, it stirred a lot of angry voices from the spokesmen of the press and student leaders. The National Student Center of Thailand issued a communique protesting the act, saying it was the regime's intention to suppress rights and freedom of expression, among other things, guaranteed by the constitution. The three organizations of Thai newspapers in Bangkok mutually agreed to fight to the end in resisting the National Security Act, which would empower the executive branch of government to suppress the people and newspapers. The act contained several articles allowing politicians to overstep the power of the judicial branch of government. According to the act, the administration was given the power to silence and punish the press in a number of ways similar to the Anti-Communist Act of 1952 and Announcement No. 17 of 1958. A confiscation of all publishing instruments belonging to any newspaper picked up by the government was permitted by the Act (*Prachachart,* 9 Sept. 1975). The National Security Act proved to be highly unpopular among the political public, especially amongst student leaders, who campaigned for the public's support in protesting it. Kukrit, in response to unfavorable criticism, told the press that changes could always be made in the details of the act (*Prachachart,* 9 Sept. 1975). But, in contrast, the Chief of the Army General Staff was quoted as saying that "we should not be over-concerned about rights and freedom." He emphasized that "national security" should be regarded as more important than rights and freedom of the individual (*Prachachart,* 9 Sept. 1975).

By late 1975, the coalition government of Prime Minister Kukrit had not yet taken any definite step in its endeavor to establish political stability for his government at the expense of press freedom. However, Kukrit himself often talked of a press council as a method of press control. The idea of a press council was not new to Thailand; it had been discussed in the 1950s when Police General Phao Sriyanondh, a rival of Sarit and Phibulsongkhram, had some power. The press council idea was also discussed during Thanom's administration but was not accepted by many outstanding critics, who believed that it was Thanom's plan to control Thai newspapers by other machinery (*Reporter Association of Thailand,* 1973). In the Kukrit administration, a new Press Act was written. According to it, the press would set up a committee of 17 to 21 members who were empowered to control newspapermen in various ways. This press council has four main duties: first, to promote educational and professional progress; second, to control journalists by the principle of professional ethics; third, to promote unity and dignity among its members; and fourth, to lead the public towards a better awareness of journalism. If passed as law, two-thirds of the total committee would be elected from regular members of the council, whereas one-third would be chosen by the regular members of the council as honorable members of the committee. The honorable members of the committee must not, said the Press Act, be selected from those who are working for government agencies. Empowered to administer newspaper licenses, this press council was to take over the responsibility of the government press officer in issuing new newspaper licenses. The press council would also have power to exercise moral sanctions, by fines and other means, upon journalists who violated the Press Act (*Square Weekly*, 28 Aug. 1975, pp. 50-51). This Press Act was written, interestingly, by government officials and some spokesmen of the press in August 1975. Analytically speaking, the new Press Act was very democratic in its original intention. It was certainly the most sensible pattern of press control, favoring the growth of political democracy in this country. The major questions were: will this Press Act be passed by the parliamentarians whose majority is controlled by the coalition government of Kukrit? And, will another Act which contradicts this Press Act, if effective, be passed by Parliament at some later date?

Whatever the pattern of press control in Thailand was to be, the case of Kukrit as prime minister seemed to be an apparent paradox: a great journalist who once steadfastly fought for press freedom in the dark years of military dictatorship was later the leader of a government which had attempted to restrict press freedom by a method frequently used by his former enemies. It is perhaps true, as pointed out by a veteran journalist, that the government leader and the press in Thailand have always had a relationship similar to that of the teeth and the tongue. The teeth sometimes bite the tongue but the two can never exist without each other (*Siam Rath*, 25 Aug. 1975).

3.10.5 Towards The Future: An Overview

It is quite clear that the development pattern of the Thai press since its earliest history has been intimately knitted to a broad context of social changes, simultaneously manifested in Thai political institutions. The political status quo in this country, at a given time, has generally thought of the newspapers as its opposition. The notion of the press as a watchdog of government has rarely been accepted, not to mention respected, by the political establishment. The power brokers since the "revolution" of 1932, have more often than not, expanded a tradition established in the Thai press in the age of absolute monarchy to manipulate and abuse newspapers to suit their own political whims. The idea of democracy (sophisticated and foreign as it is) proclaimed as the official political ideology since 1932, has appeared to clash with the authoritarian cultural heritage of the Thais. This is precisely why democracy in Thailand has taken so long a time to flourish. The concept of a free and responsible press, entwined with the concept of political democracy, hence, has also taken over a century of uneven experiences to rise with some significance.

The students' revolt of October 1973 symbolizes that after all those years of military dictatorship, the Thai political public had finally outgrown the political institution in this country. This political lag resulted in the most serious revolution Thailand has ever known. Alongside the new political process inevitable because of "The Ten Days," Thai newspaperdom has entered another stage of development, much more complicated than any other past experiences. Thailand has become a dynamic society to a point that the new generation of journalists, with a new level of political consciousness has stepped onto the scene and made itself heard by the old guard, calling the writing of the latter, "dinosaur journalism," meaning a journalism style that lags behind the age.

Apparent changes in the Thai press since the October revolution are fundamentally threefold: on the part of politicians, the new atmosphere has forced them to liberalize not only their political views in conformity to the new political forces, but also their perceptions of the Thai press as a social institution; on the part of the general public, changes in their political thinking, liberated by the psychological influence of "The Ten Days," have forced them to modify their traditional "spectator role" (a notion explained by a scholar as an orientation which permits the individual "only to view impersonally the content of communications without much sense of involvement and without any impulsion to act") (*Pye,*

1963, p. 225) towards a role more active, involved and critical; and on the part of journalists, the swift occurrence of a political vacuum since "The Ten Days" has persuaded the old guards of "journalisme à la siamoise" to be exceedingly partisan in their political viewpoints on the one hand and, on the other hand, has allowed the new generation of journalists to launch their journalistic endeavors in a fashion that claims to be the extreme opposite of "journalisme à la siamoise."

The future direction of Thai journalism rested for a while in the ever-changing political tides in Thailand in the middle of the 1970s. The state of political flux which characterized Thailand in 1973-75 makes it premature to foresee any clear pattern of the future trend of Thai journalism. A highly conscientious student leader noticed soon after "The Ten Days," that there existed a possibility that Thailand may turn towards one of the two extremes: left-wing dictatorship or right-wing dictatorship (*Zimmerman,* 1974, p. 521). Another student leader declared that when another military *coup d'état* arrives, "the only course for us may be armed resistance and Thailand will have a civil war" (*Prizzia,* 1975, p. 251). In the important second-year celebration of the October revolution in 1975, an eminent young intellectual emphasized that "the people's victory of the October revolt was unashamedly stolen." He ended his powerful article by saying that "we must remember that painful lesson to be retold to our sons and grandsons for them to be brave and to fight confidently in order that all social injustices be eliminated from this land." "Blood," he noted, "must be exchanged by blood" (*Prachachart,* 14 Oct. 1975). Alongside the tone of extreme disappointment in the present structure of the political establishment there are also the voices of those holding power. For example, an influential military man in the country, Lieutenant General Pramarn Adireksarn, in an interview with the press: "I adore domocracy. Why would you say I will stage a *coup d'état*? A person like myself needs no *coup d'état*. I am the Deputy Prime Minister and Minister of the Army. Launching a *coup d'état* so that I will be the Prime Minister? There is no use" (*Prachachart,* 5 Oct. 1975).

On this threshold of political turmoil, Thailand is not only launched towards a permanency of constitutionalism but also a freer and more responsible press. The old style of journalism will have to diminish in the course of time as Thailand enters a new stage of political development. In its place, the "New Journalism" will emerge as the mainstream of newspapers in Thailand. By then, Thai newsmen will not have to be slapped by politicians who offer them little gifts.[3] The provincial press, which has remained basically unchanged since its foundation (*Mitchell in Lent*, 1971, pp. 230-232), will gradually improve to serve the needs of people in the provinces as the Thai economy develops and as the political power is increasingly decentralized. Amidst all these potential changes, the government's mass media may be the slowest to cope with the democratic tendency now widespread in the country, but changes will be continuously forced by the progressive elements, as the military and bureaucracy slowly lose their political bargaining power.

As for the foreign language press in Thailand, scheduled changes in foreign policy will play a dominant role in deciding its future. If Thailand can manage to pursue a more neutral foreign policy in the future, the foreign language press will be more diversified. With such an atmosphere, Thailand may, for the first time since the nineteenth century when its contacts with the West were increasingly accelerated, manage to live in the world with a new consciousness, as contrasted to the one-sided relationship with the West.

The 1970s has indeed been a period of great transition in both Thai domestic and foreign affairs. Basically, however, it is practical politics in Thailand that are most crucial. With regard to Thai political history, this is probably the first time Thailand has had to face a continual choice between integration and disintegration. On this political dilemma, the future of the Thai press is dependent.

3.10.6 After 1975: Another Downswing, by John A. Lent

Even before the military coup of October, the press had reason

---

3   In October 1975, a score of newsmen were given a gift of money by the Minister of Agriculture, Tawij Klinpratum, for gambling at his residence. Condemned later by the Reporter Association of Thailand, Tawij said: "I did not know that doing such a thing was unacceptable. I did not mean to give the newsmen bribes." See *Prachachart*, 8 Oct. 1975.

to believe that 1976 was not to be its best year. First of all, the frequency of violent acts committed against reporters and newspaper offices made it hazardous to be involved in journalism. In June 1976, for example, the Thai Liberation Army threw bombs into the offices of *Ruam Prachachart* and *Athipat;* the presses of the latter paper were stopped for two weeks as a result. In fact, the number of assaults on pressmen between 1974-76 prompted Thailand's three press associations to submit a protest to the national police chief, demanding better security.

Economically, the times were not ideal for newspapers. Newsprint prices had rocketed since 1970, poor training or inadequate equipment continued to be the standard, and circulations remained relatively small. Newsprint prices had risen from Baht 180 million for the 50,000 tons imported in 1971, to Baht 280 million for 55,000 tons in 1973, and even much higher in the succeeding two years. Hundreds of newspaper licenses granted after the Revolution were not used partly because of the high newsprint prices. Seventy per cent of all presses at the nearly 2,000 registered printers used letterpress, frequently using worn-out typefaces. Many newspapers, especially those upcountry, operated on a shoestring; the 180 papers in the provinces were usually irregularly published, often appearing only when lottery results were issued, and depended heavily upon job printing for capital. Newsprint consumption by provincial papers was only a fraction of that of the 17 large Bangkok dailies, led by *Thai Rath* (circulation 370,000; 470,000 on lottery days) which printed more copies in one day than one issue of each of the 180 provincial papers. Because of these and other economic reasons, it became increasingly difficult after 1976 to sustain newspapers, especially those with specialized audiences. One such paper, *Sarn Siam,* designed for selective readers, lasted five months, during which time it lost US$250,000 (see *Lent,* 1977, pp. 49-50; *Bangkok Post* supplement, 27 Dec. 1975).

Political pressures apparently intensified as well. Early in 1976, a *Dao Siam* columnist and his editor were sentenced to three years and 14 months, respectively, for a column offensive to the queen. And in August, *Prachathipattai,* which had difficulties because of its leftist orientation, fired six ultra-left reporters, claiming their removal would improve the paper's image. When the rest of the staff protested, 33 of them were dismissed and replaced with former *Sarn Siam* personnel.

When the military seized power in the bloody coup of 6 October 1976, the constitution was suspended, all newspapers for the first time in Thai history were banned, hundreds of politicians, students and journalists were arrested as left-wing subversives, and publications considered leaning towards Communism were confiscated and burned. Almost immediately, publishers and broadcasters were summoned to command headquarters to be told the terms under which they might resume operations. They were told to apply to the junta for permission to publish. After two days, late on 8 October, the first Thai language dailies allowed to publish (those with far right and moderate views) reappeared with cautious descriptions of the coup violence. The following day, a total of 12 of the nation's leading dailies published under strict censorship guidelines, banning nearly all criticism of the authorities. The seven point censorship code barred newspapers from publishing stories and illustrations which: "Attack the monarchy; make accusations against Thailand or give a distorted, contemptuous or insulting image of Thailand or of the Thai people, or which could arouse disrespect abroad for Thailand and the Thai people; make accusations against the government or any official institutions, or present a distorted, contemptuous or insulting image of them; propagate communism; could sow fear or unease among the population to be divisive, and which would have a harmful effect on peace, public order or morality; are pornographic, obscene or coarse, or which injure the morals and culture of the nation; and which are official secrets."

One of the major papers permitted to resume on 9 October, *Dao Siam,* was banned again by 11 October, for publishing an article that might "mislead the public to distrust the policy of the administrative reform committees." Actually, *Dao Siam* had said that a return to democratic rule might be four years off. At least five radical newspapers, most of the Chinese press and *The Voice of the Nation* in English were ordered to remain closed. One of the Thai newspapers banned was *Prachatipattai,* by then not a stranger to government harassment. Concerning detained journalists, the metropolitan police chief in late October said that the police could hold journalists for 30 days, followed by an undetermined period in a rehabilitation center. If the detainees failed to recant, they were subject to 12-year prison terms (see *Lent,* 1977, pp. 49-50; see 3.1.1, 3.1.3, 3.1.4, 3.1.5). As the 1970s drew to an end, and after a brief respite for the press in 1977, newspapers and journalists were again on the defensive. In early November 1978, Thai authorities closed *Daily News* and arrested a columnist and editor on a charge of *lese majesté.* The offending item in *Daily News* was the translation of the proverb: "In the land of the blind the one-eyed man is king." Officials regarded this as a derogatory reference to King Bhumibol who is blind in one eye (London *Times,* 3 Nov. 1978, p. 8; *Bangkok Post,* 11 Nov. 1978). On 9 November 1978, the printing officer of Bangkok revoked the publication and editors' licenses of 57 dailies and threatened legal action against 32 other dailies, claiming they violated the Printing Act. The Police Department said the licenses were pulled because the dailies had never actually been printed for public distribution as required by Article 45 of the act. The 32 "dailies" facing action were charged with violating Article 29 of the act; they did not publish daily, but rather weekly (*Bangkok Post,* 10 Nov. 1978). The press associations of Thailand reacted by asking the government to revise the Printing Act and Revolutionary Announcement No. 42. The journalists said the practice of having publication licenses without printing papers for public distribution is a tradition that had been acceptable by former governments (*Bangkok Post,* 12 Nov. 1978). Earlier in October 1978, the National Legislative Assembly, in debating freedom of expression, deleted two paragraphs from Article 29 of the draft constitution which guaranteed freedom of expression. The paragraphs had read:

> The closure of a printing press or the prohibition of printing so as to restrict the liberty under this Section shall not be made except by a judgment or an order of the court closing the printing press or prohibiting the printing.
> The pre-publication censorship of a newspaper shall not be done except during the time when the country is in a state of armed conflict or war, or when a state of emergency or martial law is declared; provided that

it be done by virtue of the law enacted under paragraph
two.

On 25 January 1979, the Police Department announced that
editors of three dailies — *Siang Puangchon, Daily Mirror* and
Tawan Siam — had their licenses revoked for sensationalizing
the war in Cambodia. The papers were allowed to continue
publishing after the appointment of new editors (*Index on
Censorship*, May-Junc 1979, p. 71).

3.11 South Vietnam : Before 1975

Donald L. Guimary

When a reporter or an editor in South Vietnam was asked how much press freedom existed in his nation, he was apt to reply by citing a parable: "We cannot say we've seen an elephant, but we can report we've seen a large animal with four feet, a tail and a trunk."

Although parables are used in many societies and nations, that a South Vietnamese reporter would express the extent of press freedom — or its lack — in those terms is revealing. Such a parable was used by a journalist at a formal luncheon of the Union of Vietnamese Journalists in Saigon in 1974 when he was referring to government restrictions on the press.

The overriding concern of newspapers and other publications in South Vietnam in 1974 was freedom of the press and the ability to report on various issues without fear of government retaliation. When a group of veteran newsmen were asked that year which topics were banned by the government, they said such subjects as economics, corruption, "about everything — even the weather." While that statement was a broad generalization, such a response indicated that many newsmen and publishers indeed felt stifled by the government.

There were, obviously, historical reasons for the intense hostility between the press and government. Such a relationship was not a new phenomenon.

Donald L. Guimary is associate professor of journalism at Portland State University. During 1973, he was a lecturer at Universiti Sains Malaysia, Penang. While in Southeast Asia, he visited Saigon newspapers where he interviewed publishers and journalists.

3.11.1 Historical Perspective

The history of newspapers, by some standards, can be said to be short — about 110 years old. French colonialists introduced newspapers in the 1880s in Vietnam to publish news accounts of items concerning their home country and of interest to themselves. The first Vietnamese language newspaper is generally traced back to 1865, when *Gia-dinh Bao* (the *Journal of Gia-dinh*) was started by academician Petrus Truong Vinn Ky (*Embassy of Vietnam,* 1970, p. 2). Since that time, the number of Vietnamese newspapers has constantly fluctuated. For example, in 1974, of the 16 dailies publishing, nearly all of them were less than 15 years old.

Other early newspapers included *Phan Yen Bao* (1868); *Nhut Trinh Nam Ky* (1883); *Nong Co Min Dam* (1901); *Luc Tinh Tan Van* (1907); *An Ha Nhat Bao* (1912); *Nan Trung Nhat Bao* (1917). Under French colonial policy, newspapers were required to serve the interests of France. In 1881, French legislation required a legal deposit by publications as well as the filing of an application (*Lent,* 1971, p. 236).

It was not until the 1930s that actual Vietnamese journalists began to appear, but even during that period, publications were still hampered by colonial policies. In 1923, for example, *La Cloche Felee* (*The Cracked Bell*) was censored by the French for an article praising a moderate nationalist leader. The editor was arrested. And in 1935, Governor General René Robin, who boasted of press freedom, had suppressed 14 publications. Between 1940 and 1943, 17 newspapers and periodicals were suppressed by French police on charges of nationalism (*Buttinger,* 1967, pp. 202, 245).

According to historian Joseph Buttinger, "the Diem regime often boasted that there was no press censorship in South Vietnam. Its methods for silencing the press were indeed less overt. It abolished freedom of the press by more devious and more callous means, of which Nhu [Ngo Dinh] (of the secret police) was the inventor: mob action against criticism in the press rather than outright legal restraints. If a paper criticized the government too freely or dared to make uncomplimentary remarks about any member of the Ngo family, hoodlums hired by one of Nhu's secret services staged an outburst of 'popular indignation' which invariably ended with the wrecking of the paper's offices and plant. They lost not only permission to publish, but also much of their property. He was usually fined and jailed as well. By 1958, all opposition papers had been suppressed and applications for new ones were rejected, if answered at all" (*Buttinger*, 1967, p. 963).

Even Western news representatives were harassed by Diem's government. In early 1962, when Homer Bigart of the *New York Times* and Francois Sully of *Newsweek* wrote articles critical of the "strategic-hamlet" program, Mme. Nhu, first accused them of Communist leanings and then persuaded the government to express dissatisfaction. "Sully was called a Vietcong spy, an opium smuggler, and a participant in sex orgies." David Halberstam (Bigart's replacement), and others including Neil Sheehan of UPI, were accused of supporting the Communist conspiracy. "They were shadowed, and some of them were attacked and physically mishandled by Nhu's secret service agents. Their telephones were tapped, and they were prevented from sending uncensored dispatches out of the country" (*Buttinger*, 1967, p. 989).

One veteran Vietnamese journalist observed that Ngo Dinh Diem, from 1954 until his overthrow in 1963, placed rigid censorship on the press. But during the following five years, newspapers enjoyed a "relative free press. Each time we had a change in Cabinet or a new Premier, some five to 10 new newspapers appeared on the scene. The Premier himself, or his friends-supporters, or the newly appointed ministers would put up some new dailies to make money or to support the new cabinet."[1]

As can be seen from the above, the history of the Vietnamese press, as in other nations, has been one of constant struggle against repression. But in South Vietnam, editors, publishers and reporters have probably faced more handicaps than their counterparts in many other undeveloped countries: The colonial period under the French; World War II; harsh government measures during the French-Vietnam conflict following the war; then the escalation of

1   Personal interview, Hoang Hai Thuy, Saigon, 30 May 1974.

the United States involvement and political conflict from the early 1960s to 1975.

Through those generations of political and social turmoil, a pattern of restrictions on the press became an acceptable fact of life to many — except publishers and their employees. It would probably be impossible to document the number of instances newspapers have been confiscated, the extent of damage done to newspaper plants, the number of publishers, editors and reporters fined and jailed. Such information is not made public.

By the time the French granted independence to the nation in 1954, some form of government regulation and press supervision had become a permanent aspect to newspaper publishing. The nation's 1956 Constitution granted nominal press freedom, but it was just that, in name only.

Historically, then, there was no continuity or firm tradition of newspapers in South Vietnam. After 1963, the number of dailies and weeklies was quite fluid. In 1965, there were 10 Vietnamese, two English and one Chinese newspapers. One year later there were 23 Vietnamese papers; two French; 10 Chinese and two English papers. Under Ngo Dinh Diem's government, newspapers sympathetic to his regime received official subsidies. But after his administration, such a policy was discontinued. Newspapers then turned to former politicians, religious groups politically active, or to other organizations for support. Newspapers which opposed government policies were promptly confiscated or put out of business (*Smith et al.,* 1967, p. 286).

For example, in 1968, five Vietnamese language dailies were suspended. *Tu Do,* a daily with a circulation of 25,000, was barred for using "language of the gutter" to criticize Premier Tran Van Huoan for spending $21,000 during wartime to send an artistic group on a tour of Paris and London (AP Dispatch in Redding, California *Record-Searchlight,* 30 Oct. 1968).

In 1971, *Tin Sang (Morning News),* an opposition paper, published by Ngo Ong Duc, a Catholic politician, had been confiscated 166 times. Duc's home, office and printing plant had been vandalized and firebombed five times. In 1973, the paper was no longer publishing. "Why does the government try to muzzle opposition papers. This is dangerous. If people cannot read papers they want to read, they will listen to the Viet Cong radio. This will be damaging to the national interest," Duc said in 1971 (*Time,* 11 Oct. 1971, p. 74).

In early 1973, according to the International Press Institute, Duc had escaped from South Vietnam and received political asylum in Sweden. "Authorities had seized every other issue of his paper and eventually it was closed and Ngo Cong Duc was sentenced in his absence to three years in jail" (*IPI Report,* Jan. 1973, p. 9).

In October 1974, *Dai Dan Toc,* a daily with a circulation of 8,000 which was opposed to the Thieu government, announced on 26 October that it would suspend publication indefinitely because of lack of funds — caused by government confiscation. Vo Long Trieu, publisher of the daily which was founded in 1966, accused Information Minister Hong Duc Nha of conducting a "petty vendetta" against his publication. Trieu said that during October, his newspaper had been seized 11 times, and that each confiscation cost the publication about US$1,500, a large sum for economically fragile South Vietnamese papers. He said he "simply could not afford to keep the paper going." In a letter to readers, he promised that the newspaper would reappear "whenever the financial situation and conditions permit" (*New York Times,* 27 Oct. 1974).

3.11.2 The Press in 1974

By 1974, as noted earlier, there were 16 Vietnamese language dailies; one French newspaper; one English daily, and 10 Chinese dailies. Estimated circulation of the Vietnamese dailies was about 156,000. The Chinese dailies' circulation was about 69,000. (See Table 16).

Concerning international news, the government-owned Presse Vietnam distributed information selected from the main world wire services of Associated Press, United Press International and Reuters. These selections were then distributed to local newspapers. Such selections, obviously, tended to reflect favorably on South Vietnam.

Because of restrictions which hampered the dissemination of news and because publishers realized they would not be allowed to perform an information role in society, most papers turned to performing an entertainment function. "Most Vietnamese dailies still reserve half or over half their printing space for educational features and serialized novels that have little or nothing to do with events of the day," wrote Nguyen Ngoc Phach, a former BBC correspondent-local journalist (*Embassy of Vietnam,* 1970, p. 3). This propensity to rely on the serialization of novels to help fill their pages and sell the papers was termed "Feuilleton," a French term.

As another veteran Vietnamese journalist stated: "Many papers have large audiences not by printing news but because of some exciting Feuilletons." The continued use of such material had become something of a tradition in Vietnamese newspapers, a commodity that perhaps newspapers had become accustomed to receiving.

In addition to relying on the serialization of novels, it was not uncommon for newspapers to fill their pages with other material of questionable quality. One writer, Nguyen Trung Trinh, stated: "Others have had to resort to sex, sensationalism, or cheap romanticism as a means of subsistence." Trinh also pointed out that between 1955 and 1972, at least 37 journalists were imprisoned. "Ransacking of editorial offices and manhandling of reporters are daily occurrences. Many journalists have become jobless" (*Democratic Journalist,* Jan. 1974, p. 15).

One of the more respected newspapers in South Vietnam was *Chinh Luan (Right Opinion),* published by Dang Van Sung, a former senator. In early 1974, four issues had been confiscated for publishing articles on corruption. The newspaper was usually considered an "independent" politically. It carried editorials blaming the government for "the somber life of present society"; it criticized the cabinet, and it also graphically described how the "deteriorating economic situation" caused problems in local schools. Founded in 1964, the paper had a paid circulation of about 20,000 in 1974. In the late 1960s, its circulation was 40,000; but as most dailies, *Chinh Luan*'s circulation significantly dropped because of the cost of newsprint, inflation and other problems. In 1974, it carried 10 pages, more than most dailies. *Chinh Luan* sold for 50 piasters (US 5 cents); newspapers with six pages sold for 60 piasters (US 6 cents), and those with eight pages for 50 piasters (US 8 cents).

Table 15.   Daily Newspapers in South Vietnam in 1974

Newspaper	Publisher	Circulation	No. of Pages	Year Established
Vietnamese Language				
Chinh Luan	Dr. Dang Van Sung	20,000	10	1964
But Thep	Le Hien	18,000	8	1971
Song Than	Nguyen Thi Thai	12,000	6	1971
Hoa Binh	Father Tran Du	10,000	4	1966
Cong Luan	Sen. Ton That Dinh	8,000	8	1968
Dai Dan Toc*	Vo Long Trieu	8,000	8	1966
Dien Tin	Sen. Hong Son Dong	12,000	8	1969
Tien Tuyen	Col. Nguyen Huy Hung	5,000	4	1965
Dan Chu	Nguyen Hai Duong	10,000	8	1973
Doc Lap	Ho Quang Chau	8,000	8	1970
Tia Sang	Nguyen Trung Thanh	8,000	8	–
Trang Den	Viet Dinh Phuon	8,000	8	1967
Dong Phuong	Mrs. Phan My Truc	8,000	8	1972
Dan Luan	Thinh Quang Tran	5,000	8	1973
Quat Cuong	Hong Ha	5,000	8	1971
Thang Tien	Organ of the Council of Catholic Bishops	1,000	2	1972
	Total Circulation	156,000		
Chinese Language				
Thang Cong	Khuu Dao	10,000	10	1961
Luan Dan Moi	Phung Trac	10,000	10	1953
Vien Dong	Huynh Van Nai	10,000	10	1974
Nhan Nhan	Ly Tru	4,000	8	1972
A Chau	Ly Kiet	6,000	8	1954
Kien Quoc	Huynh Chau	8,000	10	1929
Quang Hoa	Luong Dien	4,000	8	1970
Tan Van Khoai Bao	Trieu Thi Huong	8,000	4	1950
Viet Hoa	Chung Duc N. Tihon	4,000	6	1955
Luan Dan Van Bao	Ly Trieu Quan	5,000	4	1963
	Total Circulation	69,000		
English language				
The Saigon Post	Bui Phuong The	2,000	8	1963
French Language				
Le Courrier d'Extreme Orient	M. G. Sauvezon-Gois	3,000	12	1948

* In October, 1974, Trieu announced he was closing his publication.
Source: United States Information Service, Saigon, May 1974.

The status of reporters apparently did not carry much prestige just before the Communist takeover. That reporters had a reputation of being underpaid was well known; many had second jobs. "A journalist is a man who lies to make money," says one local adage. Most journalists were secondary school graduates whose average pay was about 31,000 piasters (US$50) per month, which was about equal to a South Vietnamese Army major's salary.

Few newspapers were profitable. That many newspapers were affiliated with political or religious groups indicated that such publications received financial support other than from advertising and circulation. Since there was no national auditing organization, advertisers relied on circulation figures provided by the publication – which may or may not have been wholly accurate. Circulation figures were considered a trade secret. In 1971, only about one in 10 newspapers was estimated to be profitable (*Time,* 11 Oct. 1971, p. 74).

To standardize (and to help control) the performance of the press, in 1964, the government set up a press council. The organization was never a success and was finally allowed to expire in 1973. The council's functions included: to establish a "Press Congress to act as an official representative of the press corps"; to execute the government's press code; to contact and discuss with the government and the press, questions related to the media. Journalists were also required to have a registered press card, according to the 1969 Press Law. Earlier requirements of the 1964 council, as set forth by the government, stressing educational training for publishers, were eliminated in the 1969 Press Law.

3.11.3 Press Laws

While the South Vietnamese press traditionally was at odds with various governments, newspaper publishers, editors and reporters in the 1970s were especially opposed to a new device imposed by the government, termed "007." Decree-Law 007/YY/SLU was imposed by the Thieu government on 4 August 1972, which amended Press Law 019/69. The press law employed a device used by the French on early Vietnamese newspapers, which involved requirement of a publishing deposit. However, the severity of the 007 deposit succeeded in driving nearly two-thirds of the nation's dailies out of business. Before 007 can be discussed, reference should be made to the 1969 Press Law which was still basically in effect in mid-1974.

According to Article I of the 1969 Press Law (019):

Press Freedom is a fundamental right in the Republic of Vietnam. The exercise of press freedom shall not be harmful to personal honor, national security or traditional morality. No suspension shall be made except by judicial process.

Article 6 stated:

The publisher, editor and manager shall fulfill the following requirements: be of Vietnamese citizenship; be at least 25 years old at the time of declaration; not have been sentenced to more than three months' imprisonment for criminal or minor offenses ... not to make propaganda for Communism or to practice Communism; at least one among the three following people, the publisher, editor and manager may not be a deputy or senator. The publisher and editor must be in possession of one of the following: a degree in journalism; a university diploma; a certificate of work in an editorial staff for a period over one year; a certificate of work as a reporter for at least two years in a newspaper, information agency, radio station having legal status in Vietnam; a certificate of work as publisher or editor for at least six months (*Government of South Vietnam,* 1969).

In addition to the above requirements of Law 019, Press Law 007 created an even more severe strain on publishers — the requirement that newspaper publishers deposit 20 million piasters (US$47,000) with the government treasury. This was a measure not found in 019. Magazine publishers were required to deposit half that amount. Enactment of 007 forced 30 newspapers to close down, leaving a total of 28 papers in South Vietnam in 1972; and, as noted earlier, in late 1974, there were 16, with one scheduled to shut down.

According to the new law, 10 copies of a daily edition had to be delivered to the Ministry of Information, two copies to the

Prosecutor's Office, and two copies to the Ministry of Interior four hours prior to street delivery. This provided those government offices time to review the publications and time to press editors to delete offending sections — which frequently occurred. The law also stipulated that the press would not be used to incite people to violate domestic or external security or to commit any other crime or misdemeanor; to incite soldiers to disobey military discipline; or to praise the aforesaid offenses (*Government of South Vietnam,* 1972).

The 1972 law stated, with references to 019 in parentheses:
> With a view to safeguard national security, public order, and good morals, and in accordance with the provisions of Article 32 (paragraphs a, b, c, the press should not be used to insult the President, Vice President or other diplomatic envoys) mayors, province chiefs and the Minister of Interior may order the confiscation of the copies of a newspaper or magazine before it is distributed or while it is being distributed. Such a confiscation order may include confiscation of the printing plates and type molds used to print the confiscated publication.

Regarding the use of imported wire service material, Press Law 007 stated:
> Publications will not be prosecuted for printing translated excerpts or articles from foreign dailies and periodicals whose circulation is authorized in Vietnam provided that the translation is faithful and the publication is bona fide and that it is not harmful to personal honor, national security or good morals.

Violations of Article 32 (insulting officials) resulted in imprisonment from two months to two years or a fine ranging from 200,000 to 2 million piasters, or both. Violations of Articles 3 and 17 (failure to properly file a formal declaration to publish with the Ministry of Information), and Article 22 (libelling officials) resulted in imprisonment from six months to three years and a fine from 500,000 piasters up to 5 million piasters, or both.

Regarding libel, Article 31 stated:
Evidence of the truthfulness of statements regarded as libellous must be established. However, it is strictly forbidden to establish that truthfulness in cases when (1) libel against the President and Vice President of the Republic of Vietnam; (2) libel against chiefs of state and ambassadors . . .; (3) the facts are related to the private life of a person; (4) the facts go back more than 10 years; (5) the offense has been pardoned or eliminated, or the sentence has been expunged, either by rehabilitation or reversal. If the truthfulness of a statement regarded as libellous is established, the accused will be acquitted.

While many Vietnamese publishers and editors resented the 007 law, they did not resent some form of government restrictions. One reporter said:
We accept censorship, but we ask for an intelligent, reasonable one. The censors have all the rights and we don't have any, even the right to protest when we have been treated unfairly by the censors, or when we have different interpretation of 007 Press Act. In other words, the censors have the right to interpret the Act and we don't.[2]

Rather than exercising direct censorship, the government "advised" newspapers that certain articles should not be printed. Such articles were then deleted before being circulated. Some papers purposely left conspicuous holes or gaps in their pages to indicate which stories or paragraphs had been deleted. Editors could have closed the gaps with filler copy, but chose to leave the holes for dramatic effect.

One Vietnamese columnist, writing in the 29 May 1974 issue of *Dai Dan Toc*, stated that local journalists themselves had a "bad habit: They have an idea, and are about to express it, but then EXCISE IT BY THEMSELVES [emphasis original]. This is a bad habit, to which they have been so accustomed that it is difficult for them to get rid of it . . . . The spirit of SELF-EXCISION has impregnated the entire Vietnamese press."

2   *Ibid.*

3.11.4 Economic Problems

There were several other problems which hampered development of the South Vietnamese press: lack of transportation facilities; lack of skilled manpower; lack of technology and the availability and allocation of newsprint.

How a newspaper is distributed and circulated is only as good as its society's transportation and communication facilities. Because of the military conflict and security problems associated with transportation, circulation of South Vietnamese newspapers was centered primarily in the metropolitan Saigon area. Rural newspapers were indeed rare. This meant that South Vietnamese living in rural areas did without daily newspapers and were forced to rely more on personal communication, on announcements by local officials, or on government pronouncements.

Related to this was a newspaper distribution phenomenon probably unique to Vietnam. Newspapers were "hired out"; that is, dailies were rented out each day for about one-half of the purchase price. The rented papers were then returned to the vendor later in the day. For many potential readers, the practice of hiring out dailies was probably the most economical way to receive the day's news since the purchase price was prohibitive.

Despite that benefit, one veteran reporter-writer called the rental practice a "deadly sickness" which was "killing the dailies in South Vietnam." He believed newspapers should be sold, not rented. As noted earlier, the newspaper circulations could only be estimated. Figures ranged from 200,000 to 300,000, of which one-half were rentals. Publishers naturally preferred to sell their wares; yet the vendors continued to use the option of rentals. For newspapers which were purchased, the "pass-along" rate tended to be high. It was not uncommon for several families to share one newspaper. This significantly increased the newspaper readership, but such a figure was difficult to verify.

In addition to the above, if a newspaper publisher decided to distribute his own dailies, he had, according to Press Law 007, to apply for a separate distribution license, obtain proper identity cards for all involved in distribution and post a bond of 5 million piasters with the government. Magazine publishers were required to deposit one-half of that amount to distribute their own publications.

A commercial newspaper vendor was required to satisfy the above requirements, but he had to deposit 50 million piasters with the government. The law (Article 39) stated: "These accounts are to be opened in the name of the head of the distribution agency to guarantee the payment of fines, trial costs, and damages to plaintiffs mentioned in judgements related to violations of the provisions of this law."

The lack of manpower and technology was the result of a general shortage caused by the military situation. Many newspaper plants employed young boys — as young as 10 years old — to work six or eight hours, six days a week in the backshop. Many papers did not have mechanized typesetting equipment; instead, type was handset from the handwritten copy of reporters (who did not use typewriters). *Chinh Luan,* for example, employed 30 youths, with an average age of 15, working in its backshop. Some of the youths slept in the plant since they were orphans of the war. "We just don't have any adult manpower because of the war — as long as our present mobilization situation remains, we'll have this problem," said one of the assistant editors. *Chinh Luan* used two offset Duplex presses made in England. The presses had been confiscated by the government, and the paper, in 1974, leased them from the government. Many papers used flatbed, letterpress presses.

Ironically, as American aid to Vietnam dwindled, and as the South Vietnamese government continued to harass newspapers, an increasing number of reporters and editors found themselves out of work. In October 1974, "hungry reporters staged a national begging day to dramatize their situation. While they sincerely berated censorship and newspaper seizures, it was clear that they were equally interested in jobs" (*Los Angeles Times,* 24 Nov. 1974).

The newsprint shortage of the 1970s affected the press in Vietnam, as it did newspapers elsewhere. In 1974, the Ministry of Trade and Industry authorized the Chamber of Commerce to arrange and handle the importation of newsprint. The Publishers Association assigned its newsprint distribution committee, headed by Senator Ton That Dinh, publisher of *Cong*

Luan, to oversee distribution. Problems arose in the process. *Dai Dan Toc,* previously mentioned as an opposition paper in 1974, ceased publishing one day because it said it ran out of newsprint. The paper was allocated an extra 1,000 reams by order of the Minister of Trade and Industry. This prompted a disagreement with the distribution committee and the newspaper, which apparently felt that the minister should not have interjected himself into the issue.

In addition to distribution, newsprint cost was another problem. In early 1972, a ream of 500 pages cost about 550 piasters. Later, in 1972, it rose to 1,400 piasters and in 1973, 2,650 piasters. By April 1974, a ream sold at 4,000 piasters. In December 1973, the Publishers Association agreed to fix the number of pages of all dailies at four. Not many newspapers complied with that policy, there being only three of the 15 dailies sold on newsstands with four pages. One had six and another, eight pages.

3.11.5 Government Relationships

In 1974, the hostility with which the Thieu government viewed the press, had lessened to some extent compared to previous years — if the number of newspaper seizures can be used as a criterion. In spring 1974, the government confiscated issues on 32 occasions. Nine occurred in March when local papers carried a story about a reduction in bank deposits. The stories supposedly had violated the Press Law forbidding publication of information harmful to the nation's economy. Compared with 250 confiscations in 1970, and 718 instances in 1971, and 907 seizures in 1972, the number of papers seized during the first quarter seemed low.

The Thieu government also showed its hostility towards Western news representatives. In October 1974, three Western reporters were beaten by Saigon police as they filmed a demonstration in front of the National Assembly. Haney Howell, CBS reporter, Barry Hillenbrand of *Time Magazine,* and *Associated Press* photographer Neal Ulevich were physically assaulted, and their cameras were damaged. Earlier in the year, CBS-Television reporters, frustrated over government censorship and press restrictions, transmitted a news story to New York on the subject of press censorship. Prior to filing the story, a CBS news team was prevented'from covering a minor demonstration. "Government officials slapped grease on our camera lens, and police on motorcyles revved up their engines to block out our microphones. It worked," a CBS reporter said in frustration.[3]

Most Vietnamese journalists protested the manner in which Press Law 007 was enforced under Minister of Information Hoang Duc Nha, a cousin of President Thieu. Journalists believed Nha, a 1966 electrical engineer graduate from the University of Pittsburgh, to be too young and inexperienced for such a position.

Consequently, by September 1974, a new political faction called the "Committee for Freedom of Press and Publication" was formed to call for the ouster of Thieu. Pressure for reform and easement of press restrictions mounted and within weeks, 29 dailies announced they would suspend publication one day "to protest oppression by the Government of President Nguyen Van Thieu." The announcement was made when 300 newspaper employees held a large anti-government demonstration in downtown Saigon. The one-day suspension did not materialize. But in October 1974, Thieu had discharged 377 senior officers, including four cabinet ministers, along with his cousin, Information Minister Nha. Prior to his announcement, an alliance of newspaper publishers and press associations called on Thieu, asking him to replace Nha. On 28 November, Thieu appointed Minister of Veterans' Affairs Ho Van Cham as Minister of Information.

The lower house of the National Assembly also passed a measure which allowed the government to continue confiscation of newspapers. The Saigon Publishers Association and legislators were seeking to modify or lessen current press laws – yet both did not deny the government's right to seize newspapers. In other words, the confiscation of newspapers, per se, was not challenged. The measure, which had not yet been approved by the Senate, would reduce fines, place press trials in civil courts and most importantly, abolish the posting of large bonds. The bill was expected to be passed by the Senate. The issue of the government's right to seize newspapers appeared to be an accepted fact

3   Personal interview, Saigon, 28 May 1974.

(or hazard) of newspaper publishing in Saigon. *Los Angeles Times* writer George McArthur observed: "The process of seizure has some aspects of a bad Italian opera, with the police coming in the front door and bootleg issues going out the back. Advertisers never complain about seized issues — they know that this increases the readership of the issues that do get out, and of issues the following day explaining why the paper was seized" (*Los Angeles Times,* 24 Nov. 1974).

To illustrate how the subject of confiscation was nearly institutionalized, Ton That Thien, a former publisher of an English language, Saigon newspaper and a recipient of the Ramon Magsaysay press freedom award, had been installed as information minister in one of Thieu's early cabinets. As soon as he had been appointed information minister, Thien proceeded to seize newspapers in nearly the same manner as his predecessors had confiscated them. Out of office, Thien, in 1974, was among other journalists complaining about press restrictions.

The Thieu government was faced with another sensitive problem regarding newspapers in late 1974; the trial of *Song Thanh (Tidal Wave).* Published by Mrs. Nguyen Thi Thai, an English speaking widow, *Song Thanh* was considered an independent newspaper which occasionally supported the government. Mrs. Thai was the figurehead of an intellectual staff which included many Northern and Catholic Vietnamese. In the summer of 1974, Father Tran Huu Thanh, a 60-year-old priest in Hue publicly presented what he termed "indictment No. 1," a document which directly accused President Thieu of six counts of corruption. Thieu denied the accusations, but he did not answer them directly. *Song Thanh* published the document in its entirety and the newspaper was seized the same day and officially charged. (No charges were brought against Father Thanh.) The trial of the newspaper was scheduled for October in a military court. It was postponed and apparently was not resolved before the 1975 change of government. Nearly every well-known lawyer in Saigon volunteered to act for the defense with the number of attorneys over 200. "Father Thanh remains uncharged and his indictment No. 1 has become an underground bestseller, though, in fact, it is long on rhetoric and short on detail," according to the *Los*

Angeles Times. President Thieu was apparently reluctant to further publicize the issue, and probably hoped the matter could be quietly settled. The trial of *Song Thanh,* in late 1974, became a *cause célèbre* among journalists.

3.11.6 A Future Possible?

What could have been expected of the future of South Vietnamese newspapers in 1974? In the immediate short run, because of inflation, lack of newsprint, and lack of manpower, circulations would probably have continued to decline as they had in previous years. Yet in the long run, as literacy would have increased, as the military situation stabilized, and as journalists developed a better self-image and pride, the press would have had no choice but to develop into a viable institution.

Obviously, the future of newspapers and other publications was closely linked to government and the government's perception of the press. If the government had adopted a more liberal set of press laws, including elimination of the publishing bond require-ment, there would most likely have been an increase in the number of publications. That more secondary school graduates were studying journalism at several universities would have augured well for the improved standards of reporting and editing. The University of Dalat, Buddhist University and Mekong University were among institutions offering courses in journalism in 1974. About 500 students were enrolled in such courses that year. Occasional workshops and special seminars were held for reporters and editors. In 1966, the International Press Federation, based in Brussels, held a three-month seminar in Saigon, for which about 150 journalists applied, but only 50 were allowed to participate because of facility limitations. (Many publishers refused to release reporters from their regular duties, but the reporters, undaunted, attended.) And in 1974, the United States Information Service sponsored a week long seminar on the mass media.

Vietnamese journalist Pham Kim Pinh, foreign editor of *Chinh Luan* daily, said at a seminar in 1974 that the press was improving; he cited the following reasons: better educated young men and women would eventually demand better papers containing quality articles; strides in the worldwide development of mass communications would help cause the South Vietnamese press to keep abreast of global changes both in terms of technical and editorial content; and in 1968, the first group of journalism graduates emerged and joined both the local press corps and the government. This would eventually induce the government into developing an improved attitude towards the press, he believed (*Saigon Post,* 1 June 1974).

A professor of English literature at a Vietnamese university (who was also a student of the press) pointed out in 1974 that the press had several basic problems.

First, the ranks of reporters had been infiltrated by Communists who advocated the formation of a "third party" movement in South Vietnam;

Second, journalists lacked professional training and a sense of standards;

Third, because of the military situation, the government had the right to impose rigid controls;

Finally, "the government's stupidity" in its dealings with the press was a hindrance.

After the Thieu government imposed Press Law 007, "underground" publications emerged: ". . . The appearance of hundreds of mimeographed newsletters, newspapers and reviews, illegal or semi-legal, published by students and trade-union organizations" sprang up (*Democratic Journalist,* Jan. 1974). Yet, despite press restrictions, the press of South Vietnam probably had more freedom than its counterparts in other areas of Southeast Asia. And South Vietnamese journalists in 1974 were indeed vocal in complaining about their government's restrictions. This was not found in such nearby nations as Malaysia, Indonesia or Singapore (see *Guimary,* 1975, pp. 163-169).

3.12 Vietnam After 1975

Tran Van Dinh

3.12.1 Theoretical Underpinnings

On 1 May 1975, one day after Hanoi tanks and soldiers entered Saigon, an official announcement by the Uy Ban Quan Quan (Military Management Committee) prohibited the printing of newspapers, periodicals and books without the permission of the new revolutionary authorities.

With the collapse of the Nguyen Van Thieu administration, a press situation in South Vietnam, which could be generously characterized as "chaotic," came to an end. The Vietnamese popular saying, "Lam bao, noi lao an tien" (Journalists lie to make money), generally had reflected the state of journalism in South Vietnam from 1954-75 (*Thai* in *Lent,* 1971, pp. 235-54).

Beginning in May 1975, a new press regime emerged in South Vietnam, broadly embodying two main directions already implemented in the Democratic Republic of Vietnam (North Vietnam) since 1954.

They were:

(1) The historical Asian concept that the role of the press is "the circulation and promotion of 'correct' ideas rather than the purveying of news — the raw material for the individual opinion that collectively made up public opinion, and the

Tran Van Dinh, currently with Pan African Studies, Temple University, has published over 100 articles in newspapers and magazines and is the author of several books, the most recent being *From Bandung to Colombo: Conferences of the Non-Aligned Countries.* He has also conducted research on communications and guerrilla warfare.

furnishing of a forum for the competition of ideas" (*Lent*, 1971, p. xvi).

(2) The consistent policy on culture (in which newspapers and books play a major part) of the Indochinese Communist Party, formed in 1930 by Ho Chi Minh, who himself started his revolutionary career as a journalist in France.[1] In the *De Cuong Van Hoa Vietnam cua Dang* (Party Cultural Programme), it was clearly stated that the mission of the Marxist cultural workers is "to oppose fascist, feudalistic, reactionary, slavish, deceptive culture and to promote new democratic culture"[2] (Central Committee on Propaganda, Vietnam, 1960). The same program "set out clearly that the new culture of Vietnam should bear a triple character: national, scientific, masses, and should be led by the Party."

In 1947, one year after hostilities between the French and the Viet Minh[3] became nationwide, and at a time when the prospect of a final Vietnamese victory was far from clear in the minds of most people, the secretary general of the Indochinese Communist Party, Truong Chinh (real name, Dang Xuan Khu), wrote a series of articles in the magazine, *Su That* (Truth). In these articles, which appeared from 4 March to 1 August 1947, and were headlined, "Khang Chien Nhat Dinh Thang Loi" (The Resistance Shall Definitely Win), the author defined the strategy for the cultural front, which to him, was as important as the political, economic and military fronts. He observed that "every day, the pamphlets, books, newspapers, magazines, speeches and radio of the enemy sow their poison among our people." At the same time, he noted that on his side, "all political figures, journalists and writers are stimulating the army and people to unite for struggle." He then reiterated the guidelines in the 1943 Party Cultural Programme and emphasized that "our culture must be based on the following principles: it must be national, it must

1   In the 1920s, Ho Chi Minh edited *Paria* in Paris, and contributed articles to *l'Humanité*, organ of the Central Committee of the French Communist Party, of which he was one of the founders. See *Lacouture*, 1968.
2   Since 1951, the Indochinese Communist Party has gone by the name, Dang Lao Dong Vietnam, or Vietnam Workers Party. The change was in name only, not in leadership or policies.
3   Abbreviation of Vietnam Doc Lap Dong Minh Hoi (Association of the Allies for the Independence of Vietnam), a Communist front organization.

be scientific and it must be popular" (*Truong Chinh*, 1963, pp. 133-38).

From 1947 until 1954, when the First Indochina War ended with the Vietnamese victory at Dien Bien Phu and the signing of the Geneva Agreements temporarily partitioning Vietnam at the 17th parallel, the Viet Minh's clandestine press faithfully followed the directions proposed by Truong Chinh. After 1954, the press in North Vietnam was simply a formalization and development of the clandestine press; the change was in form and not in content. The Second Indochina War began in 1960 with the formation of the Mat Tran Dan Toc Giai Phong Mien Nam (Front for the Liberation of South Vietnam or NLF), usually called the Viet Cong, and the accelerated United States military and economic aid to South Vietnam. The NLF, as its name implied, was simply a front of the Vietnam Workers Party, a tactical maneuver "to rally all the patriotic classes and sections of the people, all patriotic parties and religious groupings, together with all individuals to oppose the US and (Ngo Dinh) Diem" (Foreign Languages Publishing House, 1963). All directives came from Hanoi whose representative in the jungles in the South was Pham Hung, a member of the Vietnam Workers Party's Politburo (see Tran Van Dinh, 1976). The NLF organized its clandestine press and radio, patterned after the Viet Minh during the 1947-54 period. The names of all publications usually began or ended with the words, "Giai Phong" (Liberation); e.g., *Can Tho Giai Phong*, a clandestine NLF newspaper circulated in the province of Can Tho; *Phu Nu Giai Phong* (Womens Liberation), etc. Radio Giai Phong went on the air on 1 February 1962, and Thong Tan Giai Phong (Liberation Press Agency) was founded a year before. These two organizations provide news and analyses for NLF publications at the regional and provincial levels and for news bulletins in foreign languages, published by a number of NLF offices abroad (*Pike*, 1966, pp. 398-412).

3.12.2 Changes after 1975

After May 1975, the press in South Vietnam not only followed the process of formalization that took place in North Vietnam after 1954, but was gradually integrated with that of the North.

For example, on 20 June 1976, Thong Tan Giai Phong (Liberation Press Agency) merged with the Hanoi Vietnam Thong Tan Xa (VNTTX). The VNTTX, was originally formed 19 September 1945 (17 days after the declaration of Vietnam independence by Ho Chi Minh), and is a government monopoly of news distribution to and from Vietnam. It maintains eight overseas bureaux — in Moscow, Peking, Paris, Vientiane, Berlin, La Havana, Cairo and Algiers — and distributes three daily bulletins in English, French and Spanish (about 6,000 words for each bulletin) for overseas embassies, besides its Vietnamese bulletins.

The population of southern Vietnam is now served by the following newspapers:[4] *Saigon Giai Phong (Liberated Saigon),* subtitled "Voice of the People of Ho Chi Minh Ville,"[5] is a four-page, evening newspaper; *Giai Phong (Liberation).* is a four-page morning daily which has continued the paper of the same name published in 1963 by the NLF. *Giai Phong* looks more austere than *Saigon Giai Phong,* its content being more ideological. Its subtitle is, "Organ of the National Liberation Front of South Vietnam." There is also a Chinese language newspaper bearing the same name with almost the same content.[6] *Tin Sang (Morning News)* is a four-page daily whose publisher-editor is Ngò Cong Duc, a former member of the National Assembly during Thieu's administration. He opposed Thieu's war policy, fled abroad and returned after 1 May 1975. Although called an independent newspaper in its nameplate, *Tin Sang*'s news comes entirely from official sources. There are also nine weeklies and three monthlies in Saigon.

The public in the South has also been served by newspapers brought in from Hanoi. In particular, they include, *Nhan Dan (People's Daily),* a four-page, austere-looking organ of the Central Committee of the Vietnam Workers Party. *Nhan Dan* was first published clandestinely on 11 March 1951, in a liberated zone at the Chinese border, during the resistance war against the French. Beginning on 20 April 1976, *Nhan Dan* published its southern edition in Ho Chi Minh Ville. *Quan Doi Nhan Dan (Vietnam*

---

4   Excluding numerous regional and provincial newspapers.
5   After 1 May 1975, Saigon became Ho Chi Minh Ville.
6   Although the government is pushing for solidarity, Chinese language papers for a foreign community are allowed in Hanoi and Ho Chi Minh Ville.

People's Army) is a daily established in 1949; it is a publication of the Vietnam People's Army under the control of the Political Department of the Army. *Tan Viet Hoa Bang* (*New Vietnam-China Relations*) is published in Chinese. The weeklies are *Tien Phong* (*Vanguard*), organ of the Federation of Ho Chi Minh Youth; *Lao Dong* (*Labour*), organ of the Federation of Labour; *Phu Nu* (*Women*), organ of Federation of Women; *Cuu Quoc* (*National Salvation*), *Mat Tran To Quoc* (*Fatherland Front*); *Van Nghe* (*Literature and Arts*), Federation of Literature and Arts; *Doc Lap* (*Independence*), Dang Dan Chu (Democratic Party); *Thieu Nien Tien Phong* (*Vanguard Children*), Federation of Ho Chi Minh Children; *The Duc The Thao* (*Gymnastics and Sports*) and *Khoa Hoc Thuong Thuc* (*Popular Sciences*). Among the 54 or so monthlies published in northern Vietnam, the most important, especially for foreign scholars, is *Hoc Tap* (*Studies*), the theoretical journal of the Political Bureau of the Central Committee of the Vietnam Workers Party.

As in the case of most socialist nations, details of circulation are not known. This author's guess is that the circulation of Vietnamese newspapers today are much higher than those of the press in South Vietnam before May 1975 because politically, the Communists are well organized in communications, and great efforts are being made by the authorities in Ho Chi Minh Ville to combat illiteracy in the South as it was nearly solved earlier in the North.

3.12.3 Questions

Perhaps, at this point, it would be prudent to see if the Vietnamese press meets the guidelines set down by Truong Chinh in 1947. First, is the press free? The 1960 constitution of the Democratic Republic of Vietnam, which will surely remain in its essentials the constitution of a reunified Vietnam, states in Article 25, "Citizens of the Democratic Republic of Vietnam enjoy freedom of speech, freedom of the press, freedom of assembly, freedom of association, and freedom of demonstration. The state guarantees all necessary material conditions for citizens to enjoy these freedoms." But as it is often explained by the leaders in Hanoi, "these freedoms are to serve the interests of the revolution, of the peoples" unlike "freedoms in the bourgeoisie press of the west."

Second, is the press national? The answer is an unequivocal yes. It is not only national in circulation, but also in content, providing information on national development and emphasizing national history and traditional culture.[7]

Third, is the press scientific? Again, an affirmative answer is in order if one uses Karl Marx', definition of science as, "All science would be superstition if outward appearance and the essence of things directly coincided." Living in a socialist state, the Vietnamese people are being taught constantly about contradictions, both at the domestic and international levels. For example, they are taught to love American people and to hate the American government and military.

Fourth, is the press popular? It is difficult to answer this question, except to say that in the North, the people being literate and members of professional and political groups, read major national newspapers and magazines as well as provincial and regional ones. However, a problem may exist among the population in the South. Unlike the North, these people were exposed to the Vietnamese "chaotic" press and to "decadent" American culture, the remedy of both being at the heart of the intense re-education campaign in South Vietnam since 1975.

3.12.4 Campaign Oriented

This author has found the press in North Vietnam very informative — not in historical details, a fact recognized by most international scholars — but in its news coverage. For example, *Nhan Dan (People's Daily)* on 28 April 1974, carried a page one story with photographs of a meeting in Hanoi, presided over by President Ton Duc Thang and other officials, during which a flag inscribed, "Thi Dua Quyet Thang" (Compete and Be Determined To Win), was presented. *Nhan Dan* reported that in his reply to the president's short address, General Van Tien Dung, chief of staff of the Vietnam People's Army, said: "Facing a new situation with a new mission, all people's armed forces are pledged to

7   For example, every issue has at least one historical background article, used to build national unity.

strongly developing their revolutionary offensive spirit, rising high the flag of 'Compete and Be Determined To Win' and to fulfilling successfully all missions entrusted to them by the Party, the government and the people." During April 1974 and after, *Quan Doi Nhan Dan (People's Army Daily)* was filled with articles and slogans on the campaign "to compete and be determined to win." From reading those articles, this author accurately predicted at that time that Hanoi intended to start a general offensive in the South to be led by General Van Tien Dung.[8]

On 19 May 1976, the birthday of Ho Chi Minh, the premier of Vietnam, Pham Van Dong, chose the occasion to write an article in the party's paper, *Nhan Dan,* attacking government officials' abuses of power, corruption and bureaucracy. The article was titled, "Let's implement the teaching of Uncle Ho," meaning, "we must keep our party very clean and pure; we must keep our party worthy of the leader, of the faithful servant of people." The article marked the beginning of the anti-corruption, anti-bureaucracy campaign in Vietnam. Unlike in China, where campaigns were started by unsigned writers in the party's paper, in Vietnam (now and before), political campaigns start with articles signed by prominent party personnel. An AFP dispatch of 25 May 1976, said that Premier Pham Van Dong's article was having the effect that officials in Hanoi were more friendly and ready to help the people. Also, after May 1975, newspapers in Ho Chi Minh Ville ran a series of articles on the history of the Vietnam Workers Party, perhaps to introduce the leadership of a unified Vietnam to the southern population.

The press could determine what was expected of it by having listened to the speech made by Le Duan, first secretary of the Vietnam Workers Party, when he addressed the unified National Assembly in Hanoi, 24 June 1976:

> The press should extend its investigative work, its studies; it should reflect the population's constructive ideas and criticize bureaucratism and the abuses by government's agencies. The citizens in our society have the right to work, to enjoy the fruits of their labor, the

---

8   For full account of General Van Tien Dung's campaign in March-April 1975, see Foreign Broadcast Service, 7 April 1976 to 27 May 1976, Excerpts printed in *New York Times,* 26, 29 April 1976.

right to vacation, the right to education, the right to their bodies, the right for the freedom of the press, freedom of speech, freedom of religion, to choose one religion or not choose any.... The Party leads, the people rule and the government administers. We must definitely combat laziness, avoidance of labor, corruption and waste. We must expose and severely criticize and must struggle against the irresponsible attitudes, the arrogance of the officials who invented all kinds of complicated and unnecessary papers and regulations.

3.12.5 Additional Information, by John A. Lent

According to one source, during the French rule of Vietnam, there were only four or five newspapers with an average circulation of 3,000 in the entire country (*Banerjee,* 1975, pp. 38-39). Another source stated there were 10 newspapers and periodicals in 1939, 64 in 1965, and 135 in the mid-1970s (*Journalists' Affairs,* 1976, pp. 3-7; see also *Interstages,* 1978, pp. 18-19). However, by early 1975, North Vietnam alone had 139 newspapers and periodicals with an average circulation of between 50,000 and 100,000. The largest North Vietnamese daily, *Nhan Dan,* had 200,000. Of the total newspapers and periodicals, 16 were published for the armed forces with an average circulation of 100,000; 62 dealt with science and technology and professional interests and 10 each, medicine and economics. Twenty-six newspapers and periodicals were of a political nature, including newspapers for youth, women, young pioneers, labor and the other two political parties, Democratic Party and Socialist Party. Twenty-eight newspapers and periodicals were published in provinces and districts outside Hanoi. In early 1975, 2,600 professional journalists worked in North Vietnam, 600 of whom were new entrants, who would become members of the Association of Vietnamese Journalists after completing two years of service (*Banerjee,* 1975, pp. 38-39; see *Hart,* 1973, pp. 8-10).

South Vietnam also had a large number of publications before 1975. In fact, Saigon was one of the very few cities in the world that could boast of having tens of newspapers publishing at various times. The number publishing usually depended upon the

authorities and how stringently they applied the press laws; as
has been indicated, under Thieu, they were enforced very strictly
and numbers of dailies were suspended. As recent as three months
before the change of government in May 1975, the Thieu government suspended five newspapers.

After 1 May 1975, *Thanh Loc* (purification of culture) took
place in the South. Journalists and writers were placed in
re-education or prison camps (*Nguyen Ho*, 1978, pp. 18-20);
literature was re-evaluated, burned or banned to fit the aims of
the cultural purge (see *Ho Truong An*, 1978, pp. 3-7); foreign
news coverage in the nation was stopped (as of May 1976);
censorship was even more effectively applied than during the
Thieu regime, and the number of media was drastically reduced.
Apart from one semi-official Buddhist and one semi-official
Catholic newspaper, *Tin Sang*, by 1976-77, was the only other
newspaper that could be classed as partly independent. Although
its staff was still composed of anti-Thieu, Third Force veterans,
headed by Ngo Cong Duc, the real power was in the hands of
political commissars (*Nguyen Ho*, 1978, p. 19).

The unification of the country also affected the press. The
South Vietnam Association of Patriotic and Democratic Journalists and the Vietnam Journalists Association (of North Vietnam)
merged 7 July 1976 to form the Association of Vietnamese
Journalists; the new organization retained the constitution of the
former North Vietnamese association. Two weeks earlier, the
news agencies of North and South Vietnam merged.

Part 4
South Asia

4.1   Freedom of the Press in South Asia

John A. Lent

The 1970s has been a harsh decade for press freedom in South Asia. Each country has had at least one unstable political situation when press freedom was all but interred. India's occurred during the Emergency of 1975-76; the gravest period in Bangladesh and Nepal was in 1975; in Afghanistan, in 1973; in Sri Lanka, 1973-74, and in Pakistan, during the past three years.

4.1.1 Afghanistan

It might be stated simply that the 1964 Constitution of Afghanistan provided for freedom of the press, while the Press Law of July 1965 qualified it substantially. Made up of eight chapters and 55 articles, the Press Law was drafted to safeguard the "fundamentals of Islam, constitutional monarchy, and other values enshrined in the Constitution" (*Dupree,* 1973, p. 600). Among the restrictive features of the Press Law is a requirement that publishers apply to the Ministry of Information and Culture for permission to publish, at the same time offering a security deposit to safeguard against possible future government action. In the application, the publisher must list the amount and sources of his periodical's capital.

Articles of the law which have been used to close newspapers are those that state the press must safeguard public security and order, the interest and dignity of the state, fundamentals of Islam, constitutional monarchy and other Constitutional values (Article 1); that rule against defamation of the principles of Islam or the king (Article 31); that warn against incitement to commit actions that are offenses (e.g., incite to disobey country's laws, disrupt public security and order, or to seek depravity) (Article 32); that state there should not be disclosure of state secrets, incitement to seek depravity (through publication of false or distorted news, obscene articles, or views which aim to divert courts from reaching correct decisions), defamation of persons or attacks upon the sanctity of private lives of individuals (Article 33); that outlaw articles that purposely weaken the state's fiscal credit or the use of false advertisements of medicines (Article 34); and that state there should be no publication of matters that would weaken the army (Article 35). Article 48 states that a paper will close if it has no editor (*Dupree*, 1973, p. 600).

A number of newspapers have been forced to close over the years (at least a dozen between 1965-72), because of their attacks on government or for a "lack of decorum." Nevertheless, there were "free" (independent of government ownership and control) newspapers in Afghanistan until the July 1973 overthrow of government. When 19 newspapers folded in that month because of government pressures, the "free" newspapers ceased to exist, having been replaced by those of the government (see 4.2).

After a Revolutionary Council seized power in May 1978, stringent controls were also placed on foreign journalists. Full scale censorship of foreign press representatives went into effect and there were reports of harassment and censorship of the wires and overseas telephone lines (*IPI Report*, June 1978, p. 16).

4.1.2 Bangladesh

Although in the late 1970s, not much was heard about infringements of press freedom in Bangladesh, the two years preceding Sheikh Mujibur Rahman's assassination on 15 August 1975, were horrid enough to have consequences on the press for years.

The culmination of this oppression came in June 1975, when 20 dailies and all political weeklies were banned, leaving only the government-owned *Observer* and *Dainik Bangla* and the previously-private *Bangladesh Times* and *Ittefaq*, the latter two taken over by the government to serve as organs of the national political party. Such drastic action seemed unnecessary since, after the daily, *Ganakantha*, was forced to close in early 1975, the entire press had capitulated. By spring, 600 journalists had applied for membership in the governing political party, and the editors had pledged allegiance to Sheikh Mujibur Rahman.

Apparently the misuse of legislation in 1973-74 to control the media was too much for journalists to bear. For example, on 19 September 1973, the Pakistani press ordinance that had been in effect since 1961 was replaced by the Printing Presses and Publications (Declaration and Registration) Act, passed by Parliament ostensibly to regulate newspapers. Under this act, newspapers were subject to prior approval by the government, requiring among other things, that all publications be licensed. Newspapers not registered with the officials were denied newsprint and/or advertising allocations. Also, publishers were fined if they failed to provide the government with four free copies of everything they published.

A Special Powers Bill of February 1974, had devastating consequences for the press, stating that "to print, publish or distribute prejudicial reports" was an offense punishable by five years' imprisonment and/or a fine. Under this legislation, newsmen were required to identify all sources of information, and the authorities were given the right to seize documents and newspapers, to ban newspapers and other publications and to search premises on the assumption they might find a document which could be classified as harmful. Pre-censorship was affected for all questions of state security and friendly relations of Bangladesh with other nations.

In less than half a year, still another legislative action, Newsprint Control Order (July 1974), was levied to control the press. Carried out through the Commerce and Foreign Trade Ministry, with the Ministry of Information and Broadcasting entrusted with implementation, this order stated that newsprint could be used only with government permission. The government stated that internal consumption of newsprint had to be controlled in this newsprint-producing nation. Although they recognized the order as a political move, the editors complied and in August, reduced the number of pages in their newspapers.

Clamps on press freedom were further tightened on 29 December 1974, when a state of emergency was declared. By then, a campaign of "down with the Western press" was in full force and issues of foreign periodicals critical of the government were regularly banned (see *Lent,* 1975a, pp. 8-10; *Lent,* 1976b, pp. 8-9).

Some of this legislation still encumbers the Bangladesh press, despite the promises of the successors of the Sheikh to make changes. To be sure, some concessions were made by succeeding governments; suspended newspapers were allowed to resume (by mid-1976, 45 were given such permission); committees and councils were set up by government to aid newspapers and journalists; and government spokesmen made for a more relaxed situation by promising a more liberal stand towards the media.

Yet, the press is still highly controlled. General censorship of all news is in effect; some journalists are in prison; management of domestic news exists in the form of omission and distortion; and few foreign journalists are permitted in the country.

In 1976, there were controversial arrests or detentions of journalists, some of whom were caught up in the politically-motivated conspiracy trials prevalent that year. One such detainee was Dutch journalist, Peter Custers, who reported that the Bangladesh press either distorted or omitted mention of the 1976 trials (*Custers,* 1977, p. 8). For example, the June arrest, subsequent acquittal and illegal detention of A. B. M. Mahmud, editor of the weekly *Wave,* was ignored except for a brief mention of the trial in *Ittefaq,* which evoked a warning from the authorities. A foreign journalist, Larry Lipschultz of *Far Eastern Economic Review,* who tried to cover the trial involving Mahmud, was expelled from Bangladesh.

Custers was held without trial or access to legal counsel for nine months (see *Contemporary South Asia News,* May 1976, pp. 1-2). When he did come to trial in September 1976, along with a number of Bangladeshi political prisoners, he was sentenced to 14 years' imprisonment by a secret military tribunal for plotting to overthrow the government. He was eventually expelled from Bangladesh when Dutch officials interceded on his behalf (*Custers,* 1979, p. 8).

4.1.3 India

Probably the severest blow to a press was that dealt by Indira Gandhi to the longstanding free newspapers of India. Some inkling of what was in store came in the early 1970s as Gandhi's government regularly accused the press of being monopolistic and in need of delinking. One government draft bill was so extreme that it risked giving control of the press to political groups in the name of press workers. The government eventually backed down on this bill (*Mankekar, 1973*). C. R. Irani of the *Statesman* said these criticisms were unwarranted as the government had a monopolies act it could use if it really believed monopolization of the press existed. He also said the keen competition of the Indian newspapers proved otherwise (*Irani, 1975*, pp. 7-8, 14-21). Other journalists in 1974 were disturbed at what they thought was an effort on the part of the government to stamp out media dissent. For example, the dismissal of B. G. Verghese, editor of *Hindustan Times,* who had been highly critical of Gandhi's policies, resulted from government pressure on the paper's management. Also, acts by regional governments to withdraw advertisements from publications such as *Searchlight* and *Pradeep* because of their oppositionist stands seemed ominous signs (*Far Eastern Economic Review, 8* Nov. 1974, pp. 33-34).

When Gandhi declared a national emergency on 26 June 1975, the press became her favorite whipping boy. Even before pre-censorship could be administered that day — the first time in free India's history — the government had taken measures to stifle newspapers. On the night of 25 June, electricity supplies were cut to many newspaper plants, stopping them from publishing. At a high level meeting on 26 June, the government decided it would restructure news agencies, allow the Press Council to die a natural death, impose pre-censorship and review all press facilities given to correspondents by the government.

During the 19 months of emergency, the four news agencies (Press Trust of India, United News of India, Hindustan Samachar and Samachar Bharati), by an act of Parliament, were merged as Samachar to control news flow; the Press Council was dissolved; 253 journalists were detained and 51 discredited; seven foreign correspondents were expelled and the entry of 29 others was barred; government and public sector advertising was denied 97 newspapers, and the media were misused for news management (*Verghese, 1977*, p. 23). The authorities also encouraged the removal of the editorial policy making functions from publishers and talked about breaking up newspaper groups. *Sorabjee* (1977) reported that three-fourths of the Indian press was muzzled and the other fourth shut down. The Registrar of Newspapers later reported that 2,600 declarations of newspapers had been cancelled by district magistrates (*Indian Press,* April 1979, p. 27). Pre-censorship was extremely harsh in that everything was subject to the censor's pencil, even pre-censorship regulations. Censorship, according to the officials, was imposed for the defense of India and civil defense, public safety, maintenance of public order and the efficient conduct of military operations (*Irani,* 1977, p. 51). After three months, pre-censorship was replaced with self-censorship, accompanied by tough guidelines from the censors that made it difficult to know anything had changed. Another almost fatal blow to the press was the enactment of the preventive action against the press, including prohibiting publication for a period not exceeding two months. "Objectionable matter" was very broadly defined.

During the first few days of Emergency, some newspapers protested by leaving their editorial columns blank, but thereafter, with a few exceptions, most newspapers meekly submitted, not willing to contest the illegality of censorship. Some newspapers, *Hindustan Times* (owned by Birla Company) and *Times of India* (owned by Jain industrial group) among them, reflected the official line because of their strong ties with government and big business (see *Grigg,* 1975, pp. 5-11). They, as well as others, kowtowed quickly because Gandhi could bring pressure against other industries they owned (*Jablons,* 1978, p. 34).

Generally, the press seemed indifferent to the Emergency (see *IPI Report,* July 1977, pp. 1, 6-8, 10-11), and journalists seemed to fall into three camps: those few who defied the authorities, those who supported and those many who acquiesced to the government. Among those few who resisted were publishers and editors of the *Indian Express, Statesman* and *Himmat.* They paid expensively for their defiance. For example, the government tried to buy *Statesman* shares at high prices to gain control; issued orders to government and public sector companies not to advertise in the *Express* or *Statesman* (see *Far Eastern Economic Review,* 15 Oct. 1976, p. 25), and tried to rip out the *Express* air conditioning system and auction it off to pay a tax bill the government said the paper owed (*Time,* 20 Dec. 1976). State banks eventually stopped credit to the *Express,* and at one time in late 1976, the government sealed its presses (see *Lifschultz,* 1976, pp. 26-28). An active underground press also functioned during the Emergency (*Hazelhurst,* 1975b, p. 4; for more on Emergency and press, see *Indian Press,* March 1976).

Censorship was lifted in January 1977, as the prime minister called for new elections in March. The victorious Janata Party in that election immediately, after 20 March, dismantled the coercive apparatus that had held the press in tow. The Prevention of Publication of Objectionable Matter Act was repealed; journalists were released; punitive action against publications was withdrawn, and papers forced to close were encouraged to resume. The Desai government seemed to bend over backwards to restore press freedom, even to the extent of removing indirect pressures. By 1978, the Press Council, through another act of Parliament, came back into existence (text in *Indian Press,* Oct. 1978, pp. 19-26), and Samachar was made into four news agencies again.

Newspapers tried to outdo each other in recounting the excesses of the Gandhi government, and among journalists, an antipathy developed between those who resisted Emergency rule and those who acquiesced (*Borders,* 1977, p. A-3). Commissions were set up to investigate the misuse of media by the government (see *Levin,* 1978; *Communicator,* Jan. 1978, pp. 13-26) and to study the adequacy of constitutional provisions and laws regarding freedom of expression. The latter — the Second Press Commission, appointed by the information minister in May 1978 — has been the subject of some controversy as journalists questioned its composition and mandate (see *Malhan,* 1978, pp. 13-15).

Despite these bright spots, some observers feared other government actions. In 1978, a court battle ensued concerning the removal of one of the mechanisms used to control the press during the Emergency. The government under Gandhi had been given the authority to set the advertising rates of publishers and to determine which publications the government and state controlled companies could advertise in (*Chinoy,* 1978, p. 30). Irani said the Desai government doggedly held onto this power, not out of sinister motives, but because it, like any government, did not like criticism. Finally, the government relinquished its hold on this advertising policy, but in 1979, it was still not very clear exactly what had been given up (*Irani,* 1979, pp. 11-17). Other fears resulted from talk by authorities of breaking up and diffusing newspaper ownerships and from the government's 1979 action to bring the printing presses under the purview of the Industries Development and Regulation Act, 1951. This, according to a report in the *Indian Press* (June 1979, p. 9), would expose the press to "the whims and fancies of the politicians in power." In 1978, the government also planned to amend the Press and Registration of Books Act to weed out more thoroughly the non-existent newspapers.

Despite the Janata Party's free press policy nationally, there were state governments in 1978-79 that were not in the mood to relax curbs. The Punjab government imposed censorship on 12 newspapers in September 1978, while the Uttar Pradesh authorities confiscated copies of two newspapers (*Media,* Dec. 1978, p. 29). At the close of the 1970s, the press seemed hesitant to get very involved in investigative reporting, still depending for most of their stories on government handouts. Self-censorship seemed to be ingrained.

4.1.4 Nepal

The Constitution of Nepal guarantees freedom of speech and expression, but laws can be made for the public good to regulate or control the exercise of these rights. Among conditions listed that warrant such restrictive laws are the preservation of the security of Nepal; maintenance of law and order, friendly relations with foreign states, good relations among people of different classes, professions or areas, good conduct, health, comfort, decency, economic interests, and morality of the people; protection of the interests of minors and women; and prevention of internal disorder or external invasion, contempt of court or Parliament and any attempt to subvert the Constitution or any law.

Legislation was passed in 1965 and 1975 that had far-reaching implications on the press. The Press and Publications Act of 1965 stated, among other things, that nothing can be printed that abets or incites to commit murder or any violent crime or to praise any person charged or convicted of a tendency to commit or abet such crimes; that diverts government employees from their duty or loyalty; that foments hatred or disrespect of the king and others; that is obscene, immoral, foments ill-will and malice among various classes, etc. Section 30-C of the act promised that the government would grant loans and facilities to newspapers that contributed to "healthy journalism, with full loyalty to the nation, the King and the Panchayat system and with the national viewpoint and national interests in mind." Among punitive actions available to the government under this act were the powers to fine, confiscate or cancel newspaper registrations; to confiscate security deposits of newspapers and require new ones, and to ban news stories the authorities thought would disturb the peace or relations Nepal had established with other nations (see 4.5.5).

The Press and Publications Act of August 1975 was rushed through Parliament, after some parts of the Nepalese press became hostile that year during discussions on the heated topic of proposed constitutional reform. The act gives the government sweeping powers against erring journalists and publishers, banning critical writing about the king, royal family, government and its agencies and diplomatic representatives. It also forbids attempts "to weaken the moral fibre of society through libellous, baseless and unwholesome comments, and use of words, symbols or illustrations and materials likely to encourage racial prejudices," and calls for prior censorship of works of foreign journalists. The government is authorized under this act to close newspapers without giving a reason. Introduced to bring about changes towards a national press, the act also promised that the government would financially support newspapers that favored "healthy journalism," the latter term defined similarly as in the 1965 act (*Indian Press,* Sept. 1975, pp. 68-69). Immediately after it was adopted, the minister of state for communication told Parliament that the act can be used to close irresponsible newspapers — that it sought to discourage and control those newspapers which are oblivious to the ethics of journalism and take "undue advantage to blackmail and harm the interests of the country" (*Indian Press,* April-May 1977, pp. 18-20, 35).

The 1975 act had a profound effect upon the Press Council of

Nepal. Originally, the council was to be a body that listened to complaints about the press made by the public. The president of the Nepal Journalists Association was to serve as council secretary and four other NJA representatives were to serve as members. Even before 1975, however, the council was serving as government mouthpiece as its membership was dominated by government officials with the government's director of information appointed as secretary. The 1975 press act deleted the citizen's ombudsman role from the council; officially made the director of information secretary, and reduced the direct representation of NJA to its president. Under the act, a member of the political body, "Go to the Village National Committee," was made a council member as were the editors of the two government-owned Gorkhapatra corporations, who were to sit alternately. The number of nominees from the press was reduced to two. The nine-member council has been given the task of drawing up a code of ethics by which the government will scrutinize the press (*Narendra*, 1975, pp. 11-12).

Newspapers are suspended in Nepal and editors are arrested for what they write. For example, two weeks after the Press and Publications Act of 1975 was passed, the government banned three dailies and four weeklies. Twice in two weeks in mid-1977, the president of the Nepal Journalists Association unsuccessfully appealed the article in the 1975 act which authorizes the government to close newspapers without stating a reason. He cited five newspapers that had been banned for a considerable time because of this article — *Dainik Nepal*, *Navin Khabar*, *Nepal Times*, *Rashtra Pukar* and *Samik Samikshya*. There have been some concessions concerning newspaper suspensions, especially after a new government comes into office. In December 1975, the new prime minister, Tulsi Giri, in an effort to gain rapport with the press, lifted the ban on all newspapers except for two dailies and two weeklies. When Kirti Nidhi Bista returned to power in 1977, he removed the bans on the remaining four, saying, "You are all free."

There is a feeling of relaxation under Bista, but a number of potentially-repressive situations, not a few of which were caused by the 1975 act, still exist (*Asiaweek*, 28 Oct. 1977, p. 49). The feeling one gets is that the government hangs as a suspended guillotine over the heads of the press. It owns or controls a part of the press through the Gorkhapatra Sansthan (publishers of *Gorkhapatra, Rising Nepal, Nepalese Perspective* and *Madhuparka*); manages news content through legislation and control of Rashtriya Samachar Simiti (the national news service which is sole distributor of foreign and domestic news), and subsidizes with loans and facilities newspapers that support "healthy journalism" and denies government advertisements to those that march to a different drummer.

4.1.5 Pakistan

The press in Pakistan, as in most of South Asia, is controlled through government ownership of some media, economic restraints, legislation and arrests of journalists and threats of suspensions of newspapers. The government ownership of print media is facilitated through the National Press Trust which has four to eight metropolitan dailies with numerous editions. The government also has the three newspapers formerly owned by former Prime Minister Zulfikar Ali Bhutto. Because the government is the single largest advertiser (in 1975-75, 57 to 89 per cent of the advertising revenue came from the government) and since 1972, the sole authority for the allocation of newsprint, economic strangleholds can be applied to the press. Under Bhutto, a newspaper earned its government advertising allotment by its "constructive policy."

A number of Pakistani laws can be applied for the control of the press, among them the Criminal Procedure Code (1898), the Security Act (1952), the Maintenance of West Pakistan Public Order Ordinance (1960), the Press and Publication Ordinance (1963) and emergency laws such as the Defence of Pakistan Rules. Pakistan has been continuously under emergency or martial law since September 1965. The Press and Publication Ordinance, established under Ayub Khan, was amended in 1975 and 1976. The prime instrument to assure that the press reflects the regime's policies, the ordinance requires, among other things, licensing and security deposits (*Williams,* 1978, pp. 54-56). All the laws are used extensively to forfeit security deposits or demand new ones, to ban newspapers, seize presses and jail editors.

Many journalists had been jailed over the years, but in March 1976, the *Far Eastern Economic Review* reported Pakistani journalists faced the most severe restrictions since the early martial law days of 1958. Between 1972-76, at least 10 editors were jailed, many others were penalized and more than three dozen publications were banned. Others, newspapers such as *Dawn,* became voices for the government. *Dawn* decided to support the authorities when the government withdrew its advertising.

Censorship and a system of "press advice" existed throughout the latter years of the Bhutto regime. For example, in October 1975, the press was prohibited for one month to publish news of a political situation in Punjab province. In fact, the order was issued by uniformed policemen who visited the newspapers. In April 1977, the government ordered censorship of all domestic news reports about the then six-week-old, violent oppositionist campaign against Bhutto (see *New York Times,* 24 April 1977).

In 1975, all newspapers had agreed to operate by press advice given usually via telephone by officials. The Pakistan Federation Union of Journalists, in a November 1975 protest, said the system of " 'press advice' had been ruthlessly and frequently used to suppress news about Opposition leaders and parties; and instead 'distorted versions' of Opposition statements have been published" (London *Times,* 6 Nov. 1975, p. 6).

Other journalism groups in 1975-76 complained about government infringements of press freedom. Newsmen in 1975 objected to the requirement that they possess "No Objection Certificates" to travel abroad. In January 1976, they joined together to form a confederation of unions to fight for common objectives, including press freedom. Later in June of the same year, the Council of Pakistan Newspaper Editors objected to governmental use of emergency powers to take action against journalists. When the National Press Commission (NPC), set up by the government, proposed in August 1976, a Court of Honour to implement a code of ethics voluntarily established by the NPC, the Pakistan Journalists' Union rejected it as an attempt "to suppress or distort facts and stifle dissension with the aim of protesting party interests."

Perhaps these protests served as a harbinger of what the government could expect in 1977-78. Ironically, pressmen protested most vehemently against General Zia ul-Haq, who, after deposing Bhutto in July 1977, promised press freedom in Pakistan. Also ironic was the issue they reacted to — Zia government harassment of the Bhutto-owned newspapers, *Musawat, Hilal-e-Pakistan* and *Nusrat.* What turned out to be the most intense confrontation between the press and government ever, began after the editor of *Musawat* was detained for a week in July 1977; no official reason was given for the detention. The government then seized the three newspapers, alleging financial irregularities, and in October 1977, forced the closure of *Musawat* when army authorities denied it access to its printing press. A number of journalists and newspaper workers went on hunger strikes in December to oppose this and other government interferences with press freedom. Some were arrested. Both the Pakistan Federation Union of Journalists (PFUJ) and All Pakistan Newspaper Employees Confederation (APNEC) joined the strikes. The authorities, in a *volte face,* conceded almost immediately to allow Mrs. Begum Nusrat Bhutto, wife of the former prime minister and chairman of the family-owned Peoples' Foundation Trust, to resume publication of *Musawat.* However, the government insisted on a new management and its own nominated editor for the daily. Journalists did not take lightly to the old staff losing their jobs.

In January and February 1978, there were a few isolated skirmishes between government and the press. In January, the editor and a printer of the *Sun* were sentenced to 10 lashes and a year of hard labor for printing an abusive line about Zia. They were pardoned within a day although the newspaper was suspended. In February, Zia was angry because the magazine published material aimed at creating public revulsion and bringing the government into contempt. As a result, the *Herald* was ordered to deposit a security payment of US$3,000.

During spring 1978, pressures grew steadily, prompting the London *Times* to print an editorial on May 12:

> Journalists now find themselves as much under attack and subject to arrest and punishment — not excluding flogging — as the corrupt politicians General Zia is determined to expose and punish.

The closing of *Musawat* again in April prompted daily hunger strikes by journalists that lasted for 29 days throughout May. And, each day strikers were arrested (over 150 in all). During the month, 11 newspapers were banned and required to deposit securities, 13 others were fined and two nationalized. The government lost the battle, however, when on 13 May, four newspaper employees were flogged in jail after being sentenced by a military court for staging a hunger strike. Protests erupted across Pakistan and there was an international backlash. What actually had started out as a defense of 600 families of *Musawat* employees who lost their jobs was escalated into a *cause célèbre* for the press (*Asiaweek,* 9 June 1978, pp. 23-24).

A settlement was reached between journalists and government in the latter part of May and *Musawat* was allowed to reappear. During June, however, the press union grew concerned at the slow pace of releasing arrested journalists, one of the conditions of the agreement.

The PFUJ and APNEC, in June, fixed deadlines for the government to resolve the freedom of press issue. Although the journalists' unions had gained substantial victories, they still had grievances about the dismissal of over two dozen union leaders from government-controlled National Press Trust newspapers, the total blackout in the press of union news and slashing attacks through official media on the union leadership. Additionally, the Karachi editions of *Musawat, Mayar* and *Alfatah* remained closed, and the unions continued to oppose the Press and Publications Ordinance (*Ali,* 1978b, p. 30).

The lull ended when hunger strikes occurred on 18 July and 30 journalists and sympathizers were arrested. To avoid further strikes, officials allowed the Karachi edition of *Musawat* and the other two newspapers to resume (*Ali,* 1978a, pp. 32-34). The strikes continued until, by September, over 270 journalists and student, peasant and worker sympathizers were arrested. Early in September, Minhaj Barna, head of both the PFUJ and APNEC, threatened to fast until death unless the government freed 90 newsmen (whom he claimed were being tortured) and reinstated the dismissed employees of National Press Trust newspapers. Later in the month, according to the London *Times,* Barna became critically ill after an eight-day fast (see *Asia 1979 Yearbook,* p. 269).

The longest press freedom fight seemed to end on 8 October,

when the government agreed to reinstate most of those who had lost their jobs and to release others from jail. While the negotiations were proceeding, the government brought sedition charges against the printers and publishers of the Karachi edition of *Musawat* and *Sadaqat,* and banned the liberal weekly, *Perbhaat.*

Another three-day strike occurred in mid-October when newspapers protested the imposition of pre-censorship, on 16 October, on newspapers and journals that published news and views considered a threat to internal peace and tranquility. Ordered to be the first of nine newspapers pre-censored was *Musawat (Akhtar,* 1978, p. 9). When the newspapers reappeared after the strike, they contained blank spaces indicating excision of news and photographs. The pre-censorship lasted until early November. Other reports followed in early 1979, claiming Zia had banned press stories, especially all details on the burial of Bhutto after his execution in April, and reimposed pre-censorship on three dailies, among them *Musawat.*

Actions such as these and the adamant nature of the journalists made one wonder in late 1979 if the pact of the previous year would last (see *Asiaweek,* 20 Oct. 1978, pp. 28, 37).

4.1.6 Sri Lanka

Until mid-1973, 95 per cent of the Sri Lanka daily press was controlled by three conglomerates – Lake House (Associated Newspapers of Ceylon), Independent Newspapers Group and Times of Ceylon Group. The government of Sirimava Bandaranaike changed all that in the course of the next two years. First, a law (Lake House Law of 1973) was passed, giving the government 75 per cent of the Lake House shares. Next, the five newspapers of Independent Newspapers Group were closed on 20 April 1974 (*IPI Report,* Aug. 1976, p. 4), and finally, a group of financiers headed by Mrs. Bandaranaike's son, Anura, and including her nephew, bought a controlling interest in the Times of Ceylon Group in 1975.

Besides gaining control of the press through ownership, the authorities used legislative and economic powers to further subjugate the press. In 1973, a law was passed which created the government-appointed Sri Lanka Press Council. Among the first actions of the council were a number of restrictions which hindered the press in its coverage of government – all sources must be revealed, matter purporting to be proceedings or decisions of the Cabinet cannot be published, etc.

Economically, newspapers were forced to rely on the state-run, monopolistic Eastern Paper Mills Corporation for their newsprint supplies, and to favor the authorities for fear of losing important government advertising. Opposition newspapers were prohibited from using the nationalized transportation system for distribution of their issues (*Jayaweera*, 1975, pp. 3-6).

In addition, editors and reporters were fired or fined frequently and blanket censorship was imposed. For example, when public service strikes spread in January 1977, all reference to strikes and to action taken by government to maintain the services were ordered deleted from the newspapers. As a result, blank spaces appeared in newspapers (see London *Times*, 11 Jan. 1977, p. 7; 12 Jan. 1977, p. 7).

Some reaction to the stringent press policies was evident during Mrs. Bandaranaike's last months in office. In early 1977, the courts of Sri Lanka revitalized most sections of the press when a reporter was acquitted after refusing to reveal his source of information; the judge in the case stated that the newspapers do and must act as watchdogs (*Media*, May 1977, p. 27). In March, the Independent Newspapers Group was permitted to reappear after a three-year lapse, and, just before the July elections, unions of J. R. Jayewardene's United National Party successfully halted Associated Newspapers, thus denying Mrs. Bandaranaike one of her key mouthpieces at a critical time.

More recent events have some parallels with what has happened in Pakistan. In both countries in mid-1977, there was a change of government and in both instances, there were promises to re-establish the independence of the media. And both Zia in Pakistan and Jayewardene in Sri Lanka were either unwilling or unable to make a complete break with press policies set down by their predecessors (see *Jayaweera*, 1978, pp. 68-77). The *Far Eastern Economic Review* (6 Jan. 1978) commented on the Sri Lanka situation:

> In the 'liberal' regime of Junius Richard Jayewardene, where the major newspaper groups are effectively State-

owned, journalists whom the government finds 'unreliable' are being fired as unceremoniously as those the left-dominated regime of Mrs. Sirimavo Bandaranaike dismissed if they were thought unlikely to toe her line.

Probably most disconcerting is that the new government in August 1977, assumed control of the Times of Ceylon Group under provisions of the Business Acquisitions Act. Jayewardene said this action was taken on behalf of employees who were in danger of losing their jobs as creditors moved in to foreclose on the assets of the bankrupt institution.

4.1.7 Brief Summary

In nearly every one of these countries, there was, in 1979, a lull in the clashes that existed between press and government during the previous half decade. However, because not much was being done to remove restrictive legislation or economic restraints, or to change ownership patterns to reflect more private investment, it was likely that there would be periodic flare-ups between the two factions.

4.2 Afghanistan

Louis Dupree

4.2.1 Press Law

In principle, the 1964 constitution of Afghanistan provided for freedom of the press. In practice, the Press Law, promulgated in July 1965, with eight chapters and 55 articles, attempted to implement this ideal. Many criticized the law as being repressive, but it did establish a code under which a free press might have conceivably developed. In a nation which has less than 10 per cent of its people literate, newspapers have little effect in the countryside, but great impact politically on the increasingly literate urban population, particularly on the impressionable students. The Press Law tried to follow a course halfway between complete freedom of the press and close government supervision. At this stage of Afghanistan's political development (in the late 1960s), total freedom for a press that too often displayed a lack of responsible reporting might have brought on anarchy and would definitely have brought in outside influences.

The Press Law, drafted to safeguard the "fundamentals of Islam, constitutional monarchy, and other values enshrined in the Constitution," gave considerable latitude to any but the most stubborn reactionaries of either the extreme left or right. Article 5 of the law spelled out the conditions under which a periodical

Louis Dupree has lived in Afghanistan for extensive periods since 1949. He is an adjunct professor of anthropology at Pennsylvania State University, research associate of the American Museum of Natural History and an associate of the American Universities Field Staff. He is author of the book, *Afghanistan,* from which a major part of this chapter was taken, with permission.

could operate: a publisher had to make application to the Ministry of Information and Culture and offer security against future government action. The security for a daily newspaper was 15,000 afghanis, for a weekly 10,000 afghanis, and for other periodicals a lesser amount. The amount and sources of the periodical's capital had also to be listed.

The following articles from the Press Law of 1965 are those under which various papers were shut down by the government in the 1960s:

Article 1: Freedom of thought and expression is immune from any encroachment in accordance with Article 31 of the Constitution of Afghanistan.

In order to implement the said article and to take into consideration the other values of the Constitution, the provisions set forth in this law organize the method of using the right of freedom of press for the citizens of Afghanistan. The goals which this law aims to secure consist of:

(1) Preparing a proper ground over which all Afghans may express their thought by means of speech, writing, pictures or the like and may print and disseminate various matters.

(2) Safeguarding public security and order and also the interest and dignity of the State and individuals from harms which they may be subjected to by the misuse of the freedom of Press.

(3) Safeguarding the fundamentals of Islam, constitutional monarchy and the other values enshrined in the Constitution.

(4) Assisting the healthy development of a press in a way so that this organ of the society may become an effective means for dissemination of knowledge, information and culture among the people of Afghanistan as well as truthfully and usefully reflecting public opinion to the society.

Article 31: The publication of matter implying defamation of the principles of Islam or defamatory to the King of Afghanistan is not allowed.

Article 32: Incitement through the press to commit

actions, the end of which is considered an offence, will also be considered an offence. Such actions may be:

    a. Incitement to disobey the country's laws.

    b. Incitement to disrupt public security and order.

    c. Incitement to seek depravity.

Article 33: Every action which is considered an offence will also be an offence if committed through the press, such actions may be:

  (1) Disclosure of state secrets such as:

      a. Secret government or parliamentary proceedings.

      b. Secret court proceedings.

      c. Military secrets.

      d. Secrets pertaining to Afghanistan's international relations.

  (2) Incitement to seek depravity by means of:

      a. Publication of false or distorted news, in spite of the knowledge that the said news is false or distorted, provided such news causes damage to the interest or dignity of the state or individuals.

      b. Publication of obscene articles or photos which tend to debase public morals. (Publication of obscene articles or photos prejudicial to good morals.)

      c. Publication of comments and views the aim of which is to divert the courts from reaching correct decisions on cases under their security.

      d. Publication of comments and views the aim of which is to divert the public prosecutor, police, witnesses or even public opinion from the correct path over a definite case.

  (3) Defamation of persons and publication of false statements about them.

  (4) Attack upon the sanctity of the private life of individuals.

Article 34: If the publication of an item causes direct and actual disruption of the country's social health or economic life, or even deceives public opinion, the editor is required to refrain from publishing it. Such action may be:

(1) Publication of items with a view to purposely weakening the state's fiscal credit.

(2) Publication of false advertisement of medicines in spite of knowledge about them.

Article 35:   Publication of matters with a view to weakening the Afghan Army is not allowed.

Article 48:   A newspaper will close down if it does not have an editor.

4.2.2 The Press Through the 1960s

Obstacles to an indigenous free press in Afghanistan appeared almost insurmountable in the 1960s. Few Afghan businessmen believed in advertising for most of their customers could not read. Newspapers had to be financed by interested individuals, and not many appeared interested. Then, too, a shortage of competent Afghan journalists existed, even on the staffs of the government controlled press.

Among other periodicals, the Ministry of Information and Culture sponsored publication of several provincial newspapers. These papers usually parroted the line of the government dailies published in Kabul: *Anis* (*Companion*; mainly in Farsi); *Islah* (*Reform*; mainly in Pashto); *Heywad* (*Homeland;* Pashto); *The Kabul Times* (English). The role of the government-controlled press remained somewhat obscure. The government proclaimed that the press could express its opinions freely, but, although occasional editorials attacked minor points of government policy, radical departures from the government line were impossible.

Shortly after the promulgation of the Press Law in 1965, six private journals sprang into existence: *Payam-i-Emroz, Khalq, Mardum, Wahdat, Afghan Mellat* and *Masawat.*

Khalq (*The Masses or The People*) was an interesting and instructive experiment. Its liberal publisher (Nur Mohammad Taraki) and editor (Bariq Shafie, a well-known leftist poet) published six issues from 11 April to 16 May 1966, before the government clamped down on 23 May. Many Afghans considered the government decision a mistake.

Number 1 and 2 of *Khalq,* printed in a single issue, proclaimed under its red ink title that it was "the publication of the democratic voice of the people." An editorial, printed in both Persian and Pashto, divided Afghanistan's problems into four categories and set forth the policy of the paper in phrases unlike the usual patterns in modern Afghan literature.

Khalq had announced that its policy would be to alleviate "the boundless agonies of the oppressed peoples of Afghanistan." Another quotation linked the policy to international communism: "The main issue of contemporary times and the center of class struggle on a worldwide basis, which began with the Great October Socialist Revolution, is the struggle between international socialism and international imperialism." Politically, *Khalq* supported the concepts of territorial integrity, political independence and the concentration of all internal power in the hands of "the people." Economically, *Khalq* favored the public over the private sector, and demanded land reform to release the Afghan peasant from "the feudal system which dominates Afghan society." Socially, the paper demanded improvements in labor conditions and "social equality." Culturally, the editor and publisher advocated universal education and social realism in art.

The first double issue, priced at 2 afghanis, sold 20,000 copies; subsequent issues sold about 10,000. The Government Press printed *Khalq* every Monday, and secondary school and university students peddled the papers in the streets. Outcries against *Khalq* rose from many quarters, particularly among the conservative religious leaders in the *Meshrano Jirgah* (Upper House, or House of Nobles), 20 of whom demanded an investigation of the paper, and on 4 May 1966, the *Wolesi Jirgah* (Lower House, or House of the People) invited the Minister of Information and Culture and the Minister of Justice to discuss the problem. This opposition delighted the staff of *Khalq,* who played a game of semantics with their detractors. Accused of being anti-Islam, anti-monarchy and anti-constitution, *Khalq* replied in an editorial that its position was not against the principles of Islam or the fundamental rights embodied in the Constitution, and that it recognized the necessity for a monarchy "at this stage of Afghanistan's development." However, *Khalq's* stand on land reform and public over private ownership was widely held to be anti-Islamic. The Attorney General's office, under Article 1 of the Press Law, banned publication on 23 May. The staff of the paper protested the injustice of the action, for under the Press Law, *Khalq* had no recourse. It had been denied its rights to publish without a day in court, and the staff now became martyrs in the eyes of many literate Afghans.

Exactly one month after *Khalq* began publication, another weekly, *Mardum*, appeared on 11 May 1966, apparently to take on *Khalq*. *Mardum* (published by Sayyid Moqades Negah and edited by Ghulam Mahayuddin Tafwiz, both respectable, pro-constitution, pro-monarchy liberals) was against corruption, for land reform, for nationalism and against any outside influence in Afghan governmental affairs. It recommended local, evolutionary solutions to local problems; it opposed the introduction of foreign ideologies, and rejected the international application of the principles of the October Revolution. As an antidote to *Khalq, Mardum* was well received. Many Afghans hoped that *Mardum* would develop specific proposals along with its general policies, but they were disappointed.

The second paper published under the new Press Law, a Persian language weekly named *Payam-i-Emroz* (started 9 February 1966), met a fate similar to that of *Khalq*. The publisher, Ghulam Nabi Khater, edited the early issues but later hired Abdul Raouf Turkmani as editor. *Payam-i-Emroz* attacked corruption, particularly among members of the Yousuf cabinet. Turkmani also demanded more consideration of the rights of minorities. The government closed the paper on 25 May, contending that *Payam-i-Emroz* had no editor as required by the Press Law; but attacks on Prime Minister Maiwandwal's person and policies may have been partly responsible for the move. Turkmani had resigned as editor a few days before the closure, but reliable sources reported that certain governmental officials had told Khater to close down, and that he had fired Turkmani to save face.

Many self-professed "modern Afghans" heartily approved the Attorney General's actions, particularly with respect to *Khalq*: "The people in the villages," they said, "will believe anything, and the brand of communism propounded by *Khalq* would have confused them and made them doubt the New Democracy."

However, the government may have set a bad precedent in the *Khalq* decision. In addition, high officials told this author that the Afghan government knew all the ultra-left-wingers well and had complete dossiers on each of them. If this is true, there would seem to have been little advantage in forcing potentially-subversive groups underground.

As if to atone for the abrupt closure of the left-wing *Khalq,* and the shutdown of *Payam-i-Emroz* on a technicality, the government permitted a proliferation of newspapers, most of which were opposition, all printed by the Government Press. Although most newspapers were anti-government, few were really anti-Shura (bicameral Parliament).

Considering the standard of the government papers, it was to be hoped that all the papers of the free press survived; for although they were not newspapers in the sense that they published news and saved editorializing for the editorial page — indeed, they were political tracts from cover to cover — until the time when government controlled papers could present a full, not a selective, news coverage, they offered an excellent counterbalance to government pap.

Probably the most influential of these new newspapers of the 1960s were *Afghan Mellat, Masawat, Parcham (The Flag),* and before it was closed on 20 July 1968, *Shu'la-yi-Jawed (The Eternal Flame). Parcham* was leftist in orientation, but more evolutionary in outlook than revolutionary. Its rival, *Shu'la-yi-Jawed,* was more Maoist and revolutionary.

Afghan Mellat, the oldest of the non-government newspapers, had been published weekly since 5 April 1966, except for a nine-month forced closure from 2 May 1967 to 20 February 1968. Its policies could be termed anti-neo-imperialist (against capitalist foreign investment, which will "strangle the society"); anti-foreign influence (it attacked the miniskirt, the German and American Peace Corps, all influence of foreign technicians, all British influence, alcoholic beverages, the sale of American and European second-hand clothing in the bazaar, etc.); and pro-"Pushtunistan." *Afghan Mellat* went farther than any other voice in calling for a "greater Afghanistan," which, as represented on a loosely drawn map printed in the paper, covered most of the eighteenth century empire of Ahmad Shah Durrani, the last great Afghan imperialist. The paper's slogan boldly proclaimed: "We want a united, free, and democratic country. And we want Greater Afghanistan to come into existence."

The publisher and editor referred to "National Democratic Socialism" as their way of life, and to many it appeared that Engineer Ghulam Mohammad Farhad (called "Papa Ghulam"), the publisher, was striving to assume the mantle of the aging Pushtun leader, Khan Abdul Ghaffar Khan. *Afghan Mellat* defined National Democratic Socialism as constitutional monarchy, Greater Afghanistan, a democratic society, no bribery, land for the landless, the prohibition of luxury imports, no foreign loans that cannot be repaid or are not needed, a progressive income tax, the restoration of Pashto as a popular language and a free "Pushtunistan" (*Afghan Mellat*, 27 Dec. 1966).

Afghan Mellat accepted advertisements, although blatantly stating that it preferred ads for locally produced products, and it undertook such causes as attacking Western-produced films that had been dubbed in Iranian Persian. The paper also supported more important causes. It attacked government corruption and, much to the discomfort of officialdom, often gave names. But it was not until the appearance of the article "How the C.I.A. Turns Foreign Students into Traitors" (which purported to expose the involvement of high-ranking government officials with the C.I.A.) in the April 1967 issue of *Ramparts* (U.S. magazine), that Papa Ghulam really got into serious trouble. The lead article in *Afghan Mellat* for 25 April 1967, was entitled "Are Our Government Officials Spies?" and the result was that the paper was closed down for the next nine months.

Few Americans bothered to read the exposé of Abdul Latif Hotaki in *Ramparts*. However, in Afghanistan, Prime Minister Maiwandwal's government was shaken, but finally remained firm. Prime Minister Maiwandwal met the threat head-on. Along with his cabinet, he faced a barrage of probing questions in the *Wolesi Jirgah,* and he came out with as clean a bill of political health as was possible under the circumstances. His eventual resignation may have had little to do with the C.I.A. episode, however, for he was genuinely ill.

After Maiwandwal's resignation, Papa Ghulam received permission to begin republication of *Afghan Mellat*. The nationalization by Maiwandwal of the electric company, of which Papa Ghulam was president, at least partly accounted for the anti-Maiwandwal attacks in *Afghan Mellat.* Incorruptible himself, Papa Ghulam had reportedly shown favoritism in granting jobs and, according to many sources, he finally found himself surrounded by ingratiating parasites. Although a public utility, the electric company had never opened its books to either the government or the public until Maiwandwal's nationalism order. Papa Ghulam had never forgiven the former prime minister, and he often used *Afghan Mellat* as his cudgel. For example, the columnist Feda Mohammad Fedayi attacked Maiwandwal's Progressive Democratic Party (PDP) as "collective dictatorship" (*Afghan Mellat,* 27 Feb. 1967). To propagate the PDP, Maiwandwal and a group of his supporters founded the weekly *Masawat* (*Equality*) in April 1967. In December 1967, it ceased publication for a few months because of enforced government pressure after Maiwandwal's resignation; but it reopened in April 1968.

Two major leftist opposition papers, which have already been mentioned, also began publication about that time: *Parcham* on 14 March 1968, and *Shu'la-yi-Jawed* on 4 April 1968. The writers for *Parcham* included such well-known socialists as Babrak Karmal and Dr. Anahita, a woman parliamentary deputy from Kabul, serving in the twelfth session — both of whom quietened down appreciably after the December 1966 *Wolesi Jirgah* fight that put Babrak in the hospital and Dr. Anahita in an embarrassing position. In a cartoon in *Afghan Mellat* on 26 December 1966, she was portrayed upside down and being beaten by other delegates. Her thighs were pointedly exposed (Papa Ghulam often attacked the miniskirt and other "obscene" Western clothing), and the caption read: "This is the condition of the aspirations of the *Wolesi Jirgah.* Here are the deputies we chose. This is the result!" Babrak, on the other hand, reportedly turned the situation to his advantage. He had a great flare for the dramatic, and when his followers demonstrated outside the hospital, he grabbed additional bandages and energetically tied them around his head before appearing to wave feebly to the spirited crowd.

In the late 1960s, however, Babrak and *Parcham* appeared to be in agreement that a milder evolutionary approach to socialism was to be preferred to violent overthrow. *Parcham* believed that all sectors of the Afghan population could contribute to the defeat of "feudalism and imperialism" and promoted the creation of a "United Democratic Front," to work for a change *within* the constitutional system. The editors called for patriotism and "a feeling of humanity" for the outside world, and the paper constantly used such slogans as "People Are Awakening!"; "The New Year Begins, a New Year of Our Sacred Struggle!" and "Long Live the Uplift of the Hardworking Women of Our Beloved Country!"

Parcham's approach drew charges of "revisionalism" from *Shu'la-yi-Jawed*, and on 13 May 1968, in the last published issue of the paper, the editor wrote: "*Parcham* is full of false propaganda and buried up to its throat in a muddy mire of revisionism." The Afghans referred to the *Parcham* evolutionists as chup- (left) and to the *Shu'la-yi-Jawed* revolutionists as chup-i-chup (left of left). In fact, the *Shu'la-yi-Jawed* group seemed to have taken over the position of "political communists," while the followers of Babrak Karmal and Dr. Anahita and those of Mir Mohammad Siddiq Farhang (a noted liberal) may have found themselves uncomfortably occupying the same position near the center — that of the "economic socialists" (in my definition), who wished to work within the existing system to bring about change.

Before it closed (possibly without adequate justification), *Shu'la-yi-Jawed* attacked not only the semi-racist groups following the "Greater Afghanistan-Pushtunistan" ideas of Papa Ghulam's *Afghan Mellat* and the evolutionary "revisionists," but also the king and his intimate advisers. This, of course, is the real reason why the paper was closed. *Shu'la-yi-Jawed* was published by the brother (Dr. Rahim Mahmudi) and nephew (Dr. Hadi Mahmudi) of Dr. Abdur Rahman Mahmudi, the well-known Afghan leader of the "Liberal Parliament" movement of 1949-52, who was jailed in May 1952 and died a few months after his release. About a month after the paper was shut down, the government arrested both Mahmudis during the mid-June 1968 workers' strike at Jangalak.

Many statements in *Shu'la-yi-Jawed*, such as "A ruling class which suppresses its own people can never free another nation" (i.e., "Pushtunistan"), certainly did not endear the already suspect Mahmudi family to the Afghan establishment. The paper attacked both the "imperialists" (the Americans) and the "reactionaries" (the Russians) and supported national liberation movements throughout the world, implying that it would support one inside Afghanistan. "Peaceful co-existence" was condemned and even such figures as Nasser of Egypt, Nehru of India and Ne Win of Burma were described as "bureaucratic capitalists who function under the name of socialism" (*Shu'la-yi-Jawed,* 9 May 1968).

One satirical weekly, *Tarjman* (*The Interpreter*) existed in the 1960s. Its cartoons were outrageously barbed, and the entire paper made extensive use of the double-entendre for which the Persian language is famous. *Tarjman* was unlike both the heavy-handed, antagonistic leftist papers and the overly-sanitized government publications. One cartoon in *Tarjman* ably expressed the dilemma of the government over the closure of *Shu'la-yi-Jawed.* No one really wanted to take the first step (although the Minister of Information and Culture finally did), and the cartoon showed the easily identifiable figures of the Ministers of Justice and of Information and Culture in soccer dress, kicking a ball (*Shu'la-yi-Jawed*) back and forth. One says to the other: "You score the goal!" The other replies, "No, you score the goal!" The incongruity of such a situation existing within the very aggressive Afghan society proved hilarious to everyone and accurately portrayed the bind in which the government found itself.

In Afghanistan, no adequate libel laws existed and the press constantly libelled the more important public figures. In open sessions of the *Wolesi Jirgah,* and in parliamentary committees, face-to-face insults flowed in a one-way direction. Such attacks often resulted in government inaction and defeated the real purpose of free speech and a free press, especially as the accusers were not held responsible for their statements and, by their criticisms, whether true or false, could prevent necessary executive action from being taken. Thus, the very antithesis of true freedom was created.

Those responsible for censorship in the Ministry of Information and Culture sometimes tended to be too sensitive. Some would have liked to close down almost all the papers of the free press, but they did not dare to make the first move without support from some higher authority, say, the Minister or the Cabinet. Often demands from the *Wolesi Jirgah* had an effect on whether or not a newspaper published or died. The censorship of incoming foreign publications sometimes occurred, although it was rare. Exaggeratedly-zealous government censors ripped out an article from the *Economist* in 1968 which called attention to the stagnation of the economy and the relatively-poor performance of the legislative branch, and which also said that some in Afghanistan predicted the monarchy might not survive much longer.

Writing in the late 1960s, this author said: A group, which by its irresponsible opposition makes certain that no alternatives are possible in government action, can, as easily as an individual, become a "dictator." Thus, an irresponsible press, encouraged by an unprincipled (or foreign influenced) group in the *Wolesi Jirgah*, could come to seem quite menacing; indeed, it could literally force the king to dissolve Parliament and possibly even to abrogate the Constitution. If this should happen, these "Red Guards" of Afghanistan, dressed in parliamentary immunity, and their companions of the press must be held partly responsible for the King's action. If the present Afghan experiment in democracy should fail, it will probably be because of an absence of the democratic spirit in the opposition, as well as suppressive activities from the right.

Increased education and communications have not brought about that oneness of Afghanistan hoped for by the intelligentsia and the King. The racist policies of *Afghan Mellat* are but one example. Others are surfacing.

4.2.3 The Press and the 1973 Coup

The experiment in democracy *did* fail, and partly because of the reasons discussed above. Other reasons included: the failure of King Mohammad Zahir to promulgate the Political Parties Law, the Provincial Councils Law and the Municipal Councils Act, all passed by Parliament; the disillusionment of the intelligentsia with both the executive and legislative branches.

On the night of 17-18 July 1973, former Prime Minister Mohammad Daoud Khan (1953-63), first cousin and brother-in-law to the king, overthrew the monarchy with the help of military and police units loyal to his person and established the Republic of Afghanistan. The publication of free press newspapers ended with the coup. A list of the free papers still being technically published at the time of the coup (and their fates) are listed in the chart below.

CHART 1. Free Press in Afghanistan at Time of 1973 Coup

Newspaper	Comments	Last Issue (1973)
Gahiz (Dawn)	Ultra Islamic. Stopped publication when editor-publisher, Mehajuddin Gahiz was murdered, Summer 1972. Began again 12 December 1972 Publisher, Maulana Rab Ahadi Wardak; editor, Lal Mohammad Aliaskhel.	1 July
Ittehad-i-Melli (National Unity)	Establishment oriented, but relatively independent; pro-Pushtun.	2 July
Afghan	Defended minority rights; favored parliamentary democracy.	26 May
Paikar (Struggle)	Middle class ideals.	10 July
Kyber	Pro-Pushtunistan and religiously conservative.	30 June
Afkar-i-Nau (New Ideas)	Middle class ideals.	17 July
Paktika (refers to Paktya)	Establishment oriented; pro-Pushtunistan.	7 July
Payam-i-Wejdan (Voice of Conscience)	Championed rights of non-Pushtun minorities and rapproachment with Iran.	9 July
Jabhai-yi-Melli (National Front)	Pro-establishment; had previously folded for financial reasons, but came back.	24 May
Tarjman (The Interpreter)	Independent satirical weekly with cartoons. Publisher, Professor Dr. Nevin, now Minister of Information and Culture.	17 July
Nida-yi-Haq (Voice of Truth)	Religiously oriented. Previously closed for financial reasons, but came back.	14 June

Newspapers	Comments	Last Issue (1973)
Afghan Mellat (Afghan Nation)	Pro-Pushtunistan; anti-Iranian.	14 June
Rozgar (Time)	Independent, generally supported constitutional processes. Anti-Iranian.	3 January
Shokhak (Clown)	Independent satirical weekly. Often banned.	15 July
Karwan (Caravan)	Most independent paper of all. Banned. Was about to republish when coup struck.	27 July
Sitar-i-Sobh (Morning Star)	Independent. Began publishing 26 November 1972. Publisher, Professor Dr. Abdurrahim Nevin; editor, Mohammad Azim Raad (dramatist). End publication with coup.	Ceased with coup
Maihan (Homeland)	Started publishing 15 February 1973. Supported king, Islam. Publisher, Khatak Mangal; editor, Sayyid Kabir Ostowar.	Ceased with coup
Payam-i-Haq (Voice of Truth)	Supported pan-Islamic ideals of Jamal ad-din al-Afghani. Began publishing 23 October 1972.	Ceased with coup
Marefat (Wisdom)	Independent. Began publishing 21 March 1973. Publisher, Ghulam Masom Ekhtar; editor, Abdur Rahim Sheikat. Suspended 4 July 1973, when editor resigned.	4 July

By February 1975, the press was limited to official government publications, the most important being three dailies published in Kabul by the Ministry of Information and Culture: *Jamhouriat* (*The Republic,* published in Dari and Pashto, began publication on 4 August 1973), the surviving *Anis* (*Companion,* mainly Dari) and *The Kabul Times,* published in English, primarily translations of articles appearing in *Jamhouriat.* Most provincial papers continued to be published, and mainly parroted the lines articulated in *Jamhouriat.*

Behind government control of the press was the predominant belief that the people must be educated to accept the ideals of the republic. But since only 5 per cent or so of the population is literate, few got the word in the press. Radio Afghanistan was and is much more effective. The result has been that Kabul's rumor quotient rose perceptibly during the first 18 months of the republic, and the regime's opponents took advantage of the situation to spread false rumors. A free press could have helped counter the situation, and kept the increasingly important middle class informed of the facts.

Instead, these urban, literate Afghans were frustrated, much in the same way they were nine years before when the new constitution failed to produce instant democracy. Both left and right had grown disgruntled, and few had outlets of expression.

In 1974, three *Shab-nameh* (*Evening History,* a play on the title of a great epic poem by Firdausi, *Shah-Nameh,* History of the Kings, written in the eleventh century A.D.) were clandestinely published and circulated. They apparently came out of the *Khalq* group, usually identified as pro-Moscow leftists. The *Shab-nameh* criticized the regime for not living up to its avowed ideals. Publication stopped after the government arrested several accused of publishing the sheets; reportedly one was executed.

When a Revolutionary Council seized power in Afghanistan in early 1978, full-scale censorship of foreign press representatives was imposed. A London correspondent reported that foreign correspondents who were allowed in the country were harassed at every turn. Phone calls overseas had "suddenly gone dead in the middle of conversations" and, according to *IPI Report* (June 1978, p. 16), reports "sent through a single machine in the capital's public telex booth were subjected to censorship. Officials blue-pencilled such phrases as 'pro-Moscow' and replaced them with 'democratic.' " The government denied it was a pro-Moscow, Communist state, and the new head of state, Prime Minister Nur Mohammad Taraki, formerly publisher of *Khalq,* declared in a radio broadcast that these were false descriptions spread by "foreign enemies," including the foreign press. The Taraki government was overthrown in September 1979.

4.3 Bangladesh

John A. Lent

4.3.1 Background

The suspension of all Bangladesh newspapers, except four government dailies, in June 1975 should not have come as a surprise to observers of that young nation's mass media situation — unless they still believed the 1971-72 press freedom promises of Prime Minister Sheikh Mujibur Rahman. After 1973, increasing government pressures in the form of press regulations, economic sanctions, emergency decrees and finally, one-party, totalitarian rule, foretold the meager chances for the preservation of a free press in Bangladesh. What happened in Bangladesh in four short years represented one of the quickest about-faces concerning press freedom executed in Asia.

Before 26 March 1971, Bangladesh (known then as East Pakistan) was the poorer half of Pakistan. The different press problems of Pakistan after World War II were magnified in East Pakistan where resources and allocated priorities were exceptionally substandard. However, between 1947-50, enough machinery was imported to allow leading newspapers to publish separately from West Pakistan and India, e.g., *Azad* and *Morning News* moved from Calcutta to Dacca, and the Pakistan (later Bangladesh) *Observer* and *Ittefaq* were founded there in 1948 and 1955, respectively (see Table 16 for establishment dates of other newspapers). As for press freedom during this period, it was restricted by the strong man, militaristic regimes of men such as Ayub Khan and Yahya Khan. Newspapers had been licensed under the Press and Publishing Law since 1961; censorship and suspension of newspapers were frequent.

During the savage war between West and East Pakistan in 1971, the Dacca press came under severe fire. Numerous East Pakistani news people, such as those on *Ittefaq, Daily Sangbad, Observer, Daily Purbadesh, Lalani, Sheelalipi, Morning News* and Pakistan Press International, were brutally tortured and killed (*IPI Report,* March 1971, pp. 1, 4), and newspapers, such as *Ittefaq* and *The People* (both supporters of the pro-separatist Awami League), were destroyed by fire. East Pakistani journalists worked under total censorship conditions imposed on 25 March 1971, and not lifted until two months later although a *de facto* censorship remained in force even then (see *Coates,* 1972, pp. 17-25; *Mohan,* 1971, pp. 163-64; *Kutty,* 1971, pp. 165-68; *Mukherjee,* 1971, pp. 171,176).

After independence, the Bangladesh government did confiscate a few newspapers, but these acts did not warrant much criticism because of the circumstances of the takeovers. For example, when the managements of *Morning News* and *Dainik Bangla* (both owned by the Press Trust of Pakistan, a central government agency) fled or were seized in 1971, the Bangladesh authorities assumed control of the papers and appointed a director-general over them. Shortly after, the Observer Group (Bangladesh *Observer, Purbadesh* and *Chitrali,* a movie magazine) also passed into government hands. Generally, however, 1972 represented a honeymoon year in Bangladesh government-press relationships. Because of Prime Minister Sheikh Mujibur Rahman's personality and "father of the nation" image, criticism of the new government was almost non-existent. The government, in turn, assured journalists of its determination to produce a free and responsible press once numerous national problems were resolved (*IPI Report,* Feb. 1972, p. 6). The few reported cases of arrests of journalists in mid-1972 resulted more from charges of wartime collaboration with the enemy than from sensitivity to press criticism on the officials' part.

As with most newly-emergent nations, the number of dailies burgeoned in the post-liberation period (1971-73), with the birth of *Dainik Bangladesh, Andolon, Dainik Michiil, Dainik Swadhinata, Bangabarta, Banglar Bani, Ganakantha, Janapad* and *Samaj.* By 1974, at least 24 dailies (Information Minister Sheikh Abdul Aziz reported 31 dailies, 135 weeklies, 13 fortnight-

lies and 76 magazines in early 1974), 18 in Bengali and six in
English, published in Dacca, Chittagong and Bogra (*Media*, Jan.
1974, p. 26). Political party affiliation was a characteristic of
many of these newspapers. Most of the pre-independence dailies,
such as *Azadi, Azad, Observer, Dainik Bangla, Morning News,
The People, Purbadesh* and *Sangbad*, were government supporters.
The importance of the press was shown by the circulation figures
as well, with *Ittefaq* listing 80,000, *Dainik Bangla*, 55,000 and
Purbadesh, Observer and *Azad* at or near the 30,000 range. These
are relatively high circulations in a nation with only 20 per cent
literacy and very low individual purchasing power.

TABLE 16. Bangladesh Dailies, 1974

Name	Founding Date	Language	Circulation	Affiliation
Bogra:				
Dainik Bangladesh	1972	Bengali	5,000	
Chittagong:				
Andolon	1973	Bengali		
Azadi	1959	Bengali	7,000	Independent, pro-govt.
Dainik Michül	1972	Bengali	3,000	
Dainik Swadhinata	1972	Bengali	3,500	
The Eastern Examiner	1952	English	5,000	
People's View	1970	English	5,000	
Dacca:				
Azad	1936	Bengali	15-30,000	Govt. administered
Bangabarta	1973	Bengali	10,000	
Bangladesh Observer	1948	English	30-45,000	Govt. administered
Banglar Bani	1971	Bengali	14-20,000	Pro-govt.
Dainik Bangla	1964	Bengali	55,000	Govt. administered
Evening Post	1959	English	5,000	
Ganakantha	1971	Bengali	10-15,000	Opposition
Ittefaq	1955	Bengali	80,000	Indep.-often opposition
Janapad	1973	Bengali	10-15,000	Indep.-pro-Indian
Morning News	1942	English	10-15,000	Govt. administered
Nabajat	1962	Bengali	1-2,000	
The People	1969	English	2-10,000	Indep.-supports govt.
Purbadesh	1969	Bengali	30,000	Govt. administered
Samaj	1972	Bengali	15,000	
Sangbad	1950	Bengali	25,000	Supports govt.

Source: *The 1974 Asian Press and Media Directory*, Manila: Press Foundation of Asia,
1974, pp. 31-36.

Other sectors of mass media were equally developed. Three national news agencies (Bangladesh Sangbad Sangstha, Bangladesh Press International and Eastern News Agency) had been set up, and trade unions on a national (Bangladesh Federal Union of Journalists) and regional levels (in Bogra, Chittagong and Dacca) appeared in 1972, as did Bangladesh Sangbadpatra Parishad, an agency to tackle developmental problems of the press. Additionally, the state-owned Radio Bangladesh, established 26 March 1971, maintained stations in Dacca (2), Chittagong, Rajshani, Sylhet, Rangpur and Khulna, and Bangladesh Television, also government-owned, operated out of Dacca, although plans called for six satellite and three relay stations by the end of the 1970s. In 1974, 34 advertising agencies sustained offices in the country (*1974 Asian Press and Media Directory,* pp. 31-36). Furthermore, mass media's key role in Bangladesh's future was emphasized as early as January 1971, when information and broadcasting were afforded ministerial status in the government.

But the progress, both in media availability and degree of freedom, was short-lived. Already in late 1972, the sensitivities of the officials to press criticism were noticeable with the arrest and removal of senior journalists such as Abdus Salaam of *Observer* and M. A. Mannan of *Morning News,* and the threat to ban others, including *The Spokesman* and four Bengali weeklies (*Index on Censorship,* Autumn 1974, p. 79; *IPI Report,* Jan. 1973, p. 9; Oct. 1972, p. 7) for publishing "fictitious, malicious, false, baseless and motivated news." As national economic conditions worsened in 1973, and the press became more critical, the two main voices of the opposition, *Ganakantha* (organ of the National Socialist Party) and the weekly *Holiday,* were among newspapers temporarily suspended (*Index on Censorship,* Summer 1974, p. i). In October 1973, the editor of the weekly *Nayabug,* Shamshul Alam, was arrested and charged under the Press and Publicity Ordinance of the Bangladesh Penal Code with "creating disaffection towards the government" (*Index on Censorship,* Autumn 1974, p. 79). The culmination came on 19 September 1973, when the Press Ordinance of the old Pakistan regime was replaced with the Printing Presses and Publications (Declaration and Registration) Act, passed by Parliament ostensibly to regulate newspapers. In effect, the act meant that publishing of newspapers would be subject to prior approval by the government, requiring, among other items, that all publications be licensed. Newspapers not registered with the officials were denied newsprint and advertising allocations. The detailed set of rules, with matching penalties, included a maximum fine of TK 500 for failing to supply the government with four free copies of every item published. Criticizing the act, the Bangladesh Federal Union of Journalists said it was no better than that under the Pakistan government because it left major publishing decisions up to the authorities, with no provision for legal challenge (*Index on Censorship*, Spring 1974; *Media*, Jan. 1974, p. 19).

4.3.2 1974-75: Repressive Years

The list of repressive legislation augmented in 1974, with the passage by Parliament on 5 February of the Special Powers Bill, the Newsprint Control Order on 9 July and the declaration of a national state of emergency on 29 December. Under the Special Powers Bill, it became an offense punishable by a maximum of five years' imprisonment and/or fine to "print, publish or distribute prejudicial reports." The bill made identification of all news sources obligatory and gave the authorities the right to seize documents and newspapers, ban newspapers and other publications and to search premises on the assumption they might find a document which could be classified as harmful. Pre-censorship was put into effect for all questions of state security, friendly relations of Bangladesh with other nations and national·security (*Index on Censorship*, Autumn 1974, p. i; *IPI Report*, Jan. 1975, pp. 18-19).

Imposition of the Newsprint Control Order was carried out through the Commerce and Foreign Trade Ministry with the Ministry of Information and Broadcasting entrusted with implementation. Basically, it meant that newsprint could only be used with government permission. In its statement on the regulation, the Ministry of Information and Broadcasting stated:

> The newspaper establishment shall have to submit to the Ministry of Information and Broadcasting, statements and returns as may be asked for, and the Government may authorize an officer to inspect or seize

documents as deemed necessary and also to collect relevant information from any person. All persons other than a producer (newsprint mill) and having in his possession any newsprint shall . within 30 days of commencement of the order submit to the Government a return showing the stock of newsprint held by him and no newsprint shall be transferred or otherwise disposed of except in such manner as the government may direct (*Data for Decision,* 5-11 Aug. 1974, p. 2141; see *Media,* Oct. 1974).

Explaining the need for the order, the prime minister said that if Bangladesh was to meet its export commitments, it must cut down on internal newsprint consumption. Before liberation, East Pakistan produced as much as 40,000 tons of newsprint yearly, enough to supply East and West Pakistan, as well as to meet export quotas. But since 1972, Bangladesh had only produced 26,000 tons. Reports in 1974 showed that the Khulna Newsprint Mills incurred a loss of TK 14.6 million (US$2 million) in 1972-73; Bangladesh Paper and Board Corporation, losses of TK 28.7 million (US$3.93 million) in 1973-74 and TK 33.5 million (US$4.58 million) in 1972-73. To increase production, the government planned two new paper mills by 1975 (*Data for Decision,* 29 July-4 Aug. 1974, p. 2118; 3-9 July 1974, p. 1928; 15-21 April 1974, p. 1766; 18-24 March 1974, p. 1675).

Journalists agreed that internal consumption had to be reduced; they disagreed, however, on the size of the cut. They feared a number of them would lose their jobs as newspaper sizes and staffs were trimmed, but more importantly, they thought the order might serve as a political weapon to stifle the independent opposition press which stood to suffer the most (*Media,* Oct. 1974). On 10 August, the Bangladesh National Editors Association (Jatiyo Sampadak Parishad) decided to cooperate by reducing newspapers to six pages daily and eight on Sunday; the Bangladesh Newspapers Association (Sangbadpatra Parishad), however, expressed concern for the newspapers without newsprint allocation which were forced to purchase on the open market (*Data for Decision,* 5-11 Aug. 1974, p. 2140).

As the government failed to check spiralling prices, revive the economy and stop corruption, rumors spread in 1974 that the parliamentary system would be junked (*Far Eastern Economic Review*, 22 July 1974, p. 22). The first stage of this development occurred when a state of emergency was declared in December, after a series of demonstrations throughout 1974. The same prime minister who had guaranteed citizen rights under the constitution three years previously now suspended them — including the right to petition the court for enforcement of fundamental rights. Activities of parties, trade unions and other associations could also be outlawed and the death penalty imposed on those associated with such organizations. The government also reserved for itself the right to make orders against "the spread of false reports or the prosecution of any purpose likely to cause disaffection or alarm, or to prejudice relations with any foreign power" (*Index on Censorship*, Summer 1975, p. 85).

Still other 1974 events which tightened the reins on the Bangladesh press included Sheikh Mujibur Rahman's reshuffling of his cabinet on 8 July, assuming five portfolios for himself, including that of information and broadcasting (*Asia 1975 Yearbook*, p. 39); the appearance of the pro-government Bangladesh *Times* with a nephew of the prime minister, Sheikh Fazlul Huq Moni, as owner-editor; an official campaign against bad news about Bangladesh in the foreign press; the development of a wage board for newspaper employees, and continued harassment of political opponents. From the time of the war for independence, Bangladesh had enjoyed a cordial relationship with the world press. But, after June 1974, the harmonic relationship showed signs of crumbling when *Newsweek*, London *Times, Daily Telegraph, The Spectator* and *Far Eastern Economic Review*, among others, carried unfavorable articles about the nation's independence dream. The authorities reacted by banning issues of these periodicals (although they were still circulated surreptitiously through typed copies and photo duplicates) and inaugurating a "down with the Western press" drive (*Far Eastern Economic Review*, 11 Oct. 1974, pp. 21-22).

The parliamentary action on a national wage board for newspaper employees, thus having a controlling influence of journalists' livelihoods, was resisted on 25 October, when newspaper and news agency employees observed a six-hour token strike to press for an interim relief from the board (*Indian Press*, Nov. 1974, p. 63;

see *Media,* March 1974, p. 23). Finally, during 1974, the prime minister stepped up his retaliatory actions against his political opponents. On 17 March, Al Malmud, editor of *Ganakantha,* was arrested for publishing seditious material (*Index on Censorship,* Autumn 1974, p. i); in May, the director of *Nayajug* was arrested for inciting readers against the government (*IPI Report,* Jan. 1975, pp. 18-19); and on 30 June, police raided the offices of *Ganakantha* and seized all copies of the July 1 edition (*Far Eastern Economic Review,* 22 July, p. 22).

As 1975 dawned, Sheikh Mujibur Rahman moved swiftly toward totalitarian control. On 26 January, parliamentary rule was abandoned as he gave up the title of prime minister and assumed absolute powers as president. Simultaneously, attacks on press freedom increased on the grounds that freedom had been abused to harm Dacca's international relations. The first newspaper to be closed was *Ganakantha.* Official pressure gained after Bangladesh was declared a one-party state (Krishak Sramik Awami League, or Peasants, Labourers and Peoples League) on 24 February, all other political organizations being banned. The rationale for a one-party state was that it would promote the fundamental principles of state policy — namely, nationalism, socialism, democracy and secularism (London *Times,* 26 Feb. 1975, p. 7). Shortly after, when a left-wing political weekly was closed and its editor arrested, the entire press capitulated, with editors meeting with Sheikh Mujibur Rahman to pledge their allegiance to him. According to the London *Times,* 600 journalists applied for party membership in spring 1975 (London *Times,* 25 June 1975, p. 6).

The eventual demise of a large portion of the nation's press was expected as early as 16 March, when the information and broadcasting ministry hinted that limiting the number of newspapers and news agencies was under consideration because a developing nation such as Bangladesh could not afford that many media outlets (*Indian Press,* May 1975, p. 50). The final axe fell in mid-June when all but four of the Bangladesh dailies were closed, these four being the already government-owned *Observer* and *Dainik Bangla* and the previously privately-owned *Bangladesh Times* and *Ittefaq,* both taken over by the authorities to serve as organs of the national political party. *Ittefaq*'s editor before the government takeover, Anwar Hossain, was made a member of the 115-man central committee of the nation's only political party in June 1975; the editor and owner of the *Bangladesh Times,* Sheikh Fazlul Huq Moni, was named a member of the 15-man executive committee of the party. More than 20 privately-owned dailies and many political weeklies were suspended, while non-political weeklies were not affected. Two news agencies — Eastern News Agency and Bangladesh Sangbad Sangstha — were allowed to continue operating. The 122 periodicals allowed to continue were mostly official organs of government departments, nationalized industries, semi-government organizations and foreign embassies in Dacca. The two most critical periodicals, *Holiday* and *Wave,* were not approved (*Majlis,* 1975). The government made plans to initiate additional dailies, under its auspices, in Chittagong, Khulna and Rajshahi. The London *Times* reported that compensation would be paid shareholders of the privately-owned papers that were confiscated, and that journalists would not go unemployed, as long as they were ready to go into rural areas to spread the message of the second revolution of Sheikh Mujibur Rahman (London *Times,* 25 June 1975, p. 6).

Simultaneously with the withdrawal of licenses to publish, the government also promulgated the "Government-Owned Newspapers Management 1975 Ordinance," a clause which stated that "all officers and employees of dissolved companies (newspaper) shall stand transferred to the government."

Thus, in four years, the press of Bangladesh had gone full cycle — from privately-owned authoritarian, to libertarian to government-owned authoritarian stages of political development.

4.3.3 Promises of Press Freedom

The enslaved, all-but-eliminated press was partly freed and rebuilt under the first two governments that succeeded Sheikh Mujibur Rahman. Suspended newspapers were allowed to resume; government spokesmen went to the podium numerous times to guarantee a more liberal stance towards the media, and committees and councils were proposed and developed to aid newspapers and journalists. Although all of the repressive publishing laws remained, media personnel generally believed by 1976 that the government was sincere in its pronouncements for press freedom, and granted that the rebuilding process would be slow, because the former government had taken the press to such low depths.

When the Mujibur Rahman government was overthrown by an army coup in August 1975, the new president, Khandaker Mushtaq Ahmed, declared a state of martial law, but announced that the constitution remained in force. Immediately after the coup, nearly all news from Dacca was blacked out (see *Ved,* 1975, p. 265). When communications were restored, the new government refused to transmit reports of foreign correspondents unless they were checked by government censors. On 22 August, the new regime announced that all Western journalists were to be expelled (London *Times,* 22 Aug. 1975, p. 4). Local media and journalists were treated more favorably. Within two weeks of the takeover, two dailies — *Sangbad* and *Ittefaq* — were returned to their owners and resumed publication (*Media,* Sept. 1975, p. 3); about the same time, Enayettula Khan, former editor of *Holiday* who had been imprisoned by Sheikh Mujib and released by him shortly before the coup, was named editor of the government operated *Bangladesh Times.* The *Times,* the nation's largest English-language daily, was previously owned and edited by Sheikh Mujib's nephew, one of the first to be killed in the coup.

By mid-September 1975, the nation was still closed to Western correspondents, but Mushtaq Ahmed had moved to restore, in his words, "an atmosphere of democracy," offering more independence to the press. In a 15 October speech, he asserted his belief in freedom of the press, but, within two weeks, he too was a victim of a coup.

The second military move in three months — a counter coup in the early hours of 3 November — left mass media temporarily silent again. On 6 November, Chief Justice Abu Mohammed Sayem, after being sworn in as president, broadcast that the Parliament and Council of Ministers were abolished and that the nation would be administered by a martial law council of 10 members. Sayem was made the chief martial law administrator; he was assisted by three deputy martial law administrators; one of whom, Army Chief of Staff Major General Ziaur Rahman, was given a number of portfolios, including that of the Ministry of Information and Broadcasting.

The martial law administrators made initial steps towards a liberalization of government-press relationships. *Holiday* (6 March 1976) reported the government was anxious to do something for the journalists, having formed or reconstituted a number of committees affecting media personnel, such as a management board, quality of newspaper improvement committee and a wage board. According to *Holiday*, "Press freedom is reiterated every now and then. There is no doubt that the government has every goodwill and good wishes for solving the problem of the press and the pressmen." Addressing the National Press Club in Dacca on 26 February 1976, Major General Ziaur Rahman asserted the government's commitment to a free press, saying, "We also believe that the freedom of the press would help in the maintenance of law and order in the country, in firmly establishing unity and also in accelerating the country's progress" (*Holiday*, 29 Feb. 1976).

A number of obstacles stood in the way of this liberalization process. For instance, despite the government's seemingly good intentions, "a super-editorial board" was working, as in the past, on the government-controlled newspapers. Although the authorities took steps to allow annulled newspapers to reappear, there hung over the heads of journalists the repressive Press Ordinance and Annulment Ordinance, which has yet to be repealed. Also, the government announced that any newspaper that wanted to publish could do so without hindrance; the difficulty, however, was that one half of the unemployed journalists were formerly associated with government-managed dailies. As *Holiday* (29 Feb. 1976) pointed out, the government had to show the way by re-establishing these journalists in the profession. The government paid TK200,000 to former employees of annulled newspapers, and efforts were made to provide some newsmen of these defunct dailies with employment in other government and autonomous agencies. The officials pointed out that they could not do much more, because the two government-owned dailies operated at financial losses and further deficits could not be endured by hiring more personnel.

As more newspapers were allowed to reappear, certain measures, construed by Dacca journalists as bureaucratic interference in their affairs, were taken. For example, as *Holiday* reported on 29 February 1976, a government committee was to be formed "for increasing circulations of newspapers, which, on the face of it, should be the concern and business of the newspaper managements themselves." *Holiday* added that "freedom is not something that can be given by one hand and taken away by the other."

In other actions, the government established a Press Commission, designed to review the infrastructure of the press, which was expected to make its report within a year. The authorities set up a Press Institute to train journalists (*Media,* Aug. 1976, p. 17), and at least one publication (*Holiday,* 7 March 1976) called for the creation of a Press Council, modelled on West European prototypes to act as an ombudsman.

By 1977-78, the press was still under the strong control of the government. Custers, who himself was held for nine months without trial in Bangladesh, reported that general censorship of all news existed and that any criticism of the martial law administration was punishable. He said a number of journalists were still held as political prisoners, among them editors and journalists of *Wave, Desh Bangla, Ganakantha* and *Ittefaq* (*Custers,* 1977, p. 8). On 16 May 1978, 22 journalists were injured and 23 others arrested when police broke up a peaceful demonstration they were staging in Dacca, demanding the restoration of freedom of the press. Reports later said all were released after protests from local colleagues.

4.3.4 The Press in 1979

As the 1980s dawned, Dacca remained the chief publishing center, although other publications appeared from Chittagong. About 336 newspapers and journals were published in Bangladesh, 34 of which were dailies and 135, weeklies. All newspapers were privately-owned, except for four dailies and three weeklies. (The 1975 law which closed all privately-owned papers was repealed in 1976.) The leading dailies, in Bengali and English, usually had eight to 10 pages and sold for the equivalent of US5 cents. Generally, contents of the Bengali press were more colorful, lively and locally oriented than English language papers which carried more international news. Although the English language press had constituted about one-third of the total dailies and weeklies in the mid-1970s, this was probably a crest, as more people turned to Bengali and as equipment, such as typewriters, has been adapted to that language.

By 1979, the Press Institute, Press Council and Press Consultative Committee were functioning, as were the two chief news agencies, Bangladesh Sangbad Sangstha (BSS) and Eastern News Agency. BSS published a weekly news bulletin highlighting events in the country, which was sent to 20 foreign nations, as well as performing its main function of screening and transmitting news from Associated Press, United Press International, Reuters and Agence France Presse. The domestic news agencies were hampered by a lack of capital resources and adequate transmission facilities to send news externally (*Sobhan,* 1979).

The newsprint industry was expanded and modernized after the mid-1970s. Under the First Five Year Plan (1973-78), it was proposed that the Khulna Newsprint Mills be modernized to attain a production of 63,000 tons annually, which was to satisfy Bangladesh's wants and allow a surplus for export. Also, in the mid-1970s, another newsprint mill (Sylhet Pulp and Paper Mills) was established at Chhatak, expected to produce 15,000 tons of pulp annually. The Newsprint Control Order, imposed in August 1974, had been repealed in April 1975, partly because production, coupled with low internal consumption and stagnant exports, had caused a glut. A newsprint oversupply had backed up, with Khulna Newsprint Mills in 1975 having a backlog of 11,000 tons, with a daily pile-up of 110 tons (*Holiday,* 20 April 1975). Certainly Bangladesh, unlike most of its neighbors, did not have a problem of shortage of newsprint.

However, other problems remained in the late 1970s. Equipment was very expensive, and newspapers, operating very marginally, had difficulties making ends meet. Many could not afford to subscribe to even one of the Bangladesh news agencies. As indicated elsewhere, laws remained that kept the press in a cautious mood. For example, editors made sure that nothing was printed that contained "adverse, critical, unfriendly, or derogatory reference" to countries with which Bangladesh maintains friendly relationships: vigilance was practiced that "none is harmed or injustice is done to the topic itself," and that credibility is retained. Editors watched for character assassination, personal vilification or slander of the head of state or contempt of court, and avoided foreign news in the "nature of polemics among nations or likely to create great controversy" (*Sobhan,* 1979).

4.4 India[*]

K. E. Eapen

Any meaningful discussion on the newspaper situation in India cannot ignore the country's size, historical background and cultural diversities. The fact that dailies appear in 20 languages, including the ancient Sanskrit, and periodicals in some 60, itself displays a press dimension not seen elsewhere.

India's present population is over 602 million, to which over a million are added every month. Usually classified as an illiterate nation, its literate population is in the neighborhood of the entire United States population. India harbors more diversities than the continents of Africa and the Americas put together. The mammoth and heterogeneous nature of the Indian subcontinent is a formidable constraint to a thorough discussion of its press problems in a few pages. The press in Kashmir in the North has little similarity with the Kerala press in the South, and to cover both of them in one sweep amounts to an over-generalization

---

* This chapter is not in lieu of what appeared before in *The Asian Newspapers' Reluctant Revolution,* edited by *John A. Lent.* The author is indebted to Roland Wolseley's chapter in that book, from which some paragraphs have been included here. Substantial information was also extracted from the *Report of the Fact Finding Committee on Newspaper Economics,* January 1975. Also, I have received considerable help from my colleague, B. A. Sridhara. It is recommended that the chapters by Wolseley and Eapen in the Lent book be consulted for historical information. For current discussion, three Delhi journals will be of help: *Communicator, Indian Press* and *Vidura.*

K. E. Eapen is professor and head of journalism at Kerala University, Trivandrum. He formerly headed the Department of Communication at Bangalore, and has been a journalist in the United States and India.

fraught with dangers. The notion of an "Indian press" itself is a dubious one.

4.4.1 Brief History

During much of its existence, the Indian press was essentially a political and propaganda tool. Only in recent years has it tended to settle down to the usual functions of newspapers; still, its main thrust is politics.

The first Indian newspaper was James Augustus Hicky's *Bengal Gazette or Calcutta General Advertiser,* which appeared in 1780, nearly 80 years before *Batavia Shimbun,* considered Japan's first newspaper in 1861. In contrast, one Japanese daily today, *Asahi Shimbun,* with its 10 million circulation, exceeds the entire circulation of all Indian dailies.

The first non-English language publication in India was in Persian — Raja Ram Mohun Roy's *Mirat-ul-Akbar,* issued about 1821. *Bombay Samachar,* in Gujarati, started as a weekly from Bombay in 1822 and converted to a daily in 1855, is the oldest existing daily. Some 20 Indian publications are over 100 years old, 11 of which are periodicals. The oldest continuing periodical is *Calcutta Review,* an English monthly started in 1844. Of the 13,320 publications today, over 92 per cent commenced publication after attainment of independence in 1947.

By 1937, only three dailies remained in British hands: *Times of India, Statesman* and the *Civil and Military Gazette.* Today, there is none. This is in contrast to the foreign investment in the press of many independent Third World countries. The *Times* appears from Ahmedabad, Bombay and Delhi, and *Statesman* from Calcutta and Delhi. The *Gazette,* Lahore, bought by a Pakistani industrialist soon after partition, ceased publication in 1964 (for more on history, see *Wolseley* in *Lent,* 1971).

4.4.2 The Present Scene

By 1976, the date of the most recent annual report of the *Registrar of Newspapers in India,* there were 13,320 newspapers in the country, compared to 12,423 in 1975 (7.2 per cent increase). Of these, 875 were dailies, compared to 835 the previous year. However, one must view with caution figures on the number of dailies. For example, the *Report of the Fact-Finding Committee on Newspaper Economics (RFCNE)*, in its survey of newspapers in 1975, showed that its communications to dailies sometimes came back undelivered with such postal remarks as "left," "press always closed," "locked," "refused" and "is not functioning." After eliminating these and other cases where circulation figures and annual reports had not been received by the Press Registrar's Office, and which had also not applied for newsprint allocation, only 534 dailies remained to be studied by the committee.

The annual report of the *Registrar of Newspapers* for 1976 painted a somewhat gloomy picture for the press, some of the gloominess attributable to the emergency that engulfed the country that year. For example, total circulation of dailies was 9,338,000, compared to 9,383,000 the previous year, and the number of small newspapers, which accounted for 53.9 per cent of all newspapers, also fell from 7,567 in 1975 to 7,188 a year later. Their total circulation was down from 15,608,000 to 14,862,000.

The report showed that Hindi newspapers increased in numbers and circulation, a trend perceivable for about a decade. In 1976, there were 3,289 Hindi newspapers (3,142 in 1975), yet, their share of the total of all newspapers fell from 25.3 per cent in 1975, to 24.7 per cent in 1976. Hindi continued to be the language with the largest number of newspapers overall and also the number of dailies (279). English newspapers claimed 20.8 per cent of the total (2,765), and there were 84 dailies in that language, compared to 100 in Urdu, 103 in Marathi and 93 in Malayalam.

English language newspapers continued to lead in circulation with a total of 7,828,000, followed closely by those in Hindi, 7,738,000. Other languages claiming at least a million circulation were Tamil, Malayalam, Gujarati, Marathi, Urdu, Bengali, Telugu and Kannada. Newspapers were published in 42 other languages (*Indian Press*, April 1979, p. 27). Another report stated that newspaper circulations soared after the 1977 elections, but specific data were not available (*Media*, March 1977).

4.4.3 Advertising

According to a 1975 national survey, India has about 350 advertising agencies with a total staff of 9,000, serving 17,000 clients and handling business worth over Rs.750 million annually (at the time Rs.8 equalled US$1). Fifty-six per cent of the advertising money is allocated to newspapers and magazines. Compared to 1968 (326 agencies and business worth Rs.440 million), the billings shot up by 70 per cent by 1974, though the number of agencies rose only by 7 per cent (*IENS*, 1975).

The first advertising agency in India was B. Dattaram & Co., Bombay, started in 1905. Its name was changed in 1971 to Dattaram Advertising Pvt. Ltd. By the mid-1970s, the company handled business worth Rs.615,000 for 74 clients. The biggest agency is Hindustan Thompson Associates, Bombay, which did about Rs.51 million worth of business yearly in the mid-1970s. It started in 1929 as a branch of J. Walter Thompson. At least 14 Indian agencies have accounts exceeding Rs.10 million. One of the largest is the Directorate of Advertising and Visual Publicity (DAVP) of the Ministry of Information and Broadcasting; it ranks third in the country. DAVP handles national advertisements and caters to over 600 clients; its budget is Rs.35 million and the agency hires 870 people. In contrast, in 1945, DAVP had a budget of Rs.205,600 and a staff of 60.

The 1975 study estimated that 90 per cent of the money spent for advertising in dailies involved only 120 publications, nearly half of which were in English. Cloth and cosmetics were among the major items advertised (*IENS*, 1975).

One of the major criticisms against Indian advertisements is their lack of "Indianness," meaning there is little of local or regional identity and character. The incongruity of news photographs appearing along with that of an automobile bonnet with a buxom girl perching, her careless thighs offered for the reader's gaze, bothers sensitive critics of consumerism.

4.4.4 Circulation

As pointed out earlier, one of the pecularities of the press of India is the many languages in which newspapers appear. Hindi, spoken by about 30 per cent of the population, in 1973 accounted for only 18 per cent of the total circulation, whereas Malayalam dailies accounted for nearly 12 per cent, though that language is spoken by only 4 per cent of the population.

Readers of the language press are, by and large, less educated than their English counterparts. Yet, many of the Indian language journalists continue to write in a literary jargon far above the understanding level of the majority of literates, some 200 million people.

Some scholars have tended to relate circulation to urbanization, literacy and income, but this generalization has not been borne out in the Indian situation. In Kerala State, for example, where Malayalam is the mother tongue, about 51 copies circulate per thousand population. Though the state is highly literate, it ranks very low on urbanization and income variables. In the Hindi belt, which sends the largest linguistic group to the national Parliament, the daily circulation per thousand has been under 11. Except for Assamese, Hindi has showed the highest percentage of increase as a newspaper language during the period, 1963-73. Of the 22 states/union territories, Kerala was surpassed in circulation per 1,000 population in 1973 only by the union territories of Chandigarh (383/1,000) and Delhi (207/1,000).

Later, in 1976, the big newspapers (50,000 and above) claimed 38.1 per cent of the total circulation. The share of the medium category (15-50,000) was 18.3, down from 19.1 in 1975, and of the small (below 15,000), 43.6 per cent, down from 46.1 in 1975.

In terms of dispersion in the early to mid-1970s, the metropolitan cities of Bombay, Calcutta, Delhi and Madras consumed four out of 10 copies, while other state capitals took a little over 18 per cent, and cities with a population of over 100,000 (excluding metropolitan cities and state capitals), over 30 per cent. The share of the rest of the country was a mere 11 per cent. If the state of Kerala were removed from the circulation scene, the spread was very thin at the grassroots level — not even one copy on the average for each of the 567,169 villages where 80 per cent of the people live.

Though the share in the circulation of dailies in towns with a population of less than 100,000 (divisional headquarters, district towns, *taluq* centers and hubs of village clusters)[1] is on the increase, the day is still far off when rural Indians can be reached directly by the printed medium, except for isolated cases such as that of Kerala. Whereas tiny Kerala has a dozen publishing points, huge states such as Bihar, Bengal and Orissa have dailies coming out of only one center each.

In comparison, in 1967, the percentage of total circulation of metropolitan dailies within the metropolis was 47.6 per cent; in 1973, it was 55.8 per cent. Whereas the percentage share in total daily circulation of metropolitan dailies was 46.5 per cent and 39.1 per cent, respectively, for 1967 and 1973, comparative figures for non-metropolitan dailies were 53.5 and 60.9.

4.4.5 Economics

The Press Commission in its report of 1954 worked out a breakdown of items which went into the cost of production of a newspaper; the cost of materials was highlighted as a significant factor. Newsprint was the main cost incurred. The commission studied 127 newspapers in 1951. It found that 18 had more than 60 per cent of their total income from advertisements. The estimated circulation of newspapers in 1951 (330 dailies) was 2.5 million and the average price per copy, 16 paise (Rs.1 equals 100 paise). At the time of the study, the price of imported newsprint was less than Rs.1,000 per ton, compared to Rs.3,500-4,000 in 1974. There was no indigenous production of newsprint then; by 1974, Indian-manufactured paper cost Rs.2,300 per ton.

In the Indian situation, the ideal proportion of news copy to advertisement is often mentioned as 60:40. Because of the complex linguistic mosaic which makes up the Indian press, some dailies use only 10 per cent of the total space for advertisements, while others use 65-70 per cent.

Large circulations normally should attract more advertisements. However, newspapers in English and the Indian languages, with the same circulations, do not attract the same amount of advertising.

---

1   India is divided into states and union territories. They, in turn, have divisions, districts, *taluqs, tahsils* and villages. Thus, a *taluq* is a sub-division of an Indian district comprising *tahsils.*

According to the *RFCNE,* more than 90 per cent of the production costs of dailies were shared by salaries/wages and cost of distribution/sale. In 1972, the newsprint component was estimated to be 35 per cent of the total cost, and more recently, even 40 per cent. A daily of standard size (2,500 sq. cms. and 10 pages), on the average, costs 33 paise to produce. The profit margin, then, is 3.3 paise per copy.

4.4.6 *Freedom of the Press*

It is customary for some of the Indian editors and assorted other leaders to get together, especially during summer months, at a hill station and talk about the state of the freedom of the press. These cliché-ridden speeches rarely reveal anything new, because freedom cannot be preserved through legal quibbling. Freedom of the press is not necessarily the articles of the constitution or relevant laws of the country, but rather the operational aspects.

This is where the quality of the man matters, whether he has to confront the advertiser, the proprietor or the government. Freedom has to be exercised by those who want to exercise it. The concept cannot be isolated from the perceptions of journalists as to their role and notion of freedom. Before Indian independence, these points were clear. They are not today. Freedom often gets equated with that of the proprietor, rather than of those responsible for the news and views disseminated. Thus, it is an institutional freedom.

Press barons in the West have their main business usually in printing; in India, this often appears to be incidental. The all-pervasive permit-quota system has its social impact. Because many of the leading dailies are owned by industrial houses, proprietor motives are more profit-oriented than service-oriented. They seem to do little to hamper their interests, and many skeletons are hidden in their cupboards. The government is aware of this but armchair summer discussions alone are unlikely to change the situation.

Sometimes, papers are started to seek government advertisements. Here, the outcome is obvious. This kind of patronage seldom comes from the central government. Government advertising is constantly under debate, yet, one hardly hears a whimper about commercial advertising. That corporate advertisers influence the press is known to the discerning and to those involved in the day-to-day production of newspapers, but the public is never made aware of this. What the reader gets is the criticism, deserving that it is, of the public sector undertakings and the government.

It is difficult to accept the opinion actively pushed by interested quarters that the government is anti-press. Until the Emergency, there was nothing in Indian press-government relationships to match former Vice President Spiro Agnew's vituperations against the U.S. press. An Indian has to travel through his neighboring countries, whether it be developed Singapore or underdeveloped Indonesia, to appreciate the freedom of the Indian situation. In the mid-1970s, that Prime Minister Indira Gandhi's election was being contested and widely reported, that Morarji Desai's Gujarat fast got top and continuous coverage (despite the fact that while chief minister of Bombay State, he had denied advertisements to the *Times of India* for criticizing some of his policies), that the Jaya Prakash Narayan movement received extra treatment despite the newsprint situation, etc., indicate that basically the Indian press has been free, though it has not always acted independently. Individual ministers (especially at the state level), and states such as Bihar, Haryana and the Punjab, have occasionally tried to tread on press freedom; this intolerant behavior, however, should not be equated with that of a government out to gag the Indian press.

4.4.7 *Press Laws*

Historically, the press of India has been in conflict with government; complete peace is unlikely to exist between the two. The disputes in the mid-1970s were of a different order, mostly over newsprint quotas, threats of ownership dispersion and restrictive emergency legislation.

During most of the years under British rule, proprietors suffered from crippling restrictions on freedom of expression; in the years when the fight for independence was at its hottest, the press was handcuffed. In an effort to avoid government interference and to regulate itself, the Indian press, after many years of consideration of the Press Commission Report of 1954, finally acquired a Press Council in July 1966. During its existence, the Council has been hampered by many problems and functionally has been ineffective. The Press Council has no mandatory powers to enforce its decisions. The mechanism of censure and publicity accompanying it — whether it be the press or the government — is an embarrassment and, thus, has a salutary effect. Some of its decisions have led to corrective steps.

Should the Council have statutory powers to enforce decisions? Some argue for putting teeth into the Council because they recognize the limitations of a moral-guardian or conscience-keeper role. Proposals were brought before the summer 1975 session of the Indian Parliament to revamp the Press Council in terms of its membership and powers, but it will be some time before action is taken.

4.4.8 Ownership

Whether it emanates from the two-decade-old *Press Commission Report* or the 1975 *Report of the Fact-Finding Committee on Newspaper Economics,* the fact that there is something rotten in the state of ownership of newspapers clearly comes through. Surprisingly, a press which debates nearly every possible issue has generally shied away from discussing its own problems of performance *vis-à-vis* ownership and control. It is not only the press; the public also has been quiet on these matters, leaving them to be tackled by journalists, proprietors and the government.

Though individual ownership accounted for over 62 per cent of the dailies in 1973, its share of the circulation was less than 16 per cent. Private limited and public limited companies with only 21 per cent of the ownership claimed almost 62 per cent of the total circulation.

Common ownership units (described as chains, groups and multiple units) own a large number of dailies. (In the Indian context, common ownership is defined as "a newspaper establishment owning two or more news-interest papers, at least one of which is a daily.") There has been a steady increase in their numbers, in the number of dailies they own, and in their circulation.

TABLE 17. Ownership Patterns of Indian Dailies, 1967 and 1973
(Figures within parentheses indicate percentage of total)

Form of Ownership	Number	
	1973	1967
Individual	516 (62.2)	322 (56.5)
Joint Stock Company	143 (17.2)	116 (19.7)
Firm and Partnership	99 (11.9)	82 (13.9)
Trust	32 (3.9)	18 (3.1)
Society/Association	29 (3.5)	31 (5.3)
Political Parties	10 (1.2)	8 (1.3)
Government (Central & State)	1 (0.1)	1 (0.2)
	830 (100.0)	588 (100.0)

TABLE 18. Number of Indian Common Ownership Units and
Number and Circulation of Dailies Owned by Them,
1967-73

Year	No. of Common Ownership Units	No. of Dailies	Circulation (in thousands)
1973	93	206	6,692
1972	95	211	6,430
1971	98	217	6,794
1970	72	182	6,069
1969	65	170	5,499
1968	64	165	4,988
1967	62	142	4,966

There are newspapers such as the *Times of India* and the *Statesman,* which come out of more than one publication center. In 1973, there were 36 such multi-edition dailies involving 91 editions. The *Indian Express,* then, had seven editions (Ahmedabad, Bangalore, Bombay, Delhi, Madras, Madurai and Vijayawada) with a combined circulation of 410,863. A year later, the paper added another point of publication, Ernakulam in Kerala State.

The ownership pattern of the Indian press is rendered complex not only by the various types of ownership but also the interlocking of businesses of various kinds. The *RFCNE* mentioned six kinds of interlinks:

(1) Different companies, all publishing newspapers from the same centre;

(2) Different companies, each at a different centre;

(3) Partnership or ownership units linked with joint stock companies;

(4) Some subsidiary non-newspaper companies related, however, to the general field of printing and publishing;

(5) Some subsidiary companies entirely unrelated to printing and publishing; and,

(6) Sometimes the same company publishes newspapers and undertakes non-newspaper activity.

Information brought out by this study revealed that some large newspaper concerns have diverted enormous funds for use unrelated to newspaper business. The Indian Express Group, for example, had major diversions and interlocking, as expressed by the report:

> The Indian Express Newspapers (Bombay) Pvt. Ltd. and its three subsidiaries namely, Indian Express (Madurai) Pvt. Ltd.; Andhra Prabha Pvt. Ltd. and Express Newspapers Pvt. Ltd. own jointly a firm known as Express Traders which dealt in Indian Iron shares. Indian Express (Madurai) has also a subsidiary of its own, namely, Ace Investment Co. Ltd. which have been holding the shares of National Company. The Indian Express's own relations appeared to be as follows:
>
> Indian Express Newspapers (Bombay) Ltd. owns all the shares of Indian Express (Madurai) Ltd. and of Andhra Prabha Pvt. Ltd. The three companies and Express Newspapers Pvt. Ltd. jointly own the firm of Express Traders. Ace Investment Pvt. Ltd. and Express Traders also own shares in Indian Iron and Steel Co. Ltd. Ace Investment Pvt. Ltd. also holds shares in the

National Company, Calcutta. The National Company, Calcutta, holds a large block of shares in the Indian Express (Bombay) Ltd. thus, completing the circle.

4.4.9 Newsprint

India's per capita newsprint consumption has been one of the lowest in the world — in the mid-1970s, 0.4 kilograms compared to 28.5 in Great Britain and 44.7 in the United States. While India normally imports only 5 per cent of its food, and two-thirds of its oil, nearly 85 per cent of its newsprint needs are met from imports.

The newsprint crisis of 1973-74 — which affected many parts of the world — gave rise to considerable turmoil in India. Dailies which averaged 12-16 pages during the decade before offered only six to eight pages during that time. In addition, they raised the prices and imposed higher advertising tariffs to stay in existence.

The government has been blamed for not taking steps to avert the newsprint crisis. Many of the licenses or letters of intent issued since the 1950s for newsprint production by the private sector, however, have remained unused. Some major newspaper owners are in every conceivable business, ranging from jute to liquor, automobiles and seed production, but not in newsprint manufacture. Yet, India is not scarce in bamboo, conifers, hardwoods and other materials necessary for pulp to make paper. Only the state-owned NEPA mills make newsprint, which in 1974, supplied about one-sixth (40,000 tons annually) of the nation's needs. The estimated annual increase in demand for newsprint is about 6 per cent, and the projected requirements for 1978-79 were in the neighborhood of 400,000 tons, the amount used by a New York daily in a year. It is evident that if newsprint production and consumption is an index of modernization, India ranks very low.

Despite the continuing crisis in India, little attention has been paid to tight copy-editing and other editorial experiments, such as cutting down on court and sports coverage and use of pictures, trying out new headline types and boiling down verbose speech stories. There have been vague debates on recycling wastepaper by de-inking, without realizing its economic and social implications. Even the metropolitan cities cannot yield daily sufficient quantities of printed wastepaper to keep a plant economically feasible. Wastepaper is the main packaging material in India and even long before World War II, the country had been importing large quantities of old British newspapers for this purpose. If a kilogram of old newspaper costs about Rs.3, it only proves its persistent demand for purposes other than recycling.

The mid-1975 price of large English dailies (10-12 pages) such as the *Hindu* and *Times of India* was 40 paise (or Rs.146 yearly) in a country where the annual per capita income is only Rs.800. These, then, are elitist newspapers, only affordable by readers from upper income groups.

All the same, the disparity with a comparable situation in the United States is evident. To highlight such gaps, another example is given. The 1973 U.S. consumption of newsprint was over 10.5 million tons − 242,000 tons more than the previous year; the difference alone is approximately the total Indian annual newsprint requirement.

4.4.10 *Readership*

Both English and Indian language dailies generally supported the freedom movement years ago. That they are now the voice of the people is not true. The discerning public is critical of the press performance, but little can be done about it. Readership studies, except for marketing surveys, have been few, but their findings pointed out the obvious, viz., that the readers are mainly urban males; the wealthier and more educated prefer English to Indian language dailies; there is significant correlation between higher levels of education and newspaper reading habits; editorials are read much less than other items, etc.

The large English language dailies have been pedestrian and very similar in content. Their readers may know more about the surface of the moon than about challenges of dry land farming in Andhra Pradesh or problems of deep sea fishing in Kerala. Some of the language dailies have stopped imitating the metropolitan English newspapers and in this process have tried to reach out to the minds of their readers.

4.4.11 Training

Though training of a sort was attempted in the 1920s, and a university department of journalism started in the Punjab in 1941, journalism education has much to gain in status (see also *Vilanilam*, 1979). No Indian Pulitzer or Newhouse has come forward to help the stunted schools. Not even the University Grants Commission, which has invested vast resources in other areas of training, has done much in this regard.

About a dozen universities and a score of private agencies are in the business of education for journalism. Some of them have fallen in line with the "communication" notion for training purposes, but here also, it has been a change in label, rather than in the quality of instruction or staff pattern. Nevertheless, many hundreds have benefitted from existing programs and adorn responsible positions in the whole gamut of media operations in the country.

4.4.12 Research and Professionalization

Journalism research, like education, is one of the neglected areas of the Indian press. Sporadic studies have been done by advertising agencies and individual newspapers, but their results are not easily available in published form. Some of the journalism departments have ventured into doing surveys and collecting data, but these have been limited by lack of funds. Research is often viewed with skepticism. Statistical concepts and sampling techniques are foreign to most people in the press industry, resulting in non-use of research and research findings for improving the quality of the profession.

During a 1967-68 study of full-time journalists working in the states of Bihar and Kerala, and the cities of Bombay and Madras, a sample of 200 people rated journalism in relation to comparative value of work to society, comparative ability to buy goods and services, and comparative intellectual attainment necessary. Respondents were ranking 10 occupations on a five-point scale, from "very high" to "very low" (*Eapen*, 1969). As for "value of work to society," the journalist was ranked with the medical doctor in this study. This, perhaps, reflected the "service" belief among the journalists interviewed about their own occupations. For "intellectual attainment necessary," the journalists awarded themselves the top rank, a step ahead of university teachers. This self perception is difficult to explain, except as a self deception based on the early intellectual origins of the Indian press. Only for the comparative "value of work to society," the farmer and university teacher were given higher ratings. It is rather intriguing that a profession, which sees its intellectual and altruistic nature superior to many others, is not generally perceived the same way by the public (*Eapen*, 1969). Maybe, what this exercise meant to the journalists was an opportunity to assert self respect by distancing from their job roles.

4.4.13 Evaluation

Among the adverse criticisms made of the Indian press have been: it is too smug and too highly concentrated in the hands of a relatively few owners, lacks journalists' initiative, permits banal and ineffective writing, shows little respect for and interest in technical excellence.

An inkling into some of the inadequacies of the India press was mirrored in a letter which a British lady wrote to the *Times of India* when it switched to a new masthead in early January 1969:

It appears the *Times of India* is basically an old fashioned institution unwilling to step into the new age and afraid to experiment and innovate. Many more changes will have to take place before you can call yourself a newspaper of 1969.

India is a throbbing, pulsating, exciting country, full of problems and promises but there is little evidence of this in your columns which are heavy with government statements, political cliches and soul-killing statistics. Bombay by itself could be a newspaperman's dream and Delhi is no less interesting and lively. Yet the *Times of India's* coverage of these cities is pitifully inadequate and unimaginative.

Your national reporting is also pedestrian . . . . The news display is without a patch of brightness on most days. As for your editorials, they may be scholarly but seem to me heavily contrived . . . .

Not long after, an Indian wrote to the *Statesman:*

The Press, radio and TV in Britain told me more about my country in the year I was a student there than I could learn in half a dozen years from our own newspapers.

Following Indira Gandhi's 1969 South American tour, the *Statesman* itself wrote:

There are all types of newsmen: those who diligently work from morn til eve and produce copy and then those who rewrite a Press handout or two to register that they are working. This classification becomes more distinct when journalists travel abroad with the P.M.

The Department of Communications has supplied us with information on the number of messages the journalists accompanying the P.M. to Latin America sent. One filed only 76 words, and another 993 during the entire trip.

The pity is that the number of those who diligently work around the clock has been dwindling in India, and the 1975 situation is no improvement on that of the 1960s.

It is unfair, however, to tar every daily with the same brush. India's press is so diverse and irregular in quality, it is possible to find numerous examples of statements that point out either faults or virtues. The compliments are for the press' fortitude in surviving through the years of revolution, wars, pressures and unstable economic conditions; for its ability, at times, to serve as a checkrein on government, and its defense of many freedoms.

Rather than dwell on what is right or wrong about the Indian press, perhaps, it is more important to consider what may be ahead for it.

4.4.14 Future

India's press is rapidly becoming more commercial and increasingly dependent upon the economic order which surrounds it. If the big business stranglehold continues, opportunities for government to twist owners' arms are bound to continue. The master-servant relationship between the proprietor and the editor may crack if the B. G. Verghese (editor, *Hindustan Times*) incident[2] takes its natural course. Trusteeship type of ownership of the huge dailies now under the umbrella of large industrial houses is a possibility. *Asahi Shimbun, Le Monde* and *Milwaukee Journal,* operating from three different continents, have ownership vested mainly among those who work for them. These are models for India.

The state of the freedom of the press in India is essentially the result of the "effects of use and disuse." If the freedom is shrunk, it is primarily because of its non-use over a quarter of a century. If the Indian press has not gone the way of the press of countries where press freedom is denied, it is not because either the public or the journalists or the owners have taken special care to tend it. It just happens to survive. India's satellite is up; the nation has gone nuclear, its agricultural universities form the vanguard in the food front; it makes its own computers; almost 100 million children are in the school stream. Yet, the press seems to let all these pass by — unaffected by technology, unaware of the literate youth, untouched by the wind of social change.

What an Indian editor said over a decade ago is more valid now than it was when he said it: "We are recipients of favors which we do little to deserve. There is a wide gap between what is attainable and what we have attained." Professional inaction cannot be wished away; nor can it be explained by finding stooges in pressure groups, such as advertisers, Banias, government or political extremists. A press cannot be better than the personnel that man it. The quality of entrants and their professional orientations have to be of a different order. Unless corrective steps are taken for better recruitment and training of potential pressmen, the Indian press is likely to continue as the preserve of the intelli-

2   The management of the *Hindustan Times,* a leading English language daily from Delhi, terminated the contract of its editor, B. G. Verghese. A committee of representation of journalists belonging to the *Hindustan Times,* as well as others, took the issue to the Press Council of India. K. K. Birla, on behalf of the management of the newspaper, went to the Delhi High Court, challenging the jurisdiction of the Press Council to hear such representations. When the Press Council was abruptly dismissed in December 1975, during the Emergency, some people believed it was done to prevent it from proclaiming its findings in the Verghese case (*Irani,* 1977, p. 52).

gentsia: stagnant, stereotyped and shrunk.

If the two estranged worlds of C. P. Snow were those of the scientist and the humanist, the Indian dichotomy is that of the literate, comparatively rich and limited urbanite, and the vast multitudes awaiting the links that communications some day might provide to help them enjoy the fruits of freedom. If the press does not take steps to reduce the gap, it will be risking its survival as a free institution.

The fascinating process of change, though slow, is evident all around. It needs no soothsayer to predict that a changing interactive, social structure will not continue to stomach for long an unchanging press.

4.4.15 An Update, by John A. Lent

Although the Indian press survived 19 months of Emergency rule (see 4.1.3), it seemed that, by the end of the 1970s, not much had changed. The main topics of debate were still the heavy dependence of newspapers upon the government; identity and credibility crises, partly brought on by the role of the press during the Emergency (see 4.1.3), and shortages or expensiveness of raw materials, especially newsprint.

Journalists still blamed the government for not taking the initiative in making newspaper production an industry. The talked-about newspaper finance corporation, which would have allowed loans to newspapers, was not established by the government; customs duties levied by the government on machinery and parts (see *Gupta, 1976,* pp. 37, 39, 55) and the price of newsprint quadrupled in the 1970s and criticism of newsprint allocations continued.

There was some encouragement for publishers concerning newsprint production and allocation. By 1979, two newsprint mills (besides NEPA) were proposed for Kerala and Mysore, and some liberalization was seen in the 1978-79 allocation policy which gave concessions to small newspapers. The 1979-80 policy said newspapers could get an additional 5 per cent of newsprint over what they consumed the previous year, and could apply for an extra allotment depending on their consumption (*Indian Press,* June 1979, p. 109).

On the negative side, however, earlier government estimates that India would be self-sufficient in newsprint production had gone far awry; by 1979, the country produced only 15 per cent of the total consumption and prospects of producing more looked dim (*Narendra,* 1979, p. 103). Also discouraging to publishers was the quality of local newsprint (very rough, unbleached, uneven in grammage and quality) (*Tiwari,* 1978, p. 16), and the procedural problems of the Indian bureaucracy regarding newsprint. Some publishers still believed favoritism was practiced in issuing newsprint, suggesting that the government, under the guise of helping small papers, had set newsprint quotas low for large papers, hindering their expansion. At the same time it gave small papers more than they needed. As a result of the latter situation, some so-called newspapers had existed merely to provide their owners with a source of newsprint to sell on the black market (*Mankekar,* 1973). Others were angry at the bad planning and panic-buying of newsprint in the early 1970s by the State Trading Corporation (STC). STC had accumulated huge newsprint stocks at high prices; in 1975, in an effort to use up the surplus, the government banned newsprint imports, forcing newspapers to buy this high-priced paper. The ban was lifted in 1976, but newspapers were required until 1978 to buy 30 per cent of their supply from STC (*Anand,* 1977, pp. 19-22; see also *Indian Press,* July 1978, pp. 26-28).

Besides newsprint, many other materials necessary for newspaper production must still be imported at high prices with taxes attached to them. In an economy move in 1979, 35 leading printers and publishers called upon the government to simplify procedures for importing second-hand, rebuilt printing machinery.

In the 1970s, India made spectacular efforts to catch up in the manufacturing of graphic arts equipment. One private company produced Web offset rotary presses, in two or four colors, with press runs of 15,000 copies per hour, while the government owned letterpress machinery built by Hindustan Machine Tools of Bangalore. (*Bhattacharjee,* 1976).

Press personnel were still undertrained and underpaid as the 1970s faded. A study, for example, of sub-editors and reporters in two towns in Punjab and Madhya Pradesh in 1977, showed 86.9 per cent had no formal journalism training. The journalism education that exists is criticized by journalists and academics alike as being far from adequate (see special issue *Indian Press,* March 1979). Journalists must take second jobs or, in some cases, corruption money to survive on their meager salaries. In 1979, a starting reporter received US$100 a month; a correspondent with 11 years' experience made US$300 a month with little hope of more (*Newman,* 1979, p. 20). Because they had not received interim pay increases, *Express* workers went on strike in 1977; shortly after, all Delhi dailies closed in support of the strike.

Because of high labor and raw material costs, coupled with shortages and credit squeezes (*Jaggi,* 1976, pp. 25-26, 42), no industry in India suffers as high a mortality rate as does the newspaper industry.

4.5 Nepal

Bhola B. Rana

4.5.1 Historical Background

The history of Nepalese journalism began with the publication of *Sudha Sagar* as a monthly in 1898. Almost three years later, the government started *Gorkhapatra* as a literary weekly. It changed to a twice-weekly paper 42 years later and became a daily in 1966. Today, this government publication has expanded and is the only national newspaper in Nepal. Indeed, the very name *Gorkhapatra* has become synonymous for a newspaper.

From 1901 to 1950, *Gorkhapatra* was the only publication of any significance to appear in Nepal. The repressive family rule of the Ranas did not provide a congenial atmosphere for the development of journalism. *Gorkhapatra* itself did not start publication by embracing the highest ideals of journalism, but as a mouthpiece of the government.

The early period of Nepalese journalism was indeed very trying. Besides facing difficulties of inadequate printing facilities and finding readerships large enough to sustain the press, newspapers faced restraints and constant threats from the autocratic regime. It is not surprising, therefore, that the Nepalese population in India was among the active promoters of Nepalese journalism. The history of Nepalese journalism would be incomplete without a brief reference to periodicals such as *Gorkha Khabar Kagajo* (*Gorkha Newspaper*), published in 1901 from Darjeeling, and *Upyanayastarangini*, published three years later in Benares.

Bhola B. Rana has been editor of *Himala Bela.*

The overthrow of the Ranas in 1950 brought with it a flood of newspapers in Nepal, the tide of which has not been properly checked to this day. The pent-up enthusiasm of youth and politicians, whether for good or evil, was channelled into journalistic pursuits. As a result, every political party, social organization and individual of any standing began to publish newspapers. The lead was taken by Hridaya Chandra Singh and Kedarnath Neupane who started the weekly *Jagran.* Within 36 hours of publication, a flood of others appeared. Literary magazines of an earlier period were quickly replaced by daily and weekly newspapers.

In the first year after the overthrow of the Ranas, as many as 12 newspapers and periodicals appeared. In the next three years, publications of this type increased to about 15 yearly, continuing to the end of the 1950s. It is difficult to enumerate all the newspapers and magazines that were published, because in the later years of the 1950s, the number increased at an alarming rate. A popular joke then (and now) was that "there were more publications than readers." Most of the newspapers of the period disappeared soon after publication, because their continuance simply was not economically feasible.

On 15 December 1960, dramatic changes took place in every aspect of Nepalese life, including journalism. The late King Mahendra dissolved Parliament, banned political parties and laid the groundwork for the *panchayat* system of government. Independent newspapers unanimously supported the king, and party papers ceased publication immediately. The role of independent newspapers also diminished considerably because the degree of freedom exercised until then was no longer possible; as a result, the role of the government paper, *Gorkhapatra,* increased almost overnight. The trend of newspapers supporting political parties exists to a large extent today. Although newspapers are not owned by political parties and big industrialists, as is the case in India, they do support different political views.

The publication of the English language daily, *Rising Nepal,* in December 1965, under the editorship of Barun Shumshere Rana, was another important milestone in Nepalese journalism. This paper is the largest circulated English language publication in Nepal, mainly reflecting government opinion. Published by the Gorkhapatra Sansthan, it acts as a publicity wing of the

Ministry of Communication (for more history, see *Lee*, 1978, pp. 16-18).

Another important development of the 1960s was the introduction of foreign news services. A contract was signed with Agence France Presse for the supply of its news services to Nepal. Until the early 1970s, AFP was the only source of international news in Nepal; a similar agreement was signed with Associated Press.

Minister for Information and Broadcasting, Shailendra Kumar Upadhyaya, in 1970, said that to own a newspaper was a fundamental right of an individual. This statement, and the subsequent liberal policy of the then-government in granting newspaper licenses, directly contributed to the newspaper proliferation in Nepal. As a result, there were, in the mid-1970s, about 26 dailies and approximately 64 weeklies, most of which were uneconomical and therefore very irregular. Among the dailies, six were published in English, one in Newari (a language spoken mainly by Newars who inhabit the Kathmandu Valley), one in Hindi and the rest in Nepali, the country's national language. Two weeklies are in English; the rest in Nepali.

An equally significant development in Nepalese journalism has been the formulation of the plan for the development of communication, which has the slogan: "Communication for Development." The formulation and subsequent implementation of this plan in 1972 was an attempt to give journalism a more meaningful purpose. The Plan was formed with the understanding that journalism can and should contribute to the development of the nation. Among other things, the Plan changed the nomenclature of the Ministry of Information and Broadcasting to the Ministry of Communication, which was to be headed by a secretary without any responsibilities to other ministries. It is not uncommon in Nepal for a secretary to head two or even three ministries, thus underscoring the importance that the government was given to the proper and speedy implementation of the Communication Plan.

Provision was made in the Plan for the classification of newspapers into different categories for the purpose of granting government loans to the press. Also, the Plan stipulated that the government was to purchase newspapers for distribution throughout the country. The establishment of a Press Council was also envisaged with functions similar to the British Press Council.

Although the Plan was generally welcomed in the beginning, impediments appeared in its implementation. The formulators of the Plan had little or no knowledge of the managerial aspects of journalism, and in drawing it up, they showed a bias against the private press by giving greater importance to the development of government newspapers. As a consequence, the first action of the government in bringing about the ideals of the Communication Plan was to stop all government advertising to the private press, naturally creating friction between the government and that part of the newspaper industry. Because of this crisis in government-press relations, the Press Council has not been able to function properly. It has been given wide-ranging powers to decide on matters affecting the press, and as a result, the government has not been able to implement those portions of the Plan directly relevant to the development of newspapers. Besides, with no provision for the granting of advertisements and loans, the financial burden on private newspapers has become overbearing. This was hardly considered by its framers.

4.5.2 Survey of the Press

Gorkhapatra is strictly an establishment-oriented, vernacular daily. The oldest existing newspaper in Nepal, it is read not only for the news and government views it carries, but also for the government notices and tenders. In 1972, its editor faced the privilege committee of the *Rashtriya Panchayat* (Parliament) for breach of privilege against a member of the House by publishing what was considered a libellous article. However, such occurrences are exceptions with *Gorkhapatra.*

Rising Nepal is another publication of the Gorkhapatra Sansthan. Although a government publication like *Gorkhapatra,* it has shown a greater degree of independence by its bold criticism of the authorities. Soon after it started publishing in 1965, *Rising Nepal* became involved in a controversy by criticizing the American ambassador, an act hardly expected of a government periodical. The government does use *Rising Nepal* occasionally to publicize its national and international views. For example, in 1967, Prime Minister Kirtinidhi Bista gave an interview to the paper in which he reflected Nepalese national aspirations by demanding the withdrawal of Indian and police personnel along Nepal's northern border with China. The interview created much ill-will between India and Nepal.

The *Commoner* is the oldest English language daily. In its editorials, this newspaper has consistently pursued a pro-Indian and pro-Soviet policy. On domestic matters, it usually took a low profile attitude, though lately, it has been very critical of the administration.

Sammeksha is a pro-Soviet vernacular weekly. After *Naya Sandesh*, it is probably the best circulated Nepalese weekly. *Matribhumi*, a pro-Chinese, vernacular weekly, is also well circulated. *The Motherland*, an English daily, has been critical of various administrations. However, it is considered a strong supporter of the *panchayat* system with its principles of the active leadership of the crown, a non-aligned foreign policy and coordination between different classes of people. In international affairs, *The Motherland* has not shown any consistency, its policies wavering from strong criticism to support of India.

Himali Bela is one of the youngest English language dailies in Nepal. In domestic affairs, it is a staunch supporter of the crown as a unifying factor, an advocate of the active leadership of the king. In international affairs, it has pursued a critical policy towards India and has been sympathetic towards China and Pakistan. *Nepal Times, Dainik Nepal* and *Nabin Khabar,* besides pursuing a distinctly pro-Indian policy in international affairs, have repeatedly shown sympathetic attitudes to the banned Nepali Congress, many of whose leaders live in self-imposed exile in India.

In summary, a list of the important Nepalese newspapers includes: *Gorkhapatra* (1901), *Naya Sandesh* (1961), *Swatantra Samachar* (1958) and *Nabin Khabar* (1971), all in Nepali; *Rising Nepal* (1965), *Himali Bela* (1970), *The Motherland* (1956) and *Commoner* (1954), all in English; *Nepali* (1958), in Hindi, and *Nepal Bhasa Patrika* (1954), in Newari.

4.5.3 Government and Private Press

The functions of the government press in Nepal is no different from the functions of government presses elsewhere. Their aims are to promote the objectives and policies of the authorities. Besides *Gorkhapatra* and *Rising Nepal,* the state controlled Gorkhapatra Sansthan (Corporation) publishes an English language monthly, *Nepalese Perspective,* and *Madhuparka.* The *Nepalese Perspective* was converted in the early 1970s from a weekly to a monthly as envisaged in the Communication Plan. *Madhuparka* is a monthly literary magazine in Nepali.

Over the years, the relationship between government and the private press has been less than cordial. The private press has had to compete with government newspapers against very great odds and the competition has by no means been fair. The government press is better staffed, has better printing facilities and is in a superior financial position, partly because the government and its agencies feed it lavishly with advertising, while ignoring the private press.

Sometimes, the private press has tried to raise an issue by pointing out that the official media have stepped out of bounds by deviating from the official line, especially in matters of foreign policy. When in March 1973, for example, the United States declared its intent to resume the sale of spare parts for American weapons to Pakistan, India reacted vehemently. *Rising Nepal* wrote a rather balanced editorial, commenting that the Indian fears were unjustified. Some Indian newspapers, the pro-Soviet *Sameeksha* and the pro-Indian *Dainik Nepal,* took the opportunity to point out that as a government newspaper of a non-aligned country, *Rising Nepal* showed a bias for and against certain countries. This point was valid, because as a government newspaper, the paper was expected to maintain a strictly neutral stance as far as developments in South Asia were concerned. Such editorials are indicative of the fruitless efforts of the government press to free itself from the reins of government control, to express opinions that are considered correct and impartial. Such efforts also indicate the attempt of the government press to promote credibility.

4.5.4 Problems

Among the main problems of the Nepalese press are: severe financial constraints, lack of advertisements, the pattern of ownership, low circulation, proliferation of newspapers and their concentration in Kathmandu, frequent shortages of newsprint, inadequate staffing of newspapers, lack of own printing presses, inability to attract adequate talent into the journalistic field, lack of good reporting and heavy dependence on a news agency whose reporting leaves a lot to be desired.

One of the main reasons that Nepalese journalism has failed to develop to the desired extent is the reluctance of individuals and groups to make heavy investments in the newspaper industry. While this is partly the result of the uncertain and sometimes hostile attitude of government towards the press, it is also based on the fact that investing in newspapers is not a very sound business proposition. This is especially true of the many vernacular dailies. Indeed, the question is often asked: How do Nepalese newspapers manage to survive?

The amount of advertising is insufficient to justify the number of newspapers in Nepal. Perhaps *Gorkhapatra* is the only economically-viable newspaper in the country. It also sustains *Rising Nepal,* which depends to some degree on government grants. Because the industrial sector still remains undeveloped, the government is the biggest source of advertisement revenue for newspapers, although most of this money goes to the government press. The government does give advertisements in the form of subsidies. This is a practice that began in the early 1960s, was discontinued for about six months in 1973 and then resumed. Closely linked to the issue of advertisements is the question of the independence of the Nepalese press. How independent can a press be under such circumstances? In Nepalese journalism, it is generally accepted that the man who controls the purse controls the policy. For example, the Indian Embassy in Kathmandu gives advertisements to those newspapers that follow a favorable policy towards India. In fact, such a policy has encouraged some newspapers to follow a strictly pro-India stance because of the financial rewards that accrue. Since the mid-1970s, the government has been pursuing the same policy.

Most newspapers in Nepal are owned by single individuals who are at the same time their editors. Such a pattern of ownership is perhaps unique, but it has its disadvantages, because one man both makes and executes policy, thus making him vulnerable to pressures. Also, it gives the illusion that he is creating and leading public opinion when, in fact, he is not.

Newspapers in Nepal generally have very low circulations, attributable partly to low literacy levels. Although figures vary, 10 per cent is generally accepted as a fair estimate of the literacy of Nepal. There are other reasons for low circulation. Since the system of transportation and communication has not developed adequately, it becomes extremely difficult to start a successful circulation drive. Therefore, newspaper circulations are limited mostly to the Kathmandu Valley. Besides, the per capita income of the country is as low as US$80, forcing people to be judicious in buying newspapers. It is not surprising, therefore, that Indian dailies that have easy access to the country are better circulated, because they have more to offer to the average reader. While Nepalese readers use national newspapers primarily for news and comments on national events, Indian newspapers are their primary source of international news. Nepalese newspapers' low circulations also happen because they have very little to offer, except their editorial comments.

As stated before, some people say there are more newspapers than readers in Nepal. Of course, this is an exaggeration; nevertheless, this statement does reflect the problem of newspaper proliferation in the country and its concentration mainly in the Kathmandu Valley, which not only seats the capital city, but has a large segment of the educated population. As long as the government continues to subsidize newspapers, irrespective of their circulation and inherent value, the proliferation of newspapers will continue. In implementing the Communication Plan, the government tried to tackle this problem, but it adopted a political rather than a practical approach. The result was that the government supported most of the newspapers that were not economically viable, thus, contributing indirectly to newspaper proliferation.

Since Nepal does not produce newsprint, its press has to depend on foreign markets, mainly China, but more recently,

Bangladesh as well. Because of the dependence on foreign markets, newspapers experience a frequent shortage of newsprint; the government had plans in the 1970s to start its own newsprint industry. Not only do newspapers lack sufficient newsprint, but they must deal with prices that have soared by as much as 60 per cent between the mid-1960s and mid-1970s. This has naturally affected the cost of production, forcing newspapers to increase their prices.

Most of the newspapers, except for a few established ones, do not have their own printing presses, and are forced to use others. Under these circumstances, the cost of production increases; newspapers become irregular and cannot meet deadlines. Provision has been made in the Communication Plan to provide loans to newspapers, but this part of the Plan remained to be fulfilled in the mid-1970s.

Newspapers in Nepal have not been able to attract talent into the field because the government invariably takes the cream of society. Very few editors have had much formal education, with the result that content suffers. Because of financial constraints, the majority of newspapers cannot maintain a large fleet of correspondents. Instead, they depend heavily on Rashtriya Samachar Simiti (RSS), the only news agency in Nepal (a monopoly protected by law), for both national and international news coverage. Under RSS's franchise, all foreign news must be filtered through this agency. This does not prohibit individual newspapers from hiring their own correspondents; they do not do so because of lack of funds. Even RSS cannot afford to maintain a huge staff. As a result, developments in the districts are not covered thoroughly and newspapers continue to concentrate on developments in the Kathmandu Valley and on foreign news. In the mid-1970s, a special effort was made to improve the reporting of RSS and to give greater attention to happenings in the districts by recruiting more reporters to cover those regions. However, it appears that Nepalese newspapers will have to depend for quite some time on the news agency as their chief source of news.

4.5.5 Press Freedom

Freedom of speech and expression is one of the fundamental

rights enshrined in the constitution of Nepal. However, this freedom can be restricted for the public good. The constitution specifically mentions that laws can be made for the sake of the public good, to regulate or control the exercise of fundamental rights. Such laws can be enforced under the following circumstances: for the preservation of the security of Nepal; the maintenance of law and order; the maintenance of friendly relations with foreign states; the maintenance of good relations among the people of different classes or professions or between people of different areas; the maintenance of good conduct, health, comfort, economic interest, decency or morality of the people in general; the protection of the interests of minors or women; the prevention of internal disorder or external invasion; the prevention of contempt of court or contempt of the *Rashtriya Panchayat* (Parliament), and the prevention of any attempt to subvert the constitution or any other law or for the prevention of any like attempt. While the freedom of speech and expression has been constitutionally guaranteed, there are severe restraints to prevent its abuse and misuse.

The Press Publications Act of 1965 further enumerates the restrictions of the press. The relevant sections of this act state that no word, symbol or direct reproduction which leads to apprehension or increase in the following, directly or indirectly, shall be printed in any newspaper, news magazine, book or other document:

a. Abetment or incitement to commit murder or any violent crime concerning life, or praise of any person, real or fictitious, charged or convicted of a tendency to commit or abet such crimes.

b. Abetment or encouragement to employees of His Majesty's Government to divert them from their duty and loyalty.

c. Fomentation of hatred or disrespect towards His Majesty or the Royal family or the diplomatic representatives of the Kingdom of Nepal in foreign countries, or the diplomatic representatives of foreign countries in the Kingdom of Nepal or the legally established government or the judicial administration, or people of any particular caste, colour, class in the

Kingdom of Nepal, or the fomentation of contempt
or malice towards His Majesty and His Majesty's
Government, or ill-feeling in the relations between
the Kingdom of Nepal and any friendly country.

d. Forcing any person to give up his property to some
other person, or to perform any action not required
to be performed under law, or preventing him from
performing any action which he is entitled to perform
under law under threat of murder or personal injury
or improper damage or through intimidation or
harassment in any other way.

e. Any crime involving the obstruction of action which
has to be taken according to law and the maintenance
of law and order, or obstruction, evasion and prevention of the collection of revenues of His Majesty's
Government such as taxes, fees, land tax.

f. Incitement to any employee of His Majesty's Government in the course of the functions assigned to him,
to perform any prohibited work, or not to perform
any work which he is required to perform, or to work
with unnecessary delay, or to resign.

g. Fomentation of mutual ill-will and malice amongst
the various classes of people in the Kingdom of
Nepal.

h. Obstruction to the training or discipline of employees
of His Majesty's Government in the course of their
appointments.

i. Expression of obscene ideas through language or
words indicative of obscenity.

j. Action tending to encourage immorality in public life
or to lower the standard of public life by means of
personal vilification.

What, then, is the sort of journalism encouraged by the
government? The answer to this question becomes clear if one
goes through Section 30C of the Press and Publication Act. It
states, "His Majesty's Government may grant or make available
loans and other facilities for the development of newspapers
and periodicals who contribute to the development of healthy
journalism, with full loyalty to the nation, the King and the

Panchayat system and with the national view-point and the national interests in mind." There is, therefore, a qualified freedom of the press in Nepal.

Closely connected with the issue of press freedom is the wide-ranging powers that the government has acquired, through legal sanctions, to fine, confiscate and cancel newspaper registrations. Under the amended Press and Publication Act of 1963, the registration of newspapers will be considered invalid after a newspaper is found guilty by a Special Bench of the Supreme Court, consisting of three judges, of having contravened any of the restrictions that have been mentioned above. The executive is also empowered to confiscate any deposits, not exceeding Rs.1,000, made on acquiring a newspaper license. The government is also empowered to ask for a fresh deposit not exceeding Rs.5,000, to be paid within 15 days of the notification, after a fine has been imposed on a newspaper. Besides these powers, the authorities also have the power to ban news stories and commentaries that they think will disturb the peace and tranquility, or the relations established between Nepal and any friendly nation or international institutions and organizations (see 4.1.4 for more recent legislation).

4.5.6 Government-Press Relations

Except for occasional periods of cordiality, the relationship between the government and the press has usually been hostile. Differences have centered around the advertisement policy, laws regulating the newspaper industry and a host of other subjects. Because of these differences, newspapers have often been banned, editors jailed, government advertisements suspended and social boycotts organized. Also, some editors have been denied passports for travel abroad.

As early as 1967, the Minister for Information and Broadcasting, Beda Nanda Jha, introduced regulations governing the size, circulation and regularity of newspapers. Explaining their objectives, the minister said they were introduced to increase the standard of Nepalese newspapers. While some agreed with this viewpoint, many thought the government was unnecessarily trying to concentrate power in its own hands, contending the rules were introduced without giving consideration to the problems of the Nepalese press. Some newspapers questioned the right of the ministry to look into the accounts of newspapers, a task newspapers rightly contended was the responsibility of the Income Tax Department. Despite the criticism, the government was adamant in implementing the regulations as amendments to the Press and Publications Act. In the process, some newspapers were banned.

Imposition of bans on newspapers by the administration has often led to friction between government and the press. Such government action has nearly always been condemned editorially and by the Nepal Journalists' Association. In 1963, the government was empowered by Article 30 of the Press Act to impose a ban on newspapers without giving any reason. This action of the government could not be appealed against. The press organized a campaign for the repeal of the act, which met with success when the government amended the act (particularly those provisions contained in Article 30) in the late 1960s.

On the plea of implementing the Communication Plan, the government in 1972, suspended advertisements to all newspapers simultaneously, without activating relevant portions of the Communication Plan which envisaged the bulk of distribution of newspapers purchased by the government. This purchase by the government of newspapers for distribution was to be made on the basis of the classification of newspapers into A, B, C categories. Not only did the government suspend its advertisements, but it sent a circular to different independent corporations, asking them not to issue any advertisements to newspapers in the private sector. This action was resented by at least two journalists who organized a campaign urging government to resume advertisements. The government remained adamant for over six months, until all newspapers from the Kathmandu Valley registered their protest by publishing, on the same day, an editorial distributed by the Nepal Journalists' Association, urging government to resume advertisements. The government realized the folly of its action, but, later, it resumed advertising only in that section of the press which was less critical of it. The consequence of this policy was the bifurcation of the Nepal Journalists' Association into groups supporting and opposing government. Those papers opposing government continued their campaign by various methods, including leaving their editorial columns blank one day in 1974, and at the same time publishing this slogan in their mastheads: "The Minister says ads have not been issued. We say it is a lie. Let it be examined impartially."

One action led to another. The Nepal Journalists' Association conducted an election to choose four representatives to the Press Council, as called for in the Communication Plan. The election was held, but not before a section of the press sympathetic to government questioned the validity of the election, by taking its complaints to the Supreme Court, which dismissed the case. The government then showed its reluctance to work with the four elected members in the Press Council. Instead, the Ministry of Communications proposed in the national legislature an amendment to the Communication Plan, which, in effect, made the Press Council a mouthpiece of government, by effectively nullifying the voice of the journalists who previously had majority membership in the Council. Still not satisfied, the government, in subsequent sessions, introduced another amendment that made the director of the Information Department the secretary of the Press Council (see *Data for Decision,* 21-27 Oct. 1974, p. 2357). In the original Communication Plan, the president of the Nepal Journalists' Association was to be the ex-officio secretary of the Council. Also, government secured the right to cancel the registration of newspapers, an action which caused further friction between the government and the press. As the *Himali Bela* commented:

> Within one year two amendments were introduced affecting the very spirit of the Communication Plan without giving a fair chance for the implementation of a Plan which was welcomed by the majority of the journalists. It is, indeed, very regrettable for the government to have introduced legislation which does not at all encourage the expression of views which was urged by His Majesty in a recent meeting of the National Development Council.

4.5.7 Prospects

The immediate prospects for journalism in Nepal are not very bright. Journalism is still not considered an honorable profession. With the private sector virtually undeveloped, the civil service still draws the cream of Nepalese society. This pattern will continue to exist for quite some time in Nepal. Besides, with the national economy developing at less than 2 per cent a year, the fourth estate in Nepal, including the private press, will continue to have serious financial problems which threaten the very survival of newspapers. Consequently, newspapers must depend heavily on the support of government, which has shown a reluctance to continue this help. Just to cite an instance, in the Communication Plan, the basic document dealing with the development of the Nepalese press, there is no provision for giving advertisements to newspapers.

Relations between government and press will continue to be a problem. Naturally, this will not contribute to the healthy and continued growth of Nepalese journalism. Journalists have themselves failed to consolidate the gains of the past, notably in securing the abrogation of Article 30 of the now amended Press Act. The result has been that government, by the mid-1970s, re-asserted its dominance over the press by amending the Press Council Act, as mentioned above, to change its composition and administration. This was a great loss for the Nepalese press for which the fourth estate and the government should be blamed.

4.5.8 Assessment

It may be because of the heavy odds against it that the Nepalese press has not really been able to come of age. The press in Nepal is not a good medium for publicity; neither is it successful in reflecting or leading public opinion. It is no exaggeration to say that radio and visual media are more effective means of communication, mainly because of the low percentage of literacy. As in other Asian countries, the press in Nepal has been giving too much attention to political developments, virtually ignoring economic and social problems. Except for editorials, which themselves are often superficial analyses of events, one rarely finds well-researched and thought-provoking articles in the newspapers. Because of the lack of stringent libel laws, libellous material often finds a place in the press.

The press of Nepal is generally free and in the exercise of this freedom, it has often clashed with different governments. Because of the clash of interests of government and the press, some newspapers have been banned and editors jailed. The real freedom of the press should be judged not on the basis of the tolerance of an administration, but on whether the rights of individuals and institutions are safeguarded by the judiciary. When judicial redress has been sought concerning government action against newspapers, the Supreme Court decisions have been favorable to the press. Sometimes, the government, in its demonstration of intolerance, seems to over-react by prosecuting editors and publishers with laws other than the prevailing Press and Publication Act. This, however, is an exception, rather than the rule.

If the Nepalese press wants to develop as a viable and more independent institution, efforts must be made to diversify its source of revenue. This is, undoubtedly, a very difficult task, but it must be given serious attention in the years ahead. There is now excessive dependence on foreign and government sources of financing. The government could help in this regard by giving prospective investors a greater sense of security.

4.5.9 An Update, by John A. Lent

Survival continued to be the problem that haunted Nepalese newspapers, especially private ones, throughout the 1970s.

In 1974, a conference of editors and publishers urged government to set up a Royal Press Commission to analyze all aspects of journalism in the country. The delegates also urged the acceptance of newspapers as an industry, impartial distribution of advertisements on a regular basis, income tax exemption on the amount spent by a party or private institution on advertisements and a regular supply of newsprint (*P.C.I. Review*, Jan. 1975, p. 10).

Advertising is in short supply (except for that of the government) because the country has virtually no industry. Distribution suffers because the mountainous nature of Nepal hinders transportation and because the only distribution agency in Kathmandu, enjoying a monopoly in the nation, is not in a hurry to distribute newspapers. For example, Indian dailies from Delhi arrive in Kathmandu at 9:30 a.m., are censored for two and a half hours and given to the distributing agency at 12:30 p.m. The agency gets around to handing out the papers in the evening. Because street hawkers do not exist, readers must pick up their copies of newspapers at the distributing agency shop (*Narendra*, 1975, p. 12).

Of course, survival is affected by the number of different newspapers published for the few literate people. In 1978, there were 22 dailies and 42 weeklies serving Kathmandu and a total of 84 newspapers in the country. The Nepal Press Council, in its annual report that year, suggested economic pressures could be alleviated if journalists pooled their resources to bring about standard newspapers. As Shreshta reported, the Council has urged the government,

> to provide financial backing for the initial establishment of better printing facilities; and the council wants to see fewer newspapers as the number is reckoned to be disproportionately larger, than available resources and readership (*Shreshta*, 1978, p. 25).

Also, the Press Council asked the press to break its concentration in Kathmandu. Of the 84 newspapers, 64 are in Kathmandu (central region), 10 in the eastern region, six in the western region and just four in the largest geographical area, the far west. The Council recommended incentives be given journalists to move from the capital and develop a "local circulation system with wide coverage of the local developments" (*Shreshta*, 1978, p. 25).

The Council report stated that except for the two main newspapers of the Gorkhapatra Corporation, which are standard size, eight-page dailies, all other newspapers are tabloids of two (and sometimes four) pages. The report pointed out that except for the logotypes, there is little difference in content of most newspapers (*Shreshta*, 1978, p. 25). Perhaps, this has come about because much of the news is supplied by Rashtriya Samachar Simiti, which mostly dispatches information of official functions.

To improve press-government relationships, which it called

"vitiated," the Council said it was necessary for the government to "take the press into its confidence" and share information on new projects, while the press must act "more responsibly" and refrain from publishing provocative and libellous material. The Council noted the irritation caused journalists by the Press Act and advocated amending it to create a "sense of greater security" among journalists (*Shreshta*, 1978, p. 25).

Two years earlier, the Council had made similar recommendations, calling for an ever-growing awareness of responsibility on the part of journalists, encouraging publication of newspapers in areas outside Kathmandu and emphasizing the need for a journalists' welfare fund, training facilities and an institute of mass communications to be headquartered at Tribhuvan University (*Indian Press*, Oct. 1976, pp. 58-59). Professionalization of journalists had been given a boost, at least on paper, when in 1974 the Nepal Press Foundation was created to do research and provide training (*Media*, March 1974, p. 24).

4.6 Pakistan

Sharif al Mujahid

4.6.1 Introduction

A discussion of the Pakistani press presents certain methodological problems. While present day Pakistan, Bangladesh and India constituted one country until 14-15 August 1947, Pakistan and Bangladesh (as West Pakistan and East Pakistan) were integral parts of a united Pakistan until 16 December 1971, when an independent Bangladesh, incorporating former East Pakistan, was hoisted onto the map.

In trying to unravel the antecedents of the present Pakistani press, one cannot, therefore, ignore the larger geographical matrix of the Indian subcontinent, or the socio-cultural context of Indic Islam, within which its progenitors had risen, and flourished or languished, as the case may be. Nor can the press in the "Pakistan" areas during the pre-1947 period be discussed on a separate level, but it has to be treated as an integral part of subcontinental journalism, since India till 1947 was one unit, geographically, politically and administratively.

Likewise, one cannot possibly ignore the influence of the East Pakistani press on its western counterpart during the united Pakistan period (1947-71). Even the natural resources and products of East Pakistan — along with its political temper and the audience, however limited, it provided — had an impact on press development in the West. To give one instance, after Bangladesh

Sharif al Mujahid is former chairman of journalism at the University of Karachi. He has been a professional journalist with media in Pakistan, India and the United States.

became a nation, Pakistan suffered a newsprint shortage because of the non-availability of Khulna (East Pakistan) newsprint, the main source since 1960. The shortage caused Pakistan papers to slice their sizes by about 50 per cent and increased their production costs considerably. Worse still, the shortage has also provided the government with yet another lever to favor or penalize publications, since it has now become the sole authority for the allocation of newsprint.

4.6.2 Historical Background

The origins of the Pakistani press are enmeshed in subcontinental journalism which began in 1780. Although the principal formative trends generated by the nature and course of press development in the subcontinent from 1780 to 1947 (see *J. Natarajan,* 1954; *S. Natarajan,* 1962) influenced the Pakistani press, yet, only some of these trends can be considered as constituting part of the Pakistani press heritage.

This may be explained in that subcontinental journalism was not an indivisible whole but the sum-total of several strands, some of them diverging, or even parallel. Out of them, three distinct, broad and somewhat parallel strands may be easily identified.

The first of these strands was represented by the Anglo-Indian press, founded and edited by the British, and dedicated to the espousal and promotion of the imperial cause. Anglo-Indian newspapers were not only the first, but also leaders in the field, being better edited and produced, highly-influential and financially-sound. They loomed large on the subcontinental journalism scene for almost 150 years but their importance waned progressively during the closing decades of British *raj* (rule) in India.

The second strand was injected during the 1820s when Indian-owned (and more specifically, Hindu-owned) papers were launched. Slow and fitful as their beginning was, they rose as a corollary to and a reaction against British-owned newspapers. The earliest Indian newspapers were almost all in vernacular languages (Bengali, Persian, Urdu, Gujerati, among others), and for the most part, Hindu-owned. It took almost 80 years before this segment of the Indian press became economically viable — though only partially — and influential. By the early decades of the twentieth century, the Hindu-owned press entered a period of consolidation, developed a tradition of its own and was branded the "nationalist" press because of its close association with the Indian National Congress, the major and best organized "nationalist" political party in undivided India. By then, its traditions became an integral part of the Indian journalistic heritage. Since it was, for the most part, established, edited and managed by the more numerous, better-educated and financially more resourceful Hindus, it espoused the viewpoint of the Hindu dominated Congress Party, which stood for *Purna Swaraj* (complete independence) and a united India. Thus, this press was in conflict with the ruling British on the first strand, and with the rather backward Muslims on the second.

The third strand was represented by the Muslim press (see *Salik,* 1963, pp. 445-67; *Feroze,* 1957, pp. 103-18) in undivided India. The Muslim press was devised as a reaction to the Hindu-owned press, since party newspapers in India were largely organized along communal lines — i.e., Hindu, Muslim, Anglo-Indian, Sikh, etc. — at least until the reorganization of the Muslim League in 1937 (*The Near East and India,* 1925, pp. 280-85). Representing the weakest link in subcontinental journalism, the Muslim press took almost a century to establish an identity of its own, and flowered only during the 1940s, when the Muslim League demanded partitioning of the subcontinent to carve out an independent Muslim state to be called Pakistan. Often called the "League press" during this period, it became, upon partition, the nucleus of the emerging Pakistan press.

4.6.3 *Muslim Press in India*

The growth and development of the press (both nationalist and Muslim) in undivided India were inextricably linked with the crystallization of political parties and demands and with increased political awakening. Although Muslim oriented newspapers, mostly in Urdu (see *Sabiri,* 1953; *Shakib,* 1952; *Lal,* 1964; especially *Shah,* 1965), had existed rather tentatively since the 1830s, they became more common around the turn of the century

(Wilber, 1964, pp. 282-83). They developed a tradition of their own only after 1910 when the Muslims increasingly engaged in political agitation. Thus, the subsequent period is marked by the rise of increasingly-vocal, politically-oriented, vastly-influential and widely-circulated newspapers. Prominent among them were *Comrade* (Calcutta/Delhi; 1911-14, 1924-26), *Hamdard* (Delhi; 1913), *Al-Hilal* (Calcutta; 1912-16, 1927), and *Zamindar* (Lahore; founded as daily, 1911; 1911-16; 1920-57), which were edited by the leading Muslim political figures of the day. Theirs was personalized journalism elevated to a national status.

While the rise of these newspapers reflected, among other things, the measure of political awakening among the Muslims, they were also highly instrumental in bringing a new awareness among both the literati and the intelligentsia — politicizing them and causing them to join the mainstream of political struggle. Thus, they were, in a sense, both the index and the agent of political awakening.

By the mid-1920s, the Muslim press had grown in both size and circulation, comprising about 220 newspapers in nine languages, including Urdu, English and Bengali *(Mott,* 1925, pp. 138-40). The Urdu press led with 120 newspapers, followed by 18 in English and 14 in Bengali. By regions, undivided Punjab (85 newspapers, all Urdu except for four in English) led, followed by Uttar Pradesh (44), Bombay including Since (37) and Madras (26). Undivided Bengal (present day Bengal and Bangladesh) had 22 newspapers, of which only six were located in the erstwhile East Pakistan (Bangladesh today), whereas (West) Punjab (i.e., Pakistani part of the Punjab) alone accounted for 61.

Most of these were financially-poor, were limited in scope, appeal and circulation, and catered to special groups and interests. Only a few, chiefly because of their political orientation and views, had a subcontinental standing and were read with interest throughout India. Besides those mentioned earlier, they included *Al-Balagh* (Calcutta), *Musalman* (Calcutta), *Muslim Rajput* (Amritsar), *Muslim Outlook* (Lahore), *Rahbar-i-Deccan* (Hyderabad), *Hamdam* (Lucknow). *Aligarh Gazette* (Aligarh), *Paisa Akhbar* (Lahore), *Qaumi Report (Madras), Al-Awam* (Delhi) and *Al-Jamiat* (Delhi).

During the 1930s, the number of Muslim-owned, English language papers declined. Although the majority of Urdu papers were edited and owned by Muslims, several such as *Ajit, Prakash, Bande Matram* and *Pratab,* all from Lahore, and *Tej* (Delhi), *Arya Musafir* (Lucknow) and *Vakil* (Amritsar), were owned and edited by Hindus and Sikhs.

Although the antecedents of the Pakistani press may be traced to these Urdu newspapers, what influenced Pakistani journalism the most during its formative stages, was the distinctive Muslim press which grew as a result of national awakening and increased political consciousness generated among the Muslims during the late 1930s. Indeed, the consolidation of the Muslim press began only when the Muslims were organized by Jinnah, later to become the founder of Pakistan. It was then they felt the need of a strong press if their case was to succeed (*Husain,* 1956, p. 216). This feeling led Jinnah to inspire the launching of a Muslim-oriented news agency (Oriented Press of India), to establish several dailies and weeklies (in English, Urdu and Gujerati), and to goad others to do the same in other parts of the country.

As a result, there appeared *Azad* (Calcutta; f. 1936) in Bengali, owned and edited by Maulana Mohammad Akram Khan, a widely-respected Muslim leader; *Manshoor* (Delhi; 1937-47), the official League daily in Urdu, edited by Maulana Hasan Reyaz; *The Star of India* (Calcutta; 1937-48) in English; *Morning News* Calcutta; f. August 1942), edited by Abdur Rahman Siddiqui, who was prominent in Muslim politics and later became governor of East Bengal; *Dawn* (Delhi), a weekly founded October 1941 by Quaid-i-Azam Mohammad Ali Jinnah to interpret the official viewpoint of the Muslim League.

Turned into a daily in October 1943, *Dawn* grew into the most powerful organ of Muslim public opinion in pre-partition India, especially under Altaf Husain's editorship. It was his crusading zeal, tireless rhetoric, dialectical approach and biting sarcasm that made *Dawn* great as an advocate of Muslim viewpoints (see *Mujahid,* 1952, Ch. 1). Thus, by the mid-1940s, a Muslim English daily and/or weekly existed in every province, and in India's capital city. Prominent among these were *Nawai-i-Waqt* (Lahore; daily; f. 1944), *The Pakistan Times* (Lahore; f. 1947), *Eastern Times* (Lahore; 1935-47), *Watan* (Bombay), *Morning Herald* (Bombay; f. 1947), *The Star* (Bombay; f. 1945), *The Muslim*

Times (Bombay; f. 1946), the *Weekly Observer* (Allahabad), *New Life* (Patna; f. 1946), *Sind Times* (Karachi; f. 1945), *Khyber Mail* (Peshawar), *Comrade* (Calcutta; f. 1946) and *Assam Herald* (Shillong). Among the notable Urdu newspapers were the old-timers, *Asr-e-Jadid* (Calcutta; f. 1923), *Roznama-i-Hind* (Calcutta), *Khilafat* (Bombay), *Sada-e-Awam* (Patna), *Hamdam* (Lucknow), and the newly established *Tanvir* (Lucknow).

Meanwhile, a large number of existing Muslim-owned dailies and weeklies were able to achieve coherence and direction and a modest circulation. This was indicated, among other things, by the convening of the first All-India Muslim Newspapers' Convention at New Delhi in May 1947 (see *Deccan Times,* Madras, 18 May 1947, pp. 3, 10), attended by about 100 editors and representatives of Muslim newspapers. The convention launched an All-India Muslim Newspapers' Association and an All India Muslim Working Journalists' Association.

By the mid-1940s, a distinct, vocal and influential — though essentially partisan — Muslim press developed in the subcontinent. Its handicaps were legion: poor finances, low circulations and meager advertising but increasingly high costs of printing and newsprint materials which, because of war, were scarce and often denied to new entrants; lack of trained personnel, press equipment, technical know-how and modern facilities; and, above all, hostile (Congress or Congress-backed) governments in nine out of 11 provinces, ready to penalize Muslim newspapers in various ways at the least provocation. During 1946-47, for instance, securities of several Muslim newspapers (*New Life, The Star, Zamindar* and *Nawa-i-Waqt,* to name only the most prominent) were confiscated more than once, resulting in the premature demise of some of them.

These circumscribing factors, in turn, denied an exceedingly large segment of the Muslim press the requisite climate for a normal and healthy growth; hamstrung it from becoming a viable economic enterprise, and made it a poor second to the nationalist press.

4.6.4 *Development of the Pakistan Press*

It is rather tempting to explain the somewhat nebulous state of

the Pakistan press in 1947-48, as well as its slow but steady
growth throughout the 1950s, in terms of Lerner's model of
modernization, based on indices of urbanization (including
industrialization), literacy, media exposure, economic participation (per capita income) and political participation (*Lerner,* 1967,
p. 46; see *Mujahid,* 1971, pp. 527-29).

Pakistani society in 1947 could be described as pre-industrial,
feudal, rural and pre-literate. These factors, enervating in themselves, were compounded by large scale dislocation in communications and economic life in wide areas, caused by communal rioting
and the greatest migration in history; hence, the anemic state and
slow growth of the press in Pakistan's early years.

Pakistan crossed the lower ceiling of the "critical minimum"
(7 per cent) of urbanization some time in the late 1950s. The
increase of over 1.94 million in the non-agricultural labor force
during 1951-61 indicated the trend towards partial industrialization. Literacy rose to 15.9 per cent in 1961, but only 9.4 per cent
of those 10 years or older were functionally literate. There was
also a corresponding rise in the per capita income, as also in the
clamor for greater participation in the political realm.

All this had an impact on press growth which was discernible
in the rise of new publications and an increase in the size of
newspapers, in the circulations of most publications, and in
advertising volume, as well as in technological improvement of
the press. For instance, the number of dailies rose from 55 in
1953 to 103 in 1958 (Pakistan. Ministry of Information, 1953-
70), after which there was a slump during the next three years —
perhaps, at least in part, because of press constraints and the
prevailing authoritarianism during the first martial law period
(1958-62). Within a year of the termination of martial law and
the return to a sort of constitutionalism in June 1962, the press
picked up its lost initiative and surged forward. Thus, the number
of dailies rose steadily from 75 in 1962 to 117 in 1970, the year
of the first general elections and one of unfettered press freedom.
This period was also characterized by the spectacular rise of
weeklies, fortnightlies and monthlies which, for the most part,
represented journals of opinion, their number having risen to
1,145 in 1970 (Pakistan. Central Statistical Office, 1972, p. 287).

Likewise, a study of the sizes of leading dailies in English,

Urdu and Bengali from both wings showed that three dailies
(West Pakistan one; East Pakistan two) had almost doubled their
size between 1948-49 and 1970, while three papers from the
West had increased by about 50 per cent. It also showed that
Pakistan Times led others with a monthly average of 17.57 pages
for September 1968, followed by *Dawn* of Karachi (16.83 pages)
for October 1966 (*Mujahid,* 1973, p. 30).

The total daily circulation tells a similar tale of steady increases
over the years. From 120,000 in 1950 (*UNESCO,* 1951, p. 91),
circulation sprang to 156,000 in 1955 (*Mujahid,* 1956, p. 38).
By 1959, nine dailies alone commanded a combined circulation
of 227,155 (Pakistan. Government of Pakistan Press, 1959,
p. 95) and by 1965, eight of these had increased their circulations
to a total of 399,250 (Pakistan Publications, 1967, p. 544).

The trend throughout the 1960s was one of rising circulations,
especially for the leading Urdu and Bengali dailies. *Imroz*
(Lahore), for example, had trebled its circulation between 1965
and 1968 (*Pakistan Times,* 21 March 1968, p. 13); the oppositionist *Nawa-i-Waqt's* circulation rose to 80,000 during the
presidential elections of 1964-65 (*The Economist,* London, 13
Feb. 1965, p. 653); and *Jang* sold over 150,000 copies (Pakistan
Publications, 1967, p. 544; East Pakistan Government Press,
1970, pp. 68-69). *Ittefaq* had likewise built up its circulation
to 33,000 by 1969 (East Pakistan Government Press, 1970,
pp. 38-39).

In view of these gains, the total daily circulation in 1970 should
have been in the neighborhood of 1 million, or a low 8.3 copies
for every 1,000 inhabitants. However, as in India and other parts
of the Third World, readership per newspaper is at least four in
cities and towns and much higher in rural areas.

During the period of united Pakistan (1947-71), dailies were
published in English, Urdu, Bengali, Sindhi, Pushto and Gujerati
and periodicals in about 10 languages. The leading papers, both
in number and circulation, were in Urdu. Dailies totalled 112
in 1971, 25 in English, 64 in Urdu, 11 in Bengali, six in Sindhi,
three in Pushto and Urdu (bilingual) and three in Gujerati
(Pakistan. Government of Pakistan, 1972). The Bengali press
was confined to East Pakistan, but some Urdu papers were

published from that wing as well. About one-third of all publications (613 out of 1,825) in 1969 were in Urdu, followed by Bengali (378) and English (361).

East Pakistan housed 20 dailies and 153 periodicals, whereas West Pakistan had 91 dailies and 992 periodicals. Upon the dismemberment of united Pakistan in December 1971, this West Pakistani press became the press of the remaining (or post-Bangladesh) Pakistan.

4.6.5 Characteristics

Information, guidance and entertainment are considered among the most crucial functions of the Pakistan press. As in the rest of the developing world, the amount of content and emphasis given to the first two functions largely depends upon the nature of the government in power and the degree of press freedom. When the government is democratic, information flow is considerably large and free, but when the country is under semi-authoritarianism, as was the case during the Ayub decade (October 1958-March 1969), even innocuous news stories are larded with "guidance." An exception to this rule was Yahya Khan's first two years (March 1969-March 1971), when the press was almost free, information flow was spontaneous and unhindered, and guidance, confined to editorials, reflected the papers', not regime's, policy.

Since 1958, there has been a tendency to emphasize the guidance function — i.e., to augment the government's capabilities in terms of Karl Deutsch's categories of mobilization of effort, unity of command and effective power of enforcement (*Deutsch* in *Friedrich*, 1954, pp. 308-33) — at the expense of the informing function. Under pressures of various kinds, increasing numbers of newspapers have been obliged to transform themselves into veritable "guidance sheets."

While this is true of newspapers of considerable standing published in the major towns of Karachi, Lahore, Rawalpindi and Peshawar, the regional press, based largely in small towns, has seldom made a distinction between the information and guidance functions, most of them donning the role of "drum-beaters" for the regime in power, if only to keep themselves alive.

4.6.6 *Ownership*

As part of its pre-1947, independence legacy, the Pakistani press has, from the beginning, been privately owned. Although some papers were considered semi-official or unofficial spokesmen for the government, the ruling Muslim League or other parties during the formative years, the first attempt at purely party control came in 1954 when *The Pakistan Standard* was launched by the then-ruling Muslim League. The party felt a need for an organ which it could depend upon for unflinching loyalty and continuing support. But the venture was short-lived, chiefly because of factional in-fighting for control of the newspaper.

During the past two decades, other party newspapers have risen, flourished for a time, and then usually declined. *Sangbad* (f. 1951) and *Sangram*, both published in Bengali and from Dacca, belonged to the National Awami Party (NAP) and Jamaat-i-Islami (JI), respectively, while *The People* (Dacca; f. weekly 1969, daily 1970) claimed that it was the spokesman for the Awami League. In West Pakistan, the *Musawat* and *Jasarat*, both founded in 1970, and *Shahbaz* (Peshawar) have been the official spokesmen of the Pakistan People's Party (PPP), JI and NAP, respectively. With the ascension of the PPP to power in December 1971, *Jasarat* fell on bad times, having been banned several times; *Shahbaz* closed because of the seizure of its press; and *Musawat* alone flourished among party papers (see 4.1.5). Party weeklies and monthlies, being primarily "viewsmagazines," have fared better, the most notable among them being *Zindagi* (JI) and *Nusrat* (PPP), both from Lahore.

When, in 1963, plans to nationalize the press, screen journalists and establish a press licensing system (see London *Times*, 6 July 1963, p. 7; 20 July 1963, p. 7; 7 Aug. 1963, p. 7; 10 Aug. 1963, p.5; 12 Aug. 1963, p. 7; 13 Aug. 1963, p. 7; 14 Aug. 1963, p. 7; 24 Aug. 1963, p. 5) aborted, and when the Press and Publication Ordinance of September 1963, amended a month later, failed to silence non-conformist papers and yield hoped for results, the Ayub regime thought of launching, or converting existing papers into, dependable organs, similar to "official" journals established in most Western countries in the seventeenth and eighteenth centuries. Thus, was floated in early 1964 the government-inspired National Press Trust (NPT), with an initial capital of about US$5.25 million, financed by 24 prominent industrialists (called "settlers") who did not participate in the management of the Trust (*Outlook,* Karachi, 25 Jan. 1964, p. 3; 15 Feb. 1964, p. 5). Avowedly set up to establish and publish newspapers with a "truly national outlook and devoted to the cause of national progress and solidarity and to acquire, promote and develop all other forms of mass information" (*Morning News,* Karachi, 6 Aug. 1964; 28 March 1964), the Trust acquired within six months 10 dailies and one weekly, including the *Morning News* (Karachi and Dacca), *Pakistan Times* and its sister publications. Former Prime Minister Ali Bhutto characterized the NPT papers as "the Marie Walewska" of the Information Ministry (*Dawn,* 25 Feb. 1967); others have compared them to "a class of paid pipers" (*Outlook,* 15 Feb. 1964, p. 5). Governmental spokesmen, however, have stoutly denied having anything to do with the Trust. This denial notwithstanding, its chairmen, nominated at times by the government and at other times by its board of governors, have included former civil servants or army generals, ruling party members and, at one time, the central minister of information himself.

4.6.7 Economics of the Press

4.6.7.1 Press Facilities

The Pakistan press started in 1947 with little or no equipment. Only the *Civil and Military Gazette* (Lahore; 1876-1963) owned a rotary press on which *Pakistan Times* was also printed until about 1950. On the other hand, *The Pakistan Observer,* in the first phase of its career (1949-52), gave the impression of being hand-composed (*Mujahid,* 1956, p. 40).

Technological improvement of the English press began in 1950 when *Dawn, Pakistan Times,* and the newly-founded *Evening Times* (Karachi) set up modern printing presses, but the *Morning News* (re-established 1953) had to be content with a flatbed press until 1966, when its new-found prosperity as a government-pampered NPT daily enabled it to import rotary presses for both its Karachi and Dacca editions. That this was the first East Pakistani daily to own a rotary machine indicated how far behind its western counterpart the eastern press was. It was the same with most vernacular language dailies.

However, since the early 1960s, an increasing number of Urdu dailies, beginning with *Jang,* have acquired modern rotary presses (for discussion of Urdu press, see *Azmi,* 1976, pp. 31-34). Circulation increases during the 1960s and 1970s have enabled all metropolitan dailies and most metropolitan weeklies to own, or at least use, rotary presses, while regional newspapers and smaller weeklies with circulations of less than 10,000, still use flatbed litho or letterpresses. This may be attributed to poor finances of the newspapers, and the country's inability to allocate scarce foreign exchange resources for the import of modern press equipment.

For some years now, offset rotary presses have been manufactured in Pakistan, *The Sun* (Karachi; f. 1970) being the first daily to use such a press. At least 28 out of 34 dailies published in Sind have presses of their own — whether modern or outdated — and the others are published on them or in commercial presses (Pakistan. Sind Government Press, 1971; also *Akhbar-i-Jahan,* Karachi, 26 June 1974, p. 4).

4.6.7.2 Capital

The usual form of financing a publication is to start a limited company with a number of industrialists subscribing capital to meet initial expenditures and costs of operating the newspaper for the first six months. Sometimes, the controlling shares are held by a single family, as was the case with the *Pakistan Times* (until its takeover by the government in April 1959) and many other dailies, such as *Dawn, Jang* and *Nawa-i-Waqt.* Party newspapers, such as *Musawat, Hilal-i-Pakistan* (Sindhi daily, Karachi), and the now defunct-*Jasarat* (Karachi; 1970-74) and *Shahbaz* (Peshawar), are financed wholly or partly from party funds and/or by affluent followers of the party.

Before the initial subscribed capital is exhausted, the newspaper is usually expected to start earning enough to meet operating costs, but in Pakistan, this seldom happens, except when governmental patronage is available. Advertising and circulation constitute the main sources of revenue, but the deficit is usually met by the initial investors or other obliging friends. Oppositionist newspapers such as *Jasarat,* and independent organs such as *Outlook* (Karachi weekly; 1962-64, 1972-74), starved of advertising from government sources, tried to survive through regular donations by friends and followers.

Most of the larger metropolitan dailies, however, have sizable annual revenues and incomes in Pakistani terms. According to the balance sheet presented to the Second Wage Board in 1969, annual revenues were: *Dawn,* US$680,000; *Morning News* (Karachi and Dacca editions), US$1,911,000; Progressive Papers Ltd. (comprising *Pakistan Times* and *Imroz*), US$2,835,000; *Jang* (Karachi), US$2,037,000; *Jang* (Rawalpindi), US$661,500, and *Nawa-i-Waqt,* US$546,000. Their incomes were: *Dawn,* US$294,000; *Morning News,* US$36,750; Progressive Papers Ltd., US$73,599; *Jang* (Karachi), US$73,500; *Jang* (Rawalpindi), US$6,615, and *Nawa-i-Waqt,* US$144,000 (Karachi Press Club, 1970). Calling for special attention is the case of *Nawai-i-Waqt.* Because of its independent stance, this paper has been almost consistently denied government advertising, and even that of non-government enterprises whose owners could not afford to displease the regime by patronizing independent publications. Yet, it was economically viable in 1969.

During the first half of the 1970s, there was considerable expansion of these enterprises, and at least some of them, besides the newly-founded, government-patronized newspapers such as *Musawat,* were making even greater profits.

The total amount spent on advertising in various media is anybody's guess, but, according to one estimate, government agencies and various semi-government corporations and bodies spent over Rs.25 million (about US$5.3 million) during 1963-64 (*Outlook,* 15 Feb. 1964, p. 5). Since government advertising at that time was estimated at being one-third of total advertising, the annual amount spent on advertising in 1963 was roughly US$16 million. In view of the hike in advertising rates; the increase in advertising volume, especially in some Urdu dailies such as *Jang;* government patronized papers, and the rupee devaluation of 1972, the amount spent on newspaper advertising in the late 1970s must have been well over $15 million. Government advertising in Sind's 30 dailies alone amounted to US$248,300 during 1972-73 (*Akhbar-i-Jahan* 16 June 1974, p. 4).

Advertising in Pakistan is highly-developed, mostly service-oriented and has a good deal of scope for future expansion, especially in consumer goods. Because of the socio-cultural milieu of Pakistani society, advertising contents are usually sober. Exceptions are advertisements for sex rejuvenation cures, especially in advertising-starved smaller Urdu papers, and night clubs, prominent in Karachi, English language, evening newspapers which largely depend on street sales.

The proportion of advertising to news content in large metropolitan dailies is usually about 1:2; *Dawn* and *Pakistan Times,* in 1975, led in advertising volume with 46.7 per cent and 43.9 per cent, respectively. But advertising volume is much less in regional dailies and in independent and opposition newspaper (whether metropolitan or otherwise) which do not qualify for government advertising.

Advertising can be placed directly with newspapers or through well-developed advertising agencies. Foreign advertising firms, once the leaders, were closed in the mid-1960s, because of shrinking business in the face of newly emerging Pakistani competitors. Most of them were taken over by Pakistanis. Industries, companies and organizations with large advertising budgets (e.g., Pakistan Tobacco and Phillips) handle their own accounts through their fully fledged advertising sections. A government proposal to set up an official advertising corporation has been alarming to private advertising agencies which feel they may be doomed if it is put into effect.

As in India, government has been the largest single advertiser in Pakistan. With the large scale nationalization policy initiated by the Bhutto regime after January 1972, it controlled at least 50 per cent of all advertising. For instance, the percentages of government advertising to total advertising volume in *Dawn, Pakistan Times* (Lahore edition) and *Jang* (Karachi edition) for January 1975, were 39.4, 65.4 and 35.4 per cent, respectively.

4.6.7.3 Capacity to Consume

Newspapers have always been expensive in terms of Pakistani wages. With the threefold rise in their price over a 15-year period in the 1960s and 1970s, the situation deteriorated all the more. A metropolitan daily, for instance, costs about 5 per cent of the wages of an average factory worker. Subscribing to a newspaper was once a status symbol; now, people usually buy a newspaper to keep informed.

Compared to the practice in Western countries or even in India, circulation figures in Pakistan are, for the most part, considered somewhat confidential, although an Adult Bureau of Circulation has been in existence since 1956. However, the trend is generally one of rising circulations, especially in the language dailies, understandable in that they cater to the growing cognitive needs of new or semi-literates. The scanty data readily available show that *Jang* increased its circulation tremendously between 1959 and 1967 (35,377 to 163,212) (Pakistan. Government of Pakistan, 1959, p. 95; Pakistan, Government of Pakistan, 1968, p. 12); *Nawa-i-Waqt* trebled its circulation between 1959 and 1965 (18,870 to 58,800), while *Pakistan Times* registered modest gains (34,850 to 42,300) for the same period (Pakistan. Government of Pakistan, 1959, p. 95; Pakistan Publications, 1967, p. 544). All these dailies had started a Rawalpindi edition in the intervening years, to which may be attributed at least some of the increase. On the other hand, *Dawn,* though a leading, national daily, has over the years remained largely at its 1959 circulation figure, its circulation for 1972-73 being 41,468 (*Akhbar-i-Jahan,* 26 June 1974, p. 4). This stability in circulation might be a result of the paper's catering to Karachi and environs where there are two other English morning papers and three evening dailies.

Despite great advances made in the 1960s and 1970s, circulations are still extremely low with about 75 per cent of the dailies having circulations of less than 10,000 each. Circulations, as in most Afro-Asian countries, are confined to urban and near urban areas, and the penetration of rural areas by print media, not to speak of dailies, is rather erratic. The considerable potential audience in these areas remains largely untapped because of the dearth of truly regional newspapers with a vested interest in local affairs and problems, and the inability of highly-educated and sophisticated journalists to understand problems of rural and semi-literate audiences and to write at their level of literacy and intelligence.

Besides the loss of these rural audiences and a high illiteracy rate, multiplicity of languages and fragmentation of readership — there are, for instance, more dailies in Karachi (21), Lahore (15), Peshawar (10) and Rawalpindi (6) than readership and economy can support — have conspired to keep circulations low.

Except for Baluchistan, where transportation facilities to outlying areas are comparatively poor, the other areas are well connected by air, rail and roads to facilitate quick and inexpensive transport of papers. Besides, over the years, metropolitan dailies have devised an efficient distribution system.

However, literacy is low, with only about 20 per cent of the people able to read and only about 50 per cent of them functionally literate. Whereas comparatively high costs of newspapers have led to borrowing or exchanging, low functional literacy rates have encouraged group listening to newspapers being read, especially in rural areas.

4.6.8 Socio-Cultural Factors and the Press

In Pakistan, dailies are published in five languages (English, Urdu, Sindhi, Pushto and Gujerati), and periodicals in about nine. Since language newspapers (except those in Gujerati) are not set in type, but are handwritten by *katibs* (scribes) on butter papers and then transferred to metal plates, this poses problems. Also, since wire service copy is in English, the copyreader's job in language newspapers is usually one of translating.

Urdu is the national language, as well as the link language between various regions. There are 75 dailies in Urdu compared to 13 in English, seven in Sindhi, and four each in Pushto and Gujerati (Pakistan. Government of Pakistan, 1973).

Although English has been progressively de-emphasized since 1947, it continues to be in a vantage position in press circles. For one thing, English is still the principal language of administration, courts, commerce and the elites, and, along with Urdu, the medium of instruction at the higher and professional levels. For another, the two leading English morning dailies, *Dawn* and *Pakistan Times,* have built a tremendous amount of goodwill and prestige and continue to be better produced and more serious in tone. Though vanquished in the race for circulation, these English dailies continue to lead in prestige and influence.

The Islamic origins and orientation of Pakistan (see *Mujahid,* 1974) are reflected in the religious features the papers carry on Fridays, the Muslim sabbath, and on other important dates in the Islamic calendar, as well as the quotes from the *Quran* and the *Hadith* (Prophet's sayings) carried by Urdu papers as *obiter dicta* below the editorial masthead.

The extreme religious sensitivity of the people has precluded free and open press discussion on issues with religious overtones. For instance, even the controversial *Marriage Commission Report* of 1956 was not fully debated in the press, although most of the elites favored it. However, religion and religious symbolism are deftly used in the press to promote different viewpoints — both to commend and condemn governmental policies and measures (see *Mujahid,* 1965, p. 291; *Mujahid,* 1971, p. 168; *Musawat,* 2-3 March 1972).

Low literacy and economic levels and the Pakistani political style, which largely precludes the prevalence of the concept of "free marketplace of ideas," have generally retarded press development, but Pakistani cultural traditions have not. During the past two decades, the press has played a crucial role in creating a new value structure — for instance, in converting people to the need for family planning and to quickening the pace of women's emancipation.

4.6.9 Content

Pakistani newspapers, like their Indian counterparts, are patterned after the British press, with an overlay of American journalism. Also, the legacy of the Muslim press in the 1940s, which functioned as a crusader for Pakistan, has somewhat conditioned their personality. The role of crusader called for a good deal of editorializing and learned argumentation, the publication of lengthy speeches by political leaders (if only to provide ammunition for the ongoing struggle) and a consuming preoccupation with national problems, mostly of a political nature. These requirements, in turn, imposed certain limitations on the tone, tenor and content of newspapers. And since, in the formative period, most senior journalists had entered the profession during the independence struggle era, the tradition of that period has left an indelible mark on the profession as a whole and on the format and content of newspapers.

As a result, most newspapers still carry rather lengthy editorials, give extensive coverage to political meetings, parliamentary debates and political polemics, and are, for the most part, deadly serious in tone and treatment of problems. All this, however, has not been an unmixed evil. For, in a society where the democratic tradition is not well entrenched; where since 1958, political dialogue has not usually been recognized as a *sine-qua-non* of a democratic dispensation and mass political participation; and where adequate facilities for such a dialogue have been sadly lacking, the focus on subjects of a political nature has served to educate people on issues and helped to establish, albeit a little indirectly, what Milton called "the liberty to know."

An analysis of three leading metropolitan dailies for January 1975 showed that over two-fifths of total space was devoted to advertising. The percentage figures for *Dawn, Pakistan Times* and *Jang* (Karachi edition) were 42.8, 44.4 and 44.5, respectively. In absolute terms, however, *Dawn* led the others, followed by *Jang* and *Pakistan Times.* Domestic news occupied about two and a half times as much space as foreign news (43.8 per cent and 18.8 per cent, respectively, in *Dawn*). Economic news predominated, followed by political, sports, cultural and foreign affairs in the metropolitan English language newspapers, whereas economic and sports news occupied a rather low position in most Urdu newspapers. On the other hand, Urdu newspapers concentrated more on local and regional affairs. English newspapers published a good deal of syndicated materials, especially on foreign affairs. The number of pictures carried by Pakistani newspapers increased considerably between the mid-1960s and mid-1970s. During January 1975, *Dawn* and *Pakistan Times* carried 209 and 163 pictures, respectively, representing 4.84 per cent and 6.4 per cent, of their respective newsholes.

4.6.10 Press Freedom

Except for the first period of martial law (1958-62), the civil war (March-December 1971), the language riots (July 1972) and the period of anti-Ahmadiyya agitation (June-September 1974), the press has enjoyed a fair measure of freedom and exhibited a considerable independence of attitude. Sometimes, the press was irresponsible, partly as a legacy of its agitational role during the pre-independence period, but never markedly worse than the press in most countries. In yet another respect, as well, the pre-independence heritage of the press has deeply affected its personality and traditions. In pre-partition India, the press developed as part of the Westernizing process. Although the subcontinent was ruled by a colonial government and the press consciously tried to imbibe British liberal traditions, following the press laws reflected a colonial or authoritarian philosophy, the press freedom pattern set by the British press. This obviously brought it into conflict with the then-British colonial government. Thus, while developing a rather well-entrenched tradition of press freedom, it also acquired the habit of being in conflict with government. This latter heritage, set in the peculiar conditions prevailing in Pakistan, especially since 1958, has not been an unmixed evil. In the final analysis, it has substantially helped in the development of a critical temper and of trade unionism among journalists and editors, the one impelling and the other enabling them to stand shoulder to shoulder in case of encroachment upon their domain.

On occasion, many newspapers have been influenced by official patronage or deterred by victimization, persecution, or threats of prosecution. This, however, is not inexplicable. For one thing, government is the single largest advertiser and since 1972, the sole authority for the allocation of newsprint, both of which can be conveniently used economically to strangle an independent newspaper. For another, government has always been armed with requisite acts, ordinances and laws to impose severe penalties on the press. More important among these are the Pakistan Security Act of 1952, the Maintenance of West Pakistan Public Order Ordinance (1960), the Press and Public Ordinance (1963) and emergency laws such as the Defence of Pakistan Rules. Except for a brief period (February-March 1969), Pakistan has been continuously under emergency and/or martial law since the Indo-Pakistan War of September 1965.

Both the 1952 act and the ordinances provide for control of information and have been extensively used for forfeiture of financial security (or demanding a new one), banning papers, seizing printing presses and jailing editors. In recent years, Defence of Pakistan Rules have been rather often invoked for the same purposes. Editors and the Pakistan Federal Union of Journalists (PFUJ), the premier journalists' body, have consistently opposed the use of Defence of Pakistan Rules, arguing that "errant" newspapers should be charged under the normal law of the land, rather than under emergency laws, so that they can seek redress against "arbitrary" executive action in a court of law[1] (see London *Times,* 15 June 1976, p. 7).

The government has based its case for continued checks and curbs on the press on the notion that the country is still passing through critical times which call for restraint and continuance of a state of emergency. Besides, the government has been suspicious of the actual role the press has played at various times. In 1973, for example, the central information minister said:

> Quite a few newspapers have failed to prove equal to the occasion. They have promoted forces of disruption . . . . Some of these papers have maligned the Head of State and sought to undermine the morale and discipline of the Armed Forces . . . . Headlines have been blown out of proportion to the actual context of the story creating wrong impressions in the public mind leading to a sense of despondency and despair (*Dawn,* 14 Feb. 1972, pp. 1, 8).

A few months later, another minister said:

> No responsible government would tolerate the kind of journalism which indulged in mudslinging among the people or in creating a situation of law and order in any part of the country . . . . (*Dawn,* 29 July 1972,

1   For instance, see the resolution of the Council of Pakistan Newspaper Editors on the suspension of *Jasarat* and the arrest of its managing editor and editor under the Defence of Pakistan Rules by the Sind government (*Dawn,* 5 July 1974, p. 5) and the PFUJ president's statement on the ban on *Outlook* (*Dawn,* 22 July 1974, p. 1).

p.1; see *Niazi,* 1972; for press reaction, see editorials in *Jasarat,* 16 Feb. 1972; *Dawn,* 16 Feb. 1972).

Infringements upon press freedom are both direct and indirect. The government does not have to invoke the laws to stop publication; it can seize a press or conveniently pressure printers into refusing to publish a paper which does not own its press. Thus, for want of a printer, *Outlook* died prematurely in August 1964, and the oppositionist *Jasarat* could not resume publication in late 1974, when the court revoked the ban imposed earlier in July of that year.

The government's capability to pressure newspapers economically increased considerably after 1972. For one thing, the scarcity of newsprint as a consequence of the loss of East Pakistan in 1971, has invested the government with the sole authority to allocate newsprint. Such authority has allegedly been used to penalize non-conformist newspapers. For another, the Bhutto regime's nationalization policy increased the amount of government advertising to 65 per cent of the total in the country. A newspaper earns this necessary government advertising on the basis of its "constructive policy." The number of newspapers that have failed in recent years to earn government advertising, or have forfeited their claim to it at least temporarily, is quite formidable, including *Dawn, Jang, Nawa-i-Waqt, Hurriyet, Jasarat, Shahbaz, Mehran, Outlook, Frontier Guardian, Pakistan Economist,* among others.

Although the government does not directly own newspapers, it controls about eight metropolitan dailies through the National Press Trust, whose chairman and the editors of the Trust newspapers, are appointed by government. Because of the extensive patronage extended to them, Trust newspapers have tended to be government mouthpieces, explaining the reasons for the insistent demands by both oppositionist political parties and journalists' organizations to disband the Trust. Of course, the government has resisted this pressure, arguing that if the Trust were to be dissolved and the newspapers turned over to private ownership, they would become organs of vested interests. This, the authorities argue, ought to be avoided if the regime is to launch and successfully implement its reforms and "revolutionary policies."

In the past, three political parties owned dailies and periodicals, but with the forced closure of *Jasarat* and *Shahbaz,* only PPP's *Musawat* and *Hilal-i-Pakistan* survived after mid-1974. The Trust and extant party newspapers not only represent about two-thirds of the metropolitan press, but are more affluent and generally better produced.

The government facilitates press coverage by issuing handouts through its well-organized Press Information Department. The handouts cover a wide spectrum, including governmental activities, government leaders' speeches, statements and press conferences and government press notes and clarifications on various issues and incidents. Press conferences and briefings are considered routine, as is press "advice." In the peculiar Pakistani context, the "advice" is usually heeded and government handouts get prominent display in almost all newspapers. Because the government has owned the premier news agency (Associated Press of Pakistan) since June 1961, it can control news at the source.

All this to the contrary, Pakistani journalists have generally shown a dedication to the cause of press freedom and have, over the years, undergone numerous trials and tribulations to promote that cause (also see 4.1.5; 4.6.12).

4.6.11 Conclusion

For years, the Pakistani press has been plagued by problems, mostly of an economic or political nature.

On the economic side have been the chronic newsprint shortages since 1971, along with the inflationary trends since 1972 that have resulted in increasingly high cost of production and distribution. These problems have undermined press economic viability and have led to an increase in the price of newspapers, thereby reversing the trend towards rising circulations.

Pakistan has more dailies than advertising and readership can support. In more advanced Western countries, the trend in recent decades has been towards mergers to maintain a sufficiently high standard; however, in Pakistan, it has been towards launching new, unwanted and insipid dailies, some to simply procure government patronage.

On the political side have been the official attempts at news management and control of the press, especially through the

National Press Trust and party newspapers, entailing serious consequences in respect of maintaining professional standards. Since ingenuity and an investigative spirit do not seem to pay in Pakistan, most newspapers have turned themselves into "handout utilizer" organs for the most part. One metropolitan daily has gone to the extreme of dispensing with the services of all reporters.

The extreme sensitivity to press criticism of the governments over the years, coupled with vast economic levers at government's disposal, and the many acts, ordinances and emergency laws, have conspired to seriously undermine "the public journal" role of the press. As a result, many independent newspapers have died, or are in the process of dying a slow, agonizing death. The fact that they have not died unmourned indicates the existence of a critical temper which represents a plus in an otherwise somber situation.

All this has resulted in a credibility gap which has been on the increase since the early 1970s. In any case, the forfeiture of the confidence of the people seems to be the greatest setback the press has suffered in recent years.

4.6.12 Since 1975, by Ann B. Radwan

The *White Paper on Misuse of Media: December 20, 1971-July 4, 1977,* published by the government in August 1978, describes in some detail how individual journalists and newspapers were manipulated to serve the purposes of the ruling party (see *Vidura,* Oct. 1978, pp. 271-74). Although it is not possible to verify all the claims contained in this White Paper, a sufficient number have been verified by the inclusion of relevant memoranda and letters (see Pakistan. Government, 1978, Appendices). Other claims have also been verified. (Interview, Ahmad Hasan Sheikh, principal information officer, Government of Pakistan, 1979, during which certain supportive documents were displayed). In sum, the Bhutto years are characterized by overt and largely successful, attempts

Ann B. Radwan is associate professor of history, University of North Florida. Her most recent research trip in South Asia was financed by the American Institute for Pakistan Studies. During that trip, 27 March-21 June 1979, she interviewed 40 government officials, journalists, editors and publishers on press-government relationship.

to prejudice journalists and newspapers of Pakistan in favor of the ruling party and officials.

The individual journalist or editor, whether employed by a Trust or independent paper, was a prime target for governmental manipulation. The techniques were the usual array of negative and positive inducements, including threats of job loss and incarceration on one hand, to all-expense-paid junkets to Europe and the U.S. and car licenses, on the other.

Publishers of weekly newspapers and journals were not ignored by the Bhutto government. Their strategy in this sector was multifaceted, with the government applying increasing pressure and sanctions until the objective of malleability was achieved. For instance, the quota of newsprint would be late or withheld entirely; the income tax returns of the paper as a corporate entity would be audited, as well as the individual returns of the owner/ publisher. In this latter instance, it could, and did, include members of the owner's family. Another form of leverage was the amount of government advertising allocated to a given publication. From 1976 until the end of Bhutto's government, this technique became increasingly important as the percentage of firms in the public sector expanded, allowing for direct govern-ment control for an ever-expanding amount of advertising decision-making. The private sector, its position becoming increasingly tenuous in this period of change, and itself dependent on the government for many licenses and approvals, was careful not to place its advertisements in publications that were in official disfavor.

Although the large English language and Urdu dailies managed to survive (and indeed some prospered throughout the Bhutto years) many journals and some important dailies either ceased publication altogether or were banned for extensive periods of time. Three outstanding examples were: *Outlook,* an independent journal published and edited by I.H. Burney, which ceased publication after the editor/publisher was harassed by the income tax authorities and other governmental agencies; *Daily Jasarat,* whose editor was jailed, and the paper itself banned for over three years, and *Frontier Guardian,* which suffered the same fate as *Outlook.*

In July 1977, when a change in government occurred and

Pakistan was once again under the control of martial law, statements were issued to the effect that the press would be freer than it was in the immediate past. It must be noted that with each governmental change in Pakistan, a similar statement has been made. There was renewed discussion regarding the disbanding of the National Press Trust and changing, or doing away with, the Press and Publications Ordinance of 1963, a document which has been used, since its passage, as the most effective tool for governmental control of the press. Unlike others, the government of CMLA-President Zia ul-Haq has gone past the pronouncement and talking stage in an attempt to replace the 1963 Ordinance. What to do with the National Press Trust is a more difficult problem as a national trust cannot legally cease to exist and even if that problem were solved, the question remains, to whom should the NPT papers revert.

In June 1979, the 1963 Press Ordinance was still in effect but a replacement had been formulated and was awaiting Cabinet approval (interview, Major General Mujib ur Rehman, information secretary, Government of Pakistan, 1979). One of the main features of this replacement law is that the declaration, a complicated and highly-politicized procedure for obtaining permission to publish and to print a paper and/or a journal, will be eliminated. In its place, the procedure will be a simple registration, requiring only a statement as to the name of the publication, the publisher and the editor.

Another important provision would be the establishment of regional press councils, whose membership would be comprised of respected citizens (such as retired Supreme Court judges) and whose duties would include, but would not be confined to acting as arbitrator and mediator in government-press and public-press relations. These councils would also have court referral rights; in other words, on their own initiative, a case involving the press could be, by the Council, placed before the judiciary. Although, at writing, no decision had been reached, it is evident that the current regime in Pakistan is making an effort to eliminate some of the most odious restraints on the press. Again, it should be remembered that all governments of Pakistan have had (and still have) many effective tools with which to control the press, such as the Defence of Pakistan Act and Official Secrets Act.

The judiciary in Pakistan has been one bulwark against the total disappearance of any visage of press freedom. Most journalists and publishers agree that in both the Bhutto and Zia eras, the courts have protected, as far as possible, the civil liberties of the fourth estate. Neither the promulgation of a new and liberal press ordinance, the dissolution of the Trust nor the protection of the courts can guarantee freedom. The press is a mirror of the society within which it functions. Consequently, without an appreciation for the necessary contribution of a "loyal opposition" by the ruling elites, the press is unable to fulfill the primary role as disinterested observer and commentator.

4.7   Sri Lanka

Shelton A. Gunaratne

The subject of the state of newspaper journalism in Sri Lanka
brings to mind a recent statement made by James C. Thomson,
curator of the Nieman Foundation at Harvard. He said:

> ... there is no 'final solution'. . . to the Government-
> media problem in a democracy, for the continuous
> tension between these two powerful institutions is a
> fundamental life sign — like blood pressure, for instance
> — within the body politic.
> One should therefore be warned against all proposed
> 'solutions' that put an end to the tension itself. As with
> blood pressure, the tension can get perilously high, also
> comatosely low . . . (*Thomson*, 1973).

The "fundamental life sign" that Thomson speaks of no longer
appears to prevail in Sri Lanka. The tension he speaks of has
become "comatosely low" and the prospect of a vigorous, investigative press in the country appears to be relatively dim.

4.7.1 Historical Background

Newspapers, in the modern sense, were introduced as a medium
of communication only after the British occupation of the island.
Ironically, the first newspapers were published in English, the
language of the British, rather than in Sinhalese, the language of

Shelton A. Gunaratne is lecturer in journalism/communication at Capricornia Institute
of Advanced Education in Australia. Previously, he taught at Universiti Sains Malaysia,
was a World Press Institute fellow in the U.S. and worked for five years on Sri Lankan
newspapers.

the large majority of the people. Obviously, the original news-papers were not intended for the masses. Hulugalle points out that "the press in Ceylon, until the middle of the nineteenth century, was published in the English language, by Englishmen, and mainly for Englishmen" (*Hulugalle*, 1969, p. 1224).

The earliest news publication was the *Government Gazette*, launched by the British administration three months after the country was declared a crown colony in 1802. In addition to government news, this publication contained marriage and death notices of prominent people and literary contributions as well. But what could be called the first newspaper, the *Colombo Journal*, was not published until 30 years later. Edited by Postmaster-General George Lee, it had the active support of Gov. Robert Wilmot Horton. This was the beginning of the island's free press.

The establishment of a free press owed much to William M. G. Colebrooke, a royal commissioner who was appointed in 1829 to inquire into the civil government. Sensing that the power of the governor to banish a person without trial could have a detrimental effect on the development of a vigorous and critical press, he recommended the repeal of that power and the encouragement of an independent press.

The *Journal* had only a short span of life because the authorities in England wanted the governor to divert his attention from the *Journal* to the official *Gazette*. However, a biweekly started in 1834 by a group of English merchants, *Observer and Commercial Advertiser*, helped fill the vacuum. The *Observer*, which has survived as the island's oldest newspaper, became a vigorous critic of the administration, so much so that Gov. Horton encouraged the launching of another newspaper, the *Colombo Chronicle* (later *Herald*), which also had a short life span.

The English mercantile interests launched two other biweeklies in 1846, the *Examiner* and the *Ceylon Times*. (While the former folded in 1900, the latter has survived as the country's second oldest newspaper under the name *Times of Ceylon*.) Meanwhile, the *Observer*, whose editorship and ownership passed on to a Scotsman, A. M. Ferguson, in 1858, became the organ of the plantation interests who were highly critical of Parliament.

Ceylonese themselves started publishing English language

newspapers later in the century. These included the first morning newspaper, published in 1881, *Ceylon Independent,* owned by Sir Hector Van Cuylenberg; *Standard; Ceylon Morning Leader,* and *Ceylonese.* Missionaries used the columns of the English language press widely to influence the country's educational policy.

A rich addition to the English language press was the *Ceylon Daily News,* started in 1918 by D. R. Wijewardene, the country's most well-known newspaper magnate who formed the Associated Newspapers of Ceylon Ltd. (ANCL), for years, the island's predominant newspaper group. Five years later, he acquired the *Observer* which Ferguson had sold to a European syndicate in 1920.

The English language press, in general, was opposed to the welfare policies of the government. According to Sumathipala, the *Times of Ceylon* was opposed to the free education bill presented to the State Council in 1938 and "even went to the extent of asking the British government not to grant self-government to Ceylon if the Bill was passed." The *Times* was also opposed to universal franchise, which it called "the most serious blot on the Ceylonese constitution." The *Daily News* too was originally opposed to "free education from kindergarten to the university," which it called a "luxury" that "cannot be maintained by a community which is not geared to a high degree of economic production" (*Sumathipala,* 1968, pp. 373, 375, 379).

Compared to the English language press, the Sinhalese press had a late start. The first Sinhalese newspaper, *Lakminipahana,* started in 1862, was followed by several weeklies — *Sarasavi Sandaresa, Sinhala Jathiya, Sinhala Bauddhaya* and *Sinhala Samaya.* The *Sandaresa* was edited by a famous Sinhalese pundit, Weragama Bandara. The Sinhalese press exuded a remarkable pronationalistic and pro-Buddhist bias, compared to the general trend of the English language press to be pro-Western and pro-Christian — a trend that continued well into the 1960s.

The country's Sinhalese press had a shot in the arm when the British administration decided in 1870 to "undertake vernacular education on a large scale" with a government school in every village.

The Sinhalese daily press emerged only after the turn of the century with *Dinamina* and *Lakmina* as the trailblazers. *Dinamina* was started in 1908 by H. S. Perera and later bought by Wijewardene, who made it the largest circulation daily newspaper in the country. A Tamil daily, *Thinakaran,* was added to the ANCL group in 1932. According to Hulugalle "D. R. Wijewardene inaugurated a new era in Ceylon journalism by sound organization and the introduction of the latest machinery for newspaper production" (*Hulugalle,* 1969, p. 1227; see *Hulugalle* in *Lent,* 1971).

By the late 1940s, the country's daily press had become a "duopoly" of the ANCL (popularly known as Lake House) and the Times of Ceylon Ltd., which in 1947 started a Sinhalese daily, *Lankadipa,* to compete with the successful *Dinamina.* (With independence, the Times' ownership had passed on to local capitalists from the hands of Englishmen.) A third company had, in 1930, started a Tamil daily, *Virakesari,* but its share in the newspaper market was negligible compared to the other two. The ANCL added an afternoon Sinhalese daily, *Janata,* in 1953, while the Times group added a morning English daily, *Morning Times,* in 1954. The latter failed to survive long, and was revived in 1961 as the Ceylon *Daily Mirror.*

An unsuccessful attempt was made in the 1950s by Swadeshi Newspapers Ltd. to capture a share of the daily newspaper market. This company was the publisher of the weekly *Sinhala Jathiya,* originally launched by Piyadasa Sirisena, a writer known for his ardent nationalistic views. The company tried out a Sinhalese daily, *Jathiya,* and an English daily, *Guardian,* both of which failed.

Backed by the financial resources of the country's largest book publishing company, M. D. Gunasena & Co. Ltd., a new newspaper group, Independent Newspapers Ltd., launched a Sinhalese daily, *Dawasa,* together with a Sunday counterpart, *Rividina* (later *Riviresa*) in 1961. The company achieved success from its very inception and surpassed the Time's group with the second largest share of the daily newspaper market. The company had the blessings of the Sirimavo Bandaranaike Government at the time of its inception, in addition to the journalistic genius of a veteran newspaperman, D. B. Dhanapala, who had earlier edited *Lankadipa* for the Times group.

4.7.2 *Press Characteristics*

4.7.2.1 Concentration

In the mid-1960s, nearly 95 per cent of the country's daily newspaper market was shared by Associated Newspapers of Ceylon
Ltd. (54 per cent), Times of Ceylon Ltd. (21 per cent) and the
Independent Newspapers Ltd. (20 per cent) (*Gunaratne*, 1970,
p. 534). On the basis of the available circulation figures for 1973,
some diffusion of the share of the market had become noticeable
with these three companies dominating only about 82 per cent,
the ANCL's share being approximately 40 per cent, Times' 17 per
cent and Independent Newspapers' 25 per cent.

The rest of the market was shared by two Tamil newspaper
companies, Virakesari Ltd. and Eelanadu Ltd., and three political
party dailies — *Aththa,* published by the Communist Party (CP)
of Ceylon Moscow Wing; *Janadina,* published by Suriya Publishers
for the Lanka Sama Samaja Party (LSSP), and *Sirilaka,* published
by the Sri Lanka People's Press for the Sri Lanka Freedom Party
(SLFP).

The ANCL published five dailies (two in Sinhalese, two in
English, and one in Tamil) and three Sunday newspapers (one in
each language). The Sinhalese newspapers, the daily *Dinamina* and
the Sunday *Silumina,* were its money spinners with the latter
having the largest circulation of any newspaper in the country.
It also published several specialized weeklies in Sinhalese dealing
with religion, culture, astrology and news of interest to women
and children.

Independent Newspapers Ltd. also published five dailies (two
in Sinhalese, two in Tamil, and one in English) and three Sunday
newspapers (one in each language). The mainstays of the company
were the Sinhalese daily, *Dawasa,* and its Sunday counterpart,
Riviresa. This company also published several specialized periodicals covering culture, literature, astrology, cinema, children's news,
etc.

The Times group published three dailies (two in English and one
in Sinhalese) and two Sunday newspapers (one each in Sinhalese
and English). Again the company was sustained by its Sinhalese
newspaper. No Tamil newspapers were published by this company,

even though its ownership has been Tamil-oriented. The company has published a weekly women's magazine and a monthly general interest magazine in Sinhalese.

Virakesari Ltd. published two Tamil dailies, their Sunday counterparts and a Tamil astrological weekly, *Jothi.* Eelanadu Ltd., located in the northern city of Jaffna, published the only daily newspaper outside the capital city of Colombo. Except for the Tamil *Eelanadu* and its Sunday edition, which have been localized for the Tamil population in the north, all other daily and Sunday newspapers have a nationwide circulation.

4.7.2.2 Ownership and Control

The country's largest newspaper publishing group, ANCL (or Lake House), ceased to be a private company in July 1973, when the government nationalized 75 per cent of its shares with the balance allocated to the "former owning family." The nationalized shares are held in trust by the "public trustee" until they are sold to the general public (as described later in this chapter) so that "in the not so very long run," the company "will again be in the ownership of persons other than the state" (*Ceylon News,* 6 Dec. 1973). However, as of the end of 1973, none of the shares had been sold to the public, because the shares had not been "valued" (*Ceylon News,* 6 Dec. 1973). Until its first annual general meeting following the "take-over," the company was run by a board of directors appointed by the "public trustee."

Before the "take-over," the company had a subscribed capital of Rs.6 million (approximately US$1 million) with four directors and their spouses owning more than two-thirds of the entire issue (Sri Lanka. Department of Government Printing, 1971). The company's 600,000 shares were owned by 42 persons with the articles of association prohibiting "any invitation to the public to subscribe for any shares or debentures or debenture stock of the company" (Sri Lanka. National State Assembly Debates, 1973a, cols. 1973-74).

While up-to-date financial information about the other newspaper publishing companies was not available when this chapter was written, the 1963 Press Commission provided the following information (Ceylon. Ceylon Government Press, 1964b, pp.

133-41):

The Times of Ceylon Ltd., a public company, had a share capital or Rs.4.2 million with 75 shareholders. However, the company was controlled by a few shareholders with the executors of the Sangarapillai Trust holding about 40 per cent of the shares. Independent Newspapers Ltd., a private company, had a share capital of Rs.1 million with 14 shareholders, who were all members of the Gunasena family. Virakesari Ltd., a private company, had a share capital of Rs.1 million with 19 shareholders. It was controlled by a board of directors comprised solely of Indian nationals. Eelanadu Ltd., a private company, had a share capital of Rs.500,000 with 28 shareholders. It was controlled by an all-Tamil directorate. Thus, each of these companies has been controlled by "a small group of persons" (Ceylon. Ceylon Government Press, 1974a, para. 10).

Following a struggle within the Times directorate in 1973, with a case pending in the courts, the deputy chairman of the company, P. A. Ediriweera, has undertaken "to see that the ownership" of the company "was broadbased so that the control of the company would not be in the hands of a few individuals." Following the policy of the Bandaranaike Government, Ediriweera indicated that "even the workers would be able to participate as shareholders and safeguard their interest" (Sri Lanka. National State Assembly Debates, 1973b, cols. 2375-76). Thus the Times newspapers, which had been very critical of the ruling coalition parties in the past, implicitly agreed to toe the line of the Bandaranaike Government.

Prime Minister Sirimavo Bandaranaike warned that she hoped Independent Newspapers Ltd. too would follow suit without forcing "the hands of the Government." Ironically, this company, which was launched with the blessings of the Bandaranaike Government, for a time was the only one of the three large newspaper publishing companies to carry on forthright criticisms of the government. "The Opposition point of view was expressed only through these newspapers," claimed a politician of the United National Party (UNP). It was also alleged that journalism today has "been reduced to a cowardly profession" with propaganda carried out by the government "being worse than that of Goebbels" (*Ceylon Daily News*, 20 Dec. 1973).

With the country's only broadcasting outlet remaining a public corporation unable to voice criticisms of government, and, since 1973, with two of the three newspaper "monopolies" tamed, freedom of the press, in terms of the libertarian theory, has been curtailed in Sri Lanka.

Assessing press freedom in 1973, the International Press Institute, wrote that "legislation for a particular publishing house" was "a dangerous precedent" and that "it is feared . . . similar measures might be taken against other Cingalese [*sic*] press groups who have continued to fight against the attacks made on press freedom by the Government" (*IPI Report,* Jan. 1974, p. 16).

4.7.2.3 Circulation and Readership

The estimated daily newspaper circulation in the mid-1970s was 615,000 copies for a population of 13 million. UNESCO figures showed that the number of daily newspaper copies per 100 people had risen from 3.6 in 1960 to 4.9 in 1970, with the consumption of newsprint per inhabitant also rising from 1.2 kilograms to 1.5 and the total newsprint consumption from 11,500 metric tons to 18,300 within the same time span (UNESCO, 1972, pp. 754, 786). If newspaper readership is considered about five times the total circulation, the country's daily newspaper readership was estimated at 3 million people.

Ceylon's socio-economic survey 1969-70 showed that 89.6 per cent of the males and 75.5 per cent of females over the age of 10 were literate. A study by Gunaratne (1972, pp. 3, 70) in four peasant communities showed that "for all practical purposes, everyone who could read accurately was also able to answer the question testing functional literacy." An island-wide survey conducted by the Audit Bureau of Circulation in 1967 reported that 58 per cent of the male population and 28 per cent of the female population claimed to read newspapers while the urban readership was more intensive than in rural areas (*Ranatunge,* 1971). The same media survey also revealed that:

* the readership of Sinhalese publications is spread evenly among all groups while English readership is confined to urban middle classes;
* there is little duplication between English and

Sinhalese publications;
* the most widely read type of publication is the morning daily and most readers spend at least 15 minutes reading it;
* Local and foreign news receive the greatest amount of attention followed by sports news and the editorial;
* borrowing and lending of newspapers is a widespread habit;
* in urban areas most people read newspapers at home because they buy every issue, but there were some who read them in their offices;
* in rural areas most people read the newspapers outside their homes — in eating houses, boutiques and community centers;
* most newspaper readers are regular readers reading every issue, but about one-fourth of the readers merely glanced through them;
* readership of morning dailies among men and women was 48 per cent and 14 per cent, respectively, compared to 15 per cent and 6 per cent for evening dailies and 43 per cent and 22 per cent for Sunday newspapers; and
* the readership of other weeklies, fortnightlies and monthlies was at a much lower level with only 20 per cent men and 12 per cent women reading the weeklies.

Gunaratne's study showed that the villagers were primarily interested in reading domestic news, short stories and verses, astrological news, police reports, cartoons and lottery results. Foreign news, letters to the editor, editorials, advertisements, radio programs and cinema news were only of secondary interest to them (*Gunaratne*, 1972, pp. 83-84).

The first newspaper readership survey conducted in the country in 1964, found that:

the reading of publications in more than one language was limited to a very small proportion of the population, almost entirely of the urban middle class . . . While 53 per cent of the men and 23 per cent of the women read some publication, 42 per cent of the men and 16 per cent of the women read only Sinhalese publications, 3 per cent of the men and 1 per cent of the women read only Tamil publications, and 3 per cent of the men and 4 per cent of the women read only English publications. Only 4 per cent of the men and 3 per cent of the women read both English and Sinhalese publications, and less than one-half of 1 per cent of the men and no detectable proportion of the women read both English and Tamil publications. The reading of both Sinhalese and Tamil publications was almost non-existent (*Kearney*, 1967, pp. 17-18).

Thus, the Sinhalese newspapers have been geared primarily to the Sinhalese Buddhists while Tamil newspapers have been oriented to the Tamil Hindus, there being hardly any Sinhalese Hindus or Tamil Buddhists. The English language newspapers have catered to the more educated elite crossing racial and religious lines.

A dip in newspaper circulation was observed in 1973. Lake House newspapers underwent "a steady drop in circulation" resulting from cuts in the newsprint quota supplied by the Eastern Paper Mills Corporation, the country's newsprint producer. A tight foreign-exchange situation forced government to severely restrict the import of newsprint, the price of which had risen to Rs.3,200 (approximately US$533) per ton by the end of 1973. The daily circulation of Lake House newspapers is estimated to have gone down by as much as 100,000 between April and December 1973 (*Ceylon News*, 6 Dec. 1973). This dip was partly because of a lower press run, resulting from the newsprint shortage, and partly because of a boycott of "nationalized" newspapers, organized by the opposition political parties.

The average daily newspaper has between four and eight pages, but the price per copy at 25 Ceylonese cents (approximately US 4 cents) is still beyond the average citizen considering a per capita annual income of about $140. This may be the primary reason why the newspaper circulation is not commensurate with the country's literacy rate.

4.7.2.4 Advertising

In the opinion of the 1963 Press Commission, "the more powerful advertisers and private capitalist interests, both foreign and local

... have a pervading and powerful influence over the newspaper organization" in the country. For instance, the commission said, the press could not afford "to be too critical of films" shown by their movie-theater advertisers because of threats to withdraw advertising, as demonstrated once by the Ceylon Theatres Ltd. The commission implied pressure from oil companies when newspaper advertising managers objected to some words used in an ad from the Ceylon Petroleum Corporation, even though the Shell company had ads designed to affect the popularity of Lanka Petrol. But it failed to substantiate the degree of pressure, if any, from heavy advertisers, such as Lever Brothers, Ceylon Tobacco Co., and Ceylon Theatres Ltd.

The commission observed that the daily newspapers and their Sunday counterparts devoted "far too much space" for advertising "while the reading content is altogether meager." On the basis of a random selection of newspapers for three months, the Sunday *Observer* devoted 61 per cent to advertising; Ceylon *Daily News,* 38.5 per cent; *Silumina,* 38.4 per cent; *Dinamina,* 36.1 per cent; Sunday *Times,* 34.4 per cent; *Lankadipa,* 31.4 per cent; *Observer,* 29.4 per cent; Sunday *Lankadipa,* 29.2 per cent; *Times of Ceylon,* 28.7 per cent; *Dawasa,* 23.7 per cent; *Daily Mirror,* 17.2 per cent; *Janata,* 5.7 per cent, and *Sawasa,* 3.2 per cent (*Ceylon. Ceylon Government Press,* 1964b, pp. 133-41).

The country's "more powerful and important advertising agencies," according to the commission, were Grants Advertising (Ceylon) Ltd., International Advertising Services, J. Walter Thompson & Co. (Private) Ltd. and Stronachs Advertising Ltd. In the mid-1970s, the advertising scene was dominated by the first two.

International Advertising Services estimated that in 1966, the "total advertising expenditure on all media was 28 million rupees" (approximately US$4.7 million), which was about 0.4 per cent of the national income. In per capita terms, advertising expenditure was about Rs. 2.60 (US$0.43). About 60 to 65 per cent of all advertising expenditure was directed to the print press, 15 per cent to radio, 5 per cent to screen advertising and 3 per cent to outdoor advertising. And much advertising space was "devoted to consumer goods," though their range and variety was rather small (*International Advertising Services,* 1968).

The severe newsprint shortage resulting in a reduction of pages in newspapers led to a loss of "considerable advertising revenue" as of 1973. Former Prime Minister Sirimavo Bandaranaike conceded that Lake House newspapers, after the "take-over," had to reduce advertising, though "still private sector advertising exceeds public sector advertising" (*Ceylon News,* 6 Dec. 1973). The country's newspapers carried less advertising in the 1970s than in the 1960s.

4.7.2.5 Press Laws

A government-appointed Press Council, details of which have been provided later in the chapter, was set up in 1973 to entertain complaints against the newspapers.

Aside from the Press Council, an aggrieved person can obtain relief in the courts "where the publication comes within the law of defamation." However, no relief is available in the courts, "where the offending publication is merely inaccurate or untrue and does not carry with it all the elements necessary to constitute the civil law of defamation." This, apparently, is where the Press Council can be helpful.

The provisions relating to the criminal law of defamation are to be found in Chapter XIX of the Penal Code. Here, the definition of the offense of defamation "is designed to punish a person who publishes an imputation concerning another person intending or knowing or having reason to believe that the imputation will harm his reputation . . ."

The law governing the civil wrong of defamation in Sri Lanka is the Roman-Dutch Law, under which (compared to the English Law) the truth of the libellous statement is not a sufficient defense; and "the defendant must, to escape liability, prove that the statement is not only true but also that its publication was in the public interest" (*Ceylon. Ceylon Government Press,* 1964b, pp. 246, 247).

4.7.2.6 Miscellaneous

The country's newspapers, in general, carry very little foreign news, which has further been affected by the continuing newsprint shortage. The vernacular newspapers and the Sunday editions of newspapers, in general, publish very little foreign news. The 1963 Press Commission reported that only four newspapers devoted over 10 per cent of their contents to foreign news, i.e., *Times of Ceylon*, 19.7 per cent; *Sawasa*, 15.3 per cent; Ceylon *Daily Mirror*, 13.5 per cent, and Ceylon *Observer*, 13.4 per cent. *Dinamina, Lankadipa* and *Janata* had less than 5 per cent (*Ceylon. Ceylon Government Press*, 1964b, app. V). However, another content analysis showed that the Ceylon *Daily News* devoted 24.3 per cent of its contents to foreign news in 1970 (*Liu and Gunaratne*, 1972, p. 38). The major source of foreign news for all the newspapers is Reuters.

Another glaring deficiency in the field of journalism is the lack of well-trained journalists. The Press Commission recommended that journalism be taught as one of the subjects in the universities until the time was ripe for the establishment of a school of journalism (*Ceylon. Ceylon Government Press*, 1964b, para. 231). In 1969, it was decided to award a diploma in mass communication to students who followed a program in one of the junior university colleges. These colleges were closed down the following year with the change of government, thereby ending the program as well. In 1973, the Vidyalankara campus of the University of Sri Lanka opened a department of mass communication.

The place of women is still undefined in the field of journalism. Top-notch positions still elude women. An exception is the case of Mrs. N. M. Wickremasinghe, a daughter of D. R. Wijewardene. She was managing director of Lake House at the time of the "take-over."

4.7.3 The Press and Politics

4.7.3.1 Before 1956: 'Kingmaker' Role

Weerawardana (1960, p. 126), in an analysis of the general election in 1956, asserts that the daily press "played a very important part in every election since 1946." With the introduction of the parliamentary system under the Soulbury constitution, just prior to the country's independence from Britain in February 1948, the Lake House press "had verily become a kingmaker." (*Ceylon. Ceylon Government Press*, 1964a, para. 17). With hardly any competition from the Times group or any other newspaper, Lake House newspapers were assumed to wield the power of moulding public opinion. From 1947 to 1956 when the country was governed by the United National Party (UNP), which had strong attachments to the local capitalists, Lake House "was almost a member of the 'inner cabinet' " as could be inferred from the revelations made by a high-level Lake House journalist, J. L. Fernando, in a book on the country's first three UNP Prime Ministers – D. S. Senanayake, Dudley Senanayake and Sir John Kotelawala (*Ceylon. Ceylon Government Press*, 1964a, paras. 19, 21).

D. R. Wijewardene, the ANCL founder, "dreaded Communism and feared the masses" (*Ceylon. Ceylon Government Press*, 1964a, para. 16) and, as a matter of course, subtly favored the UNP until his death in 1950, when the destinies of his company passed on to a trust that was to carry on the company's business until his younger son, R. S. Wijewardene, was ready to take control, which was in 1962. Meanwhile, the founder's sons-in-law – Esmond Wickremasinghe, George Gomes and Lal Gooneratne – joined the company's directorate and attempted behind-the-scene political maneuvers that helped perpetuate the impression that Lake House newspapers, as a matter of policy, supported the UNP and the local capitalist interests. Thus, Lake House press fell into disfavor with the political parties opposed to the UNP.

S. W. R. D. Bandaranaike, a cabinet minister in the UNP Government, quit in 1952 to form a middle-of-the-road political party which he named the Sri Lanka Freedom Party (SLFP). Bandaranaike assumed a socialist stance and formed a coalition with sympathetic parties[1] to fight the UNP at the 1956 general election. He also entered into a no-contest pact with the Marxist groups – the Lanka Sama Samaja Party (LSSP) and the Communist Party (CP). These political moves did not receive the sympathy of the majority of daily papers which showed their UNP-bias "not merely in the coverage given, but also in the manner of coverage" (*Weerawardana*, 1960, p. 131). Only *Lankadipa* appeared to have favored Bandaranaike.

1 The coalition was named Mahajana Eksath Peramuna (People's United Front). The partners of the coalition included K.M.P. Rajaratne's Bhasa Peramuna (Language Front) and Philip Gunawardene's Viplavakari (Revolutionary) LSSP.

In his analysis of the newspaper coverage of the election, Weerawardana said that, though "in a majority of papers the editorials were used in a generally unbiased or non-political manner," they openly used political commentaries and letters to the editor "for expressing sympathy with a party or group." While the opposition parties "received fair coverage" on the whole, taking the entire press into consideration, "the choice of headlines, the place given to different items and even 'kite-flying' were used in a manner which was somewhat partisan" (*Weerawardana*, 1960, p. 132).

The pro-UNP bias of the Lake House press came under concentrated attack during the 1956 election campaign. Adverting to the findings of an independent Buddhist commission, the supporters of the Bandaranaike coalition alleged that all daily newspapers were in the hands of Christians. A pamphlet was distributed in every Sinhalese-speaking electorate urging a Lake House boycott campaign. A vociferous group of the Buddhist clergy, the Eksath Bhikku Peramuna (United Buddhist-clergy Front), and a respected Buddhist lay leader, L. H. Mettananda, were the prime movers behind this attack. However, the taming of Lake House had to wait 17 more years.

4.7.3.2 After 1957: Government-Press Conflict

With the defeat of the UNP and the election of Bandaranaike as the country's first socialist prime minister in 1956, Lake House ceased to be a member of the "inner cabinet." The socialist policies of the Bandaranaike Government were criticized, particularly by the English language newspapers, which supposedly generated greater impact than the vernacular papers, because the country's ruling elite, including the prime minister, functioned better in English. The *Times of Ceylon* "remained reactionary and was generally opposed to almost all the governments of independent Ceylon, more so after 1956" (*Ceylon. Ceylon Government Press*, 1964a, para. 27).

The "monopoly press" came under Parliamentary discussion in February 1959, when the third member for Colombo Central, M. S. Themis, introduced a motion that "legislation should be enacted to take over from private ownership and control the

Ceylon daily newspapers and entrust the working of the system
to an independent corporation for the benefit of the people"
(*Ceylon. Ceylon Government Press,* 1964a, para. 32). This
motion, however, was not voted upon.

Bandaranaike was assassinated by a fanatical Buddhist monk
in September 1959. Following a brief period of political confusion
under Prime Minister W. Dahanayake, the country went to the
polls in March 1960, with the SLFP led by C. P. de Silva and the
UNP led by Dudley Senanayake. The results of the election were
inconclusive and Senanayake formed an interim government.
Meanwhile, the SLFP elected Sirimavo Bandaranaike, widow of
the assassinated prime minister, as its new leader; when the
country went to the polls again in July 1960, the SLFP emerged
as the clear victor.

Commenting on the role of the press during these elections,
the Press Commission, appointed later by the SLFP government,
asserted that "the press went beyond all bounds in its attempt to
do propaganda for the UNP," as evidenced by "a large number
of special articles, editorials and cartoons" produced before the
Commission; that "most of the cartoons depicting Mrs. Sirimavo
Bandaranaike . . . went beyond the limits of decency" and even
"positively vulgar"; that there was an attempt to show a "very
close connection" between the SLFP and the Soviet Union and
Communism, and that the press even went to the extent of using
astrology, the impact of which "is widespread among all classes
of people," to influence the voters to support the UNP (*Ceylon.
Ceylon Government Press,* 1964b, para. 164).

Meanwhile, concern about "the vast engines that control
opinion today" were expressed in academic circles as well. One
political scientist asserted that,

> experience of the working of the daily press in this
> country especially since 1956 has revealed how easy
> it is to disrupt a government by the pillorying of its
> leaders, by magnifying completely out of proportion
> the activities of communal extremists (*Wilson,* 1960,
> p. 6).

He also said that,

> if freedom of the press tends to disrupt national unity,
> if such freedom is utilised to promote civil commotion

and conflict between communities, religious or racial, it might become necessary for the state to introduce restrictions which might help toward restoring order or promoting unity (*Wilson*, 1960, p. 5).

Wilson argued that "the wholesale imitation of western standards by our societies" was "not altogether conducive towards the economic well-being or national unity"; that some restrictions on the press were necessary or, alternatively, "the press should draw up a code of conduct or observe a self-denying ordinance" in regard to matters affecting national unity and economic well-being; that "the right to free expression" pre-supposed "a highly politically conscious people who are not easily driven to violence"; and that in Ceylon, "the freedom of the press has in effect become the freedom of newspaper proprietors to freely malign their enemies" and to promote "conservative and reactionary" policies they support (*Wilson*, 1960, pp. 6-9). Wilson further indicted the press thus:

> In this country, though the newspapers have differed in regard to details of policy, there is no doubt that on vital matters, on fundamentals, as for instance the maintenance of the status quo, the sanctity of private property, antagonism to radical changes in the social set up, they have been united in their opposition to parties and Governments which sought to usher in changes in regard to these matters . . . (*Wilson*, 1960, p. 15).

4.7.3.3 Press Commission

The Sirimavo Bandaranaike Government announced its intention to appoint the aforementioned Press Commission in the "Speech from the Throne," read by the governor-general at the opening of Parliament on 12 August 1960. The speech also announced government's intention to introduce legislation to take over the Lake House and Times newspapers "and to vest such newspapers in statutory public corporations with unlimited share capital in which individual holdings will be restricted so as to ensure a broad-based ownership" (*Ceylon. Ceylon Government Press*, 1964a, para. 33).

Government drafted a bill to take over the newspapers, but the ruling SLFP failed to reach agreement. The 1961 throne speech failed to mention the matter at all. According to Vickery (1967, p. 426), this delay in action may have been due to two reasons: first, the emergence of Independent Newspapers Ltd., which launched a Sinhalese daily sympathetic to the government and the Buddhist Sinhalese point of view; and second, the restraint exercised by the Lake House newspapers which "often seemed inclined to say nothing at all about government." But government's suspicion that Independent Newspapers Ltd. had prior knowledge of a coup attempted in January 1962 led to an estrangement between the two. A bill "to prevent press monopolies" was announced in the 1962 throne speech. But the parliamentary debate that followed demonstrated that the SLFP itself was divided over the press takeover (*Gunaratne,* 1970, p. 536).

Several other press bills were subsequently drafted, all of which failed to receive the unanimous support of the cabinet of ministers. The 1963 throne speech again made no mention of the press, and the LSSP moved an amendment "to end the monopoly of the daily press." The government announced it had immediate plans to set up a press commission, which it appointed in September 1963, under the chairmanship of K. D. de Silva, a supreme court justice. The press claimed that the two other members of the commission were known to have anti-press sentiments and refused to cooperate with the commission, even after one of them was replaced.

A change in the composition of the government in June 1964, resulting from the coalition of the SLFP with the Marxist LSSP, based on a 14-point agreement, including one to "end the press monopoly," may have quickened the work of the Press Commission. An indictment of the anti-Marxist press was now needed more than ever. Rather than determining political biases of the newspapers through a content analysis of random samples of each, the commission depended almost entirely on the selective anti-press evidence produced before it by interested parties. Thus, some of the findings of the commission, which indicted the press both in its interim report (submitted to the governor-general on 28 July 1964) and in the final report (submitted two months later), lacked scientific objectivity. However, it served a political expediency for the government in power to justify its moves against the established press.

The commission alleged that Lake House and Times newspapers, particularly those published in English, were "chiefly responsible for the prevailing disunity of the various racial and religious groups" in the country, and that the editorial staffs of these newspapers, many of whom "had been educated in Roman Catholic missionary schools which conditioned them to accept the Greaco-Roman-Christian tradition as something superior," readily fell "into line with the wishes of the management to fight for the preservation of the undue privileges that a certain class had obtained from foreign rulers . . . ." It further alleged that the two newspaper groups "use their English language and Sinhala language newspapers, and the Lake House group its Tamil language newspaper, to preach disunity to the people and attempt to divide the nation . . ." (*Ceylon. Ceylon Government Press*, 1964b, paras. 38, 111, 200).

The commission appears to have ignored the fact that newspapers published in the three languages, albeit by the same group, may have been geared to the interests of their respective readerships as a simple matter of newspaper economics — rather than as a deliberate method of sowing racial disunity. A Tamil newspaper, extolling the interests of the Sinhalese Buddhists, for instance, would hardly have a market.

The commission recommended immediate steps to change the ownership and control of the newspaper groups, including: (1) the establishment of a state corporation to run the daily newspapers of the Lake House group; (2) broad-basing the ownership of other newspaper groups (Times, Independent Newspapers, Virakesari and Eelanadu), by restricting each shareholder to no more than one-eightieth part of the total number of shares issued (though it preferred a cooperative set-up for the Times group); (3) the setting up of a five-member Press Council "in order to safeguard the freedom of the press and the integrity on which its reputation depends, and to uphold the independence and liberty of the subject . . ." — a body which should be "independent and impervious to pressure from any direction . . ."; (4) the appointment of a five-member Press Tribunal by the Judicial Service

Commission "to deal only with matters referred to it by the Press Council," and (5) the establishment of a national news agency with extensive functions.

Following these recommendations, a bill was introduced in Parliament on 25 September 1964, to provide for the setting up of a Press Council and a Press Tribunal with a view to "exercise general supervision and control over newspaper business . . . ," to ensure "a high standard of journalistic ethics" and the presentation of. "news to the public fairly, accurately and with regard to truth" (*IPI Report,* Nov. 1964, p. 6). While the bill passed the Senate, it failed to come up for debate in the House of Representatives as a result of two opposition members gaining its sponsorship through a technicality in parliamentary standing orders.

Frustrated in its initial attempt, government introduced a bill on 15 October 1964, to nationalize Lake House and the Lake House-dominated Press Trust of Ceylon. But it turned out that the bill had not been properly presented, and to overcome this legal technicality, government decided to prorogue parliament on 13 November, and reconvene it on 20 November so that the lapsed press bills could be appropriately introduced.

Meanwhile, the newspapers and the parliamentary opposition launched a concerted attack on the government's "dictatorial tendencies." When Parliament met on 3 December to vote on the "Address of Thanks," six members of the SLFP criticized the government. Later, the SLFP's deputy leader, C. P. de Silva, himself crossed over to the opposition. An amendment to the throne speech, worded in the form of a no-confidence motion, was passed by the House, with 13 members of the governing party and one independent voting for it, thereby defeating the ruling coalition by one vote. The coalition resigned, whereupon a general election was scheduled for March 1965.

4.7.3.4 1965: Press Defeats Government

There were allegations from leftist politicians that a huge sum of money was utilized by Lake House in influencing the conduct of members of Parliament who crossed over to the opposition to defeat the SLFP-LSSP coalition government. But no proof of

526   John A. Lent *Newspapers in Asia*

such bribery was established, even though the Lake House directorate was unable to satisfactorily account for a sum of Rs.645,000 (approximately US$107,500), voted by the board of directors between 10 October 1964 and 4 March 1965, "to be utilised to safeguard the freedom of the press and the interests of the company and its shareholders from a threat of nationalization" (*Sri Lanka. Department of Government Printing*, 1971, paras. 213, 224, 238).

The Lake House directors claimed that the money was used to pay for Buddhist monks and laymen to organize large meetings "to agitate for the freedom of the press and democracy and against nationalisation of newspaper undertakings" and to conduct "propaganda work of the United National Party" (*Sri Lanka. Department of Government Printing*, 1971, para. 242). This was described as "a grim battle for their very survival." The outcome of the 1965 general election, which resulted in the victory of the UNP, headed by Dudley Senanayake, owed much to the financial resources of Lake House, even though the unpopularity of the SLFP-LSSP coalition, generated by the proposals to nationalize newspapers and proliferate toddy taverns, and its failure to bring down the cost of living, was also a significant factor.

A director of Lake House exulted that it was now possible "to breathe a little freely as we were not only able to stymy the Bill but were responsible for bringing about the defeat of the Government on the debate of the Throne Speech . . ." (*Sri Lanka. Department of Government Printing*, 1971, para. 255).

The 1965 general election also led to the emergence of the leftist, political party, daily press. Since the orthodox press, threatened by nationalization, favored the UNP, the LSSP and the CP Moscow Wing launched their own Sinhalese language dailies, *Janadina* and *Aththa*, respectively, to present the anti-UNP point of view. The SLFP added its own daily, *Sirilaka*, in 1968.

The UNP victory helped submerge the issue of press nationalization until the matter was raised again during the 1970 general election campaign. The SLFP and its leftist allies failed to provide an unambiguous answer as to whether they intended to bring the newspapers under state control. While Lake House and the Times newspapers provided an adequate forum for the opposition campaign, they openly canvassed in favor of UNP. (The Independent Newspapers Ltd., apparently giving the benefit of the doubt, favored the SLFP-LSSP-CP coalition.)

The efforts of the orthodox press to boost the UNP did not succeed in 1970. The coalition led by Sirimavo Bandaranaike won 116 out of 151 elected seats in the Parliament. Wilson surmised that "the pro-government daily press was guilty of overkill in their propaganda. It kept the opposition on its toes and gave the UNP candidates a politically fatal over-confidence" (*Wilson*, 1971, p. 140). A UNP politician observed that in backing his party, Lake House newspapers "overstepped themselves."

The throne speech of the first session of the new Parliament declared that "freedom of speech, organization, assembly will be guaranteed in law and in practice"; that "freedom of the press will be ensured"; and that "independent newspapers will be encouraged as a means to end the present domination by capitalist monopolies" (*Ceylon Daily News,* 15 June 1970, p. 5). However, the actions of the coalition government soon indicated its intention to humble the press and discredit Lake House. Legislation for a press council was announced, and a commission, under Justice T. S. Fernando, was appointed in August 1970, to inquire into the activities of Lake House during the 1960s. The commission, as documented in its report submitted in February 1971, found Lake House and its directors guilty of several contraventions of the law arising from the purchase and sale of foreign currency, the accumulation of moneys in foreign banks, tax evasion and other counts (*Sri Lanka. Department of Government Printing,* 1971, app. K).

4.7.3.5 1973: Government Defeats Press

Legislative action against the press appears to have been delayed by two major factors which diverted the energies of government: the April 1971 youth uprising that led to a long-drawn out period of press censorship, and the ruling parties' preoccupation with the drafting of a new republican constitution, which replaced the Soulbury constitution on 22 May 1972.

With the uprising quelled and the new constitution adopted, the government, backed by its sweeping parliamentary majority, was ready to defeat the "monopoly press." A bill, instituted as Sri Lanka Press Council Bill, was placed on the parliamentary agenda on 7 November 1972. But challenged by eight petitioners, the bill had to be referred to the Constitutional Court, an advisory body to the speaker, to determine its consistency with the freedom of expression guaranteed in the new constitution. Soon, there was a showdown between the government and the chairman of the Constitutional Court, Justice T. S. Fernando, who took the view that the 14-day limit, stipulated in the constitution to give its decision, was not mandatory, but directory. When the court failed to advise the speaker on the expiry of 14 days, the latter announced that the National State Assembly would proceed with the bill.

During the debate on the new "constitutional crisis," the government asserted that the constitution "nowhere recognizes any theory of separation of powers"; that the executive and judicial institutions "are not independent of the National State Assembly," which is "the supreme instrument of State power" (*Sri Lanka. National State Assembly Debates,* 1972, col. 1343). By prolonging its sittings unconstitutionally, it was argued, the court would only "produce a very valuable piece of paper which they could put into their own archives" (Sri Lanka. *National State Assembly Debates,* 1972, col. 1560). When the government withdrew the attorney general from the proceedings of the court, the court submitted its resignation.

A new development took place on 19 January 1973, when the speaker ruled that the Assembly could not debate the Press Council Bill until an opinion on its validity was first obtained from the Constitutional Court. He ruled that the court, chaired by Justice Fernando, had not been properly constituted and that the proceedings of that court were not in conformity with the provisions of the constitution (*Gunaratne,* 1973b, pp. 16, 20).

Thereafter, the bill was referred to a new constitutional court chaired by Justice Jaya Pathirana, a former politician who had been a member of SLFP from the party's inception until 1972. The court, comprising Justices Pathirana, C. V. Udalagama and T. Wijesundere, advised the speaker on 11 February that,

. . . we see nothing inconsistent in the provisions of the Bill with the provisions of the Constitution. It is not the monster that has been painted to the public from the time it was tabled ... (and) ... a Bill of this nature is essential for the proper and efficient functioning of the democratic process ... and to safeguard the rights of the common man and the Press (Sri Lanka. *National State Assembly Debates,* 22 Feb. 1973, cols. 789-90).

In the main, the petitioners had submitted that the bill's provisions were inconsistent with the articles in the constitution that deal with fundamental rights and freedoms and with the exercise of executive and judicial power. The reasons adduced by the court in dismissing the petitions were not provided at the time the bill was taken up for discussion in the Assembly on 22 February, whereupon the opposition refused to participate in the debate. Thus, on a single day, the Assembly passed the controversial Press Council Bill through all its stages by a 112:0 vote.

4.7.3.6 Press Council Law

The law created a seven-member Press Council, appointed by the president, excepting the ex-officio member, the director of information. Members include a person representing "the working journalists" (*Ceylon News,* 28 June 1973) and another representing "the interests of the employees of newspaper businesses," with each original appointee holding office for three years, and a new appointee for a vacancy holding office only for the unexpired period of his predecessor.

Clause 16 of the law, which received a barrage of criticism, makes it an offense for newspapers to publish, without official approval, any of the following types of government news:

> any matter which purports to be the proceedings ... of a meeting of the Cabinet of Ministers; any matter which purports to be the contents ... of any document sent by or to all or any of the Ministers to or by the Secretary to the Cabinet; or any matter which purports to be a decision ... of the Cabinet.

Publication of the above type of news requires the prior approval of the secretary to the Cabinet. Other types of news that cannot be published without the official approval of the Secretaries to the Ministries are:

"any statement relating to monetary, fiscal, exchange control or import control measures alleged to be under consideration by the Government or by any Ministry or by the Central Bank, the publication of which is likely to lead to the creation of shortages or windfall profits or otherwise adversely affect the economy of Sri Lanka," and "any official secret within the meaning of the Official Secrets Act or any matter relating to the military, naval, air-force or police establishments, equipment or installation which is likely to be prejudicial to the defense and security" of the country.

Clause 16 also makes it an offense to publish

"any proposal or other matter, alleged to be under consideration by any Minister or any Ministry or the Government, when it is false that such proposal or matter is under consideration . . ." Referring to the last, the Constitutional Court surmised that it "does not restrict freedom of the press in any way as it only prevents the press publishing news that is *knowingly false* . . ." (Sri Lanka. *National State Assembly Debates,* 22 Feb. 1973, cols. 779-80).

Clause 15 of the law makes it an offense to publish any profane matter, indecent or obscene matter, advertising injurious to public morality and defamatory matter as defined in the clause.

Government clarified that Clauses 15 and 16 "have really nothing to do with the Press Council itself" and that any offenses in violation of these clauses are "triable before the ordinary courts and not by the Press Council." Government further explained that the "Press Council has no powers except of an administrative and advisory character"; that its only judicial powers are under Clause 9, which states "if the Press Council receives a complaint that any statement published in a newspaper is factually false they have the right to call up the newspaper or the editor and to hold an inquiry . . ." and exercise its powers "to correct, censure and order an apology." There is, as under any other law, the "right of obtaining a writ from the Supreme Court" relating to an order from the Press Council.

Government admitted that the Press Council is "not an independent body," because its function was to implement government policy. Under Clause 10, the council may "prescribe a code of ethics ₊for journalists" and, among other things, "promote technical or other research."

The law, however, does not require the "disclosure of the source of information relating to any item of news published in any newspaper," a provision the government had included in an earlier version of the bill.

In the view of the Constitutional Court, "the Press Council is merely exercising a fact-finding function . . ." and "the decision of the Council is open to review by the Supreme Court." And, again, the magistrate who hears a case against any person tried for disobeying a *lawful order* of the council is entitled "to go into the entirety of the steps taken by the Council before a particular order was made, to determine whether the order so made was lawful" (*Sri Lanka. National State Assembly Debates,* 22 Feb. 1973, cols. 769-70).

4.7.3.7 Lake House Law

Turning next to deal with the country's largest newspaper publishing company, the government, on 18 May 1973, placed on the parliamentary agenda, a bill instituted the Associated Newspapers of Ceylon, Ltd. (Special Provisions) Bill. When, as expected, six directors and shareholders of the company challenged the legality of the bill, the matter was taken up by the Constitutional Court comprising the same judges who gave the decision on the Press Council Bill.

The petitioners claimed that the bill violated the fundamental rights of equality before the law and equal protection of the law, of freedom of association and freedom of speech. The petitioners also requested that Justice Pathirana be disqualified from sitting on the court because "he supported the change of ownership" of Lake House "both inside and outside Parliament" as an SLFP politician (*Ceylon News,* 21 June 1973, p. 5). Justice Pathirana, however, remained as chairman of the court.

The bill contained provisions to effect the following changes:

Reduce the then shareholders of the company to ownership of only 25 per cent of the total shareholding with no single shareholder owning more than two per cent of the total number of shares;

Vest the balance of 75 per cent of the shares with the Public Trustee, who will from time to time, under the directions of the Prime Minister, sell the shares he holds to members of the public (so defined as to include cooperative-societies, trade unions, working journalists and other newspaper employees) until he disposes of the entire shareholding, again on the basis that no single member of the public will hold more than two per cent of the total number of shares; and

Hand over control of the company to an interim board of directors appointed by the Public Trustee (comprising five members including a then shareholder of the company, a working journalist of the company and a qualified accountant) on an "appointed date"; and such control to pass over to a new board of directors partly elected by the shareholders at their first annual general meeting[2] (*Gunaratne,* 1973a).

Under the provisions, the "public trustee" could issue "general or special directions" to the board in matters other than "editorial policy" and "free expression of opinion," as long as he holds at least 51 per cent of the shares. When the "public trustee" holds more than 50 per cent of the shares, he can appoint three directors of the five, the other two elected by the shareholders. The number of directors the "public trustee" can appoint steadily declines with his divesting of shares, until he falls below 20 per cent, when he cannot appoint a director.

The then-directors of the company, who were found by the T. S. Fernando Commission to have contravened the law, were to be ineligible to become directors for a period of three years from the "appointed date."

The Constitutional Court, which advised the speaker on 24 June, declared that none of the provisions of the bill were inconsistent with the constitution.

---

2   On the "appointed date," 20 July 1973, a new board of directors was appointed by the "public trustee." The chairman of the Press Council, A. K. Premadasa, was also named chairman and managing director of the company. The other appointed directors were Mervyn de Silva (working journalist), C. H. Hulugalle (then shareholder), M.A.A. de Abrew and W. Siriwardena.

While the court held "that the provisions of the Bill . . . have
the effect of depriving the members of the company of their
right to freedom of speech and association" and to "freedom
of publication," it asserted that,

> On a careful consideration . . . we are of the view
> that this Bill is being enacted in the interests of national
> economy, the development of collective forms of
> property, raising the moral and cultural standards of
> the people and to eliminate economic and social
> privilege or disparity and exploitation and to ensure
> equal opportunities for all citizens, all of which come
> under the principles of State policy as set out in Article
> 16 of the constitution (Sri Lanka. *National State
> Assembly Debates,* 1973, cols. 1983-86).

The court further held that fundamental rights are "subject to
permissible limitations," as envisaged in Article 18(2) of the
constitution, and that "the equal protection clause does not take
away from the State the power to classify persons for legislative
purposes." The court was of the view that,

> The policy of the Government to broadbase the owner-
> ship of newspaper companies, the recommendation of
> the Press Commission that ANCL be acquired by a
> newspaper corporation in order to break up the concen-
> tration of ownership and the reasons given by the
> Press Commission for this, the findings of the Royal
> Commission in regard to the contravention of the
> Exchange Control Act and the Inland Revenue Act by
> ANCL . . . all justify the objects of the Bill.

While the court granted that the "Bill *ex facie* discriminates
against ANCL," it said the reasons already adduced provided "an
intelligible differentia which distinguishes this Company from
other companies" to come "within the principle of classification"
(*Sri Lanka. National State Assembly Debates,* 1973, cols. 1963-64,
1957-68, 1977-80).

The court alleged that "in the guise of claiming freedom of
publication," the petitioners were "in fact claiming rights to
property, which fundamental right is non-existent in our Constitution" (*Sri Lanka. National State Assembly Debates,* 1973, cols.
1981-82).

Displaying a lack of knowledge about the socio-psychological factors involved in public opinion formation, the court asseverated that the "wide circulation" of Lake House newspapers and the company's "power and influence" gave it "an undue advantage in moulding public opinion to its own way of thinking."

During the parliamentary debate on the bill, the opposition questioned the need to take over Lake House, when "during the last three years this newspaper company adhered to government policies to the very letter," thereby suffering a large reduction in its newspaper circulation (*Sri Lanka. National State Assembly Debates,* 18 July 1973, cols. 2488-89). Prime Minister Bandaranaike said that the reason for the nose-dive in circulation was "because the Lake House reduced the number of copies deliberately" to "prove" there was "a shortage of newsprint" (*Sri Lanka. National State Assembly Debates,* 18 July 1973, col. 2677).

The Assembly approved the bill in the early hours of 19 July, by a vote of 111 to 21. The following day, the affairs of Associated Newspapers of Ceylon Ltd. were taken over by a board of directors appointed by the "public trustee."

4.7.4 Brief Update, by John A. Lent

The heavy controls placed on the press by the Bandaranaike government in the 1970s took their toll both in press freedom (see 4.1.6) and economic stability. As the government took over the main newspaper groups, some of the best editors and journalists either left or were dismissed and were replaced by politically-oriented individuals who practiced government puffery but poor management; circulations in some cases were almost halved; and many newspapers operated in the red. Higher production costs by the mid-1970s, highlighted by a tripling of newsprint costs between 1973-75, also cut the profit-making capability of most newspapers.

The Times of Ceylon, which had published for 129 years, folded temporarily in 1975, because of economic measures by its new, government-oriented management, comprising the son and nephew of Prime Minister Bandaranaike. It resumed within a year after a transfusion of money from supporters of government. In fact, the group to which *The Times of Ceylon* belonged, bearing the same name, suffered such financial losses during the mid-1970s that it had not recovered even after the change of government in 1977. The Jayewardene government in August 1977, took over the group "in the interests of the employees" who were reportedly in danger of losing their jobs and financial dues as creditors moved in to foreclose on the bankrupt group. (Others believed the government move was a suppressive one.)

An exception was the Lake House Group, which despite a 42 per cent circulation loss in its first two years under the Bandaranaike government's broad-basing scheme, made Rs.1.2 and Rs.2.1 million in profits in 1973 and 1974, respectively. This was possible because the group had virtually little competition and was supported by government advertising and higher newsprint allocation (*Gunaratne,* 1975, p. 11).

Circulations dropped sharply in the mid-1970s because, at increasingly higher costs per copy (40-50 cents by mid-1975), newspapers were not thought to be worth the price, especially since they were primarily government bootlickers. Subscribers turned away from the major dailies that only provided government promotional information (see *Wickremesinghe,* 1977), and instead, relied on rumor or purchased and read new, smaller newspapers and periodicals which gave oppositionist views (*IPI Report,* Aug. 1976, p. 4).

Some optimism for the economic life of the press was expressed after the 1977 change of government. One report said advertisements were guaranteed to more newspapers, not just those supporting government, but also those highly critical; and journalists were once again staffing the newspapers, having replaced the politicians-turned-journalists (*IPI Report,* April-May 1978, p. 12). However, the feeling among some observers was that the economic lifeline and credibility of most major newspapers had taken such a sharp blow, that it will take years for them to regain their former vitality. There was some concern at the end of the 1970s, that the Jayewardene government was acting too slowly in making the structural changes in the press necessary to bring about this reform.

Appendices

APPENDIX I

Differences Between Urban and Rural Papers of Thailand
In Each News Category
1970

News Category	Chi Square	Level of Significance
1. Accidents, disasters, crimes, unlawful acts	.005	.98*
2. Thai government affairs: (local, national, foreign)	.0081	.80*
3. Economic activity, commerce	.0171	.80*
4. Human interest, gossip, astrology, biography, solicited advice	.0754	.80*
5. Education, educational activities	4.4147	.05
6. Labor, agriculture	4.7175	.05
7. Arts, culture, entertainment, fiction	6.2423	.02
8. Miscellaneous	7.7213	.01
9. Sports	22.4098	.001
10. Space, science, medicine (of any nation)	23.5083	.001
11. Women's news: home, fashion, domestic advice	23.6302	.001
12. Editorials, letters to the editor, religion, ethics, morals	26.8544	.001
13. Blank space	37.2047	.001
14. International, foreign news	42.7194	.001
15. Lottery, sweepstakes, related stories	47.8593	.001
16. Advertising, announcements	68.6035	.001

* No significant differences found between urban and rural papers in this category.

APPENDIX II

News Categories Ranked by Percentage of Space
in Thai Newspapers
1970

News Categories in Urban Newspapers	Percentage of space*	News Categories in Rural Newspapers	Percentage of space*
1. Advertising, announcements	22.2	Advertising, announcements	37.2
2. Arts, culture, entertainment	9.2	Arts, culture, entertainment	12.3
3. Human interest	9.0**	Human interest	8.6**
4. Sports	8.7	Blank space	8.5
5. Miscellaneous	8.6	Accidents, disasters, crimes, unlawful acts	7.7**
6. Accidents, disasters, crime, unlawful acts	7.7**	Miscellaneous	5.5
7. Editorials	6.1	Thai governmental affairs	4.7**
8. International, foreign news	5.8	Sports	3.6
9. Women's news	5.1	Lottery	2.7
10. Thai governmental affairs	4.5**	Labor, agriculture	1.6
11. Space, science, medicine	3.8	Economic activity, commerce	2.5**
12. Blank space	3.1	Education	1.5
13. Education	3.0	Editorials	1.5
14. Economic activity, commerce	2.5**	Women's news	1.2
15. Labor, agriculture	.7	Space, science, medicine	.5
16. Lottery	.05	International, foreign news	.4

*   Percentage may not sum to 100 per cent because of rounding errors
** No significant difference found

APPENDIX III

Names of the Newspapers of Thailand Content Analyzed

	Location	Number of Issues
Thai Language		
Chow Thai	(Bangkok)	14
Ban Muang	"	17
Siam Rath	"	13
Daily News	"	14
Thai Rath	"	13
Prachatipatai	"	17
Chinese Language		
Universal Daily News	"	16
Tong Fua Daily News	"	22
Sing Siang Yit Pao	"	22
Sirinakorn Daily News	"	17
English Language		
Bangkok World	"	10
Bangkok Post	"	28
The Nation	"	14
		(All provincial papers were Thai Language papers)
Issara	Pitsanulok (North)	7
Sieng Chiangmai	Chiangmai (North)	10
Khon Muang	Chiangmai (North)	7
Pandin Thai	Chiangmai (North)	14
Ekaraj	Lampang (North)	21
Prachasarn	Uttaradit (North)	9
Rachasrima	Nakorn Rajasrima (Northeast)	15
Nakorn Sarn	Nakorn Panom (Northeast)	7
Chaw Nakorn Panom	Nakorn Panom (Northeast)	3

APPENDIX IV

Summary of Respondents to Questionnaire on Thailand

Name of Newspaper*	City and/or Province and Region	Number of Respondents
Daily News	Bangkok (Central)	17
Thai Rath	Bangkok (Central)	5
Prachatibodai	Bangkok (Central)	16
Siam Rath	Bangkok (Central	10
Chow Thai	Bangkok (Central)	4
Ban Muang	Bangkok (Central)	2
*The Nation**	Bangkok (Central)	8
Allied Newspapers:		
*The Bangkok Post**	Bangkok (Central)	9
*The Bangkok World**	Bangkok (Central)	
Ow Thai	Chonburi (Central)	1
Puen Prachachan	Nakorn Sawan (Central)	3
Khon Supan	Supanburi (Central)	1
Gao Naa	Rajburi (Central)	1
Khon Muang	Chiengmai (North)	1
Ekaraj	Lampang (North)	1
Terd Thai	Nakorn Rajasrima (Northeast)	3
Nakorn Saan	Nakorn Panom (Northeast)	1
Chao Nakorn Panom	Nakorn Panom (Northeast)	1
Siang Rath	Nakorn Sri Thammarat (South)	5
Muang Tai	Nakorn Sri Thammarat (South)	3
Chao Tai	Yala (South)	1
Unnamed	–	2

* denotes English language,		Total: 95
otherwise all newspapers responding		Urban: 73
were Thai language publications		Rural: 22

Thai Tak Sin	Songkhla (South)	30
Siang Raj	Nakorn Srithammaraj (South)	14
Muang Tai	Nakorn Srithammaraj (South)	21
Pak Tai	Pattani (South)	6
Hua-Hin Sarn	Prajuab Kirikan (South)	9
Chow Thai	Yala (South)	16

Name of Newspaper*	City and/or Province and Region	Number of Respondents
Gao naa	Rajburi (Central)	8
Khon Supan	Supanburi (Central)	6
Aow-Thai	Chonburi (Central)	4
Bangsaen	Chonburi (Central)	5
Riew-Thai	Chachengsao (Central)	9
Thai Raj	Nakorn Prathom (Central)	11
Prachachon	Nakorn Sawan (Central)	4

Bibliography

This bibliography lists primarily sources cited in the text. For additional citations on Asian press, see John A. Lent, *Asian Mass Communications: A Comprehensive Bibliography* (Philadelphia: School of Communications & Theater, Temple University, 1975) and Lent, *Asian Mass Communications: A Comprehensive Bibliography — 1977 Supplement* (Philadelphia: School of Communications & Theatre, Temple University, 1978). Together, these two books contain 25,000-30,000 citations.

Abisheganaden, Felix. 1970. "From Just One Man to Staff of 620." *Straits Times* Malaysia, 15 July.

Academia, W. S. 1976. "Mass Media: Advent of the Fifth Estate." *Japan Echo*, 3, No. 3:32-43.

Adhikarya, Ronny. 1972. "The Intensification of the Communication Strategies in Family Planning Programs in Rural Java with an Emphasis on the Use of Traditional Communication Networks." Masters thesis, Cornell University.

Agassi, Judith. 1969. *Mass Media in Indonesia.* Cambridge: Center for International Studies, Massachusetts Institute of Technology, Dec.

Aird, John S. 1972. "Population Policy and Demographic Prospects in the People's Republic of China." In *People's Republic of China: An Economic Assessment.* Washington, D. C.: U.S. Government Printing Office.

Akhtar, Hasan. 1978. "Bhutto Newspaper First To Be Pre-censored by Pakistan Government." London *Times,* 18 Oct., p. 9.

Ali, Salamat. 1978a. "Saga of the Four Just Men." *Far Eastern Economic Review* (Hong Kong), 16 June, pp. 32-34.

——————————. 1978b. "Return to the Lean Times." *Far Eastern Economic Review* (Hong Kong), 23 June, p. 30.

Ali, S. M. 1977. "The Press Foundation of Asia." *Far Eastern Economic Review* (Hong Kong), 26 Aug., p. 6.

Ambalavanar, Rajeswari. 1970. "Tamil Journalism and the Indian Community in Malaya 1920-1941." *Journal of Tamil Studies* (Malaysia), Oct.

AMCB (Asian Mass Communication Bulletin) (Singapore). 1973a. "Long-range Plans To Deal with Newsprint Shortage in Asia." Sept., p. 17.

——————————. 1973b. "Newsprint Shortage in Asia Is Reaching Alarming Proportions." Sept., p. 9.

——————————. 1975. "Information Imbalance in Asia." June, pp. 1-4.

——————————. 1976a. "AMIC, IDRC Join Hands on Major Project." Dec., p. 13.

——————————. 1976b. "ASEAN News Agencies: Probing Exchange Possibilities." Dec., p. 4.

——————————. 1976c. "Linking Media Efforts in ASEAN." March-June, p. 9.

_____. 1976d. "Literary: Where Do We Stand?" March-June, pp. 13-14.

_____. 1978. "Towards an Asian News Agency." June, p. 17.

_____. 1979. "Breaking the Transmission Cost Barrier." March, pp. 5, 14.

Anand, Surinder. 1977. "Newsprint Imports: A Case for Decanalisation." *Indian Press* New Delhi), Nov., pp. 19-22.

Anant, Victor. 1968. "By Two Paths to Dignity with Freedom." *IPI Report* (Zurich), Sept.

Andelman, David. 1976a. "Indonesia's 'Fine Line' of Censorship Before the Elections." London *Times,* 29 June, p. 6.

_____. 1976b. "In Singapore, a Communist Spy Drama Features Ballerina, Peter Pan and Sister Fong." *New York Times,* 20 June, p. 13.

Anderson, Mike. 1973. "Indonesia's Press Reawakens." *Leader: Malaysian Journalism Review* (Kuala Lumpur), 3, p. 15.

Anwar, Rosihan. 1973. "Newsmen Can Take Heart When They Look Across the Border." *IPI Report* (Zurich), Nov.-Dec., p. 4.

_____. 1978. "The Sounds of Silence." *Asiaweek* (Hong Kong), 9 June, p. 90.

Arai, Naoyuki. 1966. *Sengoro Ayumi Shimbun Journalism* (The Postwar Newspaper Journalism). Tokyo: Tosho Shimbun Sha.

Arasaratnam, Sinnappah. 1970. *Indians in Malaysia and Singapore.* Bombay: Oxford University Press.

Armbruster, William. 1976. "Editor Goes Down with His Journal." *Editor & Publisher* (New York), 19 Nov., p. 19.

Arnett, Peter. 1977. "There's a Military Air, but Soldiers Are Now Builders." *Philadelphia Inquirer,* 18 March, p. 12-A.

Arpapirom, Anoot. 1974. "Thai Mass Media, Five Years Back and Five Years Ahead." *Nugkhow Yearbook* (Bangkok), March, pp. 185-204.

_____. 1975. "Newspapers Since October 14th." *Nugkhow Yearbook* (Bangkok), March, p. 213.

Asia Yearbook. Annual. Hong Kong: *Far Eastern Economic Review.*

Asian Messenger (Hong Kong). 1976a. "Criticize Media for Socialism." Autumn, p. 2.

_____. 1976b. "Rural Press To Help Eradicate Illiteracy." Spring, p. 9.

_____. 1976c. "Space Wanted." Winter, p. 8.

_____. 1977. "Exchange and Training of Journalists." Spring, p. 9.

_____. 1978a. "Newspapers." Spring, p. 6.

_____. 1978b. "Unloading Mao." Spring, p. 5.

Asiaweek (Hong Kong). 1977a. "A Man Who Couldn't Bend." 4 Nov., pp. 20-21.

_____. 1977b. "Buying a Slice of the News." 23 Dec., pp. 34-35.

_____. 1978a. "An Institution Turns '30.' " 31 March, p. 46.

_____. 1978b. "The Dark Side of the Moon." 14 April, p. 24.

_____. 1978c. "Wang and Press Politics." 8 Dec., pp. 36-39.

_____. 1979a. "A News Agency for Asia?" 2 Feb., p. 36.

_____. 1979b. "Voices from the Underground." 4 May, pp. 29-30.

Awanohara, Susumu. 1979a. "Media: In Search of a Generation." *Far Eastern Economic Review* (Hong Kong), 9 March, p. 26.

_____. 1979b. "New Blood on Older Shoulders." *Far Eastern Economic Review* (Hong Kong), 2 Feb., pp. 24-25.

Axelbank, Albert. 1963. "The Shackled Press of Formosa." *IPI Report* (Zurich), Sept., pp. 6-7.

Azmi, M. A. 1976. "Urdu Press in Pakistan." *Indian Press* (New Delhi), Aug., pp. 31-34.

Banerjee, Subrata. 1975. "Mass Media in North Vietnam." *Vidura* (New Delhi), Feb., pp. 38-39.

Bennett, Nicholas. 1974. "Planning for the Development of Educational Media in Thailand." *Educational Broadcasting International* (London), Dec.

Bhattacharjee, Arun. 1977. "Import Restrictions Check Indian Industry's Growth." *Media* (Hong Kong), April, pp. 6-7.

Birch, E. W. 1879. "The Vernacular Press in the Straits." *Journal of Malayan Branch Royal Asiatic Society,* Dec., pp. 51-54.

Blackburn, Paul P. 1971. "Communications and National Development in Burma, Malaysia, and Thailand." Ph.D. dissertation, American University.

Bonavia, David. 1975. "Activists Wage Poster War in Nanking." London *Times,* 21 Feb., p. 7.

_____. 1978. "Posters Suggest Rift in Peking Hierarchy." London *Times,* 10 April, p. 7.

_____. 1979a. "Human Rights and Wrongs." *Far Eastern Economic Review* (Hong Kong), 13 April, pp. 13-14.

_____. 1979b. "Media: Peking Feels a Breath of Spring." *Far Eastern Economic Review* (Hong Kong), 16 March, pp. 37-38.

Boonsa-ad, Supapun. 1974. *History of the Newspapers in Thailand.* Bangkok: Bhannakij Trading.

Borders, William. 1977. "India's Press Gains Verve, but There Are Some Qualms." *New York Times,* 11 May, p. A-3

Brown, Ronald G. and Jung-Bock Lee. 1977. "The Japanese Press and the "People's Right To Know." *Journalism Quarterly* (US), Autumn.

Budiardjo, Carmel. 1974. "Indonesia — Tightening the Screw." *Index on Censorship* (London), Fall, pp. 73-76.

Bunnag, Maroot. 1972. "Freedom of the Press Now and Future." *Nugkhow Yearbook* (Bangkok), March.

Burns, John. 1973. "Peking Paper Asks a Purge of Turgidities in Press." *New York Times,* 27 July.

Butterfield, Fox. 1976. "Chinese, Used to Bland News, Now Getting Sensations." *New York Times,* 13 Dec., p. 3-C.

_____. 1977a. "China Says Newspapers Are Long-Winded, Blames 'Gang of 4' and Promises 'Short, Good Stories.' " *New York Times,* 31 Jan., p. 8-C.

_____. 1977b. "246 Catholics in Subversion Rap." *Philippine Times* (Chicago), 1-15 Nov., pp. 7, 26.

_____. 1978a. "China's Press Agency Plans Own Roman Spelling." *New York Times,* 3 Dec.

_____. 1978b. "2 Big Fortune Takeovers Cited." *Philippine Times* (Chicago), 16 Dec.-31 Jan., pp. 3, 11.

Buttinger, Joseph. 1967. *Vietnam: A Dragon Embattled.* New York: Frederick A. Praeger.

Butwell, Richard. 1875. "Press and Politics in Burma." Presented at Midwest Conference on Asian Affairs, Ohio University, Athens, Ohio, 25 Oct.

Byrd, Cecil K. 1970. *Early Printing in the Straits Settlements 1806-1858.* Singapore: Singapore National Library.

Cady, John' F. 1964. *Southeast Asia: Its Historical Development.* New York: McGraw-Hill.

Campbell, Robert. 1977. "Letter from Seoul." *Far Eastern Economic Review* (Hong Kong), 25 Feb., p. 58.

Careem, Nicky. 1977a. "Dotting Hong Kong's Eye with Colour." *Media* (Hong Kong), April, pp. 3, 5.

_____. 1977b. "The *Morning Post* Expands the Most: Magazines, Books and New Looks." *Media* (Hong Kong), Jan., pp. 18-19.

Casady, Simon. 1975. "Lee Kuan Yew and the Singapore Media: 'Purging the Media.' " *Index on Censorship* (London), Autumn, pp. 3-7.

Central Committee on Propaganda of Vietnam Lao Dong Party and Committee for Study of Party's History. 1960. *Thirty Years of Struggle of the Party.* Hanoi: Foreign Languages Publishing House. Book One.

Ceylon. Ceylon Government Press. 1964a. *Sessional Paper IX — 1964: Interim Report of the Press Commission.* Colombo: Aug.

_____. 1964b. *Sessional Paper XI — 1964: Final Report of the Press Commission.* Colombo: Oct.

Chalkley, Alan. 1974. "Tea Money and the Media Men." *Media* (Hong Kong), Feb., p. 24.

Chang Kuo-sin. 1974. "The Proliferating Daily Press of Hong Kong." *IPI Report* (Zurich), Nov., pp. 8-9.

_____. 1976a. "Investigative Report Shuts Campus Paper." *IPI Report* (Zurich), Sept., p. 8.

_____. 1976b. "World News Read Only by China's Selected Few." *IPI Report* (Zurich), Feb., pp. 1, 2, 7.

Chang, Parris, trans. 1969/70. "The Confession of Wu Leng-hsi." *Chinese Law and Government, A Journal of Translations,* II, Winter.

Chao Chung. 1968. "Cultural Affairs of Communist China in 1967." *Tsukuo,* 1 April, p. 15.

Chen Mong Hock. 1967. *The Early Chinese Newspapers of Singapore, 1881-1912.* Singapore: University of Malaya Press.

Cheng, Stanway. 1964. "Free China Press Must Walk Legal Tightrope." *IPI Report* (Zurich), Nov., p. 7.

Chhabra, V. N. 1979. "Catching Up with the 'New Technology.' " *Indian Press* (New Delhi), April, pp. 15-16.

Chinoy, Michael. 1978. "The Charge for Freedom." *Far Eastern Economic Review* (Hong Kong), 11 Aug., p. 30.

Chiu, Vermier Y. n.d. "A Comparative Study of the Free Press in England and Control of Publications in Hongkong." No publisher given.

Choe Joon. 1960. *The History of the Korean Press.* Seoul: Iljogak. Korean.

Chopra, Pran. 1975. "Singapore Shows How To Control the Press — Buy It." *Media* (Hong Kong), Jan., p. 4.

Chou. 1963. *A Man Must Choose.* New York: Alfred A. Knopf.

Chowdhury, Amitabha. 1974. "The Asian Press in 1974." In *Asian Press and Media Directory 1974.* pp. 6-9. Manila: Press Foundation of Asia.

——————————. 1976. "Fiesta of Asian Press Freedom Seen at an End." *IPI Report* (Zurich), July, pp. 1-2.

——————————. 1978. "Development Reporting: 'It Gives Us the Chance to Manoeuvre with Honour?' " *IPI Report* (London), April-May, pp. 8-9.

Chu, Godwin C. and Leonard L. Chu. 1979. "Letters to the Editor They Write in China." *East-West Perspectives* (Honolulu), Summer, pp. 2-7.

Chu, James C. Y. 1975. "The PRC Journalist as a Cadre." *Current Scene,* Nov., pp. 1-13.

Chu, James. 1979. "How China's Media Train Foreign Correspondents." *Editor & Publisher* (New York), 1 Sept., p. 11.

Chu, Leonard. 1977. "1984 in 1977." *Asian Messenger* (Hong Kong), Spring, pp. 42-44.

Chulalongkorn University. 1972. "The Rural and Urban Populations of Thailand: Comparative Profiles." Bangkok: Institute of Population Studies, Chulalongkorn University. Research Report No. 8.

Chulalongkorn University. 1973, 1974. *Summary of Mass Media Surveys* (Northeastern and Southern Thailand). Bangkok: Chulalongkorn University, Communication Research Center.

Chung Hua-min. 1969. "Cultural Affairs of Communist China in 1968." *Tsukuo* (China Monthly), 1 May, p. 12.

——————————. 1970. "Cultural Affairs of Communist China in 1969." *Tsukuo,* 1 April.

Coates, Jennifer. 1972. "Bangladesh — The Struggle for Cultural Independence." *Index on Censorship* (London), Spring, pp. 17-35.

Coats, Howard. 1975. "Communications: Malaysia Gets the Message." *Media* (Hong Kong), May, pp. 9-13.

Communicator (New Delhi). 1977. "How to Improve Press Coverage? A Study." Oct., pp. 1-5.

——————————. 1978. "Training in News Agency Journalism." April. Special issue.

Contemporary South Asia News (US). 1976. "Detention of Journalist Peter Custers in Bangladesh." May, pp. 1-2.

Council for International Economic Cooperation and Development. 1973. *Taiwan: Statistical Data Book, 1973.* Taipei.

Crabbe, Robert. 1975. "S. Korea's Secret Police Cancel Ads in *Dong-A Ilbo.*" *Editor & Publisher* (New York), 15 Feb., p. 13.

Current Scene. 1970. "1969 Through Peking's Eyes: A Survey of Chinese Media." 1 Feb., p. 8.

Custers, Peter. 1977. "Bangladesh." *IPI Report* (Zurich), March, p. 8.

Dalton, Keith. 1978. "FM Cracks the Whip on Crime Reporting." *Philippine Times* (Chicago), 2-8 Sept., p. 3.

Darling, Frank C. 1960. "Marshal Sarit and Absolutist Rule in Thailand." *Pacific Affairs,* Dec.

Das, K. 1977. "Lee's TV Chiller for Malaysia." *Far Eastern Economic Review* (Hong Kong), 11 March, pp. 8-9.

Data for Decision (Manila). 1974. "11 Journalists Convicted." 1-7 July, p. 2029.

Davies, Derek. 1977a. "Traveller's Tales." *Far Eastern Economic Review* (Hong Kong), 11 March, p. 17.

——————————. 1977b. "Traveller's Tales." *Far Eastern Economic Review*, 18 March, p. 17.

——————————. 1977c. "Traveller's Tales." *Far Eastern Economic Review*, 25 March, p. 7.

——————————. 1977d. "Traveller's Tales." *Far Eastern Economic Review*, 14 Oct., p. 25.

——————————. 1977e. "Traveller's Tales." *Far Eastern Economic Review*, 2 Dec., p. 17.

D'Cruz, Filomina. 1979. "Mass Communication in Singapore." *AMCB* (Singapore), March, pp. 15-18.

DEEMAR. 1972, 1973. "Media Index." Bangkok: DEEMAR.

Deleg, G. 1974. "The Development of Journalism in the Mongolian People's Republic." *The Democratic Journalist* (Prague), No. 9, pp. 6-7.

Denoon, David B. H. 1971. "Indonesia: Transition to Stability?" *Current History* (US), Dec., pp. 337-338.

de Roy, Swadesh. 1977. "Japan Meets a 'Long-Felt Obligation.' " *Media* (Hong Kong), Feb., p. 23.

Deutsch, Karl. 1954. "Cracks in the Monolith: Possibilities and Patterns in Disintegration in Totalitarian Systems." In Carl J. Friedrich, ed. *Totalitarianism.* Cambridge: Harvard University Press.

Devcom (Philippines). 1976. "Barefoot Journalists." 1:1, p. 12.

De Voss, David. 1978. "Southeast Asia's Intimidated Press." *Columbia Journalism Review* (New York), March-April, pp. 37-39.

Dial, Roger L. 1977. "The New China News Agency and Foreign Policy in China." *Contemporary Asia Review,* 1:1, pp. 39-54.

Dicey, A. V. n.d. "Introduction to the Study of the Law of the Constitution." Pirated Taiwanese edition, no publisher or date given.

Dizard, Wilson P. 1972. "NCNA — Reporter of 'Correct' News." *Current Scene.* July.

Djajanto, Warief. 1977. "Rolling Ahead Slowly in Indonesia." *Media* (Hong Kong), April, p. 7.

Dong-A Ilbo (Seoul). 1964. *The Dong-A Ilbo.* Seoul.

Dupree, Louis. 1973. "China in Conflict over Education." *New York Times,* 13 Aug.

Eapen, K. E. 1969. "Journalism as a Profession in India: A Study of Two States (Bihar and Kerala) and Two Cities (Bombay and Madras)." Ph.D. dissertation, University of Wisconsin.

——————————. 1971. "India: An Overview." In John A. Lent, ed. *The Asian Newspapers' Reluctant Revolution.* pp. 282-297. Ames: Iowa State University Press.

——————————. 1973a. "News Agencies: The Indonesian Scene." *Gazette* (Deventer), 1, pp. 1-2.

——————————. 1973b. *The Media and Development — An Exploratory*

Survey in Indonesia and Zambia. Leicester: Centre for Mass Communication Research, University of Leicester.

East Pakistan Government Press. 1970. *Statement of Newspapers and Periodicals Printed or Published in East Pakistan During the Year 1969.* Dacca.

Effendi, Z. 1973a. "Advertising Revenue – A Large Share of Newspaper." *Jakarta Times,* 10 July.

——————. 1973b. "Newsprint and Its Problems." *Jakarta Times,* 7 July.

Ejiri, Susumu. 1973. "The Place of Research and Organization." *Vidura* (New Delhi), Feb., pp. 11-17.

——————. 1977. "Japan's Press: A Unique Structure." *Communicator* (New Delhi), April, pp. 11-16.

Ellithorpe, Harold. 1975. "The Media They Left Behind." *Media* (Hong Kong), June, p. 4.

Embassy of Vietnam. 1970. "The New Press Law of Vietnam." Washington, D. C.

Evans, Harold. 1973. "Stewardship of the Mass Media." Presented at One Asia Assembly, New Delhi, 5-8 Feb.

Everingham, John. 1975. "Censorship with a Light Touch." *Far Eastern Economic Review* (Hong Kong), 1 Aug., pp. 21-22.

——————. 1976. "Press War Creates Problems for Laos." *Far Eastern Economic Review* (Hong Kong), 23 July, pp. 18-19.

Far Eastern Economic Review (Hong Kong). 1974a. "The Death of a Newspaper." 30 Aug., p. 13.

——————. 1974b. "The Legacy of a Dead Newspaper." 13 Sept., p. 15.

——————. 1975. "The Korean 'Catch 22.' " 4 July, p. 7.

——————. 1976. "Stifling a Voice of the Liberals." 30 Jan., p. 26.

Feroze, S. M. A. 1957. *Press in Pakistan.* Lahore: National Publications.

Forbis, William. 1975. "Japan's Press in the Mid-1970s." *Montana Journalism Review,* No. 18.

Free China Review (Taipei). 1978a. "New Newspaper a Quick Success." May, p. 46.

——————. 1978b. "President Chiang Ching-kuo's Address to the Fifth Journalists' Conference." Dec., pp. 54-56.

——————. 1979a. "New Magazines Now Permissible." May, p. 55.

——————. 1979b. "Publications Must Conform to Policy." June, pp. 51-52.

Freedom at Issue (New York). 1979. "A Peking Wall Poster Calls for Democracy." May-June, pp. 50-52.

Gandelman, Joe. 1975. "Indira Gandhi's Last Press Conference." *The Quill* (Chicago), Oct., pp. 23-25.

Gaspard, Armand. 1961. "The Problem of Freedom of the Press in Formosa, Inquiry for the International Press Institute." *Nieman Reports* (US), Jan., p. 45.

Gayn, Mark. 1974. *Japan Diary.* Tokyo: Chikuma Shobo. Japanese.

Geddes, Diana. 1976. "Hongkong Partnership Offer to 'Observer.' " London *Times,* 25 Oct., p. 1.

Gerbner, George, ed. 1977. *Mass Media Policies in Changing Cultures.* New York: John Wiley and Sons.

Ghiglione, Loren. 1979a. "Newspapers in China." *Bulletin of the ASNE* (US), Dec.-Jan., pp. 12-15.

_____. 1979b. "What 34M Chinese Buy Daily." *IPI Report* (London), April, pp. 8-9, 12.

Gibson-Hill, C. A. 1953. "The Singapore Chronicle (1824-37)." Journal of Malayan Branch *Royal Asiatic Society*, 26:1, pp. 174-199.

Girling, J.L.S. 1972. "Strong-Man Tactics in Thailand: The Problems Remain." *Pacific Community*, April.

Glattbach, Jack. 1973. "South East Asia Press Centre." *Vidura* (New Delhi), Feb., pp. 19, 21.

_____, and Mike Anderson. 1971. "The Press and Broadcasting Media in Singapore." Kuala Lumpur: South East Asia Press Centre.

_____, and Vergel Santos. 1975. "News Agencies in '75: Making Good from Bad." *Media* (Hong Kong), Jan., pp. 13-18.

Goldstone, Anthony. 1974. "Suharto's Guidelines." *Far Eastern Economic Review* (Hong Kong), 4 March, pp. 27-28.

Gonzaga, Leo. 1975. "Where Timidity Is the Better Part of Valour." *Far Eastern Economic Review* (Hong Kong), 3 Oct., p. 28.

Government of South Vietnam. 1969. *Press Law 019/69*. Saigon: 30 Dec.

_____. 1972. *Decree Law 007/TT. SLU.* Modifying Law 019/69. Saigon: 4 Aug.

Grigg, John. 1975. "India's Clampdown." *Index on Censorship* (London), Winter, pp. 5-11.

Guimary, Donald L. 1975. "The Press of South Vietnam: A Recent Perspective." *Gazette* (Deventer), 21:3, pp. 163-169.

Gunaratne, Shelton A. 1970. "Government-Press Conflict in Ceylon: Freedom Versus Responsibility." *Journalism Quarterly*, Autumn.

_____. 1972. "Mass Media Information, Social Differentiation and Modernization: A Longitudinal Survey of Four Ceylonese Villages," Ph.D. dissertation, University of Minnesota.

_____. 1973a. "Public Ownership of Papers Sought in Sri Lanka." *Editor & Publisher* (New York), 26 May.

_____. 1973b. "The Sri Lanka Press Council." *Editor & Publisher* (New York), 31 March, pp. 16, 20.

_____. 1975. "Circulation Drop in Sri Lanka Under State Control." *IPI Report* (Zurich), Sept., p. 11.

Gunther, John. 1951. *The Riddle of MacArthur*. Tokyo: Jiji Press.

Gupta, P. C. 1976. "Newspaper Industry in Financial Straits." *Indian Press* (New Delhi), Sept., pp. 37, 39, 55.

Hamima Dona Mustafa. 1979. "A Comparative Analysis of the Use of Development News in Three Malaysian Dailies." In John A. Lent and John V. Vilanilam, eds. *The Use of Development News: Case Studies of Print and Broadcast Media in India, Malaysia, Ghana and Thailand*. Singapore: AMIC.

Hansen, Judy P. 1972. "Role of the Press in a Controlled Society: Comparative Functions of Chinese and English Language Newspapers in Taiwan." Presented at Association for Education in Journalism, Carbondale, Illinois, Aug.

Hansen, Judy P. and Robert L. Bishop. 1974. "A 'Mini Hundred Flowers Movement': The Rise and Fall of Press Freedom in Taiwan, 1956-1960." Unpublished paper, Ann Arbor: University of Michigan.

Hariharan, A. 1977. "The Press Breathes Easier." *Far Eastern Economic Review* (Hong Kong), 22 April, pp. 27-28.

Harris, Phil. 1977. "A Third World News Deal? Behind the Smokescreen." *Index on Censorship* (London), Sept.-Oct., pp. 27-34.

Harris, Richard. 1976. "How the Chinese Leadership Manages the News." London *Times*, 18 Oct., p. 5.

Hart, John. 1973. "The Media in North Vietnam: 'An Exchange of Views.'" *JES-COMEA Newsletter*, 30 Aug., pp. 8-10.

Hayward, Henry S. 1973. "Indonesia's Maturing Press." *Christian Science Monitor* (Boston), 3 Aug., p. 4.

Hazelhurst, Peter. 1975a. "S. Korean Paper Braves Pressure." London *Times*, 16 Jan.

―――――――――. 1975b. "Underground Press Tells Indians of Crisis." London *Times*, 7 July, p. 4.

―――――――――. 1976. "Kim Thoughts 'Increase the Fish Catch.'" London *Times*, 4 Feb., p. 8.

Henry, David. 1977. "Taiwan: Tolerant 'Rebel.'" *Index on Censorship* (London), Jan.-Feb., p. 57.

Ho Nguyen. 1978. "Erasing Vietnam's Past." *Index on Censorship* (London), Nov.-Dec., pp. 18-20.

Ho Truong An. 1978. "Vietnam's Cultural Purge." *Index on Censorship* (London), July-Aug., pp. 3-7.

Hollstein, Milton. 1961. "The Press in Burma." *Journalism Quarterly* (US), Summer.

―――――――――. 1971. "Burma." In John A. Lent, ed. *The Asian Newspapers' Reluctant Revolution*. Ames: Iowa State University Press.

Hong Kong Government. 1974. *Hong Kong 1974, Report for the Year 1973*. Hong Kong: Government Press.

―――――――――. 1976. *Hong Kong 1976: Report for the Year 1975*. Hong Kong: Government Press.

Hsiao Ping. 1954. "*Jen Min Jih Pao* — The 'People's Daily.'" *People's China* (Peking), 16 Jan.

Huang, Veronica. 1976. "Hong Kong's '007' Mixes Brazen, Bizarre in Successful Blend at 'Tonight's Paper.'" *Media* (Hong Kong), 27 Dec., p. 7.

Huffman, James L. 1977. "The Meiji Roots and the Contemporary Practices of the Japanese Press." *The Japan Interpreter*, Spring, pp. 448-446.

Hughes, John. 1967. *Indonesian Upheaval*. New York: David McKay Co.

Hulugalle, H. A. J. 1969. "Mass Media — The Press." In *Education in Ceylon — A Centenary Volume*. Colombo: Ministry of Education and Cultural Affairs.

―――――――――. 1971. "Ceylon." In John A. Lent, ed. pp. 259-267. *The Asian Newspapers' Reluctant Revolution*. Ames: Iowa State University Press.

552   John A. Lent *Newspapers in Asia*

Hung Kuei-chi. 1958. *A Study on the History of the Press in Taiwan.* Taipei: Commission on Taipei Archives. Chinese.

——————. 1962. "The Press in Taiwan Before Its Restoration." *Journalism Semi-Annually* (Taiwan), Aug., p. 72. Chinese.

Husain, Asad. 1956. "The Future of English-Language Newspapers in India." *Journalism Quarterly* (US), Spring.

IENS (Indian and Eastern Newspaper Society, New Delhi). 1975. *A Survey of Advertising Agencies in India.* New Delhi.

Index on Censorship (London). 1979. "China: Broad News." May-June, pp. 61-63.

Indian Press (New Delhi). 1977. "Newsprint: World Supply and Demand During 1976." Nov., pp. 23-26.

International Advertising Services. 1968. *Facts About Ceylon.* Colombo: Oct.

Interstages (Brussels). 1978. "Les Mass Media au Vietnam." 1 April, pp. 18-19.

IOJ (International Organization of Journalists, Prague). 1976. *Mass Media in C.M.E.A. Countries.* Prague.

IPI Report (Zurich and London). 1970. "Taipei's Press Council Has Helped Improved Standards." April-May, p. 17.

——————. 1975. "Taiwan – 'Freedom To Report.'" Aug., p. 7.

——————. 1978. "Freedom for Manoeuvre." April-May, pp. 5-7.

——————. 1979. "Political Squabbles Hit Asia Conference." March.

Irani, C. R. 1975. "The Indian Press Under Pressure." *Freedom at Issue* (New York), March-April, pp. 7-8, 14-21.

Irani, Cushrow R. 1977. "The Press Emergency in India." *Nieman Reports* (US), Summer/Autumn, pp. 49-52, 54.

——————. 1979. "Shall the 2nd Press Commission Deliver the Goods?" *Indian Press* (New Delhi), March, pp. 11-17.

Ito, Masami. 1976. "Press Freedom in Japan." Presented at Association for Asian Studies, Toronto, Canada, 20 March.

Jablons, Pamela H. 1978. "India's Press: Can It Become Independent at Last?" *Columbia Journalism Review* (New York), July-Aug., pp. 33-36.

Jackson, Karl and Johannes Moeliono. 1972. *Communication and National Integration in Sundanese Villages: Implications for Communication Strategy.* Honolulu: East-West Communication Institute.

Jain, G. P. 1979. "Future of the 'Rural Press.' " *Indian Press* (New Delhi), March, pp. 25, 27, 29.

Japan Echo. 1976. "Japanese Newspapers: Their Power and Credibility." 3:3, pp. 17-44.

Jayaweera, Neville. 1975. "Political Access to Media in Sri Lanka." *WACC Journal* (London), 1, pp. 3-6.

——————. 1978. "Mass Media and State in Sri Lanka – The Uncomfortable Juxtaposition." *Media Asia* (Singapore), 5:2, pp. 68-77.

Jenkins, David. 1978a. "Press Freedom, Military Style." *Far Eastern Economic Review* (Hong Kong), 17 Feb., p. 19.

——————. 1978b. "Pyrrhic Win for Press." *Far Eastern Economic Review* (Hong Kong), 10 Feb., pp. 13-14.

Josey, Alex. 1974a. "Judgement: A Warning for Correspondents." *Far Eastern Economic Review* (Hong Kong), 13 Dec., p. 30.

_____. 1974b. "Lee Acts To Eradicate Press 'Poison.' " *Far Eastern Economic Review* (Hong Kong), 15 Nov., pp. 17-18.

Journalists' Affairs (Prague). 1976. "Socialist Republic of Viet Nam: Unified Organization of Journalists." No. 15, pp. 3-7.

Jueng-anuwat, Panitsri. 1974. "A Life of a Newspaperman Named Kulab Saipradit." *Journal of Communication Arts* (Bangkok), Aug.

Kamm, Henry. 1978. "Indonesia Is Keeping a Tight Rein." *New York Times,* 23 April, p. 17.

Karachi Press Club. 1970. *Akhbarat Ki Aamadni Awr Akhrajat* (Newspapers' Revenues and Expenditures). Karachi: Joint Action Committee, Karachi Press Club.

Karanjia, R. K. 1976. "India's Monopoly Press." *Media* (Hong Kong), Feb., pp. 16-18.

Katz, Phillip P. 1977. "Media Perspectives." Washington, D. C.: Psyop Automated Management Information System, Foreign Media Analysis Subsystem.

Kaviya, Somkuan. 1971. *Directory of Mass Communication Resources in Thailand.* Bangkok: Thammasat University Press.

Kazer, Bill. 1978a. "Taiwan's Press Votes for Freedom." *Far Eastern Economic Review* (Hong Kong), 22 Dec., p. 23.

_____. 1978b. "The Medium Gets the Message." *Far Eastern Economic Review* (Hong Kong), 22 Sept., p. 22.

_____. 1979. "Taiwan: Pressing Ahead with Dissent." *Far Eastern Economic Review* (Hong Kong), 6 July, p. 14.

Kearney, Robert N. 1967. *Communalism and Language in the Politics of Ceylon.* Durham, N.C.: Duke University Press.

Kennard, Allington. 1970. "1845 to 1970: We're 125 Today." *Straits Times* Malaysia, 15 July.

Khatri, Tek Bahadur. 1976. *Mass Communications in Nepal.* Kathmandu: Department of Information, Ministry of Communications.

Kim Byung-Ik. 1973. "Impurity of the Newspaper Serial Novels." *Journalism Quarterly* (Seoul), Summer. Korean.

Kim Heung-Jung. 1974. "Acute Paper Lack Hits South Korea." *Depthnews* (Manila), 14 June.

Kim Sam-o. 1979. "Elite Industry or Just Another Profit-Maker?" *Far Eastern Economic Review* (Hong Kong), 18 May, pp. 59-60.

Kim Tae Ho. 1964. "Korean Press Ethics Commission." *The Bulletin of the Institute of Mass Communication.* Seoul: Seoul National University.

Kimura, Eibun. 1975. *Rokko Kikutake Sunao.* Fukuoka: Ashi Shobo. Japanese.

Kissinger, Henry. 1966. "Domestic Structure and Foreign Policy." *Daedalus* (US), Spring, pp. 503-529.

Klinsoonthorn, Jattawa, ed. 1975. *From Page 5 of "Siam Rath": M.R. Kukrit Pramoj Before His Prime Ministership.* Bangkok: Prapunsarn Press.

Koch, C. 1968. "Indonesia — Educational Broadcasting." Paris: UNESCO, Dec.

Kohli, K. D. 1979. "Scope for Manufacturing Printing Machinery in India." *Indian Press* (New Delhi), March, pp. 19-23.

Komatsubara, Hisao. 1976. "The Japanese Press and Lockheed: Speculation Without Investigation." *Media* (Hong Kong), June.

Kosaka, Masaaki, ed. 1955. *Meiji Bunkashi* (Cultural History of Meiji). Vol. 4. Tokyo: Yobun-sha. Japanese.

Kraitzer, Bill, 1975. "Hongkong Group on Expansion Trail." *Far Eastern Economic Review* (Hong Kong), 21 March, pp. 57-58.

Kulkarni, V. G. 1977. "News Flow: An East Asian Overview." Unpublished paper, Press Foundation of Asia, Hong Kong.

Kumragse, Kamchit. 1971. "Provincial Papers: A Growing Voice in the Thai Journalistic Community." *The Nation* (Bangkok), 17 Dec.

Kuo, Eddie C. Y. 1976. "Language, Nationhood and Communication Planning: The Case of a Multilingual Society." *Southeast Asian Journal of Social Science* (Singapore), 4:2, pp. 31-42.

——————. 1978. "Multilingualism and Mass Communications in Singapore." *Asian Survey* (US), Oct., pp. 1067-1083.

Kutty, K.P.K. 1971. "Covering Pakistan and Bangladesh." *Vidura* (New Delhi), May, pp. 165-168.

Lachica, Eduardo. 1974a. "How Dai Nippon Became the World's Biggest Printers." *Media* (Hong Kong), Feb., pp. 11-12.

——————. 1974b. "Japanese Press: Bucking Moves to Make Good Reporting a Crime." *Media* (Hong Kong), Sept., p. 4.

——————. 1974c. "Nelson — The Electronic Sub-editor." *Media* (Hong Kong), Feb., pp. 9-11.

Lacouture, Jeane. 1968. *Ho Chi Minh: A Political Biography.* New York: Vintage.

Lal, K. Sujan. 1964. *A Short History of Urdu Newspapers.* Hyderabad: Indo-Muslim Cultural Institute.

Lee, Daniel. 1972. "The Thai Coup." *New Left Review,* Jan.-Feb., pp. 36-43.

Lee, Jacqui. 1978. "Mass Communication in Nepal." *AMCB* (Singapore), March, pp. 16-18.

Lee Kuan Yew. 1971. "The Mass Media and New Countries." In Alex Josey, ed. *Asia Pacific Record: Basic Documents and Vital Speeches.* Vol. 11, No. 3, June, pp. 15-18.

Lee, Mary. 1978. "Looking for Quality Control." *Far Eastern Economic Review* (Hong Kong), 18 Aug., pp. 22-23.

Lee, Michael. 1976. "Air Cargo Gives Press a Quick Lift." *Media* (Hong Kong), June.

Lee-Reoma, Sandy. 1977. "News Translation in Five Asian Countries." *Media Asia (Singapore),* 4:3/4, pp. 70-76.

Lee, Thomas. 1973. *Mass Media and Communication Research in the Republic of China.* Taipei: National Chengchi University.

Lelyveld, Joseph. 1973. "Peking Politics: Old Cast, New Faces." *New York Times,* 3 Nov.

Lent, John A. 1971. *The Asian Newspapers' Reluctant Revolution.* Ames, Iowa: Iowa State University Press.

——————. 1974a. "Malaysian Chinese and Their Mass Media: History and Survey." *Asian Profile* (Hong Kong), Aug., pp. 397-412.

——————. 1974b. "Malaysian Indians and Their Mass Media." *Southeast Asian Studies* (Kyoto), Dec., pp. 344-349.

——————. 1974c. "Mass Media in Laos." *Gazette* (Deventer), 20:3, pp. 170-179.

——————. 1974d. "The Press in Laos." *Index on Censorship* (London), Autumn, pp. 31-34.

_____. 1974e. "Underground Press Fills the Gaps in the Philippines." *IPI Report* (Zurich), Dec., pp. 3-4, 9.

_____. 1975a. "An About Face Followed by New Uncertainty." *IPI Report* (Zurich), Oct., pp. 8-10.

_____. 1975b. "English-Language Mass Media of Malaysia: Historical and Contemporary Perspectives." *Gazette* (Deventer), 21:2, pp. 95-113.

_____. 1975c. "Government Policies Reshape Malaysia's Diverse Media." *Journalism Quarterly* (US), Winter, pp. 663-669, 734.

_____. 1975d. "Lee Kuan Yew and the Singapore Media: 'Protecting the People.' " *Index on Censorship* (London), Autumn, pp. 7-16.

_____. 1976a. "Most Philippines Papers Stick to Government Line Under Martial Law." *IPI Report* (Zurich), Nov., pp. 5, 12.

_____. 1976b. "Newspapers Re-open but Repressive Press Laws Remain." *IPI Report* (Zurich), Aug., pp. 8-9.

_____. 1977a. "A Third World News Deal? The Guiding Light." *Index on Censorship* (London), Sept.-Oct., pp. 17-26.

_____. 1977b. "The Burnt-Out Candle: Thailand's Brief Press Freedom." *Index on Censorship* (London), July-Aug., pp. 45-50.

_____. 1978a. "Malaysia's National Language Mass Media: History and Present Status." *Southeast Asian Studies* (Kyoto), March, pp. 598-612.

_____. 1978b. "Mass Media in Malaysia." *Asian Profile* (Hong Kong), April, pp. 153-161.

_____. 1978c. "Press Freedom in Asia: The Quiet, But Completed, Revolution." *Gazette* (Deventer), 24:1, pp. 41-60.

_____. 1978d. "True (?) Confessions: TV in Malaysia and Singapore." *Index on Censorship* (London), March-April, pp. 9-18.

_____. 1979. "The Missionary Press of Asia, 1550–1680: Precursors of Today's Journalism." In *First International Symposium on Asian Studies.* Hong Kong: Asian Research Service.

Lerner, Daniel. 1958. *The Passing of Traditional Society: Modernizing the Middle East.* New York: Free Press.

_____. 1975. "Asia in World Communications: A New Game of Show and Tell." *Media Asia* (Singapore), 1:4, pp. 11-12.

Letchmikanthan, R. 1977. "Kuala Lumpur's Computer Newsroom: The First of Its Kind East of Suez." *Media* (Hong Kong), Feb., pp. 18-19.

Levin, Bernard. 1978a. "How Mrs Gandhi Gagged the Press by a Flick of a Switch." London *Times,* 2 Aug., p. 14.

_____. 1978b. "Jail Without Trial." London *Times,* 4 Aug., p. 12.

_____. 1978c. "The Lies That Gave Mrs Gandhi Total Power." London *Times,* 1 Aug., p. 14.

Lifschultz, Lawrence. 1976. "Rolling the Presses Indira's Way." *Far Eastern Economic Review* (Hong Kong), 16 Jan., pp. 26-28.

Lim, P. Pui Huen. 1970. *Newspapers Published in the Malaysia Area.* Singapore: Institute of Southeast Asian Studies.

Lim, Richard R. S. 1970. "The 'Self-Imposed Censorship.' " *Grassroots Editor* (US), Nov.-Dec., p. 15.

Lin Shiew-sheng. n.d. "A Study of the Formosan Press with Emphasis on the Post-War Republic Period." Masters thesis, Pennsylvania State University.

Lin Yutang. 1936. *A History of the Press and Public Opinion in China.* Shanghai: Kelly & Walsh Ltd.

Liu, Alan P. L. 1966. *The Press and Journals in Communist China.* Cambridge: Center for International Studies, Massachusetts Institute of Technology.

Liu, Han C. and Shelton A. Gunaratne. 1972. "Foreign News in Two Asian Dailies." *Gazette* (Deventer), 18:1.

Liu, Melinda. 1977. "The 'Humanist' Touch Upsets the Censor." *Far Eastern Economic Review* (Hong Kong), 15 July, pp. 40-41.

───────────. 1978. "Writers Reach a Full Stop." *Far Eastern Economic Review* (Hong Kong), 14 April, p. 22.

London *Times.* 1976. " 'Wall Street Journal' To Start Asian Paper." 12 April, p. 9.

───────────. 1977a. "Chinese Press Told To Stop Official Reprints." 14 Dec., p. 7.

───────────. 1977b. " 'People's Daily' Pledge To Liven Up Its Dull Pages." 22 Jan., p. 4.

Long, Howard R. 1958. "Press Freedom in Formosa." *The Quill* (Chicago), July, p. 8.

Lowenstein, Ralph. 1967. "World Press Freedom, 1966." *Freedom of Information Center Publication No. 181* (Columbia, Mo.), June.

Lubis, Mochtar. 1968. "Mass Media and New Nations." *Horizons* (US), special reprint.

───────────. 1971. "Toward a Redefinition of the Role of the Press in Developing Societies." Presented at Third General Assembly, Press Foundation of Asia, Bali, Indonesia, 23-25 Aug.

Lucas, Christopher. 1970. "Indonesia Is a Happening." *Venture,* Dec.-Jan., p. 42.

Lyons, Louis. 1965 "Some Thoughts from Abroad." *IPI Report* (Zurich), Oct., p. 8.

Macdonald, Alexander. 1949. *Bangkok Editor.* New York: MacMillan.

MacFarquhar, Roderick. 1973. "A Visit to the Chinese Press." *The China Quarterly,* Jan.-March, p. 145.

Maeda, Yuji. 1964. *Ken Yorimo Tsuyoshi* (Mightier Than the Sword). Tokyo: Jiji Press.

Majlis, Daud. 1975. "Curbing the Role of the Press." *Far Eastern Economic Review* (Hong Kong), 27 June.

Malcolm, Andrew H. 1978. "*Asahi,* World's Largest Paper, Girds for Battle." *New York Times,* 19 March, p. F-3.

Malhan, P. N. 1977. "Role of Communication in India's Development." *Indian Press (New Delhi),* Feb., pp. 5-13.

───────────. 1978. "The Second Press Commission. Shall It Work?" *Indian Press* (New Delhi), Sept., pp. 13-15.

Malloy, Michael T. 1979. "A Racy Little Manila Newspaper Defies Rules." *The Philippine Times* (Chicago), 28 July-4 Aug., p. 9.

Mankekar, D. R. 1973. *The Press Under Pressure.* New Delhi: Indian Book Co.

Mao Tse-tung. 1967. *Selected Works of Mao Tse-tung.* Vol. 4. Peking: Foreign Language Press.

Marcuse, Jacques. 1967. *The Peking Papers.* New York: E. P. Dutton and Co.

Masuyama, Tasuke. 1972. "The Second Round of the *Yomiuri* Strike." In *Strike Struggles in Occupied Japan.* Tokyo: Rodojumpo-sha.

Mathews, Jay. 1976. "Chiang Ching Becomes Earl Butz of China." *Philadelphia Inquirer*, 22 Nov., p. 8-A.

Matsuura, Sozo. 1969. *Senryoka no Genron Dan-atsu* (Press Control Under Occupation). Tokyo: Gendai Journalism Shuppan Kai.

_____. 1975. *Senjika no Genron Danatsu* (Suppression of the Press During the War). Tokyo: Shirakawa Shoin.

McKillop, Beth. 1978. "Chinese Wall Posters." *Index on Censorship* (London), July–Aug., pp. 8-15.

Media (Hong Kong). 1974a. "Hong Kong: Towards Monopoly?" March, p. 4.

_____. 1974b. "Newsprint." Feb., p. 4.

_____. 1974c. "Newsprint: World of Want." Jan., pp. 6-10.

_____. 1974d. "PFA Initiatives Get Ball Rolling . . . Slowly." Sept., p. 21.

_____. 1975a. "Dow Jones To Raise Stake in *Review* and *SCMP*." April, p. 3.

_____. 1975b. "Fined Macao Paper Closes." April, p. 4.

_____. 1976. "New Printing Technology Comes to Asia: Rolling Ahead." June, p. 3.

_____. 1979a. "All in the Family." March.

_____. 1979b. "Graft and the Journalist." March.

_____. 1979c. "Two Views on What Makes a Free Press." April, pp. 17-18.

Media Asia (Singapore). 1975. "Newsprint and the Affluent World." 2:3.

Melegrito, Jonathan. 1977. "FM Hit on Newsman's Case." *Philippine Times* (Chicago), 16-31 March, p. 1.

Menon, R. Narayan. 1975. "Print Media Are Concentrated in Urban Areas of Asia." *Media Asia* (Singapore), 2:2.

Meor Zailan and Hassan bin Yusoff. 1975. "News Coverage of the 1974 General Election Campaigns." Unpublished paper, Universiti Sains Malaysia, Penang.

Middleton, Stuart A. 1977. "Fat Pickings Ahead for Malaysia's Advertising Men." *Media* (Hong Kong), July, pp. 19, 21.

Mijares, Primitivo. 1976. *The Conjugal Dictatorship of Ferdinand and Imelda Marcos-I*. San Francisco: Union Square Publications.

Minetrakinetra, Bancha, Kasem Sirisumpundh and John D. Mitchell. 1965. *Mass Communication Resources in Thailand*. Bangkok: Thammasat University.

Mitchell, John. 1965. "Thailand's Unexamined Media: Nondaily Newspapers and Radio-TV." *Journalism Quarterly* (US), Winter.

Mitchell, John D. 1971. "Thailand." In John A. Lent, ed. *The Asian Newspapers' Reluctant Revolution*. Ames: Iowa State University Press.

Mitchell, John L. 1976. "Training for Communications in Asia: A Reflection After 10 Years." *Korea Journal*, Dec., pp. 42-49.

Mitra, Asok. 1975. "Information Imbalance in Asia." *Communicator* (New Delhi), July, pp. 1-7.

Mohan, A. T. Chandra. 1971. "Bangladesh Coverage." *Vidura* (New Delhi), May, pp. 163-164.

Moore, Frank J. 1974. *Thailand*. New Haven: HRAF Press.

558   John A. Lent *Newspapers in Asia*

Mosel, James N. 1963. "Communication Patterns and Political Socialization in Transitional Thailand." In Lucian W. Pye, ed. *Communications and Political Development.* Princeton: Princeton University Press.

Mott, John R. 1925. "Media of Mass Communication in Pakistan." Masters thesis, Stanford University.

Mujahid, Sharif al. 1952. "Media of Mass Communication in Pakistan." Masters thesis, Stanford University.

―――――――――. 1956. "The English Press in Pakistan." *Pakistan Quarterly* (Karachi), Summer.

―――――――――. 1965. "Pakistan's First Presidential Elections." *Asian Survey* (US), June.

―――――――――. 1971a. "After Decline During Ayub Era, Pakistan's Press Thrives, Improves." *Journalism Quarterly* (US), Autumn.

―――――――――. 1971b. "Pakistan: The First General Elections." *Asian Survey* (US), Feb.

―――――――――. 1972. "*Dawn* and Muslim India. 1941-47." *Dawn Silver Jubilee Supplement,* 14 Oct.

―――――――――. 1973. "Mass Media in Pakistan (1947-71): History, Development, Problems." Presented at Conference on Communication Research Needs: Urbanization and Communication, Honolulu, 12-16 Feb.

―――――――――. 1974. *Ideology of Pakistan.* Lahore: Progressive Publishers.

Mukherjee, Basudeb. 1971. "The Death of Dacca's Daily *Ittefaq.*" *Vidura* (New Delhi), May, pp. 171, 176.

Munchzargal, Cegmidijn. 1976. "Dziennikarstwo w Mongolskiej Republice Ludowej" (Journalism in the Mongolian People's Republic). *Zeszyty Prasoznawcze* (Poland), 17:4, pp. 95-100.

Mustoffa, Sumono. 1971. "National Security and the Press in Indonesia." Presented at Third General Assembly, Press Foundation of Asia, Bali, Indonesia, 23-25 Aug.

Nakamura, Koji. 1975. "The Power of Japan's Press." *Far Eastern Economic Review* (Hong Kong), 3 Oct., p. 28.

Nam, Sunwoo. 1965. "The Theory of the Korean Press System." Unpublished paper, Stanford University.

―――――――――. 1978. "The Taming of the Korean Press." *Columbia Journalism Review* (New York), March-April, pp. 43-45. .

Narendra, K. 1975. "Why the Nepalese Press Is Tame." *Indian Press* (New Delhi), June, pp. 11-12.

―――――――――. 1979. "Precarious Newsprint Situation." *Indian Press* (New Delhi), June, pp. 103-104.

Natarajan, J. 1954. *History of Indian Journalism.* Delhi: Government of India, Publications Division.

Natarajan, S. 1962. *A History of the Press in India.* London: Asia Publishing House.

National Library of Australia. 1969. *Southeast Asian Newspapers.* Canberra.

Neill, Wilfred T. 1973. *Twentieth Century Indonesia.* New York: Columbia University Press.

New Standard, The (Indonesia). 1974. "*Press Foundation of Asia Initiatives Get Ball Rolling . . . Slowly.*" 23 Nov., p. viii.

New York Times. 1972. "Peking Press Service Seeks To Brighten Its Style." 21 Oct.

Newman, Barry. 1979. "For the Poor of India, Weighty Newspaper Usually Is Preferred." *Wall Street Journal* (New York), 6 Aug., pp. 1, 20.

_____. 1976. "Tokyo Press Slow To Dig into Graft." 11 April, p. 4.

Niazi, Maulana Kausar. 1972. "Meaning of Press Freedom." Islamabad: Ministry of Information and Broadcasting.

Nihon Shinbun Kyokai. 1956. *Nihon Shinbun Kyokai Junen-shi* (Ten Year History of Nihon Shinbun Kyokai). Tokyo.

_____. 1974-79. *The Japanese Press*. Tokyo. Annual.

Nik Ahmad bin Haji Nik Hassan. 1963. "The Malay Press." *Journal of Malayan Branch Royal Asiatic Society*. 36:1.

Niu Wu-ming. 1971. "The Future of Newspaper Advertising." *Journalism Magazine* (Taipei). Autumn. Chinese.

Nunn, G. Raymond and Dô Vân Anh. 1972. *Vietnamese, Cambodian and Laotian Newspapers: An International Union List*. Taipei: Chinese Materials and Research Aids Service Center.

Oey Hong Lee. 1971. *Indonesian Government and the Press During Guided Democracy*. Zug, Switzerland: Inter Documentation Co. AG.

Oh In-hwan. 1977-78. "Korean Journalists' Perceptions of Their Own Roles in Korean Society." *Korean Studies Forum*, Autumn-Winter, pp. 10-48.

_____, and George Won. 1976. "Journalism in Korea: A Short History of the Korean Press." *Transactions Royal Asiatic Society Korea Branch*. Vol. 51.

Oka, Mitsuo. 1969. *Kindai Nihon Shimbun Shoshi* (Short History of Modern Newspapers of Japan). Kyoto: Minerva Shobo.

O'Leary, Dennis M. 1974. "PFA Sees Waldheim on Newsprint." *Media* (Hong Kong), p. 20.

_____. 1975. "Honest Mirror of Asia: The Depthnews Story." *Media* (Hong Kong), Sept., pp. 43-48.

O'Neill, Michael. 1974. "*China Mail*, 1845-1974." *Media* (Hong Kong), Sept., pp. 22-25.

Onn Chin Kee. 1946. *Malaya Upside Down*. Singapore: Jitts and Co.

Ono, Hideo. 1922. *Nihon Shimbun Jattatsu-shi* (History of the Development of Japanese Newspapers). Tokyo: Ho Shoten.

Opletal, Helmut. 1977. "Four Observations on Chinese Mass Media." *Asian Messenger* (Hong Kong), Autumn-Winter.

Overseas Scholars (Taipei). 1973. "News Reporting and Commentaries in Taiwan." 1 Sept., p. 58. Chinese.

Pakistan. Central Statistical Office. 1972. *25 Years of Pakistan in Statistics 1947-1972*. Karachi: Central Statistical Office, Government of Pakistan.

Pakistan. Government. 1978. *White Paper on Misuse of Media: December 20, 1971-July 4, 1977*. Islamabad.

Pakistan. Government of Pakistan. 1968. *Ministry of Information and Broadcasting Year Book 1967-68, July 1967-June 1968*. Karachi: Ministry of Information and Broadcasting.

Pakistan. Government of Pakistan. 1972. *General List of Newspapers and Periodicals Published in Pakistan, December 1971*. Rawalpindi: Press Information Department, Government of Pakistan.

Pakistan. Government of Pakistan. 1973. *General List of Newspapers and Periodicals*

Published in Pakistan 1973. Rawalpindi: Press Information Department, Government of Pakistan.

Pakistan. Government of Pakistan Press. 1959. *Report of the Press Commission.* Karachi.

Pakistan. Ministry of Information. 1953-70. *General List of Newspapers and Periodicals Published in Pakistan.* Karachi: Press Information Department, Ministry of Information.

Pakistan Publications. 1967. *Twenty Years of Pakistan 1947-67.* Karachi.

Pakistan. Sind Government Press. 1971. *List of Newspapers and Periodicals Published in Sind.* Karachi.

Pardede, Samuel. 1972. "The Role of the Press in the Development of Indonesia." Honolulu: East-West Communication Institute. Unpublished paper.

Parish, Hayward Carroll, jr. 1958. "The Development of Democratic Institutions in Thailand," Ph.D. dissertation, UCLA.

Paritanondh, Kamhang. 1972. "An Interview with Chalerm Woottikosit." *Nugkhow Yearbook* (Bangkok), March.

Parker, David. 1975. "Keeping News in the Public Interest." *Far Eastern Economic Review* (Hong Kong), 20 June, pp. 31-32.

Park, Robert E. 1960. "The National History of the Newspaper." In Wilbur Schramm, ed. *Mass Communications.* Urbana: University of Illinois Press.

Peagam, Norman. 1975. "Kukrit Takes the Plunge." *Far Eastern Economic Review* (Hong Kong), 11 April.

Pelissier, Roger. 1964. *2000 Revues d'Asie.* Paris: Bibliotheque Nationale.

Phayakavichien, Pongsak. 1971. "A Comparative Content Analysis of Thai Newspapers in 1960 and 1969." Masters thesis, University of Wisconsin.

Phongpanich, Kiattichai. 1973. "The Revolution of 1932 and Changes in the Administrative Structure of Thailand." Thesis cited in *Jullasarn Krongkarn Tumra* (Bangkok), 2.

Pickerell, Albert G. 1955. "Journalism a Happy Game in Thailand." *IPI Report* (Zurich), Sept., p. 6.

_____. 1960. "The Press of Thailand: Conditions and Trends." *Journalism Quarterly* (US), 37.

Pike, Douglas. 1966. *Viet Cong.* Cambridge: Massachusetts Institute of Technology Press.

Pinch, Edward. 1977. "The Third World and the Fourth Estate: A Look at the Non-Aligned News Agencies Pool." 19th Session, Senior Seminar on Foreign Policy, Department of State, Washington, D.C.

Polsky, Anthony. 1971. "Lee Kuan Yew Versus the Press." *Pacific Community,* Oct., pp. 183-203.

Pool, Ithiel de Sola. 1963. "The Mass Media and Politics in the Modernization Process." In Lucian W. Pye, ed. *Communications and Political Development.* Princeton: Princeton University Press.

Printing and Publishing. 1977. "Printing and Publishing in Indonesia." Summer, Fall, pp. 20-28.

Prizzia, Rossario. 1968. "King Chulalongkorn and the Reorganization of Thailand Provincial Administration." *East-West Center Review* (Honolulu), March.

Prizzia, Ross. 1975. *Thailand in Transition: The Rise of a New Democracy.* Draft manuscript.

_____, and Naron Sinsawasdi. 1974. *Thailand: Student Activism and Political Change.* Bangkok: D.K. Press.

_____. 1975. "Evolution of the Thai Student Movement (1940-1974)." *Asia Quarterly,* 1.

Psinakis, Steve. 1978. "It's Not All Greek to Me." *Philippine Times* (Chicago), 25 Nov.-1 Dec., p. 5.

Purcell, Victor. 1967. *The Chinese in Malaya.* London: Oxford University Press.

Pye, Lucian W. 1978. "Communications and Chinese Political Culture." *Asian Survey* (US), March, pp. 221-246.

Quill (Chicago). 1975. "Korean Maelstrom." April, p. 8.

Race, Jeffrey. 1974. "Thailand 1973: We Certainly Have Been Ravaged by Something." *Asian Survey* (US), Feb.

_____. 1975. "Thailand in 1974: A New Constitution." *Asian Survey,* Feb.

Rampal, Kuldip. 1976. "The Concept of the Press Council." *Freedom of Information Center Report No. 350* (Columbia, Missouri), March.

Ranatunge, D. C. 1971. "Mass Communication in Ceylon." Presented at AMIC Correspondents' Meeting, Singapore, Dec.

Rao, Y. V. Lakshmana. 1977. "Media in Asia: A Time for Reflection." Presented at Seminar on Media and Society: An East/West Review of Unanswered Questions," Honolulu, 10-16 July.

Read, Hadley and John Woods. 1971. "Improving Indonesia's Rural Development Delivery Systems." Request for grant. Urbana: University of Illinois, 8 Oct.

Reporter Association of Thailand. 1973. *Problems of the Press Council.* Bangkok: 12 May.

Republic of Indonesia. 1966. "Law No. 11 of 1966 on the Basic Principles of the Press." Jakarta: Department of Information, Republic of Indonesia.

Reuter, James B. 1977. "PC-Metrocom vs. Father James B. Reuter, S.J., et al." *Philippine Times* (Chicago), 1-15 Nov., pp. 6, 19, 21.

Richardson, Michael. 1978. "Shaking Off a Dose of Flu." *Far Eastern Economic Review* (Hong Kong), 24 Feb., pp. 18-19.

Riggs, Fred W. 1966. *Thailand: The Modernization of a Bureaucratic Polity.* Honolulu: East-West Center Press.

Roff, William R. 1972. *Bibliography of Malay and Arabic Periodicals.* London: Oxford University Press.

Rosenberg, David. 1975. "Redefining Freedom: The Changing Ideology of Filipino Journalists." Presented at Midwest Conference on Asian Affairs, Ohio University, Athens, Ohio, 23-25 Oct.

_____. 1976. "Political Order in a Changing Society: A Case Study of the New Society in the Philippines." Presented at 30th International Congress of Human Sciences in Asia and North Africa, Mexico City, 3-8 Aug.

Rowley, Anthony. 1977a. "Detainee's Bid for Freedom." *Far Eastern Economic Review* (Hong Kong), 16 Dec., pp. 34-35.

_____. 1977b. "Singapore Limits Press Owners." *Far Eastern Economic Review* (Hong Kong), 17 June, pp. 112-113.

_____. 1977c. "Singapore Newspaper Bargains." *Far Eastern Economic Review* (Hong Kong), 7 Oct., pp. 120-121.

Rye, Ajit Singh and Barun Roy. 1976-77. "Above the Dark Clouds a Silver Lining." In *Asian Press and Media Directory 1976-77.* Manila: Press Foundation of Asia.

Ryu, Shintaro. 1961. "Mass Papers in Japan." *Japanese Press* (Tokyo), p. 73.

Saar, John. 1976. "Korea's Step Up Mud-Slinging To Save Face." *Philadelphia Inquirer,* 21 Nov., p. 17-A.

——————————. 1977. "In Japan, Competition's Keen and Cost Disregarded." *Philadelphia Inquirer,* 8 April, p. 4-A.

Sabiri, Imdad. 1953. *Tarikh-i-Shafat-i-Urdu* (History of Urdu Journalism). Delhi: Subhas Book Depot.

Safar Hasyim, Anne Koh and Hashim Makaruddin. 1976. "Content Analysis of the Usage of Bernama News by Three Malaysian Newspapers." Universiti Sains Malaysia, Penang, unpublished paper.

Sakurai, Yoshiko. 1975. "Japan: Circulation or Suicide." *Indian Press* (New Delhi), Sept., pp. 66-67.

——————————. 1976. "Japanese Paper Begins Massive Retrenchment." *Media* (Hong Kong), Aug., p. 16.

Salik, Abdul Majid. 1963. "Growth of Muslim Journalism." In *A History of Freedom Movement.* pp. 445-467. Karachi: Pakistan Historical Society, Vol. III, Part II.

Salonga, Jovito R. 1977. "For a Credible Rights Posture: Restore Press Freedom . . . ." *Philippine Times* (Chicago), 1-15 Sept., pp. 5, 11, 16, 27.

Samson, Allan A. 1973. "Indonesia 1972: The Solidification of Military Control." *Asian Survey* (US), Feb., pp. 128-129.

Samuttawanich, Chaianand. 1974. *October 14 — The People's Party and the Borworndet Rebellion.* Bangkok: Chulalongkorn University.

Sanders, Alan. 1975. "Mongolia: Peking's 'Poisonous Intentions.' " *Far Eastern Economic Review* (Hong Kong), 30 May, p. 30.

San Juan, E., jr. 1978. "Marcos and the Media." *Index on Censorship* (London), May-June, pp. 39-47.

Santos, Vergel. 1974. "The Missionary DEPTHNEWS." *Media* (Hong Kong), Oct., pp. 13-17.

Saravanamuttu, Manicasothy. 1970. *The Sara Saga.* Penang: Cathay Printers.

Sarkar, Chanchal. 1973. "Ten Eventful Years of PII." *Vidura* (New Delhi), Feb., pp. 9, 37.

Scandlen, Guy B. 1975. "The Thai Press: A Content Analysis." Masters thesis, California State University at Fullerton.

Schanberg, Sydney H. 1974. "Indonesian People-Pressure." *Minneapolis Tribune,* 27 Jan., p. 13-A.

——————————. 1975. "Britain Closes Embassy in Phnom Penh, Leaving US as the Only Western Mission." *New York Times,* 21 March, p. 10-C.

Schramm, Wilbur. 1964. *Mass Media and National Development: The Role of Information in the Developing Countries.* Stanford: Stanford University Press.

Schwegman, George A. 1967. *Newspapers on Microfilm.* Washington, D.C.: Library of Congress.

Shah, Muzaffar. 1975. "The Urdu Press in India." Masters thesis, University of California, Berkeley.

Shakib, Badr. 1952. *Urdu Sahafat* (Urdu Journalism). Karachi: Karwan-i-Adab.

Shaplen, Robert. 1976. "Letter from Laos." *The New Yorker* (US), 2 Aug., pp. 64-76.

Sharp, Ilsa. 1974. "Singapore Waves the Muzzle." *Far Eastern Economic Review* (Hong Kong), 15 April, p. 16.

Shen Shan. 1960. "Taiwan and Its Press." *Nieman Reports* (US), July, p. 17.

Shils, Edward. 1965. *Political Development in the New States.* The Hague: Mouton and Co.

Shreshta, Aditya Man. 1978. "Printed Words in Plenty, but Not Much Power." *Media* (Hong Kong), Dec., p. 29.

Siffin, William J. 1966. *The Thai Bureaucracy, Institutional Change and Development.* Honolulu: East-West Center Press.

Singapore. Government. 1971. *Singapore 1971.* Singapore: Government Printing Office.

Sivaram, M. 1967. "On the Upgrade." *IPI Report* (Zurich), May, p. 6.

Smith, David. 1978. "New Publisher Has Rolls-Royce Style." *Media* (Hong Kong), Sept., p. 8.

_____. 1979. "This Third World Journalist Is Disappointed with Asians." *Media* (Hong Kong), Feb., p. 16.

Smith, Harvey, Donald Bernier, Frederica Bunge, Frances Rintz, Frances Rinn-sup, Suzanne Teleki. 1967. *Area Handbook for South Vietnam.* Washington, D.C.: U.S. Government Printing Office.

Sobhan, Abdus. 1979. "Presenting Information Both Internally and Externally." Presented at World Communication Conference, Athens, Ohio, 27 April-4 May.

Sommerlad, E. Lloyd. 1966. *The Press in Developing Countries.* Sydney: Sydney University Press.

Sorabjee, Soli. 1977. *The Emergency, Censorship and the Press in India 1975-77.* London: Writers and Scholars Educational Trust.

South China Morning Post (Hong Kong). 1977. "Editors Set To Make News." 5 Dec., p. 6.

Southerland, Daniel. 1976a. "How China Public Gets World News." *Christian Science Monitor* (Boston), 14 May, p. 14.

_____. 1976b. "Indonesian Press Flexes Muscles." *Christian Science Monitor* (Boston), 19 March, p. 26.

Sri Lanka. Department of Government Printing. 1971. *Sessional Paper VIII-1971: Report of the Commission Appointed Under the Commission of Inquiry Act to Inquire into and Report on Certain Matters Affecting the Associated Newspapers of Ceylon Ltd., and Other Connected Companies.* Colombo: June.

Sri Lanka. National State Assembly Debates. 1972. "Offical Report (Uncorrected)," Vol. 4(1), No. 7, 12 Dec.

_____. 1973a. "Official Report (Uncorrected)," Vol. 6, No. 11(1), 10 July. (Decision of Constitutional Court.)

_____. 1973b. "Official Report (Uncorrected)," Vol. 6, No. 13, 17 July.

Stein, Gunther. 1945. *The Challenge of Red China.* New York: McGraw-Hill Book Co. Inc.

Stewart, Ian. 1966. "The Paper That Spreads the Cult of Mao." *New York Times Magazine*, 18 Dec., p. 66.

Stockwin, Harvey. 1976. "The Politics of Detention." *Far Eastern Economic Review* (Hong Kong), 2 July, pp. 10, 15.

Straits Echo (Penang). 1974. "Ceylonese Find There's Money in Scrap Paper." 11 Nov., p. 9.

Sukarno, S. H. 1970. "The Role of Community Press in Community Development." Presented at Third International Seminar on Communication Strategies in Community Development, Manila, Philippines, 7-19 Dec.

Sullivan, John H. 1967. "The Press and Politics in Indonesia." *Journalism Quarterly* (US), Spring.

Sumathipala, K. H. M. 1968. *History of Education in Ceylon 1796-1965.* Colombo: Tisara Prakasakayo.

Susanto, Astrid. 1977. "The Right To Communicate: The Indonesian Case." In L.S. Harms and Jim Richstad, eds. *Evolving Perspectives on the Right To Communicate.* Honolulu: East-West Center.

Sussman, Leonard R. 1974. "The Imitation of America." *Freedom at Issue* (New York), Sept.-Oct., pp. 3-7.

Taipei Journalists Association. 1971. *Press Milestones of the Republic of China.* Taipei.

Takagi, Noritsune. 1972. *Genron Tosei to Mass Media* (Press Control and Mass Media). In *Gendai Nihon to Mass Communication* (Modern Japan and Mass Communication). Vol. 2. Tokyo: Aoki Shoten.

Tasker, Rodney. 1976. "Another Censure for the Church." *Far Eastern Economic Review* (Hong Kong), 17 Dec., pp. 14-15.

——————————. 1977a. "Journalist Vindicated." *Far Eastern Economic Review* (Hong Kong), 1 July, p. 14.

——————————. 1977b. "Rebuilding the Press Foundation." *Far Eastern Economic Review* (Hong Kong), 5 Aug., pp. 24-25.

Teerawanit, Sukanya. 1974. "An Historical Account and Content Analysis of Thai Newspapers." Bangkok: Chulalongkorn University. Thai.

Teixeira, Manuel. 1965. *A Imprensa Periódica Portuguesa no Extremo-Oriente.* Macau: Notícias de Macau. Portuguese.

Teng, Yen-ping. 1966. "A Free and Prosperous Press." *Free China Review* (Taipei), March, pp. 13-18.

Thai, Nguyen. 1971. "South Vietnam." In John A. Lent, ed. *The Asian Newspapers' Reluctant Revolution.* Ames: Iowa State University Press.

Thanapornpan, Rangsan. 1973. "Mass Media and the Informal Education." *The Social Science Review* (Bangkok), Sept., pp. 18-24.

The Nation Review (Bangkok). 1977. "Revolutionary Party Leaders' Orders." 21 Oct.

The Near East and India. 1925. "Party Journalism in India." 3 Sept., pp. 280-285.

Thompson, Jack. 1975. "Thailand: The Radical Voice." *Far Eastern Economic Review* (Hong Kong), 16 May.

Thomson, James C., jr. 1973. "Government and Press — Good News about a Bad Marriage." *New York Times Weekly Review,* 25 Nov.

Thorpe, Norman. 1975a. "Press Freedom Struggle Grows Weak in S. Korea." *Editor & Publisher* (New York), 27 Sept., p. 13.

——————————. 1975b. "S. Korea and the Press." *Editor & Publisher* (New York), 12 April, p. 56.

Time (New York). 1978. "Peking's Poster Politics." 11 Dec., pp. 46, 48.

——————————. 1979. "Turning Back the Clock." 23 April, p. 41.

Ting, Wei-tung. 1965. "Freedom with Responsibility." *Free China Review* (Taipei), March, p. 16.

Ting Wing. 1967. "Communist China's Work of the Press and Publication in 1966." *Tsukuo,* 1 March.

Tiwari, Narendra. 1978. "When Procedural Hurdles and Zooming Prices Join Hands." *Indian Press* (New Delhi), Aug., pp. 15-16.

Toriumi, Yasushi. 1973. "Nihon no Gekidoki ni okeru Shimbun Hodo no arikata" (Newspaper Reporting at Times of Crisis of Japan). In *Nihon ni okeru Journalism no Tokushitsu* (Characteristics of Journalism in Japan). Tokyo: Kenkyusha.

Tran Van Dinh. 1976. "Vietnam in the Year of the Dragon." *Monthly Review,* May.

Treffkorn, Hans. 1978. "Chollima — The Pegasus of the Far East." *Democratic Journalist* (Prague), No. 9, pp. 4-6.

Truong Chinh. 1963. *Primer for Revolt* (Bernard B. Fall, ed.). New York: Praeger.

Tsai, George H. 1969. "A Comparative Study of the Vernacular and the English Language Press in Taiwan." Masters thesis, University of Missouri.

Tun, Chit. 1970. "Dateline Rangoon: Oh, To Report from a Shut-in Country." *Vidura* (New Delhi), Aug., p. 48.

UNDP (United Nations Development Program). 1973. "Indonesia Bids To Overhaul Education System." *Pre-Investment News.* Nov., p. 1.

UNESCO (United Nations Educational, Scientific and Cultural Organization). 1951. *World Communications.* Paris: UNESCO. New and rev. ed.

_____. 1952. *Press, Films, Radio, 1951.* Paris.

_____. 1964. *World Communications: Press, Radio, TV and Film.* New York: UNESCO Publications Center.

_____. 1972. *Statistical Yearbook 1971.* Paris.

_____. 1975. *World Communications: A 200 Country Survey of Press, Radio, Television, Film.* Paris: The UNESCO Press.

United Daily News (Taipei). 1971. *The 20 Years of the United Daily News.* Taipei.

Union of Burma. Directorate of Information. 1968. *A Handbook on Burma.* Rangoon: Sarpay Beikman Press.

Union of Burma. Revolutionary Council. 1966. *Report to the People by the Union of Burma Revolutionary Council on the Revolutionary Government's Budget Estimate for 1966—67.* Rangoon: Revolutionary Council.

U.S. Army. 1970. *Area Handbook for Indonesia — 1970.* Foreign Area Studies, American University. Washington, D.C.: U.S. Government Printing Office, March.

USIA (United States Information Agency). 1958. "The Press in Laos." Washington, D.C.: Office of Research and Intelligence, USIA. P-22-58.

_____. 1966. "Communication Fact Book: Burma." Washington, D.C.

_____. 1972. "Country Data: Burma." Washington, D.C.

USIS (United States Information Service). 1961. "General Population Multi-Media Habits Study." Bangkok.

_____. 1964. "General Population Multi-Media Habits Survey." Bangkok.

_____. 1967. "General Population Multi-Media Habits Survey." Bangkok.

_____. 1971. "General Population Multi-Media Habits Survey." Bangkok.

van der Kroef, Justus. 1954. "The Press in Indonesia: By-Product of Nationalism." *Journalism Quarterly* (US), 31, pp. 337-346.

Ved, Mehendra. 1975. "The First Hour." *Vidura* (New Delhi), Oct.-Dec., p. 265.

Verghese, B. G. 1977. "Black Revelations." *Asiaweek* (Hong Kong), 2 Sept., p. 23.

Vickery, Raymond E., jr. 1967. "The Ceylonese Press and the Fall of the Sirimavo Bandaranaike Government." *The South Atlantic Quarterly,* Summer.

Vidura (New Delhi). 1973. "Press Foundation of Asia and Its Evolution." Feb., pp. 3, 5, 7, 8.

_____. 1974. "Newsprint for Asia: Prospects of U.N. Action." June, pp. 609-611.

_____. 1975. "Fifty Years." Feb., p. 71.

Viénet, René. 1979. "Human Rights: What Rating for China?" *Far Eastern Economic Review* (Hong Kong), 11 May, p. 26.

Vilanilam, John V. 1979. "Journalism Studies Lightly Regarded in South Asia." *Journalism Educator* (US), July, pp. 42-44.

Vittachi, Tarzie. 1973. "The Home Grown Democracy." *Mirror* (Singapore), 5 Feb., p. 3.

_____. 1976. "The Problems Facing the Asian Press." *Devcom* (Manila), 1:1, pp. 10-11.

Vreeland, Nena and Rinn-Sup Shinn. 1976. *Area Handbook for North Korea.* Foreign Area Studies, American University. Washington, D.C.: U.S. Government Printing Office.

Wada, Yoichi. 1974. *Senjika no Journalism* (Journalism During the War in Modern Japan). Vol. 2. Tokyo: Jiji Press.

Wang Ti-wu. 1967. "The Press in Free China." *Nieman Reports* (US), 21:2, p. 26.

Weerawardana, I.D.S. 1960. *Ceylon General Election 1956.* Colombo: M.N. Gunasena and Co. Ltd.

Weintraub, Peter. 1977. "Learning To Live with Asia." *Far Eastern Economic Review* (Hong Kong), 23 Sept., pp. 35-36.

Werner, John R. 1978. "Japanese Newspapers Use Advanced Technology." *Editor & Publisher* (New York), 24 June, pp. 17-18.

Whang, Roy. 1975a. "South Korea: Dulling the Power of the Pen." *Far Eastern Economic Review* (Hong Kong), 11 April, pp. 22-23.

_____. 1975b. "South Korea: Sitting Tight in the Press Struggle." *Far Eastern Economic Review* (Hong Kong), 21 March, p. 23.

Wickremesinghe, Esmond. 1977. "A Call for Sri Lankan Free Press." *Media* (Hong Kong), June.

Wilber, Donald W. 1964. *Pakistan: Its People, Its Society, Its Culture.* New Haven: HRAF.

Williams, Francis. 1969. *The Right To Know: The Rise of the World Press.* London: Longmans, Green and Co. Ltd.

Williams, J. Melville. 1978. "The Press in Pakistan." *Index on Censorship* (London), Sept.-Oct., pp. 54-56.

Wilson, A. J. 1960. "The Press in a Democracy." Presented at Student Christian Movement Seminar, Colombo, Sri Lanka, 3 Sept.

Wilson, David A. 1962. *Politics in Thailand*. Ithaca: Cornell University Press.
Winkler, Ken and Guy B. Scandlen. 1974. "Thai Newspapers Write About Themselves." *Journal of Communication Arts*, March.
Wolseley, Roland E. 1971. "India: History and Development." In John A. Lent, ed. *The Asian Newspapers' Reluctant Revolution.* pp. 259-267. Ames: Iowa State University Press.
Wong, Eugene. 1979. "How Not To Advertise in Malaysia." *Media* (Hong Kong), May p. 25.
Worapong, Somboon. 1973. "Reaction." *Social Science Review* (Bangkok), June.
World Education Projects. 1973. "The Thailand Project: An Innovative Program in Functional Literacy and Family Life Planning." New York: Periodic Paper No. 1, May.
Yamada, Maki. 1978. "Business: The Japanese Way." *Atlas*. June, p. 27.
Yamamoto, Fumio. 1944. *Nihon Shimbun-shi* (History of Japanese Newspapers). Tokyo: Kokusai Shuppan.
Yao, Raymond. 1974a. "Macao: A Louder Voice for the Chinese." *Far Eastern Economic Review* (Hong Kong), 16 Aug., pp. 26-27.
_____. 1974b. "Macao: A Powerful Force for Status Quo." *Far Eastern Economic Review* (Hong Kong), 20 Sept., pp. 31-32.
_____. 1975. "Losing a Few Friends in High Places." *Far Eastern Economic Review* (Hong Kong), 22 Aug., pp. 25-26.
Yen Pa-chin. 1973. "A Study of the Relations Between the Growth of Advertising and That of Economy." *Journalism Magazine* (Taipei), Spring-Summer.
Yoon, Suthichai. 1974. "In My View." *Media* (Hong Kong), April, p. 27.
Yu Hong-Hai. 1972. "A Study on the Similarity of Taipei Major Newspapers Content." Taipei: National Chengchi University.
Yu, Lydia N. 1974. "Consensus-Orientation and the Indirect Style of the Japanese Press." *Philippine Journal of Public Administration* (Manila), Jan., pp. 28-39.
Zainal Abidin b. Ahmaid. 1941. "Malay Journalism in Malay." *Journal of Malayan Branch Royal Asiatic Society*, 19:2.
Zimmerman, Robert F. 1974. "Student 'Revolution' in Thailand: The end of the Thai Bureaucratic Policy?" *Asian Survey* (US), June.

Index

(Note: The alphabetical arrangement of this index is letter by letter.)